DATABASE MACHINES AND KNOWLEDGE BASE MACHINES

**THE KLUWER INTERNATIONAL SERIES
IN ENGINEERING AND COMPUTER SCIENCE**

**PARALLEL PROCESSING AND
FIFTH GENERATION COMPUTING**

Consulting Editor

Doug DeGroot

Other books in the series:

PARALLEL EXECUTION OF LOGIC PROGRAMS
John S. Conery ISBN 0–89838–194–0

PARALLEL COMPUTATION AND COMPUTERS FOR
ARTIFICIAL INTELLIGENCE
Janusz S. Kowalik ISBN 0–89838–227–0

MEMORY STORAGE PATTERNS IN PARALLEL PROCESSING
Mary E. Mace ISBN 0–89838–239–4

SUPERCOMPUTER ARCHITECTURE
Paul B. Schneck ISBN 0–89838–234–4

ASSIGNMENT PROBLEMS IN
PARALLEL AND DISTRIBUTED COMPUTING
Shahid H. Bokhari ISBN 0–89838–240–8

MEMORY PERFORMANCE OF PROLOG ARCHITECTURES
Evan Tick ISBN 0–89838–254–8

DATABASE MACHINES AND KNOWLEDGE BASE MACHINES

edited by

Masaru Kitsuregawa
University of Tokyo
Hidehiko Tanaka
University of Tokyo

KLUWER ACADEMIC PUBLISHERS
Boston/Dordrecht/Lancaster

Distributors for North America:
Kluwer Academic Publishers
101 Philip Drive
Assinippi Park
Norwell, Massachusetts 02061 USA

Distributors for the UK and Ireland:
Kluwer Academic Publishers
MTP Press Limited
Falcon House, Queen Square
Lancaster LA1 1RN, UNITED KINGDOM

Distributors for all other countries:
Kluwer Academic Publishers Group
Distribution Centre
Post Office Box 322
3300 AH Dordrecht, THE NETHERLANDS

Library of Congress Cataloging-in-Publication Data

Database machines and knowledge base machines / edited by Masaru
  Kitsuregawa.
    p. cm. — (The Kluwer international series in engineering and
computer science ; 43. Parallel processing and fifth generation
computing)
    Contains papers presented at the Fifth International Workshop on
Database Machines.
    ISBN 0-89838-257-2:
    1. Electronic digital computers—Congresses. 2. Data base
management—Congresses. 3. Expert systems (Computer science)-
-Congresses. I. Kitsuregawa, Masaru. II. Hidehiko Tanaka. III. International Workshop
on Database Machines (5th : 1987 : Tokyo, Japan) IV. Series:
Kluwer international series in engineering and computer science ;
SECS 43. V. Series: Kluwer international series in engineering and
computer science. Parallel processing and fifth generation
computing.
QA76.5.D2687 1988
004—dc19

87-29646
CIP

Printed in the United States of America

CONTENTS

v

PREFACE

This volume contains the papers presented at the Fifth International Workshop on Database Machines. The papers cover a wide spectrum of topics on Database Machines and Knowledge Base Machines. Reports of major projects, ECRC, MCC, and ICOT are included. Topics on DBM cover new database machine architectures based on vector processing and hypercube parallel processing, VLSI oriented architecture, filter processor, sorting machine, concurrency control mechanism for DBM, main memory database, interconnection network for DBM, and performance evaluation. In this workshop much more attention was given to knowledge base management as compared to the previous four workshops. Many papers discuss deductive database processing. Architectures for semantic network, prolog, and production system were also proposed.

We would like to express our deep thanks to all those who contributed to the success of the workshop. We would also like to express our appreciation for the valuable suggestions given to us by Prof. D. K. Hsiao, Prof. D. J. DeWitt, and Dr. H. Boral. The workshop was sponsored by the Information Processing Society of Japan and the Institute of New Generation Computer Technology, with the support of Japan Electronic Industry Development Association, in cooperation with the Association for Computing Machinery, Japanese Society for Artificial Intelligence, and Japan Society for Software Science and Technology. We would like to thank all those who gave us their support, including many companies which supported us financially. We are grateful for the assistance we received from the Mampei Hotel. We wish to thank Miss Y. Tasaku of Inter Group for taking care of all the arrangements for the workshop and also Mr. D. Childress and Mr. Y. Yamamoto of Kluwer Academic Publishers for publishing the proceedings. We, on behalf of the program committee, wish to express our gratitude to the many others who contributed to the success of the workshop.

Program Chairman   M. Kitsuregawa
General Chairman   H. Tanaka

I Project Research
for
Knowledge Base Machines

ICM3: Design and evaluation of an Inference Crunching Machine

Jacques Noyé, Jean-Claude Syre, et al.

ECRC - European Computer-Industry Research Centre GmbH
Arabellastr. 17 D-8000 Muenchen 81 West Germany

ABSTRACT

The ICM (Inference Crunching Machines) Project is a research project conducted at ECRC to design and evaluate the architectures of processors dedicated to Prolog. Although there is a real trend in developing co-processors for AI, little has been done to tailor the abstract Prolog machines known in the literature to the real features of existing hardware. ICM3 is one example of such an effort to modify the software Prolog machine, leading to a powerful and efficient implementation in hardware. After an introduction giving the framework of the ICM Project, we describe the modified abstract machine, then the architecture of ICM3, emphasizing its unique features (asynchronous prefetch unit, dereferencing and unification unit). Some functional and gate level simulation results follow. We conclude with comments on what we learned from ICM3, and introduce the next project under way at ECRC, in the Computer Architecture Group.

INTRODUCTION

This paper presents the architecture and performance evaluation of ICM3 (Inference Crunching Machine), a co-processor dedicated to Prolog. ICM3 is one output of the ICM research project, begun at ECRC in 1985, which also involved H. Benker, T. Jeffré, G. Watzlawik, A. Poehlmann, S. Schmitz, O. Thibault and B. Poterie as full time researchers of the Computer Architecture Group.

When we started the ICM Project, several other important research studies were under way at other places: the PSI 1 machine [12, 10] was starting running at a tremendous speed of 100 Klips (Kilo logical inferences per second), peak rate, 30 in a sustained regime, a major breakthrough compared to the conventional 1 to 3 Klips of current interpreters. Then machines running compiled Prolog were introduced. The CHI [7] machine was revealed with a peak performance of 280 Klips (OK, it was in ECL, but an interesting milestone). At about the same time, the Berkeley Group with Al Despain [5, 4] , and other people from California (Evan Tick [9]), were announcing an incredible estimate of 450 Klips (still peak performance). Most of these machines (including the more recent X-1 of Xenologic [8, 3], and to some extent too, the PSI-II of ICOT [6]) are more or less a direct mapping of the quasi "standard" WAM (Warren Abstract Machine) defined by David Warren in 1983 [11]. The achieved sustained performance, in the order of 100 to 150 Klips (already 6 to 8 times better than pure software Prolog systems), together with the idea that the hardware potentialities of the WAM were still to be explored, motivated the ICM project.

The project started by investigating the various system architectures possible by

3

associating a hardwired engine and a software Prolog environment running on a conventional Host system. We summarize below:

- In a back end processor system, the designer is free to define a format for a machine word. On the other hand, he will have to implement a complete ad-hoc software system to compile, emulate, and run the programs. While the communication with the Host system is easy, it will not allow a tightly-coupled execution (e.g. for data base or external language extensions).

- In a co-processor system, the constraints are different: the memory system being shared, the designer is faced with terrible problems of pre-defined word lengths, memory bus throughput, host compatibility, and will also face the operating system to solve his problems of communication. The software effort can be small (if the machine runs in a "one-shot" fashion, i.e. a single query is posed and completely solved by the co-processor), or it can be high, if one allows a bidirectional control of the program between the co-processor and the host system. A co-processor is more attractive for flexibility and extensions.

The ICM3 machine [4] belongs to the second class (we have another design, called ICM4 [1], corresponding to the first class of system architectures). Thus it is a co-processor, sharing the memory system of a host machine, and running compiled Prolog programs in a one-shot manner. The other requirements for ICM3 were the following:

- Achieve a peak performance of more than 400 Klips (rather easy), and a sustained performance of more than 200 (this is less easy), by really tuning the hardware design to the fundamental mechanisms involved in a Prolog execution.

- Be connectable to a 32-bit host processor, with the constraints this implies on word format, memory, ...

- Use a conventional technology.

- Be a vehicle of research to learn lessons from various design choices. In fact some of the choices were made to evaluate a feature, not really because the feature was already proven excellent.

This paper is organized as follows: Section 2 describes the abstract machine, stressing the differences with the conventional WAM where necessary. Section 3 introduces the hardware architecture of ICM3. Section 4 focusses on the Tag Flag Calculator, an important source of speed-up. Section 5 presents performance results, with comparisons, where possible, with existing Prolog systems. Section 6 gives a qualitative evaluation of ICM3, and section 7 concludes by introducing the future activities of the ICM research team, part of the Computer Architecture Group of ECRC.

ABSTRACT MACHINE

The ICAM (ICM Abstract Machine) is based on the ideas initially presented by D.H.D. Warren in ,20.. While preserving the main organization of the WAM, we modified it along two different lines. First, it was completed and enhanced. taking into account the experience of ECRC Prolog, a compiled Prolog system developed in the Logic Programming Group [9, 17]. Second, it was finely tuned to a hardware implementation. The following short description gives some examples of these two points.

Data formats

A Prolog term is represented by a 32-bit word composed of an 8-bit tag and a 24-bit value. Within the tag, the type field (4 bits) gives the type of the object, the mark field (4 bits) was reserved for future use (garbage collection).

Nine different Prolog types are defined: the bound and unbound variables, the compound terms (lists and structures) and a number of constant types (atoms, functors, 16-bit short integers, 32-bit long integers and reals). A tenth type corresponds to internally used data pointers (for instance tops of stacks).

Memory layout

The ICAM manages six memory areas:

- The Code Area statically stores compiled Prolog programs.

- The Local Stack stores the AND/OR tree corresponding to a Prolog execution, which is represented by a stack of frames, the environment frames (AND-level) and the choice point (or backtrack) frames (OR-level).

- According to the structure copy technique, the Global Stack mainly stores compound terms created during unification for argument passing purposes.

- The Trail stores the addresses of the bindings which have to be reset on backtracking.

- The Registers hold the current state of the computation (program pointers, tops of stacks, pointers to the current choice point and environment frames...) and are used for argument passing purposes. These Registers, which are the most frequently accessed objects, are actually held in hardware registers. There are 16 Argument Registers, and 9 State Registers. E points to the current environment frame, B to the current backtrack frame, T to the top of the Local Stack, TG to the top of the Global Stack, TT to the top of the Trail, GB to the Global Stack backtrack point. P is the Program Pointer, CP (Continuation Program Pointer) points to the next instruction when a clause is completed, BP points to the next instruction in case of backtracking (Backtrack Program Pointer), and S is a Structure pointer to the Global Stack used during unification.

- The PDL (Push-down List) is a small stack used by the general unification procedure. It is always empty between two ICAM instructions.

Generally, the Local and Global Stacks as well as the Trail expand towards higher addresses, as more procedures are invoked, and contract on backtracking. In addition, the Tail Recursion Optimization performs an early space recovery on the Local Stack.

Environment handling

In the WAM, when a clause comprises several goals, an environment is allocated before head unification by setting the register E (current environment) to the top of the Local Stack and pushing the continuation information (this information defines what to do next if the current goal succeeds). The bindings of the permanent variables (i.e. the variables which must survive the resolution of the first goal) are then stored in the second part of the frame during unification.

This makes it possible, as an extension to the Tail Recursion Optimization, to trim the environment. Let us suppose that a permanent variable occurs for the last time in the second goal of a clause. This clause will be compiled such that this variable will be the last one to be pushed on the Local Stack. If, before solving the second goal, this variable is still at the top of the Local Stack, the corresponding location can be recovered.

These features bring a number of drawbacks. First, each time a location is trimmed, the possibility of a dangling reference has to be checked, which is quite costly. Second, the top of the Local Stack is computed dynamically, necessitating, in a deterministic state, an access via the CP register (the continuation program pointer) to the Code Area. In a hardware implementation, this access to the Code Area disturbs the process of prefetching the next instructions. The difficulty can be circumvented, as in [7], by adding a new register holding the dynamic size of the current environment. Unfortunately, this must then be stored in the environment and choice point frames which may nullify the expected memory gain.

To overcome these drawbacks, trimming has been abandoned. As in ECRC Prolog, E points to the top of the environment frame, and T is always Max(E,B). Moreover, the allocation of environments (i.e. pushing the continuation information and setting E, now to the top of the Local Stack) can be delayed until unification has succeeded. In case of failure, unnecessary work is avoided.

Choice point handling

Three refinements (the last two inspired by ECRC Prolog) have been brought to choice point handling.

First, the backtrack program pointer BP becomes a State Register. In the same way CP is saved in the environment frame (the AND frame), BP is saved in the choice point frame (the OR frame). Additionally, both the BP and CP registers can be held in the Prefetch Unit part of the machine. This results in a notable speedup in instruction fetch, since these registers are now immediately available.

Secondly, we have introduced the management of shallow backtracking. When a clause head unification may shallow backtrack (i.e. there is at least one alternative clause), the compiler guarantees that the argument registers are not modified. In case of failure, neither the continuation (E and CP) nor the argument registers have to be restored.

The indexing scheme has been modified in order to eliminate the possibility of creating two choice point frames for the same call. This scheme saves time, and speeds up cut operations, too.

The instruction set

The kernel ICAM instruction set comprises 69 instructions, inspired from the WAM, and mostly implemented on a 32-bit word. The AND-level instructions are responsible for environment management and goal sequencing. The OR-level instructions deal with choice point management and clause sequencing as well as with the cut operation. The indexing instructions filter the candidate clauses using as a key a compiler determined argument. The get instructions perform the head unification of non-nested terms. The put instructions are responsible for argument passing of non-nested terms and the unify instructions deal with nested term unification and argument passing.

Lastly, the built-in instructions implement most of the Prolog built-in predicates as direct microcode calls. This allows register allocation optimization and extends the effectiveness of shallow backtracking.

ARCHITECTURE OF ICM3

The functional architecture of ICM3 (figure 1) looks like a conventional computer: a Prefetch Unit (PRU) is connected to a Code Cache (COCA), and an Execution Unit (EXU), is connected to a Data Cache (DACA). Thus instructions and data are separately accessed and managed, and the PRU is asynchronous to the EXU. Both units cooperate using basically two flags: NIP (Next Instruction Please) informs the PRU that the EXU has reached a point where the current instruction will run to its end without problems (such as a fail operation), so that the PRU can supply the right next instruction. PRURDY informs the EXU that this instruction is supplied in a decoded form directly executable by the EXU. Both units are separately microprogrammed.

The Execution Unit

Beside the basic Register File and the ALU, there exists a number of specific boxes dedicated to tasks involving specific Prolog operations, as shown in figure 2. The Tag Flag Calculator is described in the next section.

The Register File. This is made of AMD29334 four-port 64x32-bit register chips, and contains the Argument Registers (up to 16), the State Registers (E, B, T, TG, TT, GB, S), a 32 word PDL (or bottom of the PDL), and intermediate or scratch registers used by the microprograms.

The Register Address Control. This unit provides the register addresses for the

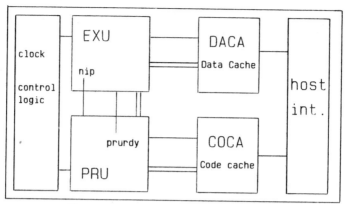

Figure 1: General organization of ICM3

four ports of the Register File. Each port can be flexibly addressed in various ways from an instruction or a microinstruction field. Another source of register addressing is the arity counter or the PDL counter. These are used and incremented in parallel, without resorting to the ALU. Many microinstructions make use of 3 registers (e.g. one to extract an address, one to store it after incrementing and the third one to extract data), thus microprograms are smaller and execution times better.

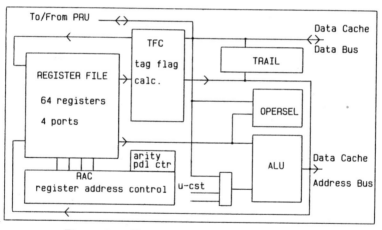

Figure 2: Diagram of the Execution Unit (EXU)

The Operand Selector. This very specialized unit implements, among other things, a feature exemplified by the environment deallocation T (the top of the Local Stack) must be set to the maximum of E (Environment Frame Pointer) and B (Backtrack Frame Pointer). In a conventional microprogrammed data path, the control would have to compare E and B in the ALU, then test the result, and decide to move E or B into T. With the OPERSEL Unit, this is done in one microinstruction. E and B are read from the Register File and compared on-the-fly The maximum value is delivered and stored back in T.

The ALU.   This is a conventional 32 bit ALU, which gets its operands from the Register File, or the Prefetch Unit. The output of the ALU is basically used to give an address, or a result to be stored back into the Register File.   Another path from the Register File provides the data for a memory operation.

The Trail Unit.   This unit is another Prolog specific device in charge of managing the trail operation that may occur after a binding is made. A trail operation is very expensive: the address of the binding must be compared with up to three registers (GB, TG and B). Instead of using the ALU, the Trail Unit is connected to a bus going to the Register File. Each time a microinstruction updates any register GB, TG or B, it also updates the latched comparators in the Trail Unit, thus always supplying the right data for a future comparison. If a binding is done, the activation of the Trail Unit will make the comparators active with the data available on the bus. The result of the comparisons is taken into account, in the same microinstruction, to enable or disable the push operation onto the Trail Stack.

The Prefetch Unit

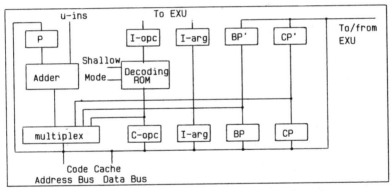

Figure 3:   Organization of the prefetch Unit (PRU)

In addition to the function that its name indicates and which will not be developed here, the PRU (figure 3) contains some unique features to optimize the execution of Prolog.

The decoding of an instruction is performed by a ROM, as usual, but the inputs for that ROM are made of two fields: the normal opcode of the incoming instruction, and the values of the two flags which may affect the semantics of that instruction: SHALLOW, giving the type of backtracking to perform in case of failure, and MODE, defining the Write or Read mode for unification. These control bits are directly handled at decode time and thus never tested at execution time.

The second feature concerns the program control: as mentioned before, the PRU contains, in addition to the conventional P register (Program Counter), the two State Registers CP and BP.   The Proceed instruction (a unit clause has succeeded, the execution proceeds to the next goal), for example, can be treated entirely in the Prefetch Unit: it consists simply in moving CP into P and reading the corresponding instruction in the code memory. This instruction can be executed in parallel with the previous instruction terminating in the EXU.

Global Data on ICM3

The Data Cache and the Code Cache each contain 16K words and use a direct mapping mode, as well as the Write-in policy. They are not the strongest features of ICM3, because of the lack of time and evaluation we had at the time of design. We now think that something much better could have been achieved (set-associative caches, or better organization to easily avoid conflicts).

The EXU has a 100 ns cycle, with a 128 bit microinstruction. The microprogram for the kernel does not exceed 2 K microwords. The PRU has a 50 ns cycle, with a simpler microprogrammed control (26 bit microinstruction, and a small microprogram). ICM3 is made of around 280 integrated circuits, and uses the AMD 29300 series of 32 bit chips.

THE TAG FLAG CALCULATOR

This strangely named unit deals with everything concerning the tags associated with the Prolog data objects. Figure 4 shows the main functions performed by the TFC.

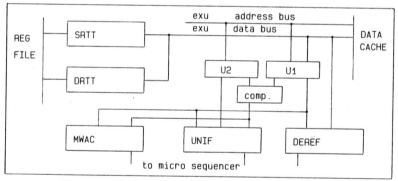

Figure 4:   Diagram of the Tag Flag Calculator (TFC)

SRTT: Source Register Tag Transcoder

This subunit allows an on-the-fly change of the original tag part of an operand extracted from the register file, a useful operation in instructions such as Get_atom or Put_variable (identical to the WAM), where a tag corresponding to a dictionary reference (DIC) or an unbound variable (FREE) must be concatenated to an address to form a Prolog object which is then written into memory.

DRTT: Destination Register Tag Transcoder

When an object is loaded into a register, its tag may be modified. This occurs in Put_value, where an unbound variable (tag FREE) must be transformed into a bound one (tag REF) before being written into the register Of course, the operation is also performed on-the-fly.

MWAC: Multi-Way Address Calculator

This unit compares a tag residing in the U1 register (one of the registers used in the general unification) with a given value, and depending on the result, outputs a 4 bit quantity which is seen as a displacement by the microsequencer of the EXU. The MWAC operates in several modes, depending on the specific operation (get, indexing, unify, and put). The MWAC is a very powerful subunit which instantly provides the right microaddress in a variety of computations involving the tags.

DEREF: Dereferencing unit

This is an important result of ICM3: the dereferencing operation, consisting of following the chain of references until something real is found, is performed in a loop of only one microinstruction. This is to be compared with a software implementation requiring at least 6 operations in the loop, or other hardware implementations using the ALU to perform the necessary operations. Basically. the register U1 is loaded with the quantity to be dereferenced. Then a single microinstruction initiates a memory operation (to follow the chain of indirections), tests the tag part of U1 to decide either to enable this memory operation if the tag denotes a REF quantity, or to stop the memory operation (the tag denotes something actually dereferenced) and jump to a microaddress which depends on that tag (thus reaching the right microsequence corresponding to that object). This operation includes some hardwired control which overrides the normal microprogrammed control.

UNIF: the Unification unit

This uses units already seen above. The first operand is dereferenced in U1, and moved to U2. The second operand is then dereferenced in U1. In parallel, a comparator constantly compares the value fields of U1 and U2. The Unification Unit provides, depending on the tags and values, the exact point where the microprogram must continue the unification. Failure is detected instantly, as is an exact match, and intermediate cases are found very rapidly. The reader familiar with the software implementation of unification will probably appreciate the gain in speed achieved by the UNIF unit.

PERFORMANCE EVALUATION

ICM3 was simulated at two different levels: A gate level simulation, based on the ICM3 schematics, allowed hardware and firmware debugging, using as a reference the outputs of a binary emulator written in C. In addition, a high level simulator, written in Lisp, was used first to validate the abstract machine and then to give coarse-grained performance evaluations, including the influence of the two caches, and using data from gate level simulation.

A whole software chain. including a compiler, an assembler, a linker as well as a number of gate level tools have been written to transform Prolog programs into the form appropriate for the different simulations.

The resulting performance evaluation is fairly accurate since all the paths internal to an ICAM instruction were considered, with most of the timings validated by the gate level simulation; both the high level and the gate level simulations give the same performance, 433 Klips, for the naive reversal of a list of 32 elements.

Comparative performance

On well-known small Prolog benchmarks ICM3 compares quite well to other computer systems executing Prolog. It is on average ten times faster than good software implementations such as BIM [3] and QUINTUS [5] (see Table 1) on SUN3 workstations (the result of BIM on nrev(30) looks like an epiphenomenon).

performance in Klips					
program	QUINTUS	ICM3	program	BIM	ICM3
nrev(30)	45	433	nrev(30)	105*	433
qsortran1(50)	29	294	qsortran2(50)	13	330
ack(3 3 X)	16	376	qsort(50)	16	207
queens(8)	28	262	fibo(17)	13	433

* with mode declarations

Table 1: Comparative performance - QUINTUS and BIM

It also seems to compare favorably with dedicated Prolog machines such as PSI-II and X-1; PSI-II reports 300 Klips on naive reverse and X-1 100 Klips. Xenologic has also studied the speed of important mechanisms such as indexing and choice point handling, they report 32 Klips on choice point handling and 232 Klips on indexing. The corresponding programs dealing with choice point creation and indexing in [2] (released to the Usenet network in 1986) respectively yield 769 and 228 Klips on ICM. These figures are however only indicative, since the benchmarks used by Xenologic are not known.

Influence of the caches

The previous figures correspond to peak performance. On ICM3, these programs are small enough to run entirely in the caches. For bigger programs, a degradation of the pure CPU performance can be observed. In order to study these problems, three programs, more representative of current Prolog applications. were simulated.

The benchmarks. Table 2 gives some information on these programs. Parser is the front-end parser of CHAT, a data base query system [19], Warplan is a plan generator [18] and Press an equation solver [13]. Note the high write/read ratios which justify the Write-in data cache policy.

The hit ratio. Table 3 gives the variation of the hit ratio on both caches with their

benchmarks	press	parser	warplan
static data			
number of Prolog clauses	137	682	64
number of ICAM instructions	1773	6484	671
dynamic data			
data memory used (words)	611	3462	2584
inferences	1533	2494	10018
number of data references	20594	44509	111933
write/read ratio	1.15	1.32	1.05
peak performance (Klips)	250	198	297

Table 2:   Benchmarks

sizes. In each case, the first figure correspond to a first run, i.e. the caches have been invalidated before running the program, and the second figure to a second run.

cache size (words)		512	1K	2K	4K	8K
data cache	press	89-89	89-89	89-89	98-98	100-100
hit ratio	parser	89-88	92-90	96-96	98-98	100-100
(%)	warplan	93-92	96-95	98-98	99-99	99-100
code cache	press	77-79	81-87	87-100	87-100	87-100
hit ratio	parser	33-33	50-52	70-76	84-94	88-100
(%)	warplan	97-98	99-100	99-100	99-100	99-100

Table 3:   Hit ratio

For this simulation, each stack has been allocated 2K in memory. Because of the direct mapping organization, there are risks of collisions on the data cache, up to 8K. Press, which uses only little data memory space, is the only program to really suffer from stack collisions. As soon as more space is necessary, the probability of collision decreases and the hit ratios are quite good, even with a small cache (92 and 96% for the parser and Warplan with 1K). This corroborates the results described in [14] on set-associative caches; only small data caches are required. However, with direct mapping, it is clear that the bigger the cache, the lower the risks of collision. The simplicity of direct mapping allowed a 16K data cache to be implemented.

As far as the code cache is concerned, satisfactory hit ratios are only reached when the size of the code cache is not far from the program size. It is believed however that bigger programs behave differently with a granularity of locality which should make a 16K code cache sufficient. Further research is needed here.

Influence of bus performance. Table 4 shows that, especially with poor hit ratios (Press and Parser examples), a slow bus leads to an unacceptable performance degradation.

performance in Klips			
bus cycle (ns)	0	800	2000
press (code 1 K - data 1K)	250	162	106
parser (code 4 K - data 1K)	198	137	94
warplan (code .5K - data 1K)	297	285	226

Table 4:   Influence of bus performance

WHAT WE LEARNED FROM ICM3

ICM3 was designed and simulated at both a functional level and a gate level. This experience allows us now to criticize the design choices.

First, the asynchronism between the PRU and the EXU is questionable. It brings an interesting micro-parallelism. The PRU executes some instructions itself, and holds the CP and BP registers. However, with this scheme, each normal instruction takes at least two cycles, which could be reduced with a better pipelined and single control. All in all, this design choice does provide a slightly better performance in some cases, but the area and silicon used for it may not be worthwhile.

Second, the SHALLOW mode introduced in ICM3 is also questionable. It speeds up shallow backtrack operations, but prevents some register optimizations. The introduction of a delayed choice point allocation, as described in [10], could make it definitely worthwhile.

Third, beside the tailorization of the CPU for Prolog, it turns out that a very important factor of performance is the memory system. It is vital for any AI machine to have a fast memory, and specially, good hit ratios in the caches. Two caches (for data and code) increase the memory bandwidth, and seem to be definitely better than one. Their implementation in ICM3 is too simple to be satisfactory: the data cache must be carefully studied to avoid overwriting entries in the active parts of the different stacks.

Another point not mentioned above is checking of stack overflows, which is an important issue since it must be often done. In ICM3, which has no virtual addressing capabilities, a hardwired mechanism is necessary to avoid all these tests. In a machine equipped with a virtual address space, this may be performed by other means (e.g. by preventing write operations in memory areas not belonging to the stacks).

The 32-bit word of current possible host machines appears to be a considerable limiting factor: the address space is reduced, the format for numbers is awkward, the hardware design itself is sometimes tricky. The current trend seems to be 40 bits (Lisp machines such as the SM45000 by Inference Machines Inc, PSI II), but this format brings its own problems, in particular a severe incompatibility with 32-bit based systems. 64 bits would probably be better, since it gives enough room to define a Prolog word with enough comfort, it gives a powerful instruction, and it preserves (to some extent) the compatibility with standard 32 bit memory systems. as well as with 32-bit word based software programs (integers and floating point numbers, "word" addressing,...).

Positive results from ICM3 include the different units dedicated to unification, tag handling, and the optimized data paths in the EXU. which can boost the performance with little hardware and clever communication The 4-port register file proved useful in most microprograms. Injecting execution control tags (such as MODE) does not complicate the decoding part and avoids unnecessary cycles, too. In the same vein, the adaptation of the WAM machine to hardware design brought us a better performance in many instructions.

CONCLUSION AND FUTURE WORK

We have presented ICM3, a Prolog coprocessor achieving a performance at least equivalent to the fastest contemporary machines. We do not pretend that we implemented the best CPU organization, nor that we have covered all the user's needs. In that respect, the PSI II system is more complete, since it is a full design including the operating system facilities. However, we believe that the trend in AI machines seems to produce fast co-processors, tighly coupled to bigger and more complete host systems. The co-processor handles parts of the Prolog application (compiled modules), while the Host would manage the non-compiled ones, as well as all the utilities dealing with the operating system, and the user's resources. However this trend still needs a lot of effort to avoid the hardware specialization of the execution being affected by the software compatibility with the host system. ICM3 takes its performance from an adapted WAM abstract machine, and from dedicated hardware units that speed up the performance in many of the fundamental Prolog mechanisms: dereferencing, unification, trailing, stack management,...

We are now involved in the successor of ICM3, called KCM (where K means Knowledge). KCM will be a Prolog/Lisp processor to be attached to a workstation. KCM, currently at the level of functional design, is a 64 bit machine with its own memory system, and implements advanced features such as constraint programming techniques. In any case, KCM will benefit from some of the features of ICM3 presented here, and also from the negative results given by ICM3. KCM will possibly be a testbed for the AI activities of the parent companies of our research centre, namely Siemens, BULL, and ICL.

References

1. H. Benker, J. Noye, G. Watzlawik. ICM4. Technical Report CA-25, ECRC, February, 1987.

2. H. Benker, J. Noye, S. Schmitz, J.C. Syre, M. Meier. Prolog Benchmark Programs. Technical Report CA-24, ECRC, February, 1987.

3. BIM. BIM_Prolog V1.12 - Technical Summary. BIM, June, 1986.

4. Computer-Architecture-Group. ICM3: Final Specification Report on a High Speed Inference Co-processor. Technical Report CA-23, ECRC, February, 1987.

5. S. Dickens and A. Bustany. Alvey Prolog Benchmarks. Imperial Software Technology, July, 1986.

6. Tep Dobry. A Coprocessor for AI; LISP. Prolog and Data Bases. Compcon 87, Xenologic, february, 1987, pp. 396-402.

7. T.P. Dobry, Y.N. Patt and A.M. Despain. Design decisions influencing the microarchitecture for a prolog machine. MICRO-17. L California Berkeley, New Orleans, 1984, pp. 217-231.

8. T.P. Dobry, A.M. Despain and Y.N. Patt. Performance Studies of a Prolog Machine Architecture. The 12th Annual International Symposium on Computer Architecture, IEEE/ACM, June, 1985, pp. 180-190.

9. K. Estenfeld and M. Meier. ECRC-Prolog User's Manual Version 1.2. Technical Report LP - 13, ECRC, September, 1986.

10. H. Nakashima, K. Nakajima. Hardware architecture of the sequential inference machine PSI II. ICOT submitted to SLP87.

11. R. Nakazaki, A. Konagaya, S. Habata, H. Shimazu, M. Umemura, M. Yamamoto, M. Yokota and T. Chikayama. Design of a High-speed Prolog Machine (HPM). The 12th Annual International Symposium on Computer Architecture, IEEE/ACM, June, 1985, pp. 191-197.

12. Randy Ribler. The Integration of the Xenologic X-1 Artificial Intelligence Coprocessor with General Purpose Computers. Compcon 87, Xenologic, february, 1987, pp. 403-407.

13. L. Sterling and E. Shapiro. *Advanced Programming Techniques.* Volume : *The Art of Prolog.* The MIT Press, 1986.

14. E. Tick. Prolog Memory-Referencing Behavior. 85-281, Standford University, September, 1985.

15. E. Tick and D.H.D. Warren. Towards a pipelined prolog processor. 1984 International Symposium on logic programming, IEEE, Atlantic City, February, 1984, pp. 29-40.

16. S. Uchida, T. Yokoi. Sequential inference machine SIM : progress report. Proc. Fifth Generation Computer Systems 1984, ICOT, November, 1984, pp. 58-69.

17. D. de Villeneuve. ECRC Prolog intermediate language PLM. Internal Report LP/LPP1/7, ECRC, September, 1986.

18. D.H.D. Warren. WARPLAN: A System for Generating Plans. memo 76, Edinburgh University, June, 1974.

19. D.H.D. Warren. Efficient processing of interactive relational database queries expressed in logic. Proceedings of the 7th International Conference on Very Large Data Bases, IEEE, September, 1981, pp. 272-281.

20. D.H.D. Warren. An abstract prolog instruction set. tn309, SRI, October, 1983.

21. M. Yokota. A personal sequential inference machine PSI. 84 workshop on HLCA, May, 1984, pp. 36.

Knowledge Base Machine Based on Parallel Kernel Language

Hidenori ITOH, Toshiaki TAKEWAKI *, Haruo YOKOTA†

ICOT Research Center
Institute for New Generation Computer Technology
Mita Kokusai Bldg., 21F, 1-4-28 Mita, Minato-ku, Tokyo 108, Japan

† *Fujitsu Laboratories Ltd. Kawasaki*
1015 Kamikodanaka, Nakahara-ku, Kawasaki 211, Japan

ABSTRACT

This paper describes a knowledge base machine (KBM) that is being researched and developed from the viewpoint of parallel logic programming. From the idea of parallel logic programming, a parallel kernel language (PKL) has been developed for the Fifth Generation Computer System (*FGCS*) project. Our KBM is based on the PKL. It has a parallel inference mechanism and a parallel retrieval mechanism which are controlled by an operating system.

INTRODUCTION

One of the principles of this research was that logic programming can become a new, unifying principle in computer science [1]. This is because logic programming will cover computer architecture, new programming styles, programming language semantics, and database processing. Logic programming will also play an important role in such fields as linguistics and artificial intelligence.

The logic programming language Prolog was selected as the research tool. From Prolog, a parallel kernel language (PKL) was developed, corresponding to a conventional machine language. The PKL is the nucleus of hardware and software systems for the Fifth Generation Computer System (*FGCS*) project. Inference mechanisms and knowledge

---

* Currently working at *Toshiba Corporation*

base mechanisms will be developed as hardware systems; basic and application software will be developed as software systems.

Development is being pursued in three stages. The first was from 1982 to 1984. We are now in the middle of the second stage, which is to end in 1988.

In the initial stage, a sequential kernel language [2] was developed with an object-oriented programming feature added to Prolog. The personal sequential inference machine (PSI) [3] was developed as an inference mechanism based on it. A relational database machine (DELTA) [4] was developed as a relational database storage and retrieval mechanism connected physically with the PSI by a LAN and logically with relational commands.

In the second stage, we are pursuing three activities.

First, the deductive database machine (PHI) is being developed. The PHI is composed of the PSI and dedicated hardware knowledge base engine (KBE) [5], connected by a bus. The technologies obtained through the development of DELTA's relational engine (RE) are integrated in the KBE. Expansion of the PHIs develops a distributed deductive database system. Second, the hierarchical memory mechanism for the global shared memory is being developed. This mechanism is composed of multi-ports and a memory unit [6, 7]. The third activity is the development of the retrieval processors [8] that communicate with inference mechanisms by data streams defined in PKL.

The hierarchical memory mechanism and retrieval processors will be integrated into the prototype of the parallel KBM model in the final stage.

PARALLEL KERNEL LANGUAGE

Guarded Horn Clauses (GHC) [9] was developed as the parallel kernel language (PKL) of the FGCS, using imposition of guards and restriction of nondeterminism where the clause which has passed the guard first is used for subsequent computation.

The pioneering works of GHC are Relational Language [10], Concurrent Prolog [11], and Parlog [12]. All of these languages are very similar and their common feature is that each has a guard part and a body part, separated by a commit operator (denoted by |). Of these languages,

GHC has the simplest syntax. Each clause written in GHC is in the following form:

```
H :- G1,...,Gm | B1,...,Bn.
```

where connectives : - and , are common to ordinary Horn clauses. The part of a clause before | is called the guard, and the part after it is called the body. The calculation results of the guard are only effective in the guard. A guarded clause with no head is a goal clause, as in Prolog.

The semantics of GHC are also quite simple. The execution of a GHC program proceeds by reducing a given goal clause to the empty clause under the following rules.

Rule 1: No piece of unification in the guard of a clause can instantiate a variable in the caller.

Rule 2: No piece of unification in the body of a clause can instantiate a variable in the guard until that clause is selected for commitment.

Rule 3: When there are several clauses of the same head predicate (candidate clauses), the clause whose guard succeeds first is selected for commitment.

Rule 1 is used for synchronization, *Rule 2* guarantees selection of one body for one invocation, and *Rule 3* can be regarded as a sequencing rule for *Rule 2*. Under the above rule, each goal in a given goal clause is reduced to new goals (or null) in parallel.

RETRIEVAL BY UNIFICATION

GHC is capable of handling parallel processes using variable bindings. A process is suspended until pieces of unification succeed or fail. This suspension is important for controlling processes running in parallel. Therefore, it is difficult to retrieve structured data containing variables with GHC. Although unification can be used for retrieving structured data in Prolog, it cannot be used the same way in GHC. If search conditions are checked in the guard part of GHC clauses, the check processes are suspended and not released. If condition checks are performed in the body part of GHC clauses, alternative clauses are never selected. To retrieve the structured data, the features described in the next section, should be added to GHC.

Since the structures in knowledge bases are expected to contain variables, special retrieval functions are required for GHC to operate knowledge bases. Moreover, GHC has no functions to update static data or to control concurrent updates. The functions are related to database operations. We introduced a model and a set of primitive operations on it to retrieve structured data containing variables [13]. The model is called a relational knowledge base. Since the model is based on a relational database model, it is easy to introduce update and concurrency control.

An object handled in a relational knowledge base is a term, a structure constructed from function symbols and variables. The definition of a term is the same as that in first order logic.

(i) 0-place function symbols and variables are terms.

(ii) If f is an n-place function symbols and $t_1,...,t_n$ are terms,
then $f(t_1,...,t_n)$ is a term.

(iii) Terms are generated only by applying the above rules.

Since GHC is based on first order logic, terms can be handled from GHC. A subset of the Cartesian products of term sets is called a term relation.

Operations on term relations are enhanced relational algebra operations. The enhancement is achieved by extending the equality check between items of ordinary relations to a unification between items of term relations. Thus, join and restriction are extended to *unification-join* and *unification-restriction*. These are called *retrieval-by-unification* (RBU) operations [13].

Not only retrieval functions but updating, definition, and other functions are also needed to handle knowledge bases in actual use. The following operations are planned for handling term relations.

- Retrieval
    Unification-join
    Unification-restriction
    Projection
    Union

- Definition
    Create a term relation
    Erase a term relation
    Make an index for an attribute
    Remove the index for an attribute

- Update
    Change items
    Insert tuples
    Delete tuples
    Add tuples

- Miscellaneous
    Count tuples

INTERFACE BETWEEN GHC AND RBU

There are two different aspects in the relationship between the GHC and RBU. As stated above, RBU is used for assisting GHC to retrieve terms as items of knowledge. GHC can control parallel retrieval processes of RBU. This section considers how to connect RBU with GHC to enhance the retrieval function of the PKL. The parallel control mechanism is described in the next section.

To use RBU from GHC, there are two approaches for the interface.

1) Provide built-in predicates for each RBU operation.

2) Provide a built-in predicate and deliver commands to the predicate as incomplete messages.

The difference between these two approaches is not very great. However, when the two systems are built independently, the interface between them in the second approach is simpler than in the first one. Therefore, we plan to use the second approach.

The interface is illustrated using a simple example. The following GHC program (Fig. 1) is an implementation of the Horn logic interpreter. Horn clauses are stored in a term relation named kb1 (Fig. 2), and retrieved by unification-restriction operations. The first attribute of a term relation is used for maintaining variable substitutions for a goal clause, the second for storing the head part of a Horn clause, and the third for storing the body part of the Horn clause.

In this case, the Horn set in kb1 pointed out the parent-ancestor relationship. The term an(x,y) indicates that y is an ancestor of x, and the term pa(x,y) indicates that y is a parent of x.

The following query is given for searching for the ancestor of "a".

```
?- solve(kb1,an(a,X),Result).
```

```
solve(KB,Goal,Result) :- true |
        loop(KB,cmd(C1,C2),[ [[Goal],[Goal]] ],Result),
        rbu(cmd(C1,C2)).
loop(KB,cmd(C1,C2),[]          ,X) :- true    | X = [], C1=C2.
loop(KB,CMD        ,[ [G,R] |L],X) :- R = []  | X = [G|Y],
        loop(KB,CMD,L,Y).
loop(KB,cmd(C1,C3),[ [G,R] |L],X) :- R \= [] |
        C1 = [unification_restriction(KB,[1=G,2=R],[1,3],S)|C2],
        merge(L,S,N),
        loop(KB,cmd(C2,C3),N,X).
```

Fig. 1. Horn Logic Interpreter Written in GHC

kb1			
	G	[an(A,B)|Tail]	[pa(A,B)|Tail]
	G	[an(A,B)|Tail]	[pa(A,C),an(C,B)|Tail]
	G	[pa(a,b)|Tail]	Tail
	G	[pa(b,c)|Tail]	Tail

Fig. 2. Example of a Term Relation

In each stage of iteration of the GHC program, the following RBU commands are generated to search the knowledge base (kb1) for clauses unifiable with the resolvents. The second argument of each item in the stream (Sn) is a resolvent of the resolution, and the first argument indicates the variable bindings for the goal clause corresponding to the resolvent.

Fig. 3 shows execution examples of RBU commands. Since S2 and S5 contain empty clauses as the resolvents, an(a,b) and an(a,c) are the answers of the query.

These iteration processes and retrieval processes can execute in parallel if the stream is long enough. That is to say, the system

```
unification_restriction(kb1,[1=[an(a,X)],2=[an(a,X)]],[1,3],S1)
   S1 = [[[an(a,X)],[pa(a,X)]],[[an(a,X)],[pa(a,C),an(C,X)]]]
unification_restriction(kb1,[1=[an(a,X)],2=[pa(a,X)]],[1,3],S2)
   S2 = [[[an(a,b)],[]]]
unification_restriction(kb1,[1=[an(a,X)],2=[pa(a,C),an(C,X)]],[1,3],S3)
   S3 = [[[an(a,X)],[an(b,X)]]]
unification_restriction(kb1, [1=[an(a,X)],2=[an(b,X)]],[1,3],S4)
   S4 = [[[an(a,X)],[pa(b,X)]],[[an(a,X)],[pa(b,C),an(C,X)]]]
unification_restriction(kb1,[1=[an(a,X)],2=[pa(b,X)]],[1,3],S5)
   S5 = [[[an(a,c)],[]]]
unification_restriction(kb1,[1=[an(a,X)],2=[pa(b,C),an(C,X)]],[1,3],S6)
   S6 = [[[an(a,X)],[an(c,X)]]]
unification_restriction(kb1,[1=[an(a,X)],2=[an(c,X)]],[1,3],S7)
   S7 = [[[an(a,X)],[pa(c,X)]],[[an(a,X)],[pa(c,C),an(C,X)]]]
unification_restriction(kb1,[1=[an(a,X)],2=[pa(c,X)]],[1,3],S8)
   S8 = []
unification_restriction(kb1,[1=[an(a,X)],2=[pa(c,C),an(C,X)]],[1,3],S9)
   S9 = []
```

Fig. 3. Execution Examples of RBU Commands

implements the OR parallel Horn logic interpreter. This is an example of RBU usage in GHC. The parallel problem solvers and parallel production systems can be built using GHC and RBU.

PARALLEL CONTROL METHODS OF RETRIEVAL PROCESSES IN GHC

This section consists of three parts. First, it describes three parallel control methods. Each method is considered as parallelism depending on the number of retrieval elements and data division. Then, meta-level control uses three parallel control methods according to the processing conditions. The last part describes the implementation of each method in GHC.

The command from inference elements is the RBU command in section 3, and is called the retrieval process. The RBU command is assigned to retrieval elements by the parallel controller and is processed. Parallel control for retrieval processes is affected by the following parameters: number of available retrieval elements, type of retrieval commands, and size of data to be handled by a command.

Parallel Control Methods and Data Division

Three parallel control methods [14] for retrieval processes are considered. The symbols n and i indicate the total number of retrieval elements and the number of available retrieval elements when the retrieval command is received.

(1) **Data non-division method (method 1):** Each retrieval command is executed by a single element, without data division. The controller receives a command, searches for an available retrieval element, and allocates the received command to its element. This method has a little overhead because of parallel control.

(2) **Data dynamic division method (method 2):** The controller receives a command, and searches for all available retrieval elements. If there are i available retrieval elements, the controller converts the command to i (variable number) sub-commands (if division of data is possible), and allocates it to i retrieval elements. This method has a lot of overhead because of parallel control, status management of retrieval elements, and data division.

24

(3) Data static division method (method 3):   This method is a combination of methods 1 and 2. The controller converts the command to n (fixed number) sub-commands (if division of data is possible). The allocation of sub-commands is much the same as method 1. This method has overhead because of parallel control and data division. The overhead of this method is between those of methods 1 and 2.

Methods 2 and 3 subdivide the grains of a process according to the division of handled data, cut down the free status of elements by using retrieval elements for details, and increase parallelism.

The data division operation of unification restriction is converted to sub-commands and executed. For example, Fig. 4 shows the process (oval) and the flow of data (arrow) performed by the data n division. The symbol L indicates the size of the data to be handled by one command.

In the unification restriction command ($ur(L)$), every ur_i corresponds to the unification restriction process in order to handle $ur_i(L/n)$, and an append corresponds to the append process for data streams after it has been restricted. The unification restriction operation of data n division needs n unification restriction processes and one append process. To remove the append process, a differential list that can partly hold a value is used. (This is a property of logical variables.) In short, the parts of unification restriction processes are fast when the number of divisions is large and an append process does not need execution time using a differential list.

The processes in the data division operations are executed along the stream of data from left to right, as shown in Fig. 4, and parallel processing of every process is possible when every process receives data.

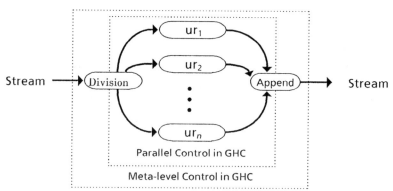

Fig. 4. Data Division Process of Unification Restriction Operation

Meta-level Control

Meta-level control uses three parallel control methods according to the retrieval processing conditions. The meta-level controller is controlled by meta-knowledge which guides the use of retrieval elements toward the best way which is usually synonymous with fast processing. Meta-level control uses meta-knowledge that satisfies the following conditions: state of the waiting queue of commands and type of commands.

First, control according to the state of the waiting queue of commands is described. If there is little traffic in the waiting queue, the meta-level controller will use method 3 because many retrieval elements are available. If there is heavy traffic in the waiting queue and the queue contains unprocessed commands, the controller will use method 1 because few retrieval elements are available. Otherwise, the controller will use method 2 for fine control.

Next, control method by command type is described. Use of the retrieval elements in parallel depends on the command type. For example, term sorting is completed during n phases. In the $i + 1$ phase, $k/2$ retrieval elements are used, whereas in the i phase, k retrieval elements are used. In the next example, unification restriction is completed in only one phase. In this case, all the idle retrieval elements can be used. When the retrieval element controller receives several types of commands at the same time, it is important to use the retrieval elements in high efficiency. All of the above items are also controlled by meta-level control.

Implementation of Methods in GHC

The implementation of each method uses the properties of logic programming, and parallel semantics of GHC and its synchronization mechanism. Each method is written in Flat GHC [9].

Fig. 5 shows the parallel controller with status management for retrieval elements under method 2. The top level predicate 'REscheduler' of the parallel controller receives a stream of RBU commands from inference elements, selects all available retrieval elements, and assigns commands to available retrieval elements. The predicate closeStream informs every retrieval element of the end of a command when a stream of commands is empty. The predicate inspect asks the free or busy status of

```
% Top level
'REscheduler'([C|T],Stream) :- true |
    availableREs(Stream, NS,Free), divide(Free,[C|T],NS).
'REscheduler'([]   ,Stream) :- true | closeStream(Stream).

availableREs(St, NS,Free) :- true |
    inspect(St,NS,Ins), checkingFree(Ins,Free).
% Inspection of REs status
inspect([]                    ,New,Ins) :- true | New=[], Ins=[].
inspect([stream(N,St)|Rest],New,Ins) :- true |
    New=[stream(N,SR)|NR], Ins=[(N,State)|IR],
    St=[ins(State)|SR], inspect(Rest,NR,IR).

divide([] ,C    ,St) :- true    |
    'REscheduler'(C,St).                        % All REs are busy.
divide(REs,[C|T],St) :- REs\=[] |               % send out C to free REs
    division(C, REs, SubC), sendOut(REs,SubC,St,NS),
    'REscheduler'(T,NS).

% 'RE' manages status of REs, SendToRE sends C to Nth RE.
'RE'(N,[term  |Cmd]) :- true | Cmd=[].          % termination
'RE'(N,[ins(C)|Cmd]) :- true |
    C=free, 'RE'(N,Cmd).                        % inspection of status
'RE'(N,[cmd(C)|Cmd]) :- true |                  % retrieval command
    sendToRE(N,C,Res), response(Res,Cmd,Next), 'RE'(N,Next).

response(end,Cmd        ,N) :- true | Cmd=N. % Process ends.
response(R   ,[ins(C)|Cmd],N) :- true | C=busy,response(R,Cmd,N).
```

Fig. 5. Parallel Controller with Status Management

every retrieval element. The predicate **checkingFree** searches for the number of available retrieval elements, and selects the available retrieval elements.

The predicate **division** generates sub-commands (third argument) by dividing the data of the command (first argument) by the number of available retrieval elements (the second argument indicates the list of retrieval elements). The predicate **sendOut** assigns sub-commands (first argument) to retrieval elements (second argument). The predicate **'RE'** handles commands from inference elements, and manages the status for retrieval elements. Arguments of the predicate **'RE'** indicate the number of elements and the stream of commands.

The predicate **sendToRE** issues a command to a retrieval element which is appointed by the first argument. This predicate instantiates the third argument to the atom **end** when a process comes to an end. If the predicate **response** receives the command **ins(C)** for an inspection of

```
metaControl([] ,                        ST, REs) :- true |
      closeStream(ST).
metaControl([cmd(C,Type,Size)|Rest], ST, REs) :- true |
      availableREs(ST, IS, Free),
      strategy(C,Type,Size,Free, Method),
      solve(Method, REs, Free, cmd(C), IS, NS),
      metaControl(REs, Rest,NewST).
solve(method1, REs, Free, C, ST, NS) :- true |
      selectRE(Free,RE), sendOut([C],[RE],ST,NS).
solve(method2, REs, Free, C, ST, NS) :- true |
      division(C,Free,SubC), sendOut(SubC,Free,ST,NS).
solve(method3, REs, Free, C, ST, NS) :- true |
      division(C,REs, SubC), sendOut(SubC,Free,ST,NS).
```

Fig. 6. Part of Program for Meta-level Control

status when an element is busy, then the atom **busy** is returned, otherwise, the atom **free** is returned by the predicate '**RE**'.

Fig. 6 shows the part of the program for meta-level control. The top level of the meta-level controller uses the predicate **metaControl** instead of the predicate '**REscheduler**' in Fig. 5. The predicate **metaControl** uses three control methods according to retrieval element conditions, command type, and the size of the data to be handled by the command. This predicate receives commands with several items of information, searches for any available retrieval elements (**availableREs**), selects the best control method from among all the methods (**strategy**), processes the command by this method (**solve**), and repeats this processing.

KNOWLEDGE BASE MACHINE MODEL

The knowledge base machine model is shown in Figs. 7 and 8.

The upper network and clusters (CLs) are also being researched and developed for a parallel inference mechanism (PIM). The PIM will be composed of about 100 CLs, each CL with about 10 processing elements.

The KBM is composed of a PIM, retrieval elements (REs), and a global shared memory (GSM). The number of REs is about one tenth of the number of CLs. Each CL has a local shared memory (LSM) for its PEs, and has a GSM connected with the lower network and REs for PEs in other CLs. The KBM has a hierarchical shared memory composed of LSM and GSM.

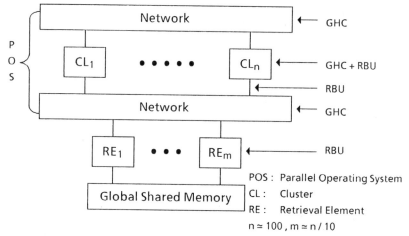

Fig. 7. Ideal Model of Knowledge Base Machine

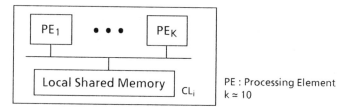

Fig. 8. Ideal Model of Inference Element Cluster

The RE receives the retrieval commands given in section 4 from CLs through the lower network. In the lower network, the destination REs of retrieval commands should be dynamically determined, as described in section 5. For this purpose, the RE parallel control method in GHC needs to be integrated into the lower network. Physically, the upper and lower networks are the same. These networks and CLs are controlled under a single parallel operating system (POS). REs are also controlled in parallel as KBM classes under the POS.

When the RE receives a retrieval command, it starts to access the global shared memory. The sets of retrieved knowledge stream into the RE. While the pairs of sets of knowledge flow into the RE, the RE sorts the knowledge in the generality defined in unifiability and detects any pairs that are unifiable. The unifiable sets of pairs are unified in a pipelined way and are sent to CLs as the response of retrieval commands [8]. The stream flowing into the RE has an affinity with the definition of the data stream in GHC.

The GSM is composed of a number of memory banks. Each bank has ports for reading and writing knowledge stored in logical page size. A logical page lies across all the banks. Each port connected to the bank can access the same page. Then the GSM mechanism permits REs to be accessed in the same logical domain at the same time [6, 15].

CONCLUSION

This paper described a knowledge base machine model based on a parallel kernel language(PKL). For the PKL, GHC has been introduced and for the knowledge base model, a term relation and its operations, named RBU, has also been introduced. We combined RBU and GHC with built-in predicates so that all solution collecting feature required in RBU were realized in GHC, which has only a don't care nondeterministic feature. The parallel control feature of GHC is effectively used for the retrieval elements, and the data-stream manipulation method has an affinity with the definition of data-stream in GHC introduced in the retrieval element. The knowledge base machine and parallel inference machine will be integrated into an FGCS prototype in the final stage of the project. To realize this aim, we accumulated technologies through research and development of a relational database machine (DELTA) in the initial stage, and a deductive database machine (PHI) based on the PSI and an experimental multi-port page shared memory mechanism in the intermediate stage. Applying these technologies, we have started to develop an experimental KBM in a parallel kernel language.

The basic functions introduced in this FGCS have been evaluated by developing some applications on it.

ACKNOWLEDGEMENTS

We would like to thank Dr. Fuchi, the director of ICOT, who contributed many useful suggestions for this research and development. We also wish to thank the members of the KBM working group and the people in industry who participated in joint research programs for their helpful discussions. We also extend our thanks to Dr. Furukawa and Dr. Uchida for their valuable comments on the KBM project.

REFERENCES

[1] K. Fuchi, "Revisiting Original Philosophy of Fifth Generation Computer Systems Project," in *Proc. of the International Conference on Fifth Generation Computer Systems*, ICOT, 1984

[2] T. Chikayama, "Unique Features of ESP," in *Proc. of the International Conference on Fifth Generation Computer Systems*, pp.292-298, ICOT, 1984

[3] M. Yokota, A. Yamamoto, et al., "The Design and Implementation of a Personal Sequential Inference Machine: PSI," *New Generation Computing*, Vol.1, pp.125-144, Ohmsha, 1984

[4] K. Murakami, et al., "A Relational Database Machine: First Step to Knowledge Base Machine," in *Proc. of 10th Annual International Symposium on Computer Architecture*, 1983

[5] M. Wada, Y. Morita, et al., "A Superimposed Code Scheme for Deductive Databases," in *Proc. of the 5th International Workshop on Database Machines*, Oct. 1987

[6] Y. Tanaka, "A Multiport Page-Memory Architecture and a Multiport Disk-Cache System," *New Generation Computing*, Vol. 2, pp. 241-260, Ohmsha, Feb. 1984

[7] H. Sakai, et al., "A Simulation Study of a Knowledge Base Machine Architecture," in *Proc. of the 5th International Workshop on Database Machines*, Oct. 1987

[8] Y. Morita, H. Yokota, et al., "Retrieval-by-Unification on a Relational Knowledge Base Model," in *Proc. of the 12th International Conference on VLDB*, Aug. 1986

[9] K. Ueda, "Guarded Horn Clauses," *Logic Programming '85*, E. Wada (ed). Lecture Notes in Computer Science 221, Springer-Verlag, 1986

[10] K. Clark, S. Gregory, "A Relational Language for Parallel Programming," in *Proc. ACM Conference on Functional Programming Languages and Computer Architecture*, pp.171-178, ACM, 1981

[11] E. Y. Shapiro, "A Subset of Concurrent Prolog and Its Interpreter," Technical Report TR-003, ICOT, 1983

[12] K. Clark, S. Gregory, "PARLOG: Parallel Logic Programming in Logic," Research Report DOC 84/4, Dept. of Computing, Imperial College of Science and Technology, 1984

[13] H. Yokota, H. Itoh, "A Model and an Architecture for a Relational Knowledge Base," in *Proc. of the 13th International Symposium on Computer Architecture*, pp.2-9, June 1986

[14] H. Itoh, C. Sakama, et al., "Parallel Control Techniques for Dedicated Relational Database Engines," in *Proc. of 3rd International Conference on Data Engineering*, 1987

[15] H. Monoi, et al., "Parallel Control Technique and Performance of an MPPM Knowledge Base Machine," Technical Report TR-284, ICOT, 1987

KEV – A Kernel for Bubba

W. Kevin Wilkinson†
Bell Communications Research
435 South St.
Morristown, NJ 07960

Haran Boral
MCC
3500 West Balcones Center Dr.
Austin, Tx 78759

Abstract

Bubba is a parallel database machine under development at MCC. This paper describes KEV, Bubba's Operating System kernel. After a brief overview of Bubba a set of requirements for KEV is presented. Our requirements are contrasted with the requirements for conventional, uniprocessor database systems as outlined by Gray, Stonebraker and others. The KEV design is then presented and its features are compared to other distributed operating systems.

INTRODUCTION

Operating systems provide users with basic resource management services. These services range from memory management, task management, and file systems to synchronization and consistency. In his ground–breaking "Notes on Database Operating Systems", Gray [1] relates the needs of data managers to some of these services by providing a detailed review of concurrency control and crash recovery protocols. He also makes a number of comments concerning time and space costs of certain services provided by general–purpose operating systems. Gray's message is that whether one chooses to use an existing operating system or design and build a new one, care must be taken to ensure that certain low–level services are provided efficiently for a data management application.

Based on his Ingres [2] implementation experience, Stonebraker [3] catalogs problems in the services provided by Unix [4] in each of five major areas: buffer management, file system, task management and scheduling, inter–process communication, and consistency management. Stonebraker's message is that, due to their generality, current operating systems do not provide the appropriate services. Real time OS's which provide minimal facilities efficiently are much better suited for use by data management systems.

A substantiation of sorts for this argument is the Britton–Lee IDM–500 back–end database machine [5,6]. The IDM–500, without the database accelerator, runs on a Z8000; yet in benchmarks, it performed quite well when compared with Ingres running on a Vax 11/750 [7]. The IDM's performance was limited not only by the relatively slow processor but also by the slow communications link between it and the host computer. Thus, its relatively "good" performance is, at least partially, due to the poor performance of Ingres which had to use a general–purpose OS (VMS in this case).††

Additional evidence to support this argument is provided by a study carried out by Hagmann and Ferrari [8] in which they compared alternative decompositions of Ingres across a front–end computer and a back–end computer. They conclude that a back–end should not run under a standard operating system. Instead a streamlined implementation of the necessary functionality should be provided.

The IDM–500 is evidence that special–purpose OS's can substantially improve performance for limited application domains. Based on this and other work [9], we feel that special

---

†Work was done while author was visiting with the Database Program at MCC.

††The implicit and highly subjective assumption underlying our argument is that the code of Ingres and the IDM–500 is roughly of the same quality.

OS's can improve system performance 2–4 times over a general–purpose OS's. Our work is an attempt to extend this result to a highly parallel environment. We are building a high performance database machine, called Bubba. Bubba differs from other database systems in many aspects and thus places a different set of requirements on the OS. Although there exist many distributed operating systems, each of which has something to offer, we feel none is suitable because Bubba's environment is substantially different. Further it will evolve as a result of experimentation. For maximum flexibility, we chose to design our own operating system rather than use an existing one.

In this paper we describe the requirements for an OS kernel in our environment and the resulting design. Most of the ideas described are not new when examined individually. The integrated ideas represent something new. Preliminary data from the two implementations of our kernel, KEV, and its usage indicate that we did a good job but more data is required for a real evaluation. We expect to change KEV as a result of further evaluation so the reader should keep in mind that KEV's design is evolving, and this paper presents a recent snapshot of the design. The paper is organized as follows. We first review previous work on the relationship between database managers and operating systems. Next we provide an overview of those Bubba features relevant to this discussion. An overview of KEV, as defined and implemented at this time is then given. We conclude with status and plans.

OPERATING SYSTEMS FOR DATABASE MANAGEMENT SYSTEMS

In this section, we state a number of design principles for database operating systems. These are based on a review of previous work in the area. Our discussion is organized as a list of topics. This list was freely plagiarized from [3] which addressed five major areas: buffer management, file system, task management, IPC, and consistency.

Buffer Management

The main question here is how much of the buffer manager should be pushed into the operating system. The consensus seems to be very little because the OS does not have knowledge of the complex algorithms used by the DBMS. For example, Stonebraker [3] states that 4 access patterns are found in most DBMS's: random/sequential vs. repeated access/accessed once. Most OS's have a single page replacement strategy so they cannot provide good performance for each type of access (see Chou and DeWitt [10] for a study of this relationship). Traiger [11] points out that when the DBMS uses write–ahead logging for recovery, either the OS must do the logging or the OS must check with the DBMS before freeing buffers. This is because a modified data buffer cannot be released until its log records have been written and the OS has no knowledge of logging activity.

Typically, the DBMS is forced to implement its own buffer manager on top of the OS memory manager (usually a page manager). For performance, the DBMS buffer manager imposes some requirements on the OS service. In particular, it needs the ability to fix buffers in memory. Otherwise, unexpected page faults will result in convoys when the blocked task is holding a critical resource [12]. An explicit unfix operation is also required. The DBMS also requires the ability to share pages among processes, for example, the lock table and data dictionary information.

File System

The major issue here is the nature of the interface between the DBMS and the disk service provided by the OS. Most DBMS's prefer a block interface which corresponds to the unit of transfer between disk and main memory. Also, the DBMS needs some control over block placement to ensure that use can be made of locality patterns inherent in applications. Usually, there is a simple mapping from block address to disk address so "close" addresses implies physical locality. The DBMS requires basic read/write service for blocks. For correctness, the write operation must have a synchronous option, i.e. control is not returned until the block is written to its correct location on disk. This is required for recovery, since, the DBMS must know when certain blocks are written. For performance, the read operation should have an asynchronous option and/or support prefetching. This is useful so the DBMS can provide good performance for sequential access.

Often, to simplify implementation, a DBMS will use the file system provided by the OS. This leads to several inefficiencies. Among these are loss of control over locality, double buffering between the file system and the DBMS and additional software and overhead to map between the file system interface (records/characters) and the blocks of the DBMS. Generally, use of the OS file system for a production DBMS seems to be a bad idea. Traiger [11], looked at using virtual memory management techniques to implement memory-mapped I/O for a DBMS. He concluded that this approach, while elegant, required adding functionality to the OS memory manager in order to support DBMS recovery services (as described above).

Process Management and Scheduling

The problem here is implementing concurrent transactions in the DBMS. Since the DBMS is a subsystem on top of the OS, it depends on the process facilities and scheduling provided by the OS. Using these, it must support concurrent transactions. If the basic OS facilities are inadequate, the result is an inefficient system. The simplest approach to implementing concurrency is to create a separate process for each transaction. Thus, each transaction runs in a protected address space and the DBMS code is simpler because it is single threaded. There is a big performance penalty, however, since the processes do not share buffers and system tables. The other extreme is to have a single DBMS process that has its own process notion and scheduler, in effect, a small operating system within the DBMS process. This has better performance but is much more complicated and a transaction is not protected from maliciousness or errors in other transactions. Stonebraker [3] discussed these approaches.

What are needed are process facilities that combine the simplicity of the first approach with the performance of the second. Thus, processes should be able to share memory, both code and buffer space.† In addition, there should be synchronization primitives to coordinate access to the shared space, e.g. semaphores. The DBMS must have some control over scheduling of processes. For example, processes in critical sections should not be preempted and processes waiting for locks should be made runnable. Also, the DBMS should be able to change the priority of a process as run–time conditions dictate. Context switches among the "light–weight" processes (which really represent transactions) should be very fast.

Whatever the process structure, Gray [1] points out that the OS should allow the DBMS to participate in "major system events". These include system shutdown and restart, dynamic reconfiguration, resetting the clock, etc. This permits the DBMS to prepare for such events in order to maintain database consistency.

---

†Of course, a process still has protected private space, i.e. stack, local variables, etc.

IPC

For those DBMS's which require inter–process communication, the cost of message passing can have a significant impact on performance. In many systems today, this cost is several thousand instructions which approaches the cost of an I/O. Thus, when deciding how to structure the DBMS, one must be wary of design decisions that simplify programming and reduce I/O at the expense of a "few" extra messages.

The other important consideration for inter–process communication is the choice of the communications protocol. For example, some protocols offer reliable connections between endpoints of communication. This simplifies programming but there is overhead associated with establishing the connection. For a DBMS with static communication channels, this may be a good choice but if the channels change frequently, a connection–less protocol may be appropriate. Some systems offer broadcast or multicast communication primitives which can significantly reduce the number of messages in a system. Systems which provide a send/receive model of communication are preferred over systems with only a remote procedure call mechanism since it is easier to initiate and control parallelism as required for two–phase commit, etc.

AN OVERVIEW OF BUBBA

Bubba is a parallel database machine designed to support a wide variety of applications. Its design incorporates decisions based on application and hardware technology projections for the 1990s.. Many of these assumptions shall remain implicit in the text. However, we emphasize the following: (1) support for a wide variety of applications will be required, (2) fault tolerance is of supreme importance, (3) IPC is more than an order of magnitude faster than disk I/O, (4) RAM is cheap and should be used to offload the cpu using classical time/space tradeoffs (see [13] for an example) but disks are here to stay as the mass storage technology, (5) there will be some amount of stable (non–volatile) RAM available for a "reasonable" cost.

Application programs running on Bubba will vary in their resource requirements – some requiring a small number of disk I/O's and less than a million cpu instructions and others requiring several hundred disk I/O's and on the order of a hundred million cpu instructions.

The interface to Bubba is a programming language designed for data intensive applications called Fad. Fad provides a powerful object model whose constituents are user–defined atomic types, tuples, and sets. An atomic type is a user–defined type, such as integer, string, array, tree, etc. with an associated interface (i.e., an abstract data type). It is the user's responsibility to provide the system with an implementation of the interface.† A tuple is a collection of named objects of arbitrary type (i.e., atomic, tuple or set) whereas a set is a collection of unnamed objects also of arbitrary types. A database is a tuple of objects. The Fad language is described in [14].

Fad provides a set of operators for object manipulation which is a superset of the relational algebra operators. It also provides the capability for defining and invoking user–supplied functions to manipulate the user–defined atomic data. Finally, Fad provides a number of control operators such as while–do and if–then–else. Thus, because Fad has more func-

---

†Clearly, the methods for the basic types that a programming language provides, such as integer and array, will be predefined for efficiency's sake. Other types, such as tree and date, will have to be defined by the user. This is similar to the ADT facility of RAD [15].

tionality than other database interfaces (e.g., relational languages) more of an application program can be off-loaded to the database system.

Bubba itself is made up of a large number of autonomous nodes which communicate via a high-speed interconnection device. A node has some processing capability, buffers and mass storage capability. Our goal is to make the nodes as small as practical in order to maximize the number of nodes and increase parallelism. As a side benefit, having many nodes reduces the performance impact of individual node failures.

A given data set is placed across many such nodes. Programs are decomposed into fragments such that each fragment runs on a given node. The idea is to bring the programs to the data rather than the data to the programs as is done traditionally. Transaction execution follows a data-flow strategy: a node begins execution of an operator as soon as enough of the needed data is available. Results are sent to nodes responsible for executing the subsequent operator. A given transaction is thus executed on multiple nodes. The degree of parallelism in executing a transaction as well as that for an individual Fad operation is controlled in two ways: the degree of data distribution (i.e., how many nodes store a fragment of a data set) and the granularity of pipelining between operators. We expect to see a wide variation in the number of nodes that participate in the execution of an application program; some applications will be serviced by a few nodes whereas others will require the services of several dozen.

Within a node, execution is based on the workspace model: a transaction's updates are temporarily stored in a private workspace. The changes become permanent at commit time and are migrated to disk in the background. This scheme makes use of stable RAM (see our technology assumptions). The concurrency control scheme allows for any protocol internal to a node but requires a transaction to execute a global validation step as part of the commit procedure.

The storage manager provides the notion of extents: a sequence of blocks in "physical proximity" to each other. The task structure is static; there is a handful of task types in Bubba. Several instantiations of a given task type may run on a node at a given instance. Several of the tasks running in a node require access to common data structures.

Since Fad supports user-defined abstract data types, some of the code in Bubba cannot be trusted, specifically, the user-supplied code that implements the abstract data types.

4 KEV† OVERVIEW

Design Considerations

Initially, it was expected that Bubba would use an existing operating system. We did not consider any of the vendor-supplied operating systems as viable alternatives. Using such a system would have saved the cost of implementing an operating system but would have tied the project to a single vendor for both hardware and software modifications. This was viewed as risky since the project was still at a very immature stage where requirements and design changes were likely to be frequent.

In contrast to the vendor-supplied systems, kernel work done at research organizations is more available. However, after some debate, it was decided to start a new design. A primary reason is the aggressive experimentation schedule called for several iterations of the

---

† KEV – Kernel for Experimental Vehicles. Bubba research prototypes are known as experimental vehicles.

system over a number of years. Thus, the effort to acquire and port any kernel to the various hardware environments would have required intimate familiarity with the chosen kernel. And many of the academic systems are research projects in their own right. They are changing and contain features and services not relevant to Bubba and not necessarily proven useful. Since we were forced into a situation requiring operating system expertise, the fastest and most flexible solution was to design something tailored to the Bubba environment.

A number of considerations influenced the KEV design. From the beginning, we decided to sacrifice functionality and generality for performance. This is in line with the recommendations in [3] and [1]. Ease of implementation was also important in that our plans call for a series of implementations, each more sophisticated (both in terms of software and hardware) and each necessitating a port of KEV on new hardware.

These considerations led to KEV becoming an amalgamation of ideas borrowed from other distributed operating systems and enhanced with features specific to the Bubba environment. Our philosophy was to provide a basic set of primitives leaving as much control as possible to the kernel user, i.e. higher layers in Bubba. High–level services such as transaction management or file systems were left out of the kernel with the intention of revisiting the decision after the system was up and running, instrumentation data became available and the software better understood. The primary contribution of KEV is not innovative features but rather in synthesizing ideas and tailoring them to a database environment. Below, we present the KEV interface in terms of its tasking, memory management, communication and exception handling facilities. We compare its features to those of other distributed operating systems. We will collectively reference them here and then refer to the systems by name in the text: Accent [16] [17], JASMIN [18] [19], Mach [20] [17], Meglos [21] [22] NOSE [23], V–Kernel [24] [25], Unix BSD 4.2 [26]. This list of systems is intended to be representative of the state of the art but is not complete.

Tasking

A KEV *task* represents a single thread of control and consists of a stack, private data space, a priority and an identifier. A KEV *clan* consists of one or more tasks that share text and global data space. Conceptually, a clan may be thought of as a "program" with concurrent threads of control. The per–task private space is made inaccessible to other tasks via virtual memory management. Tasks may be created and destroyed dynamically whereas clans are static. Tasks are scheduled non–preemptively, within a priority class.

A clan is used to embody a large body of "indivisible" code. By indivisible, we mean that a clan may not be split across nodes. Thus, tasks may take advantage of the shared global memory in a clan for data transfer. Tasks in different clans communicate only via messages. The message interface hides the interconnect so one task cannot know whether another task in a different clan is on the same processor. The intention is dual: to permit easy reconfiguration of the system by changing the assignment of clans to processors in order to run experiments; and, to provide a degree of isolation for fault tolerance reasons at the clan level.†

The task identifier is unique only within the clan. KEV users may take advantage of this by using the same task identifier for all components of the transaction at the various nodes.

---

† The choice of a clan rather than a task as the unit of isolation is dictated by efficiency concerns; task communication is through shared memory synchronized by locks – an inherently faster mechanism than message passing.

This is similar (albeit simpler and cruder) to the notion of Process Groups in the V Kernel [25]. The per-task private space allows each task to maintain separate context and identity. Conceptually, private space may be thought of as the very bottom of the stack. Since tasks in a clan differ only in their private space and stack, intra-clan task switch time is much faster than switching an entire virtual address space.

As mentioned above, clans are static. The system configuration is determined at boot time by the assignment of clans to processors. We assume there is no need to change this dynamically (except as a result of processor failure – not addressed in this paper). The number of tasks per clan varies with the load. However, to avoid the overhead of creating a task for each new transaction, KEV provides some support for primed tasks. A KEV task can change its identifier. Thus, at initialization time, a clan can create a number of idle server tasks. As requests arrive, they can be assigned to idle tasks which then change their identifier to that of the transaction.

The present implementation supports the following four functions:

id = crtask (entry_pt, task_id, priority, max_pri) – create a new task in the same clan as the invoking task but with its own stack and virtual address space. The new task shares text space and global data space with existing tasks in the clan but is given a separate copy of private space. Execution begins at the specified entry point. The task identifier is returned if crtask succeeds; otherwise, an error code is returned. Max_pri is the highest permissible priority for the task (see chpri below).

chtid (task_id) – change the identifier of the invoking task to the specified value.

chpri (task_id, priority) – change the priority of the identified task to the specified value (the caller may change its own priority). The caller may not assign the task a priority higher than its maximum priority.

rmtask (task_id, exit_code) – terminate a task.

Most distributed operating system kernels support some notion of task (single threading) and provide a way for tasks to cooperate and share data within the boundaries of a larger space (multi-threading). The larger space may be known as a module (JASMIN), team (V-Kernel), task (Mach), clan (KEV); in Nose, all tasks share the entire processor. A distinguishing feature of the systems is whether or not resources are associated with the single-threaded object or the multi-threaded object. Consider address spaces. In the V Kernel, Mach and Nose there is one address space for the entire clan. However, JASMIN and KEV a support separate address space per task. Context switches are correspondingly slower, necessitating modifications to the memory map that corresponds to the stack and the private data space, but a task's memory space is hardware protected.

Another distinguishing feature is whether the clans (modules, teams) are dynamic or static. Since Bubba is a dedicated application and only runs one program, there is no need for dynamic clan creation. This simplifies the kernel and permits certain optimizations, for example, in message routing and memory management.

Memory Management

KEV provides a virtual address space per task but does not implement virtual memory management (i.e. paging or segmentation). It supports dynamic shared space and dynamic private space with a page as the unit of allocation.

The choice of whether or not to provide virtual memory management was controversial. Virtual memory management simplifies programming for the user but adds complexity to the operating system. A primary concern is performance and the disk arm is a potential bottle-neck. Since we really have a dedicated application, we felt the user could do a better job of memory management using ad–hoc techniques than could be provided with a general-purpose algorithm implemented in the kernel. Thus, we decided against virtual memory management. However, we retained the notion of a virtual address space per task. This is needed for protection from other tasks. Recall that Bubba transactions may contain user-supplied code for atomic object manipulation so that tasks running such transactions must be protected from each other.

The dynamic private space provided by KEV is conventional. The user explicitly re-quests and releases a number of contiguous memory pages. Dynamic shared space has a different protocol. The initial request causes space to be allocated in the address space of the calling task and returns an identifier for the space. Other tasks must explicitly request that the shared space be mapped into their virtual address space. Note that the virtual address for the shared space is identical for all tasks. When a task no longer needs the space, it must be explicitly removed from its virtual address space (using *rmaddr*). When all tasks have finished with the space, it must be explicitly released back to the kernel (using *rmpubid*). However, KEV does not deallocate the space immediately. It remains "avail-able" in the free pool until the space is needed. That is the purpose of the identifier. A subsequent request to allocate shared space can use that identifier. KEV checks to see if the space is still available and if so, returns it to the task as if it had never been deallocated. If the space has been reused, KEV allocates new space and a new identifier and returns a status code indicating that the old identifier is invalid.

Although Bubba wants to see a variable length segment as the unit of memory alloca-tion, it was decided that KEV would provide a page level interface. Growable segments must be implemented by allocating a large area of memory and using a user–written routine to manage the space. If this proves to be a problem, primitives to grow and shrink dynamic space can be added to the kernel.

The present implementation supports the following four functions:

addr = crprv (size) – create a private (protected) space of a given size; the present implementation expects size to be number of bytes.

addr = crpub (size, flag, id) – create (or share) a public space of the given size. First check to see if space with the specified id has already been allocated. If so, map it into the address space of the caller. If not, allocate the requested amount of space and return a machine–wide unique identifier in id. Flag is used to indicate whether volatile or non–vola-tile memory is requested.

rmaddr (addr) – Remove the dynamic space containing the specified address from the address space of the caller. If the address is in private space, the physical memory is deallo-cated and returned to the system free pool. If the address is in public space, the space is just removed from the caller's virtual address space (but not deallocated, see rmpubid).

rmpubid (id) – Deallocate the physical memory associated with the identified public space. If the space is still is use by another task, rmpubid fails.

In the present implementation there is no support for non–volatile memory.

Most system provide some technique for managing dynamic space, although not all support both private and shared space. Dynamic private space seems to be more unusual (only because few systems support a virtual address space per task). An unusual feature of KEV shared space is that "deallocated" space may be reused if not yet reallocated.

I/O

A fundamental decision regarding disk service was whether to make the disk driver an integral part of the kernel or to have it as a separate server outside the kernel. Although elegant and flexible, making the driver a separate server means that each disk request requires at least two messages (possibly more, depending on the interface between the driver, disk controller and kernel). It was expected that a kernel call would be less expensive than a message. Also, most, if not all, Bubba nodes will have disks, anyway. So, it was decided to include the disk driver as part of the kernel.

In the present implementation extent management is handled by the database management code. The disk driver provides a block–level interface to the disk. Once we understand extent usage and implementation better we will revisit this decision.

Disk requests may be synchronous or asynchronous (blocking or nonblocking respectively). Completion of asynchronous requests is signaled via a message from the kernel. Disk arm scheduling is currently first–come–first–served but this may change in the future.

The present implementation supports the following four functions:

bread (device_no, block_no, block_cnt, io_buf) – read "block_cnt" physical blocks starting at block number block_no into the specified buffer from device (disk or tape) device_no. It is assumed (i.e. not checked) that the buffer is large enough to hold the disk blocks. The number of blocks actually transferred is returned.

bwrite (device_no, block_no, block_cnt, io_buf) – write "block_cnt" physical blocks starting at block number block_no from the specified buffer into device (disk or tape) device_no. The number of blocks actually transferred is returned.

baread (device_no, block_no, block_cnt, io_buf, port_id) – same as bread except read is asynchronous. When the operation is complete, a completion message is sent to port_id.

bawrite (device_no, block_no, block_cnt, io_buf, port_id) – same as bwrite except write is asynchronous. When the operation is complete, a completion message is sent to port_id.

Supporting extents explicitly in KEV would require incorporating an extent_id parameter into the above calls as well as new calls to allocate and deallocate extents, and blocks within extents. Note that KEV would have control of block placement within an extent.

Most distributed kernels provide no special primitives for disk and tape service. The drivers are accessed via messages as are other servers. NOSE is an exception; it offers explicit disk read/write commands. Mach provides memory–mapped I/O.

Communication

KEV uses a connection–less send/receive model of communication as opposed to the call/return or remote procedure call model. Messages are addressed to a *port* which is a triple: <C#, T#, Q#>, where C# is the destination clan identifier, T# is a task within the clan and Q# is a queue number within that task. Ports are bound to specific operations at compile time. Thus the connection is established, for all intents and purposes, by the compiler. In the present implementation each task has 30 logical message queues, lower numbered queues having highest priority. To receive a message, a task uses a bit mask to indicate the message queues it wants to wait on. In addition, there is a shared message queue for the entire clan from which any task in the clan may remove messages. For example, idle server tasks mentioned previously will wait on this queue for new transaction requests. Messages may be of arbitrary length (up to a limit of 64K bytes).

KEV attempts to minimize the number of times a message is copied in order to reduce the communications overhead. Messages are not double buffered by the kernel. Sending a message blocks the task until the message can be sent to the destination node. The message is then copied directly from the user buffer to the interconnect. On the receiver's side, the message is stored in a kernel buffer until requested by the user. At that time, the buffer containing the message is added to the virtual address space of the user rather than being copied into a user buffer. The disadvantage of this approach (aside from blocking the sender) is that the receiving task must remember to deallocate the receive buffer after it has processed the message. One idea (not implemented presently) to get around this problem, due to Livny [27], is to change the semantics of the recvmsg call to require the receiver to provide KEV with a buffer in return for the one carrying the message. This only works if message sizes are limited to, say, a memory buffer frame size.

A Bubba transaction involves several cooperating tasks, all with the same task identifier (each in a separate clan). This is an ideal situation for multicasting. Multicast messages are sent to a multicast port. Multicast ports are distinguished by a special clan number (the task number and queue number are user–specified). To receive a multicast message, a task provides KEV with a mapping from the multicast port to a local queue for the task. When a multicast message is received at a node by KEV, it is added to the appropriate receive queue for each requesting task. Note, in this case, the message is copied once for each requesting task.

The present implementation supports the following four functions:

crport (port_id, clan, task_id, queue_no) – create a message port identifier. A port_id is a triple, <CLAN#,TID,QNO>, where CLAN# is a clan number (KEV maintains a map of clan #'s to nodes), TID identifies a task running in the clan, and QNO is a queue number for that task. A task may use up to 30 different queues numbered 0 through 29. Note that this is really a macro to fill a data structure. Port identifiers are not protected kernel objects.

gport (gport_id, queue_no) – gport causes any multicast messages sent to gport_id to be received on queue queue_no for the calling task. This is the only way in which multicast messages can be received. The port, gport_id, may only be used in sendmsg. Directly receiving on gport_id is not permitted.

sendmsg (port_id, msg_buf, msg_len, flags) – send a message to the specified port. The requesting task is blocked until the message is received by the destination node (otherwise, the kernel must first copy the message into its own buffer in order to queue it for transmission). The flags parameter is used to specify options such as checking that the destination task exists.

addr = recvmsg (queue_ids, rcv_info, flags) – receive a message on one of the specified queues. The queues are specified with a bit mask in queue_ids. The rcv_info structure contains information such as the sender's identification and task id and the queue number on which the message was received. Note, the message buffer is provided by the kernel, not the user. As such, after the message has been processed, the buffer must be explicitly released by the user via rmaddr. The flags parameter may be used to specify certain options such as not blocking if no messages are pending.

Distributed operating systems widely diverge when it comes to communication facilities. Already mentioned are remote procedure call protocols (V Kernel) as opposed to send/receive (JASMIN, Mach, NOSE). Another difference is that some systems support variable-length messages (Mach, NOSE, Accent) while others (V Kernel, JASMIN) provide only fixed-length (16–32 byte) mini-messages and offer a separate move facility for long data transfers. To minimize the number of times a message is copied, Accent and Mach support a *copy-on-write* optimization. It allows the message sender and receiver to share (unknowingly) the memory segment containing the message. The message is only actually copied when either task attempts to write the memory segment. Other systems could implement this optimization, as well. Interestingly, in Accent and Mach, interprocessor communication is performed by a device driver that runs outside the kernel as a user task.

Most systems provide many-to-one communication, a few support multicast (V Kernel, Meglos) but only Meglos offers an inverse to mulicast called *readall* in which a task receives a single combined menage from a predesignated group of senders. Selective receive (or multiplexed receive, i.e. the ability to wait on a message from more than one receive queue) exists in a few systems (Meglos, JASMIN, ACCENT, Mach). In BSD 4.2, there is separate facility (*select*) to identify which input queues have pending messages; the *receive* primitive works only on a single queue.

Synchronization

Messages can be used for synchronization and many kernels offer no other primitive. However, KEV provides an additional facility, locks, for intra-clan synchronization. While we expect messages to be fast, their intended use is data transfer. When used for synchronization, they incur unnecessarily high overhead. Within a clan, data transfer will be done primarily via shared memory so there is a need for a fast synchronization facility. Locks are created and destroyed dynamically. The only permissible lock modes are exclusive or shared.

The present implementation supports the following four functions:

id = crlock ( ) – create a lock and return its identifier.

setlock (lock_id, mode) – attempt to set a lock in exclusive or share mode. Wait priority is strictly first-come, first-served. It is not possible to upgrade locks, i.e. a share lock request followed by an exclusive lock request from the same task will block that task (unless the share lock was released).

unlock (lock_id) – release the specified lock.

rmlock (lock_id) – delete the specified lock. This call fails if the lock is currently in-use.

Few systems seem to offer synchronization facilities separate from the communication primitive (NOSE is an exception). None offers a high-level primitive, like locks. Originally, KEV provided semaphores but the locking facility described above proved much more useful so it was adopted.

Exception Handling

When a task suffers an exception, KEV sends a message to an exception handler for the task. Each task may define handlers for various types of exceptions and a task inherits the exception handlers of its creator. The handler is actually identified by a port to which the exception message is sent. That port will be read by the handler task which will process the exception (i.e. kill the task, ignore the condition, etc.). The handler normally runs at a higher priority than normal tasks. The list of exceptions includes the usual address error, arithmetic fault, timeout and time slice exceeded as well as major system events such as shutdown.

The present implementation supports the following three functions (exceptions are referred to as signals):

crsignal (signal_ids, port_id, oport_id) – define a handler for the specified signals. The signals are specified in a bit mask. When any one of the exceptions identified by signal_ids occurs, send a message to the port specified by port_id. The current exception handler port, if any, is returned in oport_id. If more than one handler is defined for the list of exceptions, return the handler for the lowest numbered signal. A port_id of zero indicates no handler is defined for the exception. If no handler is defined for an exception, it is ignored.

timeout (timeval) – set a timeout for the task, in milliseconds. The timeout clock starts ticking whenever the task is blocked waiting on a system resource (setlock, recvmsg, bread, etc.) and is reset when the task becomes runnable. As such, it ticks in real time. If it expires, a timeout exception is raised and a message is sent to the signal handler, if any. A timeval of zero means an infinite timeout.

timeslice (timeval) – set a timeslice for the task, in milliseconds. The timeslice clock starts ticking when the task is dispatched and is reset when the task makes a kernel call. As such, it ticks in task virtual time. If it expires, a timeslice exception is raised and a message is sent to the signal handler, if any. A timeval of zero means an infinite timeslice.

Exceptions in the V Kernel are also handled via a message to an exception handler. Note that currently there is no need to handle hardware interrupts. All interrupts are processed by handlers inside the kernel (e.g. disk, message, clock). However, should a need arise for interrupt processing outside the kernel (e.g. software interrupts), we expect that interrupts would be treated as exceptions and the kernel would send a message to a pre–declared handler.

Services

KEV provides the usual utility services such as time–of–day, cpu usage per task, debug printing. A novel feature, however, is that the local time–of–day clocks for all nodes are guaranteed to be relatively synchronized within an implementation–defined constant.

The present implementation supports the following five functions:

time = todclock ( ) – return the current time of day (since the "epoch") in milliseconds.

time = cpuclock ( ) – return the cumulative cpu usage for the current task, in milliseconds.

prints (string) – prints the string on the system console.

prtask ( ) – print a list of all active tasks and the state of all message queues on the system co:isole.

kerr ( ) – return the error code from the previous kernel call.

Note that there are no high level services such as a name server, file server, loader or debugger. Such services can be implemented on top of the kernel and would only be incorporated in the kernel to improve performance.

STATUS

Present

Bubba is being implemented in a number of steps. The initial step provided a functional sanity check of sorts (make sure that things are working properly, that the calls have all the necessary parameters, that all needed functionality is there, etc.). Our current focus is on performance.

Our initial implementation is on a number of Sun workstations each running Unix. Where necessary, performance was sacrificed to get the code running as soon as possible. All Bubba code is written in C and C++ and makes no calls on Unix. All Operating Systems services are provided by KEV. The KEV design underwent a number of minor changes as a result of feedback during the implementation. KEV was implemented in C using the facilities of CSIM [28]. CSIM is a process–oriented simulation package for use with C programs. It provides many of the tasking and synchronization features KEV itself is supposed to provide. The KEV implementation, using CSIM, is about 3,000 lines of C code.

The value in using CSIM as an implementation base was twofold. First, it permitted a quick implementation. This was important both to make the kernel available to Bubba programmers and also to check out the functionality. It was easy to experiment with even major changes in the KEV interface. The second reason for using CSIM was to assist in instrumenting the code. CSIM can model any number of processors, any amount of memory and arbitrary devices. For example, it is a simple matter to estimate CPU usage by accumulating actual CPU usage between successive KEV calls.

Currently the Bubba software is being implemented on a 40 node Flexible Computers Flex/32 (called Seth). Each node on Seth consists of a 68020, 5 MBytes of RAM, and a high performance small disk. Nodes are connected by a bus hierarchy. KEV (as described in this paper) has been operational on Seth for about two months. The implementation has not uncovered design flaws.

Future

There are several problems in the KEV interface as well as details to be worked out ranging from the mundane, such as providing terminal input capability, to the complex and poorly understood, such as clan migration. These issues will be addressed as our understanding of the requirements, through experimentation, increases.

Naturally, we are interested whether KEV is worth the effort we put into it, both in its present form and with the additional functionality outlined in the previous section. We expect to perform extensive instrumentation of KEV and then compare its performance with that of other kernels in particular Mach [20]. We also expect to revisit several of the functions described above, primarily extents and multifetch.

ACKNOWLEDGEMENTS

Members of the Database System Architecture Team at MCC contributed to the KEV design in numerous lively discussions. In particular we wish to acknowledge Setrag Khoshafian and Patrick Valduriez – KEV's first user group. Marc Smith and Ravi Krishnamurthy read an earlier draft of the paper and provided numerous useful comments. Premkumar Uppaluru and Ming–Yee Lai studied early versions of the KEV interface and provided valuable feedback on the interprocess communication and memory management facilities. Lastly, we want to thank Larry Clay who implemented KEV on Seth.

REFERENCES

1. Gray J.N., Report RJ 2188, IBM Res. Ctr., San Jose, Calif., Feb. 1978.
2. Stonebraker M., E. Wong, P. Kreps, G. Held, *ACM TODS,* Vol. 1, No. 3, Sept. 1976.
3. Stonebraker M., *CACM,* Vol. 24, No. 7, July 1981.
4. Ritchie D., K. Thompson, *CACM,* Vol. 17, No. 7, July 1974.
5. Ubell M., *Database Engineering,* Vol. 4, No. 2, Dec. 1981.
6. Nyberg C., in [33].
7. Bitton D., D.J. DeWitt, C. Turbyfill, *Proc. of the Ninth Int'l Conf. on Very Large Databases,* 1983.
8. Hagmann R.B., D. Ferrari, *ACM TODS,* Vol. 11, No. 1, Mar. 1986.
9. Beck, M., Bitton, D., Wilkinson, W.K., to appear in the *IEEE Transactions on Computers,* 1987.
10. Chou H.-T., D.J. DeWitt, *Proc. of the Eleventh Int'l Conf. on Very Large Databases,* 1985.
11. Traiger I., October 1982.
12. Blasgen M., Gray, J., Mitoma, M., Price, T., *Operating Systems Review,* Vol. 13, No. 2, April 1979.
13. Gray J.N., F. Putzolu, Tandem Computers Technical Note, June 1985.
14. Bancilhon F., T. Briggs, S. Khoshafian, P. Valduriez, *Proceedings of the Thirteenth Int'l Conf. on Very Large Databases,* 1987
15. Osborn S.L., T.E. Heaven, "The Design of a Relational Database System with Abstract Types for Domains," *ACM TODS,* Vol. 11, No. 3, Sept. 1986.
16. Rashid R.F., G. Robinson, *Proc. 8th Symposium on Operating Systems Principles,* Dec. 1981.
17. Rashid R.F., *1986 Proc. Fall Joint Computer Conference,* Nov. 1986.
18. Lee H., U. Premkumar, Bell Communications Research Technical Memo, TM-ARH–000324, October 1984.
19. Wilkinson W.K., M.-Y. Lai, in [29].
20. Accetta, M., R. Baron, W. Bolosky, D. Golub, R.F. Rashid, A. Tevanian, M. Young, *Proc. of the USENIX Conference,* Atlanta, Ga., Summer, 1986.
21. Gaglianello R.D., H.P. Katseff, *Proc. 5th Int'l Conf. on Distributed Computer Systems,* May 1985.
22. Gaglianello R.D., H.P. Katseff, *Software Practice & Experience,* Vol. 16, No. 10, Oct. 1986.
23. DeWitt D.J., Personal Note, 1986.
24. Cheriton D., W. Zwaenepoel, *Proc. 9h Symposium on Operating Systems Principles,* Oct. 1983.
25. Cheriton D., W. Zwaenepoel, *ACM TOCS,* Vol. 3, No. 2, May 1985.
26. Sechrest S., EECS Report No. UCB/CSD 84/191, University of California–Berkeley, June 1984.
27. Livny M. – Personal Message, September 1986.
28. Schwetman H., *Proceedings 1986 Winter Simulation Conference,* Dec. 1986.
29. *IEEE Computer Society Bulletin on Database Engineering,* Vol. 9, No. 4, December 1986.

II Database Machines

IDP - A Main Storage Based Vector Database Processor -

Keiji Kojima, Shun'ichi Torii, Seiichi Yoshizumi

Central Research Laboratory, Hitachi Ltd., Kokubunji, Tokyo, Japan

ABSTRACT

A new relational database machine called an Integrated Database Processor (IDP) is presented. IDP is a main storage based database machine attached to the CPU of a general purpose computer. A database stored in a secondary storage area is dynamically rearranged into a simple vector form and placed in main storage. IDP collectively processes this vectorized database in a pipelined manner. Architecturally, IDP is regarded as an extension of a conventional pipelined vector processor. Using the extended facilities, important primitive functions in relational operations such as searching, sorting, joining, and set operations, to which conventional vector processors are difficult to apply, can be vectorized. According to measurement, IDP is more than 10 times faster than a corresponding scalar program. In this paper, we describe the design concept, architecture, hardware implementation, and performance evaluation of IDP.

1. Introduction

Relational databases have attracted wide interest in the database management community because of their plain, logical structure. Their declarative query language enables end-users to handle databases for themselves. However, Relational Database Management Systems (RDBMSs) perform poorly, which is an obstacle to their wide use.

Aiming at drastic performance improvements, database machines have been actively studied and developed for the last decade[HSIA80]. Although many researcher efforts are nearing practical use, some problems still remain. The most difficult is called the I/O bottleneck problem. Query processing in database machines tends to be I/O bound because the I/O bandwidth of disk drives are too narrow in comparison with CPU performance. Without solving this problem, powerful engines cannot be brought fully into play. Two strategies are promising, as suggested in [BORA83], for improving the I/O bandwidth. One is a parallel access of many small disk drives. Several database machines based on this idea have been proposed and implemented. GRACE [KITS83], DBC/1012 [TERA83], and GAMMA [DEWI86] are existing examples.

Another idea is the use of a large semiconductor memory, for instance, *main storage* [DEWI84]. This approach becomes very practicable due to the enormous advances in VLSI technology. In the attempt to utilize a large main storage, we have proposed a new relational database system architecture based on a vector processing method [TORI87]. In this method, necessary columns of relations are rearranged into simple vector form and

47

placed in a large main storage. Queries are processed by operating on these vectors directly. Owing to the wide bandwidth of main storage, the pipelined vector processing, which is well known by the success of supercomputers, can be efficiently applied to improve the vectorized column operation performance.

Important primitives in relational operations such as searching, sorting, and joining, however, cannot be vectorized by conventional pipelined vecotor processors, which are specialized for numerical computations. In order to vectorize these primitives, a new vector processor called *Integrated Database Processor (IDP)* was developed. IDP is a commercial product which was placed on the market at the end of 1986. It is optional hardware of Hitachi's general purpose computer, M-680H.

In this paper, the design concept, architecture, hardware implementation, and performance evaluation of IDP are described. In Section 2, basic concepts in the vectorized RDBMS are introduced. How a large main storage with a vector processor is utilized in query processing is outlined. In Section 3, the architecture of IDP is presented. We focus on the correspondence between relational primitives and IDP instructions. In Section 4, the hardware implementation is described. In section 5, results of the performance evaluation are described and discussed. Conclusions are described in Section 6.

2. Basic concepts
2.1 Granule size problem

In physical data structures of conventional RDBMSs , logical data in a table are divided into pages, usually of fixed length blocks, and are placed on disks. Data elements are stored in rows in a consecutive area of the same page (for example, in System R[DATE81]). A unit of processing is also a row, that is, each program module is designed to operate only on a single row, and processing proceeds row by row in a sequential way. Therefore, a row is the granule of processing in conventional commercial RDBMSs.

The advantages of row-wise processing are :

(1) For databases of any size, processing can be accomplished using only a few pages of main storage.

(2) For requesting access to some part of the database, only the related part needs to be accessed from the disks if the appropriate indices are available. In particular, for applications which access only a few rows at a time, this method gives a high performance.

The following is drawbacks of row-wise processing :

(1) Its pointer-based complex data structure is not suitable for collective processing by specialized hardware.

(2) For processing a heavy load query such as a join, in which a number of rows are needed to be accessed and processed at the same time, row-wise processing shows a poor performance because non-clustered disk accesses occur frequently. In such cases, overhead of miscellaneous processing such as module-calls, which occur at every row processing, is seriously increased. In conventional RDBMSs, as many implementers are aware, the overhead of module-calls cannot be ignored. In fact, the result of an experiment indicates that a commercial RDBMS consumes more than 25% of CPU time for module-calls alone.

In short, a row is the suitable granule when only a few rows are processed, but inadequate one when a number of rows are needed to be processed at a time.

On the other hand, many database machines adopt a larger granule in order to minimize the control overhead. A stream which is considered to be a set of rows [TANA82], is a good example. Systems with such a large granules show a high performance for heavy load queries. For light queries such as a single row fetch, (although their performance has not been closely examined), these systems are disadvantageous compared with conventional systems because the control overhead can no longer be ignored.

A solution to this contradiction is a *dynamic vectorization strategy*. The method is described in the following subsection.

2.2 Dynamic vectorization strategy

The system based on the dynamic vectorization strategy is illustrated in Figure 1. The

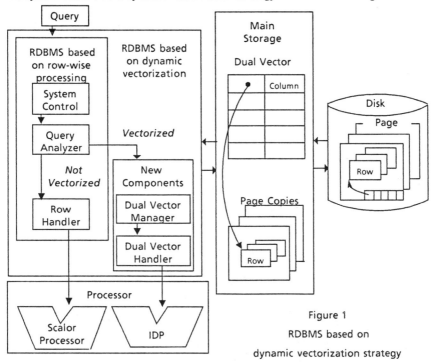

Figure 1
RDBMS based on
dynamic vectorization strategy

strategy is characterized as follows :

(1) Databases on disks are stored in the same format as conventional RDBMSs.

(2) Databases in main storage have two types of format. One is a copy of a disk page. The second is a vector of column data. The structure of the column vector is called a *dual vector*. Each element of a dual vector consists of a front and rear part. The usage of a dual vector is explained in the next section. In Figure 1, the pointer to row data is stored in the front part. The column value to be processed is stored in the rear part.

(3) The system analizes a query and judges which granule, a row or a column, is advantageous. When a row is selected as the granule, the query is processed by conventional row-wise processing. Otherwise, the column vectors are dynamically generated and collectively processed using IDP.

The best way to explain the method is to outline the query processing example. The sample query is expressed in the following SEQUEL-like command[CHAM74] :

SELECT PARTNAME, CODEA, MAKER,
    PRICE, TEL FROM A, B WHERE A.CODEA = B.CODEB.

The points listed below outline the dynamic vectorization strategy and are diagrammed in Figure 2.

(1) Dynamic vector generation.

    (a) A dual vector is built for each table, where the identification number of every row (row ID) is its rear part. The front part is empty and is filled later. Each unique row ID consists of a page number and a slot number.

    (b) For each record, the main storage address is calculated from the row ID and is stored in the front part of a dual vector.

    (c) For each record, the value of the join column is extracted according to the main storage address (obtained in the previous step) and stored into another dual vector as its rear part. In its front part, the serial number is stored.

    The data organized in conventional pointer structures are dynamically converted to vector form in the above process. This process can be regarded as collective translations from row IDs to their column values.

(2) Sorting.

    Each vector built in (1) (c) is sorted according to the value of the rear part, that is, of the join column.

(3) Joining.

    Two dual vectors, obtained in the previous step, are joined. The result is a pair of serial numbers.

(4) User interface.

    The results are returned using the serial number pairs which were obtained from the joining.Notice that the list of main storage addresses in (1) (b) has already been built .The resulting rows can be easily obtained by referring to this address list, since the serial numbers can be used as pointers for the list.

Merits of the dynamic vectorization strategy are listed below :

(1) It is possible to select the optimum granule size, according to the property of a query.

(2) The vectorized access provides an alternate access path for conventional commercial RDBMSs. In other words, the rich functions of commercial RDBMSs remain.

(3) Compared with the *static vectorization strategy*, which vectorizes all databases previously and fixes them in a main storage, the dynamic vectorization strategy can utilize the main storage more efficiently.

(4) Compared to the method which stores all relations in a *column-wise* style even on disks (for example, see [SHIB84]), no overhead is needed to compose the column values which are used to construct the final resulting rows.

For some applications the columns to be processed are known before the query is issued. In this case, by applying the static vectorization strategy only to the known columns, dynamic vector generation steps can be ommited.

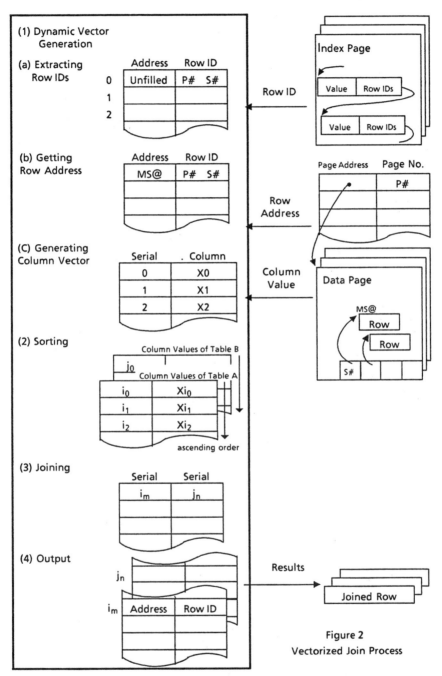

Figure 2
Vectorized Join Process

It should be noticed that the translations from row IDs to column values in (1)(a)-(c) are also carried out in the conventional RDBMS. The only difference occurs during translation . In the dynamic vectorization method, all concerned row IDs are previously translated. On the other hand, in the row-wise processing, each row ID is translated on demand. The time spent in (1)(a)-(c) approximately equals the total time of row ID translations performed in conventional RDBMSs. Therfore, no performance is lost with dynamic vector generation in comparison with conventional row-wise processing.

3. IDP Architecture

First in this section points out problems in applying conventional vector processors to our vectorization method. Second, the IDP architecture is presented as a solution to these problems. Finally, the correspondence between relational primitives and IDP instructions is discussed.

3.1 Problems with conventional vector processors

Vector processors were considered to be special purpose machines for numerical computations. Also, it is known that vector pocessors have a high potential for improving the symbolic computations performance. For instance, some symbolic processing programs were efficiently vectorized [KANA87] using fundamental vector operations (arithmetic/logical operations, move, compare, masked operations, and indirect addressing to vector elements, etc.). For database processing, however, a high vectorization ratio cannot be expected with those fundamental functions alone. Sorting is a good example. While several attempts were made to improve the sorting performance using vector processors, an efficient vectorization method is not known for important practical algorithms whose complexities are O(n log n) [ISHI87].

Architecturally, problems with conventional vector processors are summerized :
(1) Conventional vector operations are performed only between vector elements of the same index. Namely, an A(i)*B(i) type is allowed, but an A(i)*B(j) type is not. However, many popular operations in symbolic processing, such as merge, do not belong to the conventional type.
(2) It is difficult for conventional vector processors to handle flexible data structures. Tagged data, which are frequently used in symbolic processing systems, are especially difficult to represent. For example, records are often sorted by using record identifiers as tag data to key values. In the case of our vectorization strategy, row addresses are considered to be tags of column values as shown in Figure 2.

3.2 Dual vector architecture

In this subsection, the instruction format and instruction set of IDP are described. IDP is an extended vector processor dedicated for database processing. The problems described in the previous subsection are solved in the following way :
(1) IDP instructions allow operations between the vector elements of different indices. For this purpose, all vector operands have their own execution counters which are updated independently.
(2) As a new fundamental data structure, a dual vector is introduced. As we have mentioned in Section 2, each element of a dual vector has two parts, the front and rear. Dual vectors can represent arbitrary binary relations, since front and rear parts can contain different data types. Usually, tag data are stored in the front part, and key data are stored in the rear part. Some applications of dual vectors can be seen in Figure 2.

The instruction set for the IDP is obtained by adding dual vector instructions to conventional vector istructions. In the next subsection, we describe newly added IDP instructions and discuss the correspondence with relational primitives.

3.3 IDP instructions and relational operations

A list of newly added IDP instructions is listed in Table 1. Instructions for sorting,

Table 1. IDP New Instructions

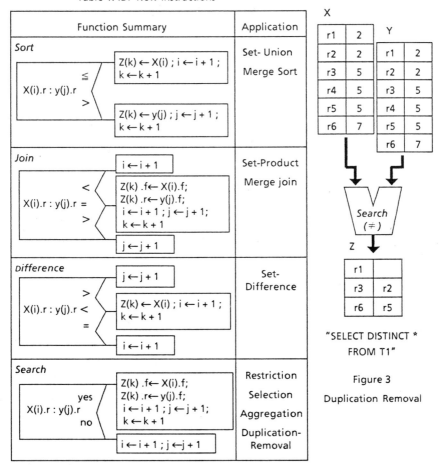

Figure 3
Duplication Removal

searching, and set operations are added. The correspondence between these instructions and relational primitives is as follows :

(1) Selection, Restriction,Sorting, and Joining

IDP instructions correspond to these operations directly. That is, The *Search* instruction corresponds to Selection and Restriction,the *Sort* instruction corresponds to Sorting, and the *Join* instruction corresponds to Joining.

(2) Duplication Removal

The *Search* instruction can be used to remove duplication in the column vector as shown in Figure 3. For removing duplication, we may compare the column vector X to the vector Y. Vector Y is specified by shifting the start address from X at a single element. Provided that X has been sorted, only the head element of each subvector, which has duplicated rear parts, is obtained in the front part of the resulting vector Z. The last elements of the subvectors are obtained in the rear parts of Z.

(3) Aggregation

Aggregation query is processed by a similar method used in duplication removal. Figure 4 shows an example. In Figure 4, we use two conventional vector instructions. One is *Vector Element Increment* instruction which stores $X_i + A_i$ as X_{i+1}. In this case, by assigning 0 to X_1 and 1 to A_i, the instruction stores the serial number in the front part of a working vector V1. Another is *Vector Elementwise Subtract*. The Vector Elementwise Subtract instruction calculates the number of duplicated elements.

As mentioned above, it is necessary to generate column vectors before performing the operations illustrated above. In other words, it is very important to vectorize the dynamic vectorization step itself in order to make the best use of IDP. New instructions shown in Table 1 also suit this purpose [TORI87].

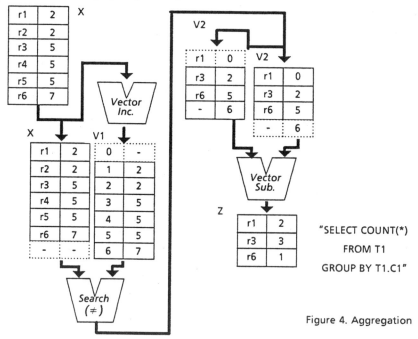

Figure 4. Aggregation

4. IDP hardware implementation

4.1 Design consideration

Database machines are classifed into *stand-alone* type, *backend* type, and *integrated* type depending on the connector interface. Stand-alone machines can independently perform all database jobs. Stand-alone machines can adopt drastic features since there are few design restrictions. However, because of high design costs, all RDBMS facilities cannot be easily supported. Backend machines are connected to host machines through channel paths or communication lines. They receive commands and return data to the host through these lines. Communication overhead is a problem with backend machines. In order to reduce communication overhead, it is necessary to establish a high level interface between the host and backend machine. As the interface level becomes higher, however, the more complicated functions become necessary. This fact also deteriorates the cost effectiveness of backend machines.

As can be seen from its name, IDP is an integrated machine. It is attached to the CPU of a host machine to improve the host machine's performance. We have adopted the integrated machine for the following reasons :

(1) There is little communication overhead.

(2) The designing cost is low compared with stand-alone machines.

(3) The most advanced hardware technologies used in general purpose computers are applicable.

Because integrated machine design depends on the host machine's construction, performance can be restricted by the host machine. First, in the following subsection, firstly, IDP hardware configuration is described briefly. Second, high acceleration ratio through cooperation with the host machine is described.

4.2 Pipelining method

IDP's host machine is Hitachi's general purpose computer, M-680H [WADA85]. Optional hardware called Integrated Array Processor (IAP) [TAKA81], a conventional vector processor, can be attached to the M-680H. The IAP is used when coventional vector instructions are necessary. Vector Element Increment and Vector Elementwise Subtract instructions in Figure 4 are IAP instructions. Implementation of IDP assumes the existence of IAP. Because much of IDP and IAP's basic logic is the same, adding IDP to the M-680H is inexpensive. In fact, the amount of IDP hardware is less than 5% of the M-680H.

Figure 5 shows the hardware configuration of IDP. Memory hierarchy of M-680H consists of three levels, *Buffer Storage (BS)*, *Work Storage (WS)*, and *Main Storage (MS)*. IDP and IAP read their vector elements from BS, the high-speed cache storage. Read/write control logic for vector elements is commonly used in both IAP and IDP. The hardware of IDP and IAP is activated and controlled by firmware stored in the Control Storage of M-680H.

Physically, IDP is a single boad on which 72 LSIs can be installed. Each LSI uses emitter coupled logic containing approximately 2 Kgates. IDP and the host machine use the same hardware technology.

Figure 6 illustrates the pipelined execution of the IDP instruction. The processing of a single element proceeds as follows :

(1) Fetch a request and update the fetch address

(2) Wait for the vector element arrival to IDP

(3) Compare vector elements and update vector counters according to the compare result

(4) Issue a store request and update the store address

Since element processing starts at every cycle, IDP generates the resulting vector element during a single cycle pitch, if execution is not disturbed by the buffer storage miss

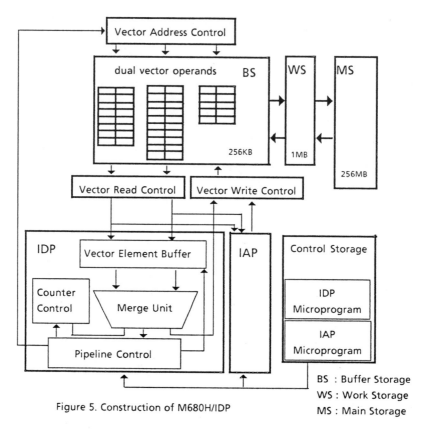

Figure 5. Construction of M680H/IDP

BS : Buffer Storage
WS : Work Storage
MS : Main Storage

hit. The inner loop of the scalar program, which has the same function as IDP, includes about 20 instructions. Consequently, IDP is a maximum of twenty times faster than the corresponding scalar program.

IDP vector element address control is more complicated than conventional vector processors. The next IDP fetch address depends on the compare result of previous element. It should be noted that the timing is late for updating of the next element address in the pipelining method. Figure 6 shows the compare result of the first element controls the seventh element address update instead of the second. Therefore, the second through sixth elements are sent to IDP regardless of compare results. This control delay is solved by the IDP vector element buffer which temporally stores overrun elements.

5. Performance evaluation

In this section, measurement results of performance improvements are described. The pereformance evaluation is devided into two stages. The first stage is an instruction level. As an instance, the performance improvement in sorting was measured. The objective of the evaluation is to measure the IDP acceleration ratio in comparison with optimized scalar programs which employ different algorithms. The relation between vector length and performance is also examined. The second stage is the RDB command level evaluation. By comparing the processing time of test queries between a conventional RDBMS and the

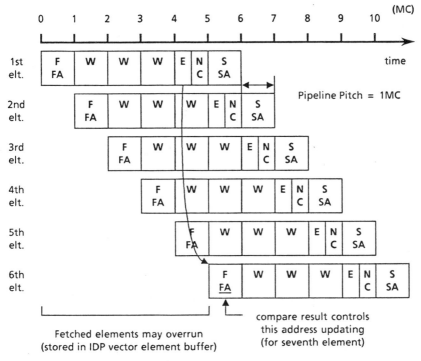

F : to issue fetch request, FA : to update fetch address,
W : to wait arrival of fetched vector element,
N : to get the next element from IDP vector element buffer,
E : Element compare,
C : to update vector counters,
S : to issue store request, SA : to update store address.

Figure 6
IDP pipelining method

new system, the effectiveness of the dynamic vectorization strategy and IDP hardware is demonstrated.

5.1 Instruction level

Figure 7 shows the performance improvement in sorting. The horizontal axis represents the number of records to be sorted. The vertical axis represents the coefficient of n log n, which is the complexity of measured sorting programs. The records are 8 byte long containing a 4 bytes key field. The records are randomly placed before sorting. The performance of IDP is compared with software sort programs such as quicksort and natural merge sort [KNUT73]. As shown in Figure 7, IDP sort is approximately 10 times faster than software sort programs. Notice that IDP performance branches where data length is greater than 10^4. As pointed out, performance degrades when vector length becomes too long for BS or WS. The lower branch shows performance when the long vectors are processed after being divided into cache size subvectors. The upper branch shows the

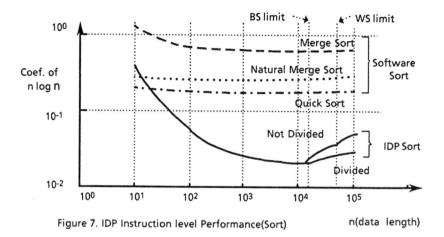

Figure 7. IDP Instruction level Performance(Sort)

performance when long vectors are processed as is. The figure shows that subvectors improve the degradation ratio.

5.2 RDB command level

For command level measurement, a sample database consisting of two relations is used. Each relation contains 6,000 rows. The length of each row is 200 bytes. As a benchmark job, the following 10 commands are used :

(1) Two join queries (join two tables without indices and return 100 rows)

(2) Seven indexed search queries (to fetch 100 rows using the index)

(3) Table scan query (to refer to 6,000 rows in a table without index and return 100 rows)

The CPU time used for processing the above ten queries was measured. The four graphs in Figure 8 shows the measurement results. The first is the total performance improvement accomplished in processing the ten queries. The second through fourth show the performance of each query. Each graph consists of three lines. The first line is the performance of a conventional RDBMS using row-wise processing. The second is the measured performance of an experimental RDBMS prototype using the dynamic vectorization. The prototype was implemented to demonstrate its efficiency [TORI87]. It should be noted that software simulation was used instead of hardware. The simulater was developed to evaluate a larger granule size. The lowest line is the performance of the IDP hardware.

Figure 8 shows the IDP, using dynamic vectorization, is approximately fifteen times faster than the conventional system. In particular, the join command is improved markedly. However, the prototype is inefficient for light load queries such as indexed searching. In indexed searching, vector length is short because candidates have been reduced with indices.

Figure 8 also lists the *vectorization ratios*. This is an important ratio to the strategy because it indicates IDP hadware applicability. The figure shows the total vectorization ratio is 70%. Vectorization ratio is defined as follows :

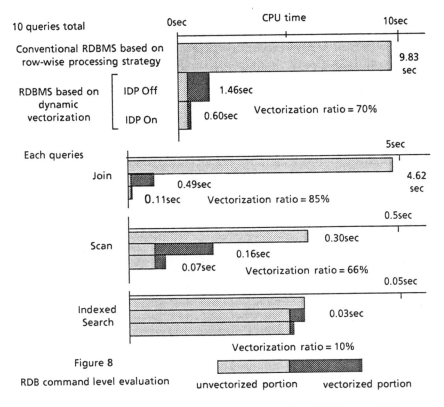

Figure 8
RDB command level evaluation

Vectorization ratio (α) = (Running time of vectorizable part / Total CPU time) ×100
Notice that the running time of the vectorizable part is IDP simulator running time. If β represents the accleration ratio of IDP hardware, performance improvement is given by the following equation.

Performance improvement = 100 / (α/β + 100 - α)

The breakdown of IDP execution time shows that execution of sort instruction accounts for more than 50% of the time [TORI87]. This indicates that accelerating the Sort instruction is crucial for the vectorization method.

6. Conclusion

A main storage based relational database processor called Integrated Database Processor, which adopts dynamic vectorization strategy, is presented. IDP extends conventional concepts of vector processing to symbolic computations.

The perfomance improvement attained by IDP was evaluated. The following results were measured :

(1) The peak execution pitch of IDP is one machine cycle. At instruction level, IDP is approximately 20 times faster than a corresponding software program.

(2) As a sort processor, IDP is approximately 10 times faster than the most efficient software sorting programs.

(3) For heavy load queries such as join, IDP is approximately 15 times faster than RDBMS which adopts conventional row-wise processing.

These results confirm the effectiveness of IDP.

7. Acknowledgement

We gratefully acknowledge Tsuneyo Chiba at Hitachi Central Research Laboratory, Shun Kawabe at Hitachi Kanagawa Works, and Masami Takahashi at Hitachi Software Works, for their continual support and valuable suggestions. We also would like to thank Akinari Watanabe at Hitachi Totsuka Works, Hideo Wada, and Shin'ichi Morita at Hitachi Kanagawa Works, for their help in implementing the IDP hardware.

8. References

[HSIA80] Hsiao, D. K. , "Data Base Computers", in Advances in Computers, Vol.19.

[KITS83] Kitsuregawa, M. et al. "Architecture and Performance of Relational Algebra Machine Grace", University of Tokyo, Technical Report, 1983.

[BORA83] Boral H. and D.J. Dewitt, "Database Machines: An Idea Whose Time has Passed," in Database Machines, edited by H.Leilich and M.Missikoff,Springer-Verlag,Proceedings of the 1983 International Workshop on Database Machines, Munich,1983.

[SHIB84] Shibayama, S. et al. "Query Processing flow on RDBMS Delta's Functionally-Distributed Architecture", Proceedings of International Conference of Fifth Generation Computer Systems, 1984.

[DEWI84] Dewitt,D.J. et al.,"Implementation Techniques for Main Memory Database Systems", Proceedings of 1984 SIGMOD Conference, Boston, MA, June, 1984.

[DEWI86] Dewitt D. J. et al., "GAMMA A High Performance Dataflow Database Machine", University of Wisconsin-Madison, Computer Sciences Technical Report #635 March 1986.

[DATE81] Date,C.J. "An Introduction to Database Systems", 3rd edition, Addison-Wesley, 1981,pp.171-180.

[CHAM74] Chamberlin,D.D. and Boyce, R. F. "SEQUEL : A Structured English Query Language", Proceedings of 1974 ACM SIGMOD Workshop on Data Description, Access and Control, 1974.

[TAKA81] Takanuki, R. et al., "Optimizing FORTRAN 77", Hitachi Review 30, 5, 1981.

[WADA85] Wada, K. et al., "Design for a High Performance Large-Scale General Purpose Computer, The HITACHI M-680H Processor", Proceedings of IEEE International Conference on Computer Design, Oct. 1985.

[ISHI87] Ishiura, N. et al., "Sorting on Vector Processors", Technical Group on computation, COMP86-88(in Japanese).

[TANA82] Tanaka, Y., "A Data Stream Database Machine with Large Capacity", Proceedings of. International Workshop on Database Machines 1982.

[TORI87] Torii S. et al. , "A Database System Architecture Based On A Vector Processing Method", Proceedings of Third International Conference of Data Engineering, Feb. 1987.

[KANA87] Kanada, Y. , "OR-parallel vector processing methods for N-queens - towards high-speed execution of logic programs on vector processors - ", Techinical Group on Programming Language, 87-PL-12 (in Japanese).

[KNUT73] Knuth, D. E., "Searching and Sorting", The Art of Computer Programming, Vol.3, Addison-Wesley, 1973.

JOIN ON A CUBE: ANALYSIS, SIMULATION, AND IMPLEMENTATION

Chaitanya K. Baru, Ophir Frieder[1], Dilip Kandlur, and Mark Segal[2]

Department of Electrical Engineering
and Computer Science
The University of Michigan
Ann Arbor, MI 48109

ABSTRACT

Our recent research effort has been in studying database processing on a cube connected multicomputer system. This paper discusses one part of our work, viz., the study of the join operation. Novel data redistribution operations are employed to improve the performance of the various database operations including join. Though a simple analysis is provided, the data redistribution operations are, in general, difficult to characterize analytically. Thus, a simulation and implementation was carried out to study the performance of these operations and the join operation. Issues involved in the simulation and implementation and a discussion of the results from both are presented in this paper.

1. Introduction

Many specialized database machines (DBM's) have been proposed in the past to solve the problem of efficient processing of moderate to large databases [BAB79, BAN79, DEW79, SCH79, SU79]. More recently there has been interest in studying more general multiprocessor/computer systems to support parallel database processing, as evidenced by [BAR86a, FUS86, HIL86, KIT84, DEW86]. Two paradigms that have evolved for general parallel architectures are, shared-memory and distributed-memory (or message-passing).

---

[1]supported by the IBM Graduate Fellowship, 1986-87. Current address: Bell Communications Research, 435 South St., Morristown, NJ 07960

[2]supported by the Faculty Research Grant, 1986-87, Rackham School of Graduate Studies, the University of Michigan, Ann Arbor, MI.

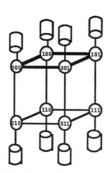
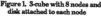

Figure 1. 3-cube with 8 nodes and
disk attached to each node

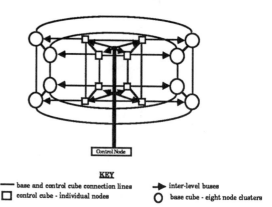

KEY

— base and control cube connection lines	➤ inter-level buses
▢ control cube - individual nodes	◯ base cube - eight node clusters

Figure 2. A 64-node system with corresponding control structure

This paper discusses a part of our recent research effort to study database processing on a specific distributed-memory parallel architecture, viz. the boolean n-cube connected multicomputer system.

This research studies novel dynamic data redistribution operations which improve the performance of the basic relational database operations in a new hypercube-based multicomputer system. A hypercube is an n-dimensional boolean cube, Q_n, defined as the cross-product of the complete graph, K_2, and the (n-1)-dimensional cube, Q_{n-1}. Each node is connected (or adjacent) to each of its $n=\log_2 N$ neighbors, where N is the number of nodes. For example, in a 4-dimensional cube, Q_4, node 0000 is adjacent to nodes 0001, 0010, 0100, and 1000. Figure 1 shows a 3-dimensional cube with a disk attached to each node.

The notion of dynamic data redistribution and algorithms for the various relational database operations in a cube-connected multicomputer system were first introduced in [BAR87]. Some issues related to the system architecture, initial data distribution, and query processing are presented in [FRI87a, FRI87b]. An analytical comparison of the performance of the nested-loop join algorithm between the cube and other recent database machines is available in [FRI87c]. This paper provides an analysis and reports some recent results from simulation and implementation of the join operation in the cube. Section 2 provides a brief overview of the proposed system architecture. An analysis of tuple balancing is provided in Section 3. The simulation is described in Section 4 and the implementation of the join algorithm on a NCUBE computer is given in Section 5. Section 6 provides a discussion of the results obtained from simulation and implementation. Finally, Section 7 is the conclusion.

2. System Architecture

This section describes the architecture of the proposed cube-connected multicomputer system. The overall system architecture, as shown in Figure 2, consists of a hierarchical, cube-controlling-cube structure. The entire database is stored in a *base cube* of dimension, say, $n = \log_2 N$. Nodes in the base cube are logically partitioned into equi-sized subcubes called the *initial storage subcubes, ISS's,* of dimension, say, k. Thus, there are 2^{n-k} ISS's of dimension k in the base cube. All the nodes in each ISS are connected via a bus to an *output collection node , OCN*. Thus, there are 2^{n-k} OCN's in the system. The OCN's themselves are interconnected in the form of a cube of dimension, $n-k$, called the *control cube, CC*. The nodes of the CC are, in turn, connected via a bus to a single *control node, CN*. The CN maintains a system-wide relation directory and implements the global query scheduling policy. It also makes routing decisions for initial and intermediate data within the cube as required by each query. The OCN's support the overlapping of the output collection with result computation. Base relations are contained entirely within an ISS, with the tuples evenly distributed among the nodes. Each database operation is, therefore, performed within an ISS's. Note that the simulation described in section 4 only simulates the functioning of a single ISS in the base cube. Similarly, the implementation on the NCUBE in section 5 represents the functioning of only one ISS and not the entire system as described above.

3. The Join Operation

All database operations that execute on intermediate relations are preceded by *data redistribution* operations which nullify the effects of uneven data distribution across parallel paths. Thus, the database operations themselves are always performed under the optimal condition of even data distribution. The *tuple balancing* operation achieves the objective of even data distribution. The *relation compaction/replication (RCR)* operation is employed to increase the available parallelism in the operation, as described below. Note that the *merging* operation discussed in [BAR87] has been renamed as the RCR operation.

3.1 Tuple Balancing

Tuple balancing is the first data redistribution operation performed preceding a join. This operation takes j steps ($1 <= j <= n = \lg N$). In each step, nodes that differ in address in the jth bit balance tuples of one relation while, simultaneously, nodes that differ in address in the $(j \bmod n)+1)^{th}$ bit balance tuples of a second relation. Nodes exchange their tuple counts, say t_1 and t_2, and the node with the larger number of tuples sends its excess tuples to the other

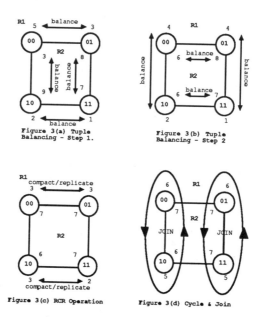

Figure 3(a) Tuple Balancing - Step 1.

Figure 3(b) Tuple Balancing - Step 2

Figure 3(c) RCR Operation

Figure 3(d) Cycle & Join

node. Thus, if $t_2 > t_1$, then the second node sends $t_2-((t_1+t_2)/2)$ or floor$((t_2-t_1)/2)$ tuples to the first. The round-off caused by the floor function can, in the worst case, result in a difference of n tuples between the maximum and minimum tuple counts *after* balancing in an n-dimensional cube, even when the number of tuples is exactly divisible by n. This discrepancy can be avoided in the following way. If the address of the node with the larger number of tuples has even (odd) parity then it sends ceil$((t_2-t_1)/2)$ tuples otherwise it sends floor$((t_2-t_1)/2)$ tuples. Figures 3(a), (b), and (c) show how tuples belonging to two relations can be balanced simultaneously in a 3-cube.

3.2 Relation Compaction/Replication

Tuple balancing is followed by the RCR operation which takes a *maximum* of n stages. In the jth stage, nodes that differ in address in the jth bit are paired together. Each node in a pair combines its tuples with those of its paired partner provided the combined set of tuples fits within a single packet. The operation stops when either any pair of nodes cannot combine tuples without violating this condition or when $j=n$ (i.e. the entire relation has been replicated in each node). The effect of this operation is to *compact* the original relation stored in Q_n into the smallest possible subcube, Q_k, without violating the above condition while, simultaneously, *replicating* the relation in 2^{n-k} Q_k subcubes.

Figure 3(d) shows the effect of the RCR operation on the smaller relation, R1, of Fig. 3(c). In this example, a packet is assumed to have a maximum size of 6 tuples, thus the RCR operation stops after a single step. The global-AND control line which is an AND-ing of local control lines from each node, is used to indicate the termination of RCR. Any pair of nodes that is unable to combine its set of tuples resets its local lines and all other nodes in the cube are intimated about this condition via the global-AND line.

3.3 Tuple Cycling

The actual joining of tuples is performed in the third and final step of the join operation, viz., *cycling*. Here, nodes in each of the 2^{n-k} subcubes communicate in a ring fashion. Tuples of the smaller relation, R1, are sent around the ring (cycled) and each node joins the received set of R1 tuples with its local set of R2 tuples. To improve the performance of the operation in the cycling step, first, a local sorting step is introduced after the balancing operation. Thus, local segments of R1 and R2 are sorted in parallel in each node. Second, relation compaction in the RCR operation is modified to perform merging (which maintains the sorted order of tuples) rather than simple concatenation. These modifications enable the use of a sort-merge rather than a nested-loop local join algorithm in the cycle step.

3.4 Some Assumptions Related to the Join Operation

The join operation is typically assumed to operate on intermediate and not base relations. Intermediate relations are assumed to be memory resident. This may not be unreasonable since hypercube nodes with 8 Mbytes of memory already exist [PET85]. Thus, for example, 128 Mbytes of memory are available in a 16-node subcube. On the other hand, the extent to which the intermediate relation distribution is skewed would be restricted by the 8 Mbyte memory at each node. If the relations are on disk, then the nodes have to read data from disk before performing tuple balancing. If the disk at each node can sustain data transfer at the communication link rate then the disk overhead should not be visible. Commercially available disks such as the one mentioned in [GAM87] can be used to meet this requirement.

An alternate join method may seem to be to use only the join attributes (rather than the entire selected and projected tuples) in the operation. This approach is, in fact, less efficient because it entails a separate tuple concatenation and result collection phase. This can involve high I/O overhead since each intermediate relation needs to be stored on disk. Additionally, in the multi-query context this can involve high communication overheads since the join may be performed by an ISS other than the ISS containing the original tuples. A discussion of issues related to intra- and inter-query concurrency is provided in [FRI87c]. This paper only discusses the performance of single join operations.

3.5. Analysis of the Tuple Balancing Operation

Tuple balancing is implemented as follows. In each of $\log_2 N$ steps, paired neighbor nodes transfer as many tuples as neccesary ($>=0$) to achieve a complete balance. The time taken in each step is proportional to the difference in tuple counts between neighboring nodes. Let R_{ij} represents the number of tuples of relation R in node i, $0<=i<N$, in the jth balancing step, $1<=j<=n$. The initial data distribution is represented by the set of values $\{R_{i1}\}$. Initially, since the data distribution is assumed to be totally random, there can be N distinct R_{i1} values. In the first step of balancing, 2^{n-1} node pairs are formed based on, say, the least significant node address bit. The pair with the largest tuple difference determines the time taken in this step. Since tuple transfer is a symmetric operation, it does not matter which of the two nodes has the larger number of tuples. After the first step of balancing, the 2^n distinct R_{i1} values are reduced to 2^{n-1} distinct R_{i2} values. Now 2^{n-1} pairs are formed based on the next to LSB but, clearly, only 2^{n-2} of these are of interest since the other 2^{n-2} are a mirror image of the first with respect to their tuple counts.

Balancing Step 1: Assume that nodes are paired with their neighbors beginning from the LSB to the MSB (right to left). In step 1, the following pairs are formed in, say, an 8 node cube, (0,1), (2,3), (4,5), and (6,7). The number of tuples transferred between nodes in each pair is, between nodes 0 & 1= $|R_{11}-R_{01}|/2$; 2 & 3= $|R_{31}-R_{21}|/2$; 4 & 5= $|R_{51}-R_{41}|/2$; and 6 & 7= $|R_{71}-R_{61}|/2$. Therefore, the time taken is

$$\text{MAX } \{ \ |R_{11}-R_{01}|/2, \ |R_{31}-R_{21}|/2, \ |R_{51}-R_{41}|/2, \ |R_{71}-R_{61}|/2 \ \}.$$

Balancing Step 2: After step1, the tuple distribution at the beginning of step 2 is as follows,

$$R_{02} = R_{12} = (R_{01}+R_{11})/2; \ R_{22} = R_{32} = (R_{21}+R_{31})/2;$$
$$R_{42} = R_{52} = (R_{41}+R_{51})/2; \ \text{and } R_{62} = R_{72} = (R_{61}+R_{71})/2.$$

The nodes are now paired based on the bit next to the LSB and the pairs are (0,2), (1,3), (4,6), and (5,7). The number of tuples transferred in each pair is, between nodes 0 & 2 (and 1 & 3): $|R_{22}-R_{02}|/2$ ($=|R_{32}-R_{12}|/2$) and between nodes 4 & 6 (and 5 & 7): $|R_{62}-R_{42}|/2$ ($=|R_{72}-R_{52}|/2$).

The time taken now is $\text{MAX } \{ \ |R_{22}-R_{02}|/2, \ |R_{62}-R_{42}|/2 \ \}$

$$\text{MAX } \{|(R_{21}+R_{31})/2 - (R_{01}+R_{11})/2|/2, \ |(R_{61}+R_{71})/2 - (R_{41}+R_{51})/2|/2\}$$

$$\text{MAX } \{ \ |R_{21}+R_{31}-R_{01}-R_{11}|/4, \ |R_{61}+R_{71}-R_{41}-R_{51}|/4 \ \}.$$

Balancing Step 3: Similarly, it can be shown that the time taken in step 3 is $\text{MAX } \{ \ |R_{41}+R_{51}+R_{61}+R_{71}-R_{01}-R_{11}-R_{21}-R_{31}|/8 \ \}$.

For a cube of dimension n, the time taken in the rth balancing step, $0 \leq r < n$, is given by,

$$\text{Time} \quad \text{MAX} \left\{ \left(\left| \sum_{s=0,\,2^{n-r}-1} \sum_{k=2^{(r-1)}+s*2^r}^{2^r-1+s*2^r} R_{kl} - \sum_{k=s*2^r}^{2^{(r-1)}-1+s*2^r} R_{kl} \right| / 2^r \right) \right\} \quad \text{--- (1)}$$

Let M_r denote the above expression for the time taken in step r of balancing. Then the total time in balancing is,

$$\text{--(2)}$$

$$\text{balancing time} = n*T_1 + \sum_{r=0}^{n-1} (K * M_r + \text{ceil}(M_r/P)*T_2)$$

where K is a constant which incorporates transmission time per tuple, etc.; P is the packet size in tuples; and T_2 is a standard packet overhead. The first term, $n*T_1$, accounts for the synchronization, message exchange, and computation required to compute the number of tuples that need to be transferred prior to actual data transfer in each dimension. Thus, in the best case, if data is evenly distributed then the summation term, incorporating the M_r's, should be zero and balancing time = $n*T_1$.

4. Join Operation Simulation

To obtain a better idea of the performance of the tuple balancing and join operations, a simulation was implemented using multiple processes on a UNIX system. The number of tuples per node before balancing is supplied as input to the simulator and the output is the total time taken in the join operation. The time to peform the actual join in each node is computed via timing equations.

4.1 The Hypercube Simulator

The simulation uses the Unix *fork* primitive to start N processes, one for each node in the cube. The main program initializes the global synchronization and communication mechanisms; the global clock; and the number of tuples per node for each of the two relations involved in the join. Finally, the main program forks the N child processes to simulate the N nodes.

4.1.1 Interprocessor Communication

Interprocessor communication is simulated using UNIX System V message queues. Each node in the cube has one message queue associated with it along with *send()* and *receive()* routines. Before a message is actually sent, the send() routine ensures that the hypercube connectivity constraints are not violated. Note that by changing the connectivity-checking function, one can simulate any interconnection scheme. Due to the way in which the underlying message queues were used, a *send()* request returns immediately while a *receive()* request blocks until a message arrives. This is also consistent with the non-blocking write and blocking read implemented in the NCUBE computer described in section 5.

4.1.2 Global Clock Mechanism

Each node (processor) is associated with a block of information referred to as its processor control structure (pcs). This structure contains information such as processor address (its ID number), tuple counts, and its local clock value. Local clocks are updated by each processing element as operations are simulated. These clocks are periodically synchronized and the global clock variable is correspondingly updated. The System V semaphores are used to guarantee mutually exclusive access to the global clock which is implemented as a shared-memory variable in Unix.

4.1.3 Cube Synchronization

In the proposed system, hardware global-AND control lines are used to synchronize nodes at various times as required by the algorithms. In the simulation, on the other hand, this is achieved by introducing a synchronization primitive known as an **event** which causes N-1 processes to wait on an event queue until the Nth one waits on the event, at which time all processes are released from the event queue and resume execution. The routine, *csync()*, implements the above using semaphores. This routine also sets all local clocks to the value of the global clock when the Nth processing element makes a call to *csync()*.

4.2 The Join Algorithm Implementation

Only tuple counts rather than actual tuples are exchanged in the tuple balancing operation. The time taken in each step is computed locally at each node. Since two relations are balanced simultaneously, the time taken by the larger of the two is used as the total balance time. The balance operation calls *csync()* at the end of each of the $\log_2 N$ steps. Tuple balancing is followed by the RCR and cycle operations. Again, no actual data are transferred between nodes in these operations. Rather, since the tuples are already balanced, independent calculations are performed at each node to compute the time taken and the number of tuples involved in these operations and the pcs data is adjusted accordingly. Thus, the main objective of the simulation was to study the tuple balancing operation.

4.3 Other Implementation Issues

This simulation was originally written for an AT&T 3B2 computer running System V Unix but was later ported to a Hewlett-Packard Model 9000/320 computer running HP-UX (a Unix work-alike). Only a small change (in pathname) was required to get the simulation running on the HP machine. Due to the large number of message queues and processes created by the simulation, the system tunable parameters of the Unix kernel had to be adjusted and the kernel regenerated to run this simulation. Even then the largest cube that could be simulated was a Q_5 with 32 nodes.

5. Implementation on the NCUBE computer
5.1 The NCUBE system

This section describes the implementation of the join operation on a NCUBE/6 computer available to us. The implementation models the functioning of a single ISS. However, note that the NCUBE *does not* provide a disk at each node. The NCUBE system at the University of Michigan has a 64 node hypercube array and a peripheral processor card with 16 I/O processors which communicate with the hypercube array. Each node consists of a 2 MIPS (0.5 Mflops) processor with 128 K bytes of local memory and 11 bi-directional serial ports, each with a 1 Mbyte/sec transfer rate, which provide the hypercube connectivity for a Q_{10} and communication with the I/O processors. User interaction with the hypercube array is via a 80286 host processor which runs a multi-tasking operating system called AXIS. AXIS supports communications between the host processor and the hypercube nodes. Communication among hypercube nodes is supported by the VERTEX communications kernel which runs on these nodes. A detailed description of the NCUBE system is available in [HAY86].

5.2 Implementation

The implementation provides a measure of the time taken by the communication-oriented activities of the join operation on the NCUBE computer. The host program first acquires a subcube of the desired size from the AXIS system. An executable image of the node program is then loaded into the host memory and is sent to each node processor which starts execution of the program. The host then sends the initial tuple counts of the two relations at each node.

5.2.1 Tuple Balancing

In tuple balancing, the transfer of tuples is emulated by sending a block of dummy data. If the number of bytes to be transferred exceeds the packet size, then multiple packets need to be sent. Ideally, the second relation is balanced concurrently with the first. However, since the VERTEX kernel does not support multi-tasking, the balancing of R1 and R2 becomes sequential. The swapping of tuple counts between a node pair is accomplished using a short message which contains only the tuple count in the data field. Parallelism in the swap operation is achieved by the use of the non-blocking **write** and blocking **read** message passing primitives of the VERTEX system:

write (count_1);   write (count_2);

read (count_2);   read (count_1);

This structure exploits the full-duplex nature of the communication links. The blocking read call provides automatic synchronization within the pair of communicating processors. This message swap construction is used repeatedly in the RCR and cycle steps where its advantages are more apparent since the volume of data transferred is high.

5.2.2 RCR

At the end of the balancing phase, the processors have to pick the smaller relation for compaction. Since, perfect tuple distribution is not always possible (see problem mentioned in section 3.1), relation R1 is chosen as the smaller one if it has n or more tuples less than R2; otherwise R2 is chosen. In the proposed system, a global-AND line is used to arrive at a consensus. Due to the inexact distribution of tuples, all processors in a subcube may not detect the end of the operation in the same step of RCR. Normally, the RCR utilizes a global-AND line to signal the end of the operation. Since the NCUBE does not have this hardware facility, this is achieved via software. The method used here is:

Step 1: Each node goes through exactly n steps of the RCR operation and remembers the tuple counts and the step at which the operation should have stopped for that node.

Step 2: The nodes pair up in a manner similar to the tuple balancing step and swap information about the step at which RCR stopped. The minimum of [stop_step1, stop_step2] is then taken as the step at which RCR should have stopped. This step is repeated n times for the different neighbors and at the end of the last step, a consensus is reached in the subcube.

Finally, the nodes determine the number of tuples they had when RCR logically stopped and use this information in the next, cycle step.

5.2.3 Cycle

In this step, rings of nodes are formed in which each ring contains all the tuples in the smaller relation. If RCR stops after k steps, then there would be 2^k rings of 2^{n-k} nodes each. A gray code scheme is used to map the 2^{n-k} nodes into a ring and tuples of the smaller

TABLE 1 - Simulation Timings

R1 - 2000 tuples of 20 bytes; R2 - 4000 tuples of 20 bytes

10 Kbyte maximum packet size; 2 MIPS CPU; 8 Mbits/sec lines

N	Data Set	Balance time	Merge time	Sort time	Cycle time	Total time
8	1	26	10	16	60	112
	2	27	10	16	60	113
	3	27	10	16	60	113
16	1	24	17	11	60	112
	2	28	17	11	60	116
	3	28	17	11	60	116
32	1	26	23	9	60	118
	2	27	23	9	60	119
	3	26	23	9	60	119

All times in milliseconds

TABLE 2 - Implementation Timings for Tuple Balancing

Data Set	N			
	8	16	32	64
1	29	14	19	13
2	21	25	19	13
3	28	22	15	12
4	25	22	13	13
5	28	15	14	14

All times in milliseconds

TABLE 3 - Implementation Timings for the RCR Operation

Data Set	N			
	8	16	32	64
1	41	36	41	45
2	23	37	41	46
3	28	35	44	46
4	25	34	42	46
5	23	35	42	47

All times in milliseconds

TABLE 4 - Implementation Timings for Cycling

Data Set	N			
	8	16	32	64
1	75	76	76	75
2	75	76	76	75
3	76	76	76	76
4	75	76	75	75
5	76	75	75	75

All times in milliseconds

relation are pipelined in the ring. Timing information on these operations was collected using the local timer on the NCUBE nodes. Since the nodes are dedicated to this program, the elapsed time directly gives the time taken for the different steps. At the end of the execution, one of the nodes sends this infomation back to the host program. Note that the time taken for the local sort and join are not computed in this implementation. The time for these steps can, however, be estimated from the parameters like CPU speed, percentage of tuples participating in the join, etc.

6. Performance Analysis

The timing values obtained from simulation and implementation are shown in Tables 1-4. Table 1 summarizes the results from simulation while Tables 2-4 show the results from implementation for the balancing, RCR, and cycling steps, respectively. The simulation parameter values were chosen to be similar to those of the NCUBE implementation. The join operates on relations R1=2000 tuples of 20 bytes and R2=4000 tuples of 20 bytes. Join selectivity has not been specified since the actual output of tuples has not been modeled either in simulation or in the implementation. In the proposed system, the OCN's will handle output collection. In all cases, the tuples of both relations are initially randomly distributed across the nodes of the cube. The maximum packet size is 10 Kbytes (due to buffer overflow problems in the NCUBE), CPU speed is 2 MIPS, the communication line rate is 8 Mbits/sec, and the packet overhead is 5 msec. Regardless of the size of the original cube, R1 is always compacted into a Q_2 (500 tuples per node or 500*20 = 10,000 bytes/packet). The simulation was run for N = 8, 16, and 32 with three input data sets for each value of N. Timings for the implementation were obtained for N = 8, 16, 32, and 64 with five random input data sets for each case.

No definite trend is seen from Table 1 for the balancing time, though the implementation results from Table 2 indicate that this time decreases with N. This is because as N increases there are fewer tuples per node and, in the random distribution case, less volume of data needs to be moved around to achieve balance. The RCR operation time increases with N (Tables 1 & 3) since more RCR steps are executed as the cube size increases. The time to sort local segments of R1 and R2 is computed via timing equations in the simulation program (Table 1). As N increases, this time should decrease. Finally, the cycle time (Table 1 & 4) should be the same in all cases since the RCR operation always compacts R1 into a Q_2. In the simulation, since every packet is assumed to return to its source, there are 4 packet transfer steps in a Q_2. Each cycle step is bound by MAX(CPU time, Communication time). In the simulation, the communication time is computed as Packet Overhead + Data Transfer Time = 15 msec to give a total cycle time of 4*15 = 60 msec.

In the implementation, on the other hand, a packet does not return to its source and, thus, there are only 3 packet transmissions. The timing from the implementation in Table 4 shows that each packet transmission in fact takes about 25 msec. The 10 msec difference between simulation and implementation is due to the time taken to copy data from user memory to the communication buffers (and vice versa) in the NCUBE system. In the NCUBE implementation, the 10 msec taken for actual data transfer is the time available for overlap with CPU operations at each node. Thus, if the local join of R1 and R2 can be performed in this time on the NCUBE then the CPU and data transfer operations are completely overlapped. The simulation was also used to compare join operation times with and without balancing. Based on the "skewness" of the initial distribution, the improvement due to balancing ranged from 20-80%. These results are reported in [FRI87c].

7. Conclusion

The concept of dynamic data redistribution was introduced in a cube-connected multicomputer system to improve the performance of relational database operations. Tuple balancing is one of the primary redistribution operations. Since the time taken in this operation is totally dependent on the (unpredictable) distribution of intermediate relations, it is difficult to analytically characterize this operation. Nonetheless, a general expression for the time taken is derived here. A much better estimation of time is obtained via simulations and implementation. A simulation using multiple processes on a uniprocessor system was implemented. The join operation was also implemented on a NCUBE computer and communication related timings were obtained. Both, the simulation and implementation, demonstrate the feasibility of the proposed approach for database processing on a cube architecture. In addition, the implementation provides us further insight into the actual timings of the various operations in the cube.

8. References

[BAB79]   Babb, E., "Implementing a Relational Database by
            Means of Specialized Hardware," *ACM Transactions on
            Database Systems*, Vol. 4, No. 1, March, 1979.

[BAN79]   Banerjee, J., Hsiao, D. K., and Kannan, K., "DBC - A
            Database Computer for Very Large Databases", *IEEE
            Transactions on Computers* , Vol. c-28, No. 6, June 1979.

[BAR86a]   Baru, C. K. and Su, S. Y. W., "The Architecture of SM3:
            A Dynamically Partitionable Multicomputer with
            Switchable Memory," *IEEE Transactions on Computers*,
            Vol.C-35, No. 9, Sept. 1986.

[BAR87]   Baru, C.K. and Frieder, O., "Implementing Relational
            Database Operations in a Cube-Connected Multicomputer
            System," to appear in the IEEE 3rd Intl.Conf. on Data
            Engineering, Los Angeles, CA, Feb 2-5, 1987.

[DEW79]   DeWitt, D. J., "DIRECT - A Multiprocessor
            Organization for Supporting Relational Database
            Management Systems", *IEEE Transactions on
            Computers,* Vol. c-28, No. 6, June 1979.

[DEW86]   DeWitt, D.J. et al, "GAMMA - A High Performance
            Dataflow Database Machine," *Proc. Intl. Conf. on Very
            Large Databases*, Aug.25-28, Kyoto, Japan, 1986.

[FRI87a]   Frieder, O. and Baru, C.K., "Issues in Query Processing
            on a   Cube-Connected Multicomputer System," *IEEE
            6th Annual Intl. Phoenix Conference on Computers and
            Communications,* Feb. 25-27, 1987, pp. 315-319.

[FRI87b]   Frieder, O. and Baru, C.K., "Data Distribution and Query Scheduling Policies for a Cube-Connected Multicomputer System," *2nd Intl. Conf. on Supercomputing Systems*, San Francisco, May 3-5,1987.

[FRI87c]   Frieder, O., "Database Processing on a Cube-Connected Multicomputer," Ph.D. Dissertation, Dept. of Electrical Engineering and Computer Science, The University of Michigan, Ann Arbor, MI 48109, 1987.

[FUS86]   Fushimi, S., Kitsuregawa, M., and Tanaka, H., "An Overview of the System Software of a Parallel Relational Database Machine GRACE," *Proc. VLDB 12th Intl. Conf. on Very Large Data Bases,* Aug.25-28, Kyoto, Japan, 1986.

[GAM87]   Gamerl, M., "Maturing Parallel Transfer Disk Technology Finds More Applications," Hardcopy, pp.41-48, Feb. 1987.

[HAY86]   Hayes, J.P. et al, "Architecture of a Hypercube Supercomputer," *Procs. Intl. Conf. on Parallel Processing,* St. Charles, IL., 1986.

[HIL86]   Hillyer, B., Shaw, D.E., and Nigam, A., "NON-VON's Performance on Certain Database Benchmarks," *IEEE Transactions on Software Engineering,* Vol.SE-12, No.4, April, 1986.

[KIT84]   Kitsuregawa, M., Tanaka, H., and Moto-Oka, T., "Architecture and Performance of the Relational Algebra Machine GRACE," *Procs. Intl. Conf. on Parallel Processing,* August, 1984.

[PET85]   Peterson, J.C., Tuazon, J.O., Lieberman, D., and Pniel, M., "The MARK III Hypercube-Ensemble Concurrent Computer," Intl. Conf. on Parallel Processing, pp.71-73, Aug. 1985.

[SCH79]   Schuster, S.A., Nguyen, H.B., Ozkarahan, E.A., and Smith, K.C., "RAP.2-An Associative Processor for Databases and its Applications," *IEEE Transactions on Computers,* Vol.C-28, No.6, June, 1979.

[SU79]   Su, S.Y.W., Nguyen, L.H., Emam, A., and Lipovski, G.J., "The Architectural Features and Implementation Techniques of the Multicell CASSM," *IEEE Transactions on Computers,* Vol.C-28, No.6, June, 1979.

Design of a HyperKYKLOS-based Multiprocessor Architecture for High-Performance Join Operations

B.L.Menezes*, K.Thadani**, A.G.Dale**, R.Jenevein**

* Dept. of Electrical and Computer Eng.
** Dept. of Computer Science
University of Texas at Austin
Austin, TX 78712
U.S.A.

ABSTRACT The traffic characteristics of various distributed join algorithms on the Hypercube are analyzed. It is shown that, regardless of which join strategy is employed, the network bandwidth requirements of the computation and collection phases are radically different. This imbalance prevents these two phases from being pipelined (overlapped). To alleviate this problem, the HyperKYKLOS Network is proposed. The topology of this network is defined and a brief description of the I/O nodes presently under construction is included.

1 Introduction

To meet the objectives of developing an external memory system commensurate with the computational power of the next generation of host machines, we have been investigating[1] and refining an architecture initially proposed in [BROW85]. As noted in that paper, the architecture lends itself to *parallel access of databases*, and to *parallel operations on data objects* that are being streamed from secondary storage toward the host.

The gross architecture of the I/O Engine is shown in Fig. 1. The architecture is partitioned into four major levels:

- Host processors, which can be either general purpose or specialized processors

---

[1]Work reported in this paper was partially supported under ONR grant N00014-86-K-0499

- A set of "Node Mappers" which make an associative translation from requested objects (eg. relation names, attribute name-value pairs and tuples) to base (I/O) nodes where the objects are stored by generating a routing tag for the Interconnection Network.

- An Interconnection Network which couples host and base(I/O) processors, and also interconnects base processors. The ICN topology proposed is based on the KYKLOS[MENE85a] multiple-tree topology. The switch nodes in this network also incorporate logic and buffering to support merge operations on data streams.

- I/O nodes each consisting of a general purpose microprocessor, associative disk cache, a sort engine, and associated conventional moving-head disks.

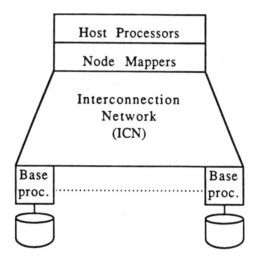

Figure 1: System Overview

The ICN topology, as discussed in Section 3 of this paper, allows the I/O nodes to be interconnected as a Hypercube, with tree connections from this level of the system to the host level.

Two features of the Hypercube topology are attractive in considering parallel database processing such as the join operation on relations that are partitioned and distributed over the I/O nodes:

1. *Topological Properties:* The average and worst case distances in the Hypercube are bounded by $n=\log_2 N$ in a cube with N nodes[2]. Also, the

---

[2] n and logN are used interchangeably

maximum traffic carried by a link under the assumption of uniform message distribution is O(N).

2. *Degrees of Freedom:* The fanout of the Hypercube is uniformly n i.e. any given node has n nearest neighbors, one per dimension. This facilitates broadcast of attribute values or relation fragments in O(log N) time by using one dimension per transmission cycle.

Although a Hypercube lends itself to efficient parallel computation of the basic relational operations (selection, projection, join, set operations), it presents major potential problems during the collection phase of database transactions when the partial results must be collected at a given node.

Section 2 of this paper analyzes the traffic properties of various join methods in a Hypercube and compares traffic loads during the compute phase of a database transaction with traffic loads generated during the collection phase. This analysis shows the existence of a serious imbalance in traffic loads between the two phases, and motivates our proposal for the HyperKYKLOS topology discussed in Section 3.

We are pursuing further studies and development of a HyperKYKLOS organized database engine. In Section 4 of this paper, we describe the architecture of a prototype I/O node which is now under development.

2 Traffic Properties of Join and Merge Operations in a Hypercube

2.1 Preliminaries

Every node in the N-cube consists of a processor, main memory and secondary storage; it has n incoming channels and n outgoing channels. It is assumed that one or more host machines is interfaced to a Hypercube node. The relational database is divided into disjoint horizontal fragments and is distributed uniformly among the N processors.

Formally, the database D_x may be viewed as a set of relations, $\{R_1, R_2, \dots, R_x\}$. Each relation R_i is partitioned int N disjoint horizontal fragments which are stored one per node. We denote by r_{ij}, the jth fragment of R_i stored at node j satisfying
$R_i = \cup_{j=0,N-1} r_{ij}$, i=1, ..., x and
$r_{ij} \cap r_{ik} = 0$, j≠k.

Evaluation of a database query proceeds in three major phases:
- *Phase 1* Transmission of the optimized query to all the processors. This is followed by access to disk or cache to obtain the desired relation(s).

- *Phase 2* (Computation Phase) Evaluation of partial results at each processor.

• *Phase 3* (Collection Phase) Transmission of the results to the host.

The transmission involved in Phase 1 is negligible and hence will not be factored into the traffic computation. Since most queries require the results to be sorted, Phase 3 requires a global sort of the partial results.

Any query can be decomposed into a sequence of selections, projections and joins. Of these, the join is the only operation that requires transmission between processors and hence will be considered in some detail.

We next discuss the details of the implementation of widely used join algorithms [VALD84] on the Hypercube. Under consideration will be the join between R_m and R_n where $|R_m| \leq |R_n|$ and the joining attribute is y. We use $|y|$ to denote the size of the join attribute. Also t_m and t_n will be used to denote the width of tuples of relations R_m and R_n. Finally, by broadcast of a data item x is meant the transmission of x from a node i to every other node in the network. An N-broadcast of a set of data items $\{X_0, X_1, \ldots, X_{N-1}\}$ is the transmission of X_j to network node j, $0 \leq j < N$. Note that a broadcast is a special case of an N-broadcast in which $x = X_i$, $0 \leq i < N$.

2.2 Join Strategies

2.2.1 Nested Loop Join

i) Every node, i, broadcasts r_{mi} using shortest path routing.

ii) At each node i:

• Compute $r_{ni} \bowtie r_{mi}$

• On receipt of r_{mj} compute $r_{ni} \bowtie r_{mj}$, $0 \leq j < N, j \neq i$.

• Compute $\cup_{j=0,N-1} [r_{ni} \bowtie r_{mj}]$.

Analysis Step i) involves communication and Step ii) involves computation. Hence the message traffic in this algorithm is due to Step i). Since broadcast of each fragment involves N-1 links and there are N such broadcasts, the average traffic through a single link in an n-cube (with Nn links[3]) is given by

$$T_{nl} = \frac{N(N-1)}{(Nn)}$$

$$= \frac{(N-1)}{n} \quad fragments/link$$

---

[3] we assume that each edge in the Hypercube is comprised of two bidirectional links or channels

Since R_m has t_m bytes/tuple and the whole relation is distributed over the N nodes of the Hypercube, the size of each fragment is $(|R_m|t_m) / N$. Hence

$$T_{nl} = \frac{(N-1)|R_m|t_m}{Nn} \quad bytes/link.$$

For $N \gg 1$,

$$T_{nl} \sim \frac{|R_m|t_m}{n} \quad bytes/link.$$

2.2.2 Sort Merge Join

This algorithm is similar to the Nested Loop Join in that fragments r_{mi} are broadcast. However, both r_{mi} and r_{ni} are sorted at each site i before step 1 of the Nested Loop Join Algorithm.

<u>Analysis</u> While the computational requirements are somewhat different, the traffic, T_{sm} for this algorithm is identical to that for the Nested Loop Join Algorithm i.e.
$T_{sm} = T_{nl}.$

2.2.3 Semi-Join based Algorithm

i) Every node, i, computes $\pi_y(r_{mi})$ and $\pi_y(r_{ni})$ and broadcasts each of these lists to every other node.

ii) At each node i:

- On receipt of $\pi_y(r_{mj})$ and $\pi_y(r_{nj})$, $j \neq i$, compute the semijoins
  $r_{ni} \ltimes \pi_y(r_{mj})$ and $r_{mi} \ltimes \pi_y(r_{nj})$

- Perform an N-broadcast of
  $\{r_{mi} \ltimes \pi_y(r_{n0}), \quad r_{mi} \ltimes \pi_y(r_{n2}), \quad \ldots, \quad r_{mi} \ltimes \pi_y(r_{nN-1})\}$

- On receiving $r_{mj} \ltimes \pi_y(r_{ni})$, $i \neq j$, compute $[r_{ni} \ltimes \pi_y(r_{mj})] \bowtie [r_{mj} \ltimes \pi_y(r_{ni})]$

- Finally compute $\cup_{j=0,N-1} \{[(r_{ni} \ltimes \pi_y(r_{mj})] \bowtie [r_{mj} \ltimes \pi_y(r_{ni})]\}$

<u>Analysis</u> Let $|y|$ be the size in bytes of the join attribute y. Part (i) of this algorithm involves a broadcast of y. Hence the average traffic through this phase, T_{SJ1} may be derived in a manner similar to that for T_{nl}

$$T_{SJ1} \sim \frac{|y||R_m|\sigma_y}{n} \quad bytes/link$$

$$where \quad \sigma_y = \frac{Number\ of\ distinct\ values\ for\ y\ in\ r_m}{|r_{mi}|}$$

i.e. $|r_{mi}|\sigma_y$ is the number of distinct attribute values for y in r_{mi}.

Part (ii) of this algorithm involves an N-broadcast. Let each of the N-1 items being broadcast traverse n' links on the average. Since there are N such broadcasts, the average traffic per link, T_{SJ2}, is

$$T_{SJ2} = \frac{(N-1)n'N}{(Nn)} \quad items/link.$$

The average distance between a pair of Hypercube nodes is

$$n' = \sum_{i=1}^{n} i \binom{n}{i}/(N-1) = \frac{Nn}{2(N-1)}$$

Upon substitution of n',

$$T_{SJ2} = N/2 \quad items/link.$$

Also each item is a semi-join output i.e. the tuples of R_m that participate in a join at another site. Hence the traffic in this phase, T_{SJ2} is given by

$$T_{SJ2} = \frac{|R_m|t_m\sigma_k}{2} \quad bytes/link.$$

where σ_k is the join selectivity

$$i.e. \quad \sigma_k = \frac{|r_{mi} \bowtie r_{nj}|}{|r_{mi} \times r_{nj}|}$$

2.2.4 Hash-based Join

This method essentially involves applying a hash function to the fragments of both relations at each node. For each relation, the function yields a set of hashed fragments, one for each node in the system.

These fragments are then N-broadcast. Since the hashing is done on the join attribute, a fragment of R_m arriving at node i joins only with fragments of R_n arriving at that node and no other.

Analysis Assuming that the hash function splits the relation fragments uniformly, each N-broadcast will involve a fragment of size

$$\frac{|R_m|t_m}{N^2} \quad or \quad \frac{|R_n|t_n}{N^2}.$$

Since the traffic for each of the 2 N-broadcasts is N/2 hash buckets per link per relation as explained in the derivation of T_{SJ2}, the traffic T_{HB} for this algorithm is

$$T_{HB} = \frac{|R_m|t_m + |R_n|t_n}{2N} \quad bytes/link.$$

2.3 The Collection Phase

Assuming a join selectivity of σ defined by

$$\sigma = \frac{|R_m \bowtie R_n|}{|R_m \times R_n|},$$

the total traffic to the host will be $\sigma^2|R_m||R_n|$ tuples. Noting that there are n connections to the host, the traffic, T_{CP} through the maximally congested links in this phase is at least

$$T_{CP} = \frac{\sigma^2|R_m||R_n|t_m t_n}{n} \quad bytes/link$$

2.4 Comparison of Traffic in Phases 2 and 3

Tables 1-3 show the ratio of traffic in Phase 3 to that in Phase 2. We have assumed tuples sizes of 208 bytes[4] and the join attribute length of 52 bytes. Finally, we have also assumed worst-case traffic in Phase 2 i.e. $\sigma_x=1$, $\sigma_y=1$. Calculations are for a Hypercube of 32 nodes (n=5). As can be seen, the traffic ratio is always greater than 1 for the range of relation sizes and selectivities under consideration. Further this is true regardless of which join strategy is employed, though this ratio is highest for the Hash-based strategy and is lowest for the semi-join based algorithm.

σ	$|R_n|=10^3$	$|R_n|=10^4$	$|R_n|=10^6$
.1	17.5	175	17,500
.2	70.0	700	70,000
.5	437.5	4375	437,500
1.0	1750.0	17,500	1,750,000

Table 1: Traffic Ratio in Nested Loop Case

Note that the traffic ratio increases linearly with relation size and quadratically with join selectivity. The fact is, that even at low selectivity and a relation size of 10,000 tuples, the traffic ratio is between 2 and 4 orders of magnitude. Also as N increases this ratio gets worse (increases) in the case of the hash-based join though the ratio in the other two cases are independent of network size.

---

[4]as in the extended Wisconsin Benchmarks [DeWI87]

σ	$|R_n|=10^3$	$|R_n|=10^4$	$|R_n|=10^6$
.1	6.36	63.6	63,600
.2	25.4	254.4	254,400
.5	159.0	1590	1,590,000
1.0	636.0	6360	6,360,000

Table 2: Traffic Ratio in Semi Join Case

σ	$|R_n|=10^3$	$|R_n|=10^4$	$|R_n|=10^6$
.1	112	1120	112,000
.2	448	4480	448,000
.5	2800	28,000	2,800,000
1.0	11200	112,000	11,200,000

Table 3: Traffic Ratio in Hash based Case

3 HyperKYKLOS: The augmented Hypercube

From the tables in Section 2, it is clear that there exists a great imbalance between maximum link traffic in the compute phase and that in the collection phase. For example, even at σ=0.1, the traffic ratio is 17.5 for only 1000 tuple sized relations. Further, this is regardless of which algorithm is actually implemented. If query processing were to be viewed as a three-stage pipeline as shown in Fig. 2, the latencies through stages 2 and 3 would be related to the maximum traffic which as explained above is severely imbalanced. The crux of the problem is that the same physical hardware viz. Hypercube links and switches are used in both stages of the pipeline while the demands, in terms of bandwidth, are radically different in the two phases. What is needed is to expeditiously collect the results of the partial joins and present them as a sorted list (of tuples) to the host.

A solution is to construct a binary tree external to the existing Hypercube with the I/O nodes of the Hypercube as the leaves. Where multiple joins have to be performed or where the bandwidth requirements of Phase 3 are not adequately met, two or more trees may be employed. The use of multiple trees (the tree replication factor is denoted r) sharing the same set of leaf nodes to improve performance and provide fault tolerance has been studied as the KYKLOS topology [MENE86,JENE86].

The advantages of such constructions are obvious: the properties of the composite topology are a superset of the properties of its constituent parts. Algorithms that require message transmission from each node to every other node would be well suited to the Hypercube; such algorithms would result in O(N) maximum traffic density. On the other hand for operations that require merging or sort-merge algorithms the use of tree structures is highly desirable. Though a tree may be mapped onto a Hypercube, a single connection

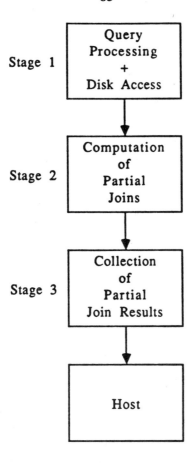

Figure 2: 3-Stage Pipeline Representation of Distributed Join Processing in Hypercube

from the root of this tree to the host could result in serious traffic bottlenecks at the root with concomitant imbalance in bandwidth utilization. This would result in a system that is network-bound (i.e. the input capacity of the host or hosts exceeds the bandwidth of the fastest link(s)) especially in the event that cartesian products or low selectivity joins be required at the host. As such, we are investigating the possibility of providing multiple trees - an alternative which seems attractive in the light of the fact that there may be many hosts and multiple queries to be processed. One such alternative is a derivation of the KYKLOS Network explained below.

A special case of the KYKLOS Network is one where r=logN (Fig. 3(a)). Because this consists of trees built on top of a Hypercube, it has been christened HyperKYKLOS.

Topology Definition We have defined KYKLOS as a multiple-tree structure sharing a set of leaf nodes. We could redraw each tree separately as a full binary tree with no link crossovers. (Fig. 3(c)). Each tree may then be characterized by a Labelling Sequence (LS) [MENE86] of leaf nodes. As an example, the LS's for each tree of Fig. 3(c) are

$L_0 = 0\ 1\ 2\ 3\ 4\ 5\ 6\ 7$

$L_1 = 0\ 2\ 4\ 6\ 1\ 3\ 5\ 7$

$L_2 = 0\ 4\ 1\ 5\ 2\ 6\ 3\ 7$

Since a HyperKYKLOS of N leaf nodes has n = logN trees, the interconnection strategy for such a structure could be defined by means of the tuple

$<L_0, L_1, \dots L_{n-1}>$

where L_i is the LS for the ith tree. We have chosen a simple interconnection strategy for the version of HyperKYKLOS presented in this paper which we call HyperKYKLOS-I. The LS's for HyperKYKLOS-I are defined below

Let $L_i(j)$ be the jth term of L_i. Then

$L_i(j) = \rho_i(j)$ where

j is an n-bit binary string and

$\rho_i(j)$ is the number obtained rotating j a total of i bits to the left.

In HyperKYKLOS, there are logN paths (through the roots of each tree) to the host. This provides a logN-fold improvement in traffic to the host especially when a low-selectivity join is to be performed with the result returning to the host. Where selectivity is low and cost considerations dominate, only a small subset of trees may be used (i.e. r < log N). In this case any subset of r LS's may be used to define the r trees.

Finally, we emphasize that if Stage 3 of the pipeline (Fig.2) is to cease to be a bottleneck it is not sufficient to merely have the extra tree(s). In fact, two requirements of the tree structure are clearly identifiable:

- High speed comparator logic at each non-leaf node to perform on-the-fly merge operations.

- High-speed links especially at the root of the tree

Given that the host may be a high-speed computer (or supercomputer), the onus of providing high performance lies with the designer of the I/O system.

As an example, consider a host like the CRAY-XMP.24. The internal channel speed of this supercomputer is 12.5 MWords/sec. With a word size of 64 bits/word, we see that the bandwidth of the fastest link should be at least 100 MBytes/sec. To achieve this bandwidth it may be necessary to multiplex the roots of the different trees.

Finally, the switching nodes should be capable of performing a merge on sorted streams of data. We envisage using special purpose ECL/CML chips. The details of the hardware are being currently worked out.

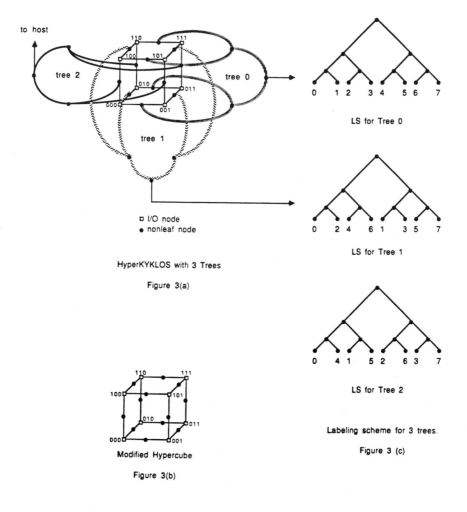

Figure 3: The HyperKYKLOS Topology

4 The Architectural Prototype

We have identified at the gross system level the two major components of the architecture viz.

- The I/O nodes linked in a Hypercube configuration

- The sort/merge trees for Phase 3.

We next present a brief description of the architecture of the I/O node prototype under construction (Fig. 4).

4.1 I/O Node Prototype

Each I/O node will be composed of the following blocks (shown in dashed lines).

    (a) Control Processor (CP)

    (b) Sort/Search/Set Engine (S^3E)

    (c) Disk System (DS) including disk cache, MC68020 and Mass Storage

    (d) Network Interface Unit (NIU)

Single I/O Node

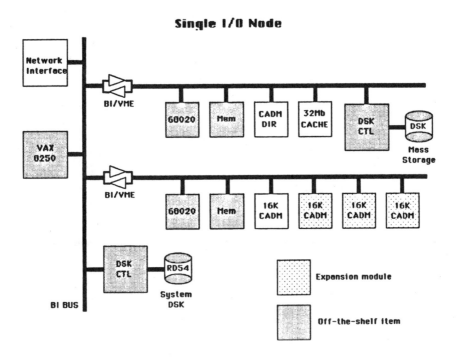

Figure 4: The Architecture of a single I/O Node

The VAX8250 (CP) with 4MByte of local memory is being used to control the I/O node system. The NIU multiplexes the log N incoming channels and routes data through the appropriate link(s). Block transfers between CP and NIU/S^3E/DS are through a high-speed BI bus which operates at 13.3 MByte DMA transfer rate. The BI bus was chosen because it uses distributed arbitration thus eliminating the need for a dedicated arbiter.

The S^3E is the heart of the I/O node design, so called because it performs <u>s</u>orting, <u>s</u>earch and set operations (union, intersection,etc.). It is being designed utilizing an array of Content Addressable Data Manager (CADM) chips designed by Advanced Micro Devices Corporation (AMD). Each CADM chip has 1 KByte of memory. We are currently building a 16K S^3E using an array of 16 CADM chips. We have made provision for S^3E expansion of upto 64K bytes (Fig. 4). The Motorola MC68020 is being used to provide the control for the CADM array's sort/search/set operations as well as for interfacing the S^3E to the CP. Our choice of the CADM chips was based on results of a simulation which indicated an expected 15-50 speedup in sorting over the VAX 11/780 and a speedup of 1.5 over software sort on the CRAY X/MP-24.

The DS will use a Disk Controller and nominally between one and four 500 MByte Disk Drives. The cache capacity has been targeted at 8% of mass storage. We are currently simulating the performance of the cache system. The actual design of this block will be driven by results of this simulation. Our tentative design envisages a track-organized design so that the minimum granularity for disk transfer is a track. The data filter can resolve the location of an object within a track residing in cache in 6 μsec. The data filter is currently being implemented in software on the MC68020.

The BI/VME converters are controllable bus interfaces between the BI and VME busses. This means that transfer through these converters occurs only by command of the CP. This bus structure will allow the cache subsystem, S^3E subsystem and CPU/NIU subsystems to function concurrently thus providing speedup due to the overlap of their respective operations.

5 Conclusion

We have shown that implementing queries on a Hypercube with horizontally fragmented data causes a serious traffic imbalance when the results are sent to the host, particularly if they are required to be sorted. The architecture proposed remedies this imbalance by having a tree structure for the collection phase. This architecture also has some other nice properties as demonstrated in [MENE85].

We strongly believe that the performance of the architecture proposed will be superior to that of a multiprocessor based purely on the Hypercube.

[BROW85] Browne, J., A.Dale, C.Leung and R.Jenevein,"A Parallel Multi-Stage I/O Architecture with a Self-Managing Disk Cache for Database Management Applications", *Proceedings of the Fourth International Workshop on Database Machines*, March 1985, pp. 330-345.

[JENE86] Jenevein, R. and B.Menezes, "KYKLOS: Low Tide High Flow" *Proceedings of the Sixth International Conference on Distributed Computing*, pp. 8-15, May 1986.

[DeWI87] DeWitt, D.J, M.Smith, H.Boral, "A Single-User Performance Utilization of the

Teradata Database Machine" *MCC Technical Report # DB-081-87*, March 5, 1987.

[MENE85] Menezes, B. and R.Jenevein, "KYKLOS: A Linear growth Fault-tolerant Interconnection Network" *Proceedings of the International Conference on Parallel Processing*, pp. 498-502, August 1985.

[MENE86] Menezes, B., R.Jenevein and M.Malek, "Reliability Analysis of the KYKLOS Interconnection Network" *Proceedings of the Sixth International Conference on Distributed Computing*, pp. 46-51, May 1986.

[VALD84] Valduriez, P. and G.Gardarin, "Join and Semi-Join Algorithms for a Multiprocessor Database Machine" *ACM TODS*, vol 9, March 1984.

Design and Implementation of High Speed Pipeline Merge Sorter with Run Length Tuning Mechanism

M.Kitsuregawa* W.Yang* T.Suzuki** M.Takagi*

* Institute of Industrial Science, The University of Tokyo
** Mitsubishi Electric Corp.

Abstract

This paper presents the design and implementation details of the pipeline merge sorter with string(run) length tuning mechanism.

Generally we lose some flexibilities at the expense of the high performance when some function is implemented by hardware. As for sorting, the length of record is the most crucial parameter. The hardware sorter can sort very efficiently the records of a given length determined by hardware. Its performance deteriorates largely, however, when the length of the input record is different from the predetermined length. For this problem, we developed the "String Length Tuning Algorithm".

In this paper, the architecture and design details of the pipeline merge sorter which implements string length tuning algorithm is presented. We have constructed the 18 stage pipeline sorter. Its memory capacity is 8 Mbytes. The sorting speed is 4MBytes/sec. 256K records can be sorted at one time.

1. Introduction

Sorting is one of the most fundamental operation and used very frequently in the computer system. Several research efforts has been devoted to improve the sorting speed. Many efficient algorithms have been developed so far. In addition to the software approach, advances in hardware technology stimulates the development of specialized hardware sorter.

In database application where large amount of data is handled, the data is stored in the disks and is staged onto main memory from disks as needed. This data transfer time becomes a large overhead time. One possible solution is to utilize this data transfer time for sorting. Several types of O(N) time sorter, which can sort the data stream in O(N) time keeping up with its flow, has been proposed so far such as pipeline bubble sorter[1], parallel enumeration sorter[2], pipeline heap sorter[3] and pipeline merge sorter[4].

Several database machines such as RDBM[5],GRACE[6], DELTA[7] and IDP[8] incorporate such hardware sorter as a key function unit.

In 1982, we constructed one stage of a pipeline merge sorter[9]. The objective was to clarify the memory management mechanism and to understand its hardware complexity. Its sorting speed attained 3 Mbytes/sec. Through the hardware

89

implementation we learned several design problems.

One of the most severe problem we faced is on record length. Generally we lose some flexibilities at the expense of the high performance when some function is implemented by hardware. As for sorting, the length of record is the most crucial parameter. The hardware sorter can sort very efficiently the records of a given length determined by hardware. Its performance deteriorates largely, however, when the length of the input record is different from the predetermined length. For this problem, we proposed the "String Length Tuning Algorithm" in [10]. After our implementation of first version of pipeline merge sorter, ICOT implemented 12-stage, 64Kbyte sorter. However no mechanism was introduced for this problem.

In this paper, the architecture and design details of the pipeline merge sorter which implements string length tuning algorithm is presented. This sorter can sort the records of any length very efficiently with memory utilization efficiency 99%. We have constructed the 18 stage pipeline merge sorter. Its memory capacity is 8 Mbytes. The sorting speed is 4MBytes/sec. 256K records can be sorted at one time.

In section 2, string length tuning algorithm is introduced with an example. Section 3 describes the merge operation of a sort element in more detail. Memory management and data structure manipulation are discussed. Hardware architecture of a sort element is given in section 4. Section 5 presents the format of the input data stream. The pilot sort system consisting 18 sort elements is described in section 6.

2. Pipeline Merge Sorter and String Length Tuning Algorithm

2.1 Pipeline merge sort algorithm

Fig.1 shows the organization of the pipeline merge sorter. If N is the number of the record to be sorted, $n(=\log_k N)$ sort elements are connected linearly. Each sort element performs k way merge operation. The i-th sort element has the memory with the capacity of $(k-1)k^{i-1}$ records. For the purpose of simplicity, 2-way instead of K-way merge sorter is used here.

The overview of the sorting process is given in Fig.2. This sorter can sort the record stream keeping up the flow of the stream. The records are given in the form of the stream. The input data stream is led

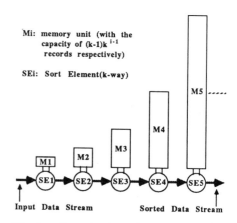

Mi: memory unit (with the capacity of $(k-1)k^{i-1}$ records respectively)

SEi: Sort Element(k-way)

Fig. 1   Organization of a Pipeline Merge Sorter

into the first sort element. The output data stream is output from the last element once all the records are given to the sorter.

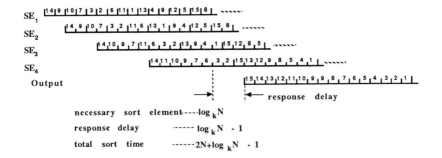

Fig. 2   Sorting Overview of a Pipeline Merge Sorter

The behavior of each sort element is very simple. The i-th element merges two strings given from the (i-1)-th element, each of which consists of 2^{i-1} records, and output the merged string of 2^i records to the (i+1)-th element. A sort element at first loads the first string in its own memory, and starts the merge processing when the first record of the second string arrives. The unit of the pipeline segment could be a record, a word, a byte and so on.

It takes $2N + \log_2 N - 1$ time to sort N records, where the second term corresponds to the flush time of the pipeline. O(N) memory space is required.

2.2   Problem on record length

The pipeline merge sorter described above can sort the records very fast in linear time, while it takes O(N log N) time in conventional uniprocessor computer system. However we usually lose some flexibility in return for the high performance if we implement some function by special hardware. In the case of sorting, the length of a record is an example of such flexibilities.

In sec 2.1, we assumed records always have some constant length, say L bytes. The first sort element has L bytes of memory. The i-th sort element has $2^{i-1} L$ bytes of memory. Nothing is stated for the case where the length of the incoming records, say X, is different from L. For example, if X > L, the first element cannot store a record of first string. Some control mechanism is required to handle arbitrary length of records.

The simple algorithm for this problem is to skip first several sort elements and to make the element which has the memory larger than X bytes a logically first sort element. If we skip first m elements, the indices of elements are incremented by m. Then the logical first element, as opposed to the physical first element, is defined as the leftmost element P_i in the linearly connected elements such that $X < 2^{i-1}L$ for given record length X. This method is very simple and no serious change of control may be necessary to implement it. But memory utilization efficiency is very low. For example, suppose X be a little bit longer than L, say 1.1L. Then we skip first element. The second sort element is a logical first element. The memory utilization efficiency becomes 55%. As described later, we

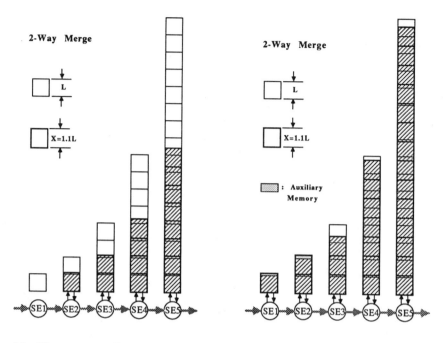

(a) The memory utilization by using the algorithm to skip first sort element when X=1.1L

(b) The optimized memory utilization by packing the space of 4-th sort element

Fig. 3   Comparison of Storage Utilization Efficiency between Simple Algorithm and String Length Tuning Algorithm

have implemented the 8 MByte hardware sorter. With this simple algorithm, about 4 Mbytes memory space is wasted. It is also very hard to use because for one record length 8 Mbytes file can be sorted using whole memory space, while for another record length only 4 Mbytes file can be sorted with half of its memory wasted.

In [10] we proposed the string length tuning (run length tuning) algorithm for this problem. With this algorithm, we can sort records of any length efficiently keeping the memory efficiency very high. The algorithm makes the number of records the sorter can sort maximal or near maximal by utilizing such unused area in the memory that would be produced by the above simple algorithm. Fig.3 shows the memory utilization efficiencies for the simple algorithm and string length tuning algorithm. You can see the efficiency is much improved by string length tuning algorithm.

2.3 String length tuning algorithm (Run length tuning algorithm)

The basic idea to improve the memory utilization efficiency is based on the following fact.

If, for some i, the i-th sort element SE_i always output to the (i+1)-th element

SE_{i+1} the longest string that SE_{i+1} can accept, that is, if SE_i always produces the string which has $\lceil 2^iL/X \rceil$ records, then the memory utilization efficiencies of all its succeeding elements are also kept ($\lceil 2^iL/X \rceil)X/2^iL$. Here we define the logical space of the i-th element as the memory space of size 2^iL. On the other hand, i-th element has the memory of $2^{i-1}L$ bytes. which we call the physical memory space of the i-th element.

So if the logical space of the i-th element is always filled up with the records as much as possible, the physical space of the succeeding elements keeps the same memory utilization efficiency as that of the logical space of the i-th element.

We call the index i optimization degree. Here i is the logical number, not physical number, of the sort element. We use 'd' to denote the optimization degree. Thus we can achieve the high memory utilization efficiency for later stages of sort elements by packing the logical space of the d-th sort element.

Our idea to realize this is to change the string length (or run length) dynamically at first d elements, which we call 'string length tuning'.

The detail algorithm of string length tuning and the expression of improved memory utilization efficiency for K-way merge sorter are given in [10]. Here we present the simplified algorithm for 2-way sorter with an example. We make 'Merge Tree' which determines the behavior of the elements. This tree is binary tree with the depth d and generated by the following procedure.

(1) label the root node with $\lceil 2^{d-1}L/X \rceil$.

(2) For all nodes, if it is labeled with H, label its left son with $\lceil H/2 \rceil$ and label its right son with $\lfloor H/2 \rfloor$.

As an example, let's make the merge tree for X=1.1L and optimization degree 3. Fig.4 shows the merge tree for this example. Suppose root node be d-th level and leaf node be first level. The label of i-th level of the tree denotes the number of records in the string that i-th sort element generates to the next element. The i-th sort element repeats merging strings whose length are successively taken from the labels at i-th level in the tree from left to right. Reaching the rightmost node, then it returns the leftmost node at the same level. The first element merges the two records when its label is two. It bypasses the incoming record to the next element if its label is one. Fig.5 shows the pipeline chart of the sorting overview of this example. As you can see, the sort element outputs dummy

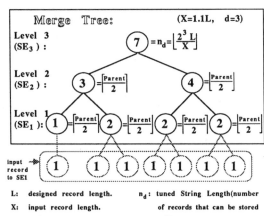

Fig. 4   Memory Tree

record in some cases.

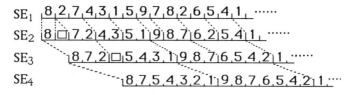

□: Dummy Record

Fig. 5   Pipeline Processing Overview

2.4 Implementation issues on string length tuning algorithm

Here we consider the implementation issues on the string length tuning algorithm, especially the difference from the ordinary pipeline merge sorter.

As you can see from the example, first element stores the record with the length X(=1.1L). Thus first d elements must have additional memory. As for the precise amount of memory, please refer to [10]. The amount of this additional memory is known to be less than L for first d elements, SE_1, SE_2,.., SE_{d-1}, SE_d, which is very small in comparison with total amount of memory.

In ordinary pipeline merge sorter, the length of the string does not change during the operation. So we simply used counters to manage strings in our previous design[9]. On the other hand, the sorter using string length tuning algorithm changes the length of the string dynamically. This is done by putting flags at the head of the record. The sort element performs merge operation following the flags which represent the sequence given by the merge tree defined at section 2.3. The flags themselves are generated by the sort driver which activates the sort operation.

As you can see in Fig.5, there arize the time slot where no record is output to the next element. These irregular patterns of pipeline are also controlled by flags.

3. Merge Operation and Memory Management in a Sort Element

3.1 Merging operation in a sort element

In sec 2.1, the original pipeline merge sort algorithm is given. In order to clarify the memory management problem, here we see the merge processing in a sort element in a little bit more detail.

Each element iterates the merge operation of the strings given by the preseeding element. This operation can be decomposed into the following three phases.

Phase 0:

In this state the records of the first string given by the preseeding element are stored in its memory. After receiving the whole first string, internal state transits to phase 1.

Phase 1:

In this state, an element merges the incoming second string with the first string stored in its memory, and outputs the merged string to the next element. After receiving the whole second string, internal state transits to phase 2.

Phase 2:

In this state, an element continues to merge two strings which remain in its memory, and at the same time stores the next string in its memory which is being given by the preseeding element. After receiving the whole next first string, internal state transits to phase 1.

3.2 Memory management in a sort element

As shown in the previous section, the behavior of an element can be clarified using three states and transition between them. During the merge operation, that is, in phase 1 and 2, an element inputs one record, compares two records from two strings, and outputs the larger or smaller record to the next element. Thus an element inputs one record and outputs one record in each pipeline segment. Therefore the necessary memory space is constant during the operation. But it is not sufficient just to store the incoming record in the memory area previously occupied by the current output record. Since the sequence to fetch the head records of the two strings is random, some mechanism to keep the sorted sequence in the memory is required.

In [10], we have presented three kind of memory management algorithms for pipeline merge sorter:Double Memory Method, Block Division Method, and Pointer Method. For this implementation, we adopted pointer method which maintains the sequence of the records as a linked list by providing the pointer at the end of each record. Fig.6 shows the hardware resources for memory management. The top records of the two strings are kept in the string top pointer registers, STP0 and STP1. The record body is read into the element using memory address registers, MAR0 and MAR1. The number of the records in the memory for each string is maintained in the registers, CTR0 and CTR1. In phase 2, an element inputs the next string while it merges two strings in the memory using STP0 and STP1. MARW has the memory address to store this incoming string. STP2 and CTR2 keeps the head address and the number of records of this string respectively.

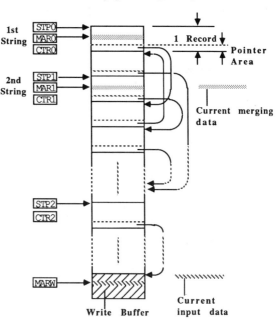

Fig. 6   Memory Management in a Sort Element

Let's see the register manipulation. Suppose a record of the first string is output. Navigating the pointer, the contents of STP0 and MAR0 are updated by the address of the next record. Since the area occupied by the output record is used to store the next input record, the address in STP0 is transferred to MARW. The address in STP0 is also stored in the pointer area of the currently stored record of the next string. The content of STP1 does not change. MAR1 is updated by STP1. Such register manipulation is performed by microprogrammed control unit during the pointer handling time, that is, two word processing time. (see Fig.7 of the next section)

3.3   Pipeline processing

A record consists of data part of arbitrary length and pointer part of two word length. As described in section 2.1, the unit of pipeline could be a record, a word, a byte, a bit and so on. In our design, word level pipelining is adopted, where one segment of the pipeline is one word processing.

In phase 1 and phase 2, sort element reads the top words of two strings from the memory and compares them. At the same time it stores the word given by the preseeding element into the memory. Thus it is necessary to access the memory three times to process one word. The processing of one word consists three clocks, read cycle for string0(R0), read cycle for string1(R1) and write cycle for input string(W) as shown in Fig.7. In W cycle a sort element output the word of the larger(or smaller) record, which the succeeding element latches. Thus word level pipelining is adopted.

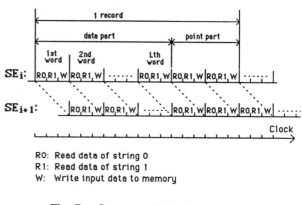

Fig. 7   Structure of Pipeline

In the previous machine developed in 1982[9], one segment consists of two clocks. While the record of either string is given as output in merge operation, the other is again used in the next merge operation. By retaining that record in the register of the sort element, the number of memory accesses can be decreased by one. That is, two cycles suffices for one word processing. A merge top register was provided in the previous design. Although this design makes the sorter run faster, we lose some flexibility, since the maximum length of the record the sorter can sort is determined by the capacity of the merge top register. Therefore we use three clocks for one segment in this design, where there is no limit for record length.

4. Architecture of a sort element

4.1 Hardware Architecture of a Sort Element

Fig.8 shows the architecture of the sort element. It consists of several address registers, counters, comparator, and so on. The function of each resource is as follows.

1) MARi(Memory Address Register for Read, 24 bits, i=0,1): Registers to have the memory address of the records of the i-th string.

2) STPi(String Top Register, 24 bits, i=0,1,2): Registers to have the top address of the i-th string.

3) MARW(Memory Address register for Write, 24 bits): A register to have the memory address of the write buffer.

4) CTRi(Counter, 20 bits, i=0,1,2): Counters to keep the number of the records of the i-th string.

5) RLC(Record Length Counter, 16 bits): A counter used to detect the end of a record

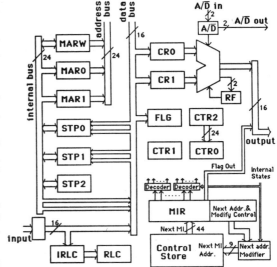

Fig. 8   Hardware Architecture of a Sort Element

6) IRLC(Initialization Register for RLC, 16bits): A register to keep the length of a record.

7) CRi(Comparison Register, 16 bits, i=0,1): Input registers to the comparator for two strings.

8) FLG(Flag Register, 3 bits): A register for the flag.

9) RF(Result Flag) (2 bits): A register to keep the result of the comparison.

These resources are controlled by the microprogrammed control unit. In the microprogrammed system, the control store and main memory are distinguished, with the former having a fairly faster access time than the latter. However, in the future, when a highly integrated circuit is realized, the sort element and the memory can be integrated on the same chip. Therefore the same memory devices are used for both control store and data memory. Horizontal microprogramming technique is adopted in stead of vertical microprogramming. One word(two bytes) is processed by three clocks. Thus the processing of one word must be realized by three microinstructions. This leads to pipelined construction of the microprogrammed control unit. Next address is provided in the instruction due to the restriction on time. Multi-way branch is supported by modifying the next address with the specified status bits.

4.2 Input and output interface of a sort element

Fig.9 shows the input and output interface of a sort element.

1) Address, Data, R/W

Address bus is 24 bits wide. Data bus is 16 bits wide. Both are connected to the external memory. Thus the maximal address space is 16Mbytes. The total capacity of the sorter can be 32Mbytes.

2) DATAin, DATAout (16 bits)

A sorting element is connected to the preseeding element and also to the succeeding element with 16 bits wide data path.

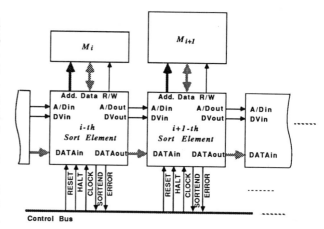

Fig. 9   Input and Output Signals of a Sort Element

3) A/Din, A/Dout (2 bits)

A/Din is given with the data at the same time, indicating ascending or descending sort. Two bits are used with one bit for each byte. Sorting order can be specified on byte boundary. A/Din signal is propagated to the succeeding sort element as A/Dout signal.

4) DVin, DVout

DVin(Data Valid in) signal indicates that the input data is valid. If this signal is low, input data on DATAin is latched on the register. This signal is used to suspend the pipeline operation when the input data stream is interrupted temporarily. DVin signal is propagated to the next sort element with three clock delay.

5) SORTEND

This signal indicates the end of the sort processing. The sort driver, which controls the input and output data stream to and from the sorter, uses the SORTEND signal of the last sort element to detect the end of the current sorted stream.

6) ERROR

A sort element can detect the error condition such as parity error and inconsistent flags. This signal indicates an error occurs.

7) HALT

This signal is used to stop all the sort elements simultaneously.

8) CLOCK

The common clock signal is supplied to all the sort elements.

9) RESET

Internal registers of a sort element is initialized with this signal.

Fig.10 shows the input and output timing of the some of the above signals, where DV signal and HALT signal are activated.

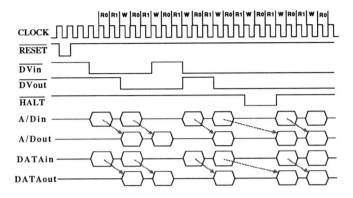

Fig.10   Timing Diagram

5. Data Format and Flags

Fig.11 shows the format of the input data stream. At the top of the stream, three words of the initialization data is sent to the sort element before the actual data. Before starting the sort operation, following various parameters must be set up in each sort element.

1) Record length

This informa-
tion is loaded in the
IRLC register.

2)   Bypass infor-
mation

If the length of
a record exceeds
that of the design
parameter L, first
several sort ele-
ments which do not
have the memory
with the capacity

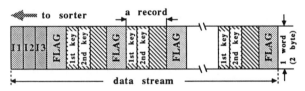

I1,I2,I3: Initial data

FLAGS: BOS: Begin of String   LS: Last String
        EOS: End of String   NMP: No Merge Pair
        SBP: Stream Bypass   DR: Dummy Record

Fig.11   Data Format of the Input Stream

larger than a record are always skipped. The information of which sort element should be skipped is given to the sorter as a bit pattern.

3)   Run length tuning information

As described in section 2, some sort elements output dummy record. These elements are notified of it with the bit pattern as a initialization data.

4)   Flag

At the top of each record, two words of flag area is attached. During this two words time, the pointer of records are manipulated. Flags handling and pointer manipulation are overlapped. There are five flags.

   *BOS flag   indicates the start of the string.
   *EOS flag   indicates the end of the string.

*NMP flag	indicates that this record has no merge pair.
*LS flag	indicates that this is the last string of the data stream.
*SBP flag	indicates stream bypass processing which is used for multi-sorter environment.

6. Organization of the Pilot System

The pilot system consists of a sort driver, 18 sort elements and memory boards as shown in Fig.12. One sort element is implemented on one multi-wire board. A sort element has 220 IC chips. At first we developed one sort element with wire wrapping. The circuits for debugging was added extensively so that almost all the registers can be monitored. On producing eighteen copies, most of debug circuits are omitted.

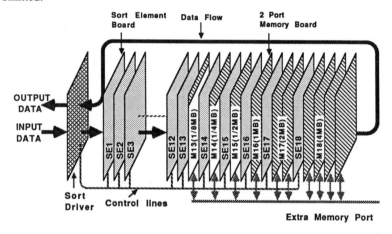

Fig.12   Organization of the Pilot System

In order to obtain some perspective on LSI implementation, the pilot system uses general purpose TTL and CMOS memory. Multi-functional LSI is not used. Fig.13 (a) shows the board of a sort element. Each board has 64 Kbytes of memory on it. The designed record length L is 32 bytes. Therefore first twelve sort elements do not need external memory boards. The sort elements after thirteenth stage use memory boards.

These external memory boards are two ported. The memory space of the sorter is mapped on that of the control processor. Thus this memory can also be used for ordinal processing in addition to sorting. Overall pilot system is shown in Fig.13(b).

The system is composed of 18 sort elements. 256K records can be sorted at one time. Total memory capacity is 8 Mbytes. The clock rate is 6MHz. The sorting speed is 4Mbytes/sec.

(a) A sort element　　　　　　　　(b) The sorter system

Fig.13　Overview of the Pilot System

Table.1　Features of a sorter

Number of sort element	18
Total capacity of memory	8M bytes
The number of records which can be sorted	256 K records
Sorting speed	4 M bytes/sec.
Clock speed	6 MHz
Tuning degree	11

7. Conclusion

In this paper, we presented the architecture and the implementation details of 18 stage sorter. One of the distinguished features is its run length tuning mechanism. The sorter can sort the file of records of any length efficiently with this mechanism. For any length of records, the efficiency of the memory utilization attains 99 percent.

Currently the sorter is being connected to the system bus of the host computer(MELCOM-80) in one experiment. Software driver of the sorter is developed under UNIX environment. Sort utility is modified to use hardware sorter. Index generation speed is much accelerated. Overall performance will be reported in another paper.

The sorter is also integrated into the disk cache system in the other experiment. We are now implementing a sort element on one VLSI chip. Several results will be presented in the future paper.

References

1] Kung,H.T.:The Structure of Parallel Algorithms, Advances in Computer 19,Academic Press,1980.

2] Yasuura,H.:The Parallel Enumeration Sorting Scheme for VLSI, IEEE, Trans. Comput. Vol.C-31, No.12, 1983.

3] Tanaka,Y. et.al.:Pipeline Searching and Sorting Modules as Components of a Data Flow Database Computer, IFIP 80,1980

4] Todd,S.:Algorithm and Hardware for Merge Sort Using Multiple Processors, IBM J.R&D, 22,5,1978.

5] Zeidler, H:Data handling and dedicated hardware for the sort problem, Database Machines, Springer Verlag, 1983(Proc. of IWDM-83).

6] Kitsuregawa,M. et.al:Architecture and Performance of Relational Algebra Machine GRACE, Int.Conf.on Parallel Processing 84,1984

7] Kakuta,T. et.al:The design and implementation of Relational Database Machine Delta, Database Machines Fourth International Workshop, Springer Verlag, 1985.

8] Torii,S. et.al.:A Relational Database System Architecture Based on Vector Processing Method, Proc. of 3rd Int. Conf. on Data Engineering, 1987.

9] Kitsuregawa,M.et.al:Organization of Pipeline Merge Sorter, Trans, IECE Japan, J66-D, 1983. Its English translation is available in scripta electronica japonica III, vol.14, 1983.

10]Kitsuregawa,M. et.al:Memory Management Algorithms in Pipeline Merge Sorter, Database Machines Fourth International Workshop, Springer Verlag, 1985.

ALGORITHMS
FOR SORTING AND SORT-BASED DATABASE OPERATIONS
USING A SPECIAL-FUNCTION UNIT [*]

C. LEE, S. Y. W. SU, H. LAM

Database Systems Research and Development Center
University of Florida, Gainesville, FL. 32611

Abstract:

This paper presents the design of a Special Function Unit for DataBase operations (SFU-DB), which is used as a backend database machine for performing sort and sort-based database operations. This machine implements a most-significant-digit-first radix sort algorithm by using a special hardware device called Automatic Retrieval Memory (ARM). The ARM performs an efficient content-to-address mapping to sort the data. Without performing any comparisons in the sorting process, the SFU-DB avoids the lower bound constraint on comparison-based sorting algorithms and achieves a complexity of $O(n)$ for both execution time and main memory size. Based on the sorting algorithm, the SFU-DB also performs other primitive database operations such as relational join, elimination of duplicates, set union, set intersection, and set difference with a complexity of $O(n)$. The capacity of the SFU-DB is limited by the size of its main memory rather than by the number of special processing elements as in most sorting machines. Hence, the SFU-DB has a better cost/performance and is more suitable for processing very large databases. Currently, a prototype SFU-DB system is under construction.

INTRODUCTION

Sorting is one of the most fundamental and frequently used operations in computer systems. Many algorithms for sorting have been developed. Recently, due to the great improvement of semiconductor technology, several specialized hardware sorters have been designed and implemented; however, most of the designs implement a comparison-based sort algorithm [1,2,3,4,5]. These comparison-based sorting machines have an inherent constraint, i.e., a serial algorithm that performs sorting by comparison requires at least $O(n\log(n))$ comparisons for n records [6].

In this paper, the design and implementation of a backend database machine called

---

[*] This project is supported by NSF Grant #ECS-8402252.

103

the Special Function Unit for DataBase operations (SFU- DB) is presented. The SFU-DB provides efficient hardware support for sorting and other sort-based database operations such as join, elimination of duplicates, set union, set intersection, and set difference. The SFU-DB presented in this paper extends our previous work [7] by introducing the stack architecture and recursive algorithms.

The algorithm implemented by the SFU-DB is a most-significant-digit-first radix sort algorithm (each digit is one byte in the SFU-DB). By using a special hardware device called Automatic Retrieval Memory (ARM), the SFU-DB can physically and effectively "shrink" the size of a database. The special-purpose device ARM in the SFU-DB is used as a "filter" as well as a "ranker", which can shrink the size of the data file and sort it at the same time. The irrelevant data elements are discarded when the sorting operation is being performed.

Without performing any comparisons in the sorting process, the SFU-DB easily avoids the lower bound constraint on comparison-based sorting algorithms and successfully achieves a complexity $O(n)$ utilizing only a single processor with a serial algorithm.

The capacity of the SFU-DB is limited by the size of the main memory instead of by the number of processing elements, as in many sorting machines [1,3]. The main memory in the SFU-DB is implemented by using commercially available RAMs. Because of the inherent density of the RAMs, the capacity of the SFU-DB is inherently larger than one whose capacity is limited by the number of processing elements. The first advantage of this large capacity is that in a very large database environment, a large capacity machine requires less I/O transmissions and less iterations in such operations as external merge sort, nested-loop join, etc. The second advantage is that the memory in the SFU-DB can be used by the host computer for other purposes when the SFU-DB is not in use.

This paper is organized as follows. In section 2, the architectures of the Special Function Unit (SFU-DB) and the Automatic Retrieval Memory (ARM) are described. Section 3 presents the sorting algorithm; a summarization of the result of a performance study and the features of the system are also given in this section. Algorithms for other important database operations such as duplicate elimination, join, and set operations are presented in section 4. Section 5 describes the prototype implementation of the SFU-DB. Finally, a conclusion is given in section 6.

SYSTEM CONFIGURATION

One possible organization of a multiprocessor system using the SFU-DB is a network of processing nodes interconnected by a system global bus, as shown in Figure 1. Each node contains a number of general-purpose processors and special-function units.

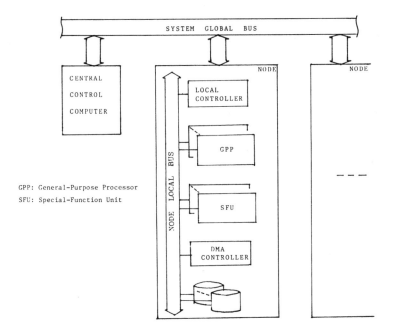

Figure 1. System Configuration.

These processors and some secondary storage devices are connected by a local bus. General-purpose processors are used to perform tasks such as compiling, scheduling, memory paging, memory access controlling, etc. Special-function units are used to perform primitive database operations. The SFU-DB works as a special-function processor to efficiently perform relational database operations.

The Architecture of the SFU-DB

The SFU-DB is an independent subsystem suspended off the local bus of a node, as shown in Figure 2. It can efficiently execute relational database operations in parallel with other SFU-DBs. Within the SFU-DB are its own local bus and the following components:

(1) an interface unit between its own local bus and the node local bus,

(2) a local processor,

(3) an instruction memory (ROM or EPROM), which stores the decoded micro-instructions of all SFU-DB sort-based operations, and a micro-engine, which controls the execution of these operations,

(4) an Automatic Retrieval Memory (ARM), which is the key component of the SFU-DB and is capable of performing sorting,

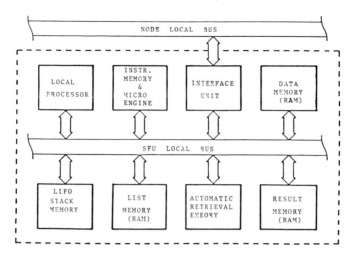

Figure 2. Architecture of the SFU.

(5) a Data Memory (DM), implemented in RAM, which stores the initial data to be processed,

(6) a List Memory (LM), implemented in RAM, which maintains a list of pointers required when sorting data with duplicate values,

(7) a LIFO Stack Memory (SM), used to handle the ARM overflow,

(8) a Result Memory (RM), implemented in RAM, which stores the final processed data.

Functionally, the SFU-DB operates as follows. The local controller of a node sends a task, which may be a part of a complex query received from the control computer, to the SFU-DB specifying the database operations to be executed and the location of the data in the secondary storage. Upon receiving the command, the SFU-DB loads the data into its Data Memory (DM) under the control of a DMA controller. Processing of the data can then be performed by using the ARM, LM, and SM. Finally, the result of the database operation is stored in the Result Memory (RM) of the SFU-DB.

The Architecture of the Automatic Retrieval Memory

As shown in Figure 3, the ARM consists of a RAM unit (the ARM-RAM) and an Automatic Retrieval Unit (ARU). Within the ARU there is a stack which is formed by L pages of mark-bit registers, each of which contains 256 one-bit registers; L is a design parameter. These one-bit registers are used to mark corresponding data in the ARM-

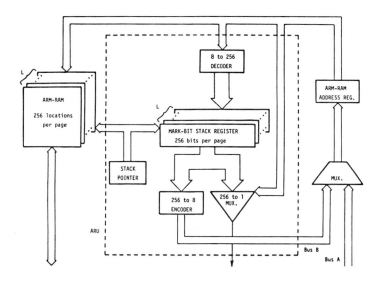

Figure 3.   Hardware organization of the ARM.

RAM during processing. Correspondingly, the ARM-RAM is also a stack containing L pages of RAMs, each of which contains 256 memory locations. These memory locations store flags and pointers that are necessary for processing data. Only the top pages of the ARU and the ARM-RAM are used when processing data, i.e., one-byte data value can be processed at a time.

There are two primary operations in the ARM: ARM Write and ARM Retrieval. For the ARM Write operation, a one-byte data value fetched from the Data Memory is used as an address to locate an entry in the ARM. Using this value, an 8-to-256 decoder marks a corresponding mark-bit in the top page of the ARU. At the same time, a pointer, whose function will be discussed in detail in section 3, is also stored in the corresponding memory location in the top page of the ARM-RAM. The mark-bit is used to indicate that the incoming byte value satisfies (or does not satisfy) a search condition or that there has been some other value(s) mapped to that address. For the ARM Retrieval operation, all the data in the top page of the ARM-RAM whose corresponding mark-bits are set are read sequentially from the lowest address to the highest address. This is accomplished by using an embedded priority encoder whose function is to encode the currently highest priority mark-bit on the top page of the stack that is set and to generate a corresponding address. This address is used to read the stored information in the ARM-RAM. This process is repeated for each of the mark-bits that is set, bypassing the unmarked ones. In this manner, the data retrieved from the ARM is automatically in sorted order. More importantly, the ARU allows only the marked words to be accessed as if they physically form a dense list of memory words, even though unmarked words are interspersed among them. In effect, this hardware feature shrinks the memory to a smaller size.

THE SORTING ALGORITHM

Many database operations can benefit from the fact that the data files on which they operate are sorted. In this section, the sorting algorithm is presented first. The methods for handling overflow situations in the SFU-DB is presented in section 3.2. Finally, a brief description of an evaluation of the sorting algorithm and the features of the SFU-DB system are given in section 3.3.

Sorting by Content-to-Address Mapping

A very simple way to sort a list of values is to use their contents to address a large memory and store them in the addressed locations. After mapping all the data values into the memory (assuming duplicated values are taken care of by some means), the values are already in order. In this manner, no comparisons are required in the sorting process. However, there are two difficulties in implementing this simple algorithm. First, the address space will have to be very large since each value may contain many bytes. Second, empty memory locations may intersperse among those that contain values. It will take time to search through all memory locations in order to read the data out in a sorted order. The Automatic Retrieval Memory (ARM) was designed to overcome these two difficulties. We shall use a single-byte sort example to illustrate the basic sorting algorithm before presenting the general multi-byte sorting algorithm.

The Basic Sorting Algorithm. The basic sort operation uses the ARM and the following memory components: Data Memory (DM), List Memory (LM), and Result Memory (RM). A relation R to be sorted based on an attribute A is initially stored in the Data Memory (DM), as shown in Figure 4(a). The ARM is initialized by clearing all the mark-bits. The sorting process begins by reading values from the DM and storing them in the ARM; this ARM is virtually the large memory described earlier. In the example shown in Figure 4, the first value to be stored in the ARM is 9. It is used to address the ARM-RAM's memory location 9 into which a pointer (P) to the DM location D0 is stored. The corresponding mark-bit in the ARU is set to 1. The process is repeated for the rest of the attribute values. After processing the first four attribute values (9, 7, 3, and 6), the ARM's contents are shown in Figure 4(b). The next value to be written into the ARM is the value 3 in D4. However, the ARM location 3 is already occupied, which implies the existence of some duplicates. To handle this situation, a conventional link list technique is used. The List Memory (LM) is used to store a linked list of DM pointers (DMPTRs) which point to the duplicate values in DM, as shown in Figure 4(c). The special character '#' represents the end of a linked list. The List Memory

DM Address	Attribute A	Rest of Tuple
D0	9	:
D1	7	:
D2	3	:
D3	6	:
D4	3	:
D5	7	:
D6	3	:

(a) The Data in Relation R.

ARM Address	ARM-RAM Data		Mark-bit
	F	P	M
0			
1			
2			
3		D2	1
4			
5			
6		D3	1
7		D1	1
8			
9		D0	1

(b) The ARM data after the first four attributes are mapped into the ARM.

ARM Address	ARM-RAM Data		Mark-bit
	F	P	M
0			
1			
2			
3	1	L4	1
4			
5			
6		D3	1
7	1	L3	1
8			
9		D0	1
10			

LM Address	LM Data	
	DMPTR	LMPTR
L0	D2	//
L1	D4	L0
L2	D1	//
L3	D5	L2
L4	D6	L1
L5		
L6		

LMC	L5

Address	RM Data DMPTR
0	D6
1	D4
2	D2
3	D3
4	D5
5	D1
6	D0
7	

RMC	7

(c) The ARM and LM contents after all the attribute words in the DM have been mapped into the ARM.

(d) The final result in the RM

Figure 4. Illustration of the Basic ARM Sort Algorithm.

Counter (LMC) associated with the LM is used to keep track of the next available location in the LM. Correspondingly, the pointer P of that ARM-RAM location is changed to point to the head of the list in LM. The flag bit (F) of the ARM-RAM location is set to 1 to indicate the existence of duplicate values.

The technique of using a linked list to handle overflows or multiple values is a standard software technique. However, in the SFU-DB, hardware is used to assist the processing of the linked list. Thus, the flexibility of linked lists is gained without the sacrifice of the software overhead usually associated with processing linked lists.

To obtain the final sorted result, an automatic retrieval operation is performed by the ARM and all marked ARM locations are read in ascending order. If an attribute value is unique (i.e., M=1 and F=0), the DM tuple pointer obtained from the ARM-RAM location is directly stored in the Result Memory (RM). If there are duplicates (i.e., M=1 and F=1), then the linked list in the LM is traversed to obtain a set of DM tuple pointers, which is then stored in the RM. Associated with the RM is a Result Memory Counter (RMC) which keeps track of its next free location. Figure 4(d) shows the contents of RM and RMC at the completion of the sorting process.

General Multi-byte Sorting Algorithm. In the basic SFU-DB sort algorithm, we assume that the ARM address bus is wide enough to process attribute values in a single pass. However, in general, the sort attribute(s) may contain many bytes and cannot be processed in a single pass. In this case, a general multi-byte sort algorithm is required. For a detailed algorithm, refer to [10]. Here we present only the general concept behind the algorithm.

Conceptually, the general multi-byte sorting algorithm processes the values byte-by-byte and partitions the attribute values into groups based on their corresponding byte values as shown in Figure 5. In this figure, we assume that there are 31 values to be sorted, each being 4 bytes wide. The most significant byte (MSByte) values are sorted first, using the basic (single-byte) sorting algorithm and the first page of the ARM; this process is represented by ARMSORT(1) as shown in the figure. The number in the parenthesis is used to represent the sequence of processing the attribute values. Four groups of identical MSByte values, indicated by DUPL (duplicate), are formed in this example. The other values indicated by NDUPL (non-duplicate) are unique in the MSByte values.

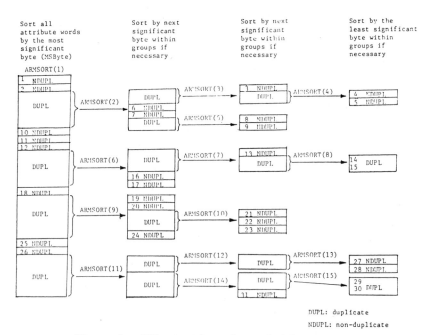

Figure 5.   Illustration of a multi-byte sort.

After the first step of processing, the MSByte values are in sorted order. If a value is unique in the list, it can be retrieved from the ARM without further processing. However, for a group of attribute values that have the same MSByte, their next byte values need to be sorted. The next step is performed on the second page of the ARM using the same basic sorting algorithm. The same process of dividing a group into sub-groups and retrieving unique values is repeated recursively until either no group within a sublist has duplicate members or all m (m=4 in this example) bytes have been processed. Note that only in the worst-case situation the sorting of all m bytes is required. In this case, the duplicate members of the group are truly duplicates and m pages of the ARM are required.

Handling of Overflow in the SFU-DB

There are two overflow situations in the SFU-DB: (1) ARM stack overflow, i.e., the width (m) of the sort attributes in bytes exceeds the number of pages (L) in the ARM, and (2) DM overflow, i.e., the number of attribute values (n) is larger than the number of DM locations.

To handle the ARM overflow, a Stack Memory (SM) is used to save the data of each group in ARM(L) (i.e., the last page of the ARM) that requires further sorting. After all the data on the ARM(L) have been processed (either stored into RM or stored into SM), the top entry of the SM data is popped and its corresponding LM list is mapped into the ARM(L) based on the next byte values. The same push and pop process is repeated until the SM is empty. There will be some degradation in performance when the ARM overflows. However, it is not a serious problem. Using the available VLSI technology, the ARM can be easily realized to contain enough pages to directly process attribute values with a "typical" width.

To handle the DM overflow, some external sorting algorithm is required. A common way to solve this problem is to bring in the large relation page-by-page from the secondary storage and to sort them internally. Then the sorted pages of records are merged into a sorted relation using either a pipelined merge or a k-way merge. Since the capacity of the SFU-DB is dependent on the size of DM and LM which are implemented in standard RAMs; whereas, the capacity of most other hardware sorters are dependent on the number of special-purpose processors and registers. (In [10], we developed a garbage collection algorithm for the LM so that only a relatively small LM (much smaller than the DM) is required.) Since the density of standard RAM is inherently greater than that of special-purpose hardware, the capacity for internal sort in the SFU-DB as compared to other sorters is also greater. The large capacity for internal sort reduces the number of levels required in the external merge. Therefore, merge-sort is one of the approaches that can be used effectively in the SFU-DB.

Another approach handling a large relation is to divide the attribute values into buckets based on some value ranges. If we have knowledge of the distribution of the attribute values, we can assign an appropriate value range to a bucket so that the sizes of the buckets are nearly equal and are smaller than the capacity of the SFU-DB. After dividing the attribute values into buckets, these buckets are externally in order. Then the internal sorting can be performed on each bucket by using the SFU-DB.

If we are not aware of the distribution of the attribute values, then an approach based on the bucket-sort algorithm introduced by Lindstrom in [8] is used. In this approach, a number of tuples (depending on the size of the DM and the size of the relation), say k tuples, are randomly selected from the original large relation. The k tuples are sorted over the sort attribute using the SFU-DB and are used to divide the original large relation into (k+1) externally sorted buckets. If the size of a bucket is smaller than or equal to the capacity of the SFU-DB, the bucket of tuples can be sorted internally in the SFU-DB. Otherwise, the pre-processing procedure is applied on that bucket recursively until every bucket can be processed directly by the SFU-DB.

Evaluation of the Sorting Algorithm

Most of the current database machines which deal with the sort problem use comparison-based algorithms. Generally, the performance of these sort algorithms is expressed in terms of the number of comparisons required to sort a data file. However, in the SFU-DB there is no comparison involved in the sorting operation. All the processes required in the SFU-DB are simply accesses to memories. Consequently, a more appropriate method to evaluate the SFU-DB operations is to calculate the number of memory accesses required to perform the database operations.

Since the number of memory accesses for performing the sorting operation in the SFU-DB is highly dependent on the nature of the data, as evident from the examples in section 3.1, it is important to characterize the data. In [9,10], we have developed an analytical model to characterize the data. Based on this model, we quantitatively analyze the sorting algorithm and derive a cost formula for the algorithm. Using this formula, the performance bounds (i.e., the best and worst cases) of the algorithm are determined. The best and worst cases for the SFU-DB algorithms are studied. They are the cases where the data contain the least and the most duplicates, respectively. Evaluation results obtained from this experiment show the following two important facts:

(1) Both the time and space complexities of the SFU-DB sorting algorithm are $O(n)$, where n is the cardinality of the relation to be processed. This is true since the SFU-DB processes data by simply reading them from the DM and storing them into the ARM (and LM, if necessary). There is no need to compare one value against the others, as in comparison-based algorithms. This feature frees the SFU-DB from the limitation of all

comparison-based sorting algorithms, i.e., a serial algorithm that sorts data by comparison requires at least $O(n\log(n))$ comparisons for n records [6].

(2) In some situations, the average number of accesses to an attribute value (or a tuple) can be less than one. This is true because the SFU- DB processes data vertically (i.e., byte-by-byte). As a simple example, assume that a file contains 64000 attribute values each being 20 bytes wide. For the best case scenario, these 64000 values are divided into 256 groups after their first byte is processed, each group containing 256 attribute values. After the second byte is processed, the 256 attribute values of each group are then uniquely sorted. No further processing is required. Obviously, the number of accesses to each attribute value is less than one, even if the accesses to the LM are counted. If each attribute value contains more bytes, the number of accesses to each attribute value is even smaller. This, again, is a special feature that does not exist in the comparison-based algorithms.

ALGORITHMS FOR OTHER SORT-BASED DATABASE OPERATIONS

In this section, algorithms for other primitive database operations, such as duplicate elimination, join, and set operations, are presented using the sorting algorithm described in the preceding section.

Projection with Duplicate Elimination

The duplicate elimination operation is one of the most important database primitives and also one of the most time consuming one. It is an implied operation in a projection or a set union operation. To perform the elimination of duplicates using the SFU-DB, the data values are mapped into the ARM just as in the sorting operation. If multiple attribute values are mapped into the same ARM location, then we conclude that they are duplicates. The ARM Retrieval operation will read only one copy of the duplicates.

The duplicate elimination algorithm is fairly straightforward. The first byte of the attribute values maps into the first page of the ARM and a number of groups of duplicates are formed. If a group contains only one member, then it is written into the RM without further sorting. If the group contains more than one element, then the sorting of the next byte is required and is processed using the next page of the ARM. Finally, for the group(s) in the last byte that contains duplicates (if there exists any), output only one copy of the duplicates into the RM. After all the DM data are processed, the RM contains a list of DM tuple pointers pointing to the DM tuples whose attribute values are unique. Note that in this algorithm only the duplicate tuples are processed completely. Non-duplicate tuples can be output as soon as they are determined to be unique.

The Join Algorithm

In this subsection, we describe how the ARM sorting operation can be exploited in the execution of an equi-join operation. We recall that in the sorting operation, data values from the DM are mapped into different locations of the ARM. When performing the equi-join operation, we map the data values of the join attribute of both relations into the ARM. If the join attribute values of both relations are mapped into the same location of the ARM, then these tuples are to be concatenated to form the result of the join.

In performing the equi-join operation, the ARM-RAM portion of the ARM is slightly changed. The flag bit (F) is replaced by two other bits, in this case a duplicate flag bit (DF) and a matching flag bit (MF). The DF bit, if set, indicates the occurrence of duplicates. However, the duplicates may or may not belong to the same relation. The MF bit, if set, indicates a match of the join attribute values in the two relations. Therefore, if MF is 1, the DF is always 1. But the converse is not necessarily true.

In order to join two relations R and S over some join attribute(s), the join attribute values of the two relations need to be "matched" for equality. With an interchanged screening process, the join algorithm avoids as much processing of redundant data as possible. The general idea is to simultaneously sort both relations byte by byte, eliminating tuples with no match at any point until finally we have the matched tuples for the join operation. The matching process is accomplished in this algorithm by taking advantage of the special address mapping feature of the ARM, i.e., the identical join attribute values from both R and S are mapped into the same ARM location. Therefore, rather than repeatedly scanning the tuples of the two relations required in a conventional join, the matching operation is "direct".

It should be noted that the above equi-join algorithm is for a binary join and is carried out by sorting the attribute values of both relations. In case of a multi-join operation over the same attribute in which N (>2) relations are involved, the same technique can be applied by simultaneously sorting the attribute value of all N relations.

Set Operations

Other important database operations to be considered in this paper are set union, set intersection, and set difference operations. They are also performed in a straightforward manner using the SFU-DB. These set operations can be performed over relations. In this case, a tuple in a relation is treated as a sort value. The union of two or more sets is accomplished by mapping the members of the sets to the ARM and using the algorithm for duplicate elimination to eliminate the duplicates. The set intersection operation can be performed by the join algorithm except that no concatenation of tuples is required. The set difference operation between two relations (e.g., R - S) processes the tuples of both relations together. This operation is also the same as a join operation except 1) the operation is on the whole tuple instead of an attribute value, 2) the R tuples are always processed first when processing a list of duplicates stored in the LM. In other words, R is always mapped to the ARM first to screen out S tuples, instead of in an interchanged order. As with the other algorithms, only the duplicate tuples need to be processed completely in these set operations.

PROTOTYPE IMPLEMENTATION OF THE SFU-DB

A prototype SFU-DB implementation is currently in progress. In order to minimize the development effort, the IBM Personal Computer was chosen as the implementation environment for this prototype SFU-DB system. The SFU RAM components are simulated by the PC's main memory, and the SFU controller is simulated with software (PASCAL). Only the ARU needs to be implemented with custom hardware.

The prototype ARU is constructed using the GE IGC-20450 CMOS gate array, which provides 120 I/O cells and a 29 by 103 array of logic cells, equivalent to 4480 two-input gates. Each array cell contains three complimentary n/p channel MOSFET pairs with 2 micron gate lengths. The chip's logic function is programmed by two custom metal layers. The design is entered into the GE CADEXEC system by specifying the placement and interconnection of predefined logic macros. Logic and performance simulations, based on best, typical and worst case parameters, are performed by CADEXEC using Calma's TEGAS simulation system. The resulting worst case access time for the ARM Retrieval is about 100 ns, equivalent to that of standard RAM. For a more detailed description of the prototype implementation, refer to [11].

CONCLUSION

In this paper, we presented the design and algorithms of a sort-based database machine, SFU-DB, which provides efficient hardware support for sorting and other sort-based operations. Algorithms for several important database operations are discussed.

Without performing any comparisons in the sorting process, the SFU-DB easily avoids the lower bound constraint of the comparison-based sorting algorithms and successfully achieves a complexity of $O(n)$ utilizing only a single processor with a serial algorithm. Unlike other sorting machines, the capacity of the SFU-DB is limited by the size of the memory units (implemented by standard RAMs) rather than by special-purpose processors. Therefore, the SFU-DB has a better cost/performance and is more suitable for processing very large data files. Furthermore, the SFU-DB is not only a sorting machine, but also provides hardware support for other primitive database operations. Without performing any comparison operations, these database operations utilize the sorting algorithm to achieve a linear order of complexity. Finally, The SFU-DB architecture is simple and RAM-intensive. It requires only a modest amount of specialized hardware, the ARU.

Future work will include the study of the parallel processing potential of the SFU-DB in two configurations: (1) multiple ARMs within a single SFU-DB subsystem and (2) multiple SFU-DBs for supporting the high performance requirements in a very large data and knowledge base environment.

References

[1] Y. Dohi, A. Suzudi, and N. Matsui, 9th Annual Symposium on Computer Architecture, Sigarch Newsletters, vol. 10, no. 3, 1982, pp. 218-225.

[2] S. Todd, IBM J. Res. Develop., vol. 22, no. 5, Sept. 1978, pp. 509-517.

[3] N. Takagi and C. K. Wang, IBM J. Res. & Dev., vol. 29, no. 1, Jan. 1985, pp. 46-67.

[4] T. C. Chen, V. W. Lum and C. Tung, Proc. 4th Int'l Conf. on and Searching, Reading, MA: Addison-Wesley, 1973.

[5] M. Kitsuregawa, S. Fushimi, K. Kuwabara, H. Tanaka, and T. Moto-oka, Trans. IECE Japan, vol. J66-d, 1983, pp. 332-339.

[6] D. E. Knuth, The Art of Computer Programming, Volume 3: Sorting and Searching, Reading, MA: Addison-Wesley, 1973.

[7] L. Rashid, T. Fei, H. Lam, and S. Y. W. Su, IEEE Trans. on Computers, vol. C-35, no. 12, 1986, pp. 1071-1077.

[8] E. E. Lindstrom and J. S. Vitter, IEEE Trans. on Computers, vol. C-34, no. 3, Mar. 1985, pp. 218-233.

[9] H. Lam, C. Lee, and S. Y. W. Su, paper submitted to IEEE Transaction on Computers, 1986.

[10] C. Lee, Master's Thesis, Dept. of Electrical Eng., Univ. of Florida, 1986.

[11] H. Lam, S. Y. W. Su, F. L. C. Seeger, C. Lee, and W. R. Eisenstadt, to appear in Int'l Conf. on Parallel Processing, Aug. 1987.

PARALLEL PARTITION SORT FOR DATABASE MACHINES

Y. Yamane, R. Take
Software Laboratory, Fujitsu Laboratories Ltd.
Kawasaki, Japan

ABSTRACT

We have been researching database machines based on parallelism using a multi-processor. In this paper, we briefly describe our database machine architecture and then we describe the parallel sort method which we are investigating based on that architecture. We discuss a new parallel sorting method, called a parallel partition sort, which transfers only a small amount of data and does not place large demands on the CPU. This method is based on the top-down partitioning of data. We experimented and evaluated our method using a multi-processor to compare our method with the block bitonic sort method.

INTRODUCTION

The use of commercial relational databases has been spreading because of their understandability, ease of use, and maintainability. However, relational database systems have worse performance than the database systems based on the network model. The requirement to improve the performance of relational database systems has motivated the research and development of database machines. Also, knowledge base and multi-media database systems have been actively explored. We believe that relational database systems are suitable for use in these systems. They process a large quantity of data, so the relational database system must have a high performance. In addition, computer environment has been shifting to distributed processing based on local area networks and workstations. The processing power of workstations is inferior to that of mainframes, so high performance database machines are required. Because of these considerations, we believe that database machines are necessary now. We are now exploring a da-

117

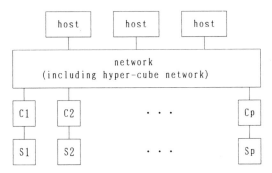

Fig. 1. This shows the horizontal architecture. Ci denotes cell i, and Si storage device i.

tabase machine architecture, called horizontal architecture, which is shown in Fig. 1.

Horizontal architecture

In this architecture, a multi-processor with p cells C_1, C_2, ..., C_p (a cell is a processing element) is used. A data storage device S_i which is main memory or secondary memory is connected to each cell C_i (i=1, 2, ..., p). A relation R is horizontally and equally partitioned into p subrelations R_1, R_2, ..., R_p; R_i is stored in S_i. All relations, input relations and resulting relations of relational operations, are partitioned in this manner. Cell C_i processes subrelation R_i. The host computers control the cells through a network. The network topology of these cells is a hyper-cube network.

The horizontal architecture is similar to some other machines, for example, the GAMMA (4) and DBC/1012 (5) have similar architectures, although their network topology is not a hyper-cube connection. Listed below are the other reasons we believe the horizontal architecture is suitable for improved relational database system performance.

Equal horizontal partitioning of data

If data must be stored in a storage device, the distribution of data into cells is an overhead, and if the resulting data is collected and stored in a storage device, the storing process is serialized, which then becomes a bottle neck. Therefore, we partition input and resulting relations. In addition, equal partitioning minimizes the processing time.

Hyper-cube network

In parallel database processing, much more data is transferred through the communication network in comparison with the other applications such as computer graphics, so the performance of the communication system is important. This is especially true in the case of all to all burst (where every cell distributes its data to all other cells simultaneously; for example, in the case where parallel hash is performed by all cells). The reasons the hyper-cube network is suitable for parallel database processing are as follows:

1) The average distance between two cells is (log p)/2, which is shorter than that of the mesh-connected network or the tree network, although longer than that of the complete graph network.

2) The number of communication links outgoing from a cell is log p, which is practical. That of a complete graph network is p-1 which is impractical.

3) There exists an all to all burst method on hypercube network which transfers data in almost the same performance as complete graph network. This method which we found will be briefly described below.

Suitability for relational operations

The implementation of relational operations on the horizontal architecture is briefly described below. In the selection operation, each cell C_i searches its subrelation R_i and stores the result in its storage device S_i. In this operation, the performance is improved p times over that of a single processor. In a parallel hash by all cells, each cell transfers tuples whose hash function value is j to cell C_j. Equijoin can be done based on parallel hash, such as in the GAMMA. As mentioned previously, using the horizontal architecture with a hyper-cube network, a parallel hash can be executed with almost the same performance as a complete graph network, so this architecture is also suitable for equijoin and other hash-based relational operations. In relational database systems, join is often performed after selection. The horizontal architecture is also suitable in this case.

To investigate our database machine architecture and parallel processing techniques of relational operations, we used a multiprocessor system. We are now investigating parallel sort methods suitable for the horizontal architecture. Therefore, in our parallel sort problem to be solved, the relation to be sorted must be equally partitioned into storage devices S_1, S_2, ..., S_p previously and the resulting relation must be also partitioned in such a fashion as shown in Fig. 2. A conventional parallel sort method suitable for the horizontal architecture is the block bitonic sort method (6). To reduce the quantity of data transfer and CPU processing, we devised a new parallel sort method, called the parallel partition sort. This method is based on top-down partitioning of data, not on merging. We experimented with these two methods to compare their performances. In this paper, we will describe the parallel partition sort, and show the results of our experiments and evaluation.

ENVIRONMENT

We implemented and analyzed parallel sorting algorithms on a cellular array processor system CAP (8). Therefore, our estimation is affected strongly by CAP's characteristics, which are described below.

Hardware

CAP is a general purpose oriented cellular array processor developed by Fujitsu Laboratories Ltd. It consists of a set of autonomous cell processors, which are connected in mesh style. CAP is still under development, and we used the latest version. It has up to 64 cells (our system had 16 cells) and each cell has an i80186 CPU and 2Mbytes RAM. A 4 by 4 mesh is equivalent to a 4-dimensional hypercube, so we regard our CAP as a hyper-cube connected system.

All of the cells and the host machine (apollo DN570) are connected to a common bus called command bus, through which they can broadcast messages. Inter-cell communication is supported by 8 bit parallel inter-cell interfaces. Each cell has four inter-cell interfaces, each of them linking the right, left, above, and below neighboring cells.

Software

Each cell has a simple operating system supporting multi-process programming. This OS schedules processes in event driven style, i.e., an event, typically a message arrival, switches a process into the ready state, and the process is queued for execution.

Programs are written in an extended Language C, which has communication facilities. Using the facilities, a process can send a message to a process specified with the cell number and process number. Messages are handed from cell to cell through inter-cell interfaces. During the movement between neighboring cells, a message travels through message buffers and FIFOs. The maximum performance of the inter-cell interface is 100Kbyte/s.

Compiling is processed on the host machine using a cross compiler. Because this compiler is a small version, we cannot address arrays larger than 64Kbytes directly in standard format (such as array[i]), so we used library functions for accessing to large arrays. These accesses are much slower than if we had used standard indexing. For reading a table and graphs, note that CAP's performance is spilt by these slow functions.

ALGORITHMS

We implemented and analyzed two parallel sort algorithms on CAP. One of them, the block bitonic sort, is well-known, it will be briefly described here. The other one, the parallel partition sort, is our new algorithm, and it will be described in detail.

In following explanation, n and p represent the number of elements (tuples) to sort, and the number of cells (processors).

Block bitonic sort

Batcher's bitonic sort (2) is suited for hyper-cube connected systems, because the distance for communication is always a power of 2 (7, 9). But, because of our hardware constraints, it is impossible for us to provide n cells for sorting n elements. Our CAP consists of a small set of large cells, and the number of cells is much fewer than the number of elements to sort. Consequently, we need some blocking method to adapt bitonic sort to CAP.

Two blocking methods, two-way merge-split (3) and merge-exchange (7), are known. In the former, the merging phase has to be finished before the splitting phase. This leads to a low concurrency and inefficiency in the use of memory space. The latter has none of these weak points, but needs an internal sort at every merge-exchange step. As we required space efficiency, and chose the merge-exchange method.

The block bitonic sort based on merge-exchange consists of log p + 1 steps. The ith step consists of an internal sort and i - 1 merge-exchanges. In case the algorithm is executed on a hyper-cube

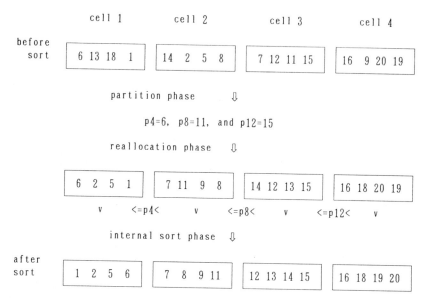

Fig. 2. Example run of parallel partition sort is shown. The values p4, p8, and p12 denote the 4th, 8th and 12th keys respectively.

connected system, all communications occur between neighboring cells, and the following holds,

    a) number of internal sorts : $\log p + 1$,

    b) time complexity of an internal sort : $O(\ n/p \log n/p\ )$,

    c) number of merge-exchanges : $1/2 \log p\ (\ \log p + 1\ )$,

    d) time complexity of a merge-exchange : $O(\ n/p\ )$.

Following above, the time complexity of the algorithm is

$$O(\ n/p \log p\ (\ \log n + \log p\ )\ )$$

Parallel partition sort

    The redundancy in data movements at block bitonic sort motivated us to develop a new algorithm called the parallel partition sort. In the block bitonic sort, all elements move $O(\ \log^2 p\ )$ times. But, $1/2 \log p$ is the mean distance between the cell where an element is initially located and the cell where the element eventually resides.

    The algorithm consists of three phases. The first is called the partition phase, where partition keys are located. In the second phase called reallocation phase, elements are moved to their proper cells according to the partition keys. In the third phase called internal sort phase, elements are sorted at each cell independently. An example run of the algorithm is shown in Fig. 2. In the example, 16 elements are sorted. First, the 4th, 8th, and 12th smallest keys are looked for. They are the partition keys. In the reallocation phase, each element is sent to a cell using the following:

if v <= 4th key then cell 1,

else if v <= 8th key then cell 2,

else if v <= 12th key then cell 3,

else cell 4,

where v is key of the element. Finally, an internal sort is done, and elements are sorted over cells.

In the algorithm, each element moves only once, and the mean distance of the movement is 1/2 log p. This parameter are now optimized, and in comparison with block bitonic sort, the traffic is reduced by a factor of log p to 1. Moreover, our algorithm needs only two internal sorts (one is the preprocessing for the partition phase, and the other is for the internal sort phase), while block bitonic sort based on merge-exchange needs log p + 1 internal sorts.

For these advantages, the algorithm has to spend cost in partition phase. The time complexity of the partition phase has a p^2 log p term, which means that this algorithm is no good for a finely granulated system. The details of the three phases are given below.

Partition phase. The algorithm to search for a partition key is a parallel version of the selection algorithm described in (1). It finds the Kth smallest key after O(log n) iterations of 4 steps, proposing local candidates, selecting a global candidate, estimating the global candidate, and making a conclusion. It needs a process to propose and estimate on every cell, and a process to select and conclude on one cell. The Kth smallest key is found in the following manner.

1) Each propose_estimate process makes an internal sort, and sets 0 as variable HEAD and (n/p + 1) as variable TAIL. This step costs O(n/p log n/p) in CPU processing.

2) Each propose_estimate process chooses (HEAD+TAIL)/2 th smallest key for the local candidate, and proposes it to the select_conclude process. (An exception is when HEAD+1 = TAIL, it proposes a NIL value.) This step costs O(1) in CPU processing, and O(p log p) in communication (p messages of O(log p) distance).

3) The select_conclude process collects local candidates (except NILs), sorts them, select the median for the global candidate, and sends it to every propose_estimate process. This step costs O(p log p) in CPU processing, and O(p log p) in communication.

4) Each propose_estimate process estimates S1 and S2. S1 is the number of keys which are less than global candidate, and S2 is the number of keys which are equal to global candidate. It sends them to the select_conclude process. This step costs O(log n/p) in CPU processing, and O(p log p) in communication.

5) The select_conclude process sums up S1s and S2s, and makes SIGMA_S1 and SIGMA_S2. In case K <= SIGMA_S1, it concludes the global candidate to be too small, and sends UP to every propose_estimate process. If K > SIGMA_S1+SIGMA_S2, the global candidate is too large, and it sends DOWN. Otherwise (SIGMA_S1 < K <= SIGMA_S1+SIGMA_S2), the global candidate is the proper Kth key, and it sends FOUND, then terminates. This step costs O(1) for CPU processing, and O(p log p) for communication.

6) Each propose_estimate process modifies HEAD or TAIL according to the conclusion. In the case of UP, it sets S1+S2+1 to TAIL, for DOWN, S1 to HEAD, and goes to step 2. In the case of FOUND, it terminates. This step costs O(1) for CPU processing.

Step 2, 3, 4, and 5 iterate O(log n) times, and we need to search p-1 partition keys; therefore the time complexity of the partition phase is O(n log n/p + p log n (p log p + log n/p)).

In the implemented program, all partition keys are searched simultaneously by p - 1 select_conclude procedures. The select_conclude procedure on cell i searchs the i*n/p th smallest key, and the procedure on cell p is idle.

Reallocation phase. In this phase, at each cell, two processes work to reallocate elements. One of them, the distribute process sends each element to the home cell according to partition keys. Elements sent leave holes in the element array. The other one, the collect process receives elements from distribute processes, and insert them into holes in the element array made by distribute process.

In case the message pattern is random, a buffer of O(n/p) size is necessary at each cell for reallocation without a deadlock. For example, suppose many distribute processes happen to send elements to one collect process, and the buffer on the cell isn't big enough to receive all of the messages. In this case, some senders must wait for the collect process to take message from the buffer into holes in the element array. However, it is possible that no holes can be made (i.e., the collect process cannot take any message from the buffer) because the distribute process on the cell is waiting for another cell's collect process to take a message from buffer. Therefore, a deadlock loop can exist, such as a distribute process waiting for a collect process waiting for the distribute process.

However, if the message pattern is coherent, the buffer can be reduced to a constant size. For example, the following protocol requires only a one element buffer.

1) set 1 to variable I;
2) set ((self_cell_number + I) mod p) to variable SEND;
3) set ((self_cell_number - I) mod p) to variable RECV;
4) cobegin

        send_elements_to_SEND;

        recv_elements_from_RECV;

   coend;

5) increment I;
6) if I <= p then goto step 2; else terminate;

This phase costs $O(n/p)$ in CPU processing, and $O(n/p \log p)$ in communication (n/p messages of $\log p$ distance).

Internal sort phase. This phase simply executes internal sort to brush up the result. It costs $O(n/p \log n/p)$ for CPU processing.

A ROUTING METHOD FOR THE HYPER-CUBE NETWORK

In this section, a class of message pattern, called a meek burst, is defined, and a method to route a meek burst on the hyper-cube network is introduced briefly (for details, see (10)).

Meek burst

The message pattern of the block bitonic sort is very well-regulated. All the messages move between neighboring cells, and no pairs of two communicating processes share one link. Therefore, there is no message conflict.

However, the message pattern of the parallel partition sort is more random compared with block bitonic. In it, a message pattern frequently appears, where every process sends messages to all other processes. This is called all-to-all burst. Without some routing method, an all-to-all burst will cause many message conflicts.

We discovered that a type of all-to-all burst, called a meek burst, can be routed on a hyper-cube network without any message conflict. The all-to-all burst in the parallel partition sort is a meek burst. The message pattern appearing in hashing on multi-processors is a meek burst also. A meek burst is defined below:

a) Each cell sends a message to every cell (including itself). Therefore, p^2 messages are delivered through the network.

b) All cells start sending messages simultaneously.

c) Messages are of constant size.

d) Each cell sends messages sequentially. Therefore, in each cell, $O(p)$ time is required to finish sending all messages.

e) The order of messages sent from a cell is not set. There are no constraints on the order, such as message M1 must be sent before message M2 is sent.

Routing method

This routing repeats a cycle consisting of p phases, where p is the number of cells. In each phase, p paths are routed coherently, and no conflicts arise. Every cell sends one message in each phase, and after p phases, all messages are delivered. Some of the phases for a 4-dimensional hyper-cube are shown in Fig. 3. Note that on each phase, no link is shared by more than one message (which means no message conflicts there), and all links are used (which means it is impossible on hyper-cube network to finish the meek burst sooner than our routing). Using the property d), any network (even a complete-graph) cannot have better performance than a hyper-cube with our router.

This routing method requires some characteristics of our network. It is necessary that each message is delivered in constant time independently of the path length. To meet the condition, we plan to adopt switch-box type router instead of normal router which buffers input messages and dispatches them to appropriate neighboring cells. In the switch-box router, links are connected directly (electrically or optically), and no delay arises at router. The connection pattern

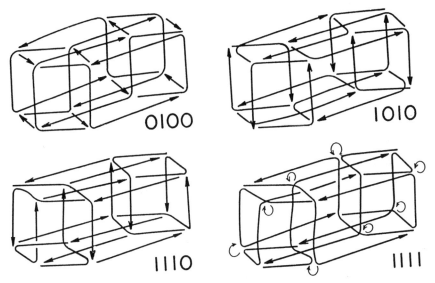

Fig. 3. Four of sixteen phases for 4-dimensional hyper-cube are shown. Note that, in each phase, no pair of paths share one link, and no links are idle.

is made by the controller, and changed at every phase. Even when the switch-box router is used, the line length (i.e. capacitance) may vary, which causes baud-rates of pathes to differ. However, we do not believe this is critical.

EXPERIMENT AND EVALUATION

We experimented with and evaluated the parallel partition sort and the block bitonic sort methods to compare their performances. Here, the results of our experiments and evaluation are described.

In our experiments, only main memory was used to store relations, since the CAP doesn't have disks, and our routing method mentioned above has not been implemented yet. Input relations were previously stored in the main memory before time measurement. Resulting relations were also stored in the main memory. The length of a tuple is 4 or 64 bytes and a 4-byte sort key was embedded in the tuple (in this paper, the word element is also used instead of tuple). The number of cells participating in the sort processing was 1, 4, or 16. The number of tuples in a relation to be sorted was 1K or 16K. In both

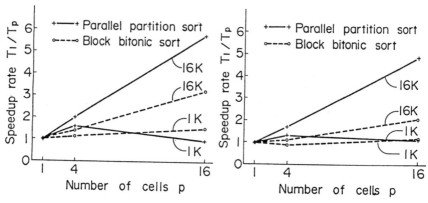

Fig. 4. This shows the performance in case that tuples
are 4-byte long.

Fig. 5. This shows the performance in case that tuples
are 64-byte long.

methods, a quick sort was used for the internal sort; Entire tuples
were exchanged in a cell, and a pointer method was not used.

Fig. 4 and 5 show the relationship between the number of cells p
and the speedup rate T_1/T_p, where T_p is the processing time using p
cells. Table 1 shows the processing time of each phase for both
methods.

From Fig. 4 and 5, we can see that the parallel partition sort is
efficient when the number of tuples of a relation is large, but not so
efficient when that is small. This is because the larger the number
of tuples becomes, the smaller the proportion of partition phase processing time becomes. From Table 1, the partition phase processing
time doesn't depend so much on the number of tuples, because its time
complexity is proportional to log n where n is the number of all tuples when the number of cells p is fixed. When the number of tuples
is comparatively large, the performance of parallel partition sort is
better than the block bitonic sort. In Fig. 4, when the number of
cells is 16 and the number of tuples is 16K, T16/T1 of parallel partition sort is 5.7 and that of block bitonic sort is 3.2. In both
methods, performance decreases when the tuple length becomes large.
This is because the quantity of data transfer through the communication network increases.

Table 1. The processing time of each phase

experiment				total elapse	CPU processing		communication		
sort method	num. of elements	element size	num. of cells	sec	sec (%)		total sec (%)	sec (%) in partition-phase	sec (%) in distribute phase
p-p	1K	4byte	4	3.21	2.28	(71.0)	0.93 (29.0)	0.64 (19.9)	0.29 (9.1)
b-b	1K	4byte	4	4.49	3.94	(87.8)	0.55 (12.2)	—	—
p-p	16K	4byte	4	50.75	47.92	(94.4)	2.83 (5.6)	1.46 (2.9)	1.37 (2.7)
b-b	16K	4byte	4	73.88	67.28	(91.1)	6.60 (8.9)	—	—
p-p	1K	64byte	4	4.92	2.87	(58.3)	2.05 (41.7)	0.68 (13.8)	1.37 (27.9)
b-b	1K	64byte	4	7.45	4.83	(64.8)	2.62 *(35.2)	— '	—
p-p	16K	64byte	4	80.92	61.04	(75.4)	19.88 (24.6)	1.51 (1.9)	18.37 (22.7)
b-b	16K	64byte	4	126.10	87.21	(69.2)	38.89 (30.8)	—	—
p-p	1K	4byte	16	5.30	0.61	(11.5)	4.69 (88.5)	3.97 (74.9)	0.72 (13.6)
b-b	1K	4byte	16	3.35	2.54	(75.8)	0.81 (24.2)	—	—
p-p	16K	4byte	16	17.87	10.65	(59.6)	7.22 (40.4)	6.25 (35.0)	0.97 (5.4)
b-b	16K	4byte	16	31.64	25.57	(80.8)	6.07 (19.2)	—	—
p-p	1K	64byte	16	5.65	0.71	(12.6)	4.94 (87.4)	4.01 (71.0)	0.93 (16.4)
b-b	1K	64byte	16	5.39	2.85	(52.9)	2.54 (47.1)	—	—
p-p	16K	64byte	16	28.16	13.41	(47.6)	14.75 (52.4)	6.30 (22.4)	8.45 (30.0)
b-b	16K	64byte	16	65.87	32.74	(49.7)	33.13 (50.3)	—	—

p-p : parallel partition sort   b-b : block bitonic sort based on merge-exchange

CONCLUSION

In this paper, we described our database machine as having a horizontal architecture, which we believe to be suitable for relational databases. We described a new parallel sort method called a parallel partition sort which is suitable for the architecture.

To solve our sort problem, the data transfer of the reallocation phase of the parallel partition sort and CPU time of its internal sort phase are necessary for any method, so the partition phase is an overhead. We found the almost optimal solution of the reallocation phase, and internal sort has been well explored. So, the main problem of parallel partition sort is the partition phase. We gave a solution to this, but there remain some problems as follows:

1) Are there more efficient parallel algorithms to find partition values ?

2) When a relation to be sorted is large, and all its sorted keys can not be loaded into main memory, we can not help using secondary memory to find partition values. In this case, are there efficient methods ?

3) How is the behavior when the number of cells is larger ?

We will explore the parallel processing methods for the operations such as selection, hash, and join for the horizontal architecture. We will then confirm the efficiency of our all-to-all burst method. In addition, we will explore total system architecture with the aim of confirming the validity of the horizontal architecture.

ACKNOWLEDGMENTS

We are indebted to Dr. A. Makinouchi, who gave us a lot of useful and helpful advice.

REFERENCES
1. Aho, A. V., Hopcroft, J. E., and Ullman, D. J., Addison-Wesley, 1974.
2. Batcher, K. E., Proc. Spring Joint Computer Conf., Vol. 32, 1968, pp.307-314.
3. Baudet, G., and Stevenson, D., IEEE Trans. Comput., C-27, No. 1, 1978.
4. Dewitt, D. J. et al., Proc. Int. Conf. on VLDB, 1986, pp.228-237.
5. Ehrensberger, M. J., Paper presented at the Minnowbrook Workshop on Database Machines, 1984.
6. Hsiao, D. C., and Menon, M. J., Tech. Rep. OSU-CISRC-TR-80-7, Computer and Science Information Dept., Ohio State Univ., Columbus, Ohio, 1980.
7. Preparata, F. P., and Vuillemin, J., Proc. 20th Sympo. Foundations of Computer Science, 1979.
8. Sato, H., et al., ACM SIGGRAPH 85, Vol. 19, No. 3, 1985, pp.95-102.
9. Siegel, H. J., Proc. 4th Annual Sympo. Computer Architecture, 1977, pp23-25.
10. Take, R., to be submitted to 25th Annual Allerton Conf. on Communication, Control and Computing.

DISTRIBUTING THE OPTIMISTIC MULTIVERSIONING PAGE MANAGER IN THE JASMIN DATABASE MACHINE

Ming-Yee Lai
W. Kevin Wilkinson
Database Research Group
Bell Communications Research
Morristown, NJ 07960

Vladimir Lanin*
Courant Inst. of Math. Sciences
New York University
NYC, NY 10012

ABSTRACT

JASMIN is a functionally distributed database machine running on multiple microcomputers that communicate with each other via message passing. The software modules in JASMIN can be cloned and distributed across computer boundaries. One important module is the Intelligent Store, which is a page manager that includes transaction management facilities. It provides an optimistic, mutliversioning concurrency control scheme. The initial implementation of the Intelligent Store deals with centralized databases only. This paper describes our experiences in modifying the JASMIN Intelligent Store module to handle distributed databases. We explore system implementation techniques in the following areas: process structure, data structures, and synchronization on data structures.

1 INTRODUCTION

JASMIN is designed as an experimental system for multiprocessor database operating system and modular data management software [1]. Its software modules run on multiple MC68000-based computers and communicate with each other via message passing kernels. The kernel also supports multi-thread control and non-preemptive scheduling. Besides the kernel, there are four major types of software modules in JASMIN: (1) File Manager (FM), (2) Intelligent Store (IS), (3) Record Manager (RM), and (4) Data Manager (DM). The FM supports the UNIX file system interface. The IS provides a page level interface and performs transaction management. The RM is an IS's client, which supports a record level interface and facilitates various access methods. The DM is an RM's client, which provides a relational level intereface and does query optimization and execution. Currently the distributed processing version has been implemented and the implementaion for distributed transactions is underway.

In this paper, we describe our experiences in modifying the IS, an optimistic, multiversioning page manager, to support distributed transactions. The IS uses a timestamp multiversion scheme for transaction management, whose implementation issues were not well studied before. This scheme allows read-only transactions to run almost without conflict checking. We outline the process structure and data structures in the JASMIN IS, and concentrate on issues related to transaction management. Synchronization on the data structures for transaction management is also discussed.

In Section 2, we briefly discuss the design and implementation of the centralized IS in JASMIN. In Section 3, the issues of migrating from the centralized IS to a distributed IS are addressed. In Section 4, we describe the operation of the distributed IS. In Section 5, the implementation issues of local IS operation are discussed.

2 THE CENTRALIZED IS

We first describe the task structure and major data structures in the centralized IS. We then describe its two major functions: (1) page management, and (2) transaction management (concurrency control and crash recovery). The detailed algorithms for read, write, commit,

---

* Work done while the author was visiting Bellcore in summer, 1986.

abort etc. are stated in [5]. In the following, we focus on the implementation issues of the centralized IS that were not discussed in [5] and are related to the distributed IS.

2.1 Task Structure

In JASMIN, the IS runs as a module, which consists of a number of tasks that share the same program and common data space. A task is not preempted until it makes a system call or until a higher priority task becomes runnable. This non–preemptive scheduling feature makes critical sections easy to implement.

The *distribution* task receives all non–administrative requests (such as allocate, free, read, write, start, commit, abort etc.) and forwards these to one of a fixed number of *request* tasks for processing. The number of request tasks is set when the IS is compiled. Thus, during its lifetime a transaction may be served by many request tasks and each request task serves any number of transactions.

Other than the request tasks, there are four other tasks in IS: the *commit task, abort task, administration task* and *retirement task*. The commit task performs the commit procedure in a critical section. The abort task performs the abort procedure in a critical section. The administration task processes administrative requests such as "restart", "shut IS", "dump IS" etc. The retirement task removes old versions of data pages written by the *retirable* transactions. A transaction T becomes retirable when all transactions that were active when T committed have themselves committed or aborted. I.e., old versions of pages updated by T are no longer needed. This task can run in the background.

2.2 Page Management

The IS models the disk as a collection of *Logical Volumes* (LV's) each consisting of a sequence of LV pages. An LV may be thought of as a disk partition, i.e. a large number of cylinders. An LV page consists of a number of contiguous disk blocks. Note that the page size and number of pages per LV are user–definable and may vary across LV's.

To provide physical locality, an LV is partitioned into a set of disjoint *cells*. A cell is just a small number of cylinders and is structured as a set of fixed–size *page frames* (abbreviated as *frames*). Each page frame holds one LV page. A page allocation request must specify an LV and may optionally specify a cell. To allocate the page, the IS first assigns it a logical page number. It then finds a free page frame (in the specified cell, if any) to hold the page using a memory resident Free–Page Bitmap. Once a page is allocated, IS keeps the page in the same cell. However, the client can explicitly move pages to different cells on a page frame available basis. A page can be freed explicitly by the client or after a transaction aborted or retired.

A logical page number in an LV is mapped into a physical page frame within a cell via a page map (PMAP), which is a single–level index. A free page has a null entry in the PMAP. The PMAP reflects a consistent database, and is carefully updated at the commit time. Currently the page maps are stored contiguously.

2.3 Data Structures

Besides the data structures for page management, the IS has the following major data structures for transaction management: transaction control block, transaction lists, public exception list, and intention list.

When a transaction starts, it is given a *transaction identifier (tid)*, which is an index into an array of *transaction control blocks (TCB)*. The TCB contains bookkeeping information like the start sequence number , various flags, etc. The IS keeps the following lists for each transaction: (a) a list of (lv #, page #) for pages read, (b) a list of (lv #, page #, cell #, frame #) for written pages, (c) a private exception list of (lv #, page #, cell #, frame #) for the PMAP entries of old versions. These lists are controlled by a general list manager to append, scan and free lists in a consistent way. They are packed into item–list blocks, which are kept in memory if possible but swapped to disk when necessary using an LRU policy. Lists are not safe over crashes.

When a transaction commits, its private exception list is added to a public area, called the public exception list. This list is used to implement multiversioning. The intention list is used to facilitate write-ahead recording for crash recovery. It consists of blocks of PMAP entries modified by the committing transactions. It is written to a reserved public place on some disk, prior to updating PMAP blocks. A transaction commits after its intention list is written onto disks.

Synchronization on the above data structures is based on simple locking and depends on the semantics of the operations on the data structures.

2.4 Concurrency Control

JASMIN uses an optimistic multiversioning scheme to ensure that transactions which run concurrently are serializable. Multiversioning means keeping a sufficiently long history of updates made by the committed transactions, so that each active transaction reads from the database state consistent with its start time. Optimistic means that transactions only do certification checking at the end of the transaction. Thus, in the optimistic approach, there is no need to do two phase locking. A transaction will never be blocked or deadlocked while accessing the database.

The actual serialization sequence produced by the centralized IS is ordered on the commit time of updating transactions and the start time of read-only transactions. The position of a committed transaction in the sequence is known as the transaction's *sequence number*. When a transaction begins, the sequence number of the latest committed transaction is noted. Reads made by the new transaction reflect (through multiversioning) that consistent database state regardless of subsequent updates by other committed transactions. This implies that read-only transactions can always succeed without any conflict checking. When an update transaction commits, it is assigned a sequence number one greater than the current largest.

Since a newly committed update transaction is always added to the end of the sequence, it does not change the database state seen by other already committed transactions. Thus, the only checking necessary at certification is that the part of the database state actually read by the certifying transaction did not change during its execution. In other words, if a certifying transaction started at (and thus read from) sequence number i and is certifying at sequence number j, certification consists of verifying that the transaction's readset does not intersect the writesets (in the public exception list) of committed transactions with sequence numbers $i+1$ through j.

The certification checking is done in two stages: the precommit stage and the commit stage. The precommit stage is done at one of the request tasks in the IS and the commit stage is done at the IS's single commit task. Thus, precommit checking of a transaction can run in parallel with precommit checking and access request processing (read, write, ...) of other transactions. However only one commit check can go on at one time. The two stage checking reduces the checking time spent in the critical section of the commit task. When a transaction precommits, it checks its readset against the writesets of the transactions committed after it started. When it commits, it checks its readset against the writesets of the transactions committed after it did precommit.

2.5 Crash Recovery

Crash recovery implies recovery from both processor failures and disk failures. Recovery from disk failures is done with mirrored disks using a novel reliable disk server scheme [4]. In the following, we only discuss recovery from processor failures.

Shadowing and Intention List are the two mechanisms used in JASMIN for crash recovery. Shadowing means when a page is written by an uncommitted transaction, a shadow page frame is created. In other words, update is not done in place. At the commit time, a careful replacement scheme is used to change the entries in the PMAP to point to the shadow page frame. Shadowing needs careful allocation of shadow pages by the cell mechanism to avoid losing physical contiguity on disks.

Careful replacement is done by using the intention list, rather than swapping a single index block atomically. A transaction is not committed until the intention list is written out to disk. The crash recovery scheme is idempotent, i.e. the centralized IS can recover from many crashes by using the saved intention list on disks.

Since pages written by uncommitted transactions are shadowed and are not installed to the database, undo is not needed in the IS. However, because transactions may commit (after writing intention list to disk) before the change is installed to the database, redo may be needed. Since no transactions read data written by uncommitted transactions in the centralized IS, no cascade aborts will occur. Also the execution sequences produced by the IS are recoverable, i.e. if Ti reads some data from Tj, then Tj must commit before Ti.

3 ISSUES IN DISTRIBUTING THE IS

In JASMIN, tasks communicate with each other through a message passing kernel which hides processor boundaries. Thus, migrating from the centralized IS to a distributed IS does not necessitate any changes to intertask communication. However, there are still many issues that need to be considered in such a system migration [3]. In this paper, we consider two major problems in moving from a centralized IS to a distributed IS: (1) distributed transaction management and (2) distributed request processing.

The design issues on distributed transaction management in JASMIN are detailed in [2], [6]. Basically, the two phase commit protocol is chosen for achieving distributed commit. A global timestamp sequencing protocol based on site identifiers and local clocks is used to synchronize access to distributed data by distributed transactions.

In two phase commit, the validation stage involves sending *prepare* messages to participant IS's for local checking and precommit preparation, receiving the votes for validation from the participants and sending *commit* or *abort* messages based on the votes. At a participant IS, a transaction is uncertain between the time its prepare message is processed and its commit or abort message is received. Such uncertain transactions create many new problems, such as deciding which version to read, what extra information is needed for crash recovery, how to validate active transactions with uncertain transactions etc. Another dimension of the complexity comes from the nature of the distributed system, such as slow messages and out-of-sync clocks. One problem associated with this is that a prepare request with a commit timstamp may show up at one site where some conflicting transactions with a younger commit timestamp has committed. In a multiversion environment using timestamp certification like JASMIN, the challenge is how to devise a correct and efficient transaction management scheme.

Distributed request processing concerns how different requests are routed to the proper sites for processing, including how subtransactions are spawned. The basic problems are security, efficiency, transparency and optimization. We consider the distributed IS clients with capabilities to: 1) involve multiple IS modules in a single transaction; 2) make access requests to the various IS modules involved in the transaction; 3) unanimously commit or abort a transaction at all the involved IS's.

There is a question of philosophy as to whether the IS client should (a) play an active, integral part in providing distribution services, or (b) explicitly request the IS to provide distribution services, or (c) remain unaware of the distribution and let the IS transparently decide when such services are needed. For example, to involve a new IS in its transaction, a client could tell the new IS all it needs to know about the transaction, or request an already involved IS to do so, or simply let an involved IS do so when it detects that the new IS is needed.

Option *a* is untenable because it allows a malicious client to violate the integrity of the database. For example, if the client were to serve as coordinator in two-phase commit, it could tell the participants to commit even though some voted to abort. Since each of options *b* and *c* has its own advantages and disadvantages, we decided to implement the union of the two options. This allows the client either to remain ignorant of distribution or to use it explicitly.

Recall a page resides in a cell, which resides in an LV. Thus, there are three choices for the unit of distribution: by LV, by cell, or by page. Distributing by page is untenable because all pages in a single cell are supposed to be physically close (as on a single cylinder). Distributing by LV is an easily implemented option, but is less desirable to the client, who would probably like to have only one LV per record type, but have records of a single type distributed. Distributing by cell is best for the client, but requires a large table at each IS to map each page number for each IS to a (cell #, IS #) pair. Other mapping alternatives are discussed in [3]. Thus, as the least of all evils, distribution by LV has been chosen. In short, an LV resides at an IS in its entirety, but may be replicated in several IS's. A table mapping LV number to IS number(s) resides in each IS.

4 DISTRIBUTED IS OPERATION

The following describes the operation of the distributed IS.

4.1 Initiating a Distributed Transaction

A transaction is started when some IS receives a *start transaction* request. The IS assigns a *start timestamp* (or *sts*) to the transaction and returns a path* to the client for sending further requests (henceforth known as the request path). The timestamp is global, i.e. the transaction will have the same timestamp at all IS's. The IS also assigns a local *transaction id* *(tid)* to the transaction. This is purely a convenience for the IS, since both the tid and the sts identify a transaction uniquely within an IS.

The IS which receives the transaction's start request is called the transaction's *home* IS. Only the home IS is capable of processing a transaction's commit, abort, or spread requests (see below). Other IS's that become involved in a transaction are called *visited* IS's.

4.2 Spreading a Transaction

A transaction spreads itself to IS's other than its home IS either explicitly by making a *spread request* or implicitly by making a request that involves a page or LV on an un-visited IS. We will call the second case an implicit spread request. Only the home IS may process a spread request.

A spread request (explicit or implicit) identifies an IS to be visited by the transaction. The home IS sends an *internal spread directive* over a private path to the IS to be visited. A network of private paths between the IS's has to be set up at boot time. Clients do not have access to these paths for security reasons. The spread directive specifies the transaction's global start timestamp.

Upon receiving an internal spread directive, an IS checks if it can provide a view of the database consistent with the start timestamp. If it can not, it sends an abort directive back to the home IS. Otherwise, it joins the set of visited IS's for the transaction. It remembers that it is not the transaction's home IS and must refuse to process a client's commit, abort, or spread requests. The newly visited IS assigns its own local tid to the transaction and replies to the home IS by sending its own request path for the transaction. All subsequent requests for that transaction to this IS come over this path.

The home IS stores this path and the visited IS's id in the transaction's control block, which contains a list of paths to all the IS's visited by the transaction. The home IS then responds to the client, sending a duplicate of the new request path and the id of the newly visited IS.

---

* A JASMIN communications channel is called a path.

4.3 The Body Of a Distributed Transaction

Requests other than start, spread, commit, and abort can be made at either the home IS or any of the visited IS's via the appropriate request path. A request to the home IS may reference a page or LV resident at any IS. If the IS has not yet been visited, the request constitutes an implicit spread request and a request path is obtained to the newly visited IS. Otherwise, the request path is simply obtained from the transaction's control block. In either case, the request is then forwarded to the visited IS. The reply path provided to the home IS by the client is sent along, so that the visited IS can respond directly to the client. Thus, the total overhead for making a request through the home IS instead of directly to the visited IS is one extra message per request.

The visited IS does not distinguish between requests coming directly from the client or indirectly through the home IS. It must refuse requests involving pages it does not have, replying with the IS id containing the page requested. This should not be too much of an inconvenience to the client: if the client had enough sophistication to send a request directly to the visited IS and not the home IS (and thus keeps track of the various IS's) it should be able to recover by making an explicit spread request at the home IS.

Thus, clients must fall into one of two groups: clients that talk only to the home IS directly and implicitly spread to visited IS's; and sophisticated clients that keep lists of the visited IS's and know precisely which IS should be contacted for which page and LV.

4.4 Terminating a Transaction: Commit and Abort

Only the home IS is capable of processing a *commit* or *abort* request, because only it has a complete list of the visited IS's. Using private paths among IS's established at the IS boot time the home IS must tell the visited IS's either that the transaction is being aborted or that its commit process is being started. In the case of a commit, the home IS assigns a global *commit timestamp (cts)* to the transaction. The entire two–phase commit process then takes place between the coordinator and participants over the private paths. Currently the home IS serves as coordinator in a two–phase commit.

A transaction is *active* at a visited IS from its start or spread up to the very end of the local validation process (or until aborted). Once validation terminates with a positive result, a record of this must be written to disk. Once this record is finished, the transaction is *uncertain* at this IS. The validation process must be atomic with respect to other validations at this IS.

If an IS crashes, all transactions active in it "abort". The uncertain transactions, however, survive the crash and remain uncertain. The committed transactions survive and remain committed, but some redo using the intention list may be needed in recovering.

If an active transaction T wants to read a page written by an older uncertain transaction, the page is made available to T. However, if the uncertain transaction is eventually aborted, T must be aborted as well. We say that T is *dependent* on the uncertain transaction. A list of dependent tid's must be kept for each uncertain transaction. T may not validate or commit until it is not dependent on any transactions.

Once a transaction becomes uncertain, a *Yes* vote is sent by a participant to the coordinator. A *No* vote would be sent if validation did not succeed or the transaction were aborted. The transaction remains uncertain until either a commit or abort directive is received from the coordinator. Once the commit directive is recorded on disk, the transaction becomes *committed*. This record takes the form of an intention list.

4.5 Global Timestamps and Certification

The reason for replacing the centralized IS's sequence numbers with explicit global timestamps (sts and cts) is that, in a distributed environment, sequence numbers will not work unless only one commit is allowed to proceed at a time in the entire distributed system.

Normally, when a cts is chosen at a transaction's home IS, it is the latest one in that IS. However, out-of-sync clocks allow the possibility that this cts is already older than another sts or cts in a different IS. Certainly, by the time a slow prepare message arrives at some visited IS, a transaction with a later cts might have already committed there, or a transaction with a later sts started. Thus, in the distributed case, a new phenomenon arises: certification of a transaction with a cts that is not the latest timestamp in the IS. This greatly complicates several processes in the distributed system.

To validate a transaction in a distributed IS, the transaction's readset must first be checked against the writesets of the committed and uncertain transactions whose cts's fall between its sts and cts. This check is analogous to the one in the centralized IS. However, there may now exist in the IS active, committed, or uncertain transactions with a younger cts or sts than the validating one. These transactions have up to now assumed a certain database state current as of the validating transaction's cts. That database state would be changed by committing the validating transaction. If any of these transactions read any of the pages written by the validating transaction, their reads would become inconsistent, which violates the guarantee of a stable view of the database. Thus, this situation must be detected by intersecting the validating transaction's writeset with the younger transactions' readsets. If the intersection is non-empty, we choose to abort the validating transaction. For read-only transactions, cts can be set equal to sts, in which case no checking is needed.

However, it is also possible to conclude that the transaction could possibly be locally validated if a later cts were issued, although definitely not on the given cts. The problem with having a participant ask for a different cts is that the two-phase commit protocol must be modified in a novel way to handle an arbitrary number of re-validate phases, each arising when one participant wants a new timestamp, thus requiring all participants to re-validate. Thus, at least for now, the participant will simply vote No in such cases.

Once certification with a non-latest cts can be handled, there is no absolute reason for the home IS to always choose the locally latest cts. For example, transactions with a very small writeset like auditing transactions may find it easier to validate with a cts equal to their sts. This, in fact, is simply a generalization of the no-checking rule for read-only transaction. For transactions with large writesets, however, the latest possible cts would probably be best. Thus, the user is allowed to specify in the commit request whether he wants the cts equal to the sts, or one that is as late as possible.

5 LOCAL IS OPERATION

This section describes the processing local to an IS for client requests, e.g. read, write, commit, abort etc. As discussed in [2], our design philosophy is optimistic even in the distributed case, which implies that a transaction can read the versions written by uncertain transactions.

5.1 Major Data Structures

The history data structure is the key data structure. It is quite different from the centralized IS due to the uncertain transactions and out-of-timestamp-order messages in the distributed environment.

The history data structure provides the database history by specifying the differences between the database state as of a certain timestamp and the "current" database state, represented by the PMAP. The PMAP is a mapping from lv-page numbers to cell-frame numbers, giving for every page the version written by the committed transaction with the highest cts. As this implies, the writes of active and uncertain transactions are not reflected in the PMAP.

Each TCB contains the following information regarding the transaction: (1) timestamp (sts, cts), (2) phase (active, uncertain, committed), (3) dependent transaction list, (4) visited site list, (5) various flags, and (6) lists describing its readset (RS) and writeset (WS). (1) – (5) and the home-IS flag have been mentioned in Section 4. The lists in (6) are kept on item-list blocks, and are elaborated below.

A transaction keeps its readset in an RS list, where each entry is simply an (lv #, page #) for each page read. The WS list records the written pages, and contains different information depending on the phase of the transaction.

The WS list of active transactions is called an Active Written Set (AWS) list. Each entry in the AWS list contains (lv #, page #, cell #, frame #), thus pointing to the block containing the version written by the transaction. The WS list of an uncertain transaction is called an AFIM (AFter IMage) list, which differs from an AWS list in that each entry contains an extra field "next BFIM pointer" (NBP). A BFIM (BEfore IMage) is a committed transaction's WS list entry (see below). The NBP points to the oldest younger BFIM entry for the same page. If no younger committed transaction wrote the page, the NBP is null. The NBP indicates where the pointer to the page version written by the uncertain transaction is to be put when it commits. Figures 1 and 2 illustrate the relationship between AFIM's and BFIM's.

The WS list of a committed transaction is called a BFIM list. Each entry is an (lv #, page #, cell #, frame #), which points not to the version written by this transaction, but to the previous committed version. The BFIM lists are analogous to the public exception lists in the centralized IS.

An attempt is made to eliminate the potentially slow scans of the various lists above by keeping the AFIM and BFIM lists sorted within each item–list block and introducing three sets of hash tables that indicate the presence or absence of a page in the lists.

A single global hash table is kept for entries in all AFIM and BFIM lists. Each bucket in the hash table is a counter, which basically indicates the number of unretired committed or uncertain transactions that wrote some pages with page number hashed into that bucket. The counter is incremented by one when a transaction becomes uncertain and is decremented by one when a transaction retires or aborts. A separate WS hash table and RS hash table are kept for each transaction. These tables have 1 bit per hash bucket and are the same size which simplifies checking of RS's and WS's.

The intention list in the distributed IS contains the following extra information: (1) the structures for identifying the head block of AFIM for recovering uncertain transactions, (2) the disk address of AFIM to recover from failures during flushing multiple intention lists for a committing transaction. These structures and functions are detailed in [3].

5.2 Database Operations on The Data Structures

The following is a description of the processing that occurs for these events: page write, page read, validate, commit, abort, retire, and recover.

Read And Write

When an active transaction writes a page, it simply adds an entry for the page version to its AWS list. When an active transaction T requests to read a page P, it first adds it to its RS list, and then determines the correct version to read. To do so:

1) T checks its own AWS list for P. If T has not written P, it proceeds to step 2.

2) T scans the AFIM lists of the uncertain transactions with cts's older than its sts in reverse time order. On the first occurrence of P in an AFIM entry, T notes the NBP in the AFIM entry. If the cts of the NBP is younger than T's sts, T gets the version written by the uncertain transaction, becoming dependent. Otherwise, T proceeds to step 3.

3) T scans the BFIM lists of the committed transactions with cts younger than its sts in time order. If T finds the page, it gets the version indicated in the BFIM entry. Otherwise, T proceeds to step 4.

4) T looks up the page in the PMAP.

In the example in Fig. 1, T3 reads P1's V2, P2's V1 and P3's V2. In step (1), T's WS hash table can be used to expedite checking. Before steps (2) and (3), it looks in the global

AFIM/BFIM hash table, which can eliminate all further tests. Before scanning any transaction's AFIM or BFIM list, it first checks the uncertain or committed transaction's WS hash table. If a scan must be made, it can proceed by binary search within each block.

Validation

A transaction may not start validation until all transactions on which it is dependent have terminated. To validate an active transaction T, the following must be done:

1) T's RS list is intersected with the BFIM's and AFIM's of the non–active transactions whose cts is between T's sts and cts. T is aborted if the intersection is non–empty.

2) T's AWS list is intersected with the RS lists of all transactions with timestamps (sts for active, cts for others) younger than T's cts. T is aborted if the intersection is non-empty.

3) If the above checking succeeds, T's AFIM list is built from the AWS list. For each page, the BFIM lists of the committed transactions with cts's younger than the validating cts must be scanned in cts order, and the NBP field set to the first matching entry.

4) T's TCB is moved in the history list from the position appropriate for its sts to one for its cts, unless the cts is equal to the sts.

5) The global AFIM/BFIM hash table is incremented for the entries in T's WS.

6) T's AFIM list is written to disk crash–resistently. Once that is done, T is uncertain.

A local read–only transaction does not need to do (1) and (4) since its sts is equal to cts. Neither does it do (2) through (3) or (5) and (6) because its WS is empty. Hence, local read–only transactions can skip the validation steps and always commit unless they depend on some uncertain transactions.

A local read–only transaction does not need to do (1) and (4) since its sts is equal to cts. Neither does it do (2) through (3) or (5) and (6) because its WS is empty. Hence, local read–only transactions can skip the validation steps and always commit unless they depend on some uncertain transactions.

For other transactions, in order to perform step (1), the potentially conflicting transactions are first identified by AND'ing the transaction's RS hash table with the WS hash tables of the committed and uncertain transactions. If any potentially conflicting transactions exist, each RS entry is checked in the global AFIM/BFIM hash table. Those in the table are assembled into a "hunk" –– a potentially large sorted array of page entries. The hunk is then intersected with the various AFIM and BFIM lists. This is done by one of several fast methods employing the sorting in the hunk and in the AFIM and BFIM blocks, the exact method depending on the relative sizes of the hunk and the block.

Steps (2) and (3) intersect T's AWS with the RS's and WS's of other transactions. Since most intersections are empty, they can be done cheaply by AND'ing the appropriate hash tables with T's WS hash table. T's AWS list is also sorted at this point to facilitate any scans that might follow.

Commit

To commit an uncertain transaction T, the following must be done:

1) T's BFIM list is built by scanning its AFIM list and modifying the PMAP and BFIM list entries pointed to by the NBP's. The disk–resident AFIM list is not changed during the process, since it must be kept safe in case of crash. For each AFIM entry, a BFIM entry is created from the page version in the target of the AFIM's NBP, and the page version in the AFIM is written to the target of the NBP. (The target is either the PMAP or another BFIM entry)

2) Since every AFIM entry must point to the next BFIM entry for the same page, the introduction of the new BFIM list of T requires the modification of older AFIM's. Thus,

the older AFIM's must be scanned and compared with T's BFIM list. For each page in the BFIM, all AFIM entries for it with an NBP younger than T must be modified to point to the new BFIM. A null BFIM pointer (i.e. indicating the PMAP) is updated in the same way.

3) The active transactions dependent on T stop being dependent on it. If they are not dependent on still other uncertain transactions, they are allowed to validate after T.

4) Using the intention list, T's updates to the PMAP and other AFIM's are made atomically. For transactions with many written pages, several intention lists may have to be written. Thus, this step may be interspersed with steps (1) through (3). In this case, however, the disk address of the disk-resident AFIM list is written to disk with the first intention list. The transaction is considered committed with the writing of the first intention list, since the disk-resident AFIM may be used for redo.

An example of (1) is shown in Figures 1 and 2 where T1 changes from uncertain to committed.

Abort, Retire, And Recover

Aborting an active transaction is easy: it must simply be deleted from the history, and its lists released. Aborting an uncertain transaction in addition requires aborting the active transactions dependent on it and updating the global AFIM/BFIM hash table by decrementing the appropriate entries. This cannot cause further cascading aborts because no one can be dependent on active transactions.

To retire a committed transaction T, not only must it be removed from the history, but the AFIM's of uncertain transactions older than T must be scanned for pointers to T's BFIM list. If such AFIM entries are found, their NBP fields must be replaced with the special "gone" tid, which indicates that no action at all is to be taken for such AFIM entries at their commit. Finally, the AFIM/BFIM hash table is updated.

A crash results in the automatic abort of all active transactions and automatic retirement of all committed transactions. The uncertain transactions survive due to their safe AFIM lists. At recovery time, the AFIM lists must be modified so that every entry with a non-null tid is replaced with a "gone" tid. Furthermore, the page versions not in the PMAP or in the safe AFIM lists must be freed.

5.3 Concurrency Control on List Blocks and History Lists

The scans described above are not atomic, since list blocks may have to be read from disk. Thus, many potential dangers exist in performing them concurrently.

Part of the solution is putting validations and commits into a single critical section by providing a validate-commit (vc) server. Although this might appear to be a severe restriction, it is not quite as bad as it seems. Validation – validation concurrency is unnecessary, since validations normally do not use disk, and overlap is impossible anyway. Commit – commit concurrency is extremely hard to achieve under any circumstances, because of the Intention List use, and was not achieved in the centralized IS. Thus, only validation – commit overlap is desirable, but is not provided now.

Reads can be performed concurrently with each other and with validations and commits (vc's). However, the vc's are dangerous when the page being read is in the WS of the transaction in the vc. This is prevented in the following manner. The tid of the transaction running in the vc task is stored in a shared variable. Prior to doing the history scans for a read, the IS checks if the page is in the WS hash table of the transaction in the vc task. If so, it waits until the end of the vc. Once it can proceed, it enters the page number being read into a shared array, and proceeds to do the scan. A vc, in turn, checks the pages already in the array against its hash table, and blocks if any are in it.

One final possible source of concurrency problems is the manipulation of the TCB linked list, i.e. insert for start, remove for retire and abort, and move (i.e. remove followed by insert) for validate. Due to non-preemption, these are atomic with respect to each other, as well as

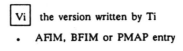

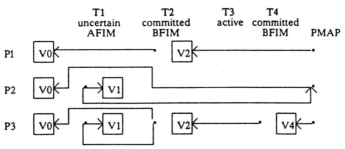

Figure 1

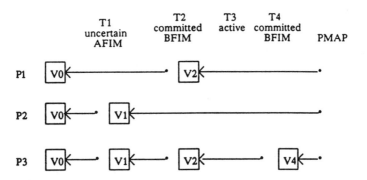

Figure 2

with respect to a scan through the linked list that does not stop at any TCB to look at its page lists. In fact, a problem could only arise if a TCB were removed (or moved) while some scanning process was stuck reading its lists. It is handled by having the removing task first flag the TCB as being about to be removed (so that now no others will stop to look at its data), and then waiting for the tasks already scanning the TCB (if any) to leave it.

6 SUMMARY

In this paper, we discuss the implementation of the centralized IS and the needed changes in migrating into a distributed IS in JASMIN. The implementation is discussed in terms of its process structure and major data structures including procedures to access and manipulate. The process structure reflects how the JASMIN message passing kernel is used in the IS and how the tasks in IS's are scheduled and communicate with each other. The major data structures and their associated operations provide a system implementation view for transaction management and page management. In addition to the schemes for concurrency control and crash recovery, synchronization on these data structures is also discussed.

7 REFERENCES

[1] Fishman D., Lai M., and Wilkinson W.K. "Overview Of The JASMIN Database Machine," *Proc. SIGMOD 84*, May 1984.

[2] Lai M. and Wilkinson W.K. "Distributed Transaction Management In JASMIN," *Proc. Very Large Database Conf.*, Aug. 1984.

[3] Lai, M., Lanin V., and Wilkinson W.K. "Distributing JASMIN's Optimistic Mulitver-sioning Page Manager," *Bell Communications Research Technical Memorandum, TM-ARH-008532*, Dec. 1986.

[4] Premkumar U. and Wilkinson W. K. "Reliable Disk Server in the JASMIN Distributed System," *Proc. 7th Intl. Distributed Computing Systems*, Sept. 1987.

[5] Roome W.D. "A Content-Addressable Intelligent Store," *Bell System Technical Journal*, Nov. 1982.

[6] Wilkinson W.K. and Lai M. "Managing Replicate Data In JASMIN," *Proc. 4th Symp. on Reliability in Distributed Software and Database Systems*, Oct. 1984.

MULTI-WAIT TWO-PHASE LOCKING MECHANISM AND ITS HARDWARE IMPLEMENTATION

K. SAISHO and Y. KAMBAYASHI

Department of Computer Science and Communication Engineering
Kyushu University 36
Hakozaki, Higasi, Fukuoka 812 Japan

INTRODUCTION

In database systems concurrency control mechanisms are essential to realize efficient systems. In this paper an efficient concurrency control mechanism called "Multi-Wait Two-Phase Locking Mechanism" is introduced. Although the mechanism realizes higher concurrency than conventional mechanisms, the mechanism itself is complicated. To reduce the overhead caused by the mechanism we have designed a hardware to realize the mechanism. The whole system is expected to realize a high performance processing by a small overhead.

In this paper we select two-phase locking mechanisms as concurrency control mechanisms, since they are used widely. In conventional two phase locking mechanisms several transactions may request locks on the already locked data. In this case to simplify the selection mechanism of the next transaction to lock that data, lock requests are managed by the lock waiting list in which the first element is the transaction currently holding the lock, second element is the transaction having the right to lock data when the currently holding transaction unlocks the data and so on. Fig. 1 shows the situation when the data A currently locked by transaction T_0 is requested by transactions $T_1, T_2, \ldots, T_m$. Instead of the representation in Fig.1 (a), we use a queue shown in Fig. 1 (b) to express the priority order.

The labels on edges show the names of requested data items. As usually there may be transactions waiting for a data item held by a transaction other than T_0, we have a graph

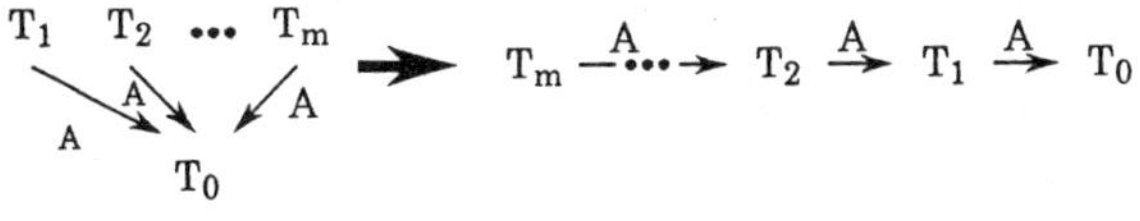

$$T_1 \quad T_2 \quad \cdots \quad T_m \quad \longrightarrow \quad T_m \xrightarrow{A} \cdots \to T_2 \xrightarrow{A} T_1 \xrightarrow{A} T_0$$

(a) (b)

Fig. 1　Management of locking order

143

showing the situation of data requests. Such a graph is called a wait-for graph. There is a deadlock if and only if there is a loop in a wait-for graph. By rolling back one of the transactions in a loop, the deadlock can be resolved.

In most papers, a transaction is assumed to be expressed by a linear sequence of operations (see Fig. 2 (a))[3, 7, 8, 9]. In such cases when transaction makes a request to use the data item which is already used by another transaction, the transaction becomes waiting state. The transaction will be active when it gets the requested data item. Thus each transaction is either in active or in waiting state. Since the transaction is expressed by a linear sequence of operations, a transaction in waiting state is requesting only one data item. Thus the wait-for graph consists of n vertices and at most n edges (each vertex can have at most one out-going edge), where n is the number of transactions.

As a generalization of the transaction model, a partial-order model as shown in Fig. 2 (b) is used. In [5], the model is used to realize efficient partial rollback. The model is also introduced in [2] in order to increase the degree of concurrency. In Fig. 2 (b), operations P_1 and P_2 can be processed in any order. Such case occurs, for example, when a transaction reads two different data items.

In the model shown in Fig. 2 (a) P_2 cannot be started before the termination of P_1, but in the model shown in Fig. 2 (b) P_2 can be started even if P_1 is waiting to hold a lock. Thus each transaction can make more than one request in the partial-order transaction model. Thus a wait-for graph of n vertices has possibly many edges. The increase of the number of edges will cause the increase of loops in a wait-for graph, and thus the possibility of deadlocks. By this reason, the conventional two-phase locking mechanism works very inefficiently for such a partial-order transaction model.

We can show that there are the following two kinds of deadlocks.

(1) A deadlock which requires a rollback of one transaction.

(2) A deadlock which can be resolved by modifying a wait-for graph without any rollbacks.

If transactions are expressed by linear sequences as the widely used model, only case (1) occurs in two-phase locking mechanisms. For transactions expressed by the partial-

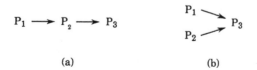

(a)   (b)

Fig. 2   Transaction model

order model, we can avoid some rollback operations by modifying wait-for graphs (case (2)).

For example, assume that T_1 and T_2 are holding locks on data items A and B, respectively, and furthermore there are two transactions T_3 and T_4, requesting both A and B. The situation can be shown in Fig, 3 (a). In this case since there is a loop, T_3 or T_4 must be rolled back. After rolling back T_4, for example, the situation becomes Fig. 3 (b). Re-execution of T_4 will not cause any problem in this case (see Fig. 3 (c)). We can see that the situations of T_4 in Fig. 3 (a) and (c) are identical, since T_4 is waiting for A and B in the both cases. This means that we need not to rollback T_4 and restart. We just need to modify the graph from Fig. 3 (a) to Fig. 3 (c).

The mechanism called Multi-Wait Two-Phase Locking Mechanism introduced in this paper can avoid that kind of rollbacks by modifying wait-for graphs.

One of the problem of Multi-Wait Two-Phase Locking Mechanism is its overhead, since it is more complicated than conventional methods. To avoid this shortcoming, we have designed a hardware to realize the function of Multi-Wait Two-Phase Locking Mechanism. We believe the total performance of the proposed method is much better than the conventional two-phase locking mechanisms.

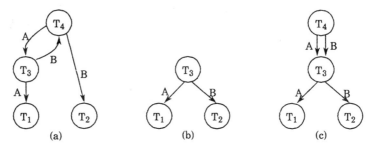

Fig. 3   Problem of the partia-order transaction model

BASIC CONCEPTS

It is assumed that the result of concurrent execution of several transactions is correct if and only if the result is the same as the one obtained by same transactions executed serially in some order.

As data conflict occurs at data access, we define transaction by a sequence of data access operations and/or their control operations. A schedule is serial if all the operations in each transaction are executed consecutively. A schedule is serializable if its result is equivalent to the result of some serial schedule.

Example 1: Lets us consider following two transactions.

T_1: Read B; Read A; A := A + B; Write A

T_2: Read A; Read B; A := A $\times$ B; Write A

Let $R_i(A)$ and $W_i(A)$ denote read and write operations of T_i to A, respectively. Possible serial schedules are T_1T_2 and T_2T_1. Thus results of serial schedules are $(A+B) \times B$ or $A \times B + B$, respectively. The result of the following schedules (1) and (2) are $A \times B + B$ and $A \times B$, respectively.

(1) $R_1(B), R_2(A), R_2(B), W_2(A), R_1(A), W_1(A)$

(2) $R_1(B), R_2(A), R_1(A), R_2(B), W_1(A), W_2(A)$

The schedule (1) is serializable because the value of A after the execution is same as serial schedule T_2T_1. As the result of the schedule (2) is not equivalent to results of both serial schedules, the schedule (2) is nonserializable.

In schedule (2), since $R_1(A)$ occurs before $W_2(A)$, T_1 reads the value of A before updated by T_2. Thus if there is a serial schedule, it should be T_1T_2. As T_1 writes A, however, just before $W_2(A)$, the result of the schedule (2) ignores $W_1(A)$. Thus the schedule cannot be equivalent to T_1T_2. To avoid such a problem we use the lock mechanism. Some order will be produced by lock operations. Lock operation on a data item can be performed only if no transaction locks the data item. We assume $L_i(A)$ denotes the lock of T_i on A and $U_i(A)$ denotes the unlock operation of T_i on A. Furthermore, we will use $L_i(A)$ and $U_i(A)$ to represent schedules. The lock sequence $L_i(A), ... , U_i(A), ... , L_j(A), ...$ makes transaction order $T_j \rightarrow T_i$ which denotes T_i precedes T_j. The schedule $L_i(A), L_j(B), U_j(B), L_i(B), U_i(A), L_j(A), ...$ is nonserializable schedule because this schedule contains inconsistent orders $T_i \rightarrow T_j$ and $T_j \rightarrow T_i$.

Two-phase locking mechanisms prevent this situation. Although there are many types of two-phase locking mechanisms, we only describe a simple two-phase locking mechanism, which uses only exclusive locks in order to simplify the discussion, although generalization (permitting shared locks) is also not difficult.

[Simple two-phase locking mechanism]

(1) A transaction is said to satisfy the two-phase locking protocol if it consists of the following two steps.

    (1-1)   Lock phase :   Transaction locks necessary data.

                                  In this phase no unlock operations are performed.

    (1-2)   Unlock phase :   Transaction unlocks locked data.

                                  In this phase there is no lock request in the transaction.

(2) In two-phase locking mechanism, all transactions are required to satisfy the two-phase locking protocol. Lock on a data item can be realized when the data item is not locked by another transaction.

In two-phase locking protocol, transaction $L_j(B)$, $U_j(B)$, $L_j(A)$, ... is not permitted because $L_j(A)$ must precede $U_j(B)$.

If the requested data item is locked by another transaction, the transaction waits till that data item to be unlocked. Deadlock is the status where transactions wait data item each other and cannot execute no more. To break deadlock we must abort and restart some transaction which contributes deadlock. This operation is called rollback.

We can detect deadlock by using the wait-for graph shown in Fig. 4. In the wait-for graph there is an edge $T_i \rightarrow T_j$ if T_i wants to get lock on the data item already locked by T_j. For the lock sequence shown in Fig. 4 (a), we can obtain the lists shown in Fig. 4 (b). By merging these lists the wait-for graph in Fig. 4 (c) without the dotted line is obtained, which is loop-free. Detection of deadlock is realized by detection of a loop in the wait-for graph. By adding $L_1(B)$ in Fig. 4 (a), lock waiting list for B is changed to $T_1 \rightarrow T_3 \rightarrow T_2$. Thus T_1 waits for T_3, T_3 waits for T_2 and T_2 waits for T_1 respectively and deadlock occurs. That is represented by the loop of the wait-for graph with the dotted edge in Fig. 4 (c).

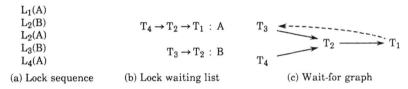

$L_1(A)$		
$L_2(B)$	$T_4 \rightarrow T_2 \rightarrow T_1 : A$	
$L_2(A)$		
$L_3(B)$	$T_3 \rightarrow T_2 : B$	
$L_4(A)$		

(a) Lock sequence   (b) Lock waiting list   (c) Wait-for graph

Fig. 4   Detection of deadlock using a wait-for graph

MULTI-WAIT TWO-PHASE LOCKING MECHANISM

In order to improve the concurrency we will use partial-order transaction model. As shown in INTRODUCTION, the possibility of loop generation will increase. How to detect the case when rollback operations are not required is discussed in this section.

If we permit concurrent executions in one transaction, we may be able to improve the efficiency by the following reasons.

(1) Efficiency improvement by concurrent execution.

(2) The total locking time will decrease by permitting concurrent execution. (For example in Fig. 2, P_1 and P_2 cannot be unlocked until P_3 is locked. Thus parallel execution of P_1 and P_2 will possibly reduce the locking periods of P_1 and P_2.).

As discussed in INTRODUCTION there is a serious disadvantage which may cancel the above advantages.

(3) The possibility of deadlock occurrence will increase.

We will show the condition when we can avoid rollbacks even if there is a loop.

148

Proposition 1: There is a loop in a wait-for graph if the following conditions are satisfied.

There exist transactions T_i, T_j and data items A, B such that

    (1) Both T_i and T_j are in queues for A and B.

    (2) In the order in the queue for A, T_i precedes T_j.

    (3) In the order in the queue for B, T_j precedes T_i.

Proof: The situation is shown in Fig. 5, where dotted lines show sequences of edges. The figure shows the existence of a loop.

Proposition 2: The loop shown in Proposition 1 can be removed by modifying the wait-for graph without rolling back of any transactions.

Proof: By exchanging the positions of T_i and T_j in queue for B, we get the wait-for graph shown in Fig. 6. Fig. 6 does not have a loop. The status of T_i (T_j) in Fig. 5 is requesting A and B and the status of T_i (T_j, respectively) in Fig. 6 is the same. Thus we need not rollback T_i or T_j.

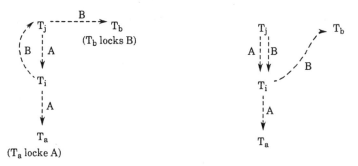

Fig. 5 Proposition 1   Fig. 6 Conversion given by Proposition 2

The remaining problem is the selection of the queue to change the order. Since the wait-for graph is dynamically modified, selection is determined by the transaction which generates the loop. For example in Fig. 5 if a loop is generated by the request to A by T_j, then the wait-for graph before the request is shown in Fig. 7 (a). In this case there is already a path from T_i to T_j, we change the direction of the edges labeled by A as shown in Fig. 7 (b), and the edge to T_a from T_i is replaced by the edge to T_a from T_j. This selection mechanism is selected to reduce the complexity of hardware implementation.

The reason why we can change the direction is that these requests are not actually executed. We call such situations to be reservations. Thus a transaction is expressed as follows.

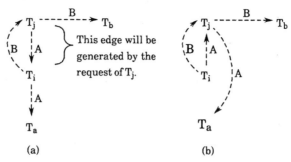

Fig. 7 Selection of edge direction

[Expression of a transaction]

(1) Each basic operation is as follows.

Reservation of A by T_i : $R_i(A)$

Lock of A by T_i : $L_i(A)$

Unlock A by T_i : $U_i(A)$

(2) There is a partial order on the set of operations.

Next we will show the Multi-Wait Two-Phase Locking Mechanism.

[Multi-Wait Two-Phase Locking Mechanism]

(1) Each transaction satisfies the following Multi-Wait Two-Phase Locking protocol.

   (1-1)   Each transaction is expressed by a partial order of reservation and unlock operations.

   (1-2)   There is no reservation operations after an unlock operation in the partial order. No data item is unlocked without reservation.

(2) Transactions are executed in the following way.

   (2-1)   Reserved data items should be locked before unlocked.

   (2-2)   No unlock operations precede lock operations.

   (2-3)   If there is a situation shown in Proposition 1, the loop is removed by using Proposition 2.

   (2-4)   If there is a loop which does not satisfy Proposition 1, then one transaction in the loop is selected to be rolled back.

METHODS TO REALIZE MULTI-WAIT TWO-PHASE LOCKING MECHANISM

Only reservation, lock and unlock operations are discussed, since these are used to represent transactions and schedules. Instead of preparing queues for all data items, we will prepare one lock waiting list to reduce redundancy. For example, the reservation sequence $R_i(A)$, $R_j(A)$, $R_i(B)$, $R_j(B)$ makes lock waiting lists $T_j \rightarrow T_i$ for A and B (see

Fig.8(a)). If reservation and lock sequence $R_j(C)$, $L_j(C)$, $R_i(C)$ follows after the above sequence, the lock waiting list on C becomes $T_i \rightarrow T_j$, so lock waiting lists on A and B must be changed to $T_i \rightarrow T_j$ (see Fig. 8 (b)) in order to avoid deadlock situation. Thus we use a "reservation set" and a "locking transaction" on each data item and one "total transaction order list".

- The set of reserving transactions $(R(x))$: This set represents the set of transactions reserving the data item x.

- The locking transaction $(L(x))$: This represent the transaction which locks data item x.

- The total waiting order list (TWO) : This list represents total order of transactions. We use this data to select transactions which can lock each data item. The order of transactions in TWO is determined by the following two conditions.

    (1) $L(x)$ precedes $R(x)$ when $L(x)$ exists.

    (2) The order of reservations by transactions determines the transaction order except the above case.

Deadlock can be detected by a wait-for graph made from $R(x)$ and $L(x)$ for all data. Edges in the wait-for graph are oriented from a reserving transaction to the transaction having a lock on x. So we introduce following additional data.

- Set of waiting transactions $(W(T_i))$: $W(T_i)$ is defined for each transaction T_i. $W(T_i)$ represents the set of transactions which must wait and is defined as follows.

$$Wd(T_i) \overset{def}{=} \bigcup_x L(x) \qquad \text{where } T_i \in R(x)$$

$$W(T_i) \overset{def}{=} \bigcup_{T_j} W(T_j) \cup Wd(T_i) \qquad \text{where } T_j \in Wd(T_i)$$

We will present methods to realize reservation, lock and unlock operations in Multi-Wait Two-Phase Locking Mechanism.

[Reservation operation]

Assume that transaction T reserves data x. As discussed before there are the following three cases.

(1) Reservation can be realized without any problems.

(2) Rolling back of T is required to resolve deadlock.

$T_j \rightarrow T_i \rightarrow T_a : A$	$T_j \rightarrow T_i \rightarrow T_a : A$	$T_i \rightarrow T_j \rightarrow T_a : A$
$T_j \rightarrow T_i \rightarrow T_b : B$	$T_j \rightarrow T_i \rightarrow T_b : B$ $\Longrightarrow$	$T_i \rightarrow T_j \rightarrow T_b : B$
	$T_i \rightarrow T_j : C$	$T_i \rightarrow T_j : C$

A and B are locked by T_a and T_b, respectivily.

T_j lockes C so we must modify lock waiting lists on A and B

(a)   (b)

Fig. 8   Modification of lock waiting lists

(3) Reordering can be used to avoid deadlock.

If there is no transaction locking x (i.e., L(x) does not exist) or no loop in the wait-for graph after appending T, reservation can be done without any problem. We must only append T to R(x). It is, however, not easy to detect a loop in the updated wait-for graph, so we use steps in the case (3) when L(x) exists. If x is locked by L(x) the cases (2) and (3) occur.

The case (2) occurs when the following condition is satisfied.

$$(L(x) \neq \phi) \wedge (T \in W(L(x)))$$

When deadlock is detected at least one transaction which contributes deadlock must be rolled back. Although there are many methods to select transactions to be rolled back, we select T for simplify. The rollback operation requires to unlock data items locked by T.

If conditions for case (1) and case (2) are not satisfied the case (3) occurs and following steps are performed.

(1) Append T to R(x).

(2) Append L(x) and members of W(L(x)) to W(T) and $W(T_i)$ where T_i waits for T.

(3) Update TWO by the following three steps.

    (3-1)   Determine the set of transactions in $L(x) \cup W(L(x))$ which are successors of T.

    (3-2)   Remove the transactions determined by step (3-1).

    (3-3)   Insert the selected transactions just before T.

[Lock operation]

This operation is realized if and only if requested data is unlocked and the requester is the first transaction in the TWO, where the transaction is a member of R(x). When this request is accepted, update of L(x) and R(x), reordering of transactions and update of $W(T_i)$ are performed by the following steps, where T_i is a member of R(x).

(1) Set T to L(x).

(2) Remove T from R(x).

(3) Update $W(T_i)$ by appending T and member of W(T) where T_i waits for T.

Transaction T stays in waiting state till there remain no transactions in $L(x) \cup R(x)$ which precede T.

[Unlock operation]

This operation updates of L(x) and all sets of waiting transactions which include T, because these sets has no indirect information and it is impossible to remove wait information only by the fact that T locks x. These updates are performed by following steps.

(1) Set L(x) to empty state (no transaction locks x).

(2) $W(T_i)$ which includes T is updated in following way.

    (2-1)   for all $W(T_i)$'s which include T do clear $W(T_i)$;

    (2-2)   for all data y do

        if $L(y) \neq \phi$ then

            for all transactions T_j in $R(y)$ and $W(T_j)$ cleared at step (2-1) do

            begin

                to $W(T_j)$ append $L(y)$ and member of $W(L(y))$;

                for every transaction T_k such the T_k waits for T_j do

                    to $W(T_k)$ append $L(y)$ and member of $W(L(y))$;

        end;

(3) If there is the transaction which is in waiting state and first transaction in the TWO being member of $R(x)$, we must give the lock on x to this transaction.

Finally we prove that algorithm presented in above arises no starvation (there are no transactions which cannot be executed forever. It is also called live lock).

Proposition 3 : There is no starvation by the above methods.

Proof : The order of T may be modified by moving successor transactions to preceding positions, only when T makes a new request. Thus if T is in waiting state and does not make any requests, then the order of T in the list will be forwarded. Eventually T can get locks on reserving data items.

THE HARDWARE PART OF MULTI-WAIT TWO-PHASE LOCKING MECHANISM

It is not easy to realize Multi-Wait Two-Phase Locking Mechanism by hardware only. Thus we divide functions of Multi-Wait Two-Phase Locking Mechanism into the hardware and software parts. The hardware part has basic functions to realize Multi-Wait Two-Phase Locking Mechanism as deadlock detection, reordering of transactions, selection of transactions to lock data items etc. The software part realizes interface between operations of transactions and functions of the hardware part and other functions not realized by the hardware part. Table 1 summarizes functions of the hardware part, with parameters to call their functions and results.

Fig. 9 shows a block diagram of the hardware part. It consists of the following four components.

(1) Control part : It controls the whole hardware.

(2) Transaction order manager : It manages the transaction order and detect the first transaction in the set of reserving transactions.

Table 1   The functions of the hardware

Functions	Input parameter	Result
Registration of data		Flags and data identifier
Registration of transactions		Flags and transaction identifier
Reservation of locks	Transaction identifier and Data identifier	Flags
Examination of lock status	Data identifier	Flags and transaction identifier
Lock data	Transaction identifier and Data identifier	Flags
Unlock data	Transaction identifier and Data identifier	Flags and Transaction identifier has the right of lock at next time
Delete data	Data identifier	
Delete transaction	Transaction identifier	

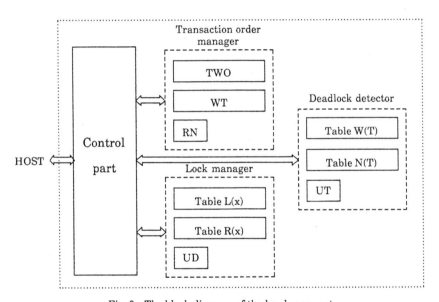

Fig. 9   The block diagram of the hardware part

(3) Lock manager : It manages the locking transaction and the set of reserving transactions on each data item.

(4) Deadlock detector : In this component, update of set of waiting transactions and deadlock detection are performed.

Component (1) control other components, thus components (2), (3) and (4) are not directly connected each other.

The transaction and the data item are identified by bit patterns to simplify management of control data. We assume that the hardware part can control n transactions and m data items. We define the data identifier (D_{id}) and the transaction identifier (T_{id}) as follows.

Each data item (transaction) have unique numbers. The software part refers to data items (transactions) by their corresponding numbers. In the hardware these identifiers are represented by bit patterns in each of which the bit corresponding to the data item (transaction) number is set to be '1' and all the other bits are set to be '0'. Thus data (transaction) identifier consists of m (n) bits. By representing the data item and the transaction by bit pattern, we can realize operations such as appending to a set, remove from a set etc. by using bit-wise **and**, **or** and **not** operations. For example, append operation is realized by **or** operation. Remove operation is realized by **not** operation and **and** operation.

Since the hardware part can manage n transactions at once, we must assign the physical transaction to the transaction identifier dynamically. Components in Fig. 9 are explained as follows.

- TWO : It is a table of T_{id}. Each element in this table is referred to by index which range is 1 to n. We assume that TWO[i] denotes i-th element of TWO and TWO[i] precedes TWO[j] if i is smaller than j.
- WT : WT stores T_{id} selected step (1) in the method of updating TWO. Each element in WT is referred to in the same way as TWO.
- RN : RN denotes the current registered transaction number. It shows the range to manage transaction order.
- Table L(x) and table R(x) : L(x) is the T_{id} of the current locking transaction for x. If no transaction locks x, L(x) is set to be zero. R(x) is the set of T_{id}'s and represented by n bit pattern in which the bit corresponding the reserved transaction is set to be '1' and all other bits are set to be '0'. We can get R(x) by **or** of all T_{id} reserving x. Each element in this table is referred to by index which range is 1 to m.
- UD : UD represents currently used data identifiers. We use this data when D_{id} is related to data item and the reconstruction of set of waiting transaction is performed.
- Table W(T) and N(T) : W(T) is the set of waiting transactions and constructed by the same way as R(x). N(T) , which denotes the current number of locked data items hold by transaction T, is used to detect the last lock operation in the transaction.
- UT : UT represents currently used transaction identifiers. We use this data same as UD.

Finally we describe how to use data defined above to realize functions in Table 1.

[Registration of a data item]

It can be realized by checking UD. The hardware returns failure flag if UD has no bit 0, otherwise the hardware returns unused D_{id}.

[Registration of a transaction]

It is identical to registration of a data item except for using UT instead of UD.

[Reservation of a lock]

Suppose that transaction T reserves lock of data x. Deadlock occur if the following condition is satisfied.

$$(L(x) \neq \phi) \wedge ((T \text{ and } W(L(x))) \neq \phi)$$

The hardware puts the failure flag on and terminates this function if deadlock is detected. Otherwise steps which are presented by reservation operation in previous section are performed. We can write these steps by following procedure.

```
if L(x) ≠ 0 then begin
    W(T) := W(T) or L(x) or W(L(x));        { update waiting list }
    for i := 1 to RN do
        if (T and W(TWO[i])) ≠ 0 then
            W(TWO[i]) := W(TWO[i]) or L(x) or W(L(x));
    i := RN; j := RN; k := RN;
    while (TWO[i] ≠ T) do begin              { reordering step (1) and (2) }
        if (TWO[i] and (L(x) or W(L(x)))) ≠ 0 then begin
            WT[j] := TWO[i]; j := j − 1;
        end else begin
            TWO[k] := TWO[i]; k := k − 1;
        end;
        i := i − 1;
    end;
    while j < RN do begin                    { reordering step (3) }
        i := i + 1; j := j + 1;
        TWO[i] := WT[j];
    end;
end;
R(x) := R(x) or T;                           { append T to R(x) }
```

[Examination of lock status]

This function returns one of the following three status and the corresponding transaction identifier.

(1) The return transaction identifier is the current locking transaction.

(2) There is no current locking transaction and the return transaction has right to lock at next time.

(3) There are no locking transactions and reserving transactions.

[Lock data]

Return flag shows whether this function is success or not. This function is success if and only if requested data is not locked and requester is first position of that data queue.

When this request is success, update of L(x) and R(x), reordering of transaction and update of $W(T_i)$ where T_i is included in R(x) are performed by the hardware.

[Unlock data]

Return flag represents whether there exists the transaction which has right to lock next. Perform steps (1) and (2) which are presented by unlock operation in previous section.

[Delete data]

This function deletes a data identifier from UD. The bit used for the data can be assigned to the other data. The execution time of reforming $W(T_i)$ is effected by the number of data items. By this function we can reduce the number of currently used data items.

[Delete transaction]

This function deletes transaction identifier from TWO and UT and decrease RN. It is executed when a transaction terminates. The bit used for the transaction can be reassigned to a new transaction.

CONCLUDING REMARKS

In this paper we showed a new algorithm to realize higher concurrency than conventional two-phase locking mechanisms. It is very important to determine how to divide functions between software and hardware. Large software part causes low execution efficiency and on the contrary small software part increases hardware complexity. We determined hardware part as simple as possible yet realizing sufficient efficiency.

REFERENCES

1. Agrawal, R., Carey M. and DeWitt D. UC Barkley, ERL Memorandum M83/3, 1983.
2. Brzozowski, J.A. and Muro, S. International Journal of Computer and Information Science, Vol.14, No.6, 1985.
3. Eswaran, K.P., Gray, J.N., Lorie, R.A. and Traiger, I.L. Comm. ACM, pp.624–633, 1976.
4. Kambayashi, Y. and Kondoh, S. AFIPS NCC Vol.53,pp.31–39, 1984.
5. Kondoh, S., Kambayashi, Y. and Yajima, S. RIMS Record 494, Kyoto University, Reseach Institute of Mathematical Sciences, pp.90–101, June 1983 (In Japanese).
6. Krishnamurthy, R. and Dayal, U. Proc. of the ACM Symposium on Principle of Database Systems, pp.293–305, 1982.
7. Papadimitriou, C.H. JACM 26, pp.631–653, 1979.
8. Papadimitriou, C.H. The Theory of Database Concurrency Control. Computer Science Press, 1986.
9. Ullman, J.D. Principles of Database Systems. Computer Science Press, 1983.

PERFORMANCE EVALUATION ON SEVERAL CAUTIOUS SCHEDULERS FOR DATABASE CONCURRENCY CONTROL

S. NISHIO*, M. WATANABE**, Y. OHIWA***, T. HASEGAWA

Department of Applied Mathematics and Physics, Faculty of Engineering
Kyoto University, Kyoto, 606 Japan

ABSTRACT: In recent studies on concurrency control of database systems, "cautious schedulers" have been developed intensively because they avoid both abortion and rollback in the process of concurrency control. In this paper, by means of simulation studies, we will evaluate the performance of three cautious schedulers: (1) cautious two-phase locking scheduling, (2) exclusive preclaimed two-phase locking scheduling, and (3) cautious conflict serializable scheduling. The performance of these cautious schedulers is compared with that of corresponding non-cautious schedulers.

Key Words: Concurrency control, Cautious scheduler,
Performance evaluation

1. INTRODUCTION

In database systems a commonly used criterion of correctness of concurrent execution of transactions is <u>serializability</u> [3, 9], and many different <u>schedulers</u> for concurrency control have been proposed to achieve serializable executions of transactions [2, 19]. In this paper the performance of several concurrency control schedulers is evaluated via simulation experiments aimed at comparing the perform-

---

* Dr. Nishio's former publications are under the name Shojiro MURO.
** Mr. Watanabe is now with the Systems Development Center, Canon Inc., 30-2, Shimomaruko 3-Chome, Ohta-ku, Tokyo, 146 Japan.
***Miss Ohiwa is now with the Central Research Laboratory, Matsushita Electric Industrial Co., Ltd., 3-15, Yagumo-Nakamachi, Moriguchi, Osaka, 570 Japan.

ance of so called cautious concurrency control schedulers (e.g., [4, 7, 8, 12, 13]; for a survey study see [14]) with that of usual (non-cautious) concurrency control schedulers.

In cautious scheduling, it is assumed that the information about the future operations of a transaction is provided to the scheduler when the first operation of the transaction arrives at the scheduler. Taking this information into account, the scheduler examines the possibility of non-serializable execution for each input operation. If any such possibility exists, the scheduler delays the execution of the operation and executes the next operation. In such a way, once the scheduler accepts the first operation of a transaction, the operations of the accepted transaction will not be roll-backed or aborted, but will be ordered as a serializable sequence. For this reason the cautious scheduler is attractive for database users. However, the conservative execution of operations reduces the degree of their concurrent execution. On the other hand, in the usual concurrency control schedulers, rollback or abortion would occur due to deadlock or non-serializable execution of operations. A recent study by Carey [5] indicates that frequent rollbacks considerably reduce system performance. Thus, a comparative study of the degradation of concurrency in cautious schedulers due to conservative execution and the degradation of throughput in non-cautious schedulers due to rollback or abortion will be of interest to the database system designer.

In this paper we consider the following three cautious schedulers: (1) cautious two-phase locking, (2) exclusive preclaimed two-phase locking [5], and (3) cautious conflict serializable scheduling [7, 8]. For performance comparison, two non-cautious schedulers corresponding to above three cautious schedulers, i.e., (4) two-phase locking [9] and (5) conflict serializable scheduling [1, 11, 17] are also considered.

On the basis of several performance criteria such as throughput and waiting time in several queues, we will evaluate the performance of these five schedulers, and discuss the characteristics of each. In particular, we will discuss the advantage of cautious schedules through the comparison of cautious and non-cautious schedulers.

2. MODEL

2.1. Transaction Model

Each transaction T_i consists of two operations such that

$$T_i = \{R_i(x_1, x_2, \cdots, x_m), W_i(y_1, y_2, \cdots, y_n)\},$$

where <u>READ</u> <u>operation</u> R_i must precede <u>WRITE</u> <u>operation</u> W_i in the execution of T_i. A READ operation $R_i(x_1, x_2, \cdots, x_m)$ returns the current values of <u>read</u> <u>set</u> $\{x_1, x_2, \cdots, x_m\}$ to T_i, and a WRITE operation $W_i(y_1, y_2, \cdots, y_n)$ updates the values of <u>write</u> <u>set</u> $\{y_1, y_2, \cdots, y_n\}$, where x_i (y_i) is a data item. We assume that write set of transaction T_i is included in read set of transaction T_i. The transaction model assumed in this paper is called "restricted two step model" (see, e.g., [17]), and it is one of the simplest mathematical transaction models.

2.2. Simulation Model

Now let us denote the number of data items in the database by N. The number of data items accessed by a transaction (i.e., data items accessed by a READ operation in our transaction model) is chosen from the values which obey a <u>binomial</u> <u>distribution</u> between DMIN and DMIN+M. The parameter WSR ($0.0 \leq WSR \leq 1.0$) determines the ratio of the number of data items of WRITE operation to the number of data items of READ operation in a transaction.

The single-site (i.e., <u>centralized</u>) database system we have considered is illustrated in Fig. 1. The system consists of two main components, <u>Transaction</u> <u>Generator</u> (TG) and <u>Database</u> <u>Management</u> <u>System</u> (DMS). The DMS is further divided into two portions, <u>Start</u> <u>Queue</u> (SQ) and <u>Concurrency</u> <u>Control</u> (CC). The DMS has a <u>Multiple</u> <u>Programming</u> <u>Level</u> (MPL), and the CC can control MPL transactions at the most.

Operations of transactions are generated by the TG. The arrival rate of transactions to the CC from the TG is given by an exponential distribution with mean $1/\lambda$. When a READ operation is generated by the TG, if the CC has MPL transactions, this operation is transferred to the tail of the SQ; otherwise, this operation enters into the CC. When a WRITE operation of transaction T_i is generated, this operation will be able to enter into the CC without waiting in queue SQ since the READ operation of T_i has already been in the CC and the number of transactions in the CC is not increased by any WRITE operations.

Normally a user executes the local computation at his terminal

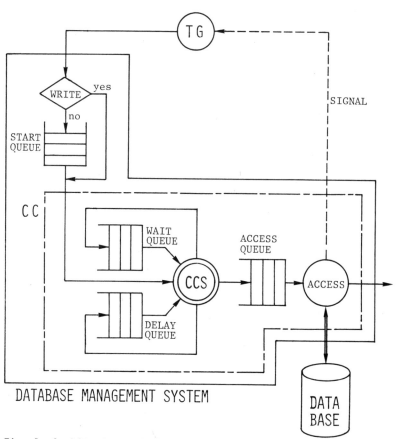

Fig. 1. Architecture of the simulation model.

after referring to the data obtained by the READ operation, and then he transfers the updation message to the database. To reflect such user behavior in our model, the WRITE operation of a transaction is issued from the TG after the completion of the READ operation (i.e., the point that the CC sends a signal to the TG). Let us refer to this point as read completion point. For each user, the interval between his read completion point and the time his WRITE operation is transmitted from his terminal to the DMS is given by the sum of C_d and the value determined by an exponential distribution with mean $1/\mu$.

The CC consists of three queues and a Concurrency Control Scheduler (CCS). The CCS examines the correctness of execution of input operations according to the type of concurrency control scheduler employed (see section 3). If the operation is permitted, it proceeds to the tail of the Access Queue (AQ); otherwise, it is transferred to the tail of the Delay Queue (DQ) or the Wait Queue (WQ). The WQ is for the operations which cannot be permitted due to the lock conflict of locking schedulings. The DQ is for the operations which cannot be executed due to cautious schedulers.

We assume that a transaction accesses the database by means of a single communication line, and that the access time of a READ operation (WRITE operation) to the database is given by C_r (C_w), respectively. Therefore, if a transaction T_i has m read data items and n write data items, it will need $m \cdot C_r$ and $n \cdot C_w$ to execute its READ and WRITE operations.

We assume that the service discipline of all queues is <u>FIFS</u> (First-In First-Served). When a transaction is committed (i.e., WRITE operation is successfully executed) or aborted, the CCS examines the possibility of execution of operations in the WQ and the DQ. We assume that the operations of the WQ has execution priority over the operations of the DQ.

In our simulation studies, we will assume that the arrival rate of transactions from the TG is so high that the CC is saturated with MPL transactions at all times, i.e., parameter λ is given by ∞.

3. CONCURRENCY CONTROL SCHEDULERS

In this section, we give five CCSs considered in this paper. Because of the space limitation, we will abbreviate their detailed description (please refer to [20] for the detailed algorithms).

3.1. Two-Phase Locking (2PL)

The 2PL algorithm obeys the following <u>two-phase</u> <u>rule</u> and it has been shown that the two-phase rule is a sufficient condition for ensuring serializability (see, e.g., [9], [19]).

<u>Two-phase rule</u>: A transaction locks all accessing data items before unlocking any one of them. []

Now we define the <u>lock conflict relation</u>. In locking algorithms a READ operation to data item x_i usually requires <u>share lock</u> (or read lock) on x_i and a WRITE operation to data item y_i usually requires <u>exclusive lock</u> (or write lock) on y_i. We say that two lock requests originating from different transactions <u>conflict</u> if the following is true: both are lock requests on the same data item, and neither are share locks. Each instance of a pair of conflicting locks is called between the corresponding transactions. If a new lock request conflicts with other lock requests, this request will be forced to wait in the WQ for the other transactions to release their lock requests.

Since the two-phase rule does not guarantee prevention of <u>dead-lock</u> problems (see, e.g., [10]), we will construct a <u>deadlock detection graph</u> [10] from the lock conflict relation among transactions in order to examine the existence of deadlock. There is no deadlock if the deadlock detection graph is acyclic (see, e.g., [10]).

In the 2PL, when a new operation arrives at the CCS, the CCS examines whether all locks required by the operation can be permitted. If not, the CCS updates the deadlock detection graph according to the lock conflict relation. Then, if the graph becomes cyclic, the CCS aborts the transaction with this operation and this transaction is removed from the system.

3.2. Cautious Two-Phase Locking (C2PL)

Based on the 2PL algorithm, we propose a cautious scheduling C2PL in our transaction model which prevents deadlocks by means of the information on the write set of the WRITE operation. This information is given to the CCS when the READ operation of the same transaction arrives at the CCS.

In the C2PL, if the first operation of a transaction is received by the CCS, the CCS can also know the write set of the transaction as well as the read set. By reflecting the lock conflict relation of write lock as well as read lock, we will construct a new dead lock detection graph in the same manner as that of the deadlock detection graph defined for the 2PL. This deadlock detection graph indicates the possibility of the occurrence of deadlocks in the future as well as the present if it is cyclic. If the graph becomes cyclic, the received operation will be transferred to the tail of the DQ; otherwise, the operation will be transferred to the tail of the WQ (AQ) if the lock request is (not) in conflict with other lock requests. When a transaction is completed, the CCS examines the possibility of execution of operations of the WQ and then of the DQ according to FIFS discipline by means of cycle check of the deadlock detection graph, and all practicable operations are transferred to the tail of the AQ successively.

3.3. Exclusive Preclaimed Two-Phase Locking (EP2PL)

In the EP2PL, the CCS examines if an arriving READ operation can lock all required data items in exclusive mode. If the operation cannot get all required locks, it is transferred to the tail of the WQ without executing any lock; otherwise, it is transferred to the tail of the AQ. In this algorithm, no WRITE operation is transferred to the tail of the WQ, since all required locks are already granted, because we are assuming the restricted two step model. The EP2PL is a kind of cautious scheduler in the sense that it does not abort any transaction.

3.4. Conflict Serializable Scheduling (CSR)

We say that two operations originating from different transactions conflict if the following is true: both operations read or write the same item, and neither are read operations. Each instance of a pair of conflicting operations is called between the corresponding transactions. Now we shall define the conflict detection graph as follows:

Conflict detection graph

(1) The vertex v_i represents a transaction T_i.

(2) We add to the graph an arc from v_i to v_j if one of next cases is satisfied.

    (a) In case that $R_i(x)$ is followed by $W_j(x)$.

    (b) In case that $W_i(x)$ is followed by $R_j(x)$ or $W_j(x)$ []

By conflict detection graph, we define the conflict serializability.

Conflict serializability [19]: A sequence is said to be conflict serializable if and only if the conflict detection graph is acyclic.

        []

The concept of conflict serializability is the same as "conflict preserving serializability" [1], "D-serializability" [17], and "WW-serializability" [11]. Papadimitriou [17] proved that the class of serializability coincides with the class of conflict serializability in the restricted two step transaction model. This means that a sequence is conflict serializable if and only if it is serializable.

In the CSR, upon receiving a operation the CCS describes the conflict detection graph. Then if the graph becomes cyclic, the CCS aborts the transaction with this operation and the transaction is removed from the system; otherwise, the operation is transferred to the tail of the AQ.

3.5. Cautious Conflict Serializable Scheduling (CCSR)

In the CCSR, upon receiving the READ operation of a transaction, the CCS updates the conflict detection graph reflecting the information of write set of the future WRITE operation of the transaction as well as read set of the received READ operation. Then, if the graph becomes cyclic, the received operation will be transferred to the tail of the DQ; otherwise, the operation will be transferred to the tail of the AQ. When a transaction is completed, the CCS examines the possibility of execution of operations of the DQ according to FIFS discipline, and all practicable operations are transferred to the tail of the AQ successively.

4. CRITERIA OF PERFORMANCE EVALUATION

Now, we shall consider nine criteria for evaluating the performance of the five CCSs.

(1) Mean transaction execution time (TET): The execution time of a transaction is the time between its entrance into the CC and its departure from the CC.

(2) Mean read completion time (RCT): The read completion time of a transaction is the time between its entrance into the CC and its read completion point.

In the restricted two step transaction model, no READ operation is aborted in the 2PL and the CSR. In cautious schedulings no operation is aborted. Thus, in the five CCSs all transactions can be executed to the read completion point. The RCT gives the mean response time for users in our assumed transaction model.

(3) Mean length of AQ (LAQ): The average length of queue AQ.

(4) Mean length of WQ (LWQ): The average length of queue WQ.

The WQ is not used for the conflict serializable schedulers; i.e., CSR and CCSR. Thus, LWQ=0.0 for these two schedulers.

(5) Mean length of DQ (LDQ): The average length of queue DQ.

The DQ is used for the cautious schedulers except for the EP2PL; i.e., C2PL and CCSR (note that the DQ has only READ operations). Thus, LDQ=0.0 for the 2PL, the CSR and the EP2PL.

(6) Average number of transactions executed without waiting (TEWW):

Table 1. Values of system parameters.

	case 1	case 2	case 3	case 4	case 5
N	100	100	100	200	100
DMIN	2	2	2	2	2
M	7	7	7	7	7
WSR	0.3	0.3	0.3	0.3	0.3
	0.5	0.5	0.5	0.5	0.5
	0.7	0.7	0.7	0.7	0.7
	1.0	1.0	1.0	1.0	1.0
MPL	7	14	7	7	7
C_r	1.0	1.0	1.0	1.0	1.0
C_w	1.0	1.0	1.0	1.0	3.0
C_d	0.0	0.0	0.0	0.0	0.0
μ	0.1	0.1	0.25	0.1	0.1

The number of transactions without waiting in queue DQ or WQ.

The TEWW is given by the value normalized by the number of all input transactions.

(7) System throughput (THRPT): The system throughput is the average number of transactions which depart from the CC after the completion of their execution in a unit of time.

(8) Average number of completed transactions (COMTRN): The average number of transactions executed without abortion.

The COMPTRN is given by the value normalized by the number of all input transactions. COMTRN=1.0 for the cautious schedulers; i.e., C2PL, EP2PL and CCSR, and COMPTRN is equal to TEWW for the CSR.

(9) Average difference between input sequence order and execution order (DIFORD): Difference between the order of a read operation entering into the CC and the order of its execution.

Assume that the operation R_2 arriving at the CC later than some read operation R_1. If R_2 will be completed earlier than R_1, then the user originating operation R_1 will be displeased. The DIFORD is a guideline for measuring such displeasure. Since no operation waits in queue DQ or WQ in the CSR, DIFORD=0.0 for the CSR.

5. NUMERICAL RESULTS AND DISCUSSION

As shown in Table 1, a total of 20 test cases consisting of 5 basic system models were examined. Case 1 is the basic system model, and each of the other four cases has a different parameter value from those of case 1; i.e., case 2 has different value of MPL, case 3 has different value of μ, and so on. As the unit time, we employ the access time of READ operation to a data item; i.e., $C_r=1.0$.

The performance of locking schedulers (conflict serializable schedulers) is considered to be seriously affected by the number of transactions with lock conflict relation (conflicting operations). Considering the fact that large values of the parameters WSR and MPL cause the high degree of these conflicting relationships, we show in Table 2~Table 4 the numerical results for the nine performance criteria introduced in section 4 with respect to the following four test cases (note that in case 1, MPL=7 and in case 2, MPL=14):

Table 2: case 1 (WSR=0.5); Table 3: case 1 (WSR=1.0);
Table 4: case 2 (WSR=0.5); Table 5: case 2 (WSR=1.0).

From the results of these tables, it becomes clear that the values of TET are about the same among the five CCSs. However, this is not true for RCT. The RCT for cautious schedulers becomes larger than that for non-cautious schedulers because of the conservative execution of READ operations. In particular, the EP2PL requires considerable time to complete read operations because their lock mode is exclusive. It is noteworthy that the EP2PL recovers such loss time until a transaction completes its execution.

As for the EP2PL, the value of WSR does not affect the values of TEWW, LWQ and DIFORD because it requires exclusive locks for read set, and for the same reason the value of LWQ is larger than that of LAQ. Such results are different from those of C2PL and 2PL.

The length of access queue (LAQ) is most sensitive to the delay of execution of operations (i.e., TET and RCT). We feel that this result is due to the assumption of single-line access to the database. From our results, the delay due to cautious schedulings does't greatly affect the total delay time.

Under the CSR and 2PL schedulings, we now consider the class of input sequences of operations which are serializable without reordering. It is proved in [17] that the class of CSR includes the class of 2PL, and in particular, that the class of CSR coincides with the class of serializability for the restricted two step transaction

Table 2. Numerical results for case 1 (WSR=0.5).

	2PL	C2PL	EP2PL	CSR	CCSR
TET	62.9867	60.8655	61.7219	58.4394	59.4975
RCT	21.2637	32.2169	41.7871	26.2785	31.6994
LAQ	2.5408	2.2137	1.4928	4.3897	3.3505
LWQ	1.5931	1.4079	2.9014	0.0000	0.0000
LDQ	0.0000	0.8232	0.0000	0.0000	1.1128
TEWW	0.2700	0.4100	0.3244	0.7396	0.6916
THRPT	0.0774	0.1052	0.1020	0.0905	0.1091
COMTRN	0.6488	1.0000	1.0000	0.7396	1.0000
DIFORD	0.1444	0.9644	1.3564	0.0000	0.5784

Table 3. Numerical results for case 1 (WSR=1.0).

	2PL	C2PL	EP2PL	CSR	CCSR
TET	77.6304	78.4246	78.5271	70.0301	77.9864
RCT	26.4592	53.5253	53.3939	32.0305	50.5224
LAQ	2.6284	1.7620	1.7170	4.4855	2.3145
LWQ	1.5878	0.6819	2.8592	0.0000	0.0000
LDQ	0.0000	2.2262	0.0000	0.0000	2.3391
TEWW	0.1180	0.3288	0.3248	0.5128	0.3924
THRPT	0.0494	0.0812	0.0794	0.0585	0.0815
COMTRN	0.4340	1.0000	1.0000	0.5128	1.0000
DIFORD	0.2256	1.2168	1.3256	0.0000	0.9380

Table 4. Numerical results for case 2 (WSR=0.5).

	2PL	C2PL	EP2PL	CSR	CCSR
TET	62.9271	59.4506	59.4652	60.1673	59.3723
RCT	25.8921	34.3418	42.7283	29.7906	34.1737
LAQ	3.4026	2.8468	2.1640	5.1447	4.2128
LWQ	1.5793	1.6258	2.8544	0.0000	0.0000
LDQ	0.0000	0.6182	0.0000	0.0000	0.9402
TEWW	0.2848	0.3908	0.3284	0.7520	0.7056
THRPT	0.0828	0.1085	0.1070	0.0916	0.1100
COMTRN	0.6788	1.0000	1.0000	0.7520	1.0000
DIFORD	0.2068	0.9088	1.3236	0.0000	0.3936

Table 5. Numerical results for case 2 (WSR=1.0).

	2PL	C2PL	EP2PL	CSR	CCSR
TET	78.4848	76.9757	77.0593	73.5287	76.8629
RCT	31.7544	54.9369	54.8278	35.8390	52.1247
LAQ	3.3532	2.2506	2.2176	5.1658	2.9918
LWQ	1.6424	0.7971	2.8513	0.0000	0.0000
LDQ	0.0000	2.1410	0.0000	0.0000	2.2245
TEWW	0.1252	0.3032	0.3292	0.5196	0.4172
THRPT	0.0526	0.0837	0.0817	0.0591	0.0843
COMTRN	0.4568	1.0000	1.0000	0.5196	1.0000
DIFORD	0.3136	1.1352	1.2996	0.0000	0.7988

model (see subsection 3.4). This theoretical result supports our simulation results on the TEWW and COMTRN; i.e., conflict serializable schedulings indicate better performance than locking algorithms for the values of TEWW and COMTRN. Papadimitriou [17] did not present any quantitative evaluation concerning the difference of the above two classes. From our results, we can see that the difference of these two classes is much larger for cases with a high degree of conflicting relationships among operations or lock requests.

As for the value of DIFORD, cautious schedulings are affected by the degree of conflicting relationships among operations or lock requests. This is due to the fact that much reordering is required to make serializable sequences for the cases with a high degree of conflicting relationships. The value of DIFORD is interrelated with the value of LDQ since queue DQ is for cautious schedulings.

Concerning the value of THRPT, all 20 test cases give the same order of performance for the five CCSs, i.e., the best is CCSR, the second is C2PL, then EP2PL, CSR, and the worst is 2PL.

Moreover, though some interesting property is observed in case 3～case 5, the basic mutual characteristics among the five CCSs are almost the same as those found in Table 2～Table 5.

Since the complexity of executing cautious schedulings employed in this paper is polynomial time (i.e., cycle check of graphs), we neglected the overhead for cautious schedulings in the above performance evaluation. However, it is interesting to evaluate the practical overhead for the execution of cautious schedulers. Thus, as the tenth performance criterion we consider the following parameter.

(10) <u>Mean scheduling execution time</u> (SET): The execution time of each scheduler is measured by the CPU time consumed for scheduling in the computer used for the simulation study.

For several cases with high degrees of conflicting relationships, we have evaluated the value of SET and the order of value of SET for CCSs is given as follows; i.e., the smallest is EP2PL, the second is 2PL, then C2PL, CSR, and the largest is CCSR.

6. CONCLUSION

In this paper we demonstrated the efficiency of performance of cautious schedulers. If we can assume that the READ operation gives the information of the WRITE set of the same transaction, cautious schedulings become very attractive since no transaction is aborted and they realize high throughput as well as about the same execution delay time as that of non-cautious schedulings. Among cautious schedulers, the EP2PL can be executed without the information of the WRITE set in the restricted two step transaction model, and we show that it realizes high throughput with very small overhead in executing the algorithm. Thus, it is shown that the EP2PL is one of the most recommedable CCSs.

Recently, multiversion two-phase locking schedulers (e.g., [6]) and multiversion conflict serializable schedulers (e.g., [16, 18]) have been proposed, and several papers discussed the performance of multiversion CCSs (see, e.g., [6, 15]). It would be interesting to investigate the performance of cautious multiversion CCSs for future study regarding the performance evaluation of cautious schedulings.

Acknowledgement

The authors wish to express their sincere appreciation to Prof. T. Ibaraki of Kyoto University for his useful comments on the simulation model. They are also highly indebted to Mr. K. Hashimoto of Sumitomo Life Insurance Company for his assistance in obtaining numerical results in section 5.

REFERENCES

1. Bernstein, P.A. and Goodman, N., ACM Comput. Surv., Vol.13, No.2, pp.185-222, June 1981.
2. Bernstein, P.A., Hadzilacos, V., and Goodman, N., "Concurrency Control and Recovery in Database Systems", Addison-Wesley, Reading, Mass. , 1987.
3. Brzozowski, J.A. and Muro, S., Inter. J. Comput. Inf. Sci., Vol.14, NO.6, pp.387-403, Dec. 1985.
4. Buckley, G.N. and Silberschatz, A., Proc. 9th Int. Conf. on VLDB, VLDB Endowment, pp.74-80, Florence, Oct.-Nov. 1983.
5. Carey, M.J., "Modeling and Evaluation of Database Concurrency Control Algorithms", Ph.D. dissertation, Computer Science Div. (EECS), University of California, Berkeley, Aug. 1983.
6. Carey, M.J. and Muhanna, W.A., ACM Trans. Computer Syst., Vol.4, No.4, pp.338-378, Nov. 1986.
7. Casanova, M.A. and Bernstein, P.A., ACTA Informatica, Vol.14, pp.195-220, 1980.
8. Casanova, M.A., "The Concurrency Control Problem for Database Systems", Lecture Notes in Computer Science Vol. 116, Springer-Verlag, Heidelberg, 1981.

9. Eswaran, K.P., Gray, J.N., Lorie, P.A., and Traiger, I.L., <u>Comm. ACM</u>, Vol.19, No.11, pp.624-633, Nov. 1976.
10. Gray, J.N., <u>In</u>: Operating Systems: An Advanced Course (Eds. Bayer, R, Graham, R.M., and Seegmüller, G.), <u>Lecture Notes in Computer Science Vol.60</u>, Springer-Verlag, Heidelberg, pp.393-481, 1978.
11. Ibaraki, T., Kameda, T., and Minoura, T., <u>Proc. 9th Int. Conf. on VLDB</u>, VLDB Endowment, pp.89-91, Florence, Oct.-Nov. 1983.
12. Ibaraki, T., Kameda, T., and Katoh, N., "Cautious Schedulers for Database Concurrency Control", TR 85-2, Dept. of Comput. Sci., Simon Fraser University, 1985.
13. Katoh, N., Ibaraki, T., and Kameda, T., <u>ACM Trans. Database Syst.</u>, Vol.10, No.2, pp.205-229, June 1985.
14. Katoh, N., Ibaraki, T., and Kameda, T., <u>Proc. Int. Seminar on Operations Research and Systems</u>, pp.193-224, Kyoto, Nov. 1985.
15. Lin, W.K. and Nolte, J., <u>Proc. 9th Int. Conf. on VLDB</u>, VLDB Endowment, pp.109-119, Florence, Oct.-Nov. 1983.
16. Muro, S., Kameda, T., and Minoura, T., <u>J. Comput. Syst. Sci.</u>, Vol.29, No.2, pp.207-224, 1984.
17. Papadimitriou, C.H., <u>J.ACM</u>, Vol.26, No.4, pp.631-653, Oct. 1979.
18. Papadimitriou, C.H. and Kanellakis, P.C., <u>ACM Trans. Database Syst.</u>, Vol.9, No.1, pp.89-91, Mar. 1984.
19. Papadimitriou, C.H., "The Theory of Database Concurrency Control", <u>Computer Science Press</u>, Rockville, Maryland, 1986.
20. Watanabe, M., "Simulation Studies on Performance of Several Database Concurrency Control", <u>Master Thesis</u>, Dept. of Applied Mathematics and Physics, Kyoto University, Feb. 1986.

THE DATABASE PROCESSOR 'RAPID'

**Pascal Faudemay, Daniel Etiemble,
Jean-Luc Bechennec, He He**

Laboratoire MASI, Université Paris 6
4 place Jussieu, 75005 Paris, France

——

Abstract:

In this paper we present RAPID, a co-processor for database operations. RAPID is a highly parallel processor, using wired algorithms, and built with several copies of a full custom VLSI component. RAPID displays several original features, such as a Sequential Partitioned Structure mixing sequential and parallel evaluation, and a full query resolution. The interfaces of RAPID with the DBMS and the host machine are quite simple. The main component of RAPID contains 16 to 32 processing elements, with sophisticated functionalities. It evaluates a 1000 tuples x 1000 join in about 3 milliseconds. The join duration is linear with the size of the source relations, even with source relations of more than one million of tuples. RAPID is presently being implemented in HCMOS3 technology.

Keywords:

Database Machine, Database Processor, Co-Processor, Parallel Evaluation, Relational Algebra, Text Retrieval, KBMS, Joins, Main Memory Database Systems, VLSI, RAPID

1. Introduction.

Much work has been devoted to database machines [e.g. KOST86, DEWI85, TANA84, HSIA83], but no architecture or processor has yet really emerged. In this paper, we describe a database co-processor, named RAPID (Relational Access

171

Processor for Intelligent Data). Such a processor may be an answer to this problem, and is presently being implemented.

The critique of database machines has been related to the usefulness of specialized processors, and to the "I/O bottleneck", which is said to make useless massive reductions in the calculus time [BORA83]. It has been said that general microprocessors always take advantage of the integration improvements ("surface improvements") to increase the memory word size and the functionalities. However, highly parallel processors, such as the one which is presented here, use the most advanced silicium technology, and turn to account the entire surface improvements. Moreover, new large main memories, from tens of megabytes to several gigabytes, will soon store in memory the data of a session or of a query and make the response times of the discs a secondary problem. With large main memories a direct access to the tuple is possible. The duration of database operations may therefore approach the transfer time of useful data within main memory. In a mono-processor environment we call it the *theoretical duration limit of database operations*.

The database operations which we consider are the set search and update operations, the text retrieval operations, the concurrency control, the management of predicate access rights, part of the multi-attribute clustering, and virtual memory management. The search operations in present databases are the relational algebra operations, extended to sorting and aggregation (e.g. the mean salary of a category of employees per region). The main relational algebra operations are the selection, the join of two relations, which is a selection on the cartesian product of two relations, the projection, which is the suppression of some attributes (or fields) of tuples (or records) of a relation (or file), and the elimination of duplicates resulting from this suppression. These operations are costly as their duration is a function of the volume of data contained in the source relation(s). With a software execution of the operation, the duration of processing a 1000 tuples x 1000 join, giving 1000 result tuples, is a few seconds. The theoretical limit for the same operation (due to main memory transfers) is presently about 0.4 ms. The prospects of approaching this limit will include the use of this operation in real time systems (with operation times about one millisecond), or the evaluation of joins or selections of one million tuples in about one second, thus allowing an interactive execution of large operations. Assertional updates will be possible in the same time span. Their duration must not be increased too much by the concurrency control. RAPID does most concurrency control by tuple level locking or by preventive certification. However, a discussion of this topic is beyond the scope of this paper.

The basis of these operations is 1:n comparisons of a tuple with n selection expression constants (each of them being relative to one attribute) or comparisons of one tuple with n tuples (join, projection, sorting), or comparisons of one word in a text with n words or character sequences. Therefore the natural architecture of such a processor is a highly parallel, associative architecture, using wired algorithms. The machine also needs a large cache to hold the tables used to access the data, which may represent about 3% of their volume. In order to make comparisons of a tuple or a word with n, the fastest solution seems to be a specialized machine with at least n processing elements (PEs). For joins up to one million tuples, the number of the RAPID PEs, and the division of large joins and projections by hashed indices with reasonable costs, always allow the above condition. In fact the number of PEs may be inferior by a ratio 3 or 4, the speed being only degraded by the same factor. The machine must be associative, i.e. give a sequence of tuple or subexpression identifiers, corresponding to tuples or subexpressions stored into the processor and verified by the evaluated tuple or equal to it. This functionality is a characteristic of associative memories. RAPID may also return the global result of an expression stored in its local memories. These two functionalities avoid the use of an external processor and support high level interfaces with the host machine. It is necessary to use wired algorithms rather than microprogrammed ones, as they return a fast result for each memory word read into the main memory. All these features characterize RAPID.

In this paper we first present the basic principles of the processor [FAUD86], then we briefly review the main search algorithms; the software and hardware interfaces with the host and the DBMS are also discussed. We then present a brief evaluation of the area and speed of the processor, and its performances; they are compared with those of optimal software algorithms, executed by a RISC processor such as CLIPPER [FAIR87] or by the Connection Machine [STAN86]. We conclude on the possible effect of the processor on a DBMS.

2. The processor organization.

2.1. the processor core.

RAPID's core is an array of processing elements (PEs), each of them evaluating a predicate. These processors receive data and control information which are broadcasted on RAPID's internal bus. Each of them recognizes its data, without any addressing. The PEs are mainly made of a local memory, which contains the predicate operand, of a 22 bit comparator, of an automaton which sequences the PE and integrates the word by word comparisons in order to obtain the result of the comparison on the whole attribute. Each PE is connected with the next ones. This allows a sequential loading of the array of PEs without addressing its elements, the management of "long predicates" whose operand does not fit in the local memory, the retrieval of ordered sequences, the management of PEs queues.

During the evaluation of an expression (or a relation) each predicate (or each relevant attribute) is evaluated by a different PE, under the condition that the number of PEs must be large enough. Each PE evaluates one predicate only. Each attribute taking part in the evaluation is broadcasted on the internal bus in one or several cycles. Each memory word broadcasted on the internal bus has 16 data bits (and 6 redundance bits, which will be presented later). Before each attribute, the control module broadcasts an attribute number, together with an "attribute number" signal on the control part of the bus. When it receives this signal, each PE compares the broadcasted data with one of the attribute numbers stored in its local memory. The second attribute number is used only in the case of an inter-attribute comparison. If the broadcasted value is equal to the relevant attribute number, the PE which is in a wait state enters a "dynamic initialization" state or an "evaluation" state. The "dynamic initialization" state only exists in inter-attribute comparisons. In this state, the PE writes the broadcasted attribute into its local memory. In the "evaluation" state, it evaluates a predicate. In this state it calculates the predicate value and keeps this value until the tuple broadcasting is finished. The tuple end is signaled on the control bus by an "end of tuple" bit. The PE then enters a wait state, until the arrival of the relevant attribute from the following tuple.

A PE is mainly made of a local memory, which contains 16 data words, each having 22 bits, and two attribute numbers on 22 bits (6 being unused), of a comparator and a sequencer (figure 1). The sequencer is mainly made of a PLA. The other elements are counters (LGAT, ADR, PROF) and registers or latches (LGINIT and others). The 3 redundance bits allow the representation of 3 special bytes: the skip (or fixed length don't care), used in text retrieval, the floor, which is the value of the low weight byte when the attribute ends in the high weight byte, the skip-floor, which is used for the beginnings and ends of sequences with variable length don't care characters. These 3 redundance bits also allow the representation of the class of character to which the current byte belongs, among 3 user defined classes. E.g. [0-9], [A-Z], may be defined as character classes. When loading the PEs local memories the character class is optional (if it is indicated, the comparison will be done on the class in place of being done on the byte); on the opposite, it is always given for each

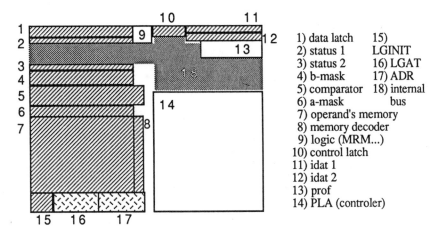

1) data latch   15)
2) status 1   LGINIT
3) status 2   16) LGAT
4) b-mask   17) ADR
5) comparator   18) internal
6) a-mask   bus
7) operand's memory
8) memory decoder
9) logic (MRM...)
10) control latch
11) idat 1
12) idat 2
13) prof
14) PLA (controler)

fig. 1. Layout of one elementary processor.

BYTE VALUE	COMPARED TO			
	skip	floor	skip-floor	usual
skip	=	>	=	=
floor	<	=	=	<
skip-floor	=	=	=	=
usual byte (0-255)	=	>	=	...

fig.2 special bytes ordering

broadcasted memory word during the evaluation phase. The comparison of broadcasted and stored memory words is done according to the rules of figure 2.

At the end of a predicate evaluation, a PE may either activate the following PE (or the next one in case of a failure), or activate the first following PE in a logical group of PEs which is set at load time by the positioning of "end of logical group" bits. In this case if no PE in the group is free, an "error" bit is positioned on the control bus. The first possibility allows to breakdown a predicate into several elementary predicates processed by several PEs. The second one allows PEs queues. These queues are used to process sequences including variable length don't care characters, using the algorithm presented in [PRAM81], or to do comparisons on hierarchically compacted or on some NF2 relations [PIST86]. An example of the interconnections between PEs is given at figure 3.

2.2 the monomial resolution.

The qualification expression (or the relation) stored into the processor is

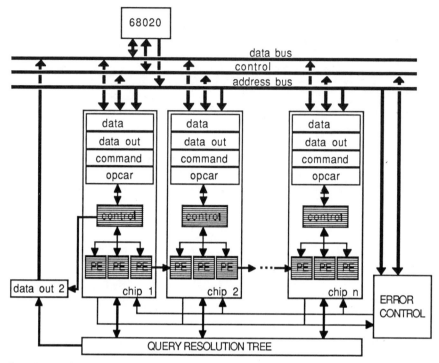

fig.3 RAPID's hardware interfaces.

divided into monomials or subexpressions (resp. tuples). Each monomial is evaluated by a logical group of Monomials Resolution Modules , each being associated to a PE and connected to the following MRM. The structure of the MRM array is an original one, which is called a "Sequential Partitioned Structure". It is a sequential structure, divided into logical groups. Each one evaluates a subexpression in parallel with the other logical groups. The logical groups are created at load time by positioning 'connectors' (and/ or) bits belonging to the qualification expression. The expression is organised into disjunctive or cunjunctive normal form, corresponding to a priority of "and" or "or", i.e. to monomials made of "ands" or of "or". In case of a priority of "and", the end of monomial is set by a connector "or", and in the other case by a connector "and".

More complex expressions may also be evaluated, they are divided into subexpressions; each subexpression is evaluated by a logical group, and is separated from the others by "ORs" in cas of a priority of "ANDs", and the converse. We shall not describe here the processing of such subexpressions.

Using a "Sequential Partitioned Structure" to evaluate subexpressions is an improvement in the evaluation of a boolean expression. The number of predicates per monomial may vary without having idle PEs or addressing the nodes of a resolution tree, as would be the case with other solutions [FAUD86, FAUD85]. The "Sequential Partitioned Structure" is also a very general structure, as will be shown in further publications. It allows a wired resolution of subexpressions, avoiding any operation of the general microprocessor except the data transfers during the processing of a set of tuples.

The MRM inputs are the signals MONIN, PRED, CONNECT, PRIO, which describe the previous value of the monomial (or of the subexpression), the current value of the predicate, the connector, the priority. The outputs are MONOUT (next value of the monomial), and FINMON, which is the value of the monomial when the current PE corresponds to an end of monomial, and is not significant in the other cases (figure 4). In some applications, as sorting, the comparison of two tuples

fig.3. Monomials
resolution module
(a) "and" priority
(b) "or" priority

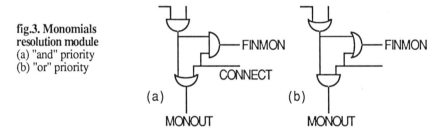

amounts to the evaluation of subexpressions such as ((Attribute_i > A) or (Attribute_i = A and Attribute_i+1 > B) or etc...). This evaluation is done in the same way as the evaluation of large predicates, which use more than one PE. When the previous PEs of the subexpression returns a result '=', it enables the evaluation of the next attribute (or the next elementary predicate) by the next PE. All PEs in the subexpression have neutral values, except the one with a '>' result. This case is the only one where the result depends on the '=' or '>' result of the comparison, and not only of the value 'true' or 'false' of the predicate. The MRM corresponding to each PE is integrated in the same micro-circuit as the PE.

2.3. the Multiple Match Resolution (MMR).

The processor has three main operation modes: the 'selection', 'join', and 'sorting' modes, each of them being characterized by a different microinstruction in the PEs and in the status register of the control module. When the processor operates in 'join' mode, each end of monomial PE having its value of monomial at 'true' delivers its monomial identifier on the internal bus. The monomials identifiers may be, e.g., tuple identifiers (TIDs) stored into the processor, or structured values such as <word identifier><word evaluation> in the vectorial selection of texts [SALT83]. However, several monomial identifiers may not be simultaneously delivered on the internal bus. An algorithm must define the sequencing of writes on this bus.

Such an algorithm called "Multiple Match Resolution" algorithm, has been defined for associative memories [MINK71, THUR75]. It is also used for some other circuits, as some binary encoders. It uses the organisation of the circuit as an array of elementary circuits, each one delivering its results on an internal bus. Each elementary circuit may transmit a control bit, called "inhibition bit", to all the elementary circuits having a superior index. Let us call INHIBIT_IN(i) the value of this bit received by the elementary circuit of index i, and INHIBIT_OUT (i) the value possibly emitted by the same circuit. We shall suppose that a circuit emitting this bit must have a bit READY(i)= TRUE. Let also INHIBIT_IN (IMAX+1) be the value of INHIBIT output by the last elementary circuit of the array. After adapting the algorithm to the case of RAPID, it becomes the algorithm of figure 5.

```
do
        for all PE i of the processor do INHIBIT_IN (i):=FALSE
        for all PE i of the processor do
                if READY(i) then begin
                        for j=i to IMAX+1 do
                        INHIBIT_IN (j):= TRUE {propagate INHIBIT_OUT(i)}
                        next j
                end
        for all PE i of the processor do
(1)        if INHIBIT_IN (i)= FALSE and READY (i)= TRUE then
                do
                write IDENTIFIER (i) on the internal bus
                READY(i):=FALSE
                end
        end
until INHIBIT_IN (IMAX+1)= FALSE
```

figure 5. Multiple Match Resolution Algorithm.

Several solutions have been presented for the inhibition bit propagation. An optimal solution has been presented by [ANDE74]. In this solution the propagation is done along a double binary tree, whose node schema is given in figure 6. In one copy the propagation is done from the leaves to the root, in the other one it is done from the root to the leaves, and the binary trees are connected at their nodes as shown at figure 7. Subtrees containing only two or four leaves may be replaced by a linear

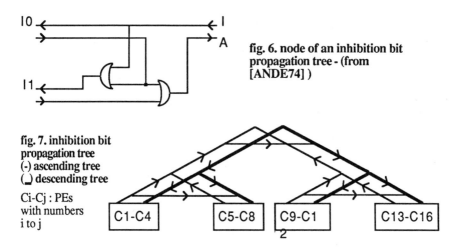

fig. 6. node of an inhibition bit propagation tree - (from [ANDE74])

fig. 7. inhibition bit propagation tree
(-) ascending tree
(‿) descending tree

Ci-Cj : PEs with numbers i to j

propagation circuit. In the solution which was proposed by Anderson, condition (1) allows the calculus of a physical address for the element which satisfies this condition. In RAPID, we write its logical address on the internal bus; the logical address is the monomial identifier, stored in the PE at load time. This logical address is common to all the PEs in the monomial, though it could also be defined only for its last PE.

2.4. the query resolution.

The query resolution receives as an input the signals which are delivered by the monomials resolution modules, the signal PRIORITY and the inhibition bit propagated by previous PEs. It delivers as an output one of the following results:

    * a bit RESULT (TRUE/ FALSE) which gives the value of the boolean expression evaluated by the processor, in the 'selection' mode.

    * a monomial identifier, in the 'join' mode

    * a number of satisfied subexpressions, in the 'sorting' mode. These subexpressions use a logical group of PEs as ordinary monomials, but are boolean binomials already presented at paragraph 2.2.

Bit RESULT is calculated by a parallel AND or OR (according to the priority) on the set of monomial results. The calculus is done by a binary tree of parallel ANDs and a binary tree of parallel ORs, one of the results being then selected (the selection may also be done in each subtree of the resolution tree, this solution has not yet been implemented). The monomial identifier is delivered by the PEs array according to the inhibition bit delivered by the MMR (see paragraph 2.3.). The couting of the number of subexpressions is done by a binary tree of adders. The circuit for query resolution is made of three hardware binary trees: the parallel AND and OR, the MMR tree, the adders tree.Both the subtrees of the query resolution and of the MMR are either implemented on the same component as the PEs, or on an interconnexion component, according to the depth level of the subtree.

2.5. the control module.

The control module has three main functions:

* it interfaces the host machine with the internal bus of processor RAPID. It calculates the bits END_OF_ATTRIBUTE and END_OF_TUPLE, and sends to the host the identifiers of the tuples which match the join condition
* it drives the memory transfers
* it drives the tuple accesses and the virtual memory mechanisms

In the first version of the processor, presently being implemented, the control module is mainly software-based. A further version will implement it in hardware.

3. Algorithms.

In this paragraph we give some precisions about the algorithms for joins, projections, text selection with automatic query enriching, and fixpoint calculus. The selection of text attributes may also include the searching of character sequences preceded (and possibly followed) by "variable don't care characters". The algorithm for these 'non anchored' sequences is presented in [PRAM81]. This algorithm is more costly than the string searching algorithm proposed by [TAKA86], but this one does not seem to allow other comparisons than equalities and inequalities, while they are needed for tuple evaluation. We shall admit that the number of non-anchored comparisons in a query is limited to tens or hundreds (more in maximal configurations of the processor).

When evaluating a join, the join expression is applied to each tuple of the 1st source relation to give a conjunctive monomial. In order to join with this tuple (i.e. to satisfy the join expression on the pair of tuples) the attributes of the current tuple of the second source relation must verify this monomial. E.g. let us evaluate the join in figure 8. The tuple identifiers (TIDs) #i are not part of the relation. They are an implicit attribute (i.e. system defined) for each relation. The system chooses relation 1 (relation REGIONS) as the smaller one; its two tuples give a selection expression composed of the two following monomials:

EMPLOYEE (NAME, REGION, SALARY)
REGION(NAME, MEANSALARY)

EMPLOYEE #	I NAME	I REGION	I SALARY
1	I DUPONT	I PARIS	I 10
2	I DURANT	I PARIS	I 20
3	I ANATOLE	I CAEN	I 20

REGION #	I NAME_REG	I MEANSALARY
1	I PARIS	I 15
2	I CAEN	I 20

RETRIEVE NAME, SALARY, REGION, MEANSALARY FROM EMPLOYEE, REGION WHERE EMPLOYEE. REGION = REGION.NAME_REG AND EMPLOYEE.SALARY ≥ REGION. MEANSALARY

figure 8. join example.

    (#1) Attribute_2= 'PARIS' and Attribute_3 ≥ 15 or

    (#2) Attribute_2 = 'CAEN' and Attribute_3 ≥ 20

To each monomial we associate a monomial identifier (between brackets), which is the identifier of the corresponding tuple. In the previous example, tuple #1 of relation EMPLOYEES does not satisfy any monomial, tuple #2 satisfies monomial #1, which gives a result tuple #2#1, and so on. A tuple of the second relation may give more than one tuple in the result relation.

    The projection may be seen in a classical way as an auto-join, however it is processed by RAPID in a slightly different way. The result relation, where the user wants to eliminate duplicates, is divided into hashing buckets either by RAPID, or by using a hashed index defined for example on a join or selection attribute, which is kept in the projection result. In a bucket each new tuple is then written in the first free PEs, and simultaneously compared with the tuples stored in the previous PEs. If the comparison shows that it was a duplicate, the "end of last tuple" tag is set back to the end of the previous tuple, and the next tuple is written at the same place. At the end the processor contains only one copy of each tuple in the bucket. The tuple identifiers, or possibly the tuple contents, are then written by RAPID in the free space of the projection result.

    The other relational database operations are the sort operation and the aggregate calculus. When sorting the processor delivers a sorting array [IVER66] of the relation tuples. Each element of index i of the array is the rank of the ith tuple of the relation in sort order. Each element value is the number of tuples previously stored in the processor, which are inferior to the current tuple (or superior, if the sort is descendant). It is possible to use this array to reorder the tuples of the result relation (or their TIDs) [FAUD86]. The agreggate calculus is done in a way similar to the projection. E.g. let us calculate the mean salary per region, using the relation in figure 8. In a 1st phase RAPID does a projection on attribute REGION and delivers the number of the current region for each tuple of the source relation. Then RAPID or the associated processor adds for each source relation tuple the salaries and the numbers of agents in elements of an auxiliary array, corresponding to a region number. At the end of the operation, this small array is sorted in the order of the regions names.

In order to evaluate recursive queries the relational algebra operations must be completed by the evaluation of least fixpoint operations [AHO79], which can be seen as relational algebra programs. Fixpoint operations are calculated by an iteration of a relational algebra expression and of the union of the new result tuples with one of the source relations. RAPID does fixpoint evaluations. The PEs array is divided into one or several areas (or subarrays), each one being used for the evaluation of one of the iterative operations. One area may evaluate both an iterative join and the union operation. RAPID may also evaluate in one operation a complex query made of several selections and a join.

An other operation similar to the least fixpoint is the vectorial selection of texts with an automatic enriching of the query. In this operation the words which are found in the selected documents, and which are more frequent in these documents than in the rest of the database, are used to enrich the query or receive an increased weight in a further evaluation of this query. This enriching is used to increase the recall and the precision of the selection, i.e. the proportion of retrieved documents among the "good" ones, and the proportion of "good" documents among the retrieved ones. To get the word frequencies the processor stores a single copy (i.e., with projection) of all the words met in the document and which do not belong to a "stop list" which is also stored in the processor. For each word RAPID delivers at the end of the document (or during the selection) the word identifier, its weight (which is null for the words which do not belong to the query) and the frequency of the word in the document (or possibly since the last frequency read of this word).

4. Interfaces.

The interface of RAPID with the DBMS is a high level and very simple one. We shall first consider the software interface with the query decomposition module of the DBMS, then say a few words about the hardware interfaces between RAPID and the general microprocessor, and end this paragraph by a few words on mixed problems which are related to both software and hardware interfaces. Due to space limitations, the problems of software interfaces with the DBMS memory manager (page faults..) and the concurrency control and recovery modules, will not be addressed in this paper. The software interface with the query decomposition module is mainly built around the two following functions:

INSTALL sends RAPID an information about its hardware configuration and that of the system

OPERATE calls the execution of any RAPID operation. Its parameters are the name of the operation, its type (number of source relations and their format), the addresses of the permanent relations referred by the TIDs of the source relations, the addresses of the source temporary relations or indices, which consist in sets of TIDs or sets of TID tuples, a pointer on the qualification expression, an address of the list of free pages available for the result relation. The operation arity may be 1 or 2. In both cases, the number of permanent relations which are referenced by the source relations may be superior to 1, as a temporary relation may be the result of several joins. A permanent relation may also be a source relation.

Regarding the hardware interfaces, RAPID is built in two versions, only the first one being presently implemented in HCMOS3. The first one is a "controller" version, in which the processor communicates with the host machine through I/O ports. The data transfers are done by a general microprocessor. This one may be e.g. a 68020. The second version is a "co-processor" version, in which RAPID receives the parameters of the OPERATE command, i.e. mainly an operation code and six addresses, and takes the control of the bus for a whole operation such as a join, or a fixpoint or a selection-join. In this case RAPID does the transfers between main memory and the I/O ports, and appears from outside much like a DMA circuit.

In the controller version, the exchanges between RAPID and the host machine are done according to an asynchronous protocol, possibly compatible with the opportunities offered by a VME bus. RAPID has three I/O ports: a control port (COMMAND), an input port (DATA), and an output port (DATA_OUT). The control port updates are always done before those of the input port; a same control word may remain valid during the processing of several successive data words. The data write on the input port is maintained as long as the corresponding value has not been read by the control module of RAPID, which informs the general processor that it has read the data by setting a signal DATA_ACK. It is also necessary that RAPID would not deliver a new result in DATA_OUT before the reading of the previous result by the general processor. In order to avoid this, the reading of DATA_OUT by the program sets a bit CLEAR in a latch of RAPID. When a data has been written in DATA_OUT and if CLEAR is not set, RAPID is halted by setting an appropriate control bit in the status register of the control module. In general, this part of the protocol is the only one which is really used, as RAPID is always faster than the general microprocessor.

The interfaces are shown at figure 2. DATA, DATA_OUT, and the control port COMMAND are replicated on each chip, together with a register OPCAR which contains the operation type (join, selection, etc..). The error control component does the time-out management. In case of a selection or sorting mode, the result is delivered in the DATA_OUT2 register.

For the co-processor version, which is under study, the main problem is to guarantee that RAPID will keep the bus for long enough times, frequently corresponding to a full relational operation. This result is obtained by a function calculus, done by a general processor or by an arithmetic co-processor, which does not interrupt the relational operation itself. Functions are calculated as calculus relations attributes. Opposite to ordinary temporary relations, these relations contain values and they are associated to the source relations. Each tuple of a source relation upon which a function is defined, is associated to a tuple of the auxiliary relation. The relational operation itself is done on TID-valued tuples, in which one TID refers the source relation and one or several TIDs refer the auxiliary relations.

5. Evaluations.

RAPID's main component, which includes several processing elements and a minimal control module, is presently being implemented in full custom, HCMOS3 technology, at MASI Laboratory. The interconnection component has a low integration level and will be implemented later in gate-array technology. The main component is designed in λ; λ is a length unit for VLSI design, and varies according to the technology and the design rules. With a value of $\lambda = 0.65 \ \mu$, the size of one PE in HCMOS3 technology will be about 1700 x 1300 $\mu2$. The number of processing elements in a 1 cm2 component will be at least equal to 16. Thus a minimum processor including 160 PEs will be built with 10 copies of the main component and 2 to 9 copies of the interconnection component (fig.1 and 2). The cycle time of a PE will be 40 ns. In case of a sequential access to data, the throughput of RAPID will thus be 50 Megabytes/ second in the co-processor version. In the most usual environments the limiting factor will be the duration of the memory cycle.

We have done comparative evaluations of the speed of a set of operations, done by RAPID and by new software algorithms assumed to be very fast and not yet implemented. When done by RAPID, the duration of the operations are about 1.750ms for a selection of 1000 tuples giving 500 tuples, 1.750 ms for a projection of 1000 tuples returning less than 1000 tuples, and 3.5 ms for a join of 1000 tuples by 1000 returning 1000 tuples. An analysis of the selection and join durations is given at fig.10 and 11. These durations are linear with the size of the source relations for the selection and the join.

elementary operation	duration
read a tuple identifier	1 R/W*
convert into a tuple address	2 R/W
* for m attributes	
access to an attribute value)	1 R/W
read a 4*n-2 bytes attribute) m times	n R/W
write the tuple identifier into the result	
relation (s= selection selectivity)	2s R/W

total	$(3+ m + mn + 2s)$ R/W

e.g. for 1 R/W= 0.25µs, m=1, n=2, s= 0.5 : 1.750 µs per source tuple
*R/W= read/writes in main memory

figure 9. duration of a selection operation, per source tuple

$$((r1 + r2).(3 + m + mn) + 2.(r1.r2.s)) \text{ R/W}$$

with s= r/ r1.r2, r, r1, r2 being the cardinalities of the result and source relations
e.g. for 1 R/W= 0.25 µs, m=1, n=2, r=r1=r2= 1000: 3.5 milliseconds

figure 10. duration of a join operation, for a 1000 tuples x 1000 join

As an illustration of RAPID efficiency, the same join needs several seconds with present DBMS. The improvement ratio is therefore above 1000 versus present implementations; this allows real time relational algebra operations, which are not possible with other methods. When compared with an evaluation of the best software algorithms, assumed to use the best existing microprocessors, RAPID is still better with an improvement ratio between 10 and 40 at least. Both these algorithms and RAPID are limited by the cycle time of memories. Thus future improvements in the cycle time will have the same effect on the response times of RAPID and on the software algorithms. The ratio between those two types of algorithms will therefore remain similar in the future; considering the speed of evolution of the cycle time for large RAM memories, and the drawbacks of some of the fastest software algorithms (update costs, projection costs in the case of some data representations), it seems that RAPID is presently the only processor allowing real time operations, or very large operations in interactive times.

For text selection with a query enrichment we have done a comparison between RAPID and the 'Connection Machine' [STAN86]. The 'Connection Machine' is a SIMD machine using 64 K processing elements. It should allow the evaluation of the compacted equivalent of 1 gigabyte of text, versus a 20000 word query, in about 4 seconds of cpu time. The same operation, versus a 5000 word query, could be evaluated in 5 seconds with an enhanced configuration of RAPID. Queries comparable to those of the Connection Machine should be evaluated by RAPID in the silicium technology following HCMOS3.

6. Conclusion.

In this paper we have presented a new highly parallel processor, which is adapted to all the database, knowledge base, and text base search operations and to some update operations. This processor does all the time consuming operations of a DBMS, including most of the concurrency control operations by locking or preventive certification, trigger firing, part of clustering operations, the management of predicate rights. Its use in a standard workstation defines a new type of database machine, specially simple to build. It will give several orders of magnitude of improvements versus present software algorithms; its improvement ratio versus software algorithms should remain important in the future. RAPID allows an evaluation of database operations on small or average relations in real time, about one millisecond, and on very large relations (about one million tuples) in one second, a time compatible with interactive utilization.

Acknowledgements. The RAPID project is supported by the Sabre Project (INRIA/ MASI Laboratory), the ACIA Project (MASI), and PRC-BD3. The MASI Laboratory is an associated unit of the Centre National de la Recherche Scientifique.

References.
[AHO79]   AHO, ULLMAN, "Universality of Data Retrieval Languages", 6th Conf. on Principles of Programming Languages, San Antonio, Texas, 1979*/

[ANDE74] ANDERSON, G.A., "Multiple Match Resolvers: A New Design Method", *IEEE Transactions on Computers* (Correspondence), dec.1974

[BORA83] BORAL, H., DEWITT, D.J., "Database Machines: An Idea Whose Time Has Passed? A Critique of the Future of Database Machines", Proc.Int. Workshop on Database Machines, Munich, Springer ed., sept.1983

[DEWI85] DEWITT, D.J., BORAL, H.,ed. *"Database Machines"*, 4th Int. Workshop on Database Machines (Grand Bahama Island, Bahamas, mars 1985), Springer, NY, 1985

[FAIR87] FAIRCHILD, *"The Clipper 32 bits Microprocessor: User Manual"*, Addison Wesley, 1987

[FAUD86] FAUDEMAY, P., *"Un processeur VLSI pour les opérations de bases de données"*, Ph.D thesis, University Paris 6, Paris, june 1986 (in french)

[FAUD85] FAUDEMAY, P., VALDURIEZ, P., "Design and Analysis of a Direct Filter Using Parallel Comparators", in [DEWI85]

[HSIA83] HSIAO, D.K., ed.*"Advanced Database Machine Architecture"*, Prentice-Hall, NJ, 1983

[IVER66] IVERSON, K.*"A Programming Language"*, Wiley, 1966

[KOST86] KOSTER, A., SONDAK, N., SULLIVAN, P., "The Application of a Geometric Arithmetic Systolic Processor to Database Machine Design", Int. Conf. on Data Engineering, Los Angeles, feb.1986

[MINK71] MINKER, J., "An Overview of Associative or Content-Adressable Memory Systems and a KWIC index to the Literature:1956-1970", *Computing Reviews,* Oct.1971

[PIST86] PISTOR, P., ANDERSEN, F., "Designing a Generalized NF2 Model with an SQL-Type Language Interface", 12th Int.Conf.on Very Large Data Bases, Kyoto, Aug. 1986

[PRAM81 PRAMANIK, S., "Hardware Organization for Non Numeric Processing", 7th. Int. Conf. on Very Large Data Bases, Cannes, France, sept.1981

[SALT86] SALTON, G., FOX, E., WU, H., "Extended Boolean Information Retrieval", *Comm.ACM*, dec.1983

[STAN86] STANFILL,C., KAHLE, B., "Parallel Free-Text Search on the Connection Machine System", *Comm.ACM,* dec.1986

[TANA84] TANAKA, Y. "Bit Sliced Algorithms for Search and Sort", 10th Int. Conf. on Very Large Data Bases, Singapore, Aug. 1984

[TAKA86] TAKAHASHI, K. et al. "A New String Search Hardware Architecture for VLSI", 13th Int. Symp. on Computer Architecture, Tokyo, Japan, june 1986

[THUR75] THURBER, K.J., WALD, L.D., "Associative and Parallel Processors", *Computing Surveys*, vol.7, n°4, dec. 1975

A BUS CONNECTED CELLULAR ARRAY PROCESSING UNIT FOR RELATIONAL
DATABASE MACHINES

M. ABDELGUERFI
Electrical Engineering Department, University of Detroit, Michigan

A.K. SOOD
Computer Science Department, George Mason University, Virginia

ABSTRACT. In this paper, an external VLSI algorithm for the
projection operation is presented. This algorithm uses a Bus
Connected cellular Array (BCA) processing unit of fixed size to
project relations of large size. The idea of incorporating a BCA
processing unit as an algorithmically specialized component into a
general purpose back-end database system is investigated. A
performance analysis in terms of the overall system parameters
shows that a significant performance improvement is acheived if the
BCA processing unit is made part of the back-end relational
database system.

INTRODUCTION

In (1, 2) it is shown that a multiple processor system
architecture utilizing the Bus Connected Cellular Array (BCA)
topology (Fig. 1) can be utilized to efficiently perform several
relational database operations (3). In this approach, a mark bit is
associated with each tuple. At each step a number of tuples are
simultaneously compared in the BCA processing unit and their
respective mark bits are manipulated according to the result of the
comparisons. The mark bits are utilized to identify the qualified
tuples. The processing of the tuples is completely overlapped with
the inputting and outputting of the tuples to and from the BCA
processing unit. It was assumed that the tuples are input to the BCA
processing unit and filtered out in a sequential fashion (Fig. 2). In
(2) is also shown that the BCA approach presents significant
advantages when compared with the approach of (4). Further, since
the tuples are input serially to the processing unit, a trivial lower
bound on the processing time of a relation of size n would be n steps

(since a least n steps are needed to input the tuples). A BCA processing unit requires 2n steps to process a relation of size n (1). Therefore, we conclude that the BCA approach is optimal up to a constant factor. The gap between the BCA processing time and the trivial lower bound can be further reduced by the use of pipelining. For example, processing m relations each of cardinality n in a pipelined way requires (m+1)n steps. Consequently, the processing of m relation on the BCA is optimal up to a constant factor $(\frac{m+1}{m})$.

The algorithms presented in (1, 2) were internal. That is, the number of tuples in the relation was assumed to be no larger than the BCA processing unit size[1]. However, in general, an entire relation cannot be processed internally by the BCA processing unit. As a consequence, it is important to design external VLSI algorithms. It is recalled that an external VLSI algorithm is one that allows a chip (or a set of chips) of fixed size to process a relation of unbounded cardinality. In general, the design of an external algorithm is more difficult than the design of an internal one. This is because external algorithms, unlike internal algorithms, are sensitive to parameters such as: data distribution, and input/output cost. On the other hand, the performance of an internal VLSI algorithm is usually determined by the size of the circuit.

The goal of this paper is to validate the idea of incorporating a BCA processing unit as an algorithmically specialized component into a general purpose back-end database system. This is done by showing that a significant performance improvement is achieved once the BCA processing unit is made part of the back-end database system. It should be noted that since the inputting and outputting of tuples to and from the BCA unit are serial, little additional overhead is necessary in order to incorporate the unit into the back-end database system. The overall system will be composed of four main components: a BCA processing unit, a back-end controller, a main memory unit, and the secondary storage. Although, the BCA processing unit can implement efficiently several relational database

---

[1]The size of a BCA unit of n cells is n.

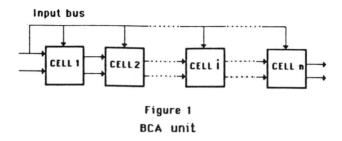

Figure 1
BCA unit

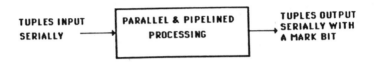

Figure 2
General approach

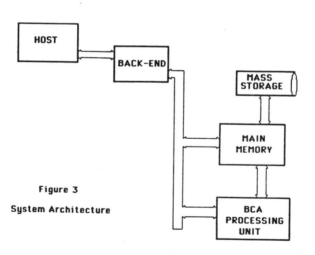

Figure 3

System Architecture

operations, our study will be limited to the projection operation. The external VLSI algorithms for the projection operation is analyzed in terms of the systems parameters. Next, the performance of the overall system with the BCA processing unit as a specialized component is analyzed for different values of the system parameters (BCA size, input/output time, main memory size, ect...). Subsequently, comparisons with existing algorithms are performed.

SYSTEM ARCHITECTURE

In this section the general architecture of the back-end database machine (Fig. 3) is presented. This back-end machine interfaces with a front-end (host) general purpose computer. The back-end database machine includes four main components: a) A BCA processing unit of fixed size devoted exclusively to database operations. b) A general purpose back-end controller. c) A primary memory. d) Mass storage.

It is recalled that the host (front-end) computer is primarilly responsible for: a) Handling all communications with the user. b) Parsing and decomposing the query. c) Sending the decomposed query to the back-end controller.

On the other hand, the back-end controller is responsible for interfacing with the host computer controlling the flow of data and control signals among the four components. The following notation will be utilized to analyze the different algorithms:

(1) n = number of tuples in a relation

(2) λ = number of tuples in a page

(3) $P = \lceil n/\lambda \rceil$ = number of pages in a relation

(4) $B+1$ = main memory size in pages

(5) c^r = time to read a page from main memory to mass storage

(6) c^w = time to write a page from mass storage to main memory

(7) V = time to move a tuple out of (into) the main memory to (from) the back-end or the BCA processing unit

(8) H = time to hash a tuple in main memory

(9) C = time to compare two tuples resident in main memory

The BCA processing unit will be assumed to be capable of internally processing up to "x" pages (of course, $x < (B+1) < P$).

THE HASH BCA PROJECTION ALGORITHM

Because of its simplicity and clustering features the hashing technique has been widely utilized in relational database machines. For example, in Grace (5), the join operation is executed in two phases. The first phase begins by partitioning the two relations into small buckets. During the second phase of the Grace algorithm a merge and sort algorithm is performed on each pair of fragments in the partition.

Our approach makes use of the hashing strategy to fragment the operand relations into small disjoint subsets that can be subsequently processed internally by a BCA processing unit of fixed size. We start by assuming that all the fragments are small enough to be processed internally by the BCA unit. Next, we present a strategy that solves the case where the fragment size exceeds the capacity of the BCA processing unit.

The algorithm.

It is recalled that the processing of projection requires the execution of two different operations. First, the relation is reduced to a vertical subrelation by discarding some columns. The second operation involves removing duplicates. In this section, we assume that the page of the relation to be projected has already been reduced to a vertical subrelation.

The hash-BCA is a divide and conquer strategy based on hashing whose aim is to fragment the relation into buckets. The bucket size is expected to be no larger than the number of cells in the BCA processing unit. However, due to data distribution some buckets might contain more tuples than the number of cells. This situation is called bucket overflow. In this section, we assume that no buffer overflow occurs, this constraint is removed in the next section . The use of hashing is attractive since it can be performed easily on the fly in hardware (6).

The hash-BCA projection algorithm consists of two phases. During the first phase, the relation is partitioned using hashing into disjoint buckets each containing an average of x pages. In the second step, each bucket is processed internally by the BCA processing unit. The partitioning or fragmentation of the relation is performed in a recursive manner until each bucket is no larger than x pages. Let J be the number of recursions needed. During the first recursion, a page of the multirelation to be projected is read into the main memory and then partitioned into B (the remaining one is used to hold the actual page) different buckets, each one will contain an average of (assuming a uniform distribution of values) P/B pages[2]. During the next recursion each bucket is itself hashed into B disjoint buckets. It is noted that a different hash function is used for each iteration. After J recursions each bucket will contain an average of x pages. Consequently,

$$\lceil P/B^J \rceil = x$$

The total number of recursions is therefore about $\lceil \ (_r) \log_B P/x \rceil$. During each recursion, the relation is read from the mass storage to the main memory. Then each tuple is moved to the back-end processor and hashed. Afterwards, the relation is stored back into the mass storage. The duration of each iteration is therefore

$$h_p = P(c^r + c^w + \lambda(2V+H))$$

Hence, the duration of phase one is $h_p \lceil \log_B P/x \rceil$.

During the second phase, the different buckets are processed internally by the BCA processing unit. If the different buckets are not processed in a pipelined way, then each one of the P/x buckets will necessitate 2x steps to be processed. Since the relation has to be read from and written back into the mass storage, the overall

---

[2]without loss of generality, P and B are assumed multiples of x.

duration of the second phase is

$$2\lambda VP + Pc^r + Pc^w$$

Therefore, the hash-BCA projection algorithm with no pipelining will require

$$h_P \lceil \log_B P/x \rceil + P(2\lambda V + c^r + c^w)$$

It is noted that the use of pipelining would require a dual port main memory. In this case, during the execution time of the second phase, the different buckets can be input and output to and from the BCA processing unit in a pipelined way. Their processing time will be therefore completely overlapped with their input-output time. Consequently, processing internally B different buckets will necessitate (P+x) steps. Hence, the second phase will require

$$\lambda(P+x)V + P(c^r + c^w)$$

time units. Therefore, the hash-BCA projection algorithm with pipelining requires

$$h_P \lceil \log_B P/x \rceil + \lambda(P+x)V + P(c^r + c^w)$$

Handling buffer overflow.

In the previous section, the hash-BCA projection algorithm has been presented. It was assumed that all the buckets are no larger than the BCA processing capacity x. In practice this is seldom the case. Our strategy to handle bucket overflow is based on an iterative use of the BCA processing unit. The strategy will be called "iterative-BCA" projection algorithm. The iterative-BCA projection algorithm will use BCA unit of fixed size (x in this case) in an iterative way to process buckets whose size is larger than x.

The iterative BCA projection algorithm works as follows: A bucket (B) whose size K is larger than x is divided into $a = \lceil 2K/x \rceil$ parts $(B_1, B_2, \ldots, B_a)$. The size of each part is $\dfrac{x}{2}$ pages or less. In the next step, each concatenation of two different parts B_i and B_j, $i \neq j = 1, 2, \ldots, a$, is transferred to the BCA processing unit for internal evaluation. In this manner, all possible pairs (B_i, B_j) $i \neq j$, are processed by the BCA unit. A total of $a(a-1)K$ steps are required to project a bucket of K $(K \geq x)$ pages when pipelining is not utlized. In case pipelining is used, the number of steps reduces to $(\frac{a(a-1)}{2}+1)K$ steps.

The iterative-BCA projection algorithm allows a BCA unit of fixed size to handle large data sets. However, it introduces a term of the order of a^2. In this section, the performance of the projection with buffer overflow is analyzed.

Let's assume first that the size K of the bucket is no larger than the size of the main memory $(x<K \leq B)$. Since the BCA processing unit can accomodate up to x pages internally and the bucket is composed of K pages, a total of $\frac{a(a-1)}{2}$ different data sets of up to x pages each are projected internally before the final result is obtained. Processing a bucket of size K will therefore necessitate

$$T = ax\lambda V(a-1) + K(c^r+c^w)$$

time units if no pipelining is used. Processing a bucket with pipelining will require

$$T' = [\frac{a(a-1)}{2}+1]x\lambda V + K(c^r+c^w)$$

When K is greater than the size of the main memory, several passes are needed. During each pass, B pages are transfered from and to the mass storage (except for the last pass during which possibly less than B pages will be transfered). Also, $\frac{B}{x}(\frac{2B}{x}-1)$ different data sets of x pages are processed internally. The number of iterations needed to process the bucket using the iterative-BCA approach will be

$$\lceil \frac{ax(a-1)}{2B(2B-x)} \rceil$$

Consequently, processing the buckets without pipelining will require

$$\frac{ax(a-1)}{2B(2B-x)}\Big\rceil\ [\frac{B(2B-x)\lambda V}{x} + B(c^r+c^w)]$$

When pipelining is used, the overall time reduces to

$$((\frac{a(a-1)}{2})+1)\lambda xV + B\frac{ax(a-1)}{2B(2B-x)}\Big\rceil(c^r+c^w)$$

COMPARISON WITH EXISTING ALGORITHMS

In order to highlight the benefits of incorporating a BCA processing unit into the back-end database system, an analysis is made of the system with no BCA unit as a component. This is done by considering algorithms used in general purpose database systems and studying their performance in the context of the back-end system of Fig. 3 (of course, the BCA unit is included). We have considered two conventional algorithms: the merge and sort and the hash and sort algorithms.

Comparison with the merge and sort algorithm.

The method consists of sorting the whole relation using the sort-merge algorithm (7). Once the relation is sorted, a single pass will be sufficient to remove the duplicate tuples. Since we do not assume that the whole relation fits entirely into the main memory, an external sort algorithm needs to be used. It is recalled that the main memory can accomodate (B+1) pages. Consequently, up to B pages can be sorted internally. Internally sorting a page requires in average $\lambda \log_2 \lambda$ comparisons and tuple moves. The average time needed to sort a page is therefore

$$S_p = (\lambda \log_2 \lambda)\ (C+2V)$$

On the other hand, merging B sorted pages on a main memory of size (B+1), requires $(B\log_2 B)\lambda$ comparisons, and $B\lambda$ tuple movements (8). The time to merge B pages is then

$$M_B = (B\log_2 B)\lambda C + 2B\lambda V + B(c^r+c^w)$$

The merge and sort method consists of internally sorting the P pages followed by several merging phases. The merging is done in an iterative way. There are about $\lceil \log_B P\rceil$ iterations. The duration of each iteration is $\dfrac{P\,M_B}{B}$. The overall duration of merging is then

$\dfrac{P}{B}\lceil\log_B P\rceil M_B$.

By adding the time for the internal sorting phase to the above quantity, we obtain the overall time needed to sort the entire relation

$$P(c^r+c^w) + PS_p + \dfrac{P}{B}\lceil\log_B P\rceil M_B$$

Next, the performance of the above algorithm is compared to that of the Hash-BCA projection algorithm. For the hash-BCA we assume that τ of the P/x buckets contain K, x<K<B, pages, and the remaining $(\dfrac{P}{x}-x)$ will contain x or fewer pages. Under this assumption the algorithm duration is

$$h_p\lceil\log_B P/x\rceil + (P+\dfrac{a^2-2a}{2}\tau x+x)\,\lambda V + P(c^r+c^w)$$

In order to examine the effect of bucket overflow on hash-BCA performance, values of a ranging from 3 to 6 have been selected, i.e, bucket size of $\dfrac{3x}{2}$, $2x$, $\dfrac{5x}{2}$, $3x$ have been considered. The four values of τ considered are $\dfrac{P}{16}$, $\dfrac{P}{8}$, $\dfrac{P}{4}$, and $\dfrac{P}{2}$. That is, up to half of the buckets were assumed to overflow. In order to compare the different algorithms, the following practical values have been selected for the different parameters: $V=113\ \mu s$, $C=10\mu s$, $H=10ms$, $\lambda=100$, and $c^r=c^w=30ms$. Some of these values have been borrowed from (9) and (10).

In Fig. 4, the ratio of the hash-BCA overall duration with that of the merge and sort has been plotted as a function of τ. In this Figure, the selected parameters are: $P=2^{10}$, $x=1$, and a ranging from 3 to 6. It can be seen that even under severe overflow conditions ($\tau=\dfrac{P}{2}$, and $a=6$) the hash-BCA is still 17% faster than the merge and sort. Of course, under more reasonable conditions, hash-BCA performs much better than merge and sort (e.g., for $\tau=P/16$, and $a=3$, the hash-BCA is 32% faster than the merge and sort). It is noted that the selected BCA size (x=1) is small compared with the relation size and the main memory size.

Comparison with the hash and sort algorithm.

The hash and sort procedure is composed of two steps. The fist step is similar to that of the hash-BCA except that the expected bucket size is B instead of x. In the second phase each bucket is projected using sorting. For the hash and sort algorithm we will assume that no bucket overflow occurs. It is emphasized that this implies that our algorithm will be compared to the hash and sort best case. For the hash and sort procedure ($\lceil \log_B P \rceil$ - 1) iterations are needed to produce the bucket (see (11)). During each iteration, the whole relation is read from and written into the mass storage. Also, all tuples are hashed and moved internally. Therefore, the duration of each step is

$$P(c^r + c^w) + (H+2v)\lambda P$$

This yields an overall duration of $P(\lceil \log_B P \rceil - 1)h_P$ time units for the first phase. The second phase consists of internally sorting each bucket. Each bucket will necessitate $BS_P + M_B$ time units. This yields an overall duration of

$$P(\lceil \log_B P \rceil - 1) \; h_P + PS_P + \frac{P}{B}M_B$$

In Fig. 5 and 6, the ratio of the hash-BCA time with that of the hash and sort best case has been plotted as a function of τ. For $P=2^{10}$, B=16, and x=1, the hash-BCA under overflow conditions ranging from $a=3$ to 6, and τ from $\frac{P}{16}$ to $\frac{P}{2}$, is still 22% faster than the hash and sort best case. When B is increased to 32, the hash-BCA is still 20% to 7% faster than the hash and sort best case for $a=3,4,5$. When $a=6$, and $\tau < \frac{P}{2}$ the hash-BCA performs 18% to 10% better. For $a=6$ and $\tau = \frac{P}{2}$, however, the hash and sort best case is 1% faster than the hash-BCA. It should be noted however, that for this case it was assumed

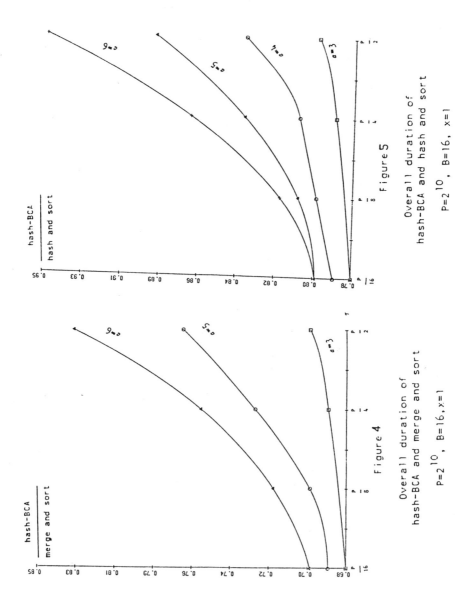

Figure 5

Overall duration of
hash-BCA and hash and sort

$P=2^{10}$, $B=16$, $x=1$

Figure 4

Overall duration of
hash-BCA and merge and sort

$P=2^{10}$, $B=16$, $x=1$

that out of the 1024 possible buckets, 512 contain 300 tuples instead of the expected 100. It is expected that situations where a large number of buckets deviates sharply from uniformity seldom occur in practice. It is also emphasized that we have compared the hash BCA under severe overflow conditions and with a very small size (x=1) against the hash and sort best case. Another important point is that since the BCA size is small compared to the size of the memory size, buckets that overflow can still in general fit entirely in the main memory. However, in the case of the hash and sort algorithm, a bucket which overflows will not fit into the main memory. Consequently, additional read and write from the mass storage are necessary to process the bucket. Thus, the hash-BCA algorithm is less sensitive to overflow than the hash and sort algorithm. As a consequence, it is expected that in practical situations the gap between the performance of the two algorithms is substantially higher than reported in this analysis.

CONCLUSION

In this paper, techniques and strategies that allow a chip of fixed capacity to process a large amount of data in the context of relational databases has been investigated. An algorithm called hash-BCA projection has been presented. This algorithm uses hashing to fragment the relation into small buckets that can be processed internally by the BCA processing unit. An algorithm called iterative BCA is used when the size of a bucket exceeds that of the BCA processing unit.

In order to realistically analyze the performances of our designs we have incorporated a BCA processing unit of fixed size in a general purpose back-end database unit. Next, the performances of the overall system with a BCA processing unit as a major component has been analyzed. This analysis takes into account major system parameters. Performances of our design have been studied first under the assumption that no bucket overflow occurs. Next, the same analysis is performed under different overflow conditions. A comparison with two other algorithms merge-sort and hash-sort, reveals that the use of a BCA processing unit leads to significant performance improvements.

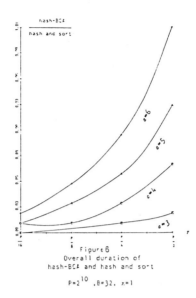

Figure 6
Overall duration of
hash-BCA and hash and sort

$P=2^{10}$, $B=32$, $x=1$

VI.REFERENCES

1. Sood, A.K., Abdelguerfi, M., International Journal of Electronics, 1985, Vol.59, No.4, pp.477-482.

2. Sood, A.K., Abdelguerfi, M., Shu, W., In:Database Machines Modern trends and Applications, Springer Verlag, 1986.

3. Codd, E.F., Comm. ACM, June 1970, pp.377-387.

4. Lehman, T.J., Kung, H.T, ACM SIGMOD International Symposium on the Management of Data, L.A., 1980, pp.105-116.

5. Kitsuregawa, M., *et al.*, New Generation Computing, Vol.1, No.1, 1983, pp.62-74.

6. Babb, E., ACM Trans. on Database Syst., Vol.4, No.1, March 1979, pp.414-429.

7. Knuth, D.E.,The Art of Computer Programming, Vol.3, Addison-Wesly, Readi g, Massachusets, 1973.

8. Menon, J., In:Database Machines Modern Trends and Applications, Springer Verlag, 1986.

9. Bitton, D., Dewitt, D.J., ACM Trans. Database Syst., 1983, No8, pp.255-265.

10. Valdurez, P., Gardarin, G., ACM Trans. Database Syst., Vol.9, No.1, March 1984, pp.412-418.

11. Giovanni, M.S., ACM Transaction on Database Systems, June 1986, Vol.11, No.2, pp.113-123.

A NETWORK ALGORITHM FOR RELATIONAL DATABASE OPERATIONS

Takanobu BABA and Hideki SAITO
Department of Information Science
Utsunomiya University
Utsunomiya 321, Japan

S. Bing YAO
Information Systems Department
University of Maryland, College Park
Maryland 20742, USA

This paper proposes a unified network algorithm for relational database operations. A popular shuffle-exchange network has been chosen to realize not only relational algebra operations but aggregation and set operations. Design issues for implementing the operations on a processor array are also presented. Microprogrammed processors were designed with two possible network organizations, called 'multistage' and 'single-stage', respectively.   Software simulation was developed to evaluate the architecture.

1. INTRODUCTION

Database machines have been the subject of considerable research for quite some time [1].   In particular, the significance of the relational data model database machines has been widely recognized.   They are expected not only to provide a high-level, non-procedural user interface but also to process input queries efficiently [2,3,4,5,6,7].

In the field of hardware, the most remarkable advance is found in the progress of VLSI processors.   New technologies have been developed to exploit parallel processable tasks and to embed application-oriented functions in a chip [8].

The requirements from the database field coupled with the hardware development naturally lead to research on VLSI processor array which supports relational database system as a specialized parallel processor. The characteristics of databases with large amount of formatted data, are advantageous for exploiting parallelism. They fit the requirement of regular structures which are desirable for the efficient VLSI fabrication [9].   There are several attempts to realize this idea [10,11,12]. Previous work designed VLSI processor arrays, where each processor contains database processing oriented functions.

Comparing with previous work, our basic motivation is to design a simple yet flexible processor array architecture which is amenable to various cost/performance requirements [13]. Thus, the design objectives of the architecture are:

1) To cover all the fundamental database operations, such as relational algebra, aggregation, and set operations by a single, popular network organization, i.e., shuffle-exchange network; and
2) To meet the users' cost/performance requirements flexibly by using a simple yet universal processor array architecture.

The first objective enables the array to cover usual operations decomposed from a given query. To attain the second goal, our shuffle-

202

exchange network processor array allows two configurations, i.e., single-stage and multistage. This is resulted from our effort to make more effective use of the processor array and to simplify system implementation. We have also adopted a microprogramming scheme to control the operations flexibly and to realize each operation as a microprogram [14].

2.   BASIC CONCEPTS

2.1 Relational database operations

A query is usually analyzed and decomposed into basic operations by a syntax analyzer. This is usually done by a host processor, and we will concentrate on the execution of the resulting operations.
     The operations we consider are as follows.

   1) Relational database operations including projection, restriction, sort, join, duplicate removal, and division;
   2) Aggregation operations including minimum, maximum, sum, count, and average; and
   3) Set operations, such as union, intersection, and difference.

     In particular, the second category is an important factor that makes a database machine realistic as these operations are known to be CPU bounded. For example, a specialized, two-dimensional processor array was proposed for this purpose in [11].

2.2 Network architecture

Parallel network algorithms have been designed for various purposes, such as sort and join processors [15,16,17,18,19]. When applying these algorithms to database operations we must pay special attention to two factors: (1) the access unit from a disk is usually a block (or a page) and it is more efficient to process tuples in blocks, and (2) each operation may require its own network organization.   Thus, if we cover all the operations by a single network architecture, we should carefully design the network as well as the processor architecture.
     There are many researches on sorting networks, which represent one of the most time consuming operations. We select to use a two-way merge split block bitonic sort as our basic algorithm [15]. This satisfies the conditions (1) and (2) above as it realizes a block sorting by a generic, shuffle-exchange network architecture. The network is so popular that it was announced as a commercially available chip [21]. It is possible to repeat a single-stage perfect shuffle and exchange operation to realize multistage operations [20].
     Therefore, our problem becomes: how can we implement various database operations described in section 2.1 on the shuffle-exchange network.

3.   RELATIONAL DATABASE OPERATIONS ON SHUFFLE-EXCHANGE NETWORK

This section describes how the database operations are realized on a shuffle-exchange network. In order to illustrate a network algorithm, we will use the following employee/department relations.

    EMPLOYEE (EMP_NAME, DEPT_NAME, AGE, OCCUP, SALARY)
    DEPT (DEPT_NAME, PLACE, MANAGER)

Queries will be expressed in SQL-like notations. The network processing
is illustrated by the data flow on the processor array, and a tuple is
represented by its attribute values.

3.1 Single-variable, single-stage operations

The following two operations may be simply done in one network stage.

(1) Projection: The projection extracts necessary attributes to make a
new relation. The following query extracts EMP_NAME, and SALARY from
relation EMPLOYEE.

    SELECT EMP_NAME, SALARY
    FROM EMPLOYEE

The processor operation extracts the attributes. A duplicate removal
operation will follow if the results should be unique.

(2) Restriction: The restriction makes a new relation by selecting the
tuples which satisfy a given condition. The following query selects
tuples from EMPLOYEE where SALARY is greater than $50,000.

    SELECT
    FROM EMPLOYEE
    WHERE SALARY > 50,000

The processor operation selects the tuples.

3.2 Single-variable, multistage operations

The following three operations basically utilize a sorting network,
slightly improved by us.

(1) Sorting: The sorting rearranges tuples so that the specified
attribute values are in ascending or decending order. Consider the
following query.

    SELECT EMP_NAME,AGE
    FROM EMPLOYEE
    ORDER BY AGE

The ORDER BY clause specifies the sorting.
     Starting from an existing bitonic method [15], we have made the
method applicable to variable number of tuples with variable lengths.
Figure 1(a) shows an example for 8 input records. For 2N inputs, $\log_2 2N$
phases of $\log_2 2N$ stages are necessary. The "0" indicates "pass the input
to the output". The "+" and "-" output smaller and larger inputs to the
upper successor, respectively. We have improved the algorithm in [15] by
deleting the first $(\log_2 2N)-1$ stages of "0"s, shaded in the figure. Thus,
the number of the network stages becomes $(\log_2 2N)^2-(\log_2 2N)+1$. Figure

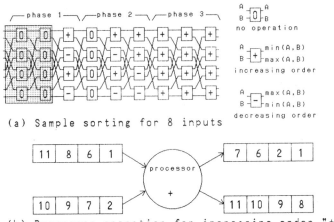

(a) Sample sorting for 8 inputs

(b) Processor operation for increasing order "+"

Fig.1 Sorting algorithm on a shuffle network

1(b) shows the internal operation of a processor for "+".

Notice that the block sorting requires input blocks be pre-sorted internally. This may be also done by the shuffle-exchange network in parallel.

(2) Duplicate removal: Duplicate removal is specified by the UNIQUE clause as follows.

```
SELECT UNIQUE AGE
FROM EMPLOYEE
WHERE OCCUP="PROGRAMMER"
```

The programmers' ages are retrieved without duplication. The removal operation is usually done by sorting tuples on the selected attribute and comparing adjacent tuple values. If we remove duplicates during the sort phase, the costs for the latter comparison can be saved. It is obvious that tuples with the same value must be compared somewhere during the sort process, and the correctness of the algorithm is intuitive.

Thus, using the same processor organization as the sorting, the operation may be implemented merely by changing the processor operations.

The duplicate removal operation covers the union operation.

(3) Aggregation: Aggregation operation performs computations on the values of a specified attribute. Typical computations include average, sum, maximum, minimum, and count. The computation may be done on a subset of a relation, specified by the GROUP BY clause.

```
SELECT DEPT_NAME, AVG(SALARY)
FROM EMPLOYEE
GROUP BY DEPT_NAME
```

This query specifies the average of salaries of the employees of a

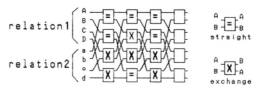

(a) Sample joining configuration for 4 blocks

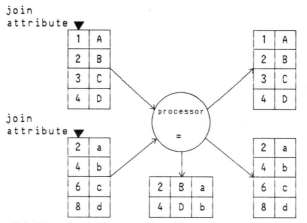

(b) Processor operation for the straight "="

Fig.2   Join algorithm on a shuffle network

specified department.

An aggregation operation may usually be applied after sorting a relation according to the name of a group. Our algorithm for the aggregation computes the sum while sorting the relation. That is, a comparison or an arithmetic operation is applied to input attribute values when the tuples are found to belong to the same group. For the maximum/minimum operations, the smaller/larger input is deleted. For the sum, average, and count, the attribute values or attribute counters are added up. Thus, the number of the stages for the aggregation is the same as the sorting.

3.3 Two-variable operations

We have developed a new, shuffle-exchange network control scheme for the following operations in order to exhaust all the pairs from two sets.

(1) Join: Join operation concatenates two tuples when they have the same value at the join attribute.

```
SELECT DEPT_NAME, EMP_NAME
FROM EMPLOYEE, DEPT
WHERE EMPLOYEE.DEPT_NAME = DEPT.DEPT_NAME
```

The example joins two relations EMPLOYEE and DEPT under the condition
that they have the same DEPT_NAME.

We perform the join by examining all the pairs of blocks from the
two relations. This is a parallel version of the nested-loop algorithm.
To do this, we need to control the processors so that at least one
combination of any pair of blocks from the two relations occurs in the
network. Figure 2(a) shows a configuration for 8 blocks. Clearly, we
need a minimum of N stages for 2N input blocks. Thus, the example gives
the smallest possible configuration. Note that the rightmost processor
array does not have output specification as it does not send outputs to
the next array. We have reported elsewhere the design of minimal N-stage
networks for N =< 128 [13].

Figure 2(b) illustrates the internal operation of one of the join
processors. Basically, it is a two-way merge split operation. However,
matched tuples are saved in the processors for result generation.

The join operation realizes the intersection operation under the
condition that all the attributes are join attributes.

3.4 Combination of the other operations

The following two operations may be implemented as a combination of the
above operations.

(1) Division: The division compares attributes of two relations, and
tests if one contains all elements of the other. The following
successive queries retrieve the employees who belong to all the
departments in the DEPT relation.

```
TR(EMP_NAME, DEPT_NAME) = (SELECT DEPT_NAME          SELECT EMP_NAME
                           FROM    EMPLOYEE)          FROM TR
                           CONTAINS
                           (SELECT DEPT_NAME
                           FROM DEPT)
```

The first division predicate, (query) CONTAINS (query), finds temporary
relation TR as the result of dividing EMPLOYEE by DEPT(DEPT_NAME) [11].
The division operation may be implemented as a combination of the
operations described above. Figure 3 shows how the operations are
combined to realize the division. After the duplicate removal
operations, the join operation yields a relation where the specified
attribute values match the second relation S. Thus, after the count
operations, if a count of an attribute value of R is same as that of
relation S, the attribute value should be included in the result.

(2) Difference: The difference may be implemented by adding a tag
manipulation operation to the above mentioned operations. First, the
duplicates in R and S are removed. Attach tags 1 and 0 to relations R
and S, respectively. While merging the relations, delete a tuple with
tag 1 if two same tuples (they should have tags 0 and 1) meet. Finally,
the deletion of tuples with tag 0 yields R - S.

3.5 Processing large databases

The network operations defined above treat a group of blocks which can be
accessed from a disk and processed in parallel. However, the size of a

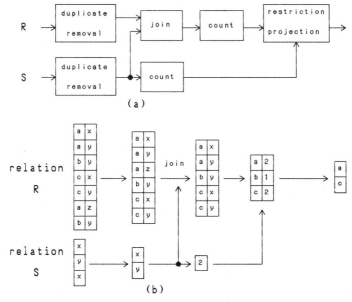

(a)

(b)

Fig.3 Division algorithm and an example

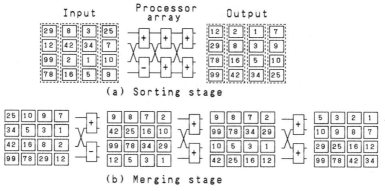

(a) Sorting stage

(b) Merging stage

Fig.4 Sorting method for a large relation

relation may be larger than the group in general. In this case, the relation should be decomposed into groups of blocks. We will describe how they are extended to be applied to such groups.

(1) Projection and restriction: The results of the operations on groups may be simply gathered to form the total results.
(2) Sorting, duplicate removal, and aggregation: We need a merge operation after the operations. Figure 4 illustrates this two-stage

operation.   The first stage sorts four groups (indicated by dotted lines)
of four blocks, i.e. intra-group sorting.   The second stage merges the
inputs to produce a totally sorted relation.
(3) Join: After joining blocks in an intra-group fashion, a nested-loop
algorithm is necessary for inter-group join.

4.   DESIGN ISSUES

Our next concern is how to implement the network algorithm on a real
processor array.   The architectural issue includes network and processing
element organization.   The results of our design, which include not only
the hardware organization but also the microprograms for the database
operations,   suggest that the network organization has two major
possibilities, while functional characteristics of the processing element
are common to the two configurations.

4.1 Network organization

The shuffle-exchange network may be implemented in either of the
following two ways:

(1) Multistage network: The first method is to realize the network
organization according to the requirement from each unique operation.
This is a natural consequence of the discussion in section 3.   It has
both time and space parallelism. The time parallelism means a pipeline
effect according to the horizontal data flow.   We may concatenate several
different operations to reduce the number of disk accesses and thus
enhance the pipeline effect.   The space parallelism is the decomposition
of data among vertically aligned processor array.   There is a further
design decision for the multistage network. That is, we may utilize a
network with the maximum stages for all the operations, or   prepare
several networks with different number of stages. The former incurs some
complicated control   mechanism to get output from an appropriate stage.
(2) Single-stage shuffle-exchange network: The network simulates the
multistage network by the repetition of a shuffle-exchange operation
[13,20].   The number of the repetition corresponds to that of network
stages.   This method makes the hardware organization simple, while
sacrificing the pipeline effect.

We will describe experimental results for each of these two methods,
which will be useful for the selection from the alternatives.

4.2 Processing element organization

The architecture of the processing element is basically independent to
the network organization.   Our design principles are as follows:

   1) The size of a processing element is small enough to be fabricated on
   a VLSI chip.
   2) The processor is controlled by microprogram to implement various
   operations flexibly yet efficiently.

The first objective is important for realizing a processor array.   As to
the second principle, we could use a conventional microprocessor, for

example Z80, MC68000, and Intel 8086, for the processing element. Based on our experimental results to be described later, we could say that even the software implementation will attain a sufficient performance.

Consequently, we have designed a processing element, which includes functional units, such as an adder and a comparator, a join buffer for saving temporary results of join, registers, flags, and a switch for controlling the outputs, i.e. cross or straight [13]. The unit of data to be processed is determined to be 1 byte as it is convenient for a variable length record processing as well as for VLSI implementation. The functional units are controlled by microprograms in a control memory. We designed a 16-bit vertical microinstruction set, and its description language [14].

The results of the design are: 1) A processor is composed of about 130 TTL ICs, which include 3430 gates; 2) The size of microprograms is 2928 bits (183-word x 16-bit) for essential operations; and 3) A machine cycle becomes 400 ns, which is decomposed into 4 phases. The first and second results above indicate that the total gate amount is small enough to be fabricated on one chip. The third machine cycle will be improved if we implemented the processor on a VLSI chip.

A data buffer should be attached to the processing element to transfer processed blocks among different network stages. We employed a double buffer mechanism to enhance the parallelism of the operations that share the same buffer. The buffer size is a design parameter to be determined according to the relationship between processing and disk access time.

5. Evaluation

5.1 Basic framework

In order to verify the logical correctness of the operations and evaluate the processor array, we have developed a microprogram simulator on a workstation (U-station model E15 [22]). The simulator fetches and executes microinstructions. Thus, we can obtain very precise results, i.e., the number of microsteps.

To evaluate the processor array, we need parameters on disk unit. We used the parameters of our workstation as an example. The access time is 28.3 ms, the transfer time is 1.229 MB/sec, and the block size is 512 bytes.

5.2 Execution steps at a processing element

Based on the analysis of microrpograms and the results of microprogram simulation, we defined equations to compute the execution microsteps of relational database operations. Division and set operations are not included, which may be computed as the combination of the other operations as described in 3.4.

The experimental results show that the number of steps s is related to the data size d by the following equation

$$s = d^c,$$

where c is 1.9 for join and around 1.0 for the rest operations. The results stem from the number of dynamically executed microprogram loops.

For the join operation, the smaller the selectivity is, the smaller the execution steps.

5.3 Processing and disk I/O times

Our basic interest here is on the effect of the number of processors in order to determine how many processors are appropriate for a given environment. We will analyze the trade-offs between processor speed and disk access time. Using the parameters for the machine cycle time of 400 ns and the disk access time in 5.1, we computed the processing and disk I/O times for a 512-byte block.

Among the operations, we selected the projection, sorting, and join as typical ones. Notice, the sorting and join have two capabilities on network organization, while it is not the case for the projection which may be performed in one network stage.

5.3.1 Projection
Figure 5 shows that the execution time for a block decreases in proportion to the number of processing elements. The disk access time is plotted by dashed lines, where n indicates that n blocks are accessed at a time. They are always higher than the execution time. This means the projection operation is a DISK-bounded operation if the processor array does just the projection and returns the result to the disk. Notice that the three lines for the execution time for n = 1, 2, and 4 overlap. This means the unit of processing does not affect the execution time for unit data.

5.3.2 Sorting
(1) Sorting on a multistage shuffle-exchange network: Figure 6 shows that under the pipeline effect of multistage network, the execution time of sorting is always under the disk I/O time.

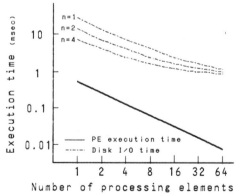

Fig.5 Execution time of block
projection operation

(2) Sorting on a single-stage shuffle-exchange network: Figure 7 shows
that for a single-stage network the difference between the execution time
and disk access time is not so large as the multistage one. The curve
for the execution time is interesting. It reaches the maximum when the
number of processors equals 4. The reason is explained as follows. For
2N input blocks, the network stages of sorting is given by $(\log_2 2N)^2-$
$(\log_2 2N)+1$. On the other hand, data are processed in parallel by N
processors. Thus, the order of the execution time is given by
$[(\log_2 2N)^2-(\log_2 2N)+1]/N$. Figure 7 reflects this equation. The unit of
processed data does not affect the execution time.

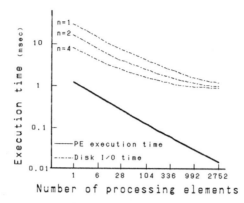

Fig.6 Execution time of block sorting
      operation on a multistage
      shuffle-exchange network

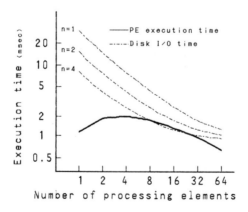

Fig.7 Execution time of block sorting
      operation on a single-stage
      shuffle-exchange network

5.3.3 Join
(1) Join on a multistage shuffle-exchange network: Figure 8 shows that
the relationship between the execution time and disk I/O time changes
depending on the selectivities. Where the selectivity is high, the
relation becomes CPU-bound.
(2) Join on a single-stage shuffle-exchange network: Figure 9 shows an
interesting result, that is, the execution time remains constant. The
reason is that the data amount to be processed in parallel increases in
proportion to the number of processors, while the network steps, which
correspond to the number of repetition for a single-stage network, also
increase in proportional to the number of processors. Thus, the increase

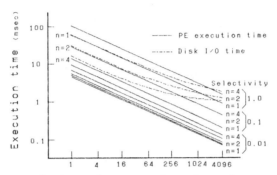

Number of processing elements

Fig.8 Execution time of block join
operation   on   a   multistage
shuffle-exchange network

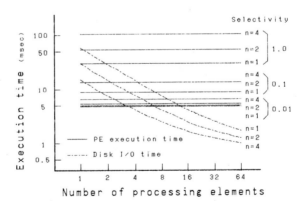

Number of processing elements

Fig.9 Execution time of block join
operation on a single-stage
shuffle-exchange network

of the processors is not advantageous for the execution time. However, the disk I/O time decreases because a large amount of data are accessed continuously.

Summing up the results, the pipeline effect of the multistage shuffle-exchange network is clear. As the number of processors increase, the execution time decreases. However, based on the assumption on the disk parameters, the single-stage network seems to attain enough performance. The choice between the two network organizations will depend on the trade-off between cost and performance.

6. CONCLUSION

This paper proposes shuffle-exchange network algorithm for relational database operations. The processor and the network are designed, and the effect is evaluated based on a microprogram simulation.

The network algorithm indicates that, for 2N input blocks, 1) projection and restriction may be performed in one stage, 2) sorting, duplicate removal, and aggregation in $(\log_2 2N)^2 - (\log_2 2N) + 1$ stages, 3) join, and union in N stages, and 4) difference and division may be performed by the combination of the other operations.

The simple network architecture makes the implementation very easy. We designed two types of network implementation, i.e. multistage and single-stage, and a microprogrammed processing element. The flexibility of microprogram control enabled us to realize various relational database operations in the processor efficiently. The gate amount proved that the processing element may be fabricated in one chip.

The experimental results show that usually we can expect the performance improvement by increasing the number of processors. However, it is not true for the join operation on the single-stage shuffle-exchange network. The balance between processing time and disk I/O time tends to be I/O bounded for the most of the operations, in particular on a multistage network. Thus, in order to balance them, our idea is 1) to perform as many operations as possible after accessing blocks from a disk, and 2) to off-load more database operations (for example, transaction processing) to a processor array.

The architecture contains several design parameters. In particular, the number of processors as well as the number of network stages may be determined based on the cost/performance requirements. Our experimental results can be used to assist making design choices.

ACKNOWLEDGMENTS

The minimum number of network stages for join operation has been obtained experimentally by T. Kumagai at Utsunomiya University. The authors would like to thank the invaluable comments of K. Okuda, and K. Yamazaki at Utsunomiya University. This research was supported in part by Japanese Ministry, Science and Culture (Grant Numbers 61550727 and 62550255), and by National Security Agency, USA.

REFERENCES

[1] C.J. Date: An Introduction to Database Systems Volume II, Addison-Wesley, p.383(1983).

[2] D.K. Hsiao: "Super database computers: Hardware and software solutions for efficient processing of very large databases," Proc. IFIP Congress 86, pp.933-944(1986).

[3] S. Sakai, M. Kitsuregawa, H. Tanaka, and T. Moto-oka: "Interconnection network for bucket distribution on relational algebra machine GRACE," Trans. IECE Japan, Vol.J68-D, No.6, pp.1272-1279(1985).

[4] Y. Tanaka: "MPDC: Massive parallel architecture for very large databases," Proc. Int. Conf. on Fifth Generation Computer Systems, pp.113-137(1984).

[5] T. Baba, S.B. Yao, and A.R. Hevner: "Design of a functionally distributed, multiprocessor database machine using data flow analysis," IEEE Trans. on Computers, Vol.C-36, No.6, pp.650-666 (1987).

[6] Y. Kiyoki, and M. Amamiya: "An execution scheme for relational database operations with eager and lazy evaluations," Trans. of Inf. Process. Soci. of Japan, Vol.26, No.4, pp.685-695(1985).

[7] S. Yoshizumi, et al: "Vector-type high-speed database processor," Proc. 32nd Annu. Conven. IPS Japan, pp.915-916 (1986).

[8] H. Yasuura, N. Takagi, and S. Yajima: "The parallel enumeration sorting scheme for VLSI," IEEE Trans. on Computers, Vol.C-31, No.12, pp.1191-1201(1982).

[9] C. Mead, and L. Conway: Introduction to VLSI Systems, Addison-Wesley (1980).

[10] Y.C. Hong: "Efficient computing of relational algebraic primitives in a database machine architecture," IEEE Trans. on Computers, Vol.C-34, No.7, pp.588-595(1985).

[11] W. Kim, D. Gajski, and D.J. Kuck: "A parallel pipelined relational query processor," ACM Trans. on Database Systems, Vol.9, No.2, pp.214-242(1984).

[12] Y. Kambayashi: "A database machine based on the data distribution approach," AFIPS Conf. Proc. NCC., Vol.53, pp.613-625(1984).

[13] H. Saito, and T. Baba: "A processor array architecture for relational database operations," Proc. 34th Annu. Conven. IPS Japan, pp.205-206(1987).

[14] T. Baba: Microprogrammable Parallel Computer, The MIT Press, p.290(1987).

[15] D. Bitton, D.J. DeWitt, D.K. Hsiao, and J. Menon: "A taxonomy of parallel sorting," Computing Surveys, Vol.16, No.3, pp.287-318(1984).

[16] S. Lakshmivarahan, S.K. Dhall, and L.L. Miller: "Parallel sorting algorithms," Advances in Computers, Vol.23, pp.295-354(1984).

[17] K.E. Batcher: "Sorting networks and their applications," AFIPS Conf. Proc., SJCC, pp.307-314(1968).

[18] M. Maekawa: "Parallel sort and join for high speed database machine operations," AFIPS Proc. NCC, Vol.50, pp.515-520 (1981).

[19] T. Feng: "A survey of interconnection networks," IEEE Computer, pp.12-27(1981).

[20] T. Lang, and H.S. Stone: "A shuffle-exchange network with simplified control," IEEE Trans. on Computers, Vol.C-25, No.1, pp.55-65(1976).

[21] Texas Instruments Inc., LSI Logic Data Book (1986).

[22] Digital Computer Ltd., U-station Users Manual(1984).

THE IMPACT OF THE INTERCONNECTING NETWORK ON PARALLEL DATABASE COMPUTERS*

DAVID K. HSIAO

Department of Computer Science, Naval Postgraduate School, Monterey, California 93943, USA

ABSTRACT

From an architectural viewpoint, the interconnecting network of the parallel database computer plays an important role. The topology of the network of parallel database processors and memories affects the overall architecture in at least two ways: the database algorithms employed for the primary operations of the computer and the reliability of the computer in interprocessor communications. This paper examines several interconnecting networks in the database computer. In the examination, the paper also relates the networks to their impact on the primary database operations and reliability of the database computer.

1. INTRODUCTION

Modern database computers are all parallel computers [1 - 6]. By parallel we mean that there are two or more database processors each of which has its own data-base store of secondary storages for the database and that the processor-store pairs are interconnected via some kind of network for multiple-data-stream-and-multiple-transaction operations. In other words, the database processors are executing multiple transactions in parallel and the database stores are reading or writing data for the transactions in parallel also. Since the parallelisms take place at the database processors, between the processors and their stores, and at the database stores, database computer architects tend to overlook the important role of the interconnecting network among the database processors. Since the interconnecting network does not involve the database stores which rely on their own data buses connected to the processors, the role of the interconnecting network is further minimized. Consequently, parallel database computers have utilized an array of diverse and distinct interconnecting networks such as the cross-bar [1], token-ring [2], double-ring [3,4], broadcast [5], and tree [6] networks. However, once the interconnecting network has been chosen for a database computer, the impacts of the chosen network on the computer become readily apparent. The impacts not only influence the database algorithms of the database computer such as sort and join operations but also affect the performance of the database computer such as reliability and degree of parallel operations. In the fol-

*The work reported herein is conducted in the Laboratory for Database Systems Research and supported by NADC, NOSC and NSGC.

lowing sections and based on the author's experience with some interconnecting networks, their impacts on database algorithms and reliability issues are expounded.

2. THE ROLE OF AN INTERCONNECTING NETWORK IN DATABASE COMPUTER

Consider Figure 1 in which we depict a database computer with four major components: the controller, the interconnecting network, the database processors and the database stores. For improving the reliability, there may be a duplicate controller. Further, since the controller is the gateway to the outside world, it may be a stand-alone computer which interfaces with the user via terminals, diskless workstations, mainframes and other host computers. If the entire database computer is dedicated to a specific host computer as its database backend, then the controller software may be integrated into the host. We may not need a controller computer. Consequently, there are three remaining components to consider for our study.

```
Database Controller : DC
Database Processor   : DP
Database Store       : DS
```

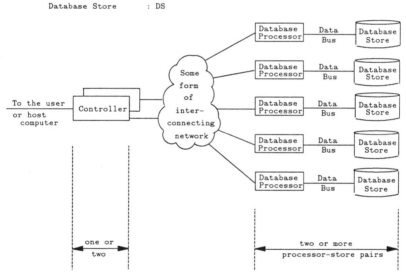

Figure 1. The Relationship of the Interconnecting
Network with Other Database Computer Components

The role of an interconnecting network in a database computer is primarily in interprocessor communications and processing. Let us expound on its issues.

3. INTERPROCESSOR COMMUNICATIONS AND PROCESSING

Parallel database processors have the need of communicating among themselves. By way of the communications, they can inform each other the progress they have made locally in processing either the meta data such as indices and keys or base data such as records and tuples. Interprocess communications are therefore necessary for the coordination and progress of the parallel processors. For example, aggregate functions such as AVG, (i.e., average) can be carried by the processors individually as subaggregates. However, when the subaggregates are ready, there is the need to perform the final stage of the aggregate function by utilizing the subaggregates. For example, if we desire to compute the average salaries of the employees and the employee records (tuples) are distributed in the secondary storages of the database stores, we can cause each database processor to access its database store for its employee records (tuples). The result will be a (sub-)average of salaries at a database processor. To compute the average of all salaries, each database processor must produce a sub-average and an employee count. With these two pieces of data from each processor the interconnecting network can either communicate them to the controller for final calculation of the average or utilize the sub-averages and counts themselves for the computation of the final average. In the former case, the interconnecting network is strictly a communication network, i.e., it has no computation capability. Such networks can be found in cross-bar, broadcasting, token-ring and double-ring networks. In the latter case, the interconnecting network has, in addition to the communications capability, the computation capability. Such network can be found in a tree-like network, known as the Y-net [6]. Let us review some of the interconnecting networks.

3.1. The Cross-Bar Network

The cross-bar network is basically a switching network for point-to-point communications as depicted in Figure 2. When a database processor desires to communicate with another processor, the message is routed through the network by opening some switches which have not been switched on for routing other on-going messages. These switches are at the intersections of the communications lines of the network. Of a m-by-n network of one controller and $(m + n - 1)$ database processors, there are $(m \times n)$ switches, since there are $(m \times n)$ possible point-to-point communications.

The cross-bar network is perhaps the most reliable network, since it has been around for a long time for interprocessor and intermemory communications. However, it is not appropriate for the parallel database computer. First, it is very costly. The cost is primarily incurred in the numerous switches. Second, it is restricted to point-to-point communications. It is not good for broadcasting purposes, i.e., one-point-to-many-points communications. For example, in order for the controller to send a transaction to all the database processors for parallel and concurrent execution of the same transaction, the controller must replicate the transaction for each database processor and send it through the network. In other words, broadcasting is not supported by the software and hardware of the network. It must be emulated via replication. The replication of messages and data is the principal delay in a parallel computer using the cross-bar switches that can not take up large amounts of messages and data simultaneously.

3.2. The Token-Ring Network

In Figure 3, we depict a database computer based on the token-ring network. The token-ring network is an inexpensive network in comparison with the cross-bar network. To communicate with others on the ring, a processor must seize or wait for the token. Conceptually, the token is circulating in the ring. At each stop, i.e., at the

Database Controller : DC
Database Processor : DP
Database Store   : DS

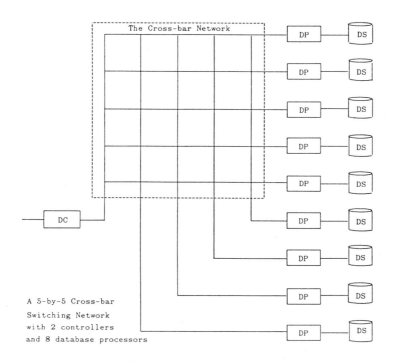

A 5-by-5 Cross-bar
Switching Network
with 2 controllers
and 8 database processors

Figure 2. Parallel Database Computer with a
Cross-bar Switching Network

site of a processor, the processor can send messages to all other processors on the ring. This is broadcasting. In fact, this is turn-taking broadcasting. In other words, it does not allow multiple, simultaneous broadcasting by multiple processors. Processors must wait for their turns. For a small number of processors on the ring, the turn-taking procedure does not hinder the parallelism of the database processors profoundly. For large numbers of processors, the turn-taking procedure can change the database processors form parallel operations into serial (or turn-taking) operations. Thus, turn-taking procedures using tokens are not suitable for parallel database computers either.

3.3. The Broadcasting Network

The architecture of a database computer utilizing the broadcasting network is depicted in Figure 4. Broadcasting network such as the Ethernet is widely used and rather inexpensive. In broadcasting, a database controller can place a message or transaction on the network which then broadcasts the message or transaction to all the database processors. This one-to-many communication capability is particularly useful in a parallel database computer where all of the database processors can receive the message or transaction simultaneously and begin their parallel operations on the

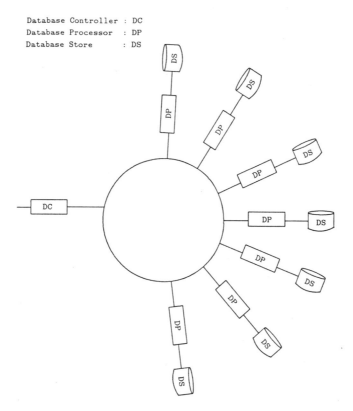

Figure 3.   Parallel Database Computer
with a Token-Ring Network

message or transaction concurrently. Furthermore, if during the broadcasting another processor desires to broadcast its message or data to all the other processors and controllers, the network has the built-in capability to resolve collisions of message traffics on the network due to multiple broadcastings in the same time-frame. Whenever a collision occurs, i.e., two messages are being placed on the network at the same time, the hardware can postpone their broadcasting momentarily, broadcast one of the two message first on the basis a random selection algorithm and send the other message next. The important feature is that the collided messages are saved in the buffer of the hardware and resending and scheduling of the new attempts are done automatically by the hardware. As long as the network is not very heavily utilized for broadcasting, collisions of messages will not cause indefinite delay.

Despite its desirability and low cost for the parallel database computer, there are important impacts on the database computer. One impact is on the database algorithms used for the architecture of this type of communication networks. The other impact is on the software reliability issue due to collision and load of the network. Let us examine them in the following:

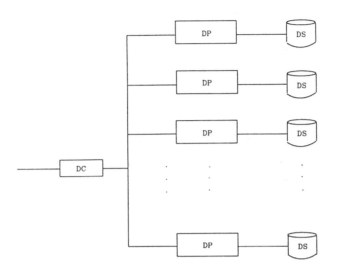

```
Database Controller : DC
Database Processor  : DP
Database Store      : DS
```

Figure 4. Parallel Database Computer
With a Broadcasting Network

A. The Impact of Broadcasting on Aggregate Functions and Sort and Merge Operations

An aggregate function such as maximum, minimum, average, sum, or count becomes a two-stage operations in a broadcasting-network-based architecture. For example, if we desire the sum of all the salaries of the employees of the employee file (relation), then each database processor accesses its own database store for the employee subfile, sum up all the employees' salaries and route the total (actually, subsum) to the controller. The controller adds up all of the totals (i.e., subsums) and produces the intended sum. Subsums as numbers are small in size (i.e., a few bytes); they are not likely to overload the network. Nevertheless, this aggregate function is carried out in two stages - first, there are the access of data, computation of subsubsums, and communication of subsums by individual processors; and second, there is the computation of the sum. We note that the first stage is a parallel operation and the second stage is not. There is considerable delay in staging the subsums.

The sort-and-merge operation and relational-join operation are similar, since they involve two files (relations). For our illustration, we consider an equi-join. In an equi-join operation there is the source relation and target relation. The resultant relation consists of tuples each of which combines a source tuple and a target tuple of identical attribute values. A typical equi-join algorithm for the broadcasting-network-based architecture is as follows:

(1) The source relation is parallelly accessed by the database processors.
(2) The join value (i.e., the attribute value to be joined) of each source tuple accessed is examined and hashed into the address of a block.
(3) The tuple is stored in the block of the address so hashed.
(4) The target relation is also parallelly accessed by the database processors.
(5) The join value of each target tuple accessed is also examined and hashed into a block address.
(6) The (target) tuple is compared with each source tuple stored in the block on their join values. If they are identical, a resultant tuple is formed. If they are different, no resultant tuple is formed.
(7) Target tuples locally accessed at each database processor are also broadcasted only once to all other database processors.
(8) All database processors handle the broadcasted target tuples in the same way as the other target tuples, i.e., repeating steps 5 and 6 on them. However, they are not to be broadcasted again.
(9) The resultant tuples at the database processors are forwarded to the controller.

It is interesting to note that unlike the aggregate functions where the controller provides some computations, the join operation does not involve the controller in any computation. Thus, all relations (i.e., source, target and resultant) are accessed, examined, and computed upon in the parallel database processors. From a complexity viewpoint, the above algorithm is the best we can devise for a parallel database computer with a broadcasting network [7].

However, the network has an important impact on the algorithm. We observe in Step 7 the target tuples (not source tuples) at each processor are being broadcasted to other processors. Although we may designate a relation with a smaller cardinality as the target relation, the amount of traffic (therefore, collisions) on the network in broadcasting the target relation may still be high. Thus, Step 7 is a time-consuming task. In this case, the topology of the communications network has an important impact on the performance of the equi-join algorithm.

There is also another impact on the database computer. This is on the reliability of the parallel operation. When several broadcastings are on-going as in the case of Step 7 of the equi-join operation, the amount of data (in this case the target tuples) may overwhelm the buffer storage of the Ethernet bus at each processor. Unless the buffered data are flushed to the virtual memory readily, some of the data may be lost. To this date, the Berkley 4.2 Unix Operating has not yet provided a set of reliable broadcasting protocols at the TCP/IP level. Consequently, any realistic, multi-point broadcasting becomes a chancy effort.

3.4. The Tree Network

The architecture of a parallel database computer utilizing a tree network is depicted in Figure 5. The tree network is a very expensive network. However, it accomplishes both communications and computations when data are being moved through the network. On communications, it is an ideal broadcasting network. In addition, at each node there is a processing unit and a memory unit. Thus, data or messages may be stored, computed, and forwarded for either broadcasting or computational purposes. To perform an aggregate function or a sorting operation it amounts to percolating the data from the database stores to the database processors and through the nodes of the tree network. By the time they arrive at the controller, i.e., the root of the tree, they become the result or answer of the function or operation. Thus, in this case, the communications net also serves as the sorting or aggregating net - the first indication of its computational versatility.

The tree network can also support the sort-and-merge operation of two files or equi-join operation of two relations. However, the algorithms are different from the ones used in the broadcast network. For the instance of an equi-join operation, both the source relation and target relation follow the following steps:

(1) The tuples of a relation are accessed by the database processors.

(2) Tuples are percolated through the tree network for the purpose of sorting them on the basis of their join values.

(3) The sorted tuples are evenly distributed in the database processors.

These three steps are first applied to the source relation then repeated for the target relation. Thus, there are six logical steps in total. The seventh step is for each database processor to combine a source tuple with a target tuple which have common attribute values.

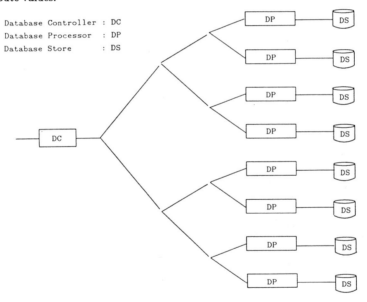

Database Controller : DC
Database Processor   : DP
Database Store   : DS

Figure 5. Parallel Database Computer
With a Tree Network

Although the percolation up and down of the tree network is similar to broadcasting in a broadcast network, there are distinct differences. One difference is that the percolation results in tuple sorting and even distribution, whereas the broadcasting does no sorting. Further, the broadcasting does not guarantee even distribution. Finally, the percolation up and down of the network does not create collision whereas multiple broadcastings do. In this case, the relational equi-join operation is accomplished via the traditional sort-and-merge operation. Because the broadcasting network cannot sort, the comparisons and merges of tuples are done locally at the database processors. Consequently, the database processors in a tree-network-based database computer may be less powerful than those of a broadcasting-network-based database computer. The lower cost of the database processors may be offset by the higher cost of the tree-network.

Not only the tree network impacts the database algorithms and computer cost, it also impacts the reliability. If any node is malfunction, the subtree rooted at the node will be out of action. Nodal malfunctions in the tree network have more devastating impact than nodal malfunctions in other type of networks.

4. CONCLUDING REMARKS

We have reviewed some common interconnecting networks for the parallel database computer. We have also assessed their cost, performance and reliability impacts on the parallel operations of the database computer. It seems to the author that the promising interprocessor networks may be either the broadcasting and tree network. At the present, the former is less expensive and less reliable and the latter is more expensive and more reliable. In either case, they have important impacts on the database algorithms and performance of the database computer.

REFERENCES

[1] DeWitt, D. J., "DIRECT - A Multiprocessing Organization for Supporting Relational Database Management Systems," *IEEE Transaction on Computers*, V.C28, No. 6, (June 1979).

[2] DeWitt, D. J., Gerber, R. H., Graefe, G., Heytens, M. L., Kumar, K. B., and Muralikrishna, M., "GAMMA - A High Performance Dataflow Database Machine," *Proceedings of 12th International Conference on Very Large Data Bases*, Kyoto, Japan, August 1986.

[3] Banerjee, J., Hsiao, D. K., and Kannan, K., "DBC - A Database Computer for Very Large Databases," *IEEE Transactions on Computers*, V. C-28, No. 6 (June 1979).

[4] Fushimi, S., Kitsuregawa, M., and Tanaka, H., "An Overview of the System of a Parallel Relational Database Machine GRACE," *Proceedings of the 12th International Conference on Very Large Data Bases*, Kyoto, Japan, August 1986.

[5] Demurjian, S. A., Hsiao, D. K., and Menon, J., "A Multibackend Database System for Performance Gains, Capacity Growth and Hardware Upgrade," *Proceedings of the 2nd International Conference on Data Engineering*, Los Angeles, CA (February 1986).

[6] "DBC/1012 Data Base Computer Concepts and Facility," Release 1.3, C02-0001-02, Terada (June 28, 1985).

[7] Tung, H. L., "Design and Analysis and Implementation of the Primary Operation, Retrieve-Common, of the Multibackend Database System (MBDS)," Master's Thesis, Naval Postgraduate School (June 1985).

DYNAMICALLY PARTITIONABLE PARALLEL PROCESSORS: THE KEY FOR COST-EFFICIENT HIGH TRANSACTION THROUGHPUT

ALEXANDROS C. PAPACHRISTIDIS

Department of Computer and Information Sciences,
University of Florida, Gainesville, Florida 32611, U.S.A.

ABSTRACT

Transaction processing on database computers which are based on multi-processor architecture usually involves a subset of the available processors for each transaction. A generic technique is proposed for partitioning this set of processors during the processing of transactions. This generic technique uses a specialized interconnection network, makes each partition set to be effectively treated as a single processor entity, allows concurrent execution of transactions, reduces resource and data contention, minimizes interprocessor communication, and provides for linear increase of transaction throughput with respect to the total number of processors. It has been implemented on DBC/1012, manufactured and marketed by Teradata Corporation.

INTRODUCTION

A *transaction* is defined as a sequence of database operations which accesses a shared database and has the property of atomicity in terms of interference with other transactions in accessing shared data

225

and in terms of the visibility of its effects in the database (1). In addition to the three basic transaction operations of *start, commit,* and *abort, locking protocols* may be used in preserving the atomicity of the transactions. In this study, a transaction is considered to consist of a number of indexed database requests of high selectivity which do not necessarily show locality of reference in terms of the individual pieces of data they access.

The problem of transaction processing in a database machine that is based on a multi-processor architecture can be considered similar to that of distributed database systems. There are some peculiarities, though, which emanate from the fact that this distributed network is within the same computer. The main differences are the high bandwidth and connectivity that can be achieved in the interconnection network due to the close proximity of the individual processors to each other, and the significant processing cost for individual *messages* as compared to the communication cost, since the individual processors are based on a microprocessor central processing unit (CPU).

Internal Bus

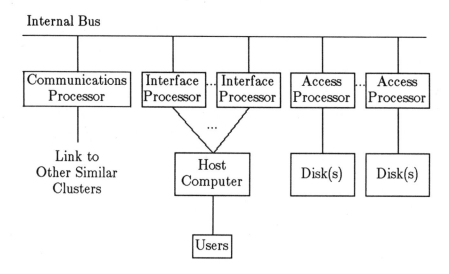

Figure 1. Distributed Function Architecture.

The justification of the use of multi-processor architecture in database machines is dealt effectively in (2), where a *distributed function architecture* is proposed. This architecture, shown in Fig. 1, is primarily comprised of two distinct types of processors, *interface* and *access*, which are interconnected through an internal high speed interconnection network. This architecture can accommodate a large number of processors efficiently, the key points of the efficiency being the distribution of the function and the nature of the interconnection network. The interface processors provide the communication with host computers, handle the tasks of session control, parse the database system *requests* which are expressed in a high level relational language to a series of database *steps* to be carried out by the access processors, and supervise the execution of the requests and transactions. The access processors have exclusive access to the disk storage attached to them, and they perform the individual database steps that are requested by the interface processors, including transaction operations. This database architecture supports the relational model for data (3). The relations are stored in horizontally partitioned fragments (4). Each fragment is stored on the disk(s) of each access processor. The partitioning criterion is the value of a hash function applied on the values of a set of attributes of a relation. This set of attributes is designated as the *primary index* of the relation during the schema definition. Index tables also have the option of being partitioned in the same way, according to the values of the indexed attributes.

The interconnection network for the distributed function architecture is the crucial element since it is its essential bottleneck (2). In (5,6,7) there is a detailed description of a viable structure for such a network. It is schematically shown in Fig. 2. Its primary functions are to prioritize messages based upon their data content and to implement a tournament sort algorithm in which the winner-message is redirected back to a single or a *predefined group* of processors (i.e., it can *broadcast;*) - whatever is designated as its destination in its data content (2). These groups are established during the system initialization phase. This network structure allows process synchronization messages and status inquiries of predefined type and format to be transmitted without any involvement of the CPUs of the processors. Also, due to the sorting of messages and the synchronized way under which the network operates, multiple acknowledgement signals from receiving processors, either a single

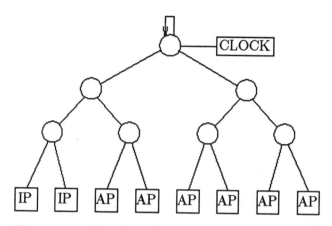

IP   : Interface Processor
AP   : Access Processor
CLOCK   : Network Timer to Synchronize Sorting

Figure 2. Interconnection Network for the Distributed Function Architecture.

one or a group, is avoided; e.g., a positive acknowledgement signal guarantees the proper reception of a message by its destination.

Under a transaction processing workload, this architecture has to minimize problems related to interprocessor communication and process synchronization, resource contention, and data contention.

PERFORMANCE ANALYSIS

Interprocessor Communication

The distributed function model architecture is an instance of a distributed database system without replication of data; it assumes that a single transaction manager/step scheduler exists per given transaction, which oversees its execution (1). Since the interface processors are the locations where session control takes place and the incoming transactions are parsed, each interface processor has its own transaction manager. These managers oversee the execution of the transactions in a centralized fashion by transmitting messages which demand the execution of specific processing steps or transaction operations on the access processors.

As a consequence, locks may be placed on data which reside on the disk(s) of access processors and additional messages may be sent to other access processors. For example, if hashed index tables are used within a transaction, the entry in the index table and the tuple(s) it points to may not be accessible on the same access processor. Also, two distinct tuples involved in a transaction may not reside on the disk(s) of the the same access processor.

Resource Contention

The situation above creates the necessity for a transaction manager to communicate with each one of the involved processors. The additional message traffic which can potentially be induced on an interface processor because of this increased demand for interprocessor communication and process synchronization, and the high cost for the processing of messages as compared to their transmission cost, reduce the throughput of an interface processor and, thus, the throughput of a given database machine configuration.

The software that can handle this additional traffic can become quite complicated since a transaction manager may need to combine execution steps generated by the parser, based solely on the available relational schema information, with additional steps generated dynamically during the runtime of a transaction due to the involvement of additional access processors in the processing of a transaction. A broadcast to a relevant predefined group of processors, which in this case would be the group of all access processors, is out of the question, as it will limit the throughput of the whole database machine by the speed that a single access processor processes a message.

One can conclude that additional interprocess communication which is induced in order to support transaction processing may seriously affect the performance of the database machine that is considered and, it can be easily argued, of any other multiprocessor architecture database machine which features a high speed communication interconnection network and microprocessor based processors.

Data Contention

The involvement of access processors in the processing of a transaction cannot always be decided before a transaction starts executing. Typical examples of this are the use of hashed indices and retrievals of tuples based on the attribute values of tuples that are previously accessed by the transaction. If the solution of a complicated transaction manager, as described in the previous section, is to be avoided, then the transaction start, commit, or abort operations have to be broadcasted to the group of all access processors. This has two undesirable side effects: The first is that the transaction throughput of the database machine is limited by the performance of a single access processor in executing the start/commit operations. The second is that there is a potential danger for placing locks on data which reside on an uninvolved access processor, making them unavailable for the processing of other transactions which will have to wait for the locks to be released (8). Finer locking granularity is sought in this case because all transactions are considered to be randomly accessing small parts of the database (9).

PROPOSED SOLUTION

Requirements

Under the light of the previous analysis, it is quite clear that a viable technique that provides for high transaction throughput has to minimize interprocessor communication to the extent that the amount of CPU resources consumed for the processing of a transaction is bound in a linear fashion with respect to the number of the processors which are involved in its processing. Moreover, it has to ensure that under normal transaction operations data contention is totally avoided.

Solution

The solution was instigated by the observation that in the distributed function architecture which is considered, any processor gets a single acknowledgement signal for any message it transmits, regardless of whether the destination is a single processor or a group of processors which are defined during the system initialization phase. Also, any database step initiated by an interface processor towards a single or all access processors creates a single response message at the time the processing of that step is completed on every access processor. This is achieved by using special status words in the identically formated high speed random access memory (HSRAM) of each processor, which is its connecting bridge/buffer with the interconnection network. The active logic which is implemented on the hardware of the network uses the information which is available on the HSRAM and automatically synchronizes the individual processes by generating special status inquiry messages without inducing any CPU cost to the processors. In summary, due to the active logic of the interconnection network and the network/processor interface, any processor may be oblivious as to whether it sends messages to a single processor or a predefined group of processors, and also ignorant of the size of these groups.

The proposal is to establish dynamically instantiated groups of processors, called *dynamic groups* and identified by unique *group ids,* so that each dynamic group is associated with a single transaction, has a life span of that transaction, and its group id is assigned before the processing of any transaction operation or a step starts executing (8); each processor of a dynamic group is able and allowed to communicate with any other processor within the group and exchange status information as it happens in the case of predefined groups.

Under the assumptions made for the structure of the transactions, an interface processor simply sends individual database requests to single processors and, at the end of the processing of the transaction, broadcasts a commit or abort operation to the relevant group of access processors. Broadcast messages to these groups do not create multiple acknowledgement messages. It is the responsibility of each involved processor to add itself to the group, whereas the interface processor is the one which makes the unique assignment of a group id to a transaction.

It is clearly seen that this technique does not create any additional message handling load on the transaction manager during the runtime that is proportional to the number of processors involved. The overall resources that are used for processing a transaction are those of the involved processors, so that the transaction throughput is not limited by the processing speed of a single processor and increases linearly with increasing number of access processors. Prerequisites for linear increase of the throughput with respect to the number of access processors are, of course, an adequate number of interface processors and absence of contention in the interconnection network.

Unique ids for the identification of individual relational database operations have been used in the parallel relational database machine GRACE (10). These unique ids are used in isolating the execution of the database operations in groups of processing modules in a similar manner as it is proposed here. That approach is different from this proposal in that it does not provide for concurrent execution of different transactions on the same processing module; the membership of a processing module to a group is specified before the execution of a database operation; and the use of at most two control modules for managing the execution of the database operations cannot avoid resource contention problems during high transaction arrival rate.

IMPLEMENTATION

This technique has been implemented on DBC/1012 (11), a database machine which is the realization of the distributed function approach. It is manufactured and marketed by Teradata Corporation.

The implementation makes use of available space in the HSRAMs of each individual processor. A pool of a large number of group ids is considered to be available for use by the database machine. Three bit words of the HSRAM are used in order to signify the *availability* of a group (1st bit), the *membership* of a processor in a group (2nd bit), and *semaphore information* (3rd bit), as described in detail in (12). Each processor can participate in many dynamic groups and many processors can be members of a single dynamic group. The consistency of the information on dynamic groups among the various HSRAMs is maintained by the active logic of the interconnection network which automatically generates process synchronization messages to this end, as in the case of the predefined groups that was discussed before. The logic of the interconnection network guarantees that messages which are broadcasted to a group are received by the current members of a group and only them. Information on the destination group is stored, of course, within a message.

Interface processors reserve an available group id or release a group id that is being used by modifying the respective group availability bit in their HSRAM. All access processors which get involved in the processing of a transaction receive a message which asks them for the particular operation they are required to perform and to what group they should assign themselves relative to the transaction. This assignment is done by modifying the respective membership bit in their HSRAM. A transaction ends with a broadcast to the processors of the group to commit/abort their relevant work. At the end of the processing of a transaction, each processor detaches itself from the group and the respective group id is freed to be used by other incoming transactions. The scheme allows the existence of multiple partitioned groups at the same time. The number of the available group ids is large enough for the system to work under any transaction load that it can carry out, the limitation being the performance of the maximum number of processors it can accommodate. The general algorithm for transaction processing as it applies in the case of a single gracefully completing transaction is shown in pseudocode in Fig. 3.

The results (13) verify the nature of the projected gains in performance made in (8) and claimed above. More specifically, the throughput of the system for transaction processing increases linearly with an increasing number of processors, whereas without the dynamic groups, it goes into saturation with a few tens of access processors. A throughput in excess of 130 transactions per second has been reported with a configuration with 104 access processors and 24 interface processors, where all processors were based on an Intel 80286 microprocessor. This figure for the throughput was obtained with a non-optimized configuration, where the number of the interface processors and the CPU processing rate of the host computer were the limiting factors. Even under that non-optimized condition the system showed an improvement to the throughput of one order of magnitude as compared to the throughput at the saturation level when dynamic groups were not used.

CONCLUSIONS

The technique of dynamically partitioning groups of processors per transaction whose processing involves them, coupled together with an intelligent, high speed, interconnection network provides for superior performance in database machines which are based on the distributed function architecture. This performance is obtained by making each processor oblivious to the fact that a given transaction may employ

Interface Processor (i) {
    Transaction Received by Interface Processor
        from Host Computer;
    Interface Processor Reserves an Available Group Id;
    Transaction is Parsed into Database Steps;
    /* the following for-loop section can use parallelism */
    for s := 1 **to** number of steps in transaction **do** {
        Send: Message with Group ID,
            Transaction Number, Step, and
            Originating Processor to Access Processor;
        Watch for: Processing Done Message
            from Access Processor;
    }
    Broadcast to All Access Processors in the Group:
        Commit Work Message;
    Wait for: Last Access Processor Done Message;
    Free the Group Id that Was Reserved;
}

Access Processor (a) {
    Receive Transaction Related Message
        from Other Processors;
    Add this Access Processor to the Group
        if not Already Added;
    Perform the Requested Step;
    if (broadcast message) and (last in completion) **then** {
        Send: Last Access Processor Done Message
        Detach this Access Processor from the Group;
        }
    else
        Send: Step Completed Message;
}

Figure 3. General Algorithm for Transaction Processing.

many access processors, and thus reducing possible resource contention by having specialized hardware to maintain the dynamic groups. The concept of the dynamic group of processors, the provision for concurrent execution of transactions, and the automatic process synchronization mechanism provided by the interconnection network drastically reduce the interprocess communication and, thus, the resource contention. On the other hand, the fact that no lock is placed by a transaction on any piece of data on any processor that does not belong to the assigned group of a transaction provides for considerable reduction of data contention. Under these conditions, provided that the transactions do not contain any database request which involves all access processors and that both interface processor and interconnection network are not utilized to their highest capacity, the throughput of the system increases in a linear fashion with increasing number of access processors.

ACKNOWLEDGEMENT

The author would like to thank P.M. Neches and the anonymous referees for their valuable comments on earlier drafts of this paper.

REFERENCES

1. Bernstein, P.A., Hadzilacos, V., and Goodman, N. Concurrency Control and Recovery in Database Systems. Addison-Wesley, Reading, Massachusetts, 1987.
2. Neches, P.M. IEEE Computer **17**:11(29-40), 1984.
3. Codd, E.F. CACM **13**:6(377-387), 1970.
4. Ceri, S. and Pelagatti, G. Distributed Databases: Principles & Systems. McGraw-Hill, New York, New York, 1984.
5. Neches, P.M., Hartke, D.H., Stockton, R.C., Watson, M.C., Cronshaw, D. and Shemer, J.E. United States Patent 4,412,285, 1983.
6. Neches, P.M. United States Patent 4,445,171, 1984.
7. Neches, P.M. United States Patent 4,543,630, 1985.
8. Papachristidis, A.C. Design Note DN-288, Teradata Corporation, Los Angeles, California, 1984.
9. Ries, D.R. and Stonebraker, M.R. ACM TODS **4**:2(210-227), 1979.

10. Fushimi, S., Kitsuregawa, M. and Tanaka, H. **In**: Proceedings of the Twelfth International Conference on Very Large Data Bases, Kyoto, Japan, 1986, pp. 209-219.
11. Shemer, J. and Neches, P. IEEE Computer **17**:11(42-56), 1984.
12. Neches, P.M., Hartke, D.H., Baran, R.J., Woodcock, D.L. and Papachristidis, A.C. United States Patent pending.
13. Higa, L.H. Design Note DN-419, Teradata Corporation, Los Angeles, California, 1986.

A High Speed Database Machine HDM

Shun-ichiro Nakamura   Harumi Minemura
Tatsuo Minohara   Kuniji Itakura[†]
Masakazu Soga

Information Systems & Electronics Development Lab.,
Mitsubishi Electric Corporation,
5-1-1 Ofuna, Kamakura City, Kanagawa, 247, Japan

[†]Mitsubishi Electric Computer Systems (Tokyo) Corporation,
572-1 Kamimachiya, Kamakura City, Kanagawa, 247, Japan

Abstract

To meet the increasing demand for the speedup of relational database processing, we are developing a prototype of HDM (it stands for a High Speed Database Machine). HDM is a relational database machine which has a simple structure with five 32-bit microprocessors, Motorola's MC 68020s. HDM can execute relational database processing very fast by the parallel processing and the best suited disk access method etc. The subset of SQL which includes almost all the basic functions is implemented on the HDM. It is still being developed, but the performance evaluation about selection, projection and join queries without indices has proved that HDM can execute these queries fairly faster than some other relational database systems. In this paper, we present the hardware and software design of HDM and the results of the performance evaluation.

1   Introduction

Recently the research for database machines seems to become very active, such as GAMMA [DeWitt 86] and GRACE [Fushimi 86]. And also several commercial base machines such as IDM500 [Britton 86] and DBC/1012 [Teradata 83] put up a good fight in the market. These are strongly related with the popularization of the relational database systems at the customer site. It becomes clear that relational databases on a general purpose computers exploit much

CPU power and also take much response time. As we thought that the relational database would become much more important in the near future, we had started the development of a database machine to overcome such problems encountered on general purpose computers.

As is known widely, relational database operation is suited for multiprocessing. Recently, marvelous progress of the semiconductor technology has been brought out, and we thought that by using high performance microprocessors for multiprocessing and attaching lots of memory to them, a high performance database machine may be made. Generally, the parallel processing is a fairly difficult problem, because it should parallelize a execution of any program that any user may submit. But for database machines, jobs to be submitted are only relational database operations. So we can classify relational database operations into some kinds and predetermine how to parallelize each kind of operations.

The design concept of the database machine HDM can be summarized as follows.

1. parallel relational database machine
2. specialized hardware and software for relational database operations
3. luxurious use of microprocessors and D-RAM
4. database optimized disk access method
5. middle sized compact and cost effective database machine using bus architecture

The item 5 is the very characteristics of the HDM. Because of the bus architecture, the number of processors in HDM may be limited around 17. Mainly the bus contention problem limits it. So HDM can't become to be a big database machine such as Teradata's DBC/1012 which allows as many as 1024 processors. Instead, because of the bus architecture, the hardware becomes fairly small. As the bus itself is simple enough, the hardware for the bus is very small, and also communication overhead between processors is small too.

We believe that the 'Bus' is the most cost effective hardware. Sometimes or frequently for the sake of bus contention, processing may be delayed. But the performance degradation is usually small in percentage of the total processing time.

In the following section, we present the hardware and software design of HDM. In section 5, we describe the result of the performance evaluation using now available SQL commands. This will show how HDM runs fast.

2   Hardware Architecture

Figure 1 shows the block diagram of the prototype HDM hardware. It consists of a master processor and four slave processors connected by a common bus.

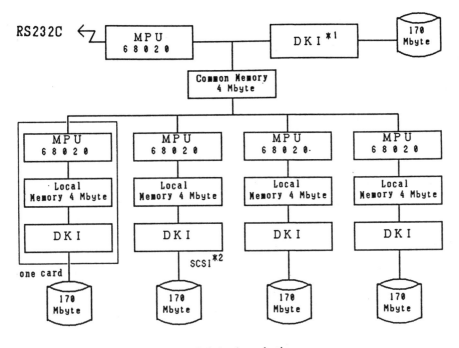

Figure 1: Block Diagram of HDM Hardware

Each processor is made of one 30cm square card, and the same card is used for both master and slave processors. Besides this, a disk drive is attached to each processor. In the processor card all the element modules are connected to the internal bus. A MC68020 CPU, a 4M byte memory module, a DMA controller, a RS-232-C controller, and a SCSI protocol controller etc. are connected to it.

By the way, in the relational database operation, small loop programs are frequently used (for search, sort, etc.). The instruction cache of MC68020 (256 byte) is very powerful in executing such small loop programs.

The memory of the master processor is used as a common memory. Namely, it is accessed by slave processors as well as accessed by the master processor for instruction fetch and operand fetch/store. Four slave processors are connected to the common memory via the common bus. Internal busses of slave processors are extended via buffer gates, and they are connected altogether to make a common bus. The access rate of the common memory is about 10M byte/second.

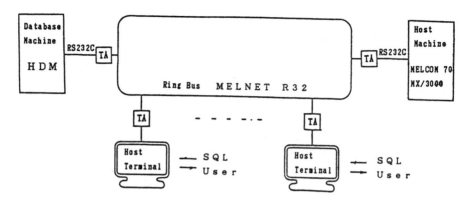

Figure 2: Operating Environment of the Prototype of HDM

Interrupt lines exist between the master processor and each slave processor bidirectionaly. Using this interrupt facility and the common memory, the master processor and a slave processor can communicate each other.

In designing the HDM hardware, we realized that although MC68020 processor was excellent, the peripheral LSIs were pretty poor in the performance aspect. They are designed to be used in various usages, and have much functions, instead the performance is not good. The DMA controller we used is also same. It is for 16 bit bus, and above all it needs 4 DMA clocks (8 machine clocks) for bus arbitration. The processor can't work well during the disk data transfer period, because the DMA takes many bus cycles for the bus arbitration. We solved this problem by adding a data buffer, so once the DMA acquires the bus cycles, burst data transfer can be executed. So the frequency of bus arbitration is diminished, and the processor can work well even if the disk is transferring data.

Each processor has an RS-232-C port and an SCSI port. A disk drive is connected to the processor via the SCSI port. The RS-232-C port of master processor connects it to a host computer. This slow line is not preferable. But while this is an experimental machine, and the fast communication with the host computer is secondary problem, we made a choice to save the cost of the hardware.

Figure 2 shows the operating environment of the prototype of HDM. HDM is connected to the host machine MELCOM 70 MX/3000 via RS-232-C. MELNET R32 ring bus system connects two RS-232-Cs (HDM and the host). A user types an SQL query from the host terminal. The host machine parses it and transfer the intermediate commands to HDM via RS-232-C. After the execution, HDM returns the result to the host machine, and the host machine displays the result to the user.

3   Query Processing Algorithms

Horizontal Partitioning In HDM, a relation is divided horizontally into even amount of fragments and stored into the slave processor – *horizontal partitioning*. The method of the partitioning a relation is as follows: If a relation has a clustered index, a tuple is inserted into a certain page of a certain processor which is determined by the value of a key of the clustered index. If the page is already full, the contents of the page are divided and stored into two pages, and one of the pages is sent to the slave processor which has the fewest tuples. On the other hand, if the relation does not have the clustered index, the tuples are inserted simply into the slave processor which has the fewest tuples, with reference to the schema in the master processor.

General Algorithm The master processor has clustered indices and non clustered indices, and schemata of relations which are implemented as keyed files. Each slave processor has the schemata and the data of the partitioned relations. The master processor checks a query by using the schema of the relation. If necessary, it investigates the index also. Then it issues the processor commands to one to four slave processors. If the query is related with a *'UNIQUE'* index, the command is issued to a certain slave processor that has a certain tuple. If the query is limited of the range by the index, the processor commands are issued to one to all slave processors accompanied with the page numbers which indicate the range. If no indices are available, an exhaustive search is executed, so the same processor commands are issued to all the slave processors.

Join Processing Basically, the join processing in HDM is executed using indices. In case one of the join attributes has no indices, the index is created temporally before the join processing. The join operation is executed as follows: The master processor gets the two indices of the attributes of the each relation for join from the disk of the master processor, and joins the indices by means of comparison. Then it issues the command for taking the record group to the slave processors according to the location information of the joined keys. Each slave processor searches the tuples and projects them, and stored them into the common memory. The master processor joins them on the common memory.

Parallel Searching In case that no indices are available for retrieve, it is necessary to execute the exhaustive search. As the relation is partitioned horizontally, each slave processor can execute the exhaustive search in parallel. So it can be done faster in proportion to the number of the slave processors. As the double buffering is used in the slave processor, while the channel transfers the data into one of the buffers, the processor makes a search operation for the

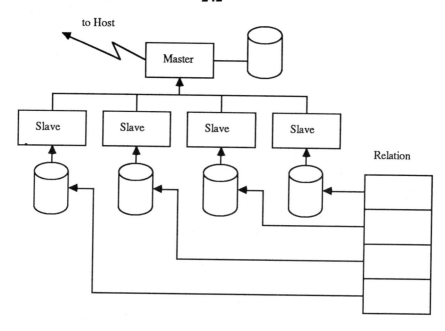

Figure 3: Horizontal Partitioning and Exhaustive Search

other buffer previously filled with data. Usually, the searching by the processor
may be finished before the termination of the data transfer. For this purpose,
we reinforced the channel hardware, so a processor can work well even if a disk
is transferring data.

Parallel Sorting   Sort operation is very important in relational database systems. Sort is necessary when *'ORDER BY'* or *'DISTINCT'* phrases are directed
or join operations or create index operations are executed. Sort operations are
executed on HDM as follows: Each slave processor loads the partial relation
from its disk to its local memory, and sorts it with the quick sort algorithm,
and then transfers the result to the master processor. The master processor
executes a merge sort upon them. Thus parallel sortings are executed among
the slave processors, a faster sort can be carried out comparing with a sort
executed by a single processor.

Parallel Multi Transaction Processing   The queries which update, append, or delete one record may be frequent in the usual typical usage of the
database. These requests are managed on one slave processor. When these
queries arrive concurrently, they may probably be scattered into all the slave
processors. Therefore, such requests are managed in parallel in the query level.

The Restricted Exhaustive Search Though the exhaustive search of HDM is processed in parallel, it is a *heavy* processing itself. But in many cases, the range of the search may be limited by a clustered index, so the exhaustive search is made on the restricted range of the relation. The tuples within such a range is physically gathered together into pages because of the clustered index. These pages may probably be distributed into whole the slave processors. So in this case the parallel search can be executed on the slave processors too.

Join with Indices If both of the keys for the join have the indices (not clustered indices), the join of the keys is executed by means of comparison of the two indices in descending order. It is important that the tuples which are indicated by the joined index are taken out from the disk of each slave processor in parallel.

4 Software Structure

The software of HDM is designed in order to make the best use of the special hardware. It manages the parallel processing in an optimized manner. Figure 4 shows the software structure of HDM. It consists of the programs on the host machine, on the master processor, and on the slave processor. MTOS-68K[1] is used as a kernel for each master and slave processor. Besides MTOS-68K, whole the software is originally made to be best suited for the relational database operation. Especially, the disk and the disk cache access method is specialized to bring out the high performance. The subset of SQL is implemented as a relational database command. It contains all the basic functions, such as CREATE/DROP TABLE/INDEX (cluster, non-cluster), INSERT, UPDATE, DELETE, selection, projection, join, and aggregate.

Software on the Host Machine The software on the host machine consists of an SQL parser, an SQL executer, and a communication program with HDM. The SQL parser converts the queries written in SQL to the format (intermediate language) for the communication with HDM. The SQL executer sends the format as a message to the communication process, receives the result from it, and displays the result. As shown in Figure 4, an SQL parser and executer process is generated for each SQL user.

Software on the Master Processor A transaction from the host machine is processed as follows: The HCP (Host Communication Program) receives the transaction from the host machine and sends it to the TCP (Transaction Control Program). The TCP checks it, and puts it into the message queue. The EXC

---

[1] MTOS-68K is a trademark of Industrial Programming, Inc.

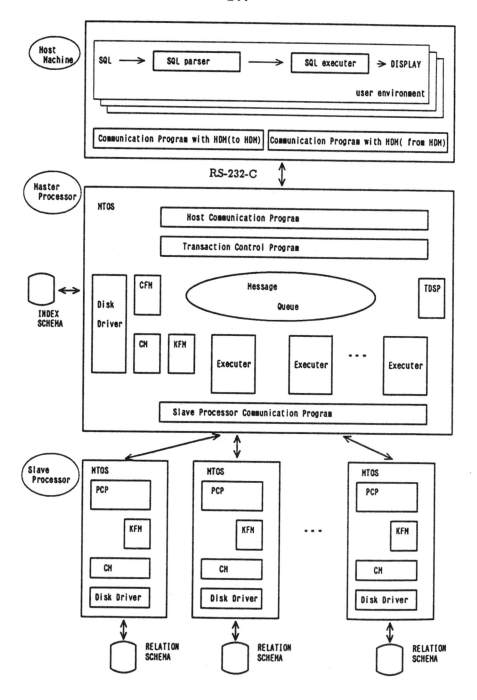

Figure 4: Software Structure of HDM

(Executer) gets it from the message queue and analyzes it. After that, it makes an execution plan, and issues the processor command to the slave processor through the SCP (Slave Processor Communication Program). The SCP sends the command to the slave processor via the mail box which is used for the message passing between the master processor and the slave processors. The slave processor sends the result to the master processor, and the SCP transfers it to the EXC. The EXC puts the result into the message queue. The TCP gets the message from the message queue, divides it into the logical communication units, and sends them to the HCP. Finally, the HCP receives the results and sends them to the host machine.

HDM receives many relational database commands that arrive in random, so it supports multi transaction processing. More than one EXC exist for the multi processing and each EXC processes a different transaction. The EXC refers the index and the schema, and decides whether to use the index or not, in order to make a processor command which is executed on the slave processor. The TDSP (Transaction Dispatcher) controls the concurrent execution of the EXC, namely it decides whether to dispatch the next transaction. The SCP manages the slave processor as a resource of the master processor, and manages synchronous processing among the slave processors. So it becomes possible for an EXC to use the slave processor without caring whether other EXC uses it.

The master processor needs a very large work area to store the intermediate data or the final data for the transaction such as join. For this purpose, the CFM (Cache File Manager) supplies other programs with the work file using a very large memory. When the CFM exhausts the memory for the work file, it uses the disk area as the work file. We also provide the disk cache on a very large memory. The CM (Cache Manager) controls it. If the accessed data is on the cache memory, the disk access won't be done. In order to decrease the disk access overhead, the CM accesses a relation by a unit of cylinder.

The files of HDM consist of the keyed files and the relation files. The schemata and the indices are keyed files, and the relations are relation files. We designed the file manager to be simple (no open and close access methods are necessary) so that the overhead of the file managing is reduced.

Software on the Slave Processor The PCP (Processor Command Processing program) accesses the relations, processes its data, and sends this result to the master processor in response to a processor command from the master processor. In some cases, one processor command is executed in parallel by the several PCP on the several slave processors. In other cases, different processor commands are executed in parallel by the several PCP on the several slave processors. The PCP directly accesses the disk cache in order to decrease the overhead.

5 Performance Evaluation

In this section, we present the performance evaluation result of HDM. It was evaluated by the Wisconsin Benchmark [Bitton 83], which is one of the most popular benchmarks for relational database systems. We also made some other tests for larger relations, such as a 100,000 tuple relation.

The database used for the evaluation is based on the relations described in [Bitton 83]. We used the relations "t1k", "t10k", and "t10ka" for the Wisconsin Benchmark, and "t10k", "t20k", ..., "t100k" for larger relation tests. The names of relations represent the numbers of tuples. Each tuple of each relation is 182 bytes long, and contains thirteen, two byte integer attributes followed by three, 52 byte character string attributes. The value of each attribute was determined by a random number generator.

All our tests were run with a host machine, an engineering workstation, ME 1200[2], which was directly connected to HDM with an RS-232-C cable. We measured the execution time on HDM itself, as well as the elapsed time at the host terminal.

5.1 The Wisconsin Benchmark

We evaluated HDM for selection, projection, and join operations without indices by a part of the Wisconsin Benchmark, i.e. the experiments shown in Tables 1, 5, and 9 in [Bitton 83]. Followings are the queries used for the evaluation:

(a) selection query with 1% selectivity
```
insert into temp select * from t10k
where unique1 between 100 and 199;
```

(b) selection query with 10% selectivity
```
insert into temp select * from t10k
where unique1 between 1000 and 1999;
```

(c) 100/10,000 projection query
```
insert into temp select distinct hundred from t10k;
```

(d) 1000/1000 projection query
```
insert into temp select distinct * from t1k;
```

(e) join AselB
```
insert into temp select t1.*, t2.* from t10k t1, t10ka t2
where t1.unique1 = t2.unique1 and t2.unique1 < 1000;
```

---

[2] ME 1200 is an engineering workstation made by Mitsubishi Electric Corp.

Table 1: Selection Queries without Indices and Projection Queries

system	selection		projection	
	(a)	(b)	(c)	(d)
U-INGRES	53.2 sec.	64.4 sec.	64.6 sec.	236.8 sec.
C-INGRES	38.4 sec.	53.9 sec.	26.4 sec.	132.0 sec.
ORACLE	53.2 sec.	72.5 sec.	29.5 sec.	117.3 sec.
IDM no dac[†]	20.3 sec.	27.2 sec.	58.9 sec.	31.5 sec.
IDM dac	19.9 sec.	23.4 sec.	33.0 sec.	22.0 sec.
DIRECT	43.0 sec.	46.0 sec.	2068.0 sec.	58.0 sec.
HDM no cache	5(1.79) sec.	4(1.81) sec.	4(2.64) sec.	5(1.73) sec.
HDM cache	3(0.65) sec.	2(0.81) sec.	3(1.50) sec.	4(1.10) sec.

[†] dac = database accelerator

Table 2: Join Queries without Indices

system	(e)	(f)	(g)
U-INGRES	10.2 min.	9.6 min.	9.4 min.
C-INGRES	1.8 min.	2.6 min.	2.1 min.
ORACLE	> 300 min.	> 300 min.	> 300 min.
IDM no dac	9.5 min.	9.2 min.	2.1 min.
IDM dac	1.4 min.	1.9 min.	0.6 min.
DIRECT	10.2 min.	9.5 min.	5.6 min.
HDM no cache	10(5.86) sec.	8(5.88) sec.	11(7.20) sec.
HDM cache	10(4.38) sec.	8(4.39) sec.	11(5.60) sec.

(f) join ABprime
```
insert into temp select t1.*, t2.* from t1k t1, t10k t2
where t1.unique1 = t2.unique1;
```

(g) join CselAselB
```
insert into temp
select t1.*, t2.* from t1k t1, t10k t2, t10ka t3
where t1.unique1 = t2.unique1 and t2.unique1 = t3.unique1
and t2.unique1 < 1000 and t3.unique1 < 1000;
```

Tables 1 and 2 show the results for these queries. In these tables, the results for the database systems other than HDM are the values measured in [Bitton 83], [Simon 85] and [Oracle].

"HDM no cache" or "HDM cache" mean the first and the second trial respectively after the cache invalidation. The benchmark on other machines might be run so that there was not caching.

For HDM, the elapsed time at the host terminal and the execution time on HDM (parenthesized) are indicated. Since a tentative RS-232-C cable is used for the communication with the host, improvement of it will make the former value closer to the latter.

These tables indicate that HDM is fairly faster than other database systems for all the evaluated queries.

5.2 Experiments for Larger Relations

Since the Wisconsin Benchmark evaluates database systems for the relations that contain at most 10,000 tuples, we carried out some other experiments in order to evaluate the performance of HDM for larger relations. Figure 5(a), (b), and (c) show the execution time on HDM itself of following five queries for relations "t10k", "t20k", ..., and "t100k".

Q1: `select unique1 from ... where unique1 = 1000;`

Q2: `select string1 from ...`
`where string1 like "%Xg%" and unique1 > 9950;`

Q3: `select string1 from ...`
`where unique1 > 9950 and string1 like "%Xg%";`

Q4: `select distinct four from ...;`

Q5: `select distinct string4 from ...;`

Here, "..." means the name of one of the relations mentioned above. In Figure 5, solid lines show the result of the "cache" case, and broken lines show the result of the "no cache" case.

As shown in Figure 5(a), processing speed in "cache" case is more than three times as fast as in "no cache" case for the query Q1. But in the case that the number of the tuples was more than 60,000, the cache lost the effect except for the directories.

The queries Q2 and Q3 select same tuples. However, since HDM doesn't optimize such queries now, the query Q2 always executes the string comparison before the integer comparison, and the execution time of the query Q2 is about four times as long as that of the query Q3 in Figure 5(b).

The queries Q4 and Q5 sort all the tuples, eliminate duplicate tuples, and select four unique tuples. Therefore, Figure 5(c) shows the sorting performance of HDM. Figure 6 shows the display screen at the host terminal when the query Q5 was executed on the relation "t100k".

5.3 Discussions

We made the performance test for larger relations (up to 100,000 tuples) in 5.2. Since the Wisconsin Benchmark tests database systems only for small relations (10,000 tuples, at most), the power of HDM submerges into the host machine

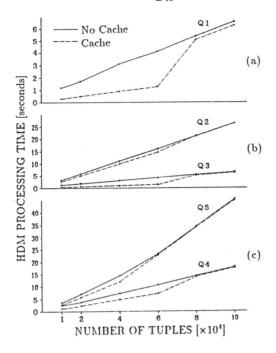

Figure 5: Performance for Larger Relations

processing time (including the communication time). As the relations become larger, the host machine overhead becomes relatively small, and the power of HDM emerges. These results demonstrate that HDM is the real "High Speed" database machine.

6 Conclusions

In this paper, we have presented the design of a new relational database machine, HDM. HDM is a compact and cost effective database machine with a simple structure using microprocessors, and it can execute relational database operations very fast by the parallel processing and the customized disk access method etc.

Though HDM is still under development, we made the performance evaluation using now available SQL commands. The results of the experiments about selection, projection, and join queries without indices show that HDM can execute such operations fairly faster than some other database systems.

Soon, the remainder of SQL commands, such as aggregate and index, will be realized.

```
Please input SQL command
select distinct string4 from t100k;
exe:  I send transaction
exe:  I received transaction

SELECT (PROJECTION) record size = 52, 4 records

string4
-----------------------------------------------------
aXXXXXXXXXXXXXXXXXXXXXXXXXXXaXXXXXXXXXXXXXXXXXXXXXXXXXa
hXXXXXXXXXXXXXXXXXXXXXXXXXXhXXXXXXXXXXXXXXXXXXXXXXXXXXh
oXXXXXXXXXXXXXXXXXXXXXXXXXoXXXXXXXXXXXXXXXXXXXXXXXXXXXo
vXXXXXXXXXXXXXXXXXXXXXXXXXvXXXXXXXXXXXXXXXXXXXXXXXXXXv

HDM: 44960[ms] COM: 47[sec] TOTAL 48[sec]
```

Figure 6: Execution of Query Q5

References

[Bitton 83]   Bitton, D., DeWitt, D.J., and Turbyfill, C., "Benchmarking Database Systems - A Systematic Approach," *Proceedings of the 18th VLDB Conference,* October, 1983.

[Britton 86]   "IDM 500 SERIES: the Logical Approach to Efficient Database Management," *Britton Lee, Inc.,* 1983.

[DeWitt 86]   DeWitt, D.J., et. al., "GAMMA - A High Performance Dataflow Database Machine," *Proceedings of the 21st VLDB Conference,* August, 1986, pp.228-237.

[Fushimi 86]   Fushimi, S., Kitsuregawa, M., and Tanaka, H., "An Overview of the System Software of a Parallel Relational Database Machine GRACE," *Proceedings of the 21st VLDB Conference,* August, 1986, pp.209-219.

[Oracle]   "Oracle Corporation Response to the DeWitt Benchmark," *Oracle Corp.*

[Simon 85]   Simon, E., "Update to December 1983 'DeWitt' Benchmark," *Britton Lee, Inc.,* March, 1985.

[Teradata 83] "Teradata: DBC/1012 Data Base Computer Concepts & Facilities," *Teradata Corp.,* Document No. C02-0001-00, 1983.

A High Performance VLSI Data Filter

K. C. Lee and Gary Herman
Bell Communications Research, Inc.
435 South Street, Morristown, NJ 07960-1961 USA

ABSTRACT

We have designed a high performance single chip VLSI data filter to perform relational algebra and simple numeric operations on a high speed input data stream. The data filter features a scalable architecture avoiding major hardware/software changes as fabrication technology evolves, a small but semantically rich instruction set, and large on-chip instruction and data buffers to maximize the query execution rate. A 2.0 micron CMOS implementation of our design should be capable of executing 20 million operations per second on a 17 megabyte per second input stream. Since this high speed data filter is programmable and supports many queries concurrently, a system utilizing tens of such data filters is capable of handling thousands of complex search requests simultaneously.

1. INTRODUCTION

The Datacycle architecture [Herm87] is a database system architecture intended to support very high levels of transaction throughput, a powerful query language, rapid execution of complex queries, and full control of concurrently executing transactions to preserve database consistency in the face of updates. The strategy in the architecture is to broadcast database contents repetitively over a very high bandwidth medium to a multitude of "listening" processors that observe the stream in parallel and use hardware filters to extract the information relevant to the transactions pending locally.

Data filters perform multiple roles in the Datacycle architecture. As in past database machine architectures, for simple queries the data filters copy records which satisfy query predicates in a single pass of the data. For complex queries (e.g., joins), filters may search the broadcast stream over multiple cycles to extract the required data. Unlike other machine architectures, in the Datacycle approach data filters are also critical to achieving efficient implementation of essentially "optimistic" mechanisms for concurrency control. That is, after a transaction has obtained its readset, data filters monitor the broadcast stream to detect relevant changes in the readset, and, once the transaction reaches the commit phase, confirm the success of the commit attempt by attempting to read the modified data items.

Because of the functional importance of data filters in the Datacycle architecture, and because of the speed and parallelism required to search data streams at the rates (gigabytes per second) required for the architecture to be useful, efficient data filtering is critical to the practicality of the architecture. To better understand the architectural and implementation issues involved, we have undertaken the design of a VLSI data filter to be used on a system prototype under construction in our laboratory. The design can be viewed as a highly optimized microprocessor featuring an instruction set customized for database search operations, pipelined instruction execution, and large on-chip data and instruction buffers. A 2.0 micron CMOS fabrication of this design should execute in excess of 20 million comparison operations per second, with 256 on-chip queries; 1.2 micron technology should improve comparison throughput by fifty percent and buffer size by a factor of 2.

In this paper, we describe the rationale and design of the data filter for the Datacycle architecture. In Section 2, we provide an overview of the operation of the Datacycle architecture, describing the role of data filters in query processing and concurrency control. In Section 3, we provide an overview of the data filter architecture. Section 4 describes both the filter instruction set in detail and the VLSI implementation of the filter architecture. Section 5 and 6 contain a discussion and a summary respectively.

2. THE DATACYCLE ARCHITECTURE

2.1 Overview

As illustrated in Figure 1, the components of the Datacycle architecture are the storage pump, the broadcast medium, the record access managers, the upstream update channel, and the record update manager. The entire contents of the database are repeatedly read from the storage pump, broadcast over the broadcast transmission channel, and observed passively and independently by many record access managers. Each access manager is associated with a host, a general purpose computing system on which applications reside.

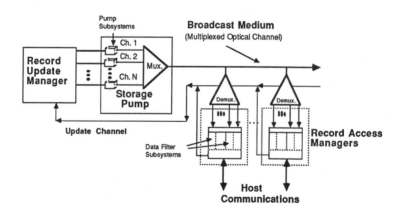

Figure 1.   The Datacycle Architecture

Each record in the database appears on the broadcast channel in a form resembling that shown in Figure 2, that is, a structured sequence of attributes. Note that, as shown in Figure 2, record attributes include both the data values associated with a database record as well as record status attributes (e.g., record ID, the time the record was last changed, the ID of the entity which last changed the record) used by the system for transaction management. Also appearing on the broadcast channel are special bit sequences used to subdivide the broadcast channel. These special patterns may serve to identify the start and end of a relation, or may be used in indexing strategies to improve search efficiency.

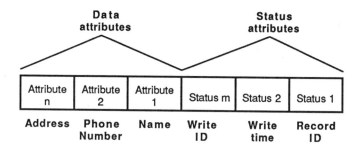

Figure 2.   A record in the Datacycle Architecture

Access managers "read" records from the broadcast stream by means of hardware data filters that compare the values of the relevant attributes of each record appearing in the stream with specifications derived from the queries submitted to the access manager by the host application. To complete a transaction and update the database, the host submits an update/commit request to the access manager. Update requests are sent from the access manager to the update manager, which accepts a serializable subset of requests and introduces the changed records into pump storage. Success of update attempts is confirmed by the access managers by reading the updated records on a subsequent broadcast cycle.

As Figure 1 indicates, each of the major system components in the architecture is constructed of a number of subsystems. To allow for flexibility in the total size of the database, implementation of the pump and the record access manager must be independent of the total transmission capacity provided in the broadcast channel. The approach is to multiplex together a number of relatively slow data streams from the subsystems in the pump, carry out the transmission at the higher aggregate rate, and then, at each access manager, demultiplex the stream into a number of slower channels, each of which operates at a rate suitable for the data filters. A need for more storage is accommodated by adding a new storage subsystem to the pump and new data filter subsystems at each of the access managers. Besides providing flexibility in database size, this approach also reduces the clock rate required within the data filter electronics.

In a prototype system currently under construction, we use framing [Chao87] and transmission electronics created for an experimental broadband communications system implemented in Bellcore [Linn86]. The storage pump comprises several semiconductor RAM storage subsystems organized similarly to video frame stores. The outputs of these subsystems drive the transmission electronics. The basic subchannel rate is 140 megabits/second, accessible for reading or writing through a 17 megabyte/second byte parallel interface provided by an integrated circuit framer. With existing time division and wavelength division multiplexors, we can transmit up to 288 separate 140 Mbps subchannels on a single fiber. Early versions of the prototype will use 4 to 16 140 Mbps subchannels.

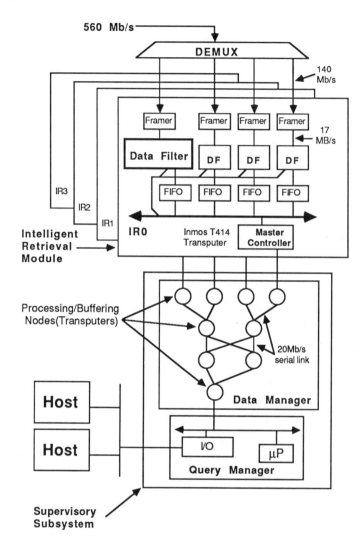

Figure 3.   Record access manager for the Datacycle prototype

As shown in Figure 3, the supervisory subsystem in the record access manager prototype includes a general purpose processor called the Query Manager as well as the Data Manager, a complex of processing nodes connected to form a network. The Data Manager controls access to the broadcast subchannels through many Intelligent Record Retrieval subsystems (IRs). Each IR consists of a processor managing four VLSI data filter units that perform the content addressable search operations over the 140 Mbps subchannels. To aid in understanding requirements for data filters in the Datacycle architecture, we describe query processing and concurrency control in more detail.

2.2 Query Processing

Queries are presented to a record access manager in a high-level database language such as SQL [Date86]. The Query Manager translates these queries into a sequence of relational algebra expressions of the form:

Select (data type) **From** (Relation) **Where** (expression) **For** (request id) .

The data type can be a record, or some fragment of a record; the expression defines the pattern to be matched and consists of simple boolean expressions relating the fields of a record and constants through operations such as equals, greater than, etc.; the request id associates the instruction with a specific query. These expressions are passed to the Data Manager. Examples are given in Section 4.

The Data Manager subsystem maps the logical data space (based on relation names and field values) to the physical data space (based on subchannels, subchannel segments, and the physical layout of records), translates the relational operations into the machine language primitives of the data filters, routes the primitives to the appropriate IRs, buffers intermediate results, and routes the results of the primitive database operations to the Query Manager.

To perform a join in this architecture, in one broadcast cycle of the database the data filters perform a hardware project over the joining attribute on the two relations to be joined. In buffers in the Data Manager, the projected values are used to build a data structure containing a count of the number of times each value appears in each of the two relations. Every value which has non-zero count for both relations will take part in the join; the count gives the size of the result exactly. If enough data filters are available, the filters are loaded with each value that will take part in the join, and in the next cycle all the desired records are retrieved. The join operation is completed at a higher level in the access manager. This join operation resembles the bit array technique in [Babb79] and the hardware-assisted semijoin approach in [Faud85].

Since the entire contents of the database are accessible to the data filters on each broadcast cycle, I/O intensive aggregate operations like **max, min, sum**, etc., can be accomplished conveniently if the data filters have the capability to perform numeric operations on the fly. Because the concurrency control mechanism in the architecture guarantees that the view of the database presented within each broadcast cycle is consistent, an on-the-fly aggregate operation in the Datacycle architecture completed in a single cycle does not require locking to guarantee a correct result.

2.3 Concurrency Control

The optimistic concurrency control mechanism in the Datacycle architecture [Herm87][Gopa87] depends on the data filter capability to decentralize much of the conflict detection for update transactions, to provide early detection of conflicts to avoid processing wasted in doomed transactions, and to confirm the success of update transactions. In a multiversion extension to the basic scheme described here, data filtering facilitates retrieval of the correct version by selecting the version of a data item with the appropriate time stamp.

Concurrency control is predicated on the assumptions that each broadcast cycle of the database has a distinct beginning and end and that the contents of the database within a single cycle are guaranteed to be consistent. In the read phase of a transaction, the access manager independently extracts records from the broadcast stream and maintains its own list of records in use, based on the records required locally. While a transaction is executing, the access manager monitors the transaction's readset. For each record on the local list of records in use, the data filter hardware scans the broadcast stream to determine if the record has been changed (updated) since it was originally read for the associated transaction. Data filters may detect changes to the readset by monitoring a record's write timestamp or even by testing each record to determine if a transaction-specific predicate constraint remains true. With this hardware testing capability and the repetitive broadcast of the database, the access manager can detect any significant modification to a pending transaction's readset, notify the host, and pass the new record values to the transaction. Based on these new values, the transaction can abort, back up, or continue. The decision is strictly local. Unlike most certification schemes, the "certification with monitoring" scheme in the Datacycle architecture permits transactions to abort as soon as a conflict is detected, reducing processing wasted on already doomed transactions [Agra85].

Each access manager subsequently determines whether the transactions with submitted update requests have committed successfully by either monitoring the actual data values or record write IDs or by examining a portion of the bandwidth used to broadcast a log of committed transactions. Commit authorization is then returned to the host.

3.0 DATA FILTER ARCHITECTURE

The Datacycle architecture is critically dependent on the efficiency of the data filtering operation. The periodic presentation of the database in the architecture requires "batching" queries at the data filters. That is, if queries arrive at an access manager at a rate of N queries per second, then the data filter must search concurrently for records specified by N*T queries, where T is the duration of the database broadcast cycle. Each query operation may require dedicating data filters for an exhaustive search of every subchannel of the database. Monitoring for concurrency control also increases the demand for data filters, as do complex queries such as joins. Finally, since the architecture has no provisions for flow control of the data on the broadcast channel, the data filters must exclude as much of the irrelevant data as possible to avoid serious buffer management problems in the access manager. As much as possible of the logical processing of records should be done at the data filter, rather than further back in the access manager.

To explore the feasibility of data filters with the characteristics required by the Datacycle architecture, we have designed a high performance data filter using a commercial VLSI design aid, Genesil^{TM}, in effect, a "silicon compiler." This tool allows us to explore architectural alternatives independently of the particular fabrication process eventually used. We can consider the area requirements and performance of different architectures, and assess the impact of including or removing functions from a specific architecture. With an architecture chosen, Genesil provides accurate predictions of performance and silicon area requirements for fabricating the design on any of the fabrication processes (currently 20+) in the system's library. Thus, we can create a

---

Genesil^{TM} is a trademark of Silicon Compiler Systems, Inc.

single architecture designed for fabrication using a 2.0 micron process, predict the performance gain and area reduction to be achieved using a 1.2 micron process, and then extend the design to exploit the opportunities created by using the smaller design rules. This is the tactic we have followed in our data filter design.

After consideration of a number of architectural alternatives for the data filter, including systolic arrays [Kung80], linear comparator arrays [Curr83], comparator with memory approaches [Faud85], as well as more traditional database machine search processors, the architecture illustrated in Figure 4 emerged. Search parallelism in our architecture is achieved by efficiently sharing the use of a single "comparator" (the micro-engine) across many queries stored in on-chip buffers. This architecture can be viewed as a highly optimized microprocessor with an application specific instruction set. The data filter accepts records from the framer in a 17 Mbytes/second 8 bit parallel stream and holds each in an internal record buffer. Records are double-buffered - one record is resident in buffer 1, while the next is arriving in buffer 2. Assuming 128 byte records, records arrive every 7 microseconds.

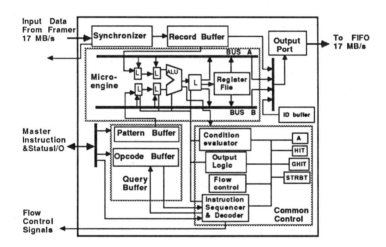

Figure 4.   Data filter internal architecture

During the time a record is resident in the record buffer, selected portions of the record are evaluated in the micro-engine (an ALU and associated logic) against a list of query patterns stored in the pattern buffer according to the query logic stored in the op-code buffer. If any of the operation sequences are evaluated to be TRUE, that is, the record satisfies a selection predicate, the record and the IDs of the queries satisfied are passed off chip to a FIFO buffer.

To maximize the execution rate, the data filter processor is highly pipelined and utilizes large on-chip instruction and data buffers. Pipelining improves the apparent execution rate by overlapping operations in different stages of the data filter, and the on-chip data and instruction buffers allow a sufficient supply of operands to let the execution unit (ALU) operate at full speed.

The filter executes an instruction in five pipeline stages including instruction fetch, instruction decode, operand fetch, execution, boolean evaluation and store. The maximum time delay of all stages is determined by the longest propagation delay of combinational logic, in this case, the delay for the ALU. This pipeline principle allows the effective speed of the processing logic in the filter to match the fastest ALU implementation by available VLSI technology.

The use of large on-chip buffers significantly improves performance. In doing a content addressable search, the same query logic is performed repetitively against the search attribute of all the records in a relation. Because the processor executes the same instruction sequence repeatedly, an on-chip instruction buffer (the pattern buffer plus the opcode buffer in Figure 4) can significantly improve the speed of instruction fetch. An on-chip instruction buffer allows the ALU to operate at maximum speed. Similarly, the on-chip record buffer also increases the data supply rate to the ALU. This buffer also allows queries which access different record attributes to be processed in the same cycle; an address field in each instruction identifies the portion of the record to which the operation is to be applied.

Referring again to Figure 4, in the remainder of this section we provide more detail on the operation and implementation of the synchronizer, micro-engine, common control, and instruction and record buffers.

3.1 Data Stream Synchronizer

The synchronizer synchronizes the arrival of incoming records, manages the double buffering of records, and provides synchronization signals to the master controller as well as the on-chip common control circuit. As in the new version of the RAP 3[Ozka86] processor, which leaves the schema to the control processor, the synchronizer detects only a few special characters like "start of record," "end of record," "start of segment," "end of segment," "start of cycle," "end of cycle," etc. On encountering any of these characters, the synchronizer outputs the appropriate boundary indicator and adjusts the address register to place the incoming information in the appropriate location. With minimal embedding of schema in the data stream, the data filter hardware is free from the run time decoding of schema information that may significantly reduce the filter processing speed. The synchronizer stores relevant boundary indicator values (e.g., relation name, segment name) for the current record, making them accessible as operands in instruction execution.

3.2 The Micro-engine

The micro-engine is a parallel datapath with a 32 bit wide ALU and a register file. As described earlier, it is highly pipelined. Two operands (e.g., a four byte query pattern and the corresponding four bytes from the specified attribute in the record buffer) are fetched into two operand receiving latches, then transferred to the ALU operand latches. By using these two close-coupled latches, the operands receive sufficient set up time for the latches at the ALU. As a result, the maximum stage delay of the pipe can be kept very close to the clock cycle time if a two phase symmetric clock is used. The result of the ALU operation is transferred from the destination latch to the register file. Note that, depending on the specific query, operands can be selected from the register file, the record buffer, or the pattern buffer. All the comparison and data movement operations are carried out through the ALU. To save translation time and register locking overhead, we use a temporary store to latch the result of the ALU and direct it to the ALU input latch if the next instruction requires it [Kate83].

Two single bits, **A** and **HIT**, are used to implement the continuous evaluation of disjunctive normal form and conditional assignment instructions (Section 4) that we use to avoid conditional branch instructions. A comparison result derived from the ALU flags and the test condition is first evaluated with a Boolean accumulator, **A**, under opcode control; then, the result of the evaluation is stored back into the accumulator. A **HIT** flag is set if the the result of the final Boolean operation is true. This **HIT** flag is used by the conditional assignment instructions. If it is set, the result of the assignment will be written into the register file; otherwise, the result is discarded.

The programmability of the ALU and ability to store intermediate results make the micro-engine more flexible and efficient in performing range search, extreme value search, and aggregate operations than are the systolic array [Kung80] and data broadcasting linear comparator array types of filters [Curr83]. The micro-engine also allows direct execution of disjunctive normal forms for the relational data model, avoiding the need for sophisticated FSA[Hask80] compilation like that used in SABRE[Gard83] and VERSO[Banc83].

3.2 Common Control

Common control circuits contain the instruction decoder, Boolean evaluation, flow control, and output control logic. Since the instruction set is fairly small and orthogonal, a few PLAs can implement a fast decoder. The sequencing of instructions is also simple because of the absence of branch instructions. Boolean evaluation of comparison results requires only a one bit accumulator with a few gates for and/or operations.

Flow control and output logic are more complex. The output logic is a finite state machine which receives inputs from the instruction decoder and executes a block move operation from the record buffer to the output port as a background task. Two types of overflow conditions are defined to deal with external buffer overflow and internal output port contention. A flow control counter is allocated to count the output traffic in terms of the number of output words per unit period of time. An external signal is also provided to indicate an external overflow. The output operation will be blocked if the counter reaches a preset value or the overflow signal is set. When both the output logic and the executing instructions want to output at the same time, contention occurs and the instructions' output (the **ID** of a **HIT** query) will be queued in the ID buffer.

3.3 Query and Record Buffers

The data filter uses both record and query buffers (the pattern and opcode blocks in Figure 4) to convert the sequential database search task into a series of random access operations. The records are double buffered in a tri-port RAM; as the next record arrives, it can be loaded into the record buffer while the current record is being examined and the previous record is being moved to the output port. The on-chip instructions are double buffered in a dual port RAM; while multiple queries are being executed against the buffered record, new instructions can be loaded into the query buffer. These query buffers consist of multiple four byte words addressable only on word boundaries.

Since the entire record is buffered, any of the fields specified by any of the instructions can be fetched and acted on according to the opcode associated with that instruction. Because of this random access capability, this data filter is more flexible and powerful for parallel content addressable search than the early stream-oriented associative processors used in CASSM [Lipo79], SURE[Leil78], and RAP 1,2 [Ozka86]. In addition, since we use VLSI technology to implement the whole data filter in one chip, the operand access time is much faster than those data filters with buffered record and instruction but separate processor and memory organization like RAP 3 [Ozka86] and RDBM [Schw83].

Buffering, combined with the synchronization capabilities just described, allows context switching among "batches" of queries. For example, if records from the same relation appear contiguously in the broadcast stream, this "segment" can be delineated by a "start of relation NAME" detected by the synchronizer. A query scheduler at the higher level in the access manager can arrange for this batch of instructions to be loaded into the chip before the records that fall into their specified search segment have arrived. The double buffering of the query (pattern and opcode) buffers facilitates fast batch context switching. While the contents of one buffer set are being executed, the other buffer set can be updated if necessary. As we discuss in Section 5.3, he throughput of the system can be increased substantially through the use of indexed search schemes, where appropriate.

4. DATA FILTER INSTRUCTION SET

The instruction set exhibits high semantic content, allows efficient pipelining, and allows output operations to proceed concurrently with instruction execution. The design of the instruction set is crucial to performance. The instruction set should be high level enough to represent high level queries in few machine instructions, but should be simple enough that one instruction can be executed in one clock cycle. As a result, instructions resemble horizontal microcode representations of the high level queries. A single instruction will perform as many actions as possible (CISC philosophy); the hardware executes the decoded instruction in a pipelined fashion.

To simplify the decoding and execution circuits in the chip, we minimized the number of instructions in the instruction set, as in RISC (c.f.,[Kate83]) architectures, but, unlike RISC, the instructions have high semantic content tailored to the data filtering application. A typical instruction can execute a test with two four byte operands (one from the record buffer and one from the pattern buffer), evaluate a Boolean operation on the current and previous test result, and output the instruction ID based on the result of the evaluation.

A query containing a complex Boolean expression is decomposed into multiple simpler disjunctive terms (i.e., the sum of products form), with each term specifying two four byte operands and the instruction opcode. In executing the chain of the terms in a query, each term generates a TRUE or FALSE flag result, to be used by one or more conditional terms that follow it. This approach not only fully utilizes the pipeline mechanism, but also significantly reduces the number of instructions required to execute a Boolean expression. For example, to evaluate a Boolean expression on a typical general purpose machine, the instructions

IF field1 > pattern1 AND field2 < pattern2, STORE ID to output port, can be translated into the pseudo machine instructions:

    COMPARE field1 with pattern1
    Branch Less to next query address
    COMPARE field2 with pattern2
    Branch Greater to next query address
    STORE ID to output port
    ...next query starts here.

Our task is to reduce the number of instructions describing this query to the minimum of two pseudo instructions, e.g.,

    If field1 > pattern1, set FLAG A
    If (field2 < pattern2) AND A, output ID.

We implement a conditional assignment instruction that allows us to eliminate branch instructions. This feature is desirable for two reasons. First, since most queries will be decomposed into two to three instructions, using a branch instruction to implement conditional assignment will lengthen the number of instructions required for each query [Henn82]. Second, frequent branch results in significant loss of execution efficiency due to pipeline flush.

An instruction set with a high semantic content saves query translation time and reduces the total number of bits required to represent the query. Therefore, the run time query translator can be implemented more easily, and the translation time will be reduced. When many instructions can be buffered on the chip to support multiple queries, the compact representation reduces the memory bandwidth requirements between the off chip memory and the data filter and also increases the number of queries that can be stored on-chip. The result is greater apparent search parallelism.

4.1 Instruction Set Definition

The primary instruction set is defined as follows:

OPr, OPa(MEM, P:MASK,ID).

OPr is the opcode for result evaluation, and OPa specifies the condition of the comparison between a four byte word addressed by MEM and the immediate operand P; a "don't care" mask indicates the bytes to be utilized in the comparison. The operand is defined as a four byte word. Most of the attributes can be encoded into four byte binary integers; longer fields that are not so encoded can be broken down into multiple words[Tana83].

A set of conditional assignment instructions designed mainly for more general aggregate and max/min operations is defined as follows:

    if HIT, OPalu(M1, M2, M3)
    if TRUE, OPalu(M1, M2, M3).

OPalu can be one of several ALU opcodes such as 'add', 'sub', 'and', 'or', etc. M1 and M2 specify the operand locations in the record buffer, the pattern buffer, or the register file; M3 is the destination, which can either specify the output port or a location in the register file. This instruction set is powerful, allowing content addressable record select, projection on a single record attribute, as well as other functions such as aggregate, extreme value selection, indirect selection, etc.

4.2 Record Select

The data filter processor is mainly designed for high speed content addressable search. This task requires the evaluation of Boolean expressions that are translated from the **from** and **where** clauses of a typical relational algebra expression. A typical high level instruction for this type of operation is as follows:

Select RECORD **From** RELATION **Where** BOOLEAN EXPRESSION **For** ID

where,

BOOLEAN EXPRESSION ::= TERM and/or BOOLEAN EXPRESSION
TERM ::= attribute OPa value
OPa ::= GT(greater than), LT(less than), EQ(equal to), GE(GT or EQ), LE(LT or EQ).

Based on a given schema, this high level language can be translated into machine instructions. For example, the simple query,

Select (RECORD)**From**(RELATION=800D)**Where** (PHONE#=7017682) **For** (Query #3)

can be translated into the following instructions:

Push A, EQ(RELATION = "800D":1111,3)
Fand A, EQ(PHONE# = "7672300":1111,3) .

In these instructions, record operands (PHONE#) are represented by their addresses relative to the start of the record. Operands which are derived from boundary indicator values (such as RELATION – see Section 3.1) are also specified as memory addresses. In executing these instructions, first the equality condition is tested between the boundary indicator value specified by RELATION and the encoded number "800D". Then, the result is stored in **A**. The second instruction will "and" its test result with the previous result in **A**. If the final result is true, a **HIT** flag is set and the query ID number, 3, will be sent to the output port.

4.3 Projection

Projection on attributes can be decomposed into multiple conditional assignment instructions where each instruction outputs a single four byte word. An example of this type of operation can be:

Get (attribute 1) **where** (attribute 2 > 20000) **for** (query 3).

To simplify the discussion, we assume that attributes 1 and 2 are each four byte attributes. The target instructions will be

Fand A, GT(ATTRIBUTE2 > "20000":1111,3)
if HIT, or(ATTRIBUTE1, NULL, output port).

The OPalu 'or' is used here to accomplish a move operation. The result returned from the data filter may be: query 3: (john), (gary), (mary), etc.

4.4 Aggregate Operations

Operations such as aggregate sums, extreme value selection, indirect search, etc., can be executed "on-the-fly" efficiently and can be incorporated into our design without changing the basic chip architecture. The cost is additional chip area for instruction decode and temporary register storage space. We decided to implement this type of instruction in the data filter.

The simplicity of adding this functionality can be illustrated by examining the similarity between instructions. For example, an aggregate operation like

Calculate the sum of checking account balances for accounts with balances
greater than $500

can be translated into a loop:

SUM=0
DO until end of relation CHECKING
   IF BALANCE>500, set flag .
   IF flag is set, BALANCE + SUM --> SUM
end DO
output SUM .

This aggregate operation is easily implemented by five machine instructions:

if TRUE, or(NULL, NULL, SUM)
Fand A, GT(BALANCE, "500":1111,3)
if HIT, add(BALANCE, SUM, SUM)
Fand A, NE(RELATION, "CHECKING",3)
if HIT, or(NULL, SUM, output port),

where BALANCE and RELATION are predefined addresses for the balance field and relation header respectively.

4.5 Synchronization Instructions

The data filter is designed as a slave processing device that communicates with its master processor via the use of synchronization instructions. Two major instructions synchronize the start and end of execution for a batch of instructions. The first instruction is

START BATCH on BOOLEAN EXPRESSION.

The other is

END BATCH on BOOLEAN EXPRESSION.

These instructions support sequential partitioning of data, permitting efficient scheduling for more improved utilization of the data filter chip. The START BATCH instruction sets an on-chip flag, **STRBT**, that enables the execution of the subsequent batch of instructions. END BATCH performs the opposite function. A typical batch of instructions containing multiple queries can be expressed in the following format:

```
START BATCH
query 0
query 1
...
query n
END BATCH.
```

5. DISCUSSION

5.1 Chip Area and Performance

The silicon compiler design tools provide generic timing and die size without requiring hand-crafting of each function block. The results of a timing and die size analysis for our data filter architecture are shown in Figure 5 for two CMOS fabrication processes, one at 2.0 microns, the other at 1.2 microns. As Table 1 shows, we estimate the total circuit size for 2.0 micron fabrication, including I/O pads, to be about 456 X 456 Mils, a large but not unreasonable size for a 2 micron CMOS fabrication process. The 1.2 micron process reduces chip dimensions to 392 X 392 Mils, despite doubling the size of the query buffers.

For a 2.0 micron fabrication process, the ALU propagation delay is about 50 ns., the dual port RAM buffer (for queries) cycle time is also about 50 ns. The instruction decoder circuit is formed by several PLAs, and the estimated propagation delay of the PLA is less than 40 ns. Consequently, we expect to execute one instruction every 50 ns.; the 2.0 micron filter throughput is approximately 20 million 4 byte comparison (or other operations) per second. The 1.2 micron process improves throughput to better than 33 million operations per second.

The data filter processor achieves high performance through balanced architecture design and a high level of integration. Buffer sizes, memory access times, and instruction execution times are well balanced. In the 7.35 microseconds between record arrivals (assuming 128 byte records) approximately 147 instructions (2.0 micron version) can be retrieved from the query buffers and executed against the stored record. The query buffers hold 256 instructions; assuming the batch context switching described in Section 4.5, 128 instructions in one half buffer can be executed against a single record while the other half buffer is being replenished. Roughly 50% of the chip area is dedicated to the data and instruction buffers required to fully utilize the micro-engine, which constitutes only 15% of the chip. Scaling the architecture to 1.2 microns yields an increase in execution rate to 200 instructions per 128 byte record, and allows doubling of query buffer size to 512 instructions. The architectural balance is preserved.

Parameters / Components	2 μm CMOS			1.2μm CMOS		
	Max. freq. (MHz)	Area (Sq. Mils)	Transistors	Max. freq. (MHz)	Area (Sq. Mils)	Transistors
Micro-engine - ALU - Register file	20	23681	3824	33	10524	3824
Query buffers - Dual Port Ram - 32 bits wide	20	88536 2 KB	134712	33	78696 4 KB	269424
Record buffer	25	18559	81272	42	8249	81272
Common Control - 4 PLAs (est.)	~30	~19928	~18400	~50	~9964	~18400
Subtotal		150704 (~388 x 388)	271886		107433 (~327 x 327)	372920
Routing			37676			26858
I/O Pads			20000			20000
Total chip area			208380 (~456 x 456)			154291 (~392 x 392)
Power			~1 W @ 20 MHz			~1.5W @ 30 MHz
Total buffered instructions			256			512
Ins./μs			20			32
Ins./7.35 μs			147			242
Ins./14.7 μs			294			484

*Input data rate = 17.04 Mbytes/sec
*Record size = 128 (256) bytes
*Processing window = record size/ data rate

Figure 5. Key design parameters

5.2 Adapting to Evolving VLSI Technology

The architecture of the data filter permits transparent performance improvement with denser and faster VLSI technologies. The size of the address and ID fields in the instruction set are specified in anticipation of increasing density of the CMOS fabrication technology. Because the architecture preserves the I/O and execution balance as the implementation technology evolves, when submicron VLSI technology becomes available, the implementable size of the data and instruction buffers will increase, and execution speed will improve. Neither the data filter architecture nor the interface to the data filter will require modification.

For example, the 10 bit address field in the current instruction set can address up to 4 kilobytes of data in the record buffer, much more than the 128 bytes physically present in our 1.2 micron design. Similarly, the 10 bit ID field allows processing of 1000 distinct on-chip queries (independent of the number of instructions per query); our 1.2 micron design has buffer space for only 512 simple queries. As a result, the current architecture for the data filter processor should effectively utilize the increase in the sizes of on-chip buffers made feasible by submicron CMOS technology.

Since the increase in speed of CMOS VLSI circuits is mainly a function of geometry and applies relatively uniformly to all the blocks (e.g., RAM, ROM, ALU, PLAs, etc.) in the data filter architecture, submicron fabrication should produce predictable speed up without need to rebalance the operand I/O bandwidth and ALU execution speed. In other words, the data path of the processor remains the same, and higher performance can be achieved by adding more on-chip instruction buffers.

5.3 Programmability and Throughput

Since the data filter is programmable, its throughput depends on the complexity of the database queries and efficiency of the batch scheduling scheme. A simple query may contain only one term (four byte word) translatable into one instruction; thus, hundreds of such queries can be served simultaneously. Complex queries may contain tens of terms. Only few of such queries can be executed at the same time.

Since the chip supports batched instruction execution with special synchronization instructions and signals, the throughput of the chip can be proportionally increased with indexing schemes until the overheads of the scheduling and indexing become dominant. For example, assume that a relation can be divided into 1000 segments based on one search key, and that the master controller is able to sort the incoming queries into 1000 batches according to the order of appearance of the segments in the broadcast data stream. Then, by loading the queries batch by batch into the data filter in synchrony with the sequence of incoming segments, this very simple scheduling scheme improves the effective data filter throughput by a factor of one thousand.

6. SUMMARY

We have presented the design of a high speed data filter for the Datacycle architecture. This 20 MIPs CMOS VLSI data filter can perform very high throughput content addressable search over a sustained 17 megabyte per second input data stream. The VLSI data filter has the following important features:

i)   Single chip CMOS VLSI implementation resulting in low power consumption and fast execution speed;

ii) Scalable architecture avoiding major hardware/software changes as fabrication technology evolves;

iii) A small but semantically rich instruction set;

iv) Large on-chip instruction and data buffers to obtain maximum execution rate.

Essentially, we have designed a reduced CISC machine based on many RISC concepts. This approach results in a very high performance application specific processor, in this case a relational data filter. Using advanced silicon compilation tools, we believe that this design methodology can also be applied to the design of other customized high performance processors. Our work has suggested that application specific processor design is no longer prohibitively expensive. In the future, we plan to investigate data placement and query processing algorithms that can fully utilize the data filter's capability, and, based on those algorithms, we will be able to make realistic cost performance comparisons against other database machines. Additionally, we would like to explore the feasibility of generalizing the design for other applications.

7. REFERENCES

[Agra85] Agrawal, R., and Dewitt, D.J., "Integrated Concurrency Control and Recovery Mechanisms: Design and Performance Evaluation," *ACM Transactions on Database Systems*, Vol. 10, No. 4, December 1985.

[Banc83] Bancilhon, F., Fortin, D., Gamerman, S., Laubin, J. M., Richard, P., Scholl, M., Tusera, D, and Verroust, A., "VERSO: A Relational Backend Database Machine." In D.K. Hsiao, ed.,*Advanced Database Machine Architectures*, Englewood Cliffs, N.J.: Prentice Hall, Inc., 1983.

[Babb79] Babb, E. "Implementing a Relational Database by Means of Specialized Hardware," *ACM Transactions on Database Systems*, Volume 4, Number 1, March 1979, pp. 1-29.

[Chao87] Chao, H. J., Robe, T. J., and Smoot, L. S., "A CMOS VLSI Framer Chip for a Broadband ISDN Local Access System." *Proceeding of 1987 VLSI Circuits Symposium*, Karuizawa, Japan, May 1987.

[Curr83] Curry, T., and Mukhopadhyay, A., "Realization of Efficient Non-Numeric Operations Through VLSI," *Proceedings of VLSI '83*, 1983.

[Date86] Date, C. J. *An Introduction to Database Systems: Volume 1, 4th Edition.* Reading: Addision-Wesley Publishing Co., 1986.

[Faud85] Faudemay, P., and Valduriez, P. "Design and Analysis of a Direct Filter Using Parallel Comparators," *Proceedings of the 4th International Workshop on Database Machines*, Grand Bahama Island, March 1985.

[Gard83] Gardarin, G., Bernadat, P., Temmerman, N., Valduriez, P., and Viemont, Y. "SABRE: A Relational Database System for a Multimicroprocessor Machine." In D.K. Hsiao, ed., *Advances Database Machine Architectures,* Englewood Cliffs, N.J.: Prentice Hall, Inc., 1983.

[Gopa87] Gopal, G., Herman, G., and Weinrib, A. "Concurrency Control in a Broadcast Database," Bell Communications Research, Technical Memorandum, 1987.

[Hask80] Haskin, R. "Hardware for Searching Very Large Text Databases," *Workshop on Computer Architectures for Non-Numeric Processing*, March 1980, pp. 49-56.

[Henn82] Hennessy, J., Jouppi, M., Baskett, F. "Hardware/Software Tradeoffs for Increased Performance," *Proceedings of the ACM Symposium on*

Architectural Support for Programming Languages and Operating Systems, Palo Alto, Calif., March 1982, pp. 2-11.

[Henn84]   Hennessy, J. "VLSI Processor Architecture," *IEEE Transaction on Computers*, Vol. c-33, No. 12, December 1984, pp. 1221-1245.

[Herm87]   Herman, G., Gopal, G. Lee, K. C., and Weinrib, A. "The Datacycle Architecture for Very High Throughput Database Systems." *Proceedings of ACM-SIGMOD 1987*, San Francisco, May 1987.

[Kung80]   Kung, H. T. and Lehman, P. L. "Systolic (VLSI) Array for Relational Database Operations," *Procceedings of ACM-SIGMOD 1980*, May 1980.

[Leil78]   Leilich, H.-O., Stiege, G., and Zeidler, H.Ch. "A Search Processor for Data Base Management Systems," *Proceedings of the 4th Conference on Very Large Databases*, June 1978, 280-287.

[Linn86]   Linnell, L. "A Wide-Band Local Access System Using Emerging Technology Components," *IEEE Journal on Selected Areas in Communications*, Vol. SAC-4, No. 4, July 1986.

[Lipo79]   Su, S. Y. W., Nguyen, L. H., Emam, A., Lipovski, G. J., "The Architecture Features and Implementation Techniques of the Multicell CASSM," *IEEE Transactions on Computers*, Vol. c-28, No. 6, June 1979.

[Kate83]   Katevenis, M. G. H., Sherburne, R. W., Patterson, D. A., and Sequin, C. H. "The RISC II Micro-Architecture," *Proceedings of VLSI '83*, 1983.

[Ozka86]   Ozkarahan, E. *Database Machine and Database Management*, pp. 236-255. Englewood Cliffs N.J.: Prentice Hall, Inc, 1986.

[Schw83]   Schweppe, H., Zeidler, H. Ch., Hell, W., Leilich, H.-O., Stiege, G., and Teich, W. "RDBM-A Dedicated Multiprocessor System for Database Management." In D.K. Hsiao, ed., *Advanced Database Machine Architectures*, Englewood Cliffs, N.J.: Prentice Hall Inc., 1983.

[Tana83]   Tanaka, Y. "A Data-Stream Database Machine with Large Capacity." In D.K. Hsiao, ed., *Advanced Database Machine Architectures*, Englewood Cliffs, N.J.: Prentice-Hall, Inc. 1983.

DESIGN, IMPLEMENTATION, AND EVALUATION OF A RELATIONAL DATABASE ENGINE FOR VARIABLE LENGTH RECORDS

F. ITOH*# K. SHIMAKAWA* K. TOGO† S. MATSUDA† H. ITOH‡ M. OBA‡

*Information and Communication Systems Laboratory, Toshiba Corporation, 2-9 Suehiro-cho, Ome, 198, Japan
†Ome Works, Toshiba Corporation, 2-9 Suehiro-cho, Ome, 198, Japan
‡ICOT Research Center, Institute for New Generation Computer Technology, Mita Kokusai Bldg., 21F, 1-4-28 Mita, Minato-ku, Tokyo 108, Japan

ABSTRACT

This paper reports the design, implementation, and evaluation of a relational database engine. The engine has special purpose hardware, the nucleus of which is a pipeline two-way merge sorter, to execute sorting and relational algebra for variable length records. In the execution of these operations, key fields are extracted from records. The engine has on-the-fly processing in which it inputs data directly from disk. The evaluation shows the characteristics of processing time, the effect of variable length records, and the effectiveness of on-the-fly processing.

INTRODUCTION

The Institute for New Generation Computer Technology (ICOT) considers that fifth generation computer systems have the integrated functions of inference and knowledge bases, and has been researching and developing inference machines (IMs) and knowledge base machines (KBMs). For KBMs, a relational database machine, Delta (1,2), was developed because the relational database is said to be suitable for logic programming which is used in IMs. In Delta, facts, as in Prolog, are stored as relations and retrieved by relational algebra. Another KBM is now under development, in which Horn clauses are stored as relations and retrieved by operations called retrieval-by-unification (RBU) (3). In RBU operations, data is selected and joined based on unifiability, in contrast to relational algebra, in which data is selected and joined based on equality. The KBM has unification engines (UEs) (4), which perform RBU operations. Although a Horn clause is represented as a structure which consists of literals and variables, UEs treat the structure as a variable length string.

With this background, we have developed a relational database engine (RDBE) with following aims.

#Currently working at Institute for New Generation Computer Technology

Processing variable length records using hardware

The RDBE performs sorting and relational algebra (RA) operations for one fixed or variable length key field in variable length records.

Efficient database processing

On-the-fly processing. To process data on disk efficiently, the RDBE has on-the-fly processing in which it inputs data directly from disk. Without on-the-fly processing, data on disk is loaded to main memory (MM) before it is input to the RDBE, then the data path in the entire processing is "disk → MM → RDBE → MM". On-the-fly processing makes the data path "disk → RDBE → MM", and achieves more effective processing.

Stream processing in the RDBE. The RDBE realizes the stream processing of sorting and RA operations.

The search processor, SHP (5), is an example of a processor which has on-the-fly processing. Examples of processors which have stream processing are VLSIs based on the systolic array (6), the RDBE in Delta (7), multiple processors for the join operation (8), and some processors for sorting, for example, a sort engine using pipeline heap sorting (9) and a pipeline merge sorter (10). An algorithm has been proposed for a sorting processor for variable length records (11), but has not been implemented yet.

Later sections discuss the design, implementation, and performance evaluation of the RDBE. Section 2 presents the basic ideas of design and features of the RDBE. Section 3 summarizes the configuration, format of data to be processed, functions, and processing. Section 4 shows the implementation of all components of the RDBE. Section 5 evaluates performance based on the design values and measurement.

BASIC IDEAS

Configuration of the Database Machine

Fig. 1 shows the configuration of the database machine. It mainly consists of a central processing unit (CPU), MM, RDBE, and database disk. Relations manipulated by the database machine have both fixed and variable length attributes. Relation schemata and data are stored in different files on disk. Data of one relation is stored in one file. One record in a file corresponds to one tuple in a relation. Fig. 2 shows the structure of a record.

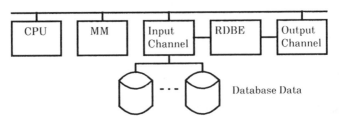

Fig. 1. Configuration of the Database Machine

A record consists of a record header (RH), fixed length fields (FFs), variable length field headers (FHs), and variable length field bodies (VFs). There are the same number of FHs and VFs, and they have one-to-one correspondence in order. The RH consists of record length (RL) and a deleting flag (DF). A DF shows whether the record is valid (logically not deleted). An FH consists of field length (FL) and field position (FP). FL denotes the length of the corresponding VF. FP means the length from the head of a record to the head of the corresponding VF. A VF has an instance of a variable length attribute. Relation data on disk is a series of records. Relation schemata include the length and the position of each FF and the position of each FH, in addition to ordinary schemata.

Data processing is shared between the RDBE and the CPU. When a query arrives at the CPU, the CPU executes a combination of the following three types of processing to obtain the answer, and returns the answer to the user.

The CPU requests the RDBE to input data from disk, process it, and output the result to MM.

The CPU requests the RDBE to input data from MM, process it, and output the result to MM.

The CPU directly processes data in MM.

The RDBE quickly performs the following processing, which is simple but time-consuming.

Sorting. Records in target data are sorted in ascending or descending order by their key values.

Duplication elimination. Records in target data are sorted in ascending or descending order. If there are two or more records which have the same key value, one is left and the others are removed.

Selection. Records are selected from target data whose key values have a specified large or small relationship to the conditional value.

Intersection and difference. Records are selected from second target data whose key values are (in intersection) or are not (in difference) included in the set of key values of first target data.

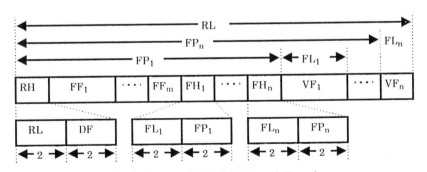

Fig. 2. Format of a Variable Length Record

Equal join. Pairs of records are made between first and second target data, each of which has the same key values. However, the creation of one record from each pair is not supported by the RDBE, but by the CPU.

The CPU performs following processing which is too complex for hardware or causes a data transfer bottleneck although the processing by hardware is quick.

Arithmetic operations, aggregate functions, and reforming records after join in the RDBE. These are too complex for hardware.

External sorting and external duplication elimination. In sorting and duplication elimination, if the volume of target data is beyond the RDBE's capacity, data is divided into several parts less than the RDBE's capacity, the RDBE sorts or eliminates duplications from each part, and the CPU performs external sorting or duplication elimination of all parts. Even if the RDBE could perform external sorting and duplication elimination, there would be a data transfer bottleneck.

Processing Methods of the Relational Database Engine

The RDBE adopts the following methods:

Stream processing by a pipeline two-way merge sorter and an RA processor. The sorting and relational algebra processing (RAP) modules are arranged in series. The sorting module consists of a pipeline two-way merge sorter (12). In the intersection, difference, and join operations, the comparison to search for equivalent or non-equivalent key values is executed more effectively by sorting key values beforehand.

Key field extraction processing. Only the key fields flow into the sorting and RAP modules. In pipeline two-way merge sorting, memories are used to store data being sorted. Different record lengths cause delays in pipeline processing. To reduce the contents of memory and the delays, the key fields are extracted from records.

Use of tags. The sorting and RAP modules use tags attached to data to execute processing. One item of information in tags indicates the end of key fields. With this information, it is not necessary to consider whether the key field length is fixed or variable.

OVERVIEW OF RELATIONAL DATABASE ENGINE

Configuration and Data Format

Fig. 3 shows the configuration of the RDBE and its data format. The RDBE consists of a controller and four modules. There are three data formats as follows,

Records. The input and output data of the RDBE is the records shown in Fig. 2. Input records are sent to the RB and IN modules simultaneously, and output records are read from the RB module. Records are input and output in two-byte units.

Key fields and record identifiers with tags. Data flowing from the IN module to the RAP module consists of key fields and record identifiers (RIDs) with tags. Key fields and RIDs flow one after the other. Each RID corresponds to the record from which the preceding key field is extracted. A one-byte tag is added to each two bytes of key fields or RIDs. Tags are used for flags and parities. Flags indicate the end of key fields and the duplication of key values. Parities are used as bit parity for data integrity. Three bytes of key fields or RIDs and tags flow in parallel.

RIDs with tags. RIDs and their tags flow between the RAP and RB modules. The content of tags is parities. Three bytes of key fields and tags flow in parallel.

Controller and Module Functions

The function of the controller and each module are as follows:

Controller. The controller interprets a command from the CPU and sets up modules. In the IN module, it determines whether key fields are of fixed or variable length, their position and length if they are of fixed length, and the position of the corresponding variable length field headers if of variable length. In the IN module, it determines the key data type (character, integer, or floating point). In the sorting module, it determines whether sorting is used in the operation processing, and whether sorting is ascending or descending. In the RAP module, it determines the kind of RA.

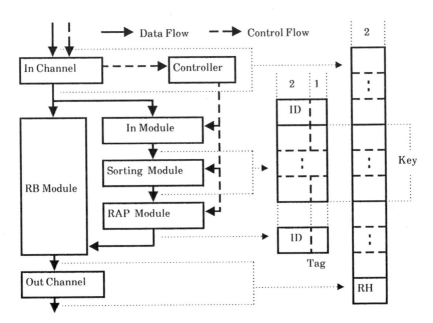

Fig. 3 Configuration and Data Format

RB module. When target data is input, the RB module stores whole records in memory, and determines the correspondence between the input serial number (used as the RID) of each record and its address in memory. When result data is output, the RB module reads the records from memory which correspond to RIDs sent from the RAP module.

IN module. The IN module extracts key fields from records, attaches RIDs, and sets key end flags. If the data type of the key is numerical (integer or floating point), it manipulates bits of key values to compare them as a character.

Sorting module. The sorting module sorts character-type key values in ascending or descending order. If there are two or more of the same key values, it sets duplication flags on all the key values other than the last one.

RAP module. The RAP module executes duplication elimination, selection, intersection, difference, and equal join operations for character-type key values. Except for selection, it requires that key values be sorted and it uses duplication flags. As a result, it outputs only RIDs.

Processing Method for Sorting and Relational Algebra Operations

Sorting and RA operations are executed with the sorting and RAP modules as follows:

Sorting. The sorting module sorts target key values. The RAP module only extracts RIDs from sorted data.

Duplication elimination. The sorting module sorts target key values. The RAP module removes redundancies from duplicated data by selecting data on which duplication flags are not set.

Selection. First, a conditional key value flows through the sorting module, and is stored in memory of the RAP module. Next, target key values flow through the sorting module, but are not sorted. The RAP module compares them in input order with the conditional key value, and extracts target RIDs whose key values satisfy the condition.

Intersection and difference. The first target key values are sorted by the sorting module and stored in memory of the RAP module. The second target key values are also sorted and flow into the RAP module. The RAP module compares the key values of the two targets and extracts the second target RIDs whose key values are (in intersection) or are not (in difference) included in the set of first target key values.

Equal join. The first target key values are sorted by the sorting module and stored in memory of the RAP module. The second target key values are also sorted and flow into the RAP module. The RAP module compares the key values of the two targets and extracts pairs of the first and the second target RIDs whose key values are equivalent.

DESIGN AND IMPLEMENTATION

Record Buffer Module and IN Module

Memory for storing whole records is one megabyte. The RID length is two bytes. In one operation, the maximum size of whole target records is one megabyte and the maximum number of target records is 64 kilobytes. A table controls the correspondence between RIDs and addresses in memory. In some operations, typically selection, result record output starts before target record input ends, thereby realizing concurrent record input and output.

Sorting Module

The pipeline two-way merge sorter consists of 12 sorting cells. The maximum number of target records in sorting is 4096 (2^{12}). Fig. 4 a) shows the configuration of a sorting cell. The memory management method is double memory (11) for ease of implementation. Memory in the 12th sorting cell is 128 kilobytes (in practice, 192 kilobytes including 64 kilobytes for the tags). Essentially, in the double memory method, two items of data to be merged are stored in district memory. However, in our implementation, they are stored in two parts of one physical memory because of the hardware size restriction.

Relational Algebra Processing Module

Fig. 4 b) shows the configuration of the RAP module. There are two memories, each of which is 128 kilobytes (in practice, 196 kilobytes). In intersection, difference, and equal join, all first target key values are stored in one memory. Comparison of the first and second target key values begins as soon as the second target key values flow into the RAP

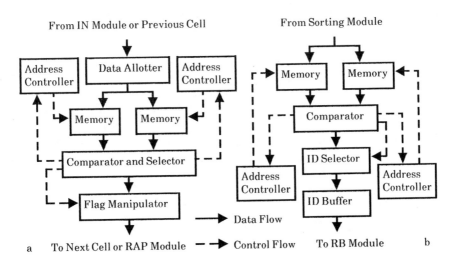

Fig.4 a) Configuration of a Sorting Cell b) Configuration of the RAP Module

module. If the speed of second target key values flowing into the RAP module is faster than the speed of the values being cast off after comparison, second target key values are stored in another memory. If another memory becomes full, the RAP module stops second target key values from flowing in until a vacancy occurs. The maximum size of first target key values and RIDs is 128 kilobytes, but the size of second target key values is not limited.

Clock Time of Data Flow

In the RDBE, data are transferred in two-byte or three-byte units, including one byte for the tag (this two or three bytes is called one word). The data path in each module is made up of registers and memories. The data transfer speed depends on memory access time because data transfer between registers and comparison of two items of data are faster than memory access.

RB module and IN module. Data input into the RB module and the IN module are synchronized. In the RB module, alternate input at word level and output to memory is adopted to realize concurrent input and output at record level. Essentially, data is input and output at a speed of one word per two clocks. In the IN module, key fields are transferred at a speed of one word per three clocks because, as described later, the sorting module receives them at that speed. Parts other than key fields are cast off without being received by the sorting module.

Then, data is input into the RB and IN module at one word per three clocks in key fields, and one word per two clocks in parts other than key fields. Data is output from the RB module at one word per two clocks or a little slower because read from memory waits if requirements of both write and read occur in the same clock.

Sorting module. To realize pipeline processing, each sorting cell must transfer data at the same speed. Consider that each sorting cell receives and sends one word for a certain time, and that there are three memory accesses in each sorting cell. Two of them are read of both words to be compared, and one is write of a word from the preceding cell. These three memory accesses are assigned every three clocks. Data is transferred at one word per three clocks.

RAP module. Essentially, it is possible to transfer data at one word per two clocks. In intersection, difference, and equal join, both words to be compared are read simultaneously because two memories are physically separated from each other, unlike the sorting module. However, for ease of implementation, data is transferred at one word per three clocks, synchronized with output from the sorting module.

Actual Implementation

The modules are controlled by transistor-transistor logic (TTL) and a programmable logic device (PLD). One clock is 250 ns.

PERFORMANCE EVALUATION

Basic Performance

The performance is evaluated when the lengths of records and keys are fixed. First, the processing time of each operation is estimated by examining the register transfer level. The processing time is from beginning input of data to ending output, and does not include the time to interpret a command from the CPU and to set up modules.

Let each record consist of only a variable length key field, and the length of the key field be 14 bytes or more, and be $2a$ bytes. The length of each record is $2a+8$ bytes, including four bytes for a record header and four bytes for a key field header.

Sorting. Let the number of target records be n (where n is a power of 2). The processing time of sorting is divided into input time, delay time, and output time. Each time is defined and summarized as follows.

Let input time be from beginning input of the first record to beginning input of the last (nth) key field. It takes eight clocks from beginning input of the first record to input of the first key field, because there are four words for the record header and key field header. The interval between inputting a key field and inputting the next key field is, essentially, $3a+8$ clocks because an a-word key and a four-word non-key (the record header and key field header of the next record) are input. The RID is transferred while the non-key is cast off. However, as stated above, because a clock where the sorting module receives a word is assigned once every three clocks, the interval becomes $3a+9$, which is the minimum multiple of three from $3a+8$ up. Then, input time is:

$$(3a+9)(n-1)+8 \ (clocks)$$

Let delay time be from beginning input of the last key field to output of the first record. It takes 91 clocks for data to flow through the engine without any processing for operations. However, the RAP module only outputs the RID ignoring the key (it takes $3a$ clocks). Then, delay time is:

$$3a+91 \ (clocks)$$

Let output time be from beginning output of the first record to ending output of the last record. The interval of the RID being output from the RAP module is $3a+3$ clocks because there are a words per key and one word per record ID. The output of one record finishes in $3a+3$ clocks because it takes $2a+8$ clocks, less than $3a+3$ clocks, assuming that $a \geq 7$. Then, output time is:

$$(3a+3)(n-1)+2a+6 \ (clocks)$$

From the above, the total time of sorting is:

$$(6a+12)n-a+93 \ (clocks)$$

The outline of other operations is as follows.

Duplication elimination. Duplication elimination is the same as sorting.

Selection. Let the record number of target data be n.

$$(3a+9)n+5a+178 \ (clocks)$$

Intersection and difference. Let the record number of first and second target data be m and n respectively (where both are a power of 2 and 4096 or less).

Minimum:

$$(6\alpha + 12)m + (6\alpha + 12)n - 4\alpha + 163 \ (clocks)$$

Maximum:

$$(9\alpha + 15)m + (6\alpha + 12)n - 4\alpha + 163 \ (clocks)$$

Equal join. Let the record number of first and second target data be m and n respectively (where both are a power of 2 and are 4096 or less). Let the record number of result data be r (where $r \geq n$).

Minimum:

$$(6\alpha + 12)m + (3\alpha + 9)n + (4\alpha + 20)r - 3\alpha + 156 \ (clocks)$$

Maximum:

Where $r \leq (\min[m,n])^2$, let r be a square number.

$$(6\alpha + 12)m + (3\alpha + 9)n + (4\alpha + 20)r + (3\alpha + 3)(m + n - 2\sqrt{r}) - 3\alpha + 156 \ (clocks)$$

Where $r > (\min[m,n])^2$, let r be a multiple of min[m,n].

$$(6\alpha + 12)m + (3\alpha + 9)n + (4\alpha + 20)r + (3\alpha + 3)(\max[m,n] - \frac{r}{\min[m,n]} - 3\alpha + 156 \ (clocks)$$

Let each record consist of more than one field. Assume the following:

A key field is the last part of a record.

The length of a key is 2α bytes, and the length of a record is 2β bytes. $\beta - \alpha$ is multiple of 3, and $3\alpha \leq 2\beta - 4$.

The number of target records is n and a power of 2.

The processing time for sorting is as follows.

$$(\alpha + 4\beta + 2)n + 4\alpha - 2\beta + 99 \ (clocks)$$

The processing time has the following characteristics.

It is linear to the number of target records.

It is linear to the key length and the record length, and depends more on the record length.

In selection, the processing time does not depend on the selectivity.

In intersection and difference, the variation in processing time depends on the number of the same key values in first and second target data. The larger the number, the shorter the processing time, because the number of comparison times in the RAP module decreases.

In join, the processing time is approximately linear to the number of result records. The variation depends on the concurrency between the comparison in the RAP module and output of the result records. If there are the same key values in first and second target data in the later part of the comparison, output of the result records continues after the end of the comparison, making the processing time longer.

Next, the real processing time is compared with the computed time. The time from beginning input of records to ending output of records is measured by a logic analyzer. The measured time is approximately equal to the computed time. Fig. 5 shows the time for sorting and selection, and Fig. 6 shows that for equal join. The difference between the measured and computed times is caused by firmware overhead in the input and output channels.

Effect of Variable Length Records

Processing time is measured for target records where record lengths, key lengths, or both are different. In sorting, the time from beginning input of records to ending output of records is measured by a logic analyzer.

Generally, it takes longer to sort variable length records than fixed length records, because the difference of processing time in each sorting cell causes a delay in the data stream. Processing time is measured for the following three cases. In each case, the number of records, the total size of records, and the total size of key fields are constant.

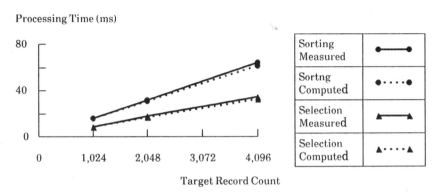

Key Length   16 Bytes (Constant)
Record Length 24 Bytes (Constant)

Fig. 5. Target Record Count Characteristic in Sorting and Selection

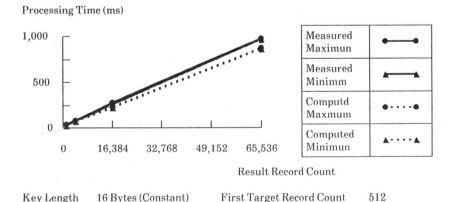

Key Length   16 Bytes (Constant)   First Target Record Count   512
Record Length 24 Bytes (Constant)   Second Target Record Count   512

Fig. 6. Result Record Count Characteristic in Equal Join

Case 1. The target records consist of only variable length key fields. The key and record lengths become gradually longer, are constant, or become gradually shorter. The gradient varies.

Case 2. The key lengths of the target records are constant. The record lengths of target records become gradually longer, are constant, or become gradually shorter. The gradient varies.

Case 3. The record lengths of the target records are constant. The key lengths of target records become gradually longer, are constant, or become gradually shorter. The gradient varies.

Fig 7 shows the measurement results in case 1. Where lengths become longer, the processing time is the same as where they are constant. However, where lengths become shorter, the greater the gradient, the longer the processing time. In cases 2 and 3, the processing time is equal among the various gradients.

Consider the last sorting cell of the sorting module. It stores the sorted first half of the keys in its memory, and when it obtains the first key of the sorted second half of the keys, it starts output of all of the sorted keys. Storage of the sorted first half of the keys begins after input of the first half of the target records to the IN module finishes. The first key of the sorted second half of the keys is obtained after input of all of the target records to the IN module finishes. Where storage of the sorted first half of keys finishes before input of all of the target records to the IN module finishes, processing time of sorting depends on the total size of the records, which is constant in all cases. However, where the key and record lengths become shorter in case 1, the total size of the first half of the keys is larger than the total size of the second half of the records, which causes longer processing time.

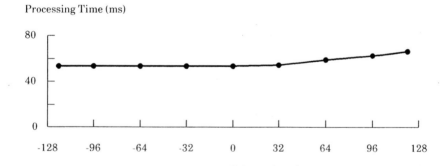

Fig. 7. Target Record Length Distribution Characteristic in Sorting

Effect of On-the-fly Processing

Processing time with and without on-the-fly processing is compared, and the effect of on-the-fly processing is evaluated. With on-the-fly processing, data on disk is directly input to the RDBE. Without it, data on disk is input to the RDBE after it is loaded to MM. Fig. 8 shows the processing time of sorting and selection with and without on-the-fly processing. On-the-fly processing reduces the processing time by about 30% in sorting and by about 40% in selection. The processing time is regarded as the time when the data is being transferred, and is measured by a logic analyzer.

The effect of on-the-fly processing is evaluated. To make the discussion simple, it is assumed that the speed of reading data from disk (disk → MM and disk → RDBE) and that of transferring data between the MM and the RDBE (MM→ RDBE and RDBE → MM) are the same.

Since the processing in the RDBE is concurrent with inputting and outputting data to it, the entire processing time is roughly estimated by the data transfer time.

In sorting, the result data is output from the RDBE almost immediately after the target data is input to it. With on-the-fly processing, there are two data transfers (disk → RDBE and RDBE → MM). Without on-the-fly processing, there are three transfers (disk → MM, MM → RDBE, and RDBE→ MM). Since the time of these data transfers is approximately the same, the processing time of sorting with on-the-fly processing is about two-thirds of that without on-the-fly processing.

In selection, input of target data to the RDBE and output of result data from it are approximately concurrent. With on-the-fly processing, there is one data transfer (disk→ RDBE → MM). Without on-the-fly processing, there are two transfers (disk→ MM and MM → RDBE→ MM). Since the time of these data transfers is approximately the same, the processing time of selection with on-the-fly processing is about half of that without on-the-fly processing.

Processing Time (ms)

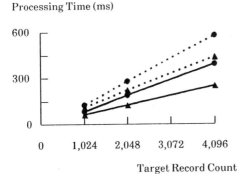

Sorting with On-the-fly	●——●
Sorting without On-the-fly	●····●
Selection with On-the-fly	▲——▲
Selection without On-the-fly	▲····▲

Target Record Count

Key Length   16 Bytes (Constant)
Record Length 64 Bytes (Constant)

Fig. 8. With and Without On-the-fly Processing in Sorting and Selection

CONCLUSION

This paper described the design, implementation, and performance evaluation of the RDBE for variable length records. To process variable length records, the key fields are extracted from records, and tags are added to them. This realizes the same algorithm for both fixed and variable length data, and reduces the delay caused by different record lengths. To execute sorting and RA operations quickly, pipeline processing by multiple processors, the nucleus of which is a two-way merge sorter, is adopted. This realizes stream processing, the concurrent execution of an operation and transfer of data. To process data on disk effectively, on-the-fly processing is used so that the RDBE inputs data directly from disk. This reduces the total processing time by about 30% in sorting and by about 40% in selection in comparison with the case where data are loaded to MM before inputting them to the RDBE.

ACKNOWLEDGMENTS

We wish to thank Dr. K. Iwata and Mr. C. Sakama of ICOT Research Center, and Mr. Y. Hoshino, Mr. S. Shibayama, and Mr. H. Sakai of Toshiba Corporation for useful discussions. We also extend our thanks to the RDBE developers for the implementation and performance measurements of the RDBE.

REFERENCES

1. Shibayama, S., Kakuta, T., Miyazaki, N., Yokota, H., and Murakami, K. New Generation Computing, Vol.2, 2:131-155, 1984.
2. Kakuta, T., Miyazaki, N., Shibayama, S., Yokota, H., and Murakami, K. In: Database Machines Fourth International Workshop (Eds. D. J. DeWitt and H Boral), Springer-Verlag, New York, 1985, pp. 193-34.
3. Yokota, H., and Itoh, H. Proc. 13th International Symposium on Computer Architecture, pp. 2-9, 1986.
4. Morita, Y., Yokota, H., Nishida, K., and Itoh, H. Proc. 12th International Conference on Very Large Data Bases, pp. 52-59, 1986.
5. Hayami, H., and Inoue, U. IPS Japan Technical Report, DB-51-2, 1986 (in Japanese).
6. Kung, H. T., et al. ACM SIGMOD, pp. 105-116, 1980.
7. Sakai, H., Iwata, K., Kamiya, S., Abe, M., Tanaka, A., Shibayama, S., and Murakami, K. Proc. of International Conference on Fifth Generation Computer Systems 1984, pp. 419-426, 1984.
8. Valduriez, P., and Gardarin, G. ACM Trans. Database Syst., Vol.9, 1:133-161, 1984.
9. Tanaka, Y., et. al. Proc. of IFIP Congress, pp. 427-432, 1980.
10. Kitsuregawa, M., Fushimi, S., Kuwabara, K., Tanaka, H., and Moto-oka, T. Trans. IECE Japan (Section J), Vol.J66-D, 3:332-339, 1983 (in Japanese).
11. Yang, W., Kitsuregawa, M., and Takagi, M. IPS Japan Technical Report, CA-63-12, 1986 (in Japanese).
12. Todd, S. IBM J. Res. Dev., Vol.22, 5:509-517, 1978.

A FILTER PROCESSOR AS PART OF AN INTELLIGENT DISK CONTROLLER

J. KREYSSIG, H. SCHUKAT, H.CH. ZEIDLER

Institut für Datenverarbeitungsanlagen
Technische Universität Braunschweig, Germany

ABSTRACT

This paper introduces a part of a research project, the concern of which was to move file management functions to an intelligent disk controller. This provides an interface to design a filter processor which supports pattern matching by special hardware and thus allows performance speed-up in non-standard applications such as office automation and knowledge base systems or engineering data processing. After some remarks concerning the state of the art and dedicated basic considerations, the design and implementation of the filter processor is described in details.

INTRODUCTION

The object of the design and implementation described is a component for searching in unstructured data - usable, for example, in non-standard applications such as office automation and knowledge base systems or engineering data processing. Pattern matching is one of the keywords, and its essential basic operation is scanning raw data in order to select substrings as fast as possible.

Although the search principle may be identical to structured data, queries of this kind are very complex, and the best solution is to process them in a high performance microprocessor, e.g. to use a software solution. Special hardware support, however, may be useful in addressing the unstructured data, e.g. marking relevant substrings of a scanned data stream. Since such substrings can start at arbitrary boundaries (byte or bit) and - with more than one argument in parallel - the history of the actual comparison must be partially considered, problems can be solved only by using special techniques; associative memories, cellular arrays and finite state automata (FSA) are known to implement such components.

STATE OF THE ART

Content addressability is the desired data access in information processing, but with the use of general purpose computers and their conventional random access memories which run todays database applications, this is possible only by reading raw data from a mass memory into the main memory and then comparing it sequentially by the central processing unit. This procedure results in performance bottlenecks of the I/O channel and in overloading the CPU with simple data qualification operations.

Navigational software such as indices and pointers may be helpful in special cases, but they are not applicable in general. The ideal solution in hardware could be a mass memory with fully parallel access which receives a query from and sends the relevant data after a minimum time delay to the CPU for further processing. Unfortunately, a highly integrated realization of such a content addressable memory (associative memory) with consequently low cost construction of semiconductor mass memories remains impossible for the present. Nevertheless, the principle retains its attractiveness for database applications, where increasingly large amounts of data have to be searched as efficient as possible.

After it became clear that fully parallel access of the required order of magnitude up to the gigabyte range is not realizable, attempts have been and are being made to develop high performance alternative constructions which, although based on byte serial access, nonetheless attain high processing speed by applying functionally designed hardware and exploiting the possibilities of parallel processing.

All previous considerations in this direction were based on the well-known "logic per track"-ideas of Slotnick (1), who proposed that rotating storage media such as magnetic disks should be furnished with additional logic at each read/write head. Such an environment allows search operations to be performed "on the fly" which means synchronized to the data transfer rate of the disk.

Using sequential searching, i.e. searching without additional reference structures, filtering of raw data can be performed according to the associative access principle, corresponding to a query of varying complexity sent from the central processor to the peripheral store, so that only relevant data have to be transferred into the main memory of the central processor. In this way, pseudo-associative mass storage characteristics can be attained.

In the course of developing hardware components, in particular for sequential searching in structured data sets, a series of aspects has crystallized which must be considered in close connection as they are of decisive importance for the efficient overall performance of a system. This means, especially, the various possibilities of connecting disks and processors (memory/processor interrelationship), synchronous or asynchronous transfer of data, search query complexity and the level of hardware support and its realization using discrete sequential networks or microprocessors (2). All these considerations have to be seen with respect to accelerating well known procedures, whereby both increasing the processing speed by faster integrated circuits and more efficient algorithms, and changing the structures by adapting to algorithms and using multilevel parallelization must be applied.

During the last decade, a lot of proposals for such search devices have been made as individual devices or as part of a database machine (e.g. see (3, 4, 5, 6, 7) and others). Most of the proposals for independent search devices didn't become successful despite of the very promising performance, especially because there was no real interface in existing databases and operating systems. The development of backends for complete database systems, the so-called database machines, which entirely offload the host of this task also suffer from great success. On the one hand there is no real proof of an acceptable cost/performance ratio, on the other hand one has to suppose that with respect to investments in conventional database systems, the idea seems to be too revolutionary. Because of that, the most successful operational areas seem to be non-standard applications. However, falling back on individual search devices, the concept of a data management kernel which was designed by an IBM research group at Böblingen/Germany (8) and which means a definable part of an operating system to be deposited to a backend, offers an excellent interface for additional components. In this way the motivation is given to start the development of a search device once again which in accordance with todays requirements mainly supports filtering of unstructured data. In this paper the basic considerations and implementation of a filter processor (FP) is described.

ENVIRONMENT AND BASIC CONSIDERATIONS

The aim of the development was to get a compact device which was to be connected to given interfaces very easily and without changing the environment. Additionally, in this case the highest priority was not dedicated to a maximum of speed - there was a standard value of about 2 MB/s transfer rate - but with regard to the functionality a maximum of flexibility had been wanted to meet a lot of actual and future applications. Therefore there was no doubt about using a fixed instruction set microprocessor (FIS) for implementing the control hardware which possibly could be supported by peripheral hardware.

First, a short overview of the filter processor's environment and its connection to the other components of the intelligent disk controller (IDC) is given (Fig. 1). For a more detailed description, see (9).

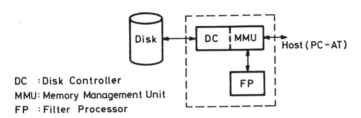

DC : Disk Controller
MMU: Memory Management Unit
FP : Filter Processor

Fig. 1: Overall Structure of the Intelligent Disk Controller (IDC)

Instruction path and data path between host and its mass memory including standard disk control have been cut and completed by additional logic. The hardware essentially encloses the whole memory management of the mass memory offloaded from the host and addressed by high-level and complex I/O-instructions. In addition to that and without any influence to the direct data path, the filter processor is adapted which is accessible only via the mass memory management unit and working asynchronously. Nevertheless, the processing speed is assumed to be fast enough to allow quasi-synchronous data processing.

Task Description and Data Formats

The filter processor as part of the whole intelligent disk controller operates as a coprocessor which executes search queries only. Updating is not allowed, but there is no problem of implementing it later on. Queries are received from the host only. They are supposed to be correct and consist of a header which contains information refering to the data to be processed and a list of pages to be scanned. It is followed by the real search program. Before execution, a query will be translated into an intermediate language (macro instruction set) which is then accepted by the filter processor. By defining search primitives, the target program can be simplified and adapted more easily to changing conditions. While executing the program, the processor demands pages of the file defined for the search in a logical order directly from the mass memory management unit and returns result pages (physical page size is 4K bytes). The last ones are sent to the host or stored in the mass memory, whereby the first mode makes sense only if a low match rate is expected.

According to sequential searching, files of structured data are stored record by record. Especially searching of unstructured data is supported, whereby ASCII - or EBCDIC-characters as well as byte oriented binary data, bit lists and integers of fixed length are allowed.

Query Language Concepts and Algorithms

An essential part of solving the task is the definition of an appropriate pattern matching language which fulfills the requirements of searching unstructured data. This means filtering and classifying raw data with a given amount of patterns which satisfy special syntactical rules. These patterns are recognized by pattern matching algorithms and realized in pure software implementations or by the aid of special hardware devices.

In this way a query consists of a source program in a special LL(1) language which is compiled into the filter processor's macro instruction set. Compared to other languages, such as SNOBOL4 (10), the semantics of the FP procedural language elements for pattern matching and control should meet a relatively low level and lack of high level structures. For special applications, a semantically preserving transformation to this low level interface can be defined.

Each program consists of a data declaration and an instruction part; in this way search arguments are known at compile time. They are restricted to fixed length just as don't cares and variables are. After execution of each instruction it is possible to get an intermediate result which is defined by a special structured data type in the program. A detailed description of the query language is provided for separate publication.

The aim of each pattern matching instruction is to find some kind of regular expressions. Underlaying instruction primitives are the Boyer-Moore algorithm for one single argument and the FSA-algorithm searching various arguments in parallel. Both algorithms had to be adapted to the FP environment. Hardware supported algorithms for pattern matching use a match-RAM as a special hardware device which is loaded with match pattern tables. Software and hardware algorithms are table driven, but each algorithm uses them with different semantics. In this way the Boyer-Moore algorithm uses a search table which contains distances to characters to the right end of the given argument, whereas for the FSA algorithm a state transition table is used. For the hardware supported algorithms the input table contains special match patterns, defining the search result. The runtime behaviour of software algorithms is described in the literature (11), whereas runtime of hardware supported search is a matter of the current evaluation.

The entire software realization is strongly influenced by the hardware available. A monitor program for running all the services just as load, compile, execute and send results is stored in the system's ROM, while the RAM is prepared for monitor's data and tables. The monitor program and compiler are coded in 'C', while the hardware drivers for interfaces and special device control are programmed in Assembler.

FILTER DESIGN

The structure of the filter processor (Fig. 2) was designed in accordance to the specification and interface interaction: A commonly used microprocessor system consisting of CPU, DRAM and ROM is completed by a cache and special hardware for searching bits and bytes in order to support the dedicated tasks. While the DRAM (capacity 128KB) represents memory space for the query consisting of instructions and data, the ROM (capacity 128KB) stores the controlling monitor program. Moreover there exists an instruction interface to the supervising system and an internal data interface to the special hardware. The latter is connected to a fast cache (capacity 32KB) which is randomly accessible by the CPU just as part of the main memory. Both special hardware for byte and bit search (read only) and the mass memory management unit as the

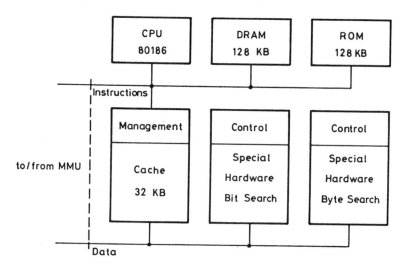

Fig. 2: Overall Structure of the Filter Processor

supervising system (write and read) are allowed to access to the cache. The priority is according to the mentioned order.

After loading a query, the search operation runs as follows: The first data page in logical order is demanded by the filter processor from the mass memory management unit and loaded into the cache. During search operation, it is addressed by a special search counter which is controlled by the CPU. In this way loading and searching can be executed simultaneously.

Selecting the CPU

Because of the provided query complexity, it was not possible to implement a fast sequential network in discrete technique. In contrast to bitslice elements a FIS-microprocessor seemed the better choice with regard to the limited space. It seemed a better idea to spend some special hardware at least in a small scale.

The main task was to select one of the many microprocessors in the market which - with respect to given preconditions - allowed best performance. Instruction set and internal structure, speed and space requirements for additional peripheral devices have been the main criteria, but also compatibility to the environment of the system and the tools available for programming and testing. The runtime of searching a 16/32 bit word (the inmost loop of comparison) finally formed one of the used speed criteria.

The evaluation of various 16-bit microprocessors (68000, 80186, 80286, Z8001) showed that the 68000 owns the largest set of internal registers which means rarely swapping, but all other processors are faster in executing string operations. With respect to 16 bit words Intel's 80286 showed the shortest execution times. Nevertheless, a lot of space is wasted in comparison to the 80186 because of necessary additional hardware. Finally, this microprocessor with a clock frequency of 8 MHz won the race. Because of its integrated DMA-, interrupt- and bus controller and clocking system it allows very compact implementation. The instruction set contains possibilities for processing data strings. There are some disadvantages in contrast to the Z8001-µP with respect to the internal register structure, however, but the compatibility to the Intel-influenced system environment was of decisive importance at last. The decision allowed to save considerable additional hardware in order to adapt the different bus philosophies, too.

Designing Special Hardware

Using special hardware means an essential increase of performance by functional adaptation, but needs extensive space and power. It is applicable over a large varying range and both extremes are using a microprocessor only or a degradation of it as a mere controller, while all processing is done in dedicated hardware. In the filter processor all real processing in the sense of pattern matching functions will be achieved relatively slowly in the CPU. So far no additional logic supporting SPAN, BREAK, LEN(i) a.o. as proposed in (12) is implemented. Instead of it, logic is designed to reduce the raw data stream by filtering as much as possible. Then the small relevant data stream can be qualified and operated further on by slower but higher level procedures. This ideas are especially relevant to unstructured data which have no directly addressable terms like records and fields, but have to be searched completely.

Both operations qualifying bytes and bits of limited length with or without masking are implemented in hardware using their own finite state automaton. Bytes of a file are qualified with one or more arguments up to a length of seven bytes; each byte may be masked, transformed or ignored. The principle is shown in Fig. 3. The kernel of the arrangement is a 256 byte match-RAM containing the state transition table with the byte positions of an argument (1 of 7 bits) and other information.

This match-RAM has to be loaded according to the demanded arguments, where byte positions with ambiguous values must have entry items in various memory words. Arguments of less than seven bytes generate "don't cares" in the remaining positions. The individual bits of the memory words according to the byte positions will be ANDed in a network which - operating similar to a shift register - switches the intermediate match result synchronously to the clock. After all seven bytes have reached a positive intermediate result, the match result is sent to the overlaying system. If an argument is longer than seven bytes, the special hardware stops the procedure and transfers it to the CPU for further processing. There a sequence of simple comparisons is necessary only. The implemented prototype contains a 4 KB match-RAM which means that up to sixteen arguments can be searched simultaneously.

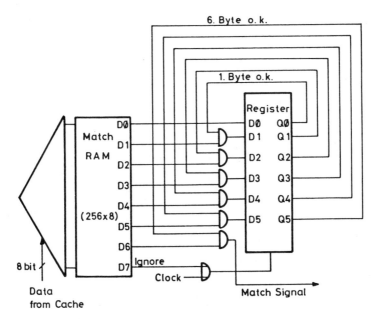

Fig. 3: Principle of Searching Bytes (1 Argument)

The qualification of bit lists allows comparing bit patterns considering all eight bit positions of a byte; various arguments are also allowed. Altogether four different arguments of up to sixteen bits can be searched for, whereby each bit is also allowed to be masked.

The principle of the implemented automaton is shown in Fig. 4. It is comparably simple, because the whole comparison window can be processed in one cycle and no feedback is necessary. Data are read from the cache in double bytes and sent to the match-RAM after passing the shift register as the entrance of the network.

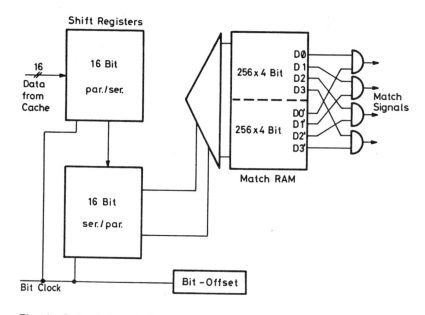

Fig. 4: Principle of Searching Bits (4 Arguments)

Before each comparison cycle, the actual part of the argument is shifted to the next byte position. A four bit-counter handles the bit offset with regard to the match evaluation. The match-RAM (capacity 2 * 256 * 4 bit) contains all data necessary for generating the match results. Its outputs are connected to a simple network which ANDs the final match results of four arguments in parallel (maximum). After sixteen shifts, reloading of the next double byte is necessary. If bit lists which are longer than sixteen bits are to be searched the special hardware is - analogous to the byte comparison - usable only for the beginning of a bit list.

CONCLUSIONS

The present contribution describes an economic solution of a filter processor which can be seen as part of an intelligent disk controller and - placed in a disk pool - is able to form highly parallel and intelligent mass memories with very high transfer rates. Using a microprocessor and asynchronous processing the device in principle allows an extensive functionality needed by complex queries. In spite of the asynchronous processing, the aim was to reach real time behaviour. Details will be found in evaluating the device.

At the time being, the filter processor has been implemented in a PC-AT environment and is being tested as part of the intelligent disk controller shown in Fig. 1. All the logic of the FP containing about one hundred integrated circuits (partially VLSI) needs a power of about 20W. The data interface allows a transfer rate of 2MB/s, the actual burst rate of the used disk is 625 KB/s. Using special hardware searching for bytes is achieved in 2.5 clock cycles in best case, which means a processing rate of 3.2 MB/s (17.5 clock cycles in worst case = 16 arguments in parallel). More detailed measurements of the system performance are under preparation.

ACKNOWLEDGEMENTS

The described filter processor is part of a joint project of IBM Germany and the Technical University of Braunschweig, Germany. Therefore, special thanks are dedicated to the IBM colleagues, J. H. Bleher, H. Diel, G. Kreissig, C. v. Krogh, B. Schoener and H. Weber.

296

Nevertheless the authors would like to thank in particular H. Auer, F. Hildebrandt and H.-O. Leilich for their inhouse support.

REFERENCES

1. Slotnick, D.L. In: Advances in Computers, Vol. 10 (ed.: J. Tou), pp. 291-297, Academic Press 1970
2. Zeidler, H.Ch., Auer, H. In: DBMS, 4th Int. Workshop (ed.: D.J. DeWitt, H. Boral) Springer NY 1985, pp. 347-366
3. Bancilhon, F., Scholl, M.
Proc. SIGMOD 1980, pp. 93-93g
4. Gonzalez-Rubio, R., Rohmer, J., Terral, D.
Proc. 11th Ann. Int. Symp. Comp. Arch. 1984, pp. 64-732
5. Leilich, H.-O., Stiege, G., Zeidler, H.Ch.
Proc. VLDB 1978, pp. 280-287
6. Mitchell, R.W. Proc. IERE Conf. System and Technology, 11/74, pp. 11-18
7. Ozkarahan, E.A., Schuster, S.A., Smith, K.C.
Proc. NCC 1975, pp. 379-387
8. Diel, H., Lenz, N., Kreissig, G., Scheible, M., Schoener, B. Proc. SIGMOD 1986, pp. 58-69
9. Diel, H., Kreyßig, J., Schukat, H., Weber, H., Zeidler, H.Ch. to be published in IBM JRD
10. Griswald, R.E. The SNOBOL4 Programming Language, Prentice Hall, 1971
11. Boyer, R.S., Moore, J.S.
CACM, No. 10, 1977, pp. 762-772
12. Mukhopadhyay, A.
IEEE TOC, Vol. C-28, No. 6, 1979, pp. 384-394

INTELLIGENT STRING SEARCH PROCESSOR
TO ACCELERATE TEXT INFORMATION RETRIEVAL

*K. TAKAHASHI, *H. YAMADA, *H. NAGAI and **M. HIRATA

*Microelectronics Research Lab. NEC Corp.
**System LSI Development Division, NEC Corp.
*1120 Shimokusawa, Sagamihara city, Kanagawa, 229 Japan

ABSTRACT

This paper describes an intelligent string search processor (ISSP) developed for faster text information retrieval and also considers its application system design concept. This ISSP has such string matching functions as anchor/non-anchor, strict/approximate, and fixed-length/variable-length don't-care matching. These functions are indispensable for getting certain given information from a full text search. Each ISSP stores 64 or less variable-length keywords to be compared with a text inputted at 10 million characters per second. A new application system design concept allows this ISSP to accumulate an increased number of user keywords. Though ISSP can always indicate the position at which the keyword appears in the text, text search time is not so short. For this reason, the ISSP is used first to check whether the user's keywords are old or new. If new, it performs a full test search, and an association is established between the keyword position and each ISSP class code output. Consequently, with the increased number of stored keywords that accompanies an increased ISSP storage capacity, it becomes possible to omit most full text scans for faster text search. Accordingly, this ISSP may be used not only for practical text retrieval systems but also for knowledge database systems.

INTRODUCTION

Advances in the use of computer terminals and word processors have resulted in the production of massive amounts of textual information. There has also been an increase in the capacity of the file memory units used to store this information. Most of these units are utilized within index search database management systems.

Such database management systems require text information to be formatted into a structure convenient for retrieval. Data formatting and keyword extraction for an index search are not so quickly accomplished as might be hoped, however, because they depend on slow and expensive manual operations. As a result, unformatted text information continues to increase year by year[1], and conventional database management systems are incapable of the retrieval of most of it. It has been proposed, therefore, to use string search hardware in stead of software index search for text information retrieval[2], but conventional string matching hardware has not been capable of quick text information retrieval[3].

The authors have developed an LSI intelligent string search processor (ISSP) for rapid text information retrieval[4][5]. This ISSP provides many kinds of string matching functions as well as a parallel string search function and thus may be used to produce text retrieval systems in which mistakenly represented keywords are used to locate desired text records.

This paper describes the required string matching functions, old and new string matching hardware architecture, our newly developed LSI chip configuration, its functions, and its application system design concept.

REQUIRED STRING MATCHING FUNCTIONS

Text information consists of character strings. User keywords for information retrieval are also character strings. Text file memory units store many text records comprised of character strings. The text is serially read out from the file memory units, and a search is made of it for user keywords (pattern strings).

String matching is a character string comparison used to locate pattern strings within text strings. Any string comparison for practical text information retrieval requires a number of string matching functions because manually produced texts are likely to contain clerical errors and because user retrieval queries may not be precise.

String search hardware must provide, therefore, the following string matching functions:

(1)　Non-anchor string matching.

(2)　Anchor string matching.

(3)   Fixed-length and variable-length don't-care string matching.

(4)   Strict-string and approximate-string matching.

(5)   Character-masked and bit-masked string matching.

STRING MATCHING HARDWARE ARCHITECTURES IN THE PAST

String matching is very easy for the human brain, but difficult for the conventional computer without sophisticated programs. In response to this, over the past 10 years a large number of string hardware algorithms have come under study.

The typical approaches may be put into 6 categories:

(a)   Software methods such as the KMP method[6] and the BM method[7]. These are well known. As a result of algorithm improvement, each pattern string can be compared with one text during one text scanning period. However, the matching of large numbers of pattern strings is very difficult.

(b)   Sort/Search methods such as CADM[8][9]. These are useful for index searches in database systems. The matching of large numbers of pattern strings can be accomplished within one text scan. Non-anchor string matching and don't-care matching, however, are not possible.

(c)   Associative memory [AM] methods using many comparators, character registers (or content addressable memory [CAM]), and shift registers[10]. These are attractive as high speed parallel string matchers. For storing variable-length pattern strings in the CAM, however, each CAM cell must have a don't-care bit comparison function. As a result, such a CAM cell becomes several times larger than a conventional RAM cell.

(d)   Cellular array [CA] methods consisting of broadcast methods[11][12][13] and systolic array methods[14]. These employ matrices of logic-in-memory cells compatible to VLSI implementation, and high density cellular array logic circuits may be looked to for the performance of many kinds of string matching functions, but current logic-in-memory cells are too large to permit storage of a large number of long pattern strings in a chip.

(e)   Finite state automaton [FSA] methods [15][16][17]. These are useful for detecting long pattern strings with many branch strings. The hardware is simply a state transition table memory whose output is fed back to the address input. This method is, however, not useful for non-anchor string matching.

(f)   Dynamic programming (DP) methods[18][19]. These make it possible to detect proximities between pattern strings and ambiguous texts with misspelled words, but current LSI circuits here are a little complex, permitting only a rather small string storage capacity.

A NEW STRING MATCHING ARCHITECTURE

None of the string matching hardwares of the past can provide all of the string matching functions required for practical text search because it has been impossible with conventional string matching hardware architecture to increase the string matching functions in a single LSI chip.

In general, a string has two aspects. The first aspect is the set of characters contained in the string. The second aspect is the occurrence sequence of matching characters. String matching hardware in the past has been intended to process simultaneously character comparison and sequence comparison. This has increased the difficulty of applying it to a variety of complex kinds of string matching comparison.

Our new hardware architecture divides string matching into two processes; i.e., character comparison and sequence comparison. Character comparison can be easily accomplished with the same content addressable memory [CAM] as that used in AM methods. Sequence comparison can be easily done by a sequential logic circuit (SLC) with the same state transition design as that in the FSA method.

Thus, since the circuit structure is simple, the sequential logic circuit can be easily expanded to implement the state transition diagram of FSA for approximate string matching.

Figure 1 shows the basic string matching hardware structure of the ISSP. This hardware consists of the CAM, the SLC, and the priority encoder. After several pattern strings have been sequentially stored in the CAM, a text string is inputted serially character by character into the CAM. Each input character of the text string is parallel compared with all characters stored in the CAM. All character comparison results are input to the SLC. The SLC checks the occurrence sequence of character matching signals 1 or 0 coming from the CAM based on the FSA method.

Figure 2 is a FSA state transition diagram for strict string matching. It shows the process of string matching by flag bit transfer. The flag bit on the i-th node of the state transition diagram indicates a matching signal for

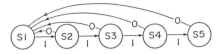

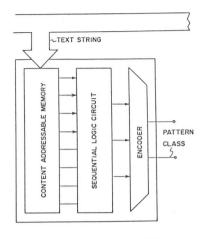

Figure 2 State transition diagram of
FSA for strict string
matching

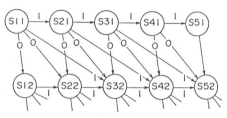

Figure 1 String matching
hardware concept

Figure 3 State transition diagram of
FSA for approximate string
matching

a character string ranging from the 1-st to (i-1)-th characters of the pattern string. Therefore, if the flag bit state on the i-th node is expressed by $S_i(t)$ and the character match signal for i-th node is expressed by $y_i(t)$,

$$S_1(t) = 1$$
$$S_i(t) = y_i(t) \times S_{i-1}(t-1) \qquad \ldots (1)$$

where $\times$ means a logical product [AND operation], and

$$y_i(t) = 1 \qquad \text{if } X(t) = X_i \qquad \ldots (2)$$
$$y_i(t) = 0 \qquad \text{if } X(t) \neq X_i \qquad \ldots (3)$$

The last node S_5, then, indicates that a string $X_1X_2X_3X_4$ was accepted.

The state transition diagram in Fig. 3 shows that nondeterministic FSA allows one character error in approximate string matching. In addition to state nodes S_{11}, S_{21}, S_{31}, S_{41}, S_{51} for exact string matching, nodes S_{12}, S_{22}, S_{32}, S_{42}, S_{52} are provided for approximate matching. That is, when a character mismatch is found, the flag bit will not immediately be returned to the start node S_{11} but will be held at either S_{12}, S_{22}, S_{32}, S_{42} or S_{52}. Therefore, a string with one character different will be accepted at the final column node S_{52}. If one more row of nodes S_{13}, S_{23}, S_{33}, S_{43}, S_{53} are added, a string with two differing characters will be accepted at node S_{53}.

Figure 4 String search processor
LSI

Figure 5 Photomicrograph
of ISSP LSI chip

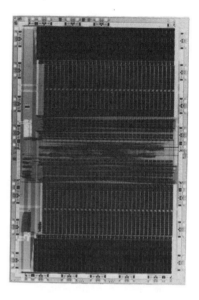

In general with to this architecture, strings with many characters differing can be handled. If the flag bit state at the i-th column and j-th row node is expressed by $S_{ij}(t)$,

$$S_{ij}(t) = y_i(t) \times S_{i-1j}(t-1) + y_i(t) \times S_{i-2j-1}(t-1) + y_i(t) \times S_{i-1j-1}(t-1) + y_i(t+1) \times S_{ij-1}(t-1)$$

where + means a logical sum [OR operation].

AN LSI CIRCUIT FOR APPROXIMATE STRING SEARCH

Figure 4 shows an intelligent string search processor LSI chip housed in a 72-pin standard pingrid-array package whose size is 2.8×2.8 cm. Figure 5 shows a photomicrograph of the ISSP LSI chip containing 217,600

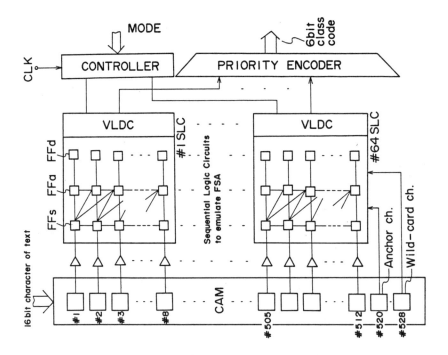

Figure 6   Blockdiagram of ISSP

transistors in an 8.62 by 12.76 mm die area. This chip was developed using
1.6μm dual-metal-layer CMOS technology. The ISSP LSI chip is operated
at 10 MHz[4]. This means that the chip can search a text at 10 Mch/sec.

This chip consists of an 8 kilobit CAM [content addressable memory]
and a 22 kilogate SLC [sequential logic circuit]. Figure 6 is a blockdiagram
of the chip. In this circuit configuration, the CAM outputs matching
character signals in parallel to the SLC as each character code is input.
Each SLC controls flag bit transfers on the register matrix using the
matching character signals. 64 SLCs, each of which checks a sequence of
eight or less characters in a string, are serially connected for variable-
length string comparison.

Let us describe the circuit configurations in more detail. The CAM
can store 16 bit×512 characters as pattern strings and can store 16 bit×16
special characters anchor and wild-card characters. The memory cell

matrix, therefore, contains a total of 8448 CAM cells or 4224 pair-bit CAM cells. Each pair-bit CAM cell employs four static RAM cells and can store don't-care bits [4].

A 16 bit character code is stored in 8 pair-bit CAM cells connected with wired AND logic. These CAM cells can be also used to store don't-care characters of fixed-length don't-care (FLDC) strings.

The SLC design is based on a nondeterministic finite state automaton (NFSA). That is, each state node of NFDS is comprised of a FFs and a FFa flip-flop, and each node connection line is comprised of AND gates.

Each SLC contains 3 rows by 8 columns of flip-flops. The flip-flop FFs on the first row are used for strict string matching. The 2nd row flip-flop FFa's are used for approximate string matching. The 3rd row flip-flop FFd's are provided for delimiter signal storage. The 1st column FFs is set to "1" if the corresponding CAM output is "1".

Variable length pattern strings are stored sequentially from the left toward the right, as seen in Fig. 6. The last character position of the pattern string is assigned by delimitter signal "1" of the corresponding FFd. The upper character position of the next string is always assigned the delimitter signal "1" of the 1st FFd in the next SLC.

A variable length don't care (VLDC) circuit between all of the SLC's and the encoder has a FFv flip-flop. If the content of the FFv is set to "1", the partial string matching signal is not output to the encoder and is used to set flag bit "1" to the 1st FFs of the next SLC. If the content of the FFv is "0", the partial string match signal is output to the encoder.

ISSP LSI CHIP FUNCTIONS

This LSI chip provides a number of string matching functions for actual text search. These functions are illustrated in Table 1~8. The top row shows an input text example. The column on the left gives examples of pattern strings stored in the CAM part of the ISSP. String match periods are indicated by solid lines in the table. The right end point of each solid line indicates the point at which signal matching was completed. The ISSP matching function is selected by giving mode signals when pattern strings are registered in the ISSP.

Table 1 Non-anchor matching mode

Text \ Pattern	ABCDEFGHIJKLMNABCD	Match signal	Class code
ABCD		11	30
CDEFG		1	1
HIJKLMN		1	2
BC		11	30

Table 2 Anchor matching mode

Text \ Pattern	ABCD EFG HIJKLMN AB CDEFG	Match signal	Class code
ABCD			
CDEFG			
HIJKLMN			
BCD		1	2
		1	0

Table 3 FLDC matching mode

Text \ Pattern	ABCDE35HIJKLMNABGDH39H	Match signal	Class code
AB?D		1	0
E??H		1	1
H2???M		1	2
2?H		11 1	03 3

Table 4 VLDC matching mode

Text \ Pattern	ABCDEFGHIJKLMNABCD	Match signal	Class code
ABC~EF		11	30
DEFG~KLM		1	1
AB~EF~LM			
A~D		1	3

Table 5 Approximate matching mode

Text \ Pattern	database system programmers	Match signal	Class code
database		1	0
data-base			
datebase			
programer		1,	3

Table 6 Masked string matching mode

Text \ Pattern	ABC?E?GHI??LMNA?C??	Match signal	Class code
ABCD		1	0
EFG		1	1
HIJKLM		1.1	3 2
GHIJK		1	0

Table 7 Masked code string matching mode

Text \ Pattern	1987 日本電気DataBaseマネジメント	match signal	Class code
DATABASE		1	3
日本電気		1	1
マネジメント		1	0
198?		1	2

Table 8 Multi-string matching mode

Text \ Pattern	VLSI memory based database	Match signal	Class code
VLSI		1	0/1
LSI			
database		1	3
base		1	2/3

FULL TEXT SEARCH APPLICATION

The 8 types of ISSP string matching modes (seen in Tables 1~8) are convenient for such full text search as technical article retrieval or patent document retrieval. Since a full text search system aims at finding desired text records by direct string comparison from all of the text, it is important to enhance text search speed.

The ISSP LSI chip can accept a text stream at 10 M characters per second. About 640 newspaper pages can be searched within 1 second. An ISSP chip can store 64 pattern strings when each user keyword is shorter than 8 characters. In this case, 64 keywords are simultaneously compared with the input text stream. Stored pattern string length can be as great as 512 characters, but then number of stored pattern strings per chip will decrease accordingly.

· Figure 7 shows a diagram of the basic application system. The ISSP is used to store user keywords. A data file contains many text records. These text records are transferred from the data file into the ISSP, where a full text search is carried out. Any text records matched are sequentially displayed or printed out after the full text search.

Figure 8 is an example of the display of a possible matching text record in Fig. 7. Matching text strings are underlined. The pattern strings were "NEC", "ISSP", a speed~per second", and "1.?μm,~CMOS".

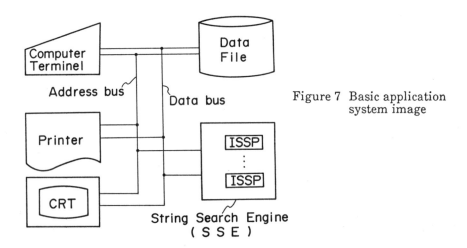

Figure 7 Basic application system image

NEC has developed an intelligent string search processor(ISSP) capable of scanning for misspelled or incorrect words and character compounds at a speed of 640 newspaper pages per second. ·On the display panel of PC98XA system, the perfectly matched, approximately matched and partially matched words and compounds are shown in red, blue, and yellow, respectively.

The ISSP was developed using 1.6um dual-metal-layer CMOS technology. The LSI chip of the ISSP has 217,000 transisters in a die area of 8.62 x12.76mm. The chip consists of an 8-kilo bit content-addressable memory and a 20-kilo gate sequential logic circuit.

Figure 8   Example of matched text

In full text information retrieval systems, the response time is taken up by the text input time. Text input time depends on input speed and text length, and it is limited by the string matching speed rather than the data transfer rate on the 1/0 bus. The ISSP can accept text at 10 Mch/sec because the string matching speed and matching functions have been that greatly much enhanced. Even when text length ranges up to 1 giga characters, input time may be as short as 100 sec.

Additionally, 1 ISSP chip can store a large number of keywords to be simultaneously compared with the input text. Text search processing capability increases with keyword storage capacity because a number of string matching operations may be conducted in parallel during a single text scanning period.

The ISSP can be used to reduce the frequency of full text search repetition, i.e., the number of times that search querries using the same keywords. By using the ISSP, after a full text search, each matched keyword can be assigned a matching text record address. Therefore, when the relationship between the keywords and the text record addresses are accumulated in ISSP and RAMs, later full text searches can be omitted.

Figure 9 shows a system configuration for reducing this full text search repeat-frequency. The output of the ISSP designates the address of RAM 1. RAM 1 outputs the scan address range of RAM 2, which stores the

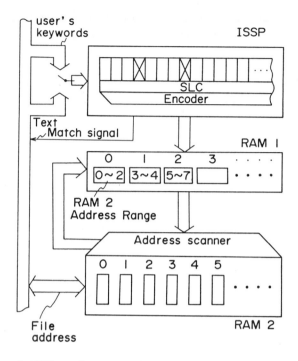

Figure 9 SSE configuration for reduced repeat frequency in full
text search

matched text record addresses sequentially. Therefore, if new keywords
match old keywords stored in the ISSP, matching text-record-addresses for
the new keywords are directly output from RAM 2 without executing full
text search operations.

Only when input keywords don't match old keywords is a full text
search executed. The new keywords thus obtained are added to the old
keywords in the ISSP. As the store of keywords increases, therefore, total
full text search times are reduced (to less than half when the hit ratio
increases to greater than 0.5).

Finally, the ISSP can be applied to AI systems. That is to say, this LSI
chip can be used in problem solving to seek required information from texts.
With conventional knowledge database systems, knowledge data must be
filed in forms, e.q. that based on the if-then rule, which are convenient for
access from inference machines. This data formatting must be done by
manual operations which are as slow as those for conventional data-base
systems. Therefore, it has been difficult to make practical knowledge
database systems.

In order to accelerate knowledge database construction speed, it is important to minimize manual data formatting operations. This may be done by using ISSPs in such a way that the knowledge data may be extracted directly from the text. The full text search system shown in Fig. 9 is useful for extracting knowledge by a learning process. Approximate string, don't-care string, and wild card string matching functions are convenient for actual text search. The text must, of course, describe comprehensible knowledge data.

In general, as VLSI technology continues its remarkable progress, the keyword storage capacity of the ISSP may be expected to increase still more. CAM capacity will reach 1 Mbit soon. As that happens, it will become possible to accumulate more user keywords in LSI chips, in which case we may expect a great expansion of the range of future ISSP applications.

CONCLUSION

This paper has described string matching hardware architecture, a newly developed intelligent string search processor [ISSP] LSI circuit configuration, ISSP functions, and its application systems.

The new string matching hardware architecture was developed by dividing the string matching process into character comparison and sequence comparison processes. With this division, the string search LSI chip may be produced with a content addressable memory and sequential logic circuit. The resultant LSI chip here has 8 types of string matching functions, including anchor/non-anchor, strict/approximate, FLDC/VLDC, masking, and multimatch. This LSI chip stores 64 keywords to be concurrently compared with the input text and is operated at 10 Mch/sec.

Many string matching functions and fast text search processing operations accelerate full text database system speed. As the input text length is increased, however, full text search time will be very long. Therefore, the authors have proposed an application system design concept to minimize full text scans. With this concept, the ISSP is used to accumulate user keywords. That is to say, user keywords are first input into the ISSP to be placed into the category of either "old" or "new." Second, new keywords are stored in the ISSP and full text search is done. The result of the search with the new keywords is stored in the RAM.

Third, when the input keywords are classified as "old", results may be learned using the RAM without carrying out a full text scan. Therefore, as user keywords stored in the ISSP increase, new keywords decrease, and the number of full text scans becomes smaller and smaller. By using this method of application, it is expected that the ISSP may be used to extract knowledge data at higher speeds directly from texts. What is needed now is to confirm the effectiveness of this application system.

AKNOWLEDGEMENT

The authors thank K. Ayaki, H. Shiraki, M. Ohta, T. Enomoto, K. Matumi, N. Chiba, and M. Yamamoto for their encouragement of this research and development effort. They also express their gratitude to K. Sugibuti, N. Yoshida, S. Itoh, and Y. Hiki for their support of ISSP LSI development.

REFERENCE

1. D. Lee & F. Lochovsky, Sec. 14 of 'OFFICE AUTOMATION' -Concepts and Tools-, Springer-Verlag, 1985.
2. L.A. Hollaar, 1979 IEEE, COMPUTER, pp. 40-50, 1979.
3. C. Faloutsos, Computing Surveys, Vol. 17(1), pp. 49-74, March, 1985.
4. H. Yamada, M. Hirata, H. Nagai & K. Takahashi, Technical Digest of ISSCC'87, FAM20.2, Feb., 1987.
5. K. Takahashi, H. Yamada, H. Nagai & K. Matumi, COMPUTER ARCHITECTURE NEWS, Vol. 14(2), pp. 20-27, June, 1986.
6. D.E. Knuth, J.H. Morris, Jr. & V.R. Pratt, SIAM J. Computer, 6(2), pp. 323-350, June, 1977.
7. R.S. Boyer and J.S. Moore, Comm. of the ACM, 20(10), pp. 762-772, Oct., 1977.
8. M. Segal, Electronic Design, pp. 85-91, June 26, 1986.
9. D.E. Knuth, The Art of Computer Programming. Vol.13, Searching and Sorting, Reading MA: Addison-Wisley, 1973.
10. F.J. Burkowski, IEEE Trans. on Computers, C31(9), pp. 825-834, Sep., 1982.
11. L.A. Hollaar, W.H. Stellhorn, Proc. of NCC'77, pp. 697-702, 1977.
12. A. Mukhopadhyay, ICCC'80, pp. 508-511, 1980.
13. A. Mukhopadhyay, Sec. 4 of 'Hardware And Software Concepts in VLSI', Edited by G. Robbat, Van Nostrand Reinhold Company, 1983.
14. M.J. Foster and H.T. Kung, IEEE COMPUTER, 13(1) pp. 26-40, Jan., 1980.
15. A.V. Aho and M.J. Corasick Comm. of the ACM, 18(6), pp. 333-340, June, 1975.
16. R.L. Haskin, SIGIR, Vol. 15(2), pp. 49-56, March, 1980.
17. R.L. Haskin, Database Engineering, 4(1), pp. 16-29, Sep., 1981.
18. P.A.V. Hall and G.R. Dowling, Computing Surveys, Vol. 12(4), pp. 381-402, Dec. 1980.
19. P.N. Yianilos, Electronics, pp. 113-117, Dec. 1983.

The Silicon Database Machine: Rationale, Design, and Results

Mary Diane Palmer Leland

Bell Communications Research
Morristown, New Jersey 07960

William D. Roome

AT&T Bell Laboratories
Murray Hill, New Jersey 07974

ABSTRACT

This paper discusses the design of the Silicon Database Machine. We show how the decisions to store the entire database in main memory and to use off-the-shelf components influenced the design of the machine, and how these decisions led to a database system that is fast, easy to implement, and easy to port to new hardware.

1. INTRODUCTION

The Silicon Database Machine (SiDBM) [11,12] is a multiprocessor, silicon memory, backend relational database machine. This paper discusses the design of the machine, the rationale behind the design decisions, and the results of implementing and testing the machine. The design started from the premise that large, non-volatile silicon memory will soon be available. Given that premise, we investigated how such memory could be used to build a backend database machine that is fast, flexible, and easy to implement.

The next section discusses the overall design of the SiDBM, concentrating on how the decision to use only main memory influenced the design. The next two sections describe the details of the processors in the SiDBM. Finally, we give performance results for various versions of the machine, and present our conclusions.

2. DESIGN DECISIONS

We had two basic requirements when designing the SiDBM. First, we insisted that it allow multiple concurrent queries, with a long-running complex query not blocking a simple one. And second, we wanted to have good response for updates. Thus we rejected any design which only allowed one query to run at a time, or any design which was optimized for retrieval at the expense of update.

2.1 Why Not A Cache Or A RAM-Disk?

Two of the obvious ways to use a large silicon memory in a backend database machine are in a large cache for a magnetic disk, or in a "silicon disk"—a disk-like storage device which uses silicon memory instead of rotating magnetic memory. An advantage is that this approach would require little, if any, change to existing database software.

However, that is the only advantage. Disks have two problems: one is that it takes a long time to access the data, and the other is that data must be accessed in large blocks. Caches and silicon disks may solve the speed problems, but they still have the block-oriented interface of a disk. Much of the complexity in disk-based database systems is devoted to disk and cache management. Consider the amount of literature devoted to managing disks and packing related data into the same disk block: clustering and indexing techniques, disk scheduling algorithms, caching methods, coping with variable delays in data access times, etc.

These techniques are incidental to the real job of a database machine, which is to store, manipulate, and retrieve application data—not disk blocks. Although a large cache or a silicon disk would speed up a database system, the system would still require software for dealing with disk blocks, clustered indices, and variable retrieval times.

Instead of using the silicon memory to mimic a disk, we felt that it would be more effective to treat the silicon memory as "main memory": a flat storage space, shared by several processors. Any processor can read any data at any time, with no appreciable delay. For example, records can be placed anywhere, and can be read and written individually. As a result, indexing, placement, locking, and access time estimation are much easier than in a disk-based system.

2.2 What Else Besides Large Memory?

A backend database machine not only stores data, but also communicates with its host computer(s) and does relational operations on its data. It also must schedule and manage its own tasks and resources. The SiDBM has multiple processors which are functionally specialized in software to perform these tasks. Each processor has its own local memory and can access the global database memory. The processors are:

- One or more Relation Managers (RMs), which are responsible for the storage of the relations, concurrency control, and crash recovery.

- One or more Query Processors (QPs), which do the high-level processing needed to answer a query, by performing relational database primitives [15].

- A Query Manager (QM), which orchestrates the actions of the RMs and QPs.

- One or more host interfaces (HIs), which communicate with the outside world.

Except for the QM, there can be one or more of each processor type. The mix of processor types can be adjusted to match the expected workload of the machine.

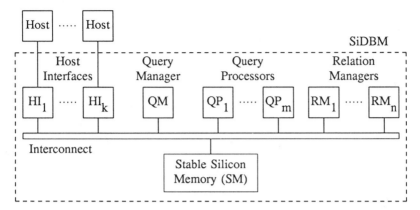

Figure 1: Logical structure of the Silicon Database Machine.

2.3 Logical Design

Figure 1 gives the logical structure of the SiDBM. The upper rectangles are computers, each with its own local memory. The HI processors can also have devices. The Stable Memory (SM) is directly addressable by all the processors. The SM holds relation data, and nothing else. Instruction text, stacks, and local data all reside in each processor's local memory, and can be accessed without using the common interconnect, keeping the interconnect from being a bottleneck.

The host connections can be anything from simple communications lines, to local area network connections, to direct connections from the host's bus to the SiDBM interconnect. The program running on the HI (or on the host) translates host-oriented queries into the format expected by the QM, and translates the results back. The QM decomposes each query into a set of primitive operations, which it assigns to the QPs and RMs. Each RM acts as the gatekeeper for a set of relations, and handles simple retrieval and update operations, and provides concurrency control and recovery. The QPs handle all other query processing operations.

In general, processors exchange pointers to records in the SM, rather than passing records themselves. Thus when asked to retrieve a set of records, an RM returns a set of pointers. A QP or HI can then access those records like ordinary data.

2.4 Tasking Kernel and Inter-Processor Communication

The software in each processor is structured as a set of tasks. A multitasking kernel, called the CTK [14], multiplexes the processor among those tasks, and allows tasks to communicate via shared memory and interrupts. Tasks are dynamic: the CTK allows tasks to be created and destroyed. The CTK is independent of the SiDBM, and hides the hardware details from the SiDBM software. This structuring of the SiDBM software has proved to be very useful. For example, it allows the QPs to be structured as a set of tasks, one per basic operation, and simplifies task creation and communication. Furthermore, porting the SiDBM to a new processor only involves porting the CTK.

The basic inter-task communication provided by the CTK is a "stream," which is a buffer in shared memory with a producer-consumer protocol implemented in a function package. Any task which knows the address of a stream can put data into it or get data from it. For example, an RM can produce a stream of record pointers which are read by a task in a QP. This stream interconnect has been easy to use, and makes it easy to create arbitrary networks of query processing primitives.

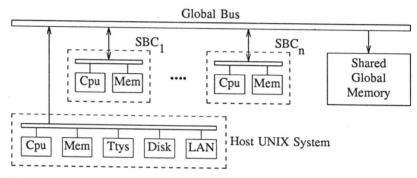

Figure 2: Physical structure of the Silicon Database Machine.

2.5 Physical Design

Figure 2 gives the physical organization of the current SiDBM hardware. The interconnect is an industry standard bus (VMEbus), the processors are off-the-shelf single board computers (SBCs), and we use ordinary memory boards for the shared memory. Currently we have five AT&T 32100-based single board computers, each with one megabyte of local, on-board memory [1], and 64 megabytes of shared memory (four 16 megabyte boards). The local memory on the processors is "dual ported", in that it can be read or written by other processors on the bus.

These boards are plugged into the VMEbus backplane of a Sun workstation, which runs the UNIX[TM] operating system. Programs running on this UNIX system, or on any other system on the local area network, can use the SiDBM. The VMEbus address space—the shared memory and the processors' local memories—is an extension of the host's local bus, and can be read and written by programs running on the host. Thus the host UNIX system also acts as a debugger and a monitor.

2.6 Experience and Rationale

Our decision to use standard hardware has proved very useful. It allowed us to get the hardware set up within a few months, and to concentrate on the problem of building the software instead of building the hardware. It also allowed us to upgrade as new hardware products became available. For example, our original system had 68000-based computers with 128 kilobytes of on-board memory, and 512 kilobyte shared memory boards. Our current system has processors which are about four times faster and have eight times the local memory, and has shared memory boards which are 32 times denser and are almost three times faster. We were able to move from one system to the other by porting the CTK, with little change to the other SiDBM software.

The decision to use a UNIX host with a direct bus connection was also very helpful. With the local area network connection, we can run the SiDBM from any machine in our local network, without needing physical access to the hardware. In fact, the backplane and boards are tucked away in a corner, and are rarely touched. The UNIX host lets us run some sophisticated monitoring tools, such as a program which monitors processor-busy and number of tasks for each of the SiDBM processors, while using the SiDBM.

The SiDBM software is written in the C programming language [8], and tasking is provided by CTK functions. An alternative would be to write the SiDBM in Concurrent C [3,6], an extension of C which provides tasking facilities at a language level. When we started on the SiDBM, Concurrent C was still in its early stages of development, and did not exist on our multiprocessor system. Since then, the Concurrent C language has stabilized, and an implementation now exists on the multiprocessor. We are considering revising the SiDBM to use Concurrent C. We think this would greatly simplify some of the software administrative details, such as setting up the network of tasks and interconnecting streams for a query.

3. THE RELATION MANAGERS

This section describes how the RMs operate, and describes the reasons behind our major design decisions. For additional details on RM operation, see [11].

3.1 Basic Description

The RMs provide transaction start, commit, and abort requests, as well as select (read) and update (write) requests. The RMs guarantee that transactions are serializable, and that commits are atomic and permanent [7]. After a crash, the RMs abort any active, uncommitted transactions. A transaction can span several RMs, in which case those RMs cooperate at transaction start and commit time to ensure serializability, atomicity, and permanence. Otherwise, each RM operates independently.

Each RM is the gatekeeper for a set of relations. An administrator (human or software) assigns each relation to one RM, and also partitions the available stable memory among the set of RMs. A client (QP or QM) directs a select or update request for a relation to the RM which owns that relation. Normally the QM hides this partitioning from the end user and/or host software; the host just specifies a relation, and the QM determines the RM.

For a select request, a client specifies a transaction, a relation, a stream, and a search expression consisting of a boolean combination of range restrictions on single fields. The RM uses that stream to return pointers to all records in that relation which match that expression. The client can use those pointers to access those records for the duration of the transaction.

If one of the fields in a search expression is indexed, the RM uses that index to locate the records. Because the RM uses binary tree indexes, the records are returned in ascending order on that field. If the search expression involves several indexed fields, the client can choose the sort order by specifying which index to use. Otherwise the RM decides which index to use. If the search expression does not involve any indexed fields, the RM tests all records in the relation.

For updates, clients do *not* directly modify records. Instead, a client first creates a new version, and then sends an update request to the RM, specifying the relation, a pointer to the current version of the record (as returned by an earlier select request), and a pointer to that new version. The RM copies the new version into stable memory, and arranges for that version to become current if and when the transaction commits. Subsequent select requests for that transaction will return a pointer to the new version.

3.2 Why Separate Relation Managers?

A fundamental design decision was to have separate RM processors, with each RM serving as the sole manager of a set of relations. All access to those relations must be mediated by that RM. This organization has several disadvantages. First, the RM in charge of a relation could become a bottleneck. Second, for a retrieval on a non-indexed field, one RM does all the work; the other RMs and QPs are idle. Third, some administrator (human or otherwise) must decide where to place each relation, and must decide how many RMs and QPs to put in the system. In spite of these disadvantages, we choose this organization because we feel that it has a number of advantages over the alternatives. To see why, consider the alternative organizations.

One alternative is to slice each relation into pieces, and assign a piece to each RM, allowing the RMs to work on a relation in parallel. However, this ''slice'' alternative requires substantial coordination between RMs, which will lead to additional overhead. For example, a select request on an indexed field will involve all the RMs. Furthermore, we expect that most databases will have many relations, and the accesses will be reasonably distributed among those relations. We do not expect the majority of references to be to one relation.

In short, we feel that the ''slice'' organization would only perform better if most queries were non-indexed retrievals from one relation. Otherwise the overhead of coordinating the RMs would outweigh any advantage of this organization. If desired, the QM could use such an organization for certain relations. The QM would do the slicing, and would keep a piece on each RM. The RMs would not know that these relations logically formed one relation.

Another alternative is to combine the QP and RM functions into each processor. Thus instead of having separate QP and RM *processors,* we would have QP and RM *layers* within each processor. The advantage would be that any processor could operate on any relation, so no one processor would become a bottleneck. Furthermore, the administrator would not have to assign relations to RMs, or decide how many RMs vs. QPs to have in a system.

However, in this alternative the RM layer becomes much more complex, and could be much slower. The RM layer has a lot of private, low-level data: indexes, free storage lists, etc. With the combined QP/RM alternative, that low-level data would be shared, and each RM layer would lock it to ensure that no other RM layer is modifying it. With our organization, each RM processor has its own set of internal data. Since the RM processor has only one task, it can access or update that data any time it wants to; no other processor can modify it. Thus we don't have the overhead of acquiring locks, or the complexity of determining when to acquire locks. Additional advantages of our organization are that it provides a clean decomposition into QP and RM components, and it simplifies testing and debugging. Only one RM can update any given section of the stable memory, and we use the memory-mapping hardware to enforce this restriction; a QP or another RM cannot do a wild store into stable memory.

To evaluate the relative performance of these two organizations, first consider a system with many concurrent update queries. In our organization, the RMs for those relations could become a bottleneck. But the alternative organization also has bottlenecks: each update request requires exclusive access to various shared data structures. The result is that for updates, neither organization is clearly superior to the other.

The only case in which the combined alternative has a clear advantage is for concurrent read-only queries which access the same relation and which do very little processing. With our organization, all the queries must go through that relation's RM, while with the alternative organization, each processor can access the relation data in parallel. However, if the queries require much additional processing of the data, this processing can be done in parallel on different QPs. If the concurrent read-only queries are to different relations, then the relative performance depends on how the relations have been assigned to RMs. If they are on different RMs, the two organizations are roughly equivalent; if they are all on the same RM, the combined alternative may be better.

Thus if we assume that updates are frequent, it appears that the two organizations give roughly the same degree of concurrency. We decided to use separate RM and QP processors because that approach had a simpler internal structure and greater robustness.

3.3 Single RM Concurrency Control

Within each RM, we use a modified form of optimistic concurrency control [10,13]. The RM allows a transaction to commit if and only if, at commit-time, every record read by that transaction is still current in the database. The modification is that the RM ensures that each transaction sees a consistent snapshot of the database, as of the time the transaction started.

The RM uses a versioning mechanism to implement this concurrency scheme. Each record has a current version, linked with zero or more old versions and new versions. The new versions are the updates for uncommitted transactions. Normally there is at most one new version for each record; if there is more than one, then only one of those transactions will be able to commit. The old versions are kept as long as they are needed to ensure that each transaction sees a consistent image of the database as of the time the transaction started. When a transaction commits, the RM atomically changes all new versions written by that transaction into current versions, and changes all current versions into old versions. The RM automatically frees old versions when they are no longer needed. Thus if there are no active transactions, there are no old or new versions.

The advantages of the optimistic concurrency control scheme are uniform response time for requests, and simplification of the RM internals. These advantages compensate for the disadvantages of transaction interference, and the extra space for the multiple versions. In particular, a conventional locking scheme prevents an RM from running a request to completion. When the RM encounters a locked record, it would have to suspend that request and run another one. This complicates the internals of the RM. A big advantage of silicon memory over disk memory is that with silicon memory, the RM can access any data at any time, and can run an operation until it reaches a natural stopping point. A conventional record locking scheme takes away that advantage.

3.4 Multiple RM Concurrency Control

A global transaction is one which spans more than one of the RMs in the SiDBM. For such transactions, the RMs use a two-phase commit protocol [7] to ensure that either all the RMs commit the transaction or else they all abort it.

For two-phase commit to work with optimistic locking, all the RMs must validate the global transactions in the same order. We do that by having one central controller task which performs the two-phase commit protocol. All commit requests for global transactions are sent to the controller task, which then sends "prepare to commit" commands to all RMs, and waits for their replies. When an RM receives this command, it validates the transaction. If successful, the RM sends a "succeeded" reply to the controller, and then waits for the controller's next command. If not successful, the RM sends an "abort" reply. Note that an RM will not accept normal requests until the controller completes the protocol. If all RMs reply successfully, the controller sends a "commit" command to each RM; if not, it sends an "abort" command. To ensure that all RMs start global transactions in the same order, all start requests for global transactions are also sent to the controller task, which forwards the request to each RM. The controller is involved only when starting or committing a global transaction. Select or update operations for global transactions are sent directly to the desired RM.

This scheme has two potential performance problems. One is that there is only one controller task, so it could become a bottleneck. The other is that each RM freezes, unable to accept other requests, until all RMs have validated the transaction. But these problems are not as significant in the SiDBM as they would be in a loosely-coupled, disk-based system. Interprocessor communication uses shared memory, and is very fast. RMs validate transactions very quickly; it takes only a few microseconds for each record that the transaction read. Also, commands from the controller have priority over other requests to the RMs. Thus there is no long delay between the two phases of the protocol, and the controller has not been a bottleneck.

3.5 Indexing and Keys

The RM uses a height-balanced binary tree for each indexed field [9]. We feel that for a silicon memory database, height-balanced binary trees are preferable to B-trees [4]. Both take roughly $\log_2 n$ comparisons, where n is the number of records in the relation. The B-tree rebalancing algorithm is simpler, but it requires rewriting an entire block. That rewriting doesn't matter in a disk-based system, but it does with silicon memory. The result is that the block-oriented properties of B-trees are very useful for a disk-based system, but are not as useful with silicon memory.

Binary trees allow the RM to handle "range" queries, and allow the RM to return records in field order. Because the QM and QPs take advantage of these features, the RM should provide binary tree indexes. The RM could also offer hashed indexes, as an administrative option, but we have not yet implemented them.

Note that the RM does not have the notion of storage order for a relation. As a result, the RM does not have "primary" or "clustered indexes" versus "secondary indexes"; it just has indexes. Index retrieval time is only a function of the number of distinct values of the indexed field.

The RM does not have the concept of a "key" as a set of fields whose value must be unique for each record. The RM could enforce such a notion, but that would be purely artificial, and only for the application's convenience. At this point, we have not added such a feature.

4. THE QUERY MANAGER AND QUERY PROCESSORS

This section describes the operation of the QPs and QM, and the rationale for the design decisions. Additional details on these processors are presented in [12].

4.1 Query Processors

Each QP performs the primitives of relational algebra [15]. These primitives are connected by streams. In general, each primitive produces one output stream to another primitive, and has one or two input streams from other primitives. The primitives use the streams to exchange pointers to database records, instead of sending the records themselves. The relational primitives include selection on fields within a record, duplicate removal, aggregate, (equi-)join, and sort. Other primitives could easily be implemented using the paradigms established for the chosen ones. The HI gets pointers to records, extracts the desired fields, and transmits those to the host. Thus the QPs do not need a project primitive (as distinct from duplicate removal).

Primitives use streams to exchange logical records. A logical record contains one or more pointers to database records, plus some optional immediate values. The format of logical records on a stream is determined when the stream is created, and the sender and receiver agree on it. For example, consider a join whose inputs are simple selects from the database. A logical record in each input stream is just a single record pointer. However, a logical record in the join's output stream consists of a pair of record pointers, one for each matching record. The primitive that gets that stream as input knows that each logical record is the concatenation of those two records.

Each primitive runs as a separate task, and the multi-tasking kernel multiplexes each processor among that processor's tasks. For example, if a QP is executing one select primitive and two sorts, that processor will have three separate tasks. The kernel handles the task scheduling.

4.2 Primitive Operations

This section summarizes the techniques we have used to implement the primitives. The select primitive has one input stream and one output stream. It gets the next logical record from the input, and tests whether that record satisfies the selection criteria. If so, it places that logical record on the output stream. If not, the select primitive "discards" the input record, by failing to output it.

The sort primitive stores the logical records in an array in local memory, and caches (part of) the major sort field in that array. It then sorts the array on the required fields, and outputs the pointers in the sorted array.

The duplicate removal primitive ensures that its output records have unique values for some set of fields. We use two strategies for this primitive. If the input is sorted by the fields on which duplicates are to be removed, the primitive outputs a record only when those fields differ from the previous record. If the input is not sorted, the primitive uses a hash table. When given a record, we look up its field values in the hash table. If they are not found, we output the record and add the values to the table. If they are found, we discard the record.

The aggregate primitives also depend on whether the input stream is sorted on the pertinent fields. If so, we calculate the aggregate value for all equal logical records, and output one logical record with the aggregrate value for that set. If the input is not sorted, we accumulate the aggregrate values for all field values in a local hash table. When all input records have been read, we output those aggregate values.

The join primitive takes two input streams. If both inputs are sorted on the join value, the primitive merges the input streams, and outputs matching records. If neither input stream is sorted, the join primitive first reads the smaller input stream (the one expected to have fewer records), stores all its record pointers in an array in local memory, and then sorts that array internally. The join primitive then reads the other input stream, looks up each record in the sorted array (using binary search), and outputs matching records. If one input stream is sorted and other isn't, the join primitive reads and stores the already sorted stream, and then reads the other relation.

Another technique for joins would be to read the smaller stream, and for each record, ask the RM to retrieve any records in the other relation which match it. This would be appropriate when joining a small relation (hundreds of records) with a large relation (millions of records) on a field that is indexed in the large relation. However, we have not as yet implemented this technique.

4.3 Query Manager

The goal of the QM is to minimize the CPU time used on the QPs while not exceeding the memory available on any QP. Our tests show that, even if processors are producing output as fast as possible, bus contention is not a serious problem [11]. Therefore, the QM does not consider the interconnect usage when assigning primitives to QPs. However, the QM does keep fairly accurate estimates of the loads on the QPs and of the added load from the current query. These estimates are used improve the utilization of the QPs.

Upon receiving a query from an HI, the QM goes through three phases to assign the query to the QPs. First, the QM translates and optimizes the query tree: it converts the user query into QP primitives and estimates the sizes of the sets involved. Then the QM groups those primitives into chunks, one per QP. And finally, the QM assigns those chunks to QPs, taking into account the current loads on the QPs. More accurate optimization and assignment could probably be done with more sophisticated techniques (e.g. having feedback between the phases). However, this method proved adequate for the SiDBM, and a more complex method could cause the QM to become a bottleneck. More details on the operation of the QM are given in [12].

The QM uses standard techniques to optimize the query tree. It moves selects and duplicate removals before joins and sorts, and combines cascaded selects or cascaded duplicate removals. The QM uses statistics kept by the RMs to estimate sizes. The QM can request the RM in charge of a relation to create and maintain a bucket histogram on a specified field of a relation. The QM can access this histogram at any time. (This histogram data is not guaranteed to be current or consistent, but it's close enough for estimates.) Using these size estimates, the QM decides which implementation of a primitive to use for each operation of the query tree. For example, the QM decides if a join should be done by sorting both inputs and merging them, or by sorting just one and doing a binary search on it. The QM also decides whether it is better to have a QP do the necessary sorting, or to request the RM to emit pointers in the specified order. The QM uses the size estimates and index information to make these decisions. Finally, in this phase, the QM splits the query tree into parallel subtrees if any of the memory-intensive operations (e.g. sorts or hashes) are estimated to be too big for the available memory of a QP. In this case, the splitting values are added to the selection criteria given to the RMs.

When grouping the optimized query tree into chunks, the QM uses simple heuristics to speed the processing of the query. Pipeline parallelism is achieved by assigning a primitive which produces its output in a (reasonably) steady stream to a different chunk than its successor. A primitive which produces output only at the end of its processing phase, such as sort, is assigned to the same chunk as its successor.

In assigning chunks to QPs, the QM uses its estimates of their current workload (both CPU and memory usage) and of the load for this query. The QM keeps its estimates of the load on each QP by using its initial estimation of the queries and by using information reported from the QPs. Each QP informs the QM when it finishes a primitive, and of the size of the outputs produced. The QM then updates its estimate of workload on that QP, and of other QPs performing later chunks of the reported query. To improve throughput, the QM processes incoming requests at higher priority than the QP information reporting. The QM does a best fit of CPU usage to current QP capacity while insuring that no QP's memory capacity is exceeded.

These simple strategies for the QM proved adequate in the tests run on the SiDBM. The QM did not become a bottleneck, and the QPs were well utilized.

5. PERFORMANCE RESULTS

The SiDBM proved to be relatively easy to create, very easy to migrate to new hardware, and very fast. Writing the original software for RM, QM, and QP took about 2 staff-years. Moving everything to new hardware took a few weeks.

We have run three of the benchmark queries described in [2] on the SiDBM. These queries use a synthetic database of relations with 10,000 records. The first two queries select 1% and 10% of the records from a 10,000 record relation, and store the selected records in another relation. The third query joins a 10,000 record relation with a 1,000 record selection from another 10,000 record relation, and produces a 1,000 record output relation ("joinAselB" [2]). Table 1 gives the times for these queries, in seconds, for the 1985 version of the SiDBM, which used 8 Mhz Motorola 68000-based processors, and for the Britton-Lee IDM-500 backend database machine. The SiDBM had five processors: one RM, one QM, and three QPs. The results depend on the index type for the fields being joined or selected. "Unindexed" means that no indexes existed. "Clustered Index" means that a primary index existed; only one field per relation can have a clustered index, and it is usually the relation's key. "Secondary Index" means that a non-clustered index existed. As mentioned earlier, the SiDBM has only one type of index, so we have reported the same results for both clustered and secondary indexes. As Table 1 shows, our first version of the SiDBM was much faster than the IDM-500.

Index Type	Query	SiDBM (1985)	IDM-500 (1983)	Ratio
Unindexed	Select 1% of 10k	4.1	21.6	5.3
	Select 10% of 10k	4.3	23.6	5.5
Clustered	Select 1% of 10k	.4	1.5	4.3
	Select 10% of 10k	3.3	8.7	2.6
	Join 10k x 1k/10k	4.8	27.6	5.7
Secondary	Select 1% of 10k	.4	3.3	9.4
	Select 10% of 10k	3.3	23.7	7.2
	Join 10k x 1k/10k	4.8	71.4	14.9

Table 1: Query times, in seconds, for prototype SiDBM and IDM-500 [2]. (Results for the unindexed join query are not available.)

DeWitt *et al.* have run these benchmarks on a Teradata database machine with 20 Access Module Processors [5]. They scaled the relations up by a factor of 10. For example, the input relations have 100,000 records, and the join query produces 10,000 records. Table 2 gives their results, along with our current results for the SiDBM. The SiDBM has five 14 Mhz AT&T 32100-based processors; as before, there are one RM, one QM, and three QPs. As can be seen, the current version of the SiDBM is much faster than the Teradata machine.

Index Type	Query	SiDBM (1987)	Teradata (1987)	Ratio
Unindexed	Select 1% of 100k	10.9	24.7	2.3
	Select 10% of 100k	26.4	108.4	4.1
	Join 100k x 10k/100k	87.0	292.4	3.4
Clustered	Select 1% of 100k	2.0	25.4	12.7
	Select 10% of 100k	18.1	107.8	6.0
	Join 100k x 10k/100k	22.9	145.5	.6.4
Secondary	Select 1% of 100k	2.0	24.8	12.4
	Select 10% of 100k	18.1	110.9	6.1
	Join 100k x 10k/100k	22.9	295.1	12.9

Table 2: Query times, in seconds, for current SiDBM and Teradata [5].

6. Conclusions

The SiDBM investigated a new way to build backend database machines. Using main memory for the entire database not only improves the machine's performance, but also simplifies its design. Because the SiDBM does not have to compensate for the limitations of disks, the SiDBM is much simpler and much faster than conventional disk-based database machines, even those with large caches and multiple processors. Also, because of its design, the SiDBM can use a variety of hardware, and can quickly take advantage of advances in technology. The SiDBM demonstrates how to build a database machine of the future.

7. ACKNOWLEDGEMENTS

Y. E. Lien and Larry Lai were involved in the early work on the SiDBM. The work on the SiDBM was done at AT&T Bell Laboratories.

REFERENCES

[1] AT&T, *WE 321SB VMEbus Single Board Computer User Manual,* Document 451-007, April 1986.

[2] Bitton, D., DeWitt, D. J., and Turbyfill, C., "Benchmarking Database Systems: A Systematic Approach," CS Tech. Rep. #526, Univ. of Wisconsin at Madison, December 1983.

[3] Cmelik, R. F., Gehani, N. H., and Roome, W. D., "Experience With Multiple Processor Versions of Concurrent C," to appear in *IEEE Trans. Software Engr,* 1988.

[4] Comer, D., "The Ubiquitous B-Tree," *ACM Computing Surveys,* 11:2 (June 1979), 121-137.

[5] DeWitt, D. J., Smith, M., and Boral, H., "A Single-User Performance Evaluation of the Teradata Database Machine," MCC Tech Report DB-081-87, March 5, 1987.

[6] Gehani, N. H., and Roome, W. D., "Concurrent C," *Software—Practice and Experience,* 16:9 (September 1986) 821-844.

[7] Gray, J. N., "Notes on Database Operating Systems," in *Operating Systems: An Advanced Course,* R. Bayer et al (ed), Springer-Verlag, 1978, pp. 393-481.

[8] Kernighan, B. W., and Ritchie, D. M., *The C Programming Language,* Prentice-Hall, Englewood Cliffs, NJ, 1978.

[9] Knuth, D. E., *The Art of Computer Programming: Volume 3/Sorting and Searching,* Addison-Wesley, 1973.

[10] Kung, H. T., and Robinson, J. T., "On Optimistic Methods for Concurrency Control," *ACM Trans. Database Systems,* 6:2 (June 1981), pp. 213-226.

[11] Leland, M. D. P. and Roome, W. D., "The Silicon Database Machine," *Proceedings of the Fifth International Workshop on Database Machines,* March, 1985.

[12] Leland, M. D. P., "Query Processing on the Silicon Database Machine," *Proceedings of ICCD '86: IEEE International Conference on Computer Design,* October, 1986.

[13] Roome, W. D., "The Intelligent Store: A Content-Addressable Page Manager," *Bell System Tech. J.,* 61:9 (November 1982), pp. 2567-2596.

[14] Roome, W. D., *The CTK: An Efficient Multi-Processor Kernel,* AT&T Bell Laboratories, October 1986.

[15] Ullman, J. D., *Principles of Database Systems,* Computer Science Press, 1980.

MARS: THE DESIGN OF A MAIN MEMORY DATABASE MACHINE

MARGARET H. EICH

Department of Computer Science and Engineering
Southern Methodist University
Dallas, Texas 75275

Abstract. The initial design of a main memory database (MMDB) backend database machine (DBM) is described. This **MA**in memory **R**ecoverable database with **S**table log (**MARS**) is designed to provide quick recovery after transaction, system, or media failure, and to also provide efficient transaction processing.

1. INTRODUCTION

Declining memory costs provides the possibility for large amounts of main memory (1-20 gigabytes) and facilitates the placement of all or major portions of databases in main memory. The investigation of these memory resident or *main memory databases (MMDB)* has recently attracted much research ([1], [3], [4], [8], [10], [14]). Due to the volatility of main memory, much of this research has centered around effective and efficient recovery techniques. Based on the results of earlier performance studies ([5], [18]), the major features impacting MMDB recovery performance have been identified: amount of stable (nonvolatile) main memory, separate processor to perform logging, and special processor to perform database checkpointing. These studies indicate that the amount of stable memory should be at least enough to store the database log, and that special processors are needed to reduce impact of logging and checkpointing overhead on transaction processing. These are the basic features of the MMDB system, MARS, proposed in this paper.

The MMDB model assumes that entire databases are memory resident and thus significant performance improvements can be found over normal database transaction processing due to the lack of I/O overhead. An *archive database* existing on secondary storage devices is used solely as a backup in the event of main memory media failure or system failure. Periodically, data must be *checkpointed* from the primary copy MMDB to the archive database. With the MMDB model, a log is needed to facilitate transaction undos, to ensure complete recoverability after system failure by providing more recent recovery information than is found in the archive database, and to provide a historical journal of transaction processing. We assume that the log exists both on a disk and in a memory buffer. Most proposed MMDB systems differ in how much stable memory exists, when and how checkpointing and logging occur, and the specific architecture involved.

There have been three MMDB proposals which assume no stable memory: IBM has implemented MMDBs in the IMS/VS Fast Path Feature ([11], [12]), researchers at the University of California at Berkeley made an initial proposal for an MMDB [3], and the design for an MMDB including data structure representation and recovery technique has been proposed at IBM for use with the Office by Example (OBE) database[1]. Three other MMDB designs assume some amount of stable memory. The HALO special logging device appears to have been the earliest design for MMDB hardware [7]. HALO intercepts all MMDB operations and performs automatic logging. HALO research has centered more around the architecture than specifics for recovery. Work at the University of Wisconsin

325

has resulted in the design of an MMDB, MM-DBMS, with an architecture design very similar to MARS [15]. The MM-DBMS work includes not only the design, but a proposal for new data structures, examination of query processing algorithms, and discussion of recovery techniques. One recent proposed MMDB system, SiDBM, assumes enough stable memory for an entire database [16]. This work includes the architecture design with some detail concerning transaction processing and recovery. Unlike the above MMDB systems, MARS is placed into a category which was identified by performance studies as the one with the greatest performance potential ([5], [18]). The major differences between MARS and previous MMDB proposals, are its technique for handling checkpointing, and the use of the shadow concept to facilitate fast transaction undo and recovery after system failure.

This paper provides an overview of the MARS architecture and processing. The next section describes the MARS architectural model and briefly compares it to previous designs. The remaining sections provide an overview of the MARS memory units, as well as transaction and recovery processing activities.

2. MARS OVERVIEW

MARS is a MAin memory Recoverable database with Stable log and functions as a backend database machine (DBM) to a host system. Figure 1 shows the proposed MARS architecture. The Database Processor (DP) receives transaction requests from the host processor, performs all database processing, and returns responses to the host. The purpose of the Recovery Processor (RP) is that of performing recovery processing activities: logging, checkpointing, and recovery from failures. The two processors function independently and, in most cases, asynchronously. Communication between the two is needed, however, to accomplish transaction termination. Each processor has its own memory unit to facilitate its own processing, and there are also two memory units which are shared by both processors: a volatile memory holding the MMDB (MM) and a nonvolatile memory with the stable log (SM). The size of the volatile memory unit must be large enough to hold the entire database (several gigabytes), while the size of the stable memory unit is large enough to hold the log. In the worst case, the size of the SM would need to be as large as MM. To avoid this problem we assume that the size of the stable memory is large enough to support most transactions, and we provide the means for graceful degradation of transaction processing in the event of log overflow. The stable memory unit can be thought of as containing shadow words for the main memory unit ⋆ [17]. Updates to permanent relations are first placed in the SM. Only when a transaction commits and any updates become clean, can the data be written into the MMDB. The archive database (AM) resides on a set of secondary storage devices. Periodically, the RP performs a fuzzy checkpoint [10] by copying dirty pages from the MMDB to AM.

Although initially appearing similar to previous MMDB techniques, MARS is quite different. As with HALO and MM-DBMS, MARS assumes enough stable memory for the log with the rest of the database being in a volatile memory. However, the structure and content of the MARS log is quite different from the logs for previous systems. The HALO, SiDBM, and MM-DBMS designs must use before image values in the log to accomplished transaction undos. This results in CPU and memory overhead to accomplished undos. MARS uses shadow words and a novel addressing scheme to ensure both efficient access of data in either the MM or SM, and no memory copies to perform transaction undo. Also, both HALO and MM-DBMS require that the database processor performing transaction processing also perform checkpoints. In our scheme the impact to transaction processing is reduced by having a separate processor perform all checkpointing functions. HALO suffers from the additional overhead of performing checkpointing for all data not just modified data. Unlike HALO and MM-DBMS we don't assume that the stable memory is error free

---

⋆ Our use of the term shadow here has almost an opposite meaning to that normally associated with shadows. A shadow page in conventional uses contains the prior database value and is used for transaction undo processing. In MARS, the shadow word contains the new value with the old value in the MM.

327

or *forever stable*. MARS can easily recover from SM media failures.

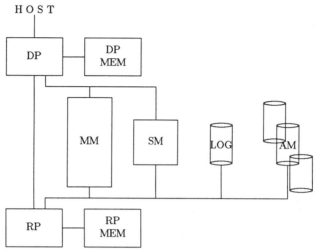

Fig. 1 - MARS Architecture

3. MEMORY UNITS

3.1. MM Structure

As with conventional segmentation/paging systems [2], MARS divides MM divides into fixed size pages and segments that are logical units consisting of a certain number of pages. Because of the potentially large size needed for MM, we add an additional level above the segment: a *partition*. Like the segment, the partition is a logical unit and consists of a number of segments. Both segments and partitions may vary in size and can be created and deleted dynamically during database processing. A segment contains a permanent or temporary relation or index and is identified by a unique name and storage structure. Different data structures have been examined to store MMDB data ([3], [14]), but as with data stored on disk there is no best storage structure for a relation in memory. The only restriction is that all data stored in the same segment use the same technique. A partition consists of potentially multiple logically related segments. (MM-DBMS uses the concept of a partition. But their partition is the same as our page.) Thus, a relation and all its indices would usually be found in the same partition.

One special MM partition always exists: the *free partition*. The free partition contains data that is temporary to a transaction as well as all free pages. The data in the free partition is not recoverable in the event of system failure since it is never checkpointed and no logging is performed on its updates. All free pages exist in a special *free segment*. Initially all pages in the free partition are placed in this free segment. During transaction processing, temporary data is maintained in special temporary segments in the free partition. At transaction termination these temporary segments are returned to the free segment or, if desired, made permanent by being placed in an existing or new partition. Updates to permanent data are always performed in the SM before being applied to MM, but updates to temporary data are always performed in MM.

3.2. SM Structure

The MARS stable memory is divided into four major areas: Shadow memory, AM directory, Checkpoint bit maps, and SM log buffer. Figure 2 shows the basic SM organization. Each entry in the shadow memory consists of the MM logical address and the after image (AFIM) value for that corresponding MM word. Data is placed and accessed in this shadow area using a set associative approach [13] based on the logical address. All AFIMs for the same transaction are also stored as a linked list. The random access is needed to access the shadow words during transaction processing, while the linked list allows efficient transaction termination processing.

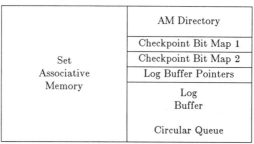

Fig. 2 - SM Organization

The two checkpoint bit maps are located at fixed locations in the SM. Each has one bit per page in MM. The first bit map inidicates all pages modified since the last checkpoint began. As a page in MM is modified, the RP updates the appropriate bit in the first bit map. The second bit map indicates the pages to be checkpointed, and thus insures that only the modified pages are checkpointed.

The AM directory contains the current structure of data on the AM disks. In the event of system failure, the directory is used to indicate which tracks contain each segment's pages. When the SM directory is updated, the appropriate directory on the AM disk is also modified.

There are three types of log records: Begin Transaction (BT), After Image Value (AFIM), and End Transaction (ET). Because of the structure and use of the shadow memory, each word updated by a transaction has only one AFIM log record regardless of the number of times that transaction changes the word. The BT and ET records either contain the Transaction ID (TID) that is used to uniquely identify that transaction, or the Checkpoint ID (ChkptID) which likewise identifies a checkpoint. Log records exist in the SM log buffer and log disk. All AFIM records for a transaction are between the BT and ET for that transaction but need not be in the same log block. The beginning and ending of a checkpoint are identified by a BT and ET containing the ID for that checkpoint. All transactions found in the log before the BT for the checkpoint have had their updates applied to main memory. Those with records between the BT and ET for the checkpoint, however, may or may not have. During recovery from system failure, a transaction consistent image of the database can be obtained by applying all AFIM records for transactions in the log between the BT and ET for the checkpoint.

A simple analytical model has been used to compare the space requirements needed by MARS and MM-DBMS. Due to the limited amount of space available for this paper we have had to omit the details of the model, but the interested reader is referred to a technical report which describes it and the results in detail [6]. MARS and MM-DBMS were found to take up a comparable amount of log space with MARS being much better when it can take advantage of the duplication of word updates. (Recall that only one AFIM value exists regardless of the number of times that a word is updated by a transaction.)

3.3. Address Translation

All MM accesses are by *logical address*: Partition number, Segment number, Page number, Offset. MARS address translation is very similar to that used in paging systems. The objective is to obtain fast access to a word of a database when the word may be in MM, SM, or even AM. There is one partition table stored at a fixed location in MM with enough entries for the maximum number of partitions possible. Each entry in the partition table points to a segment table for that partition, and each segment table entry points to a page table.

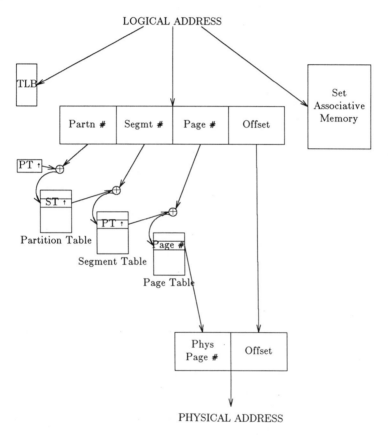

Fig. 3 - MARS Address Translation

Figure 3 shows the steps performed to accomplish logical to physical address translation. As with conventional paging address translation, we assume that special hardware is used and that a translation lookaside buffer (TLB) [2] is also needed. Three different paths for translation are performed in parallel: accessing SM, examining the TLB, and normal translation through tables located in the MM. Any address found in the shadow memory has priority over one found in the TLB, while the TLB has preference over one found through the tables. Once an address has been found in either SM or TLB, then, translation via the tables is stopped. The TLB contains the most recently referenced logical page addresses minus offset and their corresponding physical page address. The shadow memory entries contain the complete logical and physical addresses.

To speed up address translation, banks of registers are used at the partition and segment levels. Unlike the TLB, these registers do not contain physical addresses, rather they contain the address of the next table level. Just as the TLB catches localities of reference at the page level, these catch localities at the partition and segment level.

Unlike conventional paging address translation, page faults do not occur. Immediately after a system failure, however, some areas of MM may have not been reloaded. During translation, then, segment faults can occur. A special flag in each segment table entry is used to indicate if the corresponding segment is MM resident or not. If the segment being referenced is not in MM, the transaction must wait until it is reloaded from the archive disk. The fault level could be at the partition or page level, but the archive disk is designed for efficient segment level recovery.

It has been pointed out that the requirement to always access the SM could have a negative impact on the address translation process. However, this is not actually the case. We assume that if an address is found in the TLB, that MM is always accessed instead of waiting to see if the shadow memory also contains the word. Thus an address found in the shadow memory incurs one memory access, while one found in the MM incurs one memory access via the TLB and up to four through the address translation tables. This can result in an actual improvement in the expected number of memory references required for address translation, because of the fact that some of the addresses found in SM would otherwise have had to be located via the translation tables. Figure 4 shows the expected number of memory references with the percentage of TLB hits varying between 60% and 100%. The expected number of memory references required when performing normal address translation via the tables was assumed to be 2.7. The top line shows the number of references when no SM is used. The other lines indicate the number of references when 10% and 20% of the addresses are found in SM. We assumed that half of these would otherwise have been found via TLB and half via the tables. This simple graph indicates that the use of the SM does not degrade address translation performance, but can in fact improve it.

3.4. AM Structure

The placement and structure of data on the archive disk (AM) is aimed at efficient reloading of data after a system failure. The AM actually consists of multiple disk drives $(AM_1, AM_2, \cdots, AM_n)$ each having data stored with a block size equal to that of the MM page size. Data is stored on the AM by interleaving the multiple disk drives. Since the MM recoverable unit is a segment, all blocks within one track are allocated to the same segment. One AM file is associated with each MM segment and the allocation unit of the file is a track. Tracks are allocated to a file based upon the ordering of the disks. Figure 5 shows the initial structure of AM and MM given a hypothetical database consisting of three partitions: the first with two segments, second with one, and third with three. Assuming that the disk accomodates 10 pages per track, this figure shows how the AM is initially structured such that the first 10 pages of the first segment in the first partition are stored in the first track of the first disk. The next ten pages are placed on the first track of the next disk. Allocation continues in this fashion until all the disks have been allocated space, then allocation continues on the second tracks of the disks. In this fashion, each MM segment is evenly distributed across all disks. During reloading I/O is performed in parallel from each disk. Once a head is positioned on a track, all data from that track is read to reload the same segment.

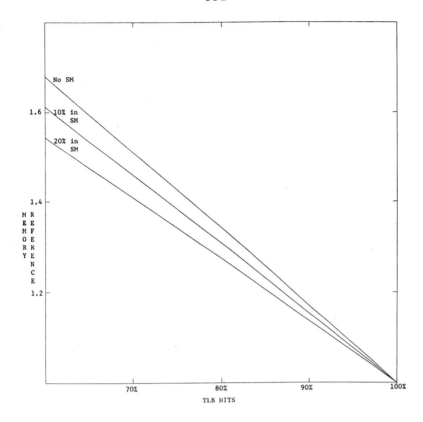

Fig. 4 - Expected Number of Memory References for Address Translation

A file directory per segment indicates the current allocation on disk for that segment. This catalog is maintained both on the AM disk and in the SM. This facilitates easy identification of placement of any MM page on the AM.

During database processing, pages may be added to or removed from a segment. Recall, however, that the AM is a backup facility and it is only updated during checkpointing. When a new page is added to a segment in MM, an additional page table entry must be created and, if needed, another track of AM allocated. If sufficient room exists in the last allocated track of a segment, this is not necessary. When allocating a new track, the first free track of the next logical AM unit is allocated to the segment file and indicated in the catalog. If entire pages are deleted in MM, then the correponding AM page is deleted. To avoid extensive overhead for garbage collection, however, the page may only be marked as such. As the database structure changes, the AM structure may become fragmented and periodic reorganizations may be needed. Since the AM must itself be periodically backed up, the backup routine should reorganize the backup as the copying is being performed. The new copy then becomes the online AM.

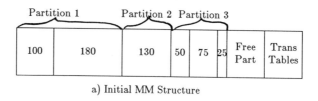

a) Initial MM Structure

P1 S1	P1 S1	P1 S1	P1 S1	P1 S1
P1 S2	P1 S2	P1 S2	P1 S2	P1 S2
P2 S1	P2 S1	P2 S1	P2 S1	P2 S1
P3 S1	P3 S1	P3 S1	P3 S1	P3 S1
P3 S2	P3 S2	P3 S2	P3 S2	P3 S2
P3 S3	P3 S3			P3 S3
Free	Free	Free	Free	Free
AM_1	AM_2	AM_3	AM_4	AM_5

b) Corresponding AM Structure

Fig. 5 - Initial AM/MM Organization for Hypothetical Database

4. DP PROCESSING

The DP has complete responsibility for processing each transaction. After receiving a transaction request from the host, the DP must perform any preprocessing (integrity, security, optimization, concurrency control, etc.), process the request, and return response to the host. Unlike other MMDB researchers we do feel that concurrency control is needed in the MMDB context. In the discussions following, we assume that locking is used at the segment level. Future research will examine other concurrency control strategies.

During transaction processing, the DP performs standard relational algebra operations. Some researchers have examined MMDB specific algorithms to perform various database operations in a MMDB context ([3], [15], [19]). For our current needs, the exact algorithms used to implement various algebra operations is not important, we assume that all database operations eventually result in database reads and writes. The DP actually performs all database updates in the SM. If a record for this address already exists in the SM, then only the AFIM value is changed. In case of processing hot spots, this reduces the size of the log data.

An analytic model similar to that used to calculate space requirements was also used to calculate transaction cost [6]. Estimating expected transaction cost by the number of memory references, it was found that MARS performed slightly better than MM-DBMS based upon transaction size and update probability. The major advantage to the shadow memory concept, however, occurs when the probabilty of transaction backout is considered. Figure 6 shows the average transaction cost based upon the number of word references as the probability for transaction undo varies between 0 and .1. The probability for transaction undo has been estimated at .03 [9].

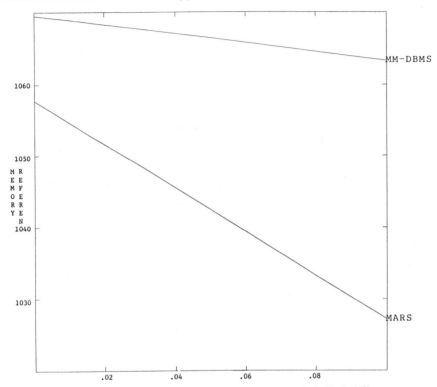

Fig. 6 - Expected Transaction Cost Based on Undo Probability

5. RP PROCESSING

The Recovery Processor has four major functions: transaction termination, checkpointing, recovery from media failure, and recovery from system failure.

5.1. Transaction Termination

When a transaction termination occurs, the DP notifies the RP throught a special interrupt. If the RP is currently in the Checkpointing state, it's processing is interrupted and resumed after the termination completes. Otherwise, the RP will process this termination immediately upon completion of it's current task. If the transaction has completed successfully then a transaction commit is performed, else a transaction UNDO is accomplished. While the RP is performing any transaction termination activities, the DP may continue processing. The only coordination between the two needed at this point is in the release of any concurrency control data. None of the modified data can be seen by subsequent update transactions until the MM has been updated. (Note that this restriction does not affect read only transactions.) A special interrupt from the RP to the DP indicates completion of transaction termination procedures.

The three main functions performed upon transaction commit are the updating of the MM, copying of log records to the output log buffer, and freeing up space in the SM shadow area. A BT log record is initially written to the first available space in the log buffer. The remaining commit processing is performed by reading the linked list for the transaction in the SM shadow area. For each AFIM record the checkpoint bit map is updated, the AFIM value is copied to MM, a corresponding log record is written into the buffer, and the shadow memory space is freed up. When the end of the transaction list is found, an ET record is added to the log buffer. As buffer blocks are filled, the RP requests that the blocks be written to the log disk in sequence.

Transaction UNDO simply requires that the RP read through the linked list for the transaction and free up the shadow memory entries. When this is accomplished, the RP notifies the DP so that any locks on the dirty items can be removed. No log records are written to the output buffer.

5.2. Checkpointing

At periodic time intervals, the RP determines that a system checkpoint must occur. Checkpointing requires that all pages modified since the last checkpoint be copied from the MM to the AM. Checkpointing is completely determined by the first checkpoint bit map located in SM. If the RP is in an idle state the checkpoint begins immediately, else it begins at the end of the current processing. The checkpointing begins by copying the first bit map to the location of the second checkpoint bit map and reinitializing the first bit map. Then, a BT record is placed into the next address in the log buffer. Checkpoint IDs are generated by a date/time stamp as to when the checkpoint was started. Once these two functions have been accomplished, checkpointing is interruptable to perform transaction undo and commit processing.

Since the bit map corresponds to physical pages, no address translation is needed to perform checkpointing. When the last bit has been examined and output complete, then the ET record can be written to the end of the output log buffer. During checkpointing, the DP processing continues as does transaction termination and undo. Thus the checkpoint is fuzzy and all transactions with AFIMs between the BT and ET records for the checkpoint must be applied to ensure a transaction consistent view. To facilitate fast recovery from system failure, when a log page containing a BT checkpoint record is written to the disk, the disk address of this record is written into a fixed location in the SM. completing an entire checkpoint.

5.3. Recovery from Media Failure

Media failure may occur on any of the memory units: MM, SM, AM, or disk log. Unlike other researchers, we do not assume that a nonvolatile memory is "error free". Thus we have prepared for recovery from error on the SM as well as the other memory units. Minor media failures may allow transaction processing to continue at a reduced rate during recovery, while more severe errors may cause a system failure or require that the system be brought down. Both types are discussed.

If an error occurs in MM, backup data exists in SM, log disk, and AM. An error occuring to a small amount of MM can be recovered by restoring the affected pages from the AM and then applying appropriate AFIMs from the disk log and SM log buffer. Any additional updates to the pages exist in the SM shadow area and need not be applied as normal address translation will uncover them. Before recovering using the AM and log, however, it should be determined if there is a copy of the affected words in the SM shadow memory. If that is the case, no recovery is needed unles the associated transaction must be undone. In this case the first alternative above is performed. During recovery from MM media failure no transactions accessing the affected area can continue. MM failures affecting the free partition result in transaction failures for the associated transactions. These transactions would then be treated as if they had failed and, after transaction undo, rescheduled. MM media failures to large portions of MM or to the translation tables are treated as complete system failures.

In response to a media failure on the AM, a checkpoint of all affected MM pages is issued. To provide an additional archive backup and to facilitate efficient recovery from system failure, we assume that periodically the AM is backed up and restructured so that the each segment is again maintained in contiguous tracks. The old AM then serves as a backup in the event of catastrophic AM failures.

Although a failure to the SM should be rare, it is advisable to ensure recoverability from problems with it. The level to which recovery is possible depends on the severity of the error. An error to the AM directory is recoverable by simply reloading the disk version. A failure to the shadow memory requires the abnormal termination of all exiting transactions and its reinitialization. An error in the log queue or checkpoint bit map is recovered by performing a checkpoint on all of main memory.

Log disk failure only affects the ability to recovery from other failures. Thus, in the event of its failure and its need for recovering from another failure, recovery to an earlier state than desired may be required. Write errors simply require that the write from the SM log buffer be retried.

Because of our concern for recovery from SM failure, our approach is unique when compared to either MM-DBMS or HALO. MM-DBMS checkpoints are performed at the page (their partition) level and are not transaction consistent. The SM is always needed to bring checkpoints up to a consistent view. If the SM is lost, there appears to be no way to easily recover. HALO also assumes that the SM is error free. However, since log records are written out to the log disk in sequence, errors could be recovered in a method similar to our approach.

5.4. Recovery from System Failure

The approach discussed in this subsection applies to any restart of the MARS system after a system failure or shut down. The approach consists of four steps:

1) Format SM and Load the AM directory into SM.

2) Format MM based upon the number of partitions, segments, and pages found in the AM directory. Also, create the needed translation tables to facilitate MM address translation.

3) Determine priority for loading segments into MM.

4) Begin reloading MM and transaction processing. The reload continues as a background lower priority process to normal RP processing.

The first task in reformatting the SM is the creation of the AM directory. At any point, the AM directory on disk must reflect the structure on disk. Thus creation of the AM directory in SM simply requires loading it from disk. Space for the first and second checkpoint bit maps are allocated in the SM. Only the first one need be formatted to all 0's. The log buffer queue needs to be formatted such that the number of buffer blocks and the location of the first empty block are known.

After the AM Directory has been built, then the MM formatting can begin. All the pages of the first segment/partition are allocated at the lowest addresses in MM. Pages of the next segment of the first partition are then allocated. After all pages of the first partition are allocated, then the second and remaining partitions can be allocated. As seen in

Figure 7, as data pages are allocated from low memory addresses the needed translation tables are allocated from high addresses. During MM recovery, space for growth of the tables is left since all tables must maintain contiguous addresses. If needed during transaction processing, new space can be allocated from the free partition and tables moved, but this processing could be time consuming and should be avoided. Once all space for the needed pages and tables have been allocated, the remaining MM space is allocated to the free segment of the free partition.

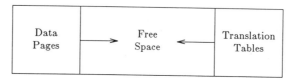

Fig. 7 - Formatting of MM after System Failure

After formatting has been completed, reloading can actually begin. This task is accomplished at the segment level based upon a priority scheme associated with each segment. In an attempt to prefetch the most used segments, priorities are assigned to each segment based upon frequency of use statistics kept during transaction processing. The segments with the highest use count are given the highest priority. A priority queue is kept in the RP memory and used to determine the order of reloading segments. This priority is modified based upon active transactions. Any transactions known to be active during the failure are rescheduled and their needed segments are given the highest reload priority. Once this has been accomplished, the RP begins reloading segments based upon the priorities assigned. Pages within segments are reloaded in sequence. Note that the use of the translation tables is not needed since the physical placement of pages can be easily determined based upon the known structure of MM.

As segments are being reloaded into MM, the reloading of SM begins. The BT record for the checkpoint reflected on the AM is located and all AFIMs of completed transactions following that BT must be reapplied to the database to ensure a transaction consistent database. However, due to our addressing technique we can apply these AFIMs to the SM rather than the MM. Since this can be done in parallel to actual reloading of MM, it should be faster than applying these values to the MM as proposed for other MMDB projects. These AFIMS are linked together as a special recovery transaction and will later be applied to MM as the commit processing for that transaction. However, commit processing is only begun on the recovery transaction after MM is reloaded. After the SM shadow memory has been loaded, a special ET record is placed into the first location in the log buffer. This record has a TID of 0 reflecting the end of the recovery process.

Immediately after the priorities have been determined and all AFIMS applied to SM, transaction processing can begin. Initially the first transactions may be haulted due to segment faults. As soon as the needed segment is available the associated transaction can be resumed. As new transactions enter the system and are, perhaps, halted due to segment faults, priorities are modified to ensure that reload priorities for needed segments are higher than those for unneeded segments. However, once a segment has been given a high priority due to its need by a transaction, no subsequently modified segment priorities may be given a higher priority. This is done to ensure that once reloading of a segment needed by an active transaction is done, it will not be interrupted.

Our scheme for system failure recovery is quite different from that proposed for MM-DBMS [15]. With MM-DBMS, recovery is at the page level. The AM is structured with one block equal to one MM partition. During checkpointing these blocks are written to the AM in a sequential fashion. The AM is viewed as a semi-circular queue. (Pages not frequently referenced and thus not checkpointed often, are "jumped" over in this queue.) The log structure is also at the page level, so after a page has been reloaded into MM from the AM any updates from the log to that page can be applied. The log does not contain AFIMs, but operations to be performed. Thus applying the log values may be time consuming since the individual operations must be interpreted and performed. Like MARS, recovery of data needed for active transactions is given top priority. However, no attempt is made to prefetch other data based upon past needs. The HALO writeups refer to a similar system failure recovery technique as ours, but all AFIMs must be applied to the MM.

6. SUMMARY AND FUTURE RESEARCH

We have described the design of a backend MMDB DBM aimed at efficient transaction and recovery processing. The ultimate goal of the MARS project is the actual implementation of a prototype system. Prior to accomplishing this, however, we intend to perform a detailed simulation study comparing the performance of MARS to other MMDB proposals. Other future MARS research will include examination of possible concurrency control techniques, data structures for MM storage, and query processing algorithms.

7. REFERENCES

[1] Arthur C. Ammann, Maria Butrico Hanrahan, and Ravi Krishnamurthy, "Design of a Memory Resident DBMS," *Proceedings of the IEEE Spring Computer Conference*, 1985, pp. 54-57.

[2] Jean-Loup Baer, *Computer Systems Architecture*, Computer Science Press, 1980.

[3] David J. DeWitt, Randy H. Katz, Frank Olken, Leonard D. Shapiro, Michael R. Stonebraker, and David Wood, *Proceedings of the ACM-SIGMOD International Conference on Management of Data*, June 1984, pp. 1-8.

[4] Margaret H. Eich, "Main Memory Database Recovery," *Proceedings of the ACM-IEEE C/S Fall Joint Computer Conference*, 1986, pp. 1226-1231. (Also available as SMU TR 86-CSE-11).

[5] Margaret H. Eich, "A Classification and Comparison of Main Memory Database Recovery Techniques," *Proceedings of the 1987 IEEE Database Engineering Conference*, 1987, pp. 332-339. (Also available as SMU TR 86-CSE-15).

[6] Margaret H. Eich, "Comparing MMDB Systems," SMU Department of Computer Science and Engineering Technical Report 87-CSE-6, February 1987.

[7] Hector Garcia-Molina, Richard J. Lipton, and Peter Honeyman, "A Massive Memory Database System," Princeton University Department of Electrical Engineering and Computer Science Technical Report, September 1983.

[8] Hector Garcia-Molina, Richard Cullingford, Peter Honeyman, and Richard Lipton, "The Case for Massive Memory," Princeton University Department of Electrical Engineering and Computer Science Technical Report 326, May 1984.

[9] Theo Haerder and Andreas Reuter, "Principles of Transaction-Oriented Database Recovery," *Computing Surveys*, Vol. 15, No. 4, December 1983, pp. 287-317.

[10] Robert B. Hagmann, "A Crash Recovery Scheme for a Memory-Resident Database System," *IEEE Transactions on Computers*, Vol. C-35, No. 9, September 1986, pp.839-843.

[11] IBM, *IMS/VS Version 1 Fast Path Feature General Information Manual*, GH20-9069-2, April 1978.

[12] IBM World Trade Systems Centers, *IMS Version 1 Release 1.5 Fast Path Feature Description and Design Guide*, G320-5775, 1979.

[13] Glen G. Langdon, Jr., *Computer Design*, Computeach Press Inc., 1982.

[14] T. Lehman and M. Carey, "Query Processing in Main Memory Database Management Systems," *Proceedings of the 1986 International Conference on Management of Data*, 1986.

[15] Tobin Jon Lehman, *Design and Performance Evaluation of a Main Memory Relational Database System*, PhD Dissertation University of Wisconsin-Madison, August 1986.

[16] M.D.P. Leland and W.D. Roome, "The Silicon Database Machine," *Database Machines Fourth International Workshop*, Springer-Verlag, 1985, pp.169-189.

[17] Raymond A. Lorie, "Physical Integrity in a Large Segmented Database," *ACM Transactions on Database Systems*, Vol. 2, No.1, March 1977, pp. 91-104.

[18] Kenneth Salem and Hector Garcia-Molina, "Crash Recovery Mechanisms for Main Storage Database Systems," Princeton University Department of Computer Science technical report CS-TR-034-86, April 1986.

[19] Leonard D. Shapiro, "Join Processing in Database Systems with Large Main Memories," *ACM Transactions on Database Systems*, Vol. 11, No. 3, September 1986, pp. 239-264.

MACH : Much Faster Associative Machine

Ryohei Nakano

Minoru Kiyama

NTT Communications and Information Processing Laboratories
1-2356, Take, Yokosuka, Kanagawa, 238-03 Japan

ABSTRACT

This paper proposes a new database machine architecture called MACH (Much Faster Associative Machine), the goal of which is to improve relational performance by two orders. This architecture is aimed mainly at the knowledge processing field, where such high performance is required. The design principles are first presented along with an overview of MACH architecture. After which, the main characteristics of MACH architecture are described in detail, including its memory resident database, fixed-length encoding, sophisticated data storing, and hash-based algorithms for main relational algebra operations. Experiment results gained from encoding databases in practical use are also shown. Tests conducted in the initial implementation of MACH1 showed that its performance exceeds any disk-based machine or system by more than one order.

1. Introduction

The architectures of database machines proposed up until now have provided few solutions to the I/O bandwidth problem[1]. Both their architectures and performances have been greatly influenced and restricted by the nature of disks. Moreover, data management overhead, e.g., the extracting of values from tuples or the generating/deleting of derived relations, can not be ignored with these machines[2]. Due to these shortcomings, then, existing database machines show their best performance (of several seconds) only in simple retrievals when indices are used[3]. However, the knowledge processing field, which has recently come to attract wide attention, requires database processing performance of at least two orders higher, when executing inferences based on facts stored in databases. Moreover, the unpredictable usage of databases in this field prevents such pre-localizing techniques as indexing or clustering, which are widely used in pure database fields. Breaking away from the normal form is also necessary in the knowledge engineering field[4,5]. Finally, recent semiconductor technologies offer a great possibility to revolutionize database machine architectures.

With these points in mind, this paper proposes MACH (Much Faster Associative Machine) architecture, whose goal is to improve the performance of database operations by two orders. The first of these database machine architectures, MACH1, features a memory resident database, fixed-length encoding, sophisticated data storing, and hash-based algorithms for join and projection. Section 2 describes the design principles and gives an overview of MACH architecture. Section 3 explains the algorithm and gives tested results on rooted tree encoding of variable-length strings to fixed-length codes. Section 4 presents a sophisticated method of data storing which, by employing a perfectly balanced tree together with attribute-wise storing, enables addressing by calculation and solves the derived(temporary) relation overflow problem. Section 5 describes the hash-based algorithms for join and projection, along with a method for storing the derived relations. Finally, section 6 describes the MACH1 implementation environment and provides performance results derived from Wisconsin benchmark test[3].

2. Overview of MACH Architecture

2.1 Goal of MACH Architecture

339

The goal of MACH architecture can be summarized as follows: Under the following conditions, MACH architecture should be able to exceed disk–based architectures by two orders of magnitude in the processing time of relational algebra operations.

These conditions are

a) that the database be up to several giga bytes in scale,

b) that pre–localizing techniques, such as indexing or clustering, not be used,

c) that the architecture be easily extendible to the nested(unnormalized) model, and

d) that semiconductor technologies be actively employed.

2.2 Design Principles

The following principles were incorporated in the MACH architecture design.

(1) Starting from zero

Radical improvement required drastic reform of database processing principles. Starting over from the beginning, a new foundation was set, and appropriate techniques and algorithms introduced. This new foundation encompasses a memory resident database and fixed–length encoding, while the appropriate techniques and algorithms include the fixed–length encoding algorithm, sophisticated data storing and hash–based algorithms for relational algebra.

(2) Memory resident database

In order to satisfy the aim of MACH architecture, stress must be laid on solving the I/O bandwidth problem. A memory resident database was adopted for this purpose. Compared with disk–based storage, main memory–based storage offers many important advantages[6]. First of all, performance of data access(read/write) can be greatly improved, when freed from the restrictions originating in the nature of disks. Furthermore, this storage makes such management mechanisms as data allocation control, query optimization, and transaction scheduling simpler. Mechanism simplicity will surely reduce data management overhead which, as pointed out, can not be neglected in existing systems.

On the other hand, the volatility and capacity of the main memory gives cause for some anxiety. However, the former can be solved by writing logs efficiently[7]. For systems in which rollforward time is critical, providing a duplicate database in disks and updating it asynchronously will suffice. The latter problem has become less serious because of rapid progress of late in semiconductor technologies, which will make a real main memory space of several giga bytes available in the near future.

Thus, a memory resident database is chosen for this architecture.

(3) Fixed–length encoding

If every value in a database were made to be of a fixed–length, database processing principles would become much simpler. This can be realized through encoding variable–length strings into fixed–length codes. Since the user interface employs variable–length strings, an encoding/decoding mechanism is placed between the user and the fixed–length kernel machine of this system.

(4) Database storing for high speed data access

Now that the database can be stored in the main memory, a storing method should be pursued which allows much faster data access(read/write) than do disks. Hence a storing method was adopted which makes quick value addressing possible using simple calculations. Sophisticated management of derived relations will greatly reduce the time to generate/delete derived relations and solve the derived relation overflow problem.

(5) Relational algebra

The set of MACH operations includes relational algebra, which embodies relational operations in a more straightforward way than does relational calculus[8]. Since, however, calculus–based interfaces including SQL[9] prevail as user interfaces, we investigated algorithms which reduce a relational calculus alpha to an optimal algebraic expression[10,11].

Moreover, in order to apply this architecture to the knowledge engineering field, its data model will be extended to the nested one[12,13]. This extension will be reported in the future and is not addressed further in this paper.

(6) Breaking away from pre–localizing techniques

Since pre-localizing techniques are not expected in the knowledge engineering field, scanning of object values can not be avoided. Heavy load (order N*N, where N denotes the cardinality of a relation) operations, such as join and projection, must be reduced to order N operations. Therefore, a hashing technique is mainly employed in this environment where no dedicated hardware is used. To improve performance even further, CAM(content addressable memory)[14] with a capacity that will soon amount to a hundred kilobits per chip will also be used.

(7) Two step verification of architecture

As shown in Fig.1, we will verify soundness of MACH architecture roughly by two steps. The first implementation of MACH1 operates on a general purpose machine and supports the first normal form model. An evaluation of MACH1 performance tells that this approach is reasonable. This will be covered later in the paper. After implementing MACH1, running two approaches in parallel may now be possible; that is, MACH1E will extend the normal form model to the nested model, while MACH2 will adopt dedicated hardware, such as CAM, to improve performance by one more order. Finally, MACH2E will merge the advantages of these two approaches.

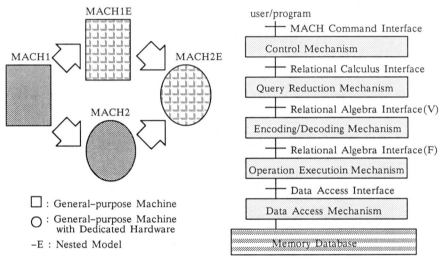

: General-purpose Machine

○ : General-purpose Machine with Dedicated Hardware

-E : Nested Model

Fig. 1. Stepwise Verification of MACH Architecture

Fig. 2. Abstract of MACH Architecture

2.3 Outline of MACH Architecture

An abstract of MACH architecture is shown in Fig.2, and the main components and interfaces are described below.

(1) Control mechanism: This consists of a user interface control mechanism and execution control mechanism. The former interprets MACH commands issued from the user or the program directly and translates them into execution forms. The latter controls the execution of MACH commands while managing system resources.

(2) Query reduction mechanism: This mechanism reduces the relational calculus alpha input by the user into a succinct optimal relational algebraic expression. Interface between this mechanism and the control mechanism is provided through relational calculus.

(3) Encoding/decoding mechanism: This mechanism encodes a variable-length string to a fixed-length code, or decodes conversely. Interface between this mechanism and the query reduction mechanism is provided through relational algebraic expressions including various length values.

(4) Operation execution mechanism: This mechanism executes operations, including relational algebra. Interface between this mechanism and the encoding/decoding mechanism is provided through relational algebraic expressions using only fixed–length values.

(5) Data access mechanism: This mechanism manages large amounts of main memory space and reads/writes data values in the memory database at high speed. Interface between this mechanism and the operation execution mechanism is provided through the data access (read/write) interface.

3. Fixed–length Encoding/Decoding

3.1 Background

Fixed–length encoding not only simplifies database processing principles, but also allows the compaction and encryption of databases. Fixed–length encoding is a well–known technique for compilers or interpreters, in which the number of objects(strings) is relatively small(up to only several hundred) which makes static encoding possible. On the other hand, the number of distinct strings in databases is extremely large (sometimes, in the millions) and increases, which necessitates dynamic encoding. Therefore, the best method for encoding large amounts of data is not totally clear. A similar approach[15] uses set type encoding(that will be described later); however, this paper introduces rooted tree encoding.

3.2 Requirements to Encoding

The requirements to database encoding are listed below. Note that we focus only on encoding of strings, because numerical data need not be encoded.

(1) Fixed–length code: Compact coding techniques, such as Huffman code, are well known mainly in compact databases. In our application, however, these codes are not appropriate because we desire, rather, to get fixed–length codes.

(2) One to one mapping: Obviously, both the source (string) and target (code) of encoding have to be mapped in a one to one relationship. For example, if the string "database machine" is encoded 12345, then other strings should not be encoded with the same number, and, of course, other occurrences of this string should always be encoded 12345.

(3) Method for order comparison: Since a code inherits little information contained in the original string, an order comparison(> ,<, etc.) between strings would seem difficult. In database encoding, maintaining order–preserving nature is quite difficult because any amount of data should be able to be added. One solution[15] to this problem is to first find the set of codes which satisfy an order comparison condition and then to search an encoded database using the set. For our application, though, simply decoding codes and comparing strings may be more effective, since a) decoding can be performed sufficiently fast because it only traces pointers to areas where sub–strings are stored, b) an order comparison of the first few characters will usually decide which string is greater, and c), as encoding information (domain) is singular, the cardinality of the code set which satisfies an order comparison condition may become unexpectedly large due to the existence of much noises.

(4) Method for partial comparison: Partial comparisons for the original string would also seem difficult to handle. Here too, simply decoding and partially comparing the original string may be most effective. A fast pattern matching algorithm[16] will shorten operation time.

3.3 Rooted Tree Encoding

This paper proposes rooted tree encoding[17] with which encoding information is managed using a rooted tree to decrease its volume. Since our objective is to locate all encoding information in the main memory to speed up the encoding operation, a reduction of encoding information is desirous.

Rooted tree encoding is outlined as follows. An entry (our term for a rooted tree node) contains n($\geq$1) characters. The system designer decides the value of n. Strings of n characters are cut up starting from its first character. Then sub–strings sequences are represented in a rooted tree where each sub–string is assigned one entry, as shown in Fig.3 (where n = 4). Sub–strings sequences that are the same from the first character can share entries, which results in a decrease in encoding information. The code of a string, then, is

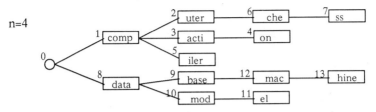

Fig. 3. Rooted Tree Representation of Strings

nothing but the address of the entry containing the last sub-string of the string. In traversing the rooted tree from the top, if the tree is found not to contain a remaining part of the sub-strings sequence, then the corresponding entries are added to the tree, and the address of the entry containing the last sub-string becomes the string code.

The decoding procedure is quite simple. The string code is merely the address of the entry containing both the last sub-string and the pointer to the entry containing the prior sub-string. Tracing the pointer, then, leads to the prior sub-string. This cycle is iterated to reach the entry which contains both the first sub-string and the null pointer. Thus, the original string is restored in order from the last to first sub-string.

Another encoding scheme is set type encoding[15]. With this scheme, distinct strings are handled separately just as distinct elements of a set. Therefore, generally speaking, the amount of encoding information with this scheme is much larger than with the rooted tree encoding.

In Itano's work[18] n(the number of characters contained in an entry) is always set at 1. In this case, the number of traversing entries is equal to the string length and increases as the length grows; therefore, a larger n, for instance of 4 or 8, would surely speed up traversing.

3.4 Implementation by Dynamic Hashing

There are two promising approaches for implementing rooted tree encoding: CAM and hashing. The former is faster, but presents restrictions in capacity and price. From the view of capacity, implementation by hashing was adopted. Since, as mentioned above, it should be possible to handle any amount of added data, static hashing is not suitable. On the other hand, as hashing techniques which can extend the number of buckets, dynamic hashing[19] and linear hashing[20] are well known. We, then, adopt dynamic hashing because it always exhibits a stable loading factor even when seriously unbalanced hashing exists. Figure 4 shows a dynamic hashing for the strings in Fig.3.

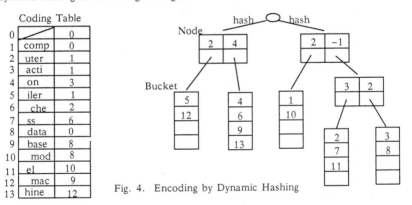

Fig. 4. Encoding by Dynamic Hashing

When traversing nodes, a random bit generator is necessary. We have used the slightly modified version of the random bit generator[21]. First, the left shift operator was changed to the right shift, since the lower bits are more significant, and second, exclusive or is always executed regardless of the overflow bit to gain randomness.

3.5 Results of Encoding Real Databases

By way of experiment, we encoded two databases in practical use: the Tokyo Metropolis yellow pages database and the NTT Yokosuka Research Center library database. The former comprises one relation containing about one million tuples and has a size amounting to 387 megabytes; the latter comprises several relations and has a size of about 10 megabytes. This experiment was carried out using a workstation (Apollo 570 turbo with 16 megabytes).

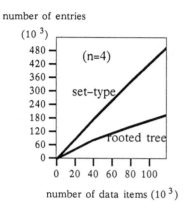

Fig. 5. Comparison of Different Encodings

Fig. 6. Amount of Main Memory versus the Number of Characters in an Entry

Figure 5 shows how rooted tree encoding can reduce the amount of main memory needed in proportion with the number of entries.

As n(the number of characters contained in an entry) increases, both the number of traversing entries and the total number of entries decrease. Hence, the amount of main memory reaches a minimum at some point when varying n. Figure 6 shows this point at $n=16$ in the library database, the average string length in the database being 20 bytes.

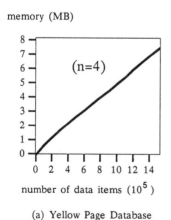

(a) Yellow Page Database

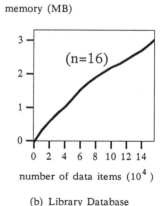

(b) Library Database

Fig. 7. Growth of Amount of Main Memory against the Number of Data Items

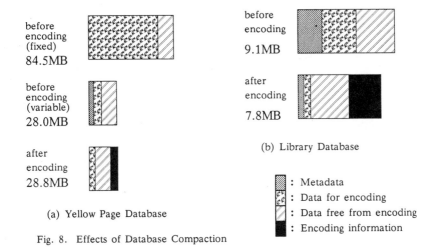

before
encoding
(fixed)
84.5MB

before
encoding
(variable)
28.0MB

after
encoding
28.8MB

(a) Yellow Page Database

before
encoding
9.1MB

after
encoding
7.8MB

(b) Library Database

▨ : Metadata
▨ : Data for encoding
▨ : Data free from encoding
■ : Encoding information

Fig. 8. Effects of Database Compaction

The encoding processes of these two databases are shown in Fig.7. A tendency toward saturation in the number of entries is seen only in the library database. However, such a tendency can be expected with any database after encoding a large amount of data, since sub-strings sharing will prevail. The amount of memory needed is 34.4 megabytes for the yellow pages database and 3 megabytes for the library database. Therefore, high-speed encoding on main memory is feasible for up to middle scale databases.

The loading factor for dynamic hashing was expected to be about 69%[19], which was shown to be correct in our experiment.

The effects of database compaction by encoding are shown in Fig. 8. They are, namely, 3/4 and 1/2 respectively for the yellow pages and library databases. The reason why the former is unexpectedly small is that this database contains many null values, without which the effect would be improved to 1/2.2. This figure also shows that the total amount of main memory is not increased even when encoding information is included.

4. Database Storing

4.1 Requirements to Database Storing

Merely locating a database on main memory without any contrivances will not bring up data access speed sufficiently. Therefore, to improve performance dramatically, a database storing method which satisfies the following conditions is indispensable.

Condition A: Since operation objects of relational algebra are represented as a set of values stored as an attribute, these values must be sequentially accessed at top speed.

Condition B: Since large variation may exist in the number of tuples, any size of relation must be stored without loss of memory.

Condition C: Since a derived relation is a subset of a basic relation, tuples of a basic relation must be randomly accessed at high speed.

Condition D: Since a relational algebraic expression generates derived relations successively, these relations must be generated and deleted using much less time. Moreover, since derived relations are located on the main memory, main memory space occupied by derived relations must be reduced. In this way, the derived relation overflow problem can be solved.

4.2 Perfectly Balanced Tree Storing

This paper adopts attribute-wise storing in order to satisfy Condition A. There are two ways of storing a relation: tuple-wise and attribute-wise. Tuple-wise storing, which has been adopted in most systems, gives natural access to tuples. On the other hand, it is inappropriate for both extracting attribute values used in operations and adding attributes. The former problem would surely stand in the way of dramatically improving performance. Attribute–wise storing provides much faster access to attribute values; however, it is weak in extracting tuples. How to overcome this problem will be mentioned soon hereafter.

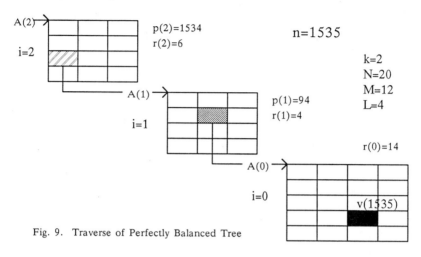

Fig. 9. Traverse of Perfectly Balanced Tree

This architecture uses the perfectly balanced tree shown in Fig.9 to store attribute values, which makes it possible to satisfy Condition B. Leaves(to be called value pages) and nodes(to be called node pages) of the tree store attribute values and pointers to lower nodes(or leaves), respectively. For example, when the capacity of a value page is set at 512, and the capacity of a node page at 64, a one–step perfectly balanced tree can store up to 32,768 values and two–step tree up to 2,097,152 values. Thus, such a tree can store relations of various sizes without loss of memory space.

To satisfy Condition C, two new concepts are introduced: tuple identification by tuple number and value addressing by calculation. The previous attribute–wise addressing method[22] attaches a tuple id to each tuple and applies clustering to both attribute values and tuple id's to make each of their accesses fast. This approach, however, has two defects: an increase in storage by attaching tuple id's and slowness in extracting tuples(due to selection using tuple id). Therefore, tuple identification by tuple number instead of tuple id is adopted. Tuple numbers require no extra storage. Moreover, an attribute value with a given tuple number can be addressed by a calculation as simple as the one described below. Thus, both of the defects stated above can be eliminated.

The following method gives the address of an attribute value $v(n)$ corresponding to tuple number n. First, we use the following notations:

$\quad$ k: depth(steps) of the present perfectly balanced tree,
$\quad$ N: the capacity of a value page,
$\quad$ M: the capacity of a node page,
$\quad$ L: the length of an attribute value,
$\quad$ $q(i)$: $M^{**}(i-1)^{*}N$, $\qquad$ where $i = k,...,1$,
$\quad$ [x]: integer part of x.

Then, $r(i)$, the entry number of i–th step of the tree corresponding to n, is given by the following equations:

$\quad$ $p(k) = n-1$,
$\quad$ $r(k) = [p(k)/q(k)]$,
$\quad$ $p(i-1) = p(i) - q(i)^{*}r(i)$, $\qquad$ where $i = k,...,2$,
$\quad$ $r(i-1) = [p(i-1)/q(i-1)]$,

$$r(0) = p(1) - q(1)^*r(1).$$

Finally, $v(n)$ can be accessed by the following memory accesses:

$$A(j-1) = word(A(j) + 4^*r(j)), \quad \text{where } j = k,...,1,$$
$$v(n) = word(A(0) + L^*r(0)),$$

where "word" denotes the content of the present entry.

4.3 Storing of Derived Relations

A value in any derived relation is basically represented by both a tuple number and an attribute number of a basic relation. Selected tuple numbers of an attribute in any derived relation are stored using a perfectly balanced tree, as before. In most cases, derived relations are temporarily generated and immediately deleted in successive algebraic operations and so saving a derived relation for later use needs a change of relation mode from derived to basic.

Attributes in a derived relation may often have the same tuple number data. To make good use of this fact, attributes of a derived relation are divided into owner attributes and branch attributes. The former really manages tuple numbers selected for a derived relation, while the latter is only provided with a pointer to the owner attribute which manages tuple numbers on its behalf. For example, in a derived relation selected from a basic relation, only one owner attribute will suffice and the rest are branch ones. Figure 10 illustrates this case. Other examples will be presented soon hereafter. Of course, owner management is also applied to relations as derived from other derived relations. An owner attribute and its branch attributes share both the original basic relation and all the operations carried out so far.

Since the number of branch attributes may be much larger than that of the owner attributes, owner management does much in satisfying Condition D; that is, the storage needed for derived relations is greatly decreased and their generation/deletion accelerated. For example, consider a derived relation of 1,000 tuples generated after selecting a basic relation of 20 attributes. Compared with 80 kilobytes memory(for only data) in the alternative storing using real attribute values, the present storing requires only 4 kilobytes ,reduced to 1/20, because there is only one owner attribute. In general, storage reduction is realized in a ratio of the number of owner attributes to the total number of attributes in a derived relation.

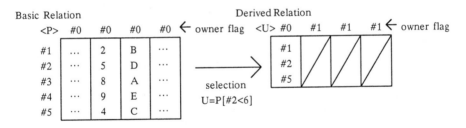

Fig. 10. Owner Status in Selected Relation

5. Algorithms for Main Relational Algebra Operations

5.1 Algorithm for Join

For memory resident databases, hashing is known to be a promising method for equi-join or natural-join[7,23]. When applying hashing, care must be taken not to cause serious conflicts. Furthermore, since the number of objects for hashing is very large, the hashing load should be made as light as possible. For a variable-length attribute, the hashing load is normally heavy because the permutation of strings must be considered. For example, hashing function should point to different buckets in the case of such permuted strings as "ABCD", "BCDA".

For MACH1, in which variable–length strings are encoded to fixed–length codes, experiments showed that the following simple hashing function suffices:

$$v >> 2 \qquad mod\ W,$$

where, v: value to be hashed,

    >> 2: right shift by 2 bits,

    $W = [c*n/e]*e + 1,$

    c: coefficient for the number of buckets,

    n: the number of tuples engaged in join,

    e(=12): entry length of coding table,

    [x]: integer part of x.

The right shift cuts off the lowest 2 bits since every code(address) has a 4 byte boundary. A slightly complicated modulo W prevents conflicts which might arise from the regularity of a code(address) in e=12 increments. A test showed the following good result where conflicts are negligible(less than 2 %):

    S = 1,000   K = 0,

    S = 10,000   K = 121,

    S = 100,000   K = 1,582,

where,   S: the number of unique strings(52 bytes),

    K: the number of conflicts.

Therefore, it is seen that encoding has a good effect on hashing.

Hashing can not be used in general theta–join operations. Therefore, an ordered merge approach would seem appropriate in this case. Dedicated hardware, such as CAM, will surely bring about performance improvement.

How to store a joined relation is described below from the viewpoint of owner management. In short, if one of the relations to be joined is a basic one, derived owner/branch relationships are generated as explained in section 4.3 above. On the other hand, if one is derived, the joined relation will inherit its owner/branch relationships. An example is shown in Fig.11. Note that attributes in distinct owner/branch groups should not be merged into one group, even if they share the same basic relation. Note also that tuple numbers in a joined relation are always those of the basic relations, even when joining derived relations.

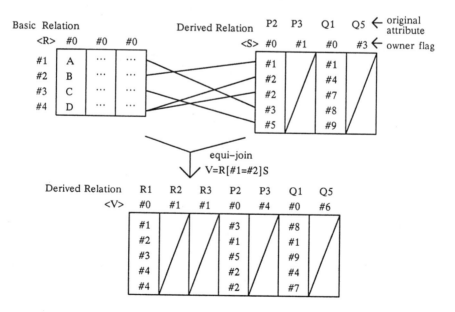

Fig. 11. Owner Status in Joined Relation

5.2 Algorithm for Projection

The most difficult problem in projection is removing duplicates which arise from extracting attributes. To accomplish this, MACH1 applies hashing again. If it is known that there is a unique key attribute among the projected attributes, only that attribute will need to be hashed. Since this is not generally expected, we do not apply such an assumption. The more attributes that are used in hashing, the less serious conflict becomes; however, the hashing load increases. Therefore, the extent of conflict and hashing load are in a trade-off relationship.

Since serious conflicts intensively worsen performance, we use every projected attribute in hashing:

$$a1^*v1 + a2^*v2 + \ldots + an^*vn \qquad mod\ W,$$

where, ai: random number,
vi: a value of the i-th attribute,
W: the same as in join.

The heart of this hashing function lies in multiplying random numbers before addition, which keeps conflicts from becoming serious. In one test, this contrivance reduced the number of equality checks from 114,478 to 1,017, shortening the processing time to 3/11.

Owner management of a projected relation is slightly intricate, as shown in Fig.12. In a single scan of projected attributes, it can handle the situation in which a branch attribute may become an owner after projection. This owner management is operated as follows. First, scan the projected attributes list {att(i)} one by one from the top. Get the owner flag w(i) of the j-th element att(i).

1) If w(i) = 0, namely, att(i) is the owner before projection, then check the rep. table as to whether there is an entry having the left value "i". If not, the attribute continues to be the owner, so add to the rep. table an entry whose left value = i and right value = j; otherwise, the attribute will become a branch, with the right value of the entry as its owner pointer.

2) If w(i) > 0, namely, att(i) is a branch before projection, then check the rep. table as to whether there is an entry having the left value "w(i)". If not, the attribute becomes the owner, so add to the rep. table an entry whose left value = w(i) and right value = j; otherwise, the attribute continues to be a branch, with the right value of the entry as its owner pointer.

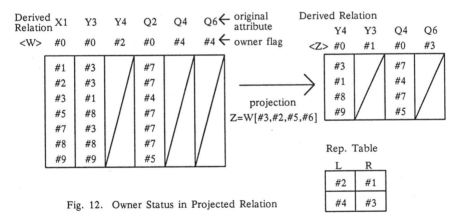

Fig. 12. Owner Status in Projected Relation

6. Performance of MACH1

6.1 Implementation Environments

MACH1 uses no dedicated hardware, and it was implemented on a workstation environment (Apollo DN570 turbo, 20MHz MC68020 with 16 megabytes main memory). Its encoding/decoding mechanism, operation execution mechanism, and data access mechanism were coded in the C programming language; while, its query reduction mechanism was prototyped in prolog[10,11]. Since benchmarks are algebraic, query reduction is not used in the following performance evaluation.

6.2 Performance Evaluation

The Wisconsin benchmark[3] is a well–known, equitable performance test for database machine/systems. We used the single user test.

Table 1 shows the result of the selection tests. MACH1 is 2.0 to 9.6 times faster than the quickest disk–based machine(IDM dac with indices). Comparison with the performance of another memory resident approach SiDBM[6] is also interesting. The machine embodies parallelism of the unique shared memory multiprocessor. It gives better performance than MACH1 when the number of selected tuples is small and indices are used, but in other conditions MACH1 exceeds. The selection time of MACH1 is in proportion to the problem size (the cardinalities of the source and target relations). For example, selection of 1,000 tuples from 100,000 requires 9.6 sec, and selection of 10,000 from 100,000 requires 11.4 sec. Various experiments revealed that the average time to read and compare a tuple is about 0.094 msec, and the time to generate a tuple is about 0.16 msec.

Table 1. Selection Queries

(sec)

System	100/10000		1000/10000	
Indices	without	with	without	with
U_INGRES	53.2	7.7	64.4	27.8
C_INGRES	38.4	3.9	53.9	18.9
ORACLE	194.2	16.3	230.6	130.0
IDMnodac	31.7	2.0	33.4	9.9
IDMdac	21.6	1.5	23.6	8.7
DIRECT	43.0	43.0	46.0	46.0
SiDBM	4.1	0.4	4.3	3.3
MACH1	0.8		0.9	

Table 2. Join Queries

(sec)

System	joinAselB		joinABprime		joinCselAselB	
Indices	without	with	without	with	without	with
U_INGRES	611	126.5	581	99.5	563	544.5
C_INGRES	109	54.0	156	103.0	127	64.0
ORACLE	>18000	476.4	>18000	433.2	>18000	826.8
IDMnodac	>18000	31.0	>18000	35.5	>18000	44.5
IDMdac	>18000	23.5	>18000	27.5	>18000	35.0
DIRECT	612	612.6	570	568.2	336	337.2
MACH1	1.9		1.2		3.5	

Table 2 shows the result of equi–join tests. MACH1 exceeds the same fastest disk–based machine by between 10.0 and 22.9 times. While L(the number of tuples in a joined relation) is small, the joining time of MACH1 is also in close proportion to the number of tuples in relations to be joined. For example, a joinABprime test which generates 10,000 tuples from 2 relations of 100,000 and 10,000 tuples requires 13.4 sec. As L gets larger, the joining time of MACH1 becomes dominated by the time to generate a joined relation. For example, in joining 10,000 and 10,000 tuples, joining time is 1.5 sec for L=0, and 4.9 sec for L=10,000. From this experiment, the average time required to merge two tuples is estimated at about 0.34 msec. The remaining time is for hashing and comparing, which depends on the distribution of hashed values.

Table 3 summarizes the result of projection tests. MACH1 exceeds the fastest disk–based machine(IDM dac) by from 6.9 to 32.7 times. The same as with selection, projection time of MACH1 is also in proportion to the problem size. For example, projection of 1,000 tuples from 100,000 requires 29.0 sec and projection of 10,000 from 10,000 requires 20.4 .

Table 3. Projection Queries

(sec)

system	100/ 10000	1000/ 1000
U_INGRES	64.6	236.8
C_INGRES	26.4	132.0
ORACLE	828.5	199.8
IDMnodac	29.3	122.2
IDMdac	22.3	68.1
DIRECT	2068.0	58.0
MACH1	3.3	2.1

Performance analysis reveals that most processing time is spent in memory access (read /write). Therefore, speedup of the memory access mechanism, for example multiprocessor approach[24] will be the main point in further improving performance.

7.Conclusions

This paper has proposed MACH architecture, whose goal is set at performance improvement by two orders of magnitude. This architecture is aimed mainly at the knowledge processing field, which requires performance on this level. The design principles and an overview of MACH architecture were first provided. They were followed by an explanation of the main characteristics of MACH architecture; a memory resident database, fixed–length encoding, sophisticated data storing, and hash–based algorithms for relational algebra operations. Encoding experiments conducted on databases in practical use revealed that high–speed encoding on the main memory is feasible for up to middle scale databases. Benchmark tests of the first implementation MACH1 showed that MACH1 exceeds any disk–based machine/system by more than one order, and that further improvement of the memory access mechanism is needed to raise performance by an additional order.

Acknowledgments

We wish to thank Dr.Akihiro Hashimoto and Dr.Kunio Murakami for their continuing guidance and encouragement. We are also grateful to Mr.Kiyoshi Yoshida and Mr.Kiyonori Konishi for their helpful discussions.

352

References

[1] Agrawal,R. and DeWitt,D.J.,"Whither Hundreds of Processors in a Database Machine?," Int'l Workshop on High-Level Architecture,Los Angeles,Cal.,1984.

[2] Fushimi,S.,Kitsuregawa,M.,and Tanaka,H.,"An Overview of the System Software of a Parallel Relational Database Machine GRACE," Proc.12th VLDB, Kyoto, Japan, May 1986.

[3] Bitton,D.,DeWitt,D.J.,and Turbyfill,C.,"Benchmarking Database Systems: A Systematic Approach," CS Tech. Rep. #526 Univ. of Wisconsin-Madison,Dec. 1983.

[4] Yokota,K.,"Deductive Approach for Unnormalized Model," SIG Notes IPS Japan, 87-DB-58, Mar. 1987 (in Japanese).

[5] Nakano,R.,and Kiyama,M.,"Frame Calculus," Sig Notes IPS Japan,87-AI-50, 1987 (in Japanese).

[6] Leland,M.D.P.,and Roome W.D.,"The Silicon Database Machine," Proc. 4th IWDM, Grand Bahama Island ,March 1985.

[7] DeWitt,D.J.,et al.,"Implementation Tecniques for Main Memory Database Systems," SOGMOD'84 Boston,MA, pp.1-17,June 1984.

[8] Codd,E.F.,"Relational Completeness of Data Base Sublanguages," in Data Base Systems, Courant Computer Symposium 6,Prentice Hall, 1972.

[9] ISO/TC97/SC21,"Database Language SQL," ISO/TC97/SC21/WG 5-15, 1985.

[10] Nakano,R.,and Saito,K.,"Rule-Based Reduction From Relational Calculus to Succinct Relational Algebraic Expression," Sig Notes IPS Japan,86-DB-54, 1986 (in Japanese).

[11] Nakano,R.,and Saito,K.,"Reduction of Aggregate Functions in Relational Calculus to Optimal Algebraic Expressions," Sig Notes IPS Japan,87-DB-57, 1987 (in Japanese).

[12] Jaeschke,G. and Schek,H.-J.,"Remarks on Algebra of Non First Normal Form Relations," Proc. ACM Symposium on Principles of Database Systems, Calif., Mar. 1982.

[13] Schek,H.-J. and Pistor,P.,"Data Structures for an Integrated Data Base Management and Information Retrieval System," Proc. 8th VLDB, Mexico City,Mexico, Sep. 1982.

[14] Ogura,T.,et al.,"A 4-Kbit Associative Memory LSI,"IEEE J. Solid State Circuits, SC-20,6,pp.1277-1282 ,1985.

[15] Tanaka Y.,"A Data-Stream Database Machine with Large Capacity," in Advanced Database Machine Architecture, D.K.Hsiao (ed.), Prentice-Hall,pp.168-202 ,1983.

[16] Boyer,R.S. and Moore,J.S.,"A Fast String Searching Algorithm," Comm.ACM, 20, 10, pp.762-772, 1977.

[17] Nakano,R.,and Kiyama,M.,"Experiment of Encoding Databases," Sig Notes IPS Japan, 87-FI-4, 1987 (in Japanese).

[18] Itano K.,et al.,"A Pipelined String Search Algorithm Based on an Associative Memory," Trans.IPS Japan,26,6,pp.1152-1155 ,1985 (in Japanese)

[19] Larson,P.-A,"Dynamic Hashing," BIT,18,2,pp.184-201 ,1978.

[20] Litwin,W.,"LINEAR HASHING:A New Tool for File and Table Addressing," Proc. 6th VLDB, pp.212-223, 1980.

[21] Knuth,D.E.,"The Art of Computer Programming,Vol.2:Semi-numerical algorithms," Addison-Wesley,Reading, Mass. ,1973.

[22] Murakami,K.,et al.,"A Relational Database Machine: First Step to Knowledge Base Machine,"Proc. 10th Symposium on Computer Architecture,June 1983.

[23] Lehman,T.J.,and Carey,M.J.,"Query Processing in Main Memory Database Systems," SIGMOD'86 Washington,DC, pp.239-250 ,March 1986.

[24] Nakano,R.,and Kiyama,M.,"Full Associative Processing for Relational Operations," 34th Annual Convention IPS Japan,3C-1 ,March 1987 (in Japanese).

A DISTRIBUTED, MAIN-MEMORY DATABASE MACHINE
Research Issues and a Preliminary Architecture

Martin L. Kersten

Centre for Mathematics & Computer Science, Department of Algorithmics & Architecture, Kruislaan 413, 1098 SJ Amsterdam

Peter M.G. Apers, Maurice A.W. Houtsma, Erik J.A. van Kuyk, Rob L.W. van de Weg

University of Twente, Computer Science Department, Postbus 217, 7500 AE Enschede

INTRODUCTION

The PRISMA project is a large-scale research effort in the design and implementation of a highly parallel machine for data and knowledge processing. The PRISMA database machine is a distributed, main-memory database management system implemented in an object-oriented language that runs on top of a large message-passing multi-computer system. A knowledge-based approach is used to exploit parallelism and query processing. Moreover, it has both an SQL and a logic programming language interface. To improve the overall performance a generative approach is used to customize the relation managers.

The need for such an architecture stems from the processing requirements put by systems that use explicit knowledge to organize their data and which apply explicit knowledge to the manipulation of large amounts of data. In the first phase of this project a parallel architecture is developed that supports both data and knowledge processing separately; resulting in a database machine and an experimental machine for parallel inferencing. The database machine is the focus of this paper.

State of the Art

The design and construction of database machines to improve non-numeric processing has attracted many researchers during the last two decades. At one end of the spectrum they have reduced the amount of data to be manipulated by filtering records as they are transferred from disk to main-memory [25, 31] and using several functional computers

The work reported in this document was conducted as part of the PRISMA project, a joint effort with Philips Research Eindhoven, partially supported by the Dutch "Stimuleringsprojectteam Informaticaonderzoek (SPIN)."

353

linked into a network [11,15,21]. The other end of the spectrum is characterized by attempts to harness the processing power and storage capacity offered by large scale integration [29,19].

Despite the many research efforts, few database machines are currently commercially available (ICL/CAFS, Britton-Lee IDM, Teradata DBC-1024). This situation can be attributed to provision of partial solutions, rapid evolution of hardware technology, and monolithic architecture of most database systems.

Current relational database machines fall short by providing a fixed set of primitive data types, i.e. integer, float, and fixed/variable length strings. Although these data types suffice for most business-like database applications, the fixed set of operators, their storage layout, and their use within the query optimizer makes it difficult to accommodate new application areas such as statistical database, CAD/CAM, and office automation. An alternative approach is to build an *extensible* database system. Such a system provides a mechanism to introduce new data types with their associated operators, a mechanism to enhance the query optimizer and storage techniques. Extensible relational system do not yet exist. However, attempts in automating the construction of the physical storage handler are currently undertaken [23,6,28].

Another observation is that no single database management system will efficiently supports all database applications in the future. There arises a need for a variety of facilities, providing the proper level of abstraction, user interface, and functionality. For example, integration of micro-computers with main-frames pushes the need for cooperative database systems and interfaces with low-end database systems, such as spreadsheet packages. The consequence is that future database systems should be designed with distribution in mind. That is, a database system comprises a set of database managers, each providing part of the required overall functionality and coordinated by a distribution manager.

The cost for main memory drops rapidly. Therefore, it becomes feasible and cost-effective to keep a major portion of the database in main memory [12,14]. Since one may not assume that a 1 GigaByte is managed by a single processor, due to hardware and performance limitations, it is mandatory to design it as a distributed system from scratch. Moreover, since dealing with physical limitations is a costly affair, such a new system should have no provisions to handle, for example, memory overflow (except for recognition of that event). In fact, if the database does not fit in the available memory then the user should construct a distributed database. It is assumed that a distribution manager takes care of proper duplication of information to guarantee continual service and reconstruction of the database. For example, by keeping a copy of the database modifications on a (slow) disk drive.

The PRISMA database machine is an attempt to gain experience and knowledge concerning these issues through the construction of a running prototype.

PRISMA Project

The long term objective of the PRISMA project is to obtain a flexible architecture for a machine that stores and manipulates both data and knowledge. This long term objective translates into the following goals:

- The construction of a message-passing multi-computer system, consisting of a large number of 32-bit processors, each containing 8-16 Mb words of main memory;
- The definition and efficient implementation of an object-oriented language (called POOL-X); POOL-X is an extension of POOL-T [1], which hides the multi-computer system and serves as an implementation language;
- The design and implementation of a main-memory database system in POOL-X with an SQL and a logic programming interface;
- The design and implementation of an expert system shell in POOL-X that exploits parallelism for inferencing;
- To investigate the usage of coarse grain parallelism, the integration of data and knowledge processing, and the evaluation of the machine, among other things.

The project started in October 1986 and is scheduled until September 1990. The project team consists of members of the Philips Research Laboratory in Eindhoven and several Dutch academia. Currently approximately 30 people are directly involved. The PRISMA machine, its operating system, and the language POOL-X are developed by Philips Research Laboratory Eindhoven and the University of Amsterdam; the design of the expert system shell is conducted at the Centre for Mathematics and Computer Science; the theoretical issues related to parallel processing in general are studied by Philips Research Eindhoven, the University of Utrecht, and the University of Leiden; the design and the development of the database system on top of the PRISMA machine is a joint effort between the University of Twente and the Centre for Mathematics and Computer Science.

This paper mainly discusses the database activities in the PRISMA-project. In section 2 the key research topics are highlighted and in section 3 the overall architecture of the PRISMA database machine software is given. We conclude with a summary and status report.

KEY ISSUES IN THE PRISMA DATABASE MACHINE

The most important ideas behind the design of the PRISMA database machine are summarized below:

- it is designed as a tightly coupled distributed system;
- it provides an SQL and a logic programming interface;
- it uses a knowledge-based approach to exploit parallelism;
- it uses a generative approach for data managers;

- it uses a very large main-memory as primary storage;
- it is implemented in an object-oriented language;
- it runs on a large message-passing multi-computer.

In the following sections we will discuss these issues, and related topics, in more detail. The presentation is purposely sketchy, because many issues pointed out still belong to the realm of active research. Both within the PRISMA project and within the database research projects elsewhere.

Design Philosophy for a Database Machine

Most database management systems are built as tightly coupled programs. Moreover, they are designed to cope with all limitations and shortcomings of their software/hardware environment. Often, a DBMS uses its own disk buffer management, its own screen manipulation, its own parsing technique, etc.. Moreover, the requirement of good performance often results in making systems more tightly coupled than advisable for software maintainability.

At the same time we see a trend towards the use of distributed database management systems. They provide an economic alternative for otherwise large investments of centralized computing centers and communication facilities. Since the theory of distributed database systems has passed its infancy, it becomes also possible to apply these techniques within a single database management system as well. That is, one may view a traditional DBMS as a tightly coupled distributed system.

Since high performance remains a key issue in the design of a database system (dynamic), compilation techniques are used on a regular basis now. For example, SQL/DS uses dynamic compilation and linkage of access routines to obtain the best performance [10]. Similar techniques are currently explored in INGRES and POSTGRES [30].

A more ambitious track is to generate large portions of a DBMS itself. Such a step is feasible, because sufficient interpretative relational systems have been developed over the last decade. Moreover, a database system compiler is assumed to be smaller and easier to maintain than a large system [22].

In the PRISMA database machine project we take these approaches one step further by generating prototypical relation managers from specifications and using a knowledge-based approach to exploit the potential parallelism in the resulting distributed system. To summarize, the design philosophy of the PRISMA database machine is based on four observations, listed below:

- Designing a DBMS is a large software engineering project;
- Off-the-shelve hardware is often more cost effective than special purpose hardware for most components in a system;
- The storage and processing in a DBMS should be distributed by content and functionality;

The effectiveness of a DBMS is largely determined by the proper level of interpretation -to obtain flexibility- and compilation -to guarantee efficiency-.

Interfaces to the PRISMA Database Machine

The database machine supports three user interfaces; an SQL interface, a POOL-X programming language interface, and a logic programming language interface. An implementation of the SQL standard has been chosen to accommodate existing application environments relatively easy. Moreover, its large user base simplifies early experimentation. The POOL-X interface, the system implementation language, enables tool developers to bypass the SQL parser, query optimizers, and possibly the transaction monitor as well. The benefit is improved performance, provided the tools behave properly. Since the ultimate goal of the PRISMA project is a single machine for data and knowledge processing, the database machine also supports a logic programming interface. The importance of this interface warrants a more detailed description.

More and more one can see the need to represent domain-specific knowledge in a declarative way. Often this type of knowledge is scattered over applications running on top of a database. Changing this knowledge requires rewriting many applications. One way to solve this problem is to interface a relational DBMS with Prolog. The data is stored in the database and the knowledge is represented in Prolog programs. Several papers have appeared on this topic [8,17]. One of the main drawbacks of this solution is the inefficiency of query processing. Another solution is to extend a DBMS with Prolog-like facilities. Many papers on recursion and Datalog have appeared [2,13,18,33,5,9] The advantage of this approach is that optimizing queries involving recursion is left to the database query optimizer. In PRISMA the latter approach is adopted.

The language that is defined in PRISMA is called PRISMAlog and has an expressive power similar to Datalog and LDL [32]. It is based on definite, function-free Horn clauses and its syntax is similar to Prolog. The statements can be divided into three groups: facts, rules, and queries. *Facts* are n-ary predicates ($n>0$) in which every argument is a constant. *Rules* are composed of two parts, a left-hand side (LHS) and a right-hand side (RHS), which are separated by an arrow. The LHS consists of an n-ary predicate ($n>0$) with as arguments either constants or variables (there should be at least one variable). The RHS consists of predicates connected by boolean connectives (logical 'and' and logical 'or'); again all arguments should be constants or variables. Every predicate that is used in the RHS of a rule should itself be a fact or the LHS of a rule. To have a meaning, every variable used in the the LHS of a rule should be bound in the RHS. *Queries* are rules without a LHS that start with a question mark.

The semantics of PRISMAlog is defined in terms of extensions of the relational algebra. Facts correspond to tuples in relations in the database. Rules are view definitions. The LHS forms a virtual relation and the RHS describes the computation in terms of joins on relations and μ-calculus expressions [3]; the latter are used for recursion. So, one of the main differences between Prolog and PRISMAlog is that the latter is set-oriented, which makes it more suitable for parallel evaluation.

The approach taken for LDL is to define a very rich language and to start implementing a restricted version of it. Here we take the opposite approach. We start off with a language very similar to Datalog and consider extensions for inclusion based on a clear semantics and a foreseeable efficient implementation. The semantics of an extension will be the translation to an operation of the relational algebra or an extension of it. Currently, the following extensions are considered:

- *Negation*. Negation will be allowed if it can be translated to the set difference operation. Stratification, as in LDL, is considered.

- *Evaluable predicates*. Evaluable predicates are considered, to allow for a simple form of arithmetic. Candidates are arithmetic comparison, average, sum, count, min, and max.

- *Sets*. Allowing sets as arguments is similar to allowing results of relational expressions as values of attributes [27].

- *Complex objects*. This leads to non-normalized relations for which an efficient implementation has to be found.

Exploiting Parallelism and a Knowledge-based Approach to Query Optimization

Having a large pool of processors available does not naturally lead to their efficient use in a database machine. Using all these processors to achieve parallelism both within the DBMS and in query processing is a non-trivial task. One dimension of the problem is the grain size of parallelism: coarse or fine grain. In the PRISMA-project the coarse grain approach is taken, because we expect to gain more performance from it in our multi-computer architecture. First, possible applications of parallelism are discussed and then the knowledge-based approach to query optimization is presented.

Parallelism will be used both within the DBMS and in query processing. Within the DBMS this will be obtained by running several occurrences of components of the DBMS in parallel. Examples of these components are the parsers, the query optimizer, the transaction monitor, and the data managers for intermediate results. For each query or update a new occurrence is created, possibly running on its own processor, depending on the work load. This means that evaluation of several queries and updates can be done in parallel, except for accesses to the same copy of base fragments of the database.

Applying parallelism to query processing is done in a similar way as in distributed databases. However, local processing cost cannot be neglected compared to transmission cost, as is done in traditional distributed databases. So, new optimization objectives are needed in the multi-computer environment. Parallelism can be applied by splitting up the relations into fragments and locating them at different processors. In this way the selection and join operators can be computed in a distributed way.

For example, let R be a relation located on one processor. In this case no parallelism can be applied to compute a selection on R. If, on the other hand, R is split into two fragments F_1 and F_2, each located at their own processor, the selections on F_1 and F_2 can be computed in parallel. Obviously, obtaining the result of the selection on R requires the computation of the union of the selections on its fragments. Determining the optimal size of the fragments depends on a number of factors, e.g. local processing cost and transmission cost. Besides the size of a fragment, also the fragmentation criterion is important as the following example shows.

Let $R = F_1 \cup F_2$ and $S = G_1 \cup G_2$. Then computing the join between R and S is the same as computing

$$F_1 \bowtie G_1 \cup F_1 \bowtie G_2 \cup F_2 \bowtie G_1 \cup F_2 \bowtie G_2,$$

which shows that the number of joins grows quadratically in the number of fragments. If R and S are fragmented in a random way nothing can be done about this. If, however, both R and S are split according to the same fragmentation criterion, computing $F_1 \bowtie G_2$ and $F_2 \bowtie G_1$ is not necessary. Our goal is to integrate the ideas of optimal fragment sizes and still using a fragmentation criterion.

Applying parallelism to the computation of recursive queries is a new research area [26]. In [4] an indication is given how this can be done. Algorithms for parallel evaluation of the transitive closure operation are under development.

Exploiting all this parallelism in a coherent way in an environment where system parameters are still unknown, because the multi-computer system is still under development, designing a query optimizer, which implements one specific strategy, is not the right thing to do. Therefore, to allow for as much flexibility as possible, a knowledge-based approach to query optimization is taken. The knowledge base contains rules concerning logical transformations, estimating sizes of intermediate results, detection of common subexpressions, and applying parallelism to minimize response time [20].

A Generative Approach to Customize Relation Managers

Most (software) database management systems are large pieces of software which provide an interpretative environment for the task at hand; namely maintaining a relational database. This software complexity is needed to obtain an efficient system and to cope effectively with the many parameters involved, such as managing a multi-level memory hierarchy, supporting a wide-variety of user requests, dealing with concurrent access and an unreliable environment. In a sense, relational database managements system are prepared for the worst, namely avoiding unacceptable performance even for unexpected user requests.

One way to deal with this complexity is to develop an 'open architecture' for relational systems. The prime advantage is that proper software organization simplifies hardwiring critical portions of the system. Moreover, it is envisioned that a proper software architecture is mandatory for future functional enhancements. The latter is the focus of the EXODUS project [7].

In the PRISMA database machine project we pursue this line of research. The system is developed-up as a locally distributed system from scratch. Moreover, we think that there is sufficient experience with relational systems, both in theory and practice, that it becomes possible to generate a customized database management system for each individual relation. Therefore, unlike existing DDBMSs, we assume that each local DBMS can only support a single fragment of a relation. Such a database management system

will be called a One-Fragment-Manager (or OFM). It contains all functions encountered in a full-blown DBMS; such as local query optimizer, transaction management,
markings and cursor maintenance, and (various) storage structures. More specifically, it
supports a transitive closure operator for dealing with recursive queries. It is assembled
from a collection software libraries. The only aspect standardized throughout the system
is the functional interface to OFMs.

Ideally, it should be possible to generate a new OFM for each relation once needed.
That is, the relation structure is reflected in the DBMS code during compilation. However, this would place an unnecessary burden on the performance of the implementation
language compiler and its linkage editor. Moreover, a limited form of interpretation is
unavoidable and does not severely threaten the overall performance. Therefore, we
assume that there are a few default OFMs implementations. The transaction monitor
selects one of the OFMs necessary for the operation at hand and creates a new instance
parameterized with the relation structure and integrity constraints.

The potential gains from our approach are summarized as follows:

- *Performance.*
  A substantial portion of the interpretation overhead is removed during compilation and OFM assemblage. Moreover, a mini-compiler allows dynamic compilation of a large class of (simple) operations.

- *Processing flexibility.*
  Each OFM is equipped with the right amount of tools for their role within the
  processing of a query and the maintenance of the database.

- *Function extensibility.*
  A generative approach simplifies the construction of a federated system in which
  new OFMS can be integrated, because the system is, to a larger extend, devoid
  from hidden implementation constraints.

The Primary Database Store is Main-Memory

The PRISMA database machine differs from traditional database machines by assuming that the database and the temporaries fit in main-memory. The role of disks is
reduced to a level where conventionally one finds tape-drives, i.e. as persistent storage for
recovery purposes. Our motivations for this attitude are as follows:

- *Economics.* It has been recognized for some time that the reduction of prices for
  main-memory enables a cost-effective solution to medium-sized databases.

- *Simplicity.* Moving the database into main-memory simplifies the data management task, because one level in the memory hierarchy need not be dealt with any
  more. In particular when the system is designed with the memory limitation as a
  given fixed boundary.

- *Improved performance.* Running a database from main-memory is likely to be faster than its disk-based counterpart. Just because the hardware has better performance and less CPU cycles are needed to access and maintain the storage structures.

A few caveats are in place here as well. Due to hardware limitations it is not possible to place a large memory under the control of a single processor. Simply adding processors, besides posing coordination problems, does not help either, because the high rate of memory references may cause communication (bus contention) problems. Therefore, a distributed approach is mandatory for a main-memory database machine.

Clearly, keeping the database in main memory improves its performance over that of a traditional disk-based system. However, the straightforward technique of providing a conventional system with sufficient memory to hold the database does not work well. Performance studies of uni-processor database system [16] show that most system are short on CPU power, which is not immediately resolved by providing a larger memory bank. Therefore, such a system should be designed from scratch.

We feel that a main-memory database system is more critical to programming errors and that the database is more threatened by hardware errors. The gap between main-memory and disks in traditional systems also provides a natural protection boundary. It is less likely that errors propagate to disk, thus permanently corrupting the database. Complementary, in a main-memory system the data structures should have built-in redundancy to recover quickly.

Last, but not least, a distributed approach is essential to accommodate the ever increasing demand for maintaining databases that do not fit in a one Giga-byte main-memory system.

Some important research issues related to large-scale, uncommitted use of main-memory are listen below;

- *Storage structures.*
  Placing the database in main-memory requires a re-evaluation of the database storage structures. In general they are not suited for the new environment, because they optimize access to the disk at considerable overhead in CPU processing.

- *Code versus data tradeoffs.*
  Since both database and DBMS are stored within in the same place it is possible to trade space normally used for data structures against enlarged code fragments. A preliminary study has shown that with judicious use of code expansion it is possible to store relational tables in minimal space and still providing the best performance.

- *Reliable storage structures.*
  Given the vulnerability of the database store it is crucial to quickly determine what portion of the database has been corrupted. Moreover, it should be possible to quickly rebuild a portion from stable storage.

- *Main-memory management.*
  Hardware support for memory management is essential. It not only provides a cheap mechanism to protect the database and database management system, it also simplifies the mapping of the database to the physical memory pages.

A Parallel Object-Oriented Implementation Language

Another innovative aspect of the PRISMA project is to develop a parallel object-oriented language and to use it as an implementation language for some non-trivial applications. The database software being one of them.

This language, called POOL-X, is an outgrowth and enhancement of the language POOL, which is being developed in a companion ESPRIT project, called the DOOM project [24]. All objects in POOL are implemented as processes with message passing the only means to establish cooperative behavior. Unlike most object-oriented languages POOL is augmented with a firm static verification scheme. The prime reason being the unpredictable nature of a highly parallel system and the expected improved performance by avoiding runtime checks. Moreover, it hides the underlying distributed hardware from the application programmer, i.e. objects are allocated to processing nodes automatically.

In the PRISMA project POOL is extended to obtain a language that is better suited as an implementation language. In particular, it has been extended with an exception handling mechanism, a more flexible typing scheme, floating point arithmetic, and a series of standard classes. Three concepts are introduced to simplify the implementation of a database management and to improve its performance.

- *Tuples*

  Primitives have been included to simplify the construction of tuples from standard primitive data types. Tuples can be passed around, copied freely, and portions can be extracted through a projection operator. They cannot, however, be partially modified.

- *Tuple types*

  A strong typing scheme stands in the way of an efficient implementation of a database system, because the structure and type of a relation are known after the program has been written. Therefore, a mechanism is included to construct type descriptors and to code the runtime type checks explicitly.

- *Mini compiler*

  Since interpretation of the same expression for many tuples in a relation is expensive, a dynamic compiler is included in the runtime system. It takes the structure of a relation and a syntax tree of a selection expression and compiles it into a boolean routine. This routine can subsequently be called for each candidate tuple.

- *Control over object placement*

  In a distributed database system automatic object placement is unacceptable, because it could render all optimizations useless. Therefore, the POOL-X implementation also provides the means to place objects near others. That is, place two objects on the same physical site. In combination with an enquire function (what is the site of an object) and a migration facility we think to have the facilities needed to obtain an efficient implementation of the PRISMA database machine.

The PaRallel Inference and Storage MAchine

The hardware configuration of the PRISMA machine is based on state-of-the-art and mostly off-the-shelf components. The prototype machine is based on processor (M68020, M68030), memory (8-16 Megabyte), and communication processor triplets that are connected with a network of point-to-point connections. The prototype machine is a 64 node system.

Although our aim is the development of a main-memory database system, this multi-computer system will be equipped with several disks as well. They are primarily used to boot the system and to provide persistent storage.

The following issues are dealt with:

- *Communication processor*
  The novel hardware is the communication processor, developed in a companion DOOM project, that will improve the communication between POOL objects residing on different machines.

- *Operating system*
  The operating system should support fast context switching, because the work is distributed over many thousands of small processes, which communicate by sending messages.

- *Stable storage*
  Stable storage is used to store checkpointed relations and log information. The language POOL-X provides an interface with stable storage. Also, less frequently used relations may reside on stable storage. These relations must be loaded in main memory before they can be accessed.

THE PRISMA DATABASE MACHINE ARCHITECTURE

This section describes the preliminary architecture of the PRISMA Database Machine by listing the components and shortly describing their functionality. Their interaction is described by considering a query in execution.

A Preliminary Architecture

Fig. 1 shows the Global Data Handler, several One-Fragment Managers, and their components. The two main internal interface are the XRA (eXtended Relational Algebra) and POOL-X. XRA is an extension of the relational algebra to capture the meaning of both SQL and PRISMAlog. One of the new features of XRA is the inclusion of recursion. The functionality of each component is described briefly.

SQL and PRISMAlog parser. The function of these interfaces has been described above. The task of the SQL parser is to translate SQL to XRA. Similar, the PRISMAlog parser compiles the logic programming statements into XRA.

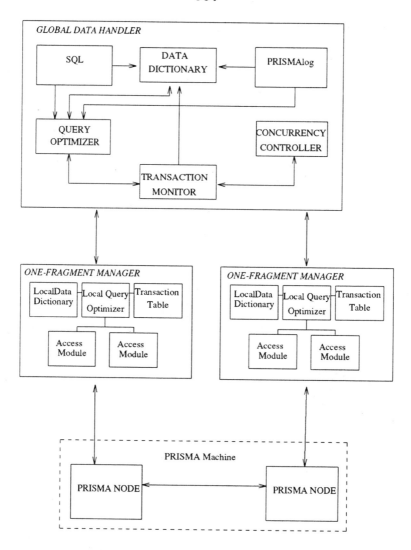

Figure 1: The PRISMA Database Architecture

Data Dictionary. The Data Dictionary is the prime repository for system wide information about the contents of the database. It contains the description of the schema of the relations, domain information, constraints, sizes and allocation of relations, etc.. As such, the Data Dictionary is used by the interface subsystems, query optimizer, and transaction monitor to obtain information about the current state of affairs.

Query Optimizer. The Query Optimizer is a global query optimizer. It takes a query in XRA and removes recursion by replacing it by while-loops. The remaining query is optimized by taking the allocation of the involved relations into account. The result of the Query Optimizer is a schedule containing subqueries for One-Fragment Managers and transmissions in between One-Fragment Managers. The objective is to minimize response time.

Transaction Monitor. The Transaction Monitor initiates and controls the execution of a schedule produced by the Query Optimizer. This may involve the creation of new One-Fragment Managers to store the intermediate results. Furthermore, the Transaction Monitor requests locks from the Concurrency Controller and handles rollback or commit.

Concurrency Controller. To provide the database with the functionality that several users may access the data simultaneously, a concurrency control based on two-phase locking, will be provided.

A *One-Fragment Manager.* provides full-fledged database management facilities for a single occurrence of a (logical) relation fragment. The interface with the Global Data Handler is formed by XRA. The storage capabilities take into account the resources available on the PRISMA node it operates on. From a database management system point of view the One-Fragment Managers form the smallest granularity for parallelism and data distribution. The functionality of each component is described shortly.

Local Data Dictionary. In the Local Data Dictionary information concerning the current state of the fragment is kept. This information is used internally for query optimization and administration of intermediate results. It is interrogated by its users for actual cost parameters and statistics about its behavior.

Transaction Table. The Transaction Table describes the concurrent running transactions. It partially replicates the information contained in the Concurrency Controller. This way it can deal with transaction failures more effectively.

Local Query Optimizer. The Local Query Optimizer takes an XRA request and selects the access paths and algorithms for evaluation. Moreover, it allocates local storage for the intermediate result. Unlike the Query Optimizer, this optimizer focuses on CPU and main-memory resource usage to obtain the minimum response time.

Access Modules. The Access Modules contain the actual code and free space to maintain the database storage structures. A variety of main-memory storage techniques are being used, such as linear lists, balanced-trees, and encoded tables. The One-Fragment Manager provides a simple scheme to keep partial results for a while, such as table markings. The facilities for this are largely independent of the relation definition and, therefore, grouped together in an access module.

Query Execution

In this section the interaction between the components of the Global Data Handler and the One-Fragment Managers are discussed, by showing what happens when a PRISMAlog query is executed.

A PRISMAlog query is accepted by an occurrence of the PRISMAlog parser. Besides the syntax of the query also the references to database predicates and other predicates (view definitions) are checked. This is done by accessing the Data Dictionary. When the query is syntactically and semantically correct it is translated to an XRA program.

The XRA query is passed on to an occurrence of the Query Optimizer, which, based on information in the Data Dictionary, produces a parallel schedule. This schedule is then handed over to an occurrence of the Transaction Monitor. It creates the OFMs for storage of the intermediates and controls the execution of the schedule. This Transaction Monitor communicates with the Concurrency Controller to guarantee a consistent view of the database. Furthermore, it communicates with the One-Fragment Managers of the involved relations or fragments to inform them about their task. Query execution may either be done in a data flow or demand driven way. The result of the query is managed by a One-Fragment Manager as well. The latter may be created for this purpose during query analysis. Finally, the result is passed to the user or kept for further query processing.

In case of an update (e.g., from SQL), the One-Fragment Manager affected should ensure stability, i.e. log information is saved before the update transaction is committed. This is done by storing the old and new version of affected tuples in a special One-Fragment Manager, which is sent to stable storage.

SUMMARY

The PRISMA project is a large scale research effort of Philips Research Laboratory in Eindhoven and Dutch academia. One of its goals is to design and implement a distributed, main-memory database machine. In this paper we have given an overview of the major innovative ideas behind the PRISMA Database Machine, which are 1) designing a tightly coupled distributed system running on a large message-passing multi-computer. 2) providing a logic programming interface, 3) exploiting parallelism using a knowledge-based approach, 4) providing several types of One-Fragment-Managers, each having their own characteristics, 5) storing all data in a distributed main-memory, and 6) using an object-oriented language as implementation language.

Since the project is just 8 months on its way, we have only been able to provide a rationale for the approach taken and to present a preliminary architecture. By the time this paper is published the functional design will be completed and prototypes of the key software components are being implementation.

Acknowledgements

We wish to thank the project members for providing a challenging environment and productive cooperation with the teams from Philips Research Eindhoven and the University of Amsterdam to develop this database machine. In particular, we wish to thank dr. A.J. Nijman from Philips Research Laboraties for bringing academia and industry together, dr. H.H. Eggenhuisen from Philips Research Laboraties for providing good project management and for stimulating the interaction between the various subprojects, and P. America for his work on the definition of POOL-X.

References

[1] America, P.H.M., "Design Issues in a Parallel Object-Oriented Language," *Proc. Parallel Computing 85*, 1986, North-Holland.

[2] Apers, P.M.G., Houtsma, M.A.W., and Brandse, F., "Processing Recursive Queries in Relational Algebra," *Proceedings IFIP TC2 working conference Knowledge and Data (DS-2)*, November 3-7, 1986.

[3] Apers, P.M.G., Houtsma, M.A.W., and Brandse, F., "Extending a relational interface with recursion," *Proceedings of the 6th Advanced Database Symposium*, pp.159-166, Aug. 29-30, 1986.

[4] Apers, P.M.G., Houtsma, M.A.W., and Brandse, F., "Extending a relational interface with recursion," *Proceedings of the 6th Advanced Database Symposium*, pp.159-166, Aug. 29-30, 1986.

[5] Bancilhon, F., "Naive evaluation of recursively defined relations," pp. 165-178 in On Knowledge Base Management Systems, ed. M.L Brodie and J. Mylopoulos, Springer-Verlag, New York (1986).

[6] Batory, D.S., "GENESIS: A Project to Develop an Extensible Database Management System," *Proceedings Int. Workshop on Object-Oriented Database Systems*, pp.206-207, Sep 1986.

[7] Carey, M.J., DeWitt, D.J., FRabk, D., Graefe, G., Muraliksihna, M., Richardson, J.E., and Shekita, E.J., "The Architecture of the EXODUS Extensible DBMS," *Proc. Int. Workshop on Object-Oriented Database Systems*, pp.52-65, Sep 1986.

[8] Ceri, S., Gottlob, G., and Wiederhold, G., "Interfacing relational databases and Prolog efficiently," *Proc. First International Conference on Expert Database Systems*, pp.141-153, April 1-4, 1986.

[9] Ceri, S., Gottlob, G., and Lavazza, L., "Translation and optimization of logic queries: the algebraic approach," *Proceedings of the 12th International Conference on Very Large Data Bases*, pp.395-402, August 25-28, 1986.

368

[10] Chamberlin, D.D., Gilbert, A.M., and Yost, R.A., *A History of System R and SQL/Data System.* Proc. 7-th Int. Conf. on Very Large Databases, Sep 1981.

[11] DeWitt, D.J., "DIRECT - A Multiprocessor organization for Supporting Relational Database Management," *IEEE Transactions on Computers*, vol. C-28, no. 6, pp.395-406, June 1979.

[12] DeWitt, D.J., Katz, R.H., Olken, K., Shapiro, L.D., Stonebraker, M.R., and Wood, D., "Implementation Techniques for Main Memory Database Systems," *Proceedings ACM SIGMOD*, pp.1-8, 1984.

[13] Emde Boas, G. van and Emde Boas, P. van, "Storing and evaluating horn-clause rules in a relational database," *IBM, Journal of Research and Development*, vol. 30, no. 1, January 1986.

[14] Garcia-Molina, H., Lipton, R.J., and Honeyman, P., "A Massive Memory Database System", Techn. Report 314, Dep. of Comp Sci. Princeton Univ., Sep 1983.

[15] Gardarin, G., Bernadat, P., Temmerman, N., Valduriez, P., and Viemont, Y., "Design of a Multiprocessor Relational Database System," *IFIP World Congress*, Sep. 1983.

[16] Hawthorn, P. and Stonebraker, M., "Performance Analysis of a Relational Data Base Management System," *Proceedings ACM SIGMOD*, pp.1-12, 1979.

[17] Jarke, M., Clifford, J., and Vassiliou, Y., "An Optimizing Prolog Front-End to a Relational Query System," *Proc. ACM-SIGMOD*, June 18-21, 1984.

[18] Jarke, M., Linnemann, V., and Schmidt, J.W., "Data constructors: on the integration of rules and relations," *Proceedings 11th International Conference on Very Large Data Bases*, pp.227-240, August 21-23, 1985.

[19] Katuka, T., Miyazaki, N., Shibayama, S., Yokota, H., and Murakami, K., "The Design and Implementation of Relational Database Machine Delta," pp. 13-34 in Proc. of the 4-th Int. Workshop on Database Machines, ed. H. Boral, Springer Verlag (1985).

[20] Kuijk, H.J.A. van, "A Knowledge-based Approach to Query Optimization," *Technical Report INF-86-37*, December 1986, Twente University of Technology.

[21] Leland, M.D.P. and Roome, W.D., "The Silicon Database Machine," pp. 169-189 in Proc. of the 4-th Int. Workshop on Database Machines, ed. H. Boral, Springer Verlag (1985).

[22] Maryanski, F., Bedell, J., Hoelscher, S., Hong, S., McDonald, L., Peckman, J., and Stock, D., "The Data Model Compiler: A Tool for Generating Objec-Oriented Database Systems," *Proceedings Int. Workshop on Object-Oriented Database Systems*, pp.73-84, Sep 1986.

[23] Maryanski, F., Bedell, J., Hoelscher, S., Hong, S., McDonald, L., Peckman, J., and Stock, D., "The Data Model Compiler: A Tool for Generating Objec-Oriented Database Systems," *Proceedings Int. Workshop on Object-Oriented Database Systems*, pp.73-84, Sep 1986.

[24] Odijk, E.A.M., "The Philips Object-Oriented Parallel Computer," in Fifth Generation Computer Systems, ed. J.V. Woods, North Holland (1985).

[25] Ozkarahan, E.A., Schuster, S.A., and Smith, K.C., "RAP- An Associative Processor for Database Management," *Proceedings of the National Computer Conference* , vol. 45, pp.379-387, 1975.

[26] Raschid, L. and Shu, S.Y.W., "A parallel strategy for evaluating recursive queries," *Proceedings of the 12th International Conference on Very Large Data Bases*, pp.412-419, August 25-28, 1986.

[27] Schek, H.-J. and Scholl, M.H., "The relational model with relation-valued attributes," *Information Systems*, vol. 11, no. 2, pp.137-147, 1986.

[28] Schwarz, P., Chang, W., Freytag, J.C., Lohman, G., McPherson, J., Mohan, C., and Pirahesh, H., "Extensibility in the Starburst Database System," *Proceedings Int. Workshop on Object-Oriented Database Systems*, pp.85-92, Sep 1986.

[29] Shaw, D., "Knowledge-Based Retrieval on a Relational Database Machine", Ph.D. Department of Computer Science, Stanford University, 1980.

[30] Stonebraker, M., "Object Management in POSTGRES Using Procedures," *Proceedings Int. Workshop on Object-Oriented Database Systems*, pp.66-72, Sep 1986.

[31] Su, S.Y.W., Nguyen, L.H., Emam, A., and Lipovski, G.L., "The Architectural Features and Implementation Techniques of a Multicell CASSM," *IEEE Transactions on Computers*, vol. C-28, no. 6, June 1979.

[32] Tsur, S. and Zaniolo, C., "LDL: a logic-based data-language," *Proceedings of the 12th International Conference on Very Large Data Bases*, pp.33-41, August, 1986.

[33] Ullman, J.D., "Implementation of logical query languages for databases," *ACM Transactions on Database Systems*, vol. 10, no. 3, pp.289-321, September 1985.

A SINGLE USER EVALUATION OF THE GAMMA DATABASE MACHINE

David J. DeWitt, Shahram Ghandeharizadeh, Donovan Schneider, Rajiv Jauhari,
M. Muralikrishna, and Anoop Sharma

Computer Sciences Department, University of Wisconsin, Madison, WI., USA

Abstract

This paper presents the results of an initial performance evaluation of the Gamma database machine based on an expanded version of the single-user Wisconsin benchmark. In our experiments we measured the effect of relation size and indices on response time for selection, join, and aggregation queries, and single-tuple updates. A Teradata DBC/1012 database machine of similar size is used as a basis for interpreting the results obtained. We analyze and interpret the results of these experiments based on our understanding of the system hardware and software, and conclude with an assessment of the strengths and weaknesses of the two machines.

1. Introduction

In this report we present the results of an initial evaluation of the Gamma database machine [DEWI86, GERB86]. As a basis of comparison we have used results from a similar study [DEWI87] of the Teradata DBC/1012 database machine [TERA83, TERA85a, TERA85b]. Our objective in writing this paper was to compare the storage organizations and multiprocessor algorithms of the two database machines and **not** to compare their absolute performance. In interpreting the results presented below, the reader should remember that Gamma is not a commercial product at this time and, as such, its results may look slightly better for some queries. The most obvious deficiency in Gamma is that full recovery capabilities have not yet been implemented although distributed concurrency control is provided.

While we have so far limited our efforts to single user tests, we plan on conducting multiuser experiments in the near future. For the most part this work is based on the benchmarking techniques described in [BITT83] (what is popularly known as the "Wisconsin benchmark"), extended to utilize relations commensurate in size with the capabilities of these database machines.

In Sections 2 and 3, respectively, we describe the Teradata and Gamma configurations that were evaluated. Section 4 presents an overview of the benchmark relations used and a discussion of the types of indices used during the benchmark process. Four types of tests were conducted: selections, joins, aggregates, and updates. A description of the exact queries used and the results obtained for each query are contained in Sections 5 through 8. Our conclusions are presented in Section 9. See Appendix I in [DEWI87] for the SQL version of the queries used in the benchmark.

2. Teradata Hardware and Software Configuration

The Teradata machine tested consists of 4 Interface Processors (IFPs), 20 Access Module Processors (AMPs), and 40 Disk Storage Units (DSUs). The IFPs communicate with the host, and parse, optimize, and direct the execution of user requests. The AMPs perform the actual storage and retrieval of data on the DSUs. IFPs and AMPs are interconnected by a dual redundant, tree-shaped interconnect called the Y-net [TERA83, NECH83]. The Y-net has an aggregate bandwidth of 12 megabytes/second. Intel 80286 processors were used in all IFPs and AMPs.

Each AMP had 2 megabytes of memory and two[1] 8.8", 525 megabyte (unformatted) Hitachi disk drives (model DK 8155). The host processor was an AMDAHL V570 running the MVS operating system. Release 2.3 of the database machine software was used for the tests conducted on this configuration. While [DEWI87] also evaluated a similar Teradata configuration but with 4 megabytes

---

[1] The software actually treats the drives as a single logical unit.

of memory per processor, we have used the results obtained with the 2 megabyte/AMP configuration as each processor in Gamma also has 2 megabytes of memory.

All relations on the Teradata machine are horizontally partitioned [RIES78] across multiple AMPs. While it is possible to limit the number of AMPs over which relations are partitioned, all 20 AMPs were used for the tests presented below. Whenever a tuple is to be inserted into a relation, a hash function is applied to the primary key[2] of the relation to select an AMP for storage. Hash maps in the Y-net nodes and AMPs are used to indicate which hash buckets reside on each AMP.

Once a tuple arrives at a site, that AMP applies a hash function to the key attribute in order to place the tuple in its "fragment" (several tuples may hash to the same value) of the appropriate relation. The hash value and a sequence number are concatenated to form a unique tuple id [TERA85a, MC^{2}86]. Once an entire relation has been loaded, the tuples in each horizontal fragment are in what is termed "hash-key order." Thus, given a value for the key attribute, it is possible to locate the tuple in a single disk access (assuming no buffer pool hits). This is the only physical file organization supported at the present time. It is **important** to note that given this organization, the only kind of indices one can construct are dense, secondary indices. The index is termed "dense" as it must contain one entry for each tuple in the indexed relation. It is termed "secondary" as the index order is different than the key order of the file. Furthermore, the rows in the index are themselves hashed on the key field and are **NOT** sorted in key order. Consequently, whenever a range query over an indexed attribute is performed, the **entire** index must be scanned.

3. Overview of the Gamma Database Machine

In this section we present an overview of the Gamma database machine. After describing the current hardware configuration, we present an overview of the software techniques used in implementing Gamma. Included in this discussion is a description of the alternatives provided by Gamma for partitioning relations plus an overview of query execution in Gamma. More detailed descriptions of the algorithms used for implementing the various relational operations are presented in Sections 5 through 8 along with the performance results obtained during the benchmarking process. For a complete description of Gamma see [DEWI86, GERB86].

3.1. Hardware Configuration

Presently, Gamma consists of 17 VAX 11/750 processors, each with two megabytes of memory. An 80 megabit/second token ring developed for the Crystal project [DEWI84b] by Proteon Associates [PROT85] is used to connect the processors to each other and to another VAX 11/750 running Berkeley UNIX. This processor acts as the host machine for Gamma. Attached to eight of the processors are 333 megabyte Fujitsu disk drives (8") which are used for database storage. One of the diskless processors is currently reserved for query scheduling and global deadlock detection. The remaining diskless processors are used to execute join, projection, and aggregate operations. Selection and update operations are executed only on the processors with disk drives attached.

3.2. Software Overview

Physical Database Design

All relations in Gamma are **horizontally partitioned** [RIES78] across all disk drives in the system. The Gamma query language (gdl - an extension of QUEL [STONE76]) provides the user with four alternative ways of distributing the tuples of a relation: round robin, hashed, range partitioned with user-specified placement by key value, and range partitioned with uniform distribution. As implied by its name, in the first strategy when tuples are loaded into a relation, they are distributed in a round-robin fashion among all disk drives. This is the default strategy in Gamma for relations created as the result of a query. If the hashed strategy is selected, a randomizing function is applied to the key attribute of each tuple (as specified in the partition command of gdl) to select a storage unit. Since the Teradata database machine uses this technique, all the tests we conducted used this tuple distribution

---

[2] The primary key is specified when the relation is created.

strategy. In the third strategy the user specifies a range of key values for each site. Finally, if the user does not have enough information about his data file to select key ranges, he may elect the final distribution strategy. In this strategy, if the relation is not already loaded, it is initially loaded in a round robin fashion. Next, the relation is sorted (using a parallel merge sort) on the partitioning attribute and the sorted relation is redistributed in a fashion that attempts to equalize the number of tuples at each site. Finally, the maximum key value at each site is returned to the host processor.

Query Execution

Gamma uses traditional relational techniques for query parsing, optimization [SELI79, JARK84], and code generation. The optimization process is somewhat simplified as Gamma only employs hash-based algorithms for joins and other complex operations [DEWI85]. Queries are compiled into a tree of operators. At execution time, each operator is executed by one or more operator processes at each participating site.

After being parsed and compiled, the query is sent by the host software to an idle scheduler process through a dispatcher process. The dispatcher process, by controlling the number of active schedulers, implements a simple load control mechanism based on information about the degree of CPU and memory utilization at each processor. The scheduler process, in turn, activates operator processes at each query processor selected to execute the operator. The result of a query is either returned to the user through the ad-hoc query interface or through the embedded query interface to the program from which the query was initiated.

In the case of a multisite query, the task of assigning operators to processors is performed in part by the optimizer and in part by the scheduler assigned to control the execution of the query. For example, the operators at the leaves of a query tree reference only permanent relations. Using the query and schema information, the optimizer is able to determine the best way of assigning these operators to processors. The root node of a query tree is either a **store** operator in the case of a "retrieve into" query or a **spool** operator in the case of a retrieve query (ie. results are returned to the host). In the case of a **Store** operator, the optimizer will assign a copy of the query tree node to a process at each processor with a disk. Using the techniques described below, the **store** operator at each site receives result tuples from the processes executing the node which is its child in the query tree and stores them in its fragment of the result relation (recall that **all** permanent relations are horizontally partitioned). In the case of a **spool** node at the root of a query tree, the optimizer assigns it to a single process; generally, on a diskless[3] processor.

In Gamma, the algorithms for all operators are written as if they were to be run on a single processor. As shown in Figure 1, the input to an Operator Process is a stream of tuples and the output is a stream of tuples that is demultiplexed through a structure we term a **split table**. After being initiated, a query process waits for a control message to arrive on a global, well-known control port. Upon receiving an operator control packet, the process replies with a message that identifies itself to the scheduler. Once the process begins execution, it continuously reads tuples from its input stream, operates on each tuple, and uses a split table to route the resulting tuple to the process indicated in the split table. Consider, for example, the case of a selection operation that is producing tuples for use in a subsequent join operation. If the join is being executed by N processes, the split table of the selection process will contain N entries. For each tuple satisfying the selection predicate, the selection process will apply a hash function to the join attribute to produce a value between 1 and N. This value is then used as an index into the split table to obtain the address (e.g. machine_id, port #) of the join process that should receive the tuple. When the process detects the end of its input stream, it first closes the output streams and then sends a control message to its scheduler indicating that it has completed execution. Closing the output streams has the side effect of sending "end of stream" messages to each of the destination processes. With the exception of these three control messages, execution of an operator is completely self-scheduling. Data flows among the processes executing a query tree in a dataflow fashion.

---

[3] The communications software provides a back-pressure mechanism so that the host can slow the rate at which tuples are being produced if it cannot keep up.

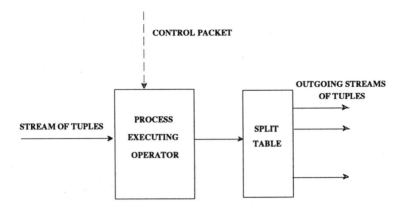

CONTROL PACKET

OUTGOING STREAMS
OF TUPLES

STREAM OF TUPLES

PROCESS

EXECUTING

OPERATOR

SPLIT
TABLE

Figure 1

To enhance the performance of certain operations, an array of bit vector filters [BABB79, VALD84] is inserted into the split table. In the case of a join operation, each join process builds a bit vector filter by hashing the join attribute values while building its hash table using the outer relation [BRAT84, DEWI85, DEWI84a, VALD84]. When the hash table for the outer relation has been completed, the process sends its filter to its scheduler. After the scheduler has received all the filters, it sends them to the processes responsible for producing the inner relation of the join. Each of these processes uses the set of filters to eliminate those tuples that will not produce any tuples in the join operation.

Operating and Storage System

Gamma is built on top of an operating system developed specifically for supporting database management systems. NOSE provides multiple, lightweight processes with shared memory. A non-preemptive scheduling policy is used to help prevent convoys [BLAS79] from occurring. NOSE provides reliable communications between NOSE processes on Gamma processors and to UNIX processes on the host machine. The reliable communications mechanism is a timer-based, one bit stop-and-wait, positive acknowledgment protocol [TANE81]. A delta-T mechanism is used to re-establish sequence numbers [WATS81]. File services in NOSE are based on the Wisconsin Storage System (WiSS) [CHOU85]. Critical sections of WiSS are protected using the semaphore mechanism provided by NOSE.

The file services provided by WiSS include structured sequential files, byte-stream files as in UNIX, B^+ indices, long data items, a sort utility, and a scan mechanism. A sequential file is a sequence of records. Records may vary in length (up to one page in length), and may be inserted and deleted at arbitrary locations within a sequential file. Optionally, each sequential file may have one or more associated indices. The index maps key values to the records of the sequential file that contain a matching value. Furthermore, one indexed attribute may be used as a clustering attribute for the file. The scan mechanism is similar to that provided by System R's RSS [ASTR76] except that predicates are compiled into machine language.

4. Description of Benchmark Relations

The benchmark relations used are based on the standard Wisconsin Benchmark relations [BITT83]. Each relation consists of thirteen 4-byte integer attributes and three 52-byte string attributes. Thus, each tuple is 208 bytes long. In order to more meaningfully stress the two database machines, we constructed 100,000 and 1,000,000 tuple versions of the original 1,000 and 10,000 tuple benchmark relations. As in the original benchmark, the unique1 and unique2 attributes of the relations are generated in a way to guarantee that each tuple has a unique value for each of the two attributes and that there is no correlation between values of unique1 and unique2 within a single tuple. Two copies of each relation were created and loaded. The total database size is approximately 464 megabytes (not including indices).

For the Teradata machine all test relations were loaded in the NO FALLBACK mode. The FALLBACK option provides a mechanism to continue processing in the face of disk and AMP failures by automatically replicating each tuple at two different sites. Since we did not want to measure the cost of keeping both copies of a tuple consistent, we elected not to use the FALLBACK feature.

Except where otherwise noted, the results of all queries were stored in the database. We avoided returning data to the host because we were afraid that we would end up measuring the speed of the communications link between the host and the database machine or the host processor itself. By storing all results in the database, these factors were minimized in our measurements. Of course, on the other hand, we ended up measuring the cost of storing the result relations.

Storing the result of a query in a relation incurs two costs not incurred if the resulting tuples are returned to the host processor. First, the tuples of each result relation must be distributed across all processors with disks. In the case of the Teradata database machine (in which the result relation for a query must be created as a separate step), since unique1 was used as the primary key of both the source and result relations, we had expected that no communications overhead would be incurred in storing the result tuples. However, since the low-level communications software does not recognize this situation, the execution times presented below include the cost of redistributing the result tuples. Since, the current version of Gamma redistributes result tuples in a round-robin fashion, both machines incur the same redistribution overhead while storing the result of a query in a relation.

The second cost associated with storing the result of a query in a relation is the impact of the recovery software on the rate at which tuples are inserted in a relation. In this case, there are substantial differences between the two systems. Gamma provides an extended version of the query language QUEL [STON76]. In QUEL, one uses the construct "*retrieve into result_relation ...* " to specify that the result of a query is to be stored in a relation. The semantics of this construct are that the relation name specified must not exist when the query is executed. If for some reason the transaction running the query is aborted, the only action that the recovery manager must take is to delete all files associated with the result relation.

The query language for the Teradata database machine is based on an extended version of SQL. In order to execute an SQL query that stores the result tuples in a relation, one must first explicitly create the result relation. After the result relation has been created one uses the syntax:

> *insert into result_relation*
> *select * from source_relation where ...*

Since in some cases the result relation may already contain tuples (in which case the insert acts more like a union), the code for *insert into* must log all inserted tuples carefully so that if the transaction is aborted, the relation can be restored to its original state. Since the Teradata insert code is currently optimized for single tuple and not bulk updates, at least 3 I/Os are incurred for each tuple inserted (see [DEWI87] for a more complete description of the problem). A straightforward optimization would be for the the "insert into" code to recognize when it was operating on an empty relation. This would enable the code to process bulk updates much more efficiently (by, for example, simply releasing all pages in the result relation if the "insert into" is aborted).

Since the Teradata machine provides "more functionality" than Gamma when inserting result tuples from a query into a relation, for those queries which produce a significant number of result tuples, we present the measured execution time of the query plus the estimated execution time of producing the result relation without the cost of either redistributing or actually storing the tuples in the result relation. Our technique for estimating the cost of redistributing and storing the result tuples is described in the following section.

All queries were submitted in scripts. Six query scripts were used: one for each of three relation sizes tested for both indexed and non-indexed cases. For each query submitted, the two machines report the number of tuples affected and the elapsed time. The times reported below represent an average for a set of similar queries using the techniques described in [BITT83]. The benchmark is designed to minimize the effect of the buffer pool on the response time of queries in the same test set in spite of their similarity.

5. Selection

5.1. Overview

The performance of the selection operator is a crucial element of the overall performance of any query plan. If a selection operator provides insufficient throughput, it can become a bottleneck, limiting the amount of parallelism that can effectively be applied by subsequent operators. Both Gamma and Teradata use horizontally partitioned relations and closely coupled processor/disk pairs to achieve parallelism within a selection operator.

Although parallelism improves the performance of the selection operator, it cannot be used as a complete substitute for indices. Gamma provides both clustered and non-clustered B-tree organizations as alternative index structures whereas Teradata offers only dense, secondary indices. As will be shown in the next section, a clustered B-tree organization significantly reduces the execution time for range selection queries even in a parallel database machine environment.

5.2. Performance

The selection queries were designed with two objectives in mind. First, we wanted to know how the two machines would respond as the size of the source relations was increased. Ideally, given constant machine configurations, the response time should grow as a linear function of the size of input and result relations. Second, we were interested in exploring the effect of indices on the execution time of a selection on each machine while holding the selectivity factor constant.

Our tests used two sets of selection queries: first with 1% selectivity and second with 10% selectivity. On Gamma, the two sets of queries were tested with three different storage organizations: a

Table 1
Selection Queries
(All Execution Times in Seconds)

Query Description	Number of Tuples in Source Relation					
	10,000 Teradata	10,000 Gamma	100,000 Teradata	100,000 Gamma	1,000,000 Teradata	1,000,000 Gamma
1% nonindexed selection	6.86	1.63	28.22	13.83	213.13	134.86
10% nonindexed selection	15.97	2.11	110.96	17.44	1106.86	181.72
1% selection using non-clustered index	7.81	1.03	29.94	5.32	222.65	53.86
10% selection using non-clustered index	16.82	2.16	111.40	17.65	1107.59	182.00
1% selection using clustered index	-	0.59	-	1.25	-	7.50
10% selection using clustered index	-	1.26	-	7.27	-	69.60
single tuple select	-	0.15	1.08	0.15	-	0.20

heap (no index), a clustered index on the key attribute (index order = key order), and a non-clustered index on a non-key attribute (index order ≠ key order). On the Teradata machine, since tuples in a relation are organized in hash-key order, it is not possible to construct a clustered index. Therefore, all indices, whether on the key or any other attribute, are dense, non-clustered indices.

In Table 1, we have tabulated the results of testing the different types of selection queries on three sizes of relations (10,000, 100,000, and 1,000,000 tuples). Two main conclusions can be drawn from this table. First, for both machines the execution time of each query scales in a linear fashion as the size of the input and output relations are increased. Second, as expected, the clustered B-tree organization provides a significant improvement in performance.

As discussed in [DEWI87], the results for the 1% and 10% selection using a non-clustered index (rows three and four of Table 1) for the Teradata machine look puzzling. Both of these queries selected tuples using a predicate on the unique2 attribute, an attribute on which we had constructed a non-clustered index. In the case of the 10% selection, the optimizer decided (correctly) not to use the index. In the 1% case, the observed execution time is almost identical to the result obtained for the nonindexed case. This seems to contradict the query plan produced by the optimizer which states that non-clustered index on unique2 is to be used to execute the query.

A partial explanation of the above paradox lies in the storage organization used for indices on the Teradata machine. Since the index entries are hash-based and not in sorted order, the entire index must be scanned sequentially instead of scanning only the portion corresponding to the range of the query. Thus, exactly the same number of attribute value comparisons is done for both index scans and sequential scans. However, it is expected that the number of I/Os required to scan the index is only a fraction of the number of I/Os required to scan the relation. Apparently, the response time is not reduced significantly because while the index can be scanned sequentially, each access to the relation requires a random seek.

Gamma supports the notion of non-clustered indices through a B-tree structure on top of the actual data file. As can be seen from Table 1, in the case of the 10% selection, the Gamma optimizer also decides not to use the index. In the 1% case, the index is used. Consider, for example, a scan with a 1% selectivity factor on a 10,000 tuple relation: if the non-clustered index is used, in the worst case 100(+/- 4) I/Os will be required (assuming each tuple causes a page fault). On the other hand, if a segment scan is chosen to access the data, with 17 tuples per data page, all 588 pages of data would be read. The difference between the number of I/Os is significant and is confirmed by the difference in response time between the entries for Gamma in rows 3 and 4 of Table 1.

Gamma also supports the notion of clustered index (the underlying relation is sorted according to the key attribute and a B-tree search structure is built on top of the data). The response time for 1% and 10% selection through the clustered index is presented in rows five and six of Table 1. Since the tuples in the actual data are sorted (key order = index order), only that portion of the relation corresponding to the range of the query is scanned. This results in a further reduction of the number of I/Os compared to the corresponding search through a file scan or a non-clustered index. This saving is confirmed by the lower response times shown in Table 1.

One important observation to be made from Table 1 is the relative consistency of the cost of selection using a clustered index in Gamma. Notice that the response time for both the 10% selection from the 10,000 tuple relation and the 1% selection from the 100,000 tuple relation using a clustered index is 1.25 seconds. The reason is that in both cases 1,000 tuples are retrieved and stored, resulting in the same amount of I/O and CPU costs.

The selection results reveal an important limitation of the Teradata design. Since there are no clustered indices, and since non-clustered indices can only be used when a relatively small number of tuples are retrieved, the system must resort to scanning entire files for most range selections. While hash files are certainly the optimal file organization for exact-match queries, for certain types of applications, range queries are important. In that case, it should be possible for the database administrator to specify the storage organization that is best suited for the application.

In the final row of Table 1 we have presented the times required by both machines to select a single tuple and return it to the host. For the Teradata machine, the key attribute is used in the selection condition. Thus, after hashing on the constant to select an AMP, the AMP software will hash again on the constant to select the hash bucket that holds the tuple. In the case of Gamma, a clustered index on the key attribute was used. While we only ran this test for the 100,000 tuple relation on the Teradata machine, we would expect comparable times for the 10,000 and 1,000,000 tuple tables. These results indicate that clustered indices have comparable performance with hash files for single tuple retrieves while providing superior performance for range queries.

As discussed in Section 4, since the semantics of QUEL and SQL are different, the results presented in Table 1 are slightly misleading and the times for the two machines are not directly comparable. This is largely due to the fact that Teradata provides full recovery for the resulting relation, whereas Gamma does not need to provide this level of functionality. Furthermore, Teradata treats each insertion as a separate operation [DEWI87] (rather than as part of a bulk update), while Gamma pipelines the output of the selection result handling it as a bulk update. Thus, in the Teradata machine the time required to insert tuples into a result relation accounted for a significant fraction of the execution time of the query. We calculated the rate at which tuples can be redistributed and inserted by dividing the difference in the number of tuples selected by the difference between the time to select 10% of the tuples and the time to select 1% of the tuples. For example, on the Teradata machine, the 10% nonindexed selection on a 1,000,000 tuple relation takes 1106.86 seconds and inserts 100,000 tuples into the result relation. The 1% selection takes 213.13 seconds and inserts 10,000 tuples. Since the time to scan the million tuple relation is the same in both cases, we concluded that the time to redistribute and insert 90,000 tuples is 893.73 seconds. This is an average rate of insertion of 100.7 tuples/second using all 20 disk drives or approximately 5.0 tuples/second/drive. We calculated the insertion rate for relations of different sizes on each machine and then calculated the overall average. The average number of tuples inserted per second for the Teradata machine was 104.08 tuples/sec (5.2 tuples/sec/drive), whereas in the case of Gamma, the average insertion rate was 2096.23 tuples/sec (262.03 tuples/sec/drive).

Since the insertion rate is such a dominant factor in the Teradata results, we decided to separate the processing time for the queries from the time to insert tuples into the result relations. To get a measure of the processing time alone, we subtracted the approximate time to redistribute and store the result relation (number of tuples retrieved multiplied by the average cost of insertion per tuple) for each entry in Table 1 to come up with Table 2. As a result of these calculations, some inconsistencies became apparent (e.g., 10% nonindexed selection on 100,000 tuple relation for Teradata shows a lower response time than 1% nonindexed selection on that same relation). These are largely due to the fact that we used a single constant insertion rate for all our calculations for each machine.

As can be seen from Table 2, for the 100,000 and 1,000,000 tuple relations, the two machines have comparable times for the non-indexed selections. In fact, in the case of 1% nonindexed selections on the million tuple relations the Teradata system is faster than Gamma. The reader should, however, remember that the Teradata machine is running with more than twice as many CPUs and disk drives (Gamma uses 8 disks and 8 CPUs for the selections, whereas the Teradata machine used 20 CPUs and 20 disk drives[4]).

6. Join Queries

The second series of tests consists of a collection of join queries. The Teradata machine uses four alternative join algorithms [TERA85a, MC^{2}86]. One computes an outer-join, while two others are used only in special cases (for example, when the inner relation contains a single tuple). The fourth and most common way in which the Teradata executes join queries involves redistributing the two source relations by hashing on the join attribute. As each AMP receives tuples, it stores them in temporary files sorted in hash key order. After the redistribution phase completes, each AMP uses a conventional sort-merge join algorithm to complete the join. For our test queries, the Teradata used only this fourth join algorithm.

Gamma also partitions its source relations by hashing but instead of using sort-merge to effect the join, it uses a distributed hashing algorithm (see [KITS83, DEWI85, DEWI86, GERB86]). The algorithm works in two phases. During phase one, Gamma partitions the smaller source relation and

---

[4] Recall that although the Teradata machine actually had 40 disk drives, the 2 drives on each AMP are treated as one logical unit and thus seeks are not overlapped.

Table 2
Adjusted Selection Queries
(All Execution Times in Seconds)

Query Description	Number of Tuples in Source Relation					
	10,000 Teradata	10,000 Gamma	100,000 Teradata	100,000 Gamma	1,000,000 Teradata	1,000,000 Gamma
1% nonindexed selection	5.90	1.58	18.61	13.43	117.71	130.08
10% nonindexed selection	6.36	1.63	14.88	12.67	152.66	134.02
1% selection using non-clustered index	6.85	0.98	20.33	4.84	127.23	49.10
10% selection using non-clustered index	7.21	1.68	15.32	12.88	153.39	134.30
1% selection using clustered index	-	0.54	-	0.78	-	2.73
10% selection using clustered index	-	0.78	-	2.50	-	21.90

builds main-memory hash tables. During phase two, Gamma partitions the larger source relation and uses the corresponding tuples to immediately probe within the hash tables built in phase one. Note that as the second source relation is being partitioned its tuples are **not** stored in temporary files but rather are used immediately to probe the hash tables. This data pipelining gives Gamma much of its superior performance.

Of course, whenever main-memory hashing is used there is a danger of hash table overflow. To handle this phenomenon, Gamma currently uses a distributed version of the Simple hash-partitioned join algorithm described in [DEWI85]. Basically, whenever a processor detects hash table overflow it spools tuples to a temporary file based on a second hash function until the hash table is successfully built. The query scheduler then passes this function used to subpartition the hash table to the select operators producing the probing tuples. Probing tuples corresponding to tuples in the overflow partition are then spooled to a temporary file; all other tuples probe the hash table as normal. The overflow partitions are recursively joined using this same procedure until no more overflow partitions are created and the join has been fully computed. As previous analytical models [DEWI85] predicted and the following test results show, this method degrades drastically when the size of the building relation is significantly larger than the hash table size. For this reason, we will implement the distributed Hybrid hash-join algorithm [DEWI85] in the near future.

Gamma can actually run joins in a variety of configurations. The selection operators will of course run on all disk sites but the hash tables may be built on the processors with disks, the diskless processors or both sets of processors. These alternatives are referred to as Local, Remote, and Allnodes, respectively. Initial results [DEWI86] showed that offloading the join operators to diskless processors can be done inexpensively freeing the processors with disk for performing operations requiring access to the disk. Future multiuser performance tests will determine the validity of this assumption. The results for all join queries reported below are based on the Remote configuration (8 disk nodes, 8 nondisk nodes and 1 scheduler) in which the joins are done only on the diskless processors.

Queries

Three join queries formed the basis of our join tests. The first join query, joinABprime, is a simple join of two relations: A and Bprime. The A relation contains either 10,000, 100,000 or 1,000,000 tuples. The Bprime relation contains, respectively, 1,000, 10,000, or 100,000 tuples. The second query, joinAselB, performs one join and one selection. A and B have the same number of tuples and the selection on B reduces the size of B to the size of the Bprime relation in the corresponding joinABprime query. For example, if A has 100,000 tuples, then joinABprime joins A with a Bprime relation that contains 10,000 tuples, while in joinAselB the selection on B restricts it from 100,000 to 10,000 tuples and then joins the result with A.

The third join query, joinCselAselB contains two joins and two restricts. First, A and B are restricted to 10% of their original size (10,000, 100,000, or 1,000,000 tuples) and then joined with each other. Since each tuple joins with exactly one other tuple, this join yields an intermediate relation equal in size to the two input relations. This intermediate relation is then joined with relation C, which contains 1/10 the number of tuples in A. The result relation contains as many tuples as there are in C. As an example assume A and B contain 100,000 tuples. The relations resulting from selections on A and B will each contain 10,000 tuples. Their join results in an intermediate relation of 10,000 tuples. This relation will be joined with a C relation containing 10,000 tuples and the result of the query will contain 10,000 tuples.

The first variation of these three queries that we tested involved no indices and used a non-key attribute (unique2D or unique2E) as the join attribute and selection attributes. Since all the source relations were distributed using the key attribute, the join algorithms of both machines required redistribution (partitioning) phases. The results from these tests are contained in the first 3 rows of Tables 3.

The second variation of the three join queries used the key attribute (unique1D or unique1E) as the join attribute. (Rows 4 through 6 of Table 3 contain these results.) Since, in this case, the relations are already distributed on the join attribute the Teradata demonstrated substantial performance improvement (25-50%) because the redistribution step of the join algorithm could be skipped. Since Table 3 shows the "Remote" configuration of Gamma all data must still be redistributed to the diskless processors.

Although we are not entirely sure why Gamma showed improvement it is probably due to the fact that, in this second set of queries, the redistribution step maps all tuples from processor 1 (with a disk) to processor 9 (without a disk), and from processor 2 to processor 10, etc. In [GERB86], Bob Gerber showed that, when all Gamma processors send to all other sites in synchronization, the network interfaces can become a temporary bottleneck. The effect of the different Gamma configurations will be discussed in more detail below.

From the results in Table 3, one can conclude that the execution time of each of the queries increases in a fairly linear fashion as the size of the input relations are increased. Given the quadratic cost of the join operator, this is an impressive result. Gamma does not exhibit linearity in the million tuple queries because the size of the building relation (20 megabytes) far exceeds the total memory available for hash tables (4.8 megabytes) and the Simple hash partition overflow algorithm deteriorates exponentially with multiple overflows. In fact, the computation of the million tuple join queries required six partition overflow resolutions on each of the diskless processors. To demonstrate how costly overflow resolution is, we ran the joinAselB query with 400K of hash table memory per node instead of 600K. The query then required ten partition overflow resolutions and the time rose from the listed 737.7 seconds to 1016.1 seconds.

Bit Vector Filters in Gamma

In [DEWI85], bit vector filtering was analyzed and shown to be extremely effective for a wide spectrum of multiprocessor join algorithms (including distributed sort-merge); the primary benefit being the elimination of nonqualifying probing tuples at their selection sites - saving the costs of sending them over the network and subsequent processing in the join computation. Table 5 show the effects of bit vector filtering for the joinABprime query in Gamma as the configuration is changed. As you can see all three configurations performed substantially better with bit filters.

Table 3
Join Queries
(All Execution Times in Seconds)

Query Description	Number of Tuples in Source Relation					
	10,000 Teradata	10,000 Gamma	100,000 Teradata	100,000 Gamma	1,000,000 Teradata	1,000,000 Gamma
joinABprime with non-key attributes of A and B used as join attribute	34.9	6.5	321.8	46.5	3,419.4	2,938.2
joinAselB with non-key attributes of A and B used as join attribute	35.6	5.1	331.7	36.3	3,534.5	703.1
joinCselAselB with non-key attributes of A and B used as join attribute	27.8	7.0	191.8	38.4	2,032.7	731.2
joinABprime with key attributes of A and B used as join attribute	22.2	5.7	131.3	45.6	1,265.1	2,926.7
joinASelB with key attributes of A and B used as join attribute	25.0	5.0	170.3	36.9	1,584.3	737.7
joinCselAselB with key attributes of A and B used as join attribute	23.8	7.2	156.7	37.9	1,509.6	712.8

Table 4
Adjusted Join Queries
(All Execution Times in Seconds)

Query Description	Number of Tuples in Source Relation					
	10,000 Teradata	10,000 Gamma	100,000 Teradata	100,000 Gamma	1,000,000 Teradata	1,000,000 Gamma
joinABprime with non-key attributes of A and B used as join attribute	25.3	6.0	225.7	41.7	2,458.6	2,890.5
joinAselB with non-key attributes of A and B used as join attribute	25.9	4.6	235.6	35.8	2,573.7	655.4
joinCselAselB with non-key attributes of A and B used as join attribute	18.2	6.5	95.7	37.9	1,071.9	683.5
joinABprime with key attributes of A and B used as join attribute	12.6	5.2	35.2	45.1	304.3	2,878.9
joinASelB with key attributes of A and B used as join attribute	15.4	4.5	74.2	32.1	623.5	689.9
joinCselAselB with key attributes of A and B used as join attribute	14.2	6.7	60.6	33.1	548.8	665.1

Table 5
Bit Vector Filtering in Gamma
JoinABprime - 100K Tuple Relations - No Indices - Join on Non-Key Attrs
(All Execution Times in Seconds)

	Local	Remote	Allnodes
without bit filters	56.31	46.53	51.69
with bit filters	42.12	35.26	39.07
%speedup	25%	24%	24%

The joinAselB and joinCselAselB queries show no improvement from bit filtering because the Gamma optimizer is clever enough to propagate the selection predicates for these queries and thus no non-joining tuples will participate in the join (this explains why joinAselB ran significantly faster than joinABprime in Tables 3 and 4). Performance gains similar to those in Table 5 did not occur for the million tuple joinABprime queries because at the present time only a single 2K page is used to hold the bit vectors from all building sites. After deducting the space for the communication protocol header, this corresponds to only 122 bytes (976 bits) for the bit filter for each site. If one assumes that the partitioning phase results in uniformly distributing the 100,000 tuple relation across the 8 building sites, each site will end up with 12,500 tuples; thus overwhelming the bit filters and rendering them useless.

Join Performance of Alternative Gamma Configurations

The choice of Gamma configuration also directly affects the response time of join queries. Gamma's "Local" configuration corresponds most closely to Teradata's configuration. When the join attributes are also the partitioning attributes, no data packets will be sent over the network, i.e. all building relation tuples will be put in their respective local hash tables and all probing tuples will only probe their respective local hash tables. In Table 6, the performance of the joins on the 100K tuple relations with the join attributes being the partitioning attributes is shown. In order to determine the effects of data transmission on the three Gamma configurations we turned off bit vector filtering for the queries. Since the joinABprime query handles the most data its entry will be most interesting. As the joinABprime query results show, shipping large numbers of data packets remotely can be costly. Although the results reported in [DEWI86] showed that remote joins were as cheap as local joins there is no contradiction with these results. In the earlier paper, the relations were range-partitioned on their key attribute instead of hash-partitioned and thus repartitioning was required in every configuration. Its obvious that local joins are very attractive if the source relations are partitioned on their join attributes.

Table 6
Effect of Alternative Gamma Configurations on Join Execution Time
100K Tuple Relations - No Indices - Join Attributes are Partitioning Attributes
(All Execution Times in Seconds)

	Local	**Remote**	**Allnodes**
joinAselB	37.14	35.93	37.24
joinABprime	38.24	45.55	42.19
joinCselAselB	43.01	37.86	42.29

The observant reader may have noticed that the Teradata can always do joinABprime faster than joinAselB but that just the opposite is true for Gamma. We will explain the difference by analyzing Table 3 with the 100,000 tuple joins. Selection propagation by the Gamma optimizer will reduce joinAselB to joinselAselB. This means that although both 100,000 tuple relations will be read in their entirety only 10% of each of the relations will be sent over the network and participate in the join.

Although joinABprime only reads a 100,000 and a 10,000 tuple relation it must send the entire 100,000 tuples over the network and probe with all these tuples (assuming no bit filters). Recall that Table 5 shows that approximately 24% speedup can be obtained just by reducing the number of probing tuples via bit filters. Thus the costs to distribute and probe the 100,000 tuples outweigh the difference in reading a 100,000 and a 10,000 tuple file. On the other hand, the Teradata database machine will compute joinABprime by reading and sorting a 10,000 tuple relation and a 100,000 tuple relation and then merging them. JoinAselB will read two 100,000 tuple relations and then sort and merge a 10,000 and a 100,000 tuple relation. Thus joinAselB will be slower by the difference in reading the 100,000 and 10,000 tuple relations.

Join Summary

As shown by the very high response times for the million tuple joins in Table 3, Gamma must find an alternative for its present use of Simple hash for join overflow resolution. Also, the size of the bit filters should be increased in order to help with very large joins.

Teradata should strongly consider incorporating bit vector filtering techniques and selection propagation. The implementation costs are very low and the potential gains very high. In fact, every page of tuples eliminated via bit filtering saves two disk I/O's in a conventional sort-merge algorithm. Selection propagation definitely improves performance for these join queries by reducing the number of tuples in the join computation. How often selection propagation can be applied in the "real world" is an open question, though.

Finally, after analyzing Tables 3 and 4, and keeping in mind the selection costs reported in Section 5, it is obvious that hash-join outperforms sort-merge when no partition overflow is encountered. This substantiates the analytical results reported in [DEWI85].

7. Aggregate Queries

The third set of queries includes a mix of scalar aggregate and aggregate function queries. The first query computes the minimum of a non-indexed attribute. The next two queries compute, respectively, the sum and minimum of an attribute after partitioning the relation into 100 subsets. The results from these tests are contained in Table 7. Since each query produces only either a single result tuple or 100 result tuples, we have not bothered to display the query times adjusted by the time to store the result relation.

By treating a scalar aggregate query as an aggregate function query with a single partition, the Teradata machine uses the same algorithm to handle both types of queries. Each AMP first computes a piece of the result by calculating a value for each of the partitions. Next the AMPs redistribute the partial results by hashing on the partitioning attribute. The result of this step is to collect the partial results for each partition at a single site so that the final result can be computed.

Table 7
Aggregate Queries
(All Execution Times in Seconds)

| Query Description | Number of Tuples in Source Relation | | | | | |
	10,000 Teradata	10,000 Gamma	100,000 Teradata	100,000 Gamma	1,000,000 Teradata	1,000,000 Gamma
MIN scalar aggregate	4.21	1.89	18.29	15.53	127.86	151.10
MIN aggregate function (100 partitions)	8.66	2.86	27.06	19.43	175.95	184.92
SUM aggregate function (100 partitions)	8.94	2.89	24.79	19.54	175.78	185.05

Gamma implements scalar aggregates in a similar manner although the hashed redistribution step discussed above can be skipped. Each disk-based processor computes its piece of the result and then sends it to a process on the scheduler processor which combines these partial results into the final answer. Aggregate functions are implemented almost exactly like in the Teradata machine. As with scalar aggregates, the disk-based processors compute their piece of the result but now the partial results must be redistributed by hashing on the partitioning attribute.

Some relational database systems have special cased the computation of scalar aggregates over indexed attributes by considering just the index as opposed to the base relation. Teradata would benefit little from such a special case operator since its indices are not maintained in key order. On the other hand, Gamma could improve performance but the potential gains were deemed to be less than the implementation costs.

8. Update Queries

The last set of tests included a mix of append, delete, and modify queries. The Teradata machine was executing with full concurrency control and recovery, whereas Gamma used full concurrency control and partial recovery for some of the operators; hence the performance results from the two machines are not directly comparable. The results of these tests are presented in Table 8.

The first query appends a single tuple to a relation on which no indices exist. The second appends a tuple to a relation on which one index exists. The third query deletes a single tuple from a relation, using an index to locate the tuple to be deleted (in the case of Teradata, it is a hash-based index, whereas in the case of Gamma, it is a clustered B-tree index, for both the second and third queries). In the first query no indices exist and hence no indices need to be updated, whereas in the second and third queries, one index needs to be updated.

Table 8
Update Queries
(All Execution Times in Seconds)

	Number of Tuples in Source Relation					
	10,000	10,000	100,000	100,000	1,000,000	1,000,000
	Teradata	Gamma	Teradata	Gamma	Teradata	Gamma
Append 1 Tuple (No indices exist)	0.87	0.18	1.29	0.18	1.47	0.20
Append 1 Tuple (One index exists)	0.94	0.60	1.62	0.63	1.73	0.66
Delete 1 tuple. Using the Key attribute	0.71	0.44	0.42	0.56	0.71	0.61
Modify 1 tuple using the Key attribute	2.62	1.01	2.99	0.86	4.82	1.13
Modify 1 tuple Modified attribute is odd100 - a non-indexed attribute. The key attribute is used to locate the tuple to be modified.	0.49	0.36	0.90	0.36	1.12	0.36
Modify 1 tuple using a non-key attribute with non-clustered index	0.84	0.50	1.16	0.46	3.72	0.52

The fourth through sixth queries test the cost of modifying a tuple in three different ways. In all three tests, a non-clustered index exists on the unique2 attribute on both machines, and in addition, in the case of Gamma, a clustered index exists on the unique1 attribute. In the first case, the modified attribute is the key attribute, thus requiring that the tuple be relocated. Furthermore, since the tuple is relocated, the secondary index must also be updated. The fifth set of queries modify a non-key, nonindexed attribute. The final set of queries modify an attribute on which a non-clustered index has been constructed, using the index to locate the tuple to be modified.

As can be seen from Table 8, for the fourth and sixth queries, both machines use the index to locate the tuple to be modified. Since modifying the indexed attribute value will cause the tuple to move position within the index, some systems avoid using the index to locate the tuple(s) to be modified and instead do a file scan. While one must indeed handle this case carefully, a file scan is not a reasonable solution. Gamma uses deferred update files for indices to handle this problem[5]. We do not know what solution the Teradata machine uses for this problem.

Although Gamma does not provide logging, it does provide deferred update files for updates using index structures. The deferred update file corresponds only to the index structure and not the data file. The overhead of maintaining this functionality is shown by the difference in response times between the first and second rows of Table 8.

In examining the results in Table 8, one will notice that the cost of performing an update operation in Teradata is sometimes effected by the size of the relation being updated, whereas this is not the case in Gamma. For example in Teradata the time to append a single tuple in a relation with no indices increases as the size of the relation increases.

9. Conclusions & Future Directions

In this report we presented the results of an initial evaluation of the Gamma database machine by comparing its performance to that of a Teradata DBC/1012 database machine of similar size. From this comparison, one can draw a number of conclusions regarding both machines. With regard to Gamma, its most glaring deficiencies are the lack of full recovery features and the extremely poor performance of the distributed Simple hash-join algorithm when a large number of overflow operations must be processed. In the near future we intend on rectifying these deficiencies by implementing a recovery server that will collect log records from each processor and a distributed version of the Hybrid hash join algorithm. Since the Simple hash-join algorithm has superior performance when no overflows occur, the query optimizer will select the appropriate join algorithm based on the expected size of the smaller input relation.

Based on these results a number of conclusions can also be drawn about the Teradata database machine. First, the significantly superior performance of Gamma when using clustered indices indicates that this search structure should be implemented. Second, Teradata should incorporate bitvector filtering and a pipelined join strategy into their software. While the current sort-merge join algorithms always provide predictable response times, our results indicate that there are situations (ie. no overflows) when hash-join algorithms can provided significantly superior performance.

We are planning a number of projects based on the Gamma prototype during the next year. First, we intend to thoroughly compare the performance of parallel sort-merge and hash join algorithms in the context of Gamma. While the results presented in this paper indicate what sort of results we expect to see, doing the evaluation on one database machine will provide a much more reasonable basis for comparison. Second, since Gamma provides four alternative ways of partitioning relations across the processors with disks, we intend to explore the effect of these different partitioning strategies on the performance of selection and join queries in a multiuser environment. While for any one query there will always be a preferred partitioning of the relations referenced, we are interested in determining the tradeoff between response time and throughput in a multiuser environment as a function of the different partitioning strategies.

---

[5] This problem is known as the Halloween problem in DB folklore.

10. Acknowledgements

Like all large systems projects, a large number of people beyond those listed as authors made this paper possible. Bob Gerber deserves special recognition for his work on the design of Gamma plus his leadership on the implementation effort. Goetz Graefe made a number of contributions to the project including the first version of a SARGable predicate compiler. Joanna Chen was responsible for completing the predicate compiler and deserves special thanks for being willing to debug the machine code produced by the compiler. Finally, we would like to thank the Microelectronics and Computer Technology Corporation for their support in funding the study of the Teradata machine described in [DEWI87]. Without this earlier work, this paper would not have been possible.

This research was partially supported by the Defense Advanced Research Projects Agency under contract N00039-86-C-0578. by the National Science Foundation under grants DCR-8512862, MCS82-01870, and MCS81-05904, and by a Digital Equipment Corporation External Research Grant.

11. References

[ASTR76] Astrahan, M. M., et. al., "System R: A Relational Approach to Database Management," ACM Transactions on Database Systems, Vol. 1, No. 2, June, 1976.

[BABB79] Babb, E., "Implementing a Relational Database by Means of Specialized Hardware" ACM Transactions on Database Systems, Vol. 4, No. 1, March, 1979.

[BITT83] Bitton D., D.J. DeWitt, and C. Turbyfill, "Benchmarking Database Systems - A Systematic Approach," Proceedings of the 1983 Very Large Database Conference, October, 1983.

[BLAS79] Blasgen, M. W., Gray, J., Mitoma, M., and T. Price, "The Convoy Phenomenon," Operating System Review, Vol. 13, No. 2, April, 1979.

[BRAT84] Bratbergsengen, Kjell, "Hashing Methods and Relational Algebra Operations" Proceedings of the 1984 Very Large Database Conference, August, 1984.

[CHOU85] Chou, H-T, DeWitt, D. J., Katz, R., and T. Klug, "Design and Implementation of the Wisconsin Storage System (WiSS)" Software Practices and Experience, Vol. 15, No. 10, October, 1985.

[DEWI84a] DeWitt, D. J., Katz, R., Olken, F., Shapiro, D., Stonebraker, M. and D. Wood, "Implementation Techniques for Main Memory Database Systems," Proceedings of the 1984 SIGMOD Conference, Boston, MA, June, 1984.

[DEWI84b] DeWitt, D. J., Finkel, R., and Solomon, M., "The Crystal Multicomputer: Design and Implementation Experience," to appear, IEEE Transactions on Software Engineering, August 1987.

[DEWI85] DeWitt, D., and R. Gerber, "Multiprocessor Hash-Based Join Algorithms," Proceedings of the 1985 VLDB Conference, Stockholm, Sweden, August, 1985.

[DEWI86] DeWitt, D., Gerber, B., Graefe, G., Heytens, M., Kumar, K. and M. Muralikrishna, "GAMMA - A High Performance Dataflow Database Machine," Proceedings of the 1986 VLDB Conference, Japan, August 1986.

[DEWI87] DeWitt, D., Smith, M., and H. Boral, "A Single-User Performance Evaluation of the Teradata Database Machine," MCC Technical Report Number DB-081-87, March 5, 1987.

[GERB86] Gerber, R., "Dataflow Query Processing using Multiprocessor Hash-Partitioned Algorithms," PhD Thesis and Computer Sciences Technical Report #672, University of Wisconsin-Madison, October 1986.

[JARK84] Jarke, M. and J. Koch, "Query Optimization in Database System," ACM Computing Surveys, Vol. 16, No. 2, June, 1984.

[KITS83] Kitsuregawa, M., Tanaka, H., and T. Moto-oka, "Application of Hash to Data Base Machine and Its Architecture," New Generation Computing, Vol. 1, No. 1, 1983.

[MC²86] Measurement Concepts Corp., "C³I Teradata Study," Technical Report RADC-TR-85-273, Rome Air Development Center, Griffiss Air Force Base, Rome, NY, March 1986.

[NECH83] Neches, P.M., et al., U.S. Patent No. 4,412,285, October 25, 1983.

[PROT85] Proteon Associates, Operation and Maintenance Manual for the ProNet Model p8000, Waltham, Mass, 1985.

[RIES78] Ries, D. and R. Epstein, "Evaluation of Distribution Criteria for Distributed Database Systems," UCB/ERL Technical Report M78/22, UC Berkeley, May, 1978.

[SELI79] Selinger,P. G., et. al., "Access Path Selection in a Relational Database Management System," Proceedings of the 1979 SIGMOD Conference, Boston, MA., May 1979.

[STON76] Stonebraker, Michael, Eugene Wong, and Peter Kreps, "The Design and Implementation of INGRES", ACM Transactions on Database Systems, Vol. 1, No. 3, September, 1976.

[TANE81] Tanenbaum, A. S., **Computer Networks**, Prentice-Hall, 1981.

[TERA83] Teradata Corp., *DBC/1012 Data Base Computer Concepts & Facilities*, Teradata Corp. Document No. C02-0001-00, 1983.

[TERA85a] Teradata Corp., *DBC/1012 Data Base Computer System Manual, Rel. 2.0*, Teradata Corp. Document No. C10-0001-02, November 1985.

[TERA85b] Teradata Corp., *DBC/1012 Data Base Computer Reference Manual, Rel. 2.0*, Teradata Corp. Document No. C03-0001-02, November 1985.

[VALD84] Valduriez, P., and G. Gardarin, "Join and Semi-Join Algorithms for a Multiprocessor Database Machine" ACM Transactions on Database Systems, Vol. 9, No. 1, March, 1984.

[WATS81] Watson, R. W., "Timer-based mechanisms in reliable transport protocol connection management" *Computer Networks 5*, pp. 47-56, 1981.

PERFORMANCE PROJECTIONS
FOR A RELATIONAL QUERY PROCESSOR

J.N. Kemeny   D.W. Lambert   F.J. Maryanski

ABSTRACT

The Hercules Relational Query Processor (HRQP) is a special purpose hardware device designed to accelerate database retrievals. A set of performance equations describing the selection and join operations of HRQP has been developed and used to compare and contrast HRQP with other database architectures. The equations have been parameterized with various configurations and database sizes in order to explore the performance range of HRQP. The results show that for its intended environment HRQP exhibits better performance than the closest competing architecture.

INTRODUCTION

The Hercules Relational Query Processor (HRQP) is a special purpose hardware device employing parallel searching and caching along with straightforward data structures to speed up database retrievals. It is intended to work in environments with medium-sized databases. HRQP can only deal with fixed-length, formated records. But a given field can have an arbitrary length, allowing HRQP to be used with predicable-length compressed databases. In this paper a set of performance equations, similar to those developed by D.J. De-Witt and P.B. Hawthorn [1], are defined for HRQP. These performance equations are used to compare HRQP's performance with other generic database architectures.

Two types of queries are considered: Simple selection and selection with join. These query types are involved in the great majority of retrieval requests. The performance equations used for these query types were parameterized in a variety of ways. The results presented represent a minicomputer configuration close to HRQP's intended application space. A number of database sizes, including very large databases, are examined to explore the performance range of HRQP.

Hercules is the name of an experimental distributed database management system targeted for command and control environments where availability and reliability are at a premium [8]. It runs on three DEC PDP 11/73 computers connected by DECnet under the RSX-11M Plus real-time operating system. In the current Hercules system all the functions of a distributed DBMS, including a relational algebra query manager and disk storage interface, are implemented in software (Pascal, in particular).

Early performance projections, confirmed by recent measurements, indicated that query processing would be the dominant bottleneck in the system. As a consequence, a separate effort was initiated to build a special purpose "back-end" query processor. The approach chosen was to use VLSI technology to build a processor (the HRQP) to directly process data from mass storage "on the fly."

The HRQP is intended to support very general ad hoc retrieval requests from a relational database system. Communication to the host DBMS is via a relational algebra interface. The purpose of the hardware is to provide both a flexible query capability and high-speed performance. The performance can be used to provide a fast response time and/or to increase the level of sharing possible in the DBMS.

RELATED RESEARCH

High performance is a key objective of any system which seeks to share a resource among a large community of consummers. Database systems are no exception. While relational databases provide a uniquely simple and general purpose model for real world information, poor performance has often been cited as a reason for not using a relational approach in practice. Attempts to offload database processing into dedicated back-end machines have been made in the past [2].

An early design which used a special architecture for implementing a relational database was CAFS [3]. It was one of the first to recognize that the usefulness of the relational model depends on the efficient implementation of the join operation. Previous architectures for high speed searching, such as the processor-per-track approach, were inadequate for interfile comparisons (i.e. joins).

DIRECT [4] represents a multiprocessor approach which did address joins in a straightforward fashion. The Multi-Processor Cache (MPC) architecture described in this paper is essentially a model for DIRECT. The straightforward approach compares every record with every other record. A more elaborate approach is to partition like records using a hashing algorithm. This was the original idea in CAFS, and there have been variations, for example, the work reported by Hong [5].

Software algorithms generally use another technique altogether; namely, they sort and merge files in order to join them. GRACE [6] represents an attempt to combine partitioning by hashing and hardware sort/merging into a very elegant database machine. Various other specialized processors have been proposed for database systems. Kim, Gajski, and Kuck [7] proposed a design for a pipelined relational query processor that had VLSI amenability as a design objective.

Many "systolic array" type architectures depend on VLSI systems where the number of processing elements is of the same order of magnitude as the number of data elements. We make no attempt at comparisons to such systems since the HRQP effort has a more near term focus.

ARCHITECTURE

This paper does not explore the detailed design of the proposed hardware. A schematic view is sufficient in order to explain the analytical equations we used in the modeling. However, to better explain the rationale behind the architecture, we will touch upon some tangential issues.

The Hercules Relational Query Processor is a hardware device that processes a data stream read in from mass storage (e.g., disk). A double buffering arrangement matches the input transfer rate to the processing rate. The processor is specified to process data at least as fast as it is presented by the data stream. This means that while one buffer is being loaded with data, the processor can complete computing on the other buffer.

Standard mass storage devices limit the speeds attainable with this model. It might be possible, however, to attain much higher performance by using storage with faster transfer rate capability. It is conceivable that the price of high-speed RAM will fall enough in the near future to be practical for mass storage. However, this paper compares architectures based on existing mass storage devices.

The data stored by a relational database system consists of files of fixed length records, also known as relations of tuples. The records are composed of fields. The query processor is able to lexically compare the fields within a record (it has no arithmetic capability - it can only match bit strings) and decide if the record meets a qualification condition based on the comparisons (for example: $field_1 = field_2$ and $field_3 > field_4$).

This filtering process is simple selection. If this were the sole capability of the HRQP, it would be limited to processing one relation at a time. Queries involving multiple relations require the use of a join operation. Logically, a join involves taking a subset from a cartesian product of two relations. Conventional computers usually do this by sorting both relations on the fields to be compared and then merging the two files. Other solutions involve using hashing to partition the relations, and then joining appropriate partitions.

The simplest way to do join, and therefore the one we adopted, is called a "nested iteration" algorithm. It involves the straightforward creation of a cartesian product by concatenating each record of one relation with each record of the other. The concatenated records are then passed to the comparison engine for evaluation. If the two relations are of size N, this algorithm is order N^2 with respect to I/O. Nevertheless, our models show a surprisingly good performance characterization, as compared to alternative architectures.

The descriptive power of a relational query language, such as relational algebra, comes from its ability to compose operations. The result of one operation is often used as the input to another. Thus, the result of a selection, for example, is not the data the user wants retrieved, but an intermediary result. Intermediary results may be needed several times in the course of a query. It would obviously be inefficient to recompute them each time. However, if an intermediary result is a large subset of a large join, it may not be possible to store it back to mass storage.

Hercules has a unique treatment for intermediary results. A special data structure called a "normal" is used to store this information. The normal has, at most, one bit for each record. (In certain circumstances it can be compressed further.) The bit indicates whether or not the record participates in the result. For example, the selected subset of a file containing N records can be represented by a bit string of length N. This bit string is a dynamically created "index" into the file, and represents the result of a single selection operation.

Arbitrarily complex compositions of operations using the relational algebra can also be represented this way. Intermediary results can be stored as normals. Unlike indices, these normals are never updated. Normals are only retained for the duration of a single transaction, which may, of course, involve multiple queries. During the life of a complex transaction a normal functions in precisely the same fashion as a database index. Figure 1 is a query illustrating the use

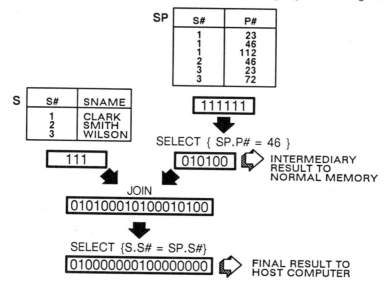

Figure 1: Query Illustrating Use of Normals

of normals for intermediary results. Relation S is a supplier file, with name and number; and relation SP is a supplier-parts file listing supplier numbers along with the parts they supply. The query asks, "What are the names of the suppliers who supply part number 46?" Computing the result involves a simple selection followed by a selection which is part of a natural join. The results of the first selection are saved in a special memory and used to do the second selection. This report will only examine simple queries where the use of normals for intermediary results has no performance impact. A future report will examine complex queries, where the effect of normals on performace can be explored. Figure 2 shows a data flow diagram for HRQP. The Reader

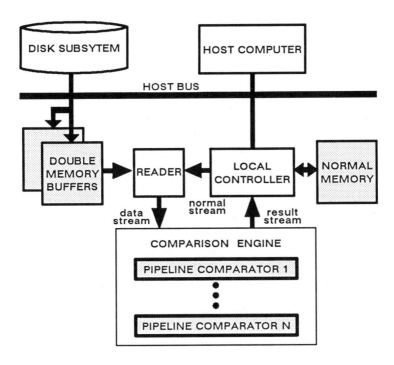

Figure 2: Dataflow of Hercules Query Processor

section extracts information from the double-buffered memory. This includes all the fields required by the comparison engine. Fields are not aligned on byte boundaries, nor are they multiples of bytes in length (there is no point in storing a one bit response in an eight bit field, for example). As a result, the comparison engine must deal with unaligned arbitrary length fields. The simplest way to handle this is to serialize the data stream. The Reader serializes the data stream and passes it to the Pipeline subsystem for comparison.

If a join is being done, the Reader concatenates the appropriate fields from the different files found in the memory (the allocation of memory to relations is discussed later). When processing an intermediary result, a normal bit stream is delivered by the Local Controller, allowing the Reader to skip records. Normals also tell the disk controller which blocks to read and which to skip.

Comparators are set up in parallel so that multiple conditions can be tested (for example, compare $field_1$ to $field_2$ and $field_3$ to $field_4$). The results are passed to the Local Controller to be stored as a normal in the local Normal Memory. There is also access to the Host bus for retrieved results.

PERFORMANCE ANALYSES

Several sets of parameters were utilized to describe the characteristics of CPU and disk operations. The set in Table 1 is intended to reflect the mini micro environment toward which Hercules is oriented. The values in Table 1 are based upon the configurations (PDP 11/73 with RL02 disks) used in the original Hercules software prototype. They are representative of medium-sized database application environments. The tuple size is assumed to be 100 bytes.

As in [1], the precise values in the table represent a combination of available measurements and some "back of the envelope" calculations. The results described, however, are not sensitive to either tuple size nor the model parameters.

Parameter	Description	Value	
BSIZE	Block Size	512.	bytes
DCYL	Blocks per Cylinder	40.	
T_{IO}	Block Read/Write Time	1.	msec
T_{DAC}	Average Access Time	67.	msec
T_{SK}	Track Seek Time	15.	msec
T_{SC}	CPU Time to Scan 1 Block	0.95	msec
T_{BLK}	CPU Time for Complex Operation	9.	msec
T_{OIO}	CPU Time to Initiate an I/O	4.	msec
$T_{CODE-GEN}$	CPU Time to Generate Code	52.	msec
T_{MSG}	CPU Time to Send/Receive Msg	4.	msec
T_{BT}	Transfer Time from Backend	0.25	msec

Table 1: System Parameters

Other sets of evaluations were made so that HRQP projections could be compared against other architectures. Since, except for some variations at the extreme end point (i.e., join of billion record relations) the results were similar, only those obtained using the parameters of Table 1 are presented.

Simple Selection

The architecture of the software version of Hercules fits the general model presented by DeWitt and Hawthorn. Their equation is utilized to describe the performance of the software version of Hercules. A comparison for a simple selection is then made with the hardware assisted Hercules, the Multi-Processor Cache architecture as defined in [1], and a software approach using indices.

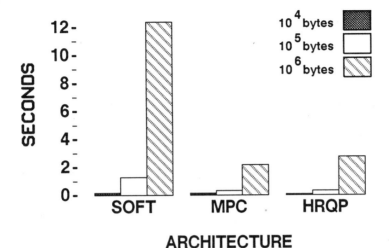

Figure 3: Selection Without Indexing

Software Only. A selection operation on a conventional computer involves an initial code generation (or set up) time, followed by a direct access of the first block in the relation. If the relation spans multiple tracks, additional seek time will be incurred for each extra track. Finally, for each block in the relation, a block transfer and scan will be required. This algorithm is described by:

$$T_{\text{SEL-SOFT}} = T_{\text{CODE-GEN}} + T_{\text{DAC}} + \left(\left\lceil \frac{|R|}{\text{DCYL}} \right\rceil - 1\right) T_{\text{SK}}$$

$$+ |R| \left(T_{\text{IO}} + T_{\text{OIO}} + T_{\text{SC}}\right)$$

Hercules Hardware. When a hardware query processor is added to Hercules, the block transfers and scans of a query will be performed in an overlapped fashion. Hence only the I/O times for each block are considered plus one initial I/O operation and one final scan. Selection performance is given by the following equation:

$$T_{\text{SEL-HRQP}} = T_{\text{CODE-GEN}} + T_{\text{DAC}} + \left(\left\lceil \frac{|R|}{\text{DCYL}} \right\rceil - 1\right) T_{\text{SK}}$$

$$+ T_{\text{OIO}} + |R| \, T_{\text{IO}} + T_{\text{SC}}$$

MPC Architecture. DeWitt and Hawthorn also evaluated the performance of four other generic database machine architectures in their study. Of

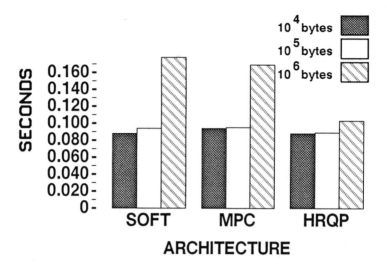

Figure 4: Selection With Indexing

these, the Multi-Processor Cache (MPC) yielded the best join performance and is the only architecture of the four in the study using conventional disk technology. For these reasons, the MPC architecture is included in this evaluation. MPC is capable of supporting an index structure as well as linear searches. Two sets of equations are used to described MPC performance. Non-indexed selection for MPC is given by:

$$T_{\text{SEL-MPC}} = T_{\text{CODE-GEN}} + 2T_{\text{MSG}} + T_{\text{DAC}} + T_{\text{BT}}$$
$$+ \max \left\{ \begin{array}{l} (|R|\text{SF} - 1)(T_{\text{MSG}} + T_{\text{BT}}), \\ \left\lceil \frac{|R|}{N} \right\rceil T_{\text{SK}} + (|R| + 1) T_{\text{IO}} + T_{\text{SC}} \end{array} \right\}$$

where N is the number of processors, and SF is the selection factor.

An MPC configuration consists of a collection of processors and RAM memory caches and one standard disk. Data is transferred from the cylinder to the caches in a serial manner, but then processors may read from their individual caches in parallel. Execution of the selection criteria can be overlapped with the loading of the cache with new tuples.

Indexed Queries. Queries on predefined indices can be handled by both conventional software systems and the Multi-Processor Cache architecture. HRQP does not support explicit indices, but does contain a dynamic index facility (normals) which can be utilized in complex transactions. The access time equations for the three approaches are presented below. Note that these equations consider only processing time and do not factor in the additional cost of the space required for the maintenance of the index structures.

Furthermore, the frequency of the index-based retrievals is highly application dependent, thus increasing the difficulty of performing a balanced comparison of the alternative techniques. As a general rule of thumb, indexed structures are viable in an established schema in which the most commonly used queries are well known. For more dynamic situations, the costs of these additional storage structures outweigh their benefits.

The equations for the indexed queries differ from those presented previously only in that both the number of blocks transferred and the number of cylinders searched are both reduced by an index selection factor. This modeling technique was originally described in [1].

$$T_{\text{SEL-SOFT-IND}} = T_{\text{CODE-GEN}} + T_{\text{DAC}} + \left(\left\lceil \frac{|R|\, \text{SF}}{\text{DCYL}} \right\rceil - 1 \right) T_{\text{SK}}$$

$$+ |R|\, \text{SF}(T_{\text{IO}} + T_{\text{OIO}} + T_{\text{SC}})$$

$$T_{\text{SEL-MPC-IND}} = T_{\text{CODE-GEN}} + 2T_{\text{MSG}} + T_{\text{DAC}} + T_{\text{BT}}$$

$$+ \max \left\{ \begin{array}{l} (|R|\text{SF} - 1)(T_{\text{MSG}} + T_{\text{BT}}), \\ \left\lceil \frac{|R|SF}{N} \right\rceil T_{\text{SK}} + (|R| + 1)\, T_{\text{IO}} + T_{\text{SC}} \end{array} \right\}$$

$$T_{\text{SEL-HRQP-IND}} = T_{\text{CODE-GEN}} + T_{\text{DAC}} + \left(\left\lceil \frac{|R|\, \text{SF}}{\text{DCYL}} \right\rceil - 1 \right) T_{\text{SK}}$$

$$+ T_{\text{OIO}} + |R|\, \text{SF}\, T_{\text{IO}} + T_{\text{SC}}$$

Comparison. Initially, the selection performance of the architecture was evaluated for non-indexed retrievals. The MPC architecture has an awkward implementation when the block size is small as with the DEC RL/02 disks. The total cache space of 200K must be distributed among all processors. A wide range of values were evaluated with 400 representing the median value. The results of this first evaluation are pictured in Figure 3. Both hardware configurations provide superior performance as the number of tuples in the target relation increase. MPC is slightly better than HRQP (2.16 secs, to 2.75 secs.).

However, HRQP is cheaper since MPC in this case involves 400 processors. As the number of bytes increases beyond 10^6, the time required by all three systems increases linearly. Unless otherwise noted, this behavior is true for all graphs presented in the paper.

For queries utilizing indices, as in Figure 4, HRQP offers better performance than either the software based scheme or the augmented MPC architecture. It should be noted that the normals used by HRQP in queries of this type would only be available in multi-step transactions.

Join

As described previously, the HRQP join algorithm differs significantly from those normally utilized in the other architectures. In this study, the hardware version of Hercules, a conventional software-only system executing a sort-merge join algorithm, and the Multi-Processor Cache architecture were modeled.

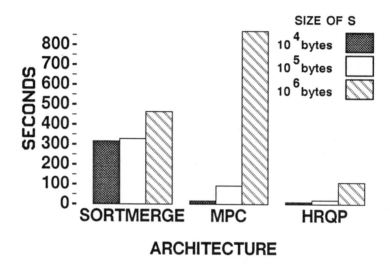

Figure 5: Join with 10^6 Bytes in R

Hercules Hardware. The HRQP join strategy uses N one block buffers: $N - 1$ of which are filled with tuples from relation S. The remaining buffer holds a block from R. The R tuples are matched against those from S and then the next R block is read. When all of R has been processed, the next $N - 1$ blocks of S are read until all tuples have been checked. A simple comparison is employed throughout. As in the previous situation, processing and I/O activity are overlapped. The following equation describes joins on HRQP:

$$T_{\text{JOIN-HRQP}} = T_{\text{CODE-GEN}} + 2 \left\lceil \frac{|R|}{(N-1)} \right\rceil (T_{\text{DAC}} + T_{\text{OIO}}) + T_{\text{SC}}$$

$$+ \left(\left\lceil \frac{|R|}{(N-1)} \right\rceil \left(\left\lceil \frac{|S|}{\text{DCYL}} \right\rceil - 1 \right) \right) T_{\text{SK}}$$

$$+ \left(|R| + \left\lceil \frac{|R|}{(N-1)} \right\rceil |S| \right) T_{\text{IO}}$$

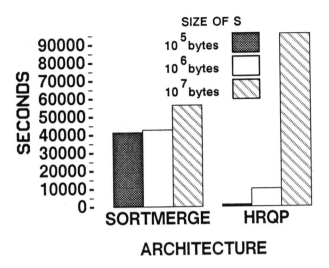

Figure 6: Join with 10^8 Bytes in R

Conventional Software. A four-way external merge sort on both relations is performed in the first phase of the sort-merge join. Then the joined relation is formed by merging the two sorted relations. It is assumed that the relations exist on different cylinders. The merging, therefore, incurs accessing penalties as it bounces between the relations. The overall join equation [1] for relations R and S is:

$$T_{\text{JOIN-CS}} = T_{\text{CODE-GEN}} + T_{\text{SORT-R}} + T_{\text{SORT-S}} + T_{\text{MERGE}}$$

The cost of sorting a relation with X blocks is:

$$T_{\text{SORT-X}} = 2\log_4(X) \left\{ T_{\text{DAC}} + X\left(T_{\text{IO}} + T_{\text{OIO}}\right) \right.$$

$$\left. + \left(\left\lceil \frac{X}{\text{DCYL}} \right\rceil - 1 \right) T_{\text{SK}} + \left(\frac{X}{4} \right) T_{\text{BLK}} \right\}$$

Merging is described by:

$$T_{\text{MERGE}} = \left(|R| + |S| \right) \left(T_{\text{DAC}} + T_{\text{OIO}} + T_{\text{IO}} + \left(\frac{T_{\text{BLK}}}{2} \right) \right)$$

Multi-Processor Cache. The MPC architecture is a back-end database system with a standard host processor and N special purpose database pro-

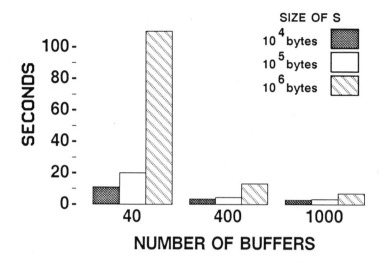

Figure 7: Effect of Buffersize (10^6 Bytes in R)

cessors. Each of the back-end processors is given a different block of R to initiate the join processing. The blocks of S are then broadcast sequentially to the processors where a 2-way merge is performed. When the size of R is larger than the number of processors, the process must be repeated until all blocks of R have been handled.

After the join is executed, the results are transmitted back to the coordinating processor. This transmission is overlapped with continued join processing. Join performance is as specified below. In the third equation, "JSF" represents the join selectivity factor. For the example considered (and most situations), the JSF factor is insignificant because executing the join consumes much more time than transmitting the results.

$$T_{\text{JOIN}-\text{MPC}} = T_{\text{CODE}-\text{GEN}} + 2T_{\text{MSG}} + T_{\text{BT}}$$

$$+ \max\{T_{\text{EXEC}-\text{JOIN}}, T_{\text{SEND}-\text{RESULT}}\}$$

where

$$T_{\text{EXEC}-\text{JOIN}} = \left\lceil \frac{|R|}{(N-1)} \right\rceil \left(2T_{\text{DAC}} + (N+3)T_{\text{IO}} + |S|T_{\text{BLK}} \right.$$

$$\left. + \left(\left\lceil \frac{|S|}{\text{DCYL}} \right\rceil - 1 \right) T_{\text{SK}} \right)$$

and

$$T_{\text{SEND}-\text{RESULT}} = (|R||S|\,\text{JSF} - 1)(T_{\text{MSG}} + T_{\text{BT}})$$

Comparison. The join equations were exercised to yield three types of evaluations. First relation R was given 10^6 tuples, and the performance of the three architectures is projected for joins against the relation S with a varying number of tuples. The number of tuples is then increased in both relations. In this second comparison, only sort-merge and HRQP are considered as the performance of the MPC architecture is far inferior to the other two. Finally, the effect upon the Hercules architecture of increasing the number of available buffers is studied. Figure 5 shows the performance projections when the participating relations are up to a megabyte in size. This is the most likely situation in Hercules' target environment. HRQP performs very well in this domain. Note the linear join time increments of the MPC architecture, while the sort-merge join increases much more slowly.

This behavior becomes more pronounced when the relations sizes are increased to the 100 megabyte range, as illustrated in Figure 6. At this point, HRQP's performance becomes a linear function of the number of tuples in S, while sort-merge continues to increase in a logarithmic fashion. However, HRQP is expected to offer the best join performance in all except the largest case.

The Hercules approach is essentially an N^2 algorithm in that each tuple in R must be compared against each tuple in S. Through the use of I/O and CPU overlap and careful buffering strategies, the full effect of the N^2 algorithm can be dampened until the relations become very large. MPC is also N^2 but it falls into the squared behavior more quickly than does HRQP which uses a less complex join algorithm. Thus, while MPC and HRQP both overlap processing and I/O, MPC is limited by the processing speed while HRQP is limited by the I/O transfer rate. In effect, MPC performs I/O for "free" while HRQP does the processing "free."

Sort-merge, as described here, has an $N \log_4 N$ behavior. In fact, except in the case of joining large square relations, the performance of the sort-merge join is dominated by the time required to sort the large relation. Thus, the time for the join is not affected by increases in the size of S wherever S is small in comparison to R. This discrepancy between performance projections for specific situations and theroretical complexity limits is similar to that obtained by Bitton et al [9] in their study of parallel sorting algorithms.

Figure 7 displays the effect of increasing the buffer size, and hence the amount of parallelism, upon HRQP join performance. The figure shows that after 400 buffers (of 512 bytes each) the performance improvements begin to level off. This behavior indicates that, at some point, the overhead of setting up the join cannot be compensated for by additional parallelism.

CONCLUSION

The performance equations for database architectures developed by DeWitt and Hawthorn [1] are extended to describe the architecture of the Hercules

Relational Query Processor (HRQP). Comparisons are made against a conventional system using commonly employed algorithms and the Multi-Processor Cache architecture which is a parallel back-end system. The results obtained for a variety of relation sizes are generally favorable to HRQP. This is particularly true for mid-size databases which are expected to be prevalent in the command and control environment toward which HRQP is targeted. Since HRQP is designed to be a low cost database machine, it is expected to exhibit a favorable cost/performance ratio.

The special case of queries on an index was included in the analyses presented here. While Hercules does, through its normals feature, provide a dynamic indexing mechanism, it does not explicitly support predefined indices. However, it is important to note that the models employed in this study consider only the run time cost of the queries and do not compute the storage cost of the indices and no consideration given to the relative frequency of index-based queries. Nor are other costs of indexing, such as update cost and impact on recovery algorithms included.

The HRQP processor is proceeding through prototype development. Four VLSI chips, incorporating two styles of comparison engines, have been designed, fabricated and tested. These have been assembled into a prototype processor which uses a single board computer as the Local Controller. This prototype is serving as a testbed to validate the analytical models presented. Finally, the analyses are being extended, e.g., we are investigating the impact of using hashing algorithms.

REFERENCES

[1] DeWitt, D.J., and P.B. Hawthorn, *Proceedings of the VLDB Conference.* October 1981.

[2] Maryanski, F.J., *ACM Computing Surveys.* V.12, N.1, March 1980.

[3] Babb, E., *ACM Transactions on Database Systems.* V.4, N.1, March 1979.

[4] DeWitt, D.J., *IEEE Transactions on Computers.* V.28, N.6, June 1979.

[5] Hong, Y.C., *IEEE Transactions on Computers.* V.34, N.7, July 1985.

[6] Kitsuregawa, M., H. Tanaka and T. Moto-oka, *Journal of Information Processing.* V.6, N.3, 1983.

[7] Kim, W., D. Gajski and D.J. Kuck, *ACM Transactions on Database Systems.* V.9, N.2, June 1984.

[8] Lambert, D.W., R.C. Hanckel, J.N. Kemeny, E.H. Leclair and R.M. Monzillo, MITRE MTP-258, August 1986. The MITRE Corporation, Burlington Rd., Bedford, MA 01730.

[9] Bitton, D., H. Boral, D.J. DeWitt and W.K. Wilkinson, *ACM Transactions on Database Systems.* V.8, N.3, September 1983.

ANALYTICAL PERFORMANCE EVALUATION OF RELATIONAL DATABASE MACHINES

J. S. LIE, G. STIEGE

Institut für Betriebssysteme und Rechnerverbund,
Technische Universität Braunschweig,
Bültenweg 74/75, D-3300 Braunschweig, West Germany

ABSTRACTS
The main intention of this paper is to show the use of queueing network models for analytical performance evaluation of relational database machines.

For the existing database machine RDBM the performance measures are presented. Then an alternative configuration of RDBM is shown which yields better throughput of the special purpose processors. Another concept based on data flow for relational database machines is discussed also. The performance of these models is evaluated and finally all results are compared.

INTRODUCTION

For the development of complex computer architectures a more sophisticated methodology for the performance analysis and evaluation is needed. One way to get performance measures is to use queueing networks for modelling the system architecture. Open queueing networks (Jackson Theorem) will be used for the performance analysis and evaluation of the relational database machine RDBM. The next section gives an overview of this database machine which has a heterogeneous multiprocessor system. Then the system model and the considered synthetic workloads are described. The results of the evaluation for the implemented RDBM prototyp will be discussed. Afterwards an alternative concept for relational database machines will be introduced and evaluated. Finally the results will be compared.

RELATIONAL DATABASE MACHINES WITH HETEROGENEOUS MULTIPROCESSOR SYSTEM

This database machine architecture is charaterized by functionally specialized processor classes, where each processor class consists of one or several processors capable of performing a specialized task. This architecture has the advantage, that systems can be tailored and optimized for specific workloads by building a special multiprocessor configuration which consists of the necessary number of specialized processors. I. e. the system can be adapted to the database applications. On

401

the other side, it has the disadvantage that every processor class is only capable of performing a specific task and therefore other workload distributions will cause idle time in some processors and thus decrease the possible performance.

Now we look at one of these database machine systems in more detail, namely the one which was developed and implemented at the Technical University of Braunschweig. An overview of the RDBM system configuration is given in fig. 1. Here only the most important aspects of the RDBM for the modelling are shown. A detail description of the RDBM is found in ref. 1 and 4.

The components of the RDBM multiprocessor system are interconnected via a bus system, which consists of separate lines for data, instructions and status informations. The transfer rates for these lines are 8 MB/sec, 4 MB/sec and 1MB/sec respectively.

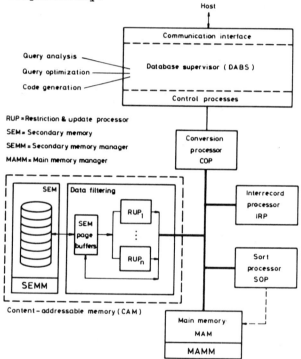

Fig. 1. RDBM System Configuration

The content-adressable memory consists of the **secondary memory** (SEM) and its **memory manager** (SEMM), which uses a set of data filters (**RUPs**) to allow data access by contents. The data·of a relation can be subdivided in data segments. Each segment consists of one or more data pages, which contain the tuples of the relation. The page size is 16 KB. The **main memory** (MAM) together with its

manager (MAMM) is the central component of the multiprocessor system. It is the common data memory for all
processors. The **sort processor** (**SOP**) is based on a
hardware structure specially tailored to the sorting
algorithm employed, a 4-way merge sort. The **conversion
processor** (**COP**) is the connecting component between the
RDBM data bus and the database supervisor. The
interrecord processor (**IRP**) performs operations working
on several tuples, these include aggregation functions
and the interrelation operations (i.e. joins).

ANALYSIS AND EVALUATION OF RDBM CONCEPT
System Model

The multiprocessor system of RDBM can be modelled as
an open queueing network with 6 service stations (fig.
2). The RUPs have 3 servers in the implemented RDBM
prototyp. The modelling is based on the Jackson Theorem,
which assumes the independence of the service stations
having negativ exponential service rates μ_i and arrival
rates λ_i and which gives an exact analysis of the
queueing networks (see also ref. 2).

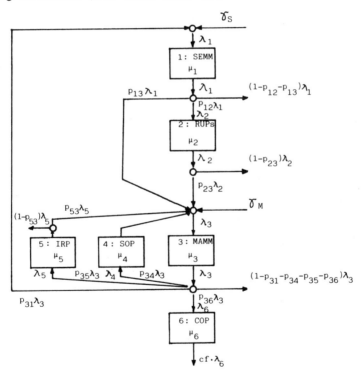

Fig. 2. Model of RDBM Multiprocessor System
The service stations are:
1 : SEMM (secondary memory manager)
2 : RUP with 3 servers(restriction and update processors)

3 : MAMM (main memory manager)
4 : SOP (sort processor)
5 : IRP (interrecord processor)
6 : COP (conversion processor)

The used symbols have following meaning :

γ_S : external arrival rate of data segments from secondary memory

γ_M : external arrival rate of shadow segments, which are created in main memory

p_{12} : probability that data segments are transfered to RUPs for qualification

p_{13} : probability that data segments are placed in the main memory

$(1-p_{12}-p_{13})$: probability that data segments are placed in the secondary memory

p_{31} : probability that data segments are replaced from main memory

p_{34} : probability that data segments will be sorted

p_{23} : probability that data segments will be qualified

p_{35} : probability that interrecord and interrelation operations will be performed

p_{36} : probability that data segments flow to the converter processor

$(1-p_{31}-p_{34}-p_{35}-p_{36})$: probability that data segments will be deleted after end of database transactions

p_{53} : probability that data segments from the interrecord processor go to main memory

$(1-p_{53})$: probability that data segments are not transfered to the main memory

cf : factor for the decrease of data segments (cf<1) because of the permutation and deletion of attribute in the COP and for the increase of them (cf>1) because of restructuring of data between external and internal formats.

For performance reasons insert operations will be performed as mass data inserts. Therefore the insert data flow is neglected in the model. The formulas for are given as:

$$\lambda_1 = \gamma_S + p_{31}\lambda_3$$
$$\lambda_2 = p_{12}\lambda_1$$
$$\lambda_3 = \gamma_M + p_{13}\lambda_1 + p_{23}\lambda_2 + p_{34}\lambda_3 + p_{53}\lambda_5$$
$$\lambda_4 = p_{34}\lambda_3$$
$$\lambda_5 = p_{35}\lambda_3$$
$$\lambda_6 = p_{36}\lambda_3$$

The parameter λ_1, λ_4, λ_5 and λ_6 can be deducted from λ_3 and λ_2 from λ_1 respectively. This system of equations can be solved and it yields:

$$\lambda_1 = (p_{31}\gamma_M + (1-p_{34}-p_{53}*p_{35})\gamma_S)/a$$

$$\lambda_2 = (p_{12}*p_{31}\gamma_M + (p_{12}-p_{12}*p_{34}-p_{12}*p_{53}*p_{35})\gamma_S)/a$$

$$\lambda_3 = (\gamma_M + (p_{13}+p_{23}*p_{12})\gamma_S)/a$$

$$\lambda_4 = (p_{34}\gamma_M + (p_{34}*p_{13}+p_{34}*p_{23}*p_{12})\gamma_S)/a$$

$$\lambda_5 = (p_{35}\ \gamma_M + (p_{35}\ *p_{13} + p_{35}\ *p_{23}\ *p_{12}\ )\ \gamma_S\ )/a$$

$$\lambda_6 = (p_{36}\ \gamma_M + (p_{36}\ *p_{13} + p_{36}\ *p_{23}\ *p_{12}\ )\ \gamma_S\ )/a$$

$$a = 1 - p_{13}\ *p_{31}\ -p_{23}\ *p_{12}\ *p_{31}\ -p_{34}\ -p_{53}\ *p_{35}$$

In the equilibrium state the data flow in the system is defined by parameter values of the transition probabilities, which reflect the system workload. So we get the arrivals rates of the service stations and with these measures the global system performance behavior can be determined. The bottlenecks of the systems can be also found.

Synthetic Workloads

The system performance is depended on the workloads which will put on the considered system. In the performance evaluation of the system the workload will be variated so, that a principle rule for the system performance can be derived the workload-dependent performance. For the investigations three synthetic workloads have been chosen. The first one reflects a database application, which only consists of retrieval operations. The second workload represents an active database application, which includes update, interrecord and interrelation operations. The last workload gives a good utilization for the implemented RDBM multiprocessor system. The following parameter values are chosen for the investigations:

	workload profile I	workload profile II	workload profile III
p_{12}	1.	0.9	1. (*)
p_{13}	0.01 (*)	0.05	0. (*)
p_{23}	0.5	0.05	0.1
p_{31}	0.	0.1	0. (*)
p_{34}	0.5	0.6	0.5
p_{35}	---	0.15	0.2
p_{36}	0.5	0.15	0.3
p_{53}	---	0.5	0.5
γ_S	10 (*)	10 (*)	10 (*)
γ_M	0	2	1
cf	1.5	1.0	1.0

Table 1. Workload profiles. (*): values will be variated

Investigations

Now we are going to present the results of the investigations. Fig. 3. shows the expected values of the service times for every processor class as a function of the number of tuples in each segment. These values are based on measured elementary processor operations. Increasing the number of tuples yields a higher service time and a low corresponding service rate. The shown service time does not include the access times for the common main memory. This access time depends on the utilization of the MAMM, which in turn depends on the system's transition probilities and external arrival rates. The expected service times per segment for the processor classes SEMM, RUPs, MAMM and SOP are in the milliseconds range, whereas the service times for the COP and IRP are in the range of seconds.

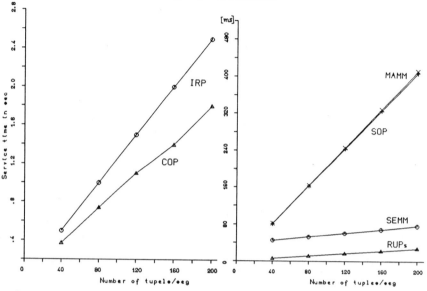

Fig. 3. Expected service times

For the workload profile I the processors' utilizations are shown in fig. 4.

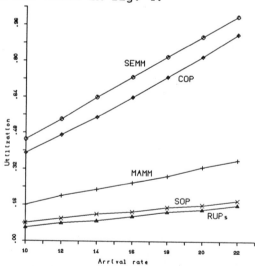

Fig. 4. Processors' utilizations over external rate γ_s

The chosen parameter values are given in table 1. Starting with the external arrival rate of 10 data segments per second, this value has been increased in steps of 2 data segments/sec. Each segment includes an average number of 40 tuples. The average length of the tuples is 200 bytes. For the probability that tuples qualify the values 0.01 (1%), 0.05 (5%), 0.1, 0.2, 0.3, 0.4 and 0.5 have been taken. If all tuples qualify the MAMM will be totally overloaded, because of the many necessary main memory accesses. As can be seen in fig. 4, the RUPs and the SOP are scarcely loaded.

The update operations are essential in the workload profile II. They are represented in the external arrival rate γ_M. The expected value for this arrival rate is chosen to be 2 segments/sec. The hit probability is chosen to be 0.1. The processors' utilization are shown in fig. 5. The MAMM is very busy with update operations, because the shadow segments additionally occupy the main memory. The SEMM is also loaded up to 97%, but the RUPs and SOP are only half utilized (γ_S = 20 segments/sec). From this it appears, that both of the memory managers will be bottlenecks in the system if many update operations will be done and therefore many page replacements are necessary.

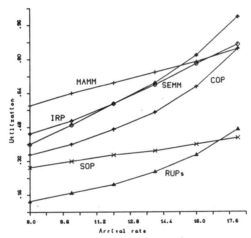

Fig. 5. Processors' utilization as function of external arrival rates γ_S

The workload profile III has principally a similar workload as the both investigated before. Here in this investigations the transition probability are variated. The variations will be done in 2 steps:
1. With or without paging. Paging causes an additional workload for the system. The necessary communication and management overhead is not neglectible.
2. Hit probability 0.1 and 0.2. These probabilities are sufficient to reflect a great number of standard database applications.

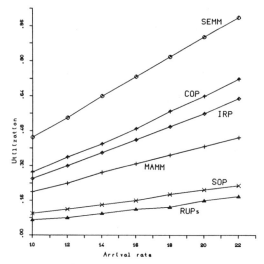

Fig. 6. Processors' utilization as functions of external arrival rates γ_S

Fig. 6 shows the utilizations of the processors with a hit probability of 0.1, a transition probability to the SOP of 0.5, to the IRP of 0.2, to the COP of 0.3, and without replacement. With γ_S =22 segments/sec the SEMM is totally busy and the other processors are only half utilized. For all workload profiles the SEMM is always strongly loaded; which shows, that here this is a system bottleneck.

The average waiting and residence times (in ms) are listed in the table 2, where γ_S = 16 segments/sec.

	SEMM !	RUPs !	MAMM !	SOP !	IRP !	COP !
waiting times	162	12	312	55	3895	1364
residence times	208	35	394	137	4740	2049

Table 2. Average waiting and residence times

For the processor classes with higher service rates the waiting time is low in comparison to processor classes with lower service rate (see Table 2). For example, the waiting times in the IRP and the COP are more than half of the whole residence times. The SEMM, MAMM, SOP and RUPs have service times in the same range; so that they can process the data in pace with the others. The IRP and COP have longer service times and therefore the waiting and residence times are many times longer.

If the probability of hits is doubled (p_{23} =0.2), all processors will be saturated. If paging is done, the SEMM will have a full utilization (γ_S =20 segments/sec). In that case there will be no equilibrium state any more which means, that the throughput of the multiprocessor system decreases. Caused by overloading in MAMM (γ_S =20 segments/sec) the waiting time for main memory access will be higher. This leads to higher waiting times in other processors, i. e. the RUPs, and therefore to a delay.

For all considered workload profiles it is cleary to be seen, that the main bottleneck is the MAMM, if paging has to be done. The system throughput is bounded on the one side by disk speed, on the other side by the SEMM service rate. This maximum throughput will be reached by Υ_S = 20 segments/sec.

Now we investigate an alternative configuration of the RDBM, where the data rate on the disk is assumed to be 8 MB/sec and the service rates of the processor classes are increased, so that all the processors can process the data in step. For this modified configuration a high performance SEMM is assumed and in any case one more IRP and one more COP will be added. The average service rate for SEMM is increased by a factor of 3 and and the service rate of the COP and the IRP by a factor 2 each. The ability to connect more processors of a processor class to the system is given by the RDBM concept by using a common bus system. The modification could be managed in the IRP by the distribution of independent IRP instructions among the same kind of processors (multiple instruction multiple data) and in the COP by the distribution of the tuples among the processors (single instruction multiple data).

Investigations have been made with this modified configuration. The results show that the augmented processors' capacities eliminate the bottlenecks which exist in the real configuration. For details see ref. 3.

ALTERNATIVE CONCEPT FOR RELATIONAL DATABASE MASCHINES: DATA FLOW ARCHITECTURE

The availability of virtual memory means a unlimited memory capacity. But the system throughput decreases, if paging occurs frequently. Another concept for the multiprocessor system of a relational database machine will be suggested (s. fig. 7), without a central main memory and its manager. Instead of them, the processors get a big enough local memory. In fact the processor classes with high service rates need not very much memory compared to processor classes with low service rates. It is important, that in the equilibrium state the data flow within the multiprocessor in the equilibrium state is not slowed down due to a memory bottleneck. The memory size needed depends on the service rate of the processor classes. Each processor has the ability to send data segments into secondary memory when it needs free memory. The connection between the processors can be by a global bus system or by connection matrix. Thus the system stays flexible and extendable and it still represents a heterogenous distributed system.

The segments which circulate in the processor contain not only to qualifying and process data, but they contain also following informations:

- which processors will be passed
- for which segment must be waited before the processing
  can begin

These informations are put together by the database supervisor and the segments will be supplemented with them. The data processing is very much the same as with RDBM concept. The differents are that in the RDBM concept the data flow is managed by the MAMM but it is now done by the processors themselves. The status information from each processor is sent to the supervisor, which collects all segments and puts the results together.

The concept is modelled as an open queueing network. Now we have 5 service stations and the number of connections is greater, because the MAMM doesn't exist. The formulas needed to calculate the external arrival rate is a little bit complicated.

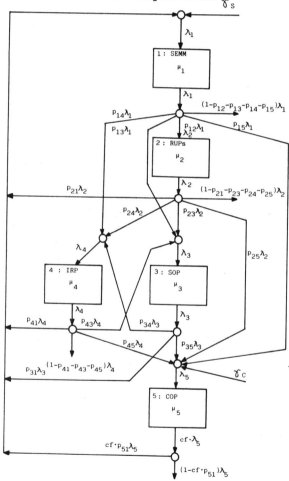

Fig. 7. Model of the data flow concept

The service stations are : 1 : SEMM
2 : RUP with 3 servers
3 : SOP
4 : IRP with 2 servers
5 : COP with 2 servers

For the modelling and performance analysis the performance values of the RDBM multiprocessor system are taken.

γ_S : external arrival rate of data segments from secondary memory

γ_C : external arrival rate of segments which are inserted into the database

p_{ij} : probability that data segments from processor class i goto processor class j

The formulas for λ_i (i=1,...,5) are as follows:

$$\lambda_1 = \gamma_S + p_{21}\lambda_2 + p_{31}\lambda_3 + p_{41}\lambda_4 + cf\,p_{51}\lambda_5$$
$$\lambda_2 = p_{12}\lambda_1$$
$$\lambda_3 = p_{13}\lambda_1 + p_{23}\lambda_2 + p_{43}\lambda_4$$
$$\lambda_4 = p_{14}\lambda_1 + p_{24}\lambda_2 + p_{35}\lambda_3$$
$$\lambda_5 = \gamma_C + p_{15}\lambda_1 + p_{25}\lambda_2 + p_{35}\lambda_3 + p_{45}\lambda_4$$

The solution of this system of equations is:

$$\lambda_1 = \frac{\gamma_S + cf\cdot p_{51}\gamma_C}{1-cf\cdot p_{51}\cdot p_{15}-cf\cdot p_{51}\cdot p_{25}\cdot p_{12} - \frac{(p_{31}+cf\cdot p_{51}\cdot p_{35})a}{1-p_{43}\cdot p_{34}} - \frac{(p_{41}+cf\cdot p_{51}\cdot p_{45})b}{1-p_{43}\cdot p_{34}}}$$

$$\lambda_2 = p_{12}\lambda_1$$

$$\lambda_3 = \frac{a\cdot\lambda_1}{(1-p_{43}\cdot p_{34})} \qquad\qquad a = p_{13}+p_{23}\cdot p_{12}+p_{43}\cdot p_{14}+p_{43}\cdot p_{24}\cdot p_{12}$$

$$\lambda_4 = \frac{b\cdot\lambda_1}{(1-p_{43}\cdot p_{34})} \qquad\qquad b = p_{14}+p_{24}\cdot p_{12}+p_{34}\cdot p_{13}+p_{34}\cdot p_{23}\cdot p_{12}$$

$$\lambda_5 = \frac{(p_{35}\cdot a+p_{45}\cdot b)\lambda_1}{(1-p_{43}\cdot p_{34})} + \gamma_C+p_{15}\lambda_1+p_{25}\cdot p_{12}\lambda_1$$

The expected values for the service rates can be derived from those of the RDBM prototyp, but the waiting time for memory access can now be neglected. The service rate are:

μ_1 = 70 segments/sec ; μ_2 = 144 segments/sec
μ_3 = 12 segments/sec ; μ_4 = 4 segments/sec ;
μ_5 = 5 segments/sec

It can be seen, that the service rates of the processor classes are different. We assume, that no paging occurs, i. e. the transition probabilities p_{21}, p_{31}, p_{41} und p_{51} have the value 0. Thus p_{13}, p_{14} und p_{15} are also equal to 0.

First we consider a database application which consists only of restriction operations. Then γ_C equals

0, because no tupel will be inserted. The parameters have the following values :

$$p_{12} = 1. \;\; ;$$
$$p_{23} = 0.08 \; ; \; p_{24} = 0.06 \; ; \; p_{25} = 0.06 \; ;$$
$$p_{34} = 0.6 \; ; \; p_{35} = 0.4 \; ;$$
$$p_{43} = 0.3 \; ; \; p_{45} = 0.2 \; ; \; cf = 1.$$

From these parameters the arrival rates of the service stations can be derived from these parameters (γ_s = 28 segments/sec):

λ_1 = 28 segments/sec ; λ_2 = 28 segments/sec ;
λ_3 = 3 segments/sec ; λ_4 = 4 segments/sec ;
λ_5 = 4 segments/sec

Fig. 8 shows the utilization of each processor class and the respective waiting and residence times are listed in table 3.

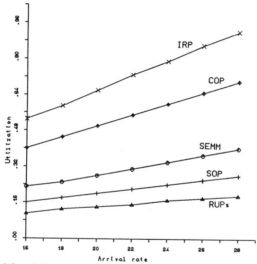

Fig. 8. utilization of processors over the external arrival rate γ_s

	waiting time		residence time	
SEMM	9.3	ms	23.5	ms
RUPs	1.7	ms	8.6	ms
SOP	31.3	ms	113.7	ms
IRP	3	sec	3.29	sec
COP	431.2	ms	617.2	ms

Table 3. waiting and residence time

There is no waiting time for memory access on the RUPs, therefore the RUPs have a higher service rate. Even higher hit rate there will be no overload of the RUPs.

Now we investigate a second database application which also consists of insert operations (γ_c = 1 segment/sec). Following transition probabilities have been chosen:

$$p_{12} = 0.9 \; ;$$
$$p_{23} = 0.08 \; ; \; p_{24} = 0.06 \; ; \; p_{25} = 0.06 \; ;$$

$$p_{34} = 0.6 \quad ; \quad p_{35} = 0.4 \quad ;$$
$$p_{43} = 0.3 \quad ; \quad p_{45} = 0.2 \quad ;$$
$$p_{51} = 0.1 \quad ; \quad cf = 1.$$

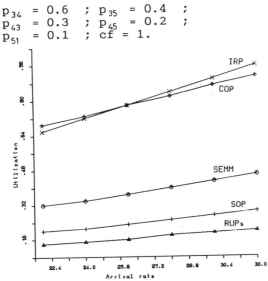

Fig. 9. Utilizations of the processors over the external arrival rates γs

Fig. 9 shows the utilizations of the processors. Because of the insert operations the utilization of the COP is higher than in fig. 8. The utilization of the SEMM is also higher, because there are a additional flow of data segments from the SEMM to the COP. It can be seen, that the data flow concept gives no significant performance enhancement, because the segments are processed like before.

DISCUSSION AND CONCLUSION

After having investigated the RDBM concept with two different configurations as well as the data flow concept for relational database machines, we are now going to compare the results. In this part we want to show the pros und cons of the two concepts. It is not the aim of the comparison to come to a decision whether one concept is better than the other. It should merely help one in the decision process determinating when a similiar concept is to be supplied in future. Above all it should be a guide to come to results analytically.

The main attention of the development of new computer systems, repectively computer architectures is directed to better performance results in comparison to already existing computer systems. This means not only more performance values in quantity, e. g. throughput, utilization, waiting time, service time, but also better quality, as to mention ergonomy, reliability, availability and servicability.

First, we want to show the commonness of the two concepts. Both use a heterogeneous system of functionally specialized processors which is flexible and extendable.

Thus, there is ability to analyze configurations for specific database applications and to connect additional processors when needed. Flexibility and the possibility of extensions are essential for aspects as reliability, availability and servicability.

Now we want to discuss the RDBM concept. This concept offers an "unlimited" main memory by using common memory for all the functionally specialized processors and their virtual memory. But this requires an expensive main memory manager as well as an expensive secondary memory manager. It requires above all a great deal of communications and transfer overhead if in case of memory bottlenecks a lot of paging is to be done. As shown in chapter 3 this overhead can not be neglected. Even if the page replacements are only 5 percent of the whole data segment flow from the MAMM, the utilization of the MAMM increases by about 50 percent. A memory bottleneck at the implemented RDBM configuration comes very quickly, because the two processors IRP and COP have service times, which are in the range of seconds. But staying rather long in memory leads to full memory and as a final result to page replacement.

This bottleneck can be removed with the modified RDBM configuration with the help of a high performance secondary memory respectively its manager and a doubled service rate of the main memory manager. Furthermore the service rates of IRP and COP have been doubled in order to avoid very slow processing in the multiprocessor system. With this modification of the configuration of the multiprocessor system the RDBM is qualified for gaining a good throughput for most of the database applications.

Even if the high performance memory manager is balanced against the aditional expenditure of paging, the transfer of pages which is not fundamentally necessary and its bus loading, cannot be removed by this concept. Consequently the second concept, the dataflow driven concept for relational database machines, has the advantage that the main bottleneck of the first concept, the main memory and its manager does not exist yet and that the data segments circulate as indepedent units in the system and can be worked on. In principle, this concept is close to the idea of distributed systems. Each data segment carries within it the information in which component of the system its data should be worked on. However this concept does not give an essential growth in power over the two versions of the common main memory.

REFERENCES
1. H.Auer et al. In: Information Systems, 6(2), 1981
2. H.Kobayashi; Modeling and Analysis. Addison Wesley, 1978
3. Lie,J.S.; Ph. D. thesis, T.U. Braunschweig, 1987
4. H.Schweppe et al. In: Proc. of 2nd IWDM (Ed. D.K. Hsiao), Prentice Hall, 1983

Algebra Operations on a Parallel Computer — Performance Evaluation

Kjell Bratbergsengen
Department of Computer Science
The Norwegian Institute of Technology
University of Trondheim

Abstract

The design of a parallel database computer is described. It contains 8 single board computers, each with a disk controller and disk. They communicate over a system of shared RAM, allowing fast communication without interference. The 8 computers are programmed and controlled from an IBM-compatible PC. The database computer is used for experimentation with relational algebra operations, sorting and numeric computations. In this paper we describe the methods used for doing relational operations, and test results are reported. The performance of the system did meet our expectations, and is quite good. The DeWitt join test was completed in 1.8 seconds. The system will be extended to 64 or 128 nodes and a brief description of the new interconnection network and an estimate of the expected performance is given.

1 Introduction

The proliferation of powerful micro processors and inexpensive mass produced powerful Winchester disks has made it technically and economically feasible to get super high performance using many of these bread and butter components together. The main challenge is to develop methods for parallel systems and not least, develop methods for effective programming and testing of highly parallel systems.

2 A brief description of the CROSS8 parallel database computer

CROSS8 is an experimental computer especially built for doing research on parallel algorithms for relational algebra operations. However it has also been used for parallel sorting and a few computational problems.

The main computer consists of 8 single board micro computers, each complete with memory, SCSI port to a hard disk controller, a small Winchester disk and a port to the combined interconnection network and host. The single board computer is running an Intel 80186 processor, clock frequency is 8 MHz, and the memory is 256 KB without wait states. The 80186 is particularly good at moving data, a much used operation in database computers. Using the Intel string move instructions, moving one word (16 bits) takes 1 microsecond, and the bus load is minimized.

Our algorithms for relational algebra operations are based on fast relocation of data between node computers. This puts special requirements on the interconnection network. Exchanging data between nodes is not allowed to become the bottleneck. The

415

capacity of the network must keep pace with increasing number of nodes. One such a network is the hypercube. Our work on the hypercube network topology goes back to 1978/79, see [BRAT80] — in that paper the hypercube was called "a k-dimensional network of intersecting rings". But up till now it has not been easy to realize hypercube networks with the required capacity for database operations. However the availability of dual port RAM chips has changed that.

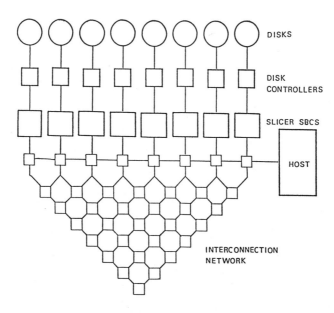

Figure 1: An outline of the CROSS8 database computer

The interconnection network topology of CROSS8 is not hypercubic, it is an all to all direct communication. The reason is that for only 8 nodes there is not much to save in components and less complexity having a hypercube network rather than a cross connected network. Cross connected networks based on dual port RAM chips gives a reasonable component count up till 12 nodes, above that hypercube topology should be used. An interconnection network board has been developed. In addition to internode communication, it is also the link between the host computer and all nodes. The host can address a single node or it can broadcast messages, data or a program to all nodes. The host can interrupt any or all nodes, and a node can interrupt the host. The effective data rate between any node and the node and host is today 0.5 M bytes pr second. Very little overhead is required, even for single byte messages, and using dual port RAMs are much more flexible than communication over serial links like FIFOs. The transfer rate is limited by the processor bus bandwidth. The developed interconnection board could — with an appropriate processor, come as high as 4 MB/sec effective transfer rate between any two nodes. This capacity can again be doubled if necessary.

However, with the 8 Intel 80186 processors the total effective relocation capacity is 4 MB/sec. The main structure of the CROSS8 database computer is shown in fig. 1.

3   Secondary storage

The database tables are stored on Winchester disks. For budget reasons we had to use inexpensive disks. As we already had some experience with Seagate ST225, used in IBM compatible PCs the choice felt on them. ST225 is a 20 MB disk, with an average access time of 65 milliseconds. The disk transfer rate is the standard 5 M bits per second. Positioning to a neighboring track takes 20 ms, and the rotation time is 16.67 ms. The disk is formatted to 512 bytes pr. sector giving 17 sectors on each track.

Our calculations had already shown that reading data from the disk would be the bottleneck. Making the most out of the disk was vital. Reading one track in one disk revolution should in theory be within reach. This gave 2 microseconds pr. byte transfer time, 50% of bus capacity. We tested several disk controllers which should be able to support 1:1 interleave, and ended up using Western Digital 1003 SCS. This controller is able to read with interleave factor 1:1, but writing data with that interleave factor was disastrous. The disk controller and node computer could not transfer data fast enough when writing. The result was that two sectors were written on each revolution. With interleave factor 1:2 both read and write worked properly, however this doubles the effective transfer time to 4 microseconds pr. byte.

4   Program development

The processor of the node computer is compatible with IBM compatible PCs. All programming has been done on PCs, also linking of modules. A special load program was used for transferring program modules to the node computers. The load program can either broadcast the module to all nodes — if they are to run identical programs, or each node can be loaded individually. MSDOS is not available at the node computers. Only a monitor program resides permanently in each node. The monitor takes care of initialization, basic I/O and debugging. All programming languages with a compiler for the IBM PC can be used for developing programs for the database computer. However if the generated programs use MSDOS functions; they can not run. We have experienced so far that there has been only small problems in *programming* the parallel computer. It has been much more difficult to *debug* programs.

A primitive development tool has been developed. All I/O normally going to the terminal generated by node computers is redirected to the host computer through the interconnection network. The host computer has a small window for each node computer, in which normal output is written. Input from keyboard is broadcast to all nodes or sent to one specified node. If the user wants to concentrate on communication with only one node, the host computer gives one full screen to this node. The other nodes are then not shown, but full size screen buffers are continuously maintained for all of them and can be flashed at any moment.

Writing messages from node computers has been the most often used debugging tool so far. But a debugger for setting breakpoints and examining memory during execution has been of great help in some hard cases. However a more elaborate development tool will be highly appreciated.

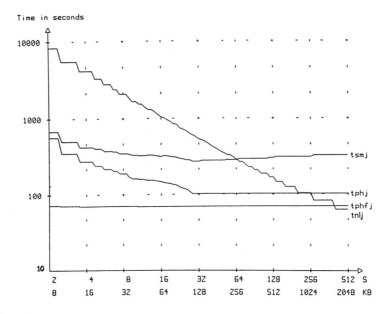

Figure 2: JOIN processing time as a function of available workspace. Monoprocessor system, pagesize is 4 KB, operands are of equal size. VAX 780 class computer. Total operand volume is 6.4 MB.

5 Relational algebra operations

The records of a database table are as evenly as possible spread out on all nodes. This is necessary to be able to search or read a table in parallel. For single record operations like insertion, update and deletion only one node is activated, the node with the record. We assume that the primary key of that record is known, otherwise a search for the record on all nodes must be undertaken. The base tables are stored as flat files and no indices have been established.

The basic operation of all relational algebra operations (except SELECTION) is to match keys, either within the same table (PROJECTION and AGGREGATION) or keys in two different tables (JOIN, INTERSECTION, UNION, DIFFERENCE). Several methods based on hashing for doing algebra operations on a monoprocessor computer has been described in [BRAT84], [MENO86] and other recent papers. The methods described in [BRAT84] are easily extended to run on multicomputer systems. Multiple computers incurs only one extra stage. After the records are read from disk they are sent to a node where all candidate matching keys are sent. The target node of each record is determined using a hash formula on the operation key (join attribute in the JOIN operation, primary key in PROJECTION, UNION, INTERSECTION, and DIFFERENCE; and grouping attributes in the AGGREGATE operation). This method was — as far as this author knows, first described in [BRAT80] and was the fundamental reason for analyzing the relocation capacity of several interconnection networks. Later similar methods were described in [GOOD81] and [KITS83]. Relocation methods called *global hash* methods are analyzed together with several other methods for parallel algebra operations in [QADA85]. DeWitt and Gerber in [DEWI85] undertakes a simulation analysis of several variants of parallel hash join algorithms.

Fast relocation of records is depending on the interconnection network capacity. Performance of the local algorithm is very much dependent on available random access memory for work space and buffers. This is analyzed in [BRAT84], and figure 2 shows some results from that work.

In figure 2 four different methods are analyzed

nlj	—	nested loop join,
smj	—	sort merge join,
phj	—	partition hash join and
phfj	—	partition hash join with filter.

We are using nested loop join, and this method is extremely good if the memory is large enough compared to the operand size. The total memory of all 8 node processors in CROSS8 is 2 MB. Memory available for buffers and workspace is about 1.5 MB. This is enough for handling operands up to about 15 MB in an optimal way as long as the smallest operand are about $\frac{1}{10}$ of the largest operand. For extremely large operands partition hash join is employed.

6   A model for performance estimation

Assume we are analyzing join of two tables A and B. There are two obvious possible bottlenecks: The disk transfer and the microprocessor bus. The bus is used during actual transfer of data between memory and disk, during relocation of data between computers, during local moves of data from I/O-buffer to record working storage and during general program execution. The two latter elements are put together and included into a local handling time for each A-record — t_A, and each B-record — t_B. Relocation and disk transfer are depending on operand volume. The following expression will approximately describe the time consumption on the local bus:

$$
\begin{array}{llll}
T_{BUS} = (& V & \times & t_d & \text{actual data transfer during disk I/O} \\
+ & V & \times & t_r & \text{relocation time} \\
+ & N_A & \times & t_A & \text{handling time for each A record} \\
+ & N_B & \times & t_B \ )/C & \text{handling time for each B record.}
\end{array}
$$

C is the number of nodes or cells. V is total operand volume, N_A is the number of A-records and N_B is the number of B-records. t_d is the time to transfer one byte from disk IO-port to memory, and is measured with an oscilloscope to be 2.0 microseconds/byte. Relocation takes 4 memory accesses. There are no waitstates, hence $t_r = 4 \times 500ns = 2.0$ microseconds. t_A and t_B can only be estimated. t_A is set to 250 microseconds and t_B to 450 microseconds. Although the times are fixed they are not quite independent of record length, but record length is assumed not to dominate the handling times.

Disk time is easier to estimate. Page size is one track. The disk is formatted with interleave factor 2, hence the disk must rotate twice for reading one track. The time between finishing reading of one track till the start of next track is so short — only 1 ms — that the disk controller will not get the next command in time to immediately read next track. Then another rotation is lost. Between cylinders at least 2 rotations are lost during positioning. On the average 3.5 rotations are used for each page read or write. After this the disk time is:

$$T_{DISK} = \frac{V \times T_{ROT} \times 3.5/V_{TRK}}{C}$$

T_{ROT} — time pr. disk rotation — 16.67 ms.

V_{TRK} — No of bytes pr. track — 8704 for our disks.

During disk operation only a fraction of the total disk time require bus service. During lost rotations and skipping of interleaved sectors the bus is free. During these disk channel pauses the CPU is active doing relocation and record handling. In the first version of the program the DeWitt test took 2.8 seconds. Later we changed our programs to work during channel pauses; and the DeWitt test ran in 1.8 seconds. All CPU activity is hidden in the channel pauses.

D	CELLS	DISK	REL	RECORD LENGTH IN BYTES						
				364	182	91	45	22	11	6
1	2	6702	2000	5187	6375	8750	13500	23000	42000	80000
2	4	3351	1000	2594	3187	4375	6750	11500	21000	40000
3	8	1676	500	1297	1594	2187	3375	5750	10500	20000
4	16	838	250	648	797	1094	1687	2875	5250	10000
5	32	419	125	324	398	547	844	1437	2625	5000
6	64	209	62	162	199	273	422	719	1312	2500
7	128	105	31	81	100	137	211	359	656	1250
8	256	52	16	41	50	68	105	180	328	625
9	512	26	8	20	25	34	53	90	164	312
10	1024	13	4	10	12	17	26	45	82	156

Table 1: Join of 2 MB as a function of number of nodes. $DISK$ gives total time for disk transfer. REL gives the relocation part of bus load. The other columns gives the total bus load as a function of different record lengths. All times are in milliseconds. Network is crossbar, all nodes connected to all. $CELLS = 2^D$.

Table 1 and figure 3 shows the estimated bus load and disk time as a function of number of nodes and record length. An operand volume of 2 MB is used, and both record length and number of records is varied such that the total operand volume is held constant. When record length is 182 bytes, $N_A = 1000$ records and $N_B = 10000$ records. These values are the same as those used in the DeWitt test, see section 7.

It is seen from table 1 and figure 3 that disk I/O is the bottleneck when records are 182 bytes or longer. For shorter records the handling of individual records becomes dominant, and bus load (or the CPU) becomes the bottleneck. These estimates are also consistent with our measured results, see figures 4, 5 and 6.

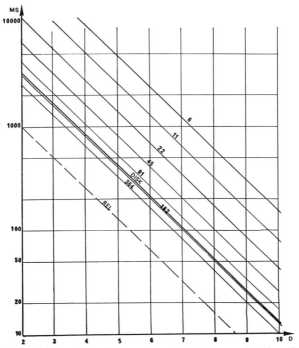

Figure 3: Estimated lower limits for JOIN execution time as a function of processing nodes and record length. Number of nodes is 2^D. Operand volume is 2 MB. Same conditions as for table 1.

7 The DeWitt JOIN test

To be able to compare CROSS8 with other systems we have run the join test described in [BITT83], the so called DeWitt join test. To be more specific, the test we have run is denoted *JoinABPrime* in [BITT83]. The two operands were without indices. The A table contains 1000 records each 182 bytes long. The other operand B contains 10000 records, also 182 bytes long. The volume of A is 182 KB, and the volume of B is 1.82 MB. Together this is quite close to 2 MB. Every key in A is found in B, such that the resulting table R will contain 1000 records. The join key is a 16 bit integer field. The result table is not written back to disk, this is also in accordance with the other tests. Writing the result file back takes about 400 milliseconds included opening and closing of the result file. The time is measured from start of operation is signaled from host, to all result records are ready in workspace. The different nodes will not finish operation exactly at the same time, but the differences are small, only 40 ms at most. These are our results:

CROSS8	1.8	seconds
TechRa on ND 540	17	seconds
TechRa on VAX 11/750	32	seconds
IDM with indices and accelerator	27.5	seconds
Ingres VAX 11/750	156	seconds

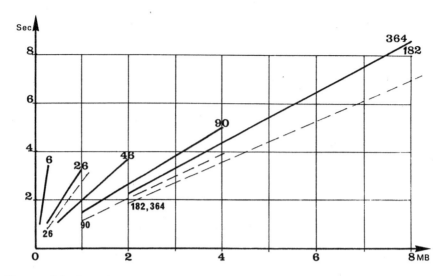

Figure 4: Join of A and B, B is 10 times larger than A. Operation time is given as a function of operand volume. The time varies with record length. Record length is written to each curve. Solid lines includes time for writing result file, dashed lines without writing result file. Result file has the same size as A.

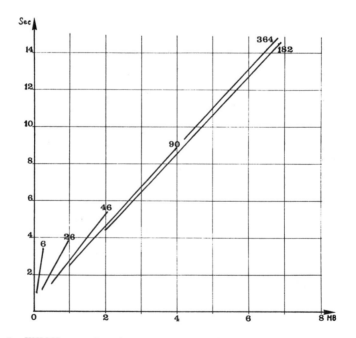

Figure 5: UNION operation time as a function of operand volume and record length. $B = 10 \times A$. Time includes writing result table to disk.

The figures for IDM and Ingres are taken from [BITT83]. TechRa [TECH84] is a commercially available system developed by a Norwegian company. The algorithms for doing relational algebra in TechRa are based on partition hash, see [BRAT84].

Why are the result so good? The hardware, both the processor and the disks on CROSS8 are much slower than ND540 and VAX 11/750. These factors are significant:

- CROSS8 runs directly on raw disks, there is no intermediate file and operating system.

- CROSS8 is programmed in assembler.

- CROSS8 is a single user system

- The CROSS8 host is not parsing and analyzing SQL statements, rather relational algebra calls are given directly to the CROSS8 database computer.

8   More extensive performance testing

We have run the join and the other algebra operations with different operand volumes, record sizes and number of records. The results are shown in figures 4, 5 and 6.

8.1   The JOIN test

The JOIN test has been run in two variants: one without writing the result records back to disk and the more extensive test which includes writing the result file. In figure 4 dashed lines are for non writing and solid lines includes writing the result file. If we compare estimated and measured results, the correspondence is good:

Record length	Estimated	Record length	Measured
22	5.75 sec.	26	6.00 sec.
91	2.19 sec.	90	2.20 sec.
182	1.68 sec.	182	1.84 sec.
364	1.68 sec.	364	1.80 sec.

8.2   Test of UNION

Figure 5 shows the test results for UNION. This operation is run only with writing of result file. Writing the result file is the only reason why this operation takes considerably longer time than JOIN. The same files as for the JOIN test has been used. All records in the A-operand is found in B and they are removed as duplicates. The result file is identical to B at least in size. Disk I/O is almost doubled compared with the JOIN operation. This is also reflected in the time used. UNION of 2 MB (record length is 182) takes 4.4 second, a little less than double 2.3 seconds as was the JOIN time for the same operands (includes time for writing result table).

8.3   Operations on large tables

All algebra operations have been run for different operand volumes, and the results are summarized in figure 6. Through all tests the number of records in B is 10 times the number of records in A. Both operands have the same record size namely 364 bytes.

The main purpose of this test was to find the effect of large operands, so large that they do not fit into workspace. The discontinuities of the curves in figure 6 reveals how many times the workspace has been filled up. Records which do not get room in workspace must be stored temporarily on disk. If a naive algorithm is used, only one A-record too much implies writing the complete B-operand on disk. However this is not necessary, a bit vector is set up for all A-records written to the temporary file. Only B-records finding a matching bit in the bit vector is saved.

The operations seem to fall in three groups: aggregation which did not fill workspace because only short records need to be stored. Join, intersection and difference-A fall in the second group. The bit vector filtering works well and not much extra work is done when work space overflows. Difference-A is R:=A-B, A is the smallest operand, and the result table is empty. The third group is union and difference-B. Both operations produce large result tables, and bit vector filtering has no effect as all records in the second operand have a matching key in the first operand. Difference-B is R:=B-A where A is the smallest operand.

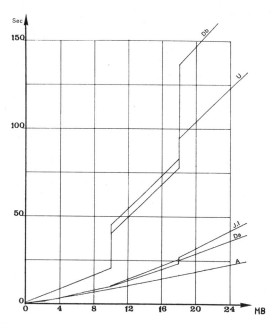

Figure 6: Execution times of relational algebra operations as function of operand volume. Record length is 364 bytes in both operands. For binary operations B is 10 times A. Operations are denoted: Db – difference R:=B-A, Da – R:=A-B, U – union, J – join, I – intersection, A – aggregation.

9   Extending the database machine to higher number of nodes

When we will increase the number of nodes to more than 12 we have to use a different interconnection network than the crossbar network used to day. The crossbar is too expensive to realize in large systems. In [BRAT80] several different homogeneous networks was analyzed. The best network was found to be "the D-dimensional network of intersected rings with 3 nodes in each ring". The second best was the same type of network with 2 nodes in each ring, or in modern language — the hypercube. As the 3 node pr. ring variant is harder to realize than the hypercube, the latter is chosen. The hypercube network we are building has a two byte wide path. When we are relocating records in the hypercube, the average number of dimensions the records have to cross is $\frac{D}{2}$. We are always assuming a uniform redistribution of records. To cross one dimension the data have to be moved twice. To cross $\frac{D}{2}$ dimensions a data word must be moved $(\frac{D}{2}+1)$ times. Each move implies two memory accesses, a load and a store. Relocation of V bytes will then take:

$$Th_{rel} = \frac{t_m V (D/2+1) 2/b}{C} = \frac{t_m V (D/2+1)}{C}$$

when b — the number of bytes per word is 2. t_m is the memory access time.

As before there are two possible bottlenecks: the disk operation time and the bus load. The hypercube adds load to the bus, as each node must handle records in transit. There are no changes to the disk operation time. For hypercubes we get the following modified formula for bus load:

$$
\begin{aligned}
TH_{BUS} = (\quad & V \quad \times \quad t_d & \text{actual data transfer during disk I/O} \\
+ \quad & V \quad \times \quad t_m \quad \times (D/2+1) & \text{relocation time} \\
+ \quad & N_A \quad \times \quad t_A & \text{handling time for each A record} \\
+ \quad & N_B \quad \times \quad t_B \quad)/C & \text{handling time for each B record.}
\end{aligned}
$$

The relation between C and D is: $C = 2D$

Our new machine will have a faster microprocessor than our current. Assume that the clock frequency is increased to 12.5 MHz. That will reduce all CPU and bus related activities with a factor $8/12.5 = 0.64$ compared to our current prototype. Hence:

t_d = 1.28 microseconds
t_m = 320 nanoseconds
t_A = 160 microseconds, and
t_B = 288 microseconds.

Using these values we get the following timing table. The operand volume is 2 MB to make it easy to compare with the numbers in table 1.

Relocation takes a significant part of the bus time for long records and high order cubes. However, for long records the system is disk bound. That can change. With faster bus and CPU the disk controller might be able to run the disk with interleave factor 1:1. The disk time would then decrease to approximately two thirds the values in the table. So very probably, the system will be CPU bound for even long records. Conclusion: get a faster microprocessor. The values of table 2 is also shown in figure 7. The observant reader will notice that relocation times for hypercubes of order less than 5 are smaller than relocation times for crossbar connections, also after adjusting for faster memory cycle time. This is due to the fact that the crossbar connection is one byte wide, while the hypercube is two bytes wide.

D	CELLS	DISK	REL	RECORD LENGTH IN BYTES						
				364	182	91	45	22	11	6
1	2	6702	480	2520	3280	4800	7840	13920	26080	50400
2	4	3351	320	1340	1720	2480	4000	7040	13120	25280
3	8	1676	200	710	900	1280	2040	3560	6600	12680
4	16	838	120	375	470	660	1040	1800	3320	6360
5	32	419	70	197	245	340	530	910	1670	3190
6	64	209	40	104	127	175	270	460	840	1600
7	128	105	22	54	66	90	137	232	422	802
8	256	52	12	28	34	46	70	117	212	402
9	512	26	7	15	18	24	36	59	107	202
10	1024	13	4	8	9	12	18	30	54	101

Table 2: Bottleneck values, disk and bus activity. *REL* is the part of bus time used for relocation. Intel 80186 12.5 MHz processor is assumed. Memory cycle time is 320 nanoseconds. Operand volume is 2 MB. All times are in milliseconds.

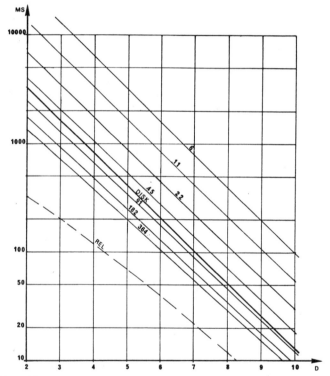

Figure 7: Disk and bus activity times as a function of cube size and record length. Operand volume is 2 MB.

10   Conclusion and future work

CROSS8 is an experimental parallel computer. We have shown that heavy database operations can be performed in parallel to reduce response time and increase throughput. Also from a cost and performance point of view it is less expensive to buy high performance through many small computers and disks, rather than through one supercomputer. Our algorithms for parallel execution are able to exploit a high degree of parallelism without degradation. Based on the same type of components the execution time will be almost inversely proportional to the number of nodes.

To further investigate our methods we are now building a new database computer which will have from 16 to 128 nodes. These computers are based on hypercubic interconnection network.

CROSS8 is also used for testing of other parallel algorithms. A test of parallel sorting is in its final stage, and with very encouraging results. A parallel database computer gives new problems and opportunities for handling concurrency, integrity and security. Also fail safe or graceful degradation of the data base system is possible and should be given special attention. The rules are simple, the more nodes in a system the higher probability of error, and a massively parallel system must have some mechanisms for graceful degradation.

11   Acknowledgments

CROSS8 is supported by NTNF, The Norwegian Government Research Agency. Many persons have contributed to the success of this research project. Tor Eivind Johansen put together most parts of the computer. Svein Arne Solbakk made the first design and realized the kernel programming system. Eirik Andresen worked hard for a long period trying to get the SCSI interface and the disk controller to become friends. Esten Erlien and Jan Grønsberg have helped getting the hardware running. Last but not least Torgrim Gjelsvik put all pieces together, he found errors, made changes and new designs, and at last both hardware and software cooperated as it should. Torgrim was also the one who improved the interrupt system and made the necessary program changes to exploit channel pauses for useful CPU work. That shaved one second off the DeWitt test time, from 2.8 seconds to 1.8 seconds. And very last, thanks to Øystein Torbjørnsen who is the last to join the CROSS8 group. As the TeXexpert of the group he transferred the manuscript from Wordstar 2000 to TeX. The result you can see for yourself. I am grateful to all of you.

References

[BITT83]   D.Bitton, D. DeWitt and Turbyfill, *Benchmarking Database Systems. A Systematic Approach*, The 9th International Conference on Very Large Data Bases, Florence Oct. 1983.

[BRAT80]   Kjell Bratbergsengen, Rune Larsen, Oddvar Risnes and Terje Aandalen: *A Neighbor Connected Processor Network for Performing Relational Algebra Operations*, The papers of the Fifth Workshop on Computer Architecture for Nonnumeric Processing, Pacific Grove, Ca, March 1980, SIGMOD Vol. X No. 4.

[BRAT84]   Kjell Bratbergsengen, *Hashing Methods and Relational Algbra Operations*, The 10th Conference on Very Large Data Bases, Singapore Aug. 1984.

[DEWI85]   David DeWitt and Robert Gerber, *Multiprocessor Hash-Based Join Algorithms*, The 11th Conference on Very Large Data Bases, Stockholm Aug. 1985.

[GOOD81]   J.R. Goodman, *An Investigation of Multiprocessor Structures and Algorithms for Database Management*, Technical Report UCB/ERL M81/33 Electronic Research Lab., College of Engineering, UCB, May 1981.

[KITS83]   M. Kitsuregawa, H. Tanaka and T. Moto-oka, *Application of Hash to Data Base Machine and Its Architecture* New Generation Computing, Vol. 1, No. 1, 1983.

[MENO86]   Jai Menon, *Sorting and Join Algorithms for Multiprocessor Database Machines* Database Machines, Modern Trends and Applications, Springer-Verlag 1986.

[QADA85]   G. Z. Qadah, *The Equi-join Operation on a Multiprocessor Database Machine: Algorithms and the Evaluation of Their Performance* Fourth International Workshop on Database Machines, Grand Bahama Islands 1985, Conference Proceedings Springer Verlag New York 1985.

[SOOD86]   A.K.Sood, M.Abdelguerfi and W.Shu, *Hardware Implementation of Relational Algebra Operations*. Database Machines, Modern Trends and Applications, Springer-Verlag 1986.

[STON76]   Stonebraker M. et al., *The Design and Implementation of INGRES*, TODS 2, sept. 1976.

[TECH84]   TECHRA User Manual. Kongsberg Vaapenfabrikk avd. Trondheim, 1984.

[VALD84]   P.Valduriez and G.Gardarin, *Join and Semi-Join Algorithms for a Multiprocessor Database Machine*, ACM Transactions on Database Systems 9, No 1, March 1984

[UBEL85]   Michael Ubell, *The Intelligent Database Machine (IDM)*, Query Processing in Database Systems, Kim, Reiner & Batory; Eds., Springer Verlag 1985.

EXPERIMENTS WITH DATA ACCESS AND DATA PLACEMENT STRATEGIES FOR MULTI-COMPUTER DATABASE SYSTEMS

J. Greg Hanson and Ali Orooji

Department of Computer Science, University of Central Florida, Orlando, Florida 32816

ABSTRACT

The software-oriented multi-computer database systems are characterized by a set of processing elements (PEs) which run identical software and operate on a partitioned database in parallel. Performance improvements and capacity growth can be achieved in this type of system by adding more PEs to the configuration and replicating the existing software on the new PEs.

In multi-computer relational database systems, realization of design goals depends largely upon mechanisms and algorithms for data access and data placement. In this paper we present our experiments with different data access and data placement strategies for one such system.

INTRODUCTION

With the recent decline in data processing hardware costs much of the research in the field of very large databases has been dedicated to exploring configurations characterized by multiple processing elements. Originally, the idea of dedicating a single, general-purpose computer (backend) to database management was explored. Studies generally indicate that this approach yields gains in performance and functionality only to a limited extent. In an effort to exploit the power of parallel processing the concept of database machines emerged as an approach to improving access to very large databases. Unfortunately, many of these architectures rely on the commercial availability of mass storage technology as well as customized microcode and VLSI components. While the processor-per-track, processor-per-head and off-the-disk designs (1) that typify the

429

database machine approach are based upon unique hardware configurations and technologies, a new software-oriented approach emerged geared towards exploiting parallel processing, while relying on conventional, off-the-shelf hardware. The multi-backend database system (MDBS), developed at The Ohio State University, typifies this approach. MDBS is a multi-backend system developed to explore the possibility of using multiple, commercially-available, minicomputers and disk drives to achieve throughput gains and response time improvement. The ultimate goal of this attribute-based system was to achieve performance gains and improvements proportional to the multiplicity of processing elements (2, 3).

The basic idea in the software-oriented approach is that all the processing elements (PEs) run identical software and they operate on a partitioned database in parallel. Performance improvements and capacity growth can be achieved in this type of system by adding more PEs to the configuration and replicating the existing software on the new PEs.

In a software-oriented multi-computer database system, realization of design goals depends largely upon mechanisms and algorithms for data access and data placement. In this paper we present our experiments with different data access and data placement strategies for one such system. A taxonomy of database systems is presented in Section 2, putting the work into perspective. In Section 3, we briefly describe the relational replicated database system (RRDS) used in the experiments. RRDS is similar in concept to MDBS, but it supports the relational data model as opposed to the attribute-based data model supported by MDBS. Sections 4 and 5 describe the strategies considered, method of analysis, and experimentation. Finally, in Section 6, we present our conclusions.

CLASSIFYING DATABASE SYSTEMS

Database systems may be categorized according to the taxonomy shown in Figure 1 (4). First, all database systems can be classified as either conventional, distributed, or backend. The backend database systems are further subdivided into those which are based upon a hardware orientation and those which are based upon a software orientation.

Conventional database systems are the common, monolithic architectures, e.g., (5), (6), (7). Distributed database systems are those featuring a collection of autonomous, geographically-dispersed systems which communicate via a long-haul communication network, e.g., (8), (9), (10), (11). The backend system concept evolved from a desire to relieve the host processor from the database management system (DBMS) activity by offloading some, or all, of the DBMS functions to some backend system. This frees host

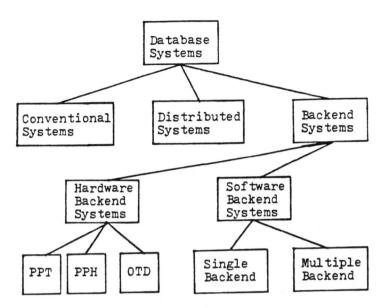

Figure 1: The Taxonomy of Database Systems

resources, making them available for other activities not directly connected with the database. These backend architectures are broken down into two categories, depending on whether the processing elements comprising the backend system are hardware based or software based. The hardware-based systems are those which utilize specialized hardware to accomplish the majority of the database management functions, e.g., (12), (13), (14), (15), (16), (17), (18), (19), (20), (21), (22), (23), (24). On the other hand, software-based backend systems are those where specialized hardware is nonexistent or held to a minimum. The DBMS functions are accomplished in software in the backend network which can consist of one, or more, processors. The single-backend systems differ from the conventional system with respect to the location of the database management functions which are implemented on an autonomous backend with exclusive access to the database on secondary storage, e.g., (25), (26), (27, 28, 29), (30). The multi-backend approach uses multiple computer systems for database management with a software-oriented database system and, usually, a central controller of various complexity, e.g., (2, 3), (31), (32), (33), (34), (35), (36).

THE EXPERIMENTAL RELATIONAL DATABASE SYSTEM

RRDS, the system used for experiments, is based upon the multi-backend approach to database management. The first step in developing an architecture for the system was to design the generic multi-backend architecture shown in Figure 2 (4). A number of design goals must be considered when developing a multi-computer database system. They include:

1) The system must be extensible.
2) The system performance must be proportional to the number of processing elements.
3) Maximum use of parallel processing, for improved throughput, should be made.
4) The system must rely on off-the-shelf hardware.

The generic architecture of Figure 2 was refined, based upon the above design goals, into the preliminary RRDS hardware configuration shown in Figure 3. The system consists of a controller connected to a number of replicated computers (RCs) via a broadcast bus. Each RC is, in turn, connected to a number of disk drives comprising the secondary storage for that RC.

The controller is responsible for receiving requests from the host, parsing them, and broadcasting them to the RCs for processing. All of the database management capability is resident on the RCs where the relational database is stored. Upon receiving a request from the controller the RCs will act accordingly on their portion of the database and send the results back to the controller where they will then be forwarded to the user (host).

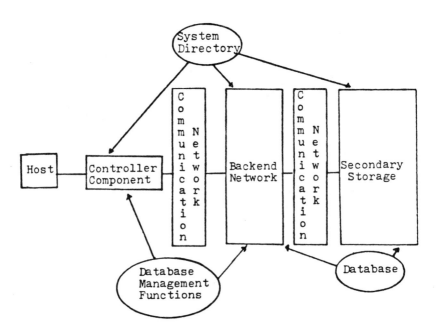

Figure 2: The Generic Multi-Backend Architecture

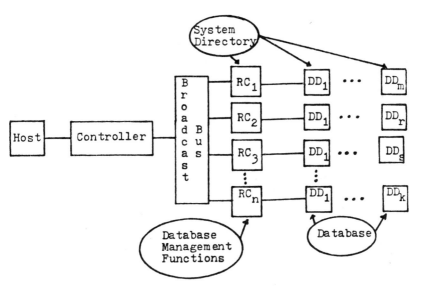

Figure 3: The Preliminary RRDS Architecture

DATA ACCESS STRATEGIES

The modes of data access considered included hashing, B+_trees, and clustering. Although an extremely fast method for look-up on a primary key, hashing performs poorly for range queries since it cannot access records easily in order of sorted key values. For this reason this approach was eliminated from further consideration.

Clustering is a technique for refining response set granularity by partitioning the database into subsets of records. Under the relational clustering strategy, each relation consists of a set of non-intersecting records, each record having all the attributes defining the relation scheme. The records in a relation are grouped into clusters based upon the attribute values, and attribute value ranges, in the records. These values and value ranges are called descriptors. By grouping the records into clusters the segment of a relation that needs to be processed, to carry out a user request, is reduced. Furthermore, distributing the records in a cluster, across the RCs, facilitates parallel processing. These benefits are offset, however, by the overhead of maintaining the clusters as well as the processing required for directory management. In addition, all the cluster directories must be replicated at each RC, making this approach costly in terms of space.

A relation information table (RIT) is required to associate each relation with its corresponding directory attribute table (DAT) and cluster table (CT). The DAT contains the attributes of the relation which serve as directory attributes (i.e., search key attributes).

For each directory attribute there is a list of descriptors maintained in a descriptor table (DT). The descriptors provide the value ranges for their respective directory attributes. The CT contains information on each cluster including a cluster identifier, a descriptor set describing the cluster, and the secondary storage addresses of the cluster records.

Data access under a clustering scheme consists of three phases. First the RIT, DAT, and DT are consulted to construct a query descriptor set. The query descriptor set contains all the descriptors which cover the value ranges specified in the query predicate(s). Second, the query descriptor set is checked against the CT to determine which clusters are required, forming a query cluster set. In the final phase, the clusters of the query cluster set are located in the CT and their corresponding addresses read.

An alternative data access strategy can be implemented using B+_trees as indices into a main file. An RIT associates each relation in the database with its corresponding DAT. Each entry in the DAT is a pointer to the B+_tree index for that attribute. Data access under this scheme consists of searching the B+_trees to locate the addresses of the records satisfying each predicate, then intersecting the results to get the records satisfying each conjunction. The union of all the query conjunction results gives the set of record addresses satisfying the query. The benefits of the B+_tree scheme are well documented in the literature and they include simplicity and adaptability to the range query environment (37), (38). Finally, the B+_tree directories need not be replicated, resulting in a space saving which could be significant for a very large database.

The cost tradeoffs, in terms of response time, for the clustering and B+_tree schemes were compared. A simulation model of the RC actions under each strategy was designed and implemented in the SLAM simulation language (39). A set of experiments was designed to examine their performance for a range of scenarios, examining the effects of database characteristics (relation size and number of directory attributes) and query characteristics (number of conjunctions, predicates, and predicate types). In addition, experiments were conducted on each strategy to observe performance for different implementations.

Results of experiments favored the B+_tree approach over clustering. The results of running Select, Join, and Insert queries on a database with relation partitions ranging from

Table 1: Average Response Time For Alternative Data Access Strategies

Query Type	Data Access Scheme	
	Clustered	B+_Tree
Select	48.01	40.16
Join	26.82	26.79
Insert	7.75	.09

100 to 100,000 records are shown in Table 1. The clustered scheme was especially sensitive to the query characteristics exhibiting severe performance degradation for Select queries as the number of predicates was increased. Queries were run on a database where the size of the relation partition was 10,000 records, with five directory attributes. The number of predicates per query was varied from 1 to 10 and response time observed. The rapid degradation of the cluster model, due to calculation of the query cluster sets, is illustrated in Figure 4.

The number of clusters per relation had a profound effect upon the response time for the clustered database. For all three query types a small number of clusters per relation (i.e., between 1 and 100) gave the best response times. A relation stored as one cluster, containing all the records (i.e., no clustering), performed better than scenarios with relations partitioned into more than 100 clusters. This is due to the fact that as the number of clusters increases the overhead of searching the CT overwhelms the benefits of the partitioning effect. Worst performance, as shown in Table 2, was observed when the relation was partitioned such that each cluster consisted of only one record.

The results of varying the degree of the B+_trees are shown in Table 3. Queries of all three types were run against a relation of 10,000 records with five directory attributes and the degree of the B+_trees varied from 10 to 100 key values per block. As the degree increased performance improved, but not dramatically, indicating that the B+_tree

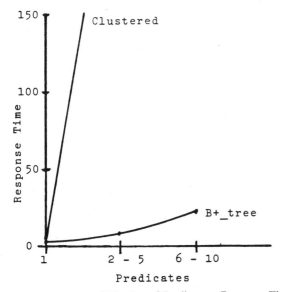

Figure 4: Increased Number of Predicates - Response Time

Table 2: Response Time for Clustering Scheme For Variable Clusters/Relation

Query Type	1	1 - 100	100 - 1000	1000 - 10000	10000
			Number Of Clusters		
Select	2.91	.644	1.99	25.54	50.45
Join	5.60	5.60	5.60	5.60	5.60
Insert	.09	.02	.11	2.01	3.51

Table 3: Effect on Response Time of Increasing B+_Tree Degree

Query Type	10 - 40	41 - 70	71 - 100
		B+_Tree Degree	
Select	7.75	4.92	4.20
Join	5.43	5.43	5.43
Insert	.27	.23	.19

Table 4: Response Time for Select Query as Degree of B+_Tree Increases and
Database Size Increases

Relation Size	10 - 40	41 - 70	71 - 100
		B+_Tree Degree	
10,000	7.75	4.92	4.20
100,000	78.90	32.84	28.05
1,000,000	768.43	486.19	417.62

approach will not degrade significantly if key values are large (i.e., long strings).

Table 4 shows the effect of increasing the size of the database and the degree of the B+_trees. Select queries were run against databases where the relation ranged from 10,000 to 1,000,000 records. As the degree of the B+_trees increased performance improved, indicating the benefits of the B+_tree approach for large database applications.

Based on the simulation results, and due to the fact that software-oriented multi-computer relational database systems are designed for large database applications and must provide efficient range query capability, the B+_tree option should be the method of data access. This simple approach eliminates the overhead of cluster management, yielding better performance. In addition the B+_tree index can be partitioned across the processing elements saving secondary storage space.

DATA PLACEMENT STRATEGIES

In a multi-backend system with a partitioned database, data placement mechanisms directly impact the degree of parallelism in query execution. The goal is to disperse the data such that all the processing elements participate equally in the execution of all queries. Two data placement strategies were considered - a simple round-robin (RR) policy, and a value-range partitioning (VRP) policy.

In RR, the simplest strategy, memory requirements are minimal. The first record of a relation is placed at an arbitrary RC. Successive records are inserted round-robin and RCs need only maintain the identifier of the next RC for insertion. The obvious advantages of this approach are simplicity and the fact that the records of each relation are distributed evenly across the system. This even distribution does not, however, guarantee parallelism in query processing. Under this policy there is no way to guarantee a query will access records on all the RCs and not a subset of the RCs.

The VRP policy, which requires more memory and processing overhead, guarantees that queries will be processed equally on all the RCs. In this scheme, similar to clustering described in the previous section, the relation is divided into value range partitions based upon descriptors. Each partition is then spread evenly across the system. For each relation there is a partitioning attribute table (PAT) which contains the attributes for which the relation is partitioned. For each entry in the PAT there is a DT which gives the descriptors delineating the value ranges of the partitions. Each relation has an associated partition table (PT) which identifies each partition of the relation, the descriptor set for the partition, and the next RC for insertion of a record in the partition (the records in a partition are inserted into the RCs in a round-robin fashion).

When a record is to be inserted into a relation, the RIT, PAT, and DT are consulted to determine the descriptor set for the record. Next, the PT is consulted to determine which partition covers the descriptor set. The record is then inserted at the RC indicated.

Table 5: Effect of Number of Partitioning Attributes on Insert Response Time

Data Placement Strategy	Partitioning Attributes		
	0 - 1.6	1.7 - 3.3	3.4 - 5
	Number of Partitions		
	1 - 10	11 - 100	101 - 1000
VRP	.392	.403	.583
RR	.389	.389	.389

Table 6: Effect of Descriptors/Partitioning Attribute on Insert Response Time

Data Placement Strategy	Descriptors Per Partitioning Attribute			
	1 - 3	4 - 6	7 - 9	10 - 12
	Number of Partitions			
	1 - 27	64 - 216	343 - 729	1000 - 1728
VRP	.395	.423	.530	.834
RR	.389	.389	.389	.389

Under this strategy, each partition of a relation is spread evenly across all the RCs. Thus, if the partitions are created based upon query characteristics, then all the RCs will participate equally in query execution. (Note that the partitioning scheme is used during record insertions and not during record retrievals. The B+_trees, and not the partitioning information, are used during record retrievals.)

An RRDS, operating under each data placement strategy, was simulated and analyzed with respect to data placement overhead during record insertions and performance improvement during record retrievals. Experiments were designed to determine whether the advantage of parallelism under the VRP policy is worth the overhead of partition maintenance. The degree of overhead incurred was determined by running Insert operations on RRDS models using each of the placement strategies. VRP characteristics, such as the number of records per partition, number of partitioning attributes, and number of descriptors per partitioning attribute were varied and response times observed.

The average response times for Insert operations, under both policies, are shown in Tables 5 and 6. As shown in Table 5, for a small number of partitions (i.e., few partitioning attributes) the overhead of the VRP strategy was not significant relative to the RR policy. However, as the number of partitioning attributes and resulting partitions increased, the cost of their maintenance, under the VRP strategy, became prohibitive.

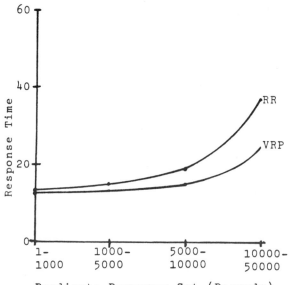

Figure 5: Effect of Degree of Parallelism and Response Set Size on Performance

Similarly, as illustrated in Table 6, few descriptors per partitioning attribute had little adverse effect on response time of VRP. However, as the number of descriptors increased, the number of partitions increased, resulting in degraded performance. Although both the number of partitioning attributes and number of descriptors per attribute affect the number of partitions, and hence the VRP performance, increased numbers of partitioning attributes had the most impact.

Select queries were run on two models of RRDS designed to simulate the degree of parallelism under both data placement strategies. Figure 5 shows the impact of degree of parallelism and query response set size on performance. The size of response sets was varied from 1 to 50,000 records and degree of parallelism for the RR policy varied from 1 to n, where n is number of RCs in the system. Simulation runs of Select queries revealed that for small response sets (1 to 1,000 records) the ratio RR/VRP was small (approximately 1.01). However, as the size of the response sets increased so did the benefit of VRP parallelism. For large response sets (10,000 to 50,000 records) the ratio RR/VRP was 1.51, a significant improvement in performance. Finally, Figure 6 illustrates the performance of different RRDS configurations under both data placement strategies, for Select queries with large response sets. As the number of RCs comprising the system increases so does the performance benefit derived from a VRP data placement strategy. However, as the number of RCs increases, the performance, under RR, fails to improve proportionally.

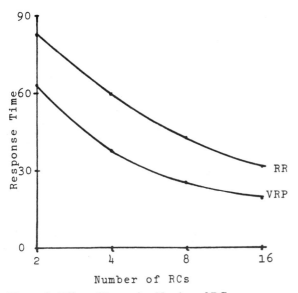

Figure 6: Effect of Increasing Number of RCs

Since the multi-computer database systems are targeted for large database applications, and improved response time is more desirable than memory savings, the VRP option should be the data placement strategy of choice. If relations are partitioned, into a few relatively large partitions, the overhead incurred during Insert operations is acceptable given the fact that complete parallelism is guaranteed, for query processing, under the VRP strategy.

SUMMARY AND CONCLUSIONS

This paper describes experiments with different data access and data placement strategies for a multi-computer database system operating on a partitioned relational database. In a systems designed for extensibility, and high-volume data, choosing proper data access and data placement strategies are major software design decisions.

Three data access schemes, hashing, clustering and B+_trees, were considered. Analysis and experimentation were conducted based upon design goals and system performance. Memory requirements, though an important factor, were secondary selection criteria. The experiments showed efficient range query capability of B+_trees.

Data placement, in a partitioned database, has a direct and profound impact on performance. Two placement strategies, round robin and value range partitioning, were considered and analyzed in terms of processing overhead during record insertions versus performance improvement during record retrievals. Though costlier in terms of processing overhead, the VRP strategy guaranteed maximum parallelism during retrieval, and it should be employed in multi-computer database systems.

REFERENCES

1. Haran, B., and DeWitt, D.J., "Database Machines: An Idea Whose Time has Passed? A Critique of the Future of Database Machines," Pages 166-187, *Database Machines,* Edited by Leilich, H.O., and Missikoff, M., Springer-Verlag, 1983.

2. Hsiao, D.K., and Menon, M.J., "Design and Analysis of a Multi-Backend Database System for Performance Improvement, Functionality Expansion and Capacity Growth (Part I)," Technical Report, OSU-CISRC-TR-81-7, The Ohio State University, Columbus, Ohio, July 1981.

3. Hsiao, D.K., and Menon, M.J., "Design and Analysis of a Multi-Backend Database System for Performance Improvement, Functionality Expansion and Capacity Growth (Part II)," Technical Report, OSU-CISRC-TR-81-8, The Ohio State University, Columbus, Ohio, August 1981.

4. Hanson, J.G., and Orooji, A., "A Taxonomy of Database Systems," Technical Report CS-TR-87-10, University of Central Florida, Orlando, Florida, June 1987.

5. Stonebraker, M., Wong, E., Krepps, P, and Held, G., "The Design and Implementation of INGRES," *ACM TODS,* 1, 3, September 1976.

6. Astrahan, M.M., et. al., "System R: A Relational Approach to Database Management," *ACM TODS*, 1, 3, September 1976.

7. Cincom Systems, "OS TOTAL Reference Manual," Cincinnati, Ohio, 1978.

8. Rothnie, J.R., et. al., "Introduction to a System for Distributed Databases (SDD-1)," *ACM TODS*, 5, 1, March 1980.

9. Stonebraker, M., and Neuhold, E., "A Distributed Database Version of INGRES," *Proceedings of the Second Berkeley Workshop on Distributed Databases and Computer Networks*, May 1976.

10. Williams, R., "R*: An Overview of the Architecture," IBM Research Report RJ3325, December 1981.

11. Stonebraker, M., "MUFFIN: A Distributed Database Machine," Memorandum No. UCB/ERL M79/28, Electronics Research Laboratory, University of California, Berkeley, May 1979.

12. Su, S.Y.W., and Lipovski, G.J., "CASSM: A Cellular System for Very Large Databases," *Proceedings of the VLDB Conference*, 1975.

13. Ozkarahan, E.A., Schuster, S.A., and Smith, K.C., "RAP - Associative Processor for Database Management," *AFIPS Conference Proceedings*, Vol. 44, 1975.

14. Lin, S.C., Smith, D.C.P., and Smith, J.M., "The Design of a Rotating Associative Memory for Relational Database Applications," *ACM TODS*, 1, 1, March 1976.

15. Smith, D., and Smith, J., "Relational Database Machines," *IEEE Computer*, March 1979.

16. Banerjee, J., Baum, R.I., and Hsiao, D.K., "Concepts and Capabilities of a Database Computer," *ACM TODS*, 3, 4, December 1978.

17. Leilich, H.O., Stiege, G., and Zeidler, H.Ch., "A Search Processor for Database Management Systems," *Proceedings of the 4th Conference on VLDB*, 1978.

18. Mitchell, R.W., "Content Addressable File Store," *Proceeding of Online Database Technology Conference*, Online Conferences Ltd., April 1976.

19. Britton Lee, Inc., "IDM 500 Intelligent Database Machine," Product Announcement, 1980.

20. Shibayama, S., Kakuta, T., Miyazah, N., Yokota, H., and Murakami, K., "A Relational Database Machine with Large Semiconductor Disk and Hardware Relational Algebra Processor," *New Generation Computing*, Vol. 2, 1984.

21. Baru, C., and Su, S., "The Architecture of SM3: A Dynamically Partitionable Multicomputer System," *IEEE Transactions on Computers*, C-35, 9, September 1986.

22. Leilich, H.O., and Missikoff, M., *Database Machines*, Springer-Verlag, 1983.

23. Schuster, S.A., Nguyen, H.B., Ozkarahan, E.A., and Smith, K.C., "RAP.2 - An Associative Processor for Databases and its Applications," *IEEE Transactions on Computers*, C-28, 6, June 1979.

24. Srinidhi, H.N., "A Relational Database Machine Using Magnetic Bubble Memories," Ph.D. Dissertation, Southern Methodist University, 1982.

25. Canaday, R.E., Harrison, R.D., Ivie, E.L., Ryder, J.L., and Wehr, L.A., "A Backend Computer for Database Management," *CACM*, 17, 10, October 1974.

26. Hutchison, J.S., and Roman, W.G., "MADMAN Machine," *Workshop on Computer Architecture for Non-Numeric Processing*, August 1978.

27. Farrell, M.W., "Concurrent Programming of a User Envelope in a Distributed Database Management System," M.S. Thesis, Computer Science Department, Kansas State University, Manhattan, Kansas, March 1979.

28. Housh, R.D., "An Implementation of a Distributed Database Management System," M.S. Thesis, Computer Science Department, Kansas State University, Manhattan, Kansas, 1978.

29. Maryanski, F.J., Fisher, P.S., Housh R.D., and Schmidt, D.A., "A Prototype Distributed DBMS," *Hawaii International Conference on System Sciences,* January 1979, Vol. 2.

30. Cullinane, J., Goldman, R., Meurer, T., and Navarawa, R., "Commercial Data Management Processor Study," Cullinane Corp., Wellesley, Mass., December 1975.

31. Teradata Corporation, "Teradata DBC 1012," Product Announcement, Los Angeles, 1986.

32. Missikoff, M., and Terranova, M., "The Architecture of a Relational Database Computer Known as DBMAC," Chapter 4, *Advanced Database Machine Architectures,* Edited by Hsiao, D.K., Prentice-Hall, 1983.

33. Auer, H., "RDBM - A Relational Database Machine," Technical Report No. 8005, University of Braunschweig, June 1980.

34. Stonebraker, M., "A Distributed Database Machine," Memorandum No. UCB/ERL M78/23, Electronics Research Laboratory, University of California, Berkeley, May 1978.

35. DeWitt, D.J., "DIRECT - A Multiprocessor Organization for Supporting Relational Database Management Systems," *IEEE Transactions on Computers,* June 1979.

36. Qada, G., and Irani, K., "A Database Machine for Very Large Relational Databases," *IEEE Transactions on Computers,* C-34, 11, November 1985.

37. Comer, D., "The Ubiquitous B-Tree," *Computing Surveys,* 11, 2, June 79.

38. Korth, H.F., and Silberschatz, A., *Database System Concepts,* McGraw-Hill, 1986.

39. Pritsker, A., and Pegden, C.D., *Introduction to Simulation and SLAM,* John Wiley and Sons, 1979.

40. Date, C.J., *An Introduction to Database Systems, Volume II,* Addison-Wesley, 1983.

41. Maryanski, F.J., "Backend Database Systems," *Computing Surveys,* 12, 1, March 1980.

Set-Oriented Memory Management
In A Multiprocessor Database Machine

Günter von Bültzingsloewen, Rolf-Peter Liedtke,
Klaus R. Dittrich

Forschungszentrum Informatik
an der Universität Karlsruhe
Haid-und-Neu-Straße 10–14
D–7500 Karlsruhe 1

Abstract: *In the past few years research in the area of database machines has been centered mainly around efficient query processing and increased I/O-bandwidth. A large variety of software and hardware mechanisms has been proposed, including various forms of filtering techniques and parallel query evaluation in multiprocessor systems. However, the issue of memory management under these new techniques has received only little attention. In this paper we analyze the effects of employing filtering techniques and set-oriented query evaluation in multiprocessor systems on memory management. We propose a set-oriented memory management method which has been designed for a multiprocessor database machine utilizing software filtering and parallel query processing under dataflow control. We also address the problem of performing updates in a set oriented environment.*

1 Introduction

Early research in the area of database machines was mainly geared towards speeding up low level DBMS operations, particularly of search operations. Most approaches include some sort of associative disk device, where specialized hardware is directly coupled to the disk (see [BoDe83] for an overview). In such configurations the connection to the host computer turned out to be a bottleneck. Moreover progress in storage device technology made this kind of approach impracticable.

For these reasons recent research has turned to investigate the efficient execution of higher level operations including complex queries with join operations. Also, new machine architectures for supporting such high level operations have been considered. The most important topics of interest include:

- multiprocessor architectures consisting either of specialized hardware devices (such as GRACE [FKTa86] or RDBM [Schw83]) or of general purpose processors (such as GAMMA [DeWi86], MDBS [HeHi83], SABRE [Gard83]);

- distributed query evaluation with intra-query parallelism, particularly parallel join algorithms (GAMMA, GRACE, SABRE [CFMT86]);

- data flow for reduced control overhead (GAMMA, GRACE);

- data partitioning with parallel disk access for increased I/O-bandwidth (GAMMA, MDBS, SABRE);

- hardware and software based filtering techniques (GAMMA, MDBS, SABRE, SCHUSS [GRTe84], VERSO [Banc83], [Kies83]).

443

Although some approaches integrate several or all of these techniques (e.g. GAMMA, GRACE) into a single system concept, database buffer management under these new conditions is not fully considered. Mostly, either conventional page based buffer management or tuple oriented pipelining is used. We feel that new approaches are needed in this area as well in order to support the new techniques appropriately.

Furthermore, all recent approaches are focussed on retrieval operations such as selection or join. The consideration of update operations leads to additional requirements.

In section 2 of this paper we analyze the effects of the techniques quoted above upon database buffer management. The question of integrating update operations is also considered. Section 3 presents the architecture of a multiprocessor database machine utilizing software filtering and parallel query processing under data flow control. In section 4 we propose a set oriented memory management method which has been designed for this database machine. It handles results of filter operations as well as sets of tuples to be updated and supports the data flow mechanism controlling the parallel execution of relational queries.

2 Requirements for Main Memory Management

In this section we discuss how the use of filter techniques and data flow control affects database buffer management in multiprocessor database machines.

Filtering is a retrieval method that scans relations sequentially and applies simple relational operations such as simple selections and projections to the tuples while they are read from disk (thus overlapping I/O operations with the first step of query evaluation). The result of a filter operation consists of those tuples satisfying the given selection expression; only these are transferred to main memory. This is in contrast to loading every page containing at least one qualified tuple as is the case with conventional page-oriented database buffers. Thus the page organization of the secondary storage cannot be maintained in main memory. Instead, we have to deal with results of filter operations which are represented by subsets of base relations.

Data driven processing of database operations poses similar requirements. A data flow program is represented by a directed graph which consists of nodes denoting elementary operations and arcs denoting the flow of data from one operation to a subsequent one. An operation is ready for execution if each of its child operations has been executed, i.e. if operand data are available on each incoming arc. Thus a data flow program directly corresponds to the operator tree of a relational query [BoDe82]. Cooperation between the modules executing the nodes of a data flow program requires that a result generated by some module is passed as an operand to the module executing the subsequent node. As the nodes of a data flow program mostly represent operations of the relational algebra or relation-oriented update operations, operands and results consist usually of tuples or tuple sets. An appropriate mechanism for representation and management of such operands and results is needed.

When considering the representation of tuple sets in main memory, two more technical issues have to be taken into account. First, to reduce response time, I/O-Operations should be avoided. Data needed to process a database operation should be loaded only once and remain in main memory until execution of the operation is finished. Even with very large main memories (tens or hundreds of MBs) becoming realistic, efficient main memory·utilization is still important, as operands and results of relational operations may reach a considerable size (e.g. a selection with low selectivity or a join leading to a high number of matching tuples). In fact, regarding operands and results within data flow programs, only those tuples really needed to process a given operation should be kept in main memory. This is just what is achieved by filtering: the loading of tuples is restricted to those qualified for further processing.

The other issue refers to message passing in a multiprocessor system. The modules executing the nodes of a data flow program may reside on different processors. Hence, the operands of a node have to be transmitted to the processor where the respective module is located unless the modules executing the nodes which produce the operands are located on the same processor. The communication overhead is determined by the total amount of data transmitted and by the number of messages. Both should be minimal. The amount of data transmitted can be minimized by only transmitting those tuples needed for further processing. This is in analogy to the efficient utilization of main memory as discussed above. To reduce the number of messages, it is necessary to combine single tuples to larger units, i.e. to tuple-sets.

We conclude that main memory management under the conditions discussed should provide the following capabilities:

- management of sets of tuples occurring as

  - operands and results within data flow programs (incl. results of filter operations);
  - messages between processors;

- management of sets of tuples independent from the pages on which the individual tuples reside on secondary storage.

Achieving efficient main memory utilization and communication with a page-oriented method would require relations to be appropriately clustered. A set-oriented method, however, is independent from any clustering and therefore from the attributes a query refers to. Furthermore, a representation mechanism for operands within data flow programs is needed anyway. An integrated approach is clearly desirable which pays regard to both types of requirements. Hence, main memory management should be set-oriented instead of page-oriented, where sets are tuple-sets resp. subrelations in the sense of the relational data model.

Strictly set-oriented main memory management, however, has to address the problems of update operations which, for reasons of uniformity, should deal with sets of tuples, too. Modify and delete operations may contain arbitrary qualifying expressions, which means that the actual update operation is preceded by a retrieval operation. As has been explained, retrieval results in a set of qualifying tuples. Accordingly, modifications have to be applied to the tuple sets yielded by the evaluation of the qualifying expression. Similarly, tuples to be inserted form a set. However, as the permanent database on disk is still organized in pages, the sets constructed by an update operation have to be mapped to the pages of the permanent database at an appropriate point of time.

After the presentation of the overall architecture of the database machine KARDAMOM which incorporates the concepts mentioned above, we will describe the functionality and the mechanisms needed for a set-oriented memory management in more detail.

3   The Architecture of the KARDAMOM Database Machine

In this section we present the architecture of the KARDAMOM multiprocessor database machine which utilizes software filtering and parallel query processing under data flow control. The system is designed as a database backend which is able to serve a number of host systems. The objectives of the design are the following:

- We want to exploit the capabilities of a multiprocessor system built from off-the-shelf microprocessors to achieve a response time better than conventional relational database systems as well as an increased transaction throughput.

- We want to be able to meet a wide range of different performance requirements, so hardware and software should be configurable in a flexible way.

The basic idea behind the software design is to decompose the database management system into a number of functional components, each implementing certain suboperations of transaction processing (relational algebra operations, software filtering, update, synchronization and recovery). The components are realized as processes that are mapped onto the processors of the multiprocessor system. The assignment of components to processors can be very flexible. It is possible to have only a single instance of some component mapped to some processor as well as to have several instances of other components which are replicated on several processors. Copies of the same component can process different operations (e.g. several centralized join operations originating from different database operations) or they can cooperate in processing a single operation (e.g. a distributed join operation originating from a single database operation). Thus we are able to obtain intratransaction parallelism for reduced transaction response times as well as intertransaction parallelism for increased throughput. Furthermore, the components can be replicated and distributed across the processors as demanded by the performance requirements of a special application.

The other concepts underlying the design were already motivated above. The operation of the functional components is controlled by data flow. Secondary storage access is accomplished via software filter techniques. Main memory management is set-oriented; only tuple sets actually needed by the functional components are retained in main memory.

Using these concepts, we can distinguish two kinds of data objects. First, we have so-called physical objects, representing the base relations defined in the schema. Second, we have tuple sets which are the results of suboperations performed by the functional components. These are called logical objects. Following this distinction, we can build two groups of functional components, thus decomposing the database management system into two subsystems, whereby all communication is via the set-oriented memory manager. The *logical system* $DBMS_{log}$ contains all functional components operating on logical objects, the *physical system* $DBMS_{phys}$ realizes all functions that map logical objects to physical objects and vice versa (see Figure 1).

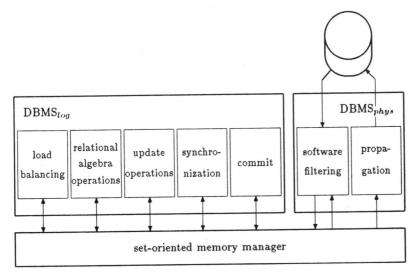

Figure 1: Architecture of the database management system

3.1 The Physical System

The physical system creates logical objects from base relations and updates base relations. As base relations are primarily held on secondary memory, the $DBMS_{phys}$ has to manage and access secondary storage. Read access, i.e. the creation of logical objects, is accomplished by software filtering. Write access integrates logical objects created by insert or update operations into the corresponding base relations (i.e. propagation [HaRe83]). As secondary storage access is page-oriented, the $DBMS_{phys}$ has to perform a transition between the set-oriented and the page-oriented representation of data objects.

Transactions exist in the $DBMS_{log}$ only. While operations of the $DBMS_{phys}$ are invoked by the $DBMS_{log}$, they are not executed in connection with a transaction. Particularly, writing updated pages to disk is performed completely independently of the transaction causing the update. Hence, the DBMS$_{phys}$ is an autonomous component and thus is able to implement optimizing access strategies supporting an efficient access of base relations.

3.2 The Logical System

The DBMS$_{log}$ contains all functional components operating on logical objects, i.e. relational algebra operations on tuple sets created by the DBMS$_{phys}$ and update operations including insertion and deletion.

Furthermore, according to the design of the DBMS$_{phys}$, the whole transaction management is included in the DBMS$_{log}$. Synchronization thus has to operate on logical objects (see e.g. [EGLT76,JBBa81]). To guarantee autonomy of the DBMS$_{phys}$, a recovery method allowing the update of base relations after commit time has to be chosen ($\neg$FORCE [HaRe83]).

Another important task of the DBMS$_{log}$ is load balancing. It distributes the operations of a relational query, i.e. of a data flow program derived from an operator tree, across processors running the appropriate functional components. The operator tree can be modified before distribution by combining consecutive nodes and by node splitting to achieve an optimal degree of parallelism. After distribution, the operations are executed under data flow control.

3.3 Data Flow Control

The load balancing component distributes operations by sending them to operation schedulers (one on each processor) that implement data flow control. Their task is to realize the firing rule for the operations they have received. It is fulfilled as soon as all operands needed for the execution of the operation are available. If the firing rule for an operation is fulfilled and a functional component implementing the operation is available, it can be sent to this component for execution. After the operation has been executed, the operation schedulers supervising succeeding nodes are informed that the corresponding operands are available. The operands themselves are directly transmitted between the functional components by means of the set-oriented memory manager.

4 Mechanisms for Set-Oriented Main Memory Management

The main task of a set-oriented memory management as proposed for the KARDAMOM database machine is to control all data objects which have to be accessed by the different functional components or to be communicated between them during the execution of database operations. Therefore, the following functions are required:

- *memory management:* allocation of space for set objects; garbage collection;

- *database buffer:* providing the physical addresses of data requested by functional components (i.e. mapping logical references to physical addresses);

- *communication:* transfer of data objects between functional components in order to realize data flow.

These functions are appropriately combined and reflected in the operations provided by the set-oriented memory manager.

In this section, we first describe the properties of set objects as processed in the evaluation of database operations by the KARDAMOM-architecture. Then we discuss the representation of such objects and the operations which are needed to deal with them. Finally, we illustrate the update problem in a set-oriented architecture.

4.1 Properties of Set Objects

All data accessed by components of the database system — primary data manipulated by database operations as well as secondary data such as access paths and auxiliary data — are considered to be set objects. They are defined to be sets of elements with common properties and serving the same purpose. More precisely, elements of the same set object must be of identical length and type. The type of an element is defined by its internal structure. Furthermore, each set object is characterized by the number of its elements.

While this notion is adopted from relations as sets of identically structured tuples, any type of data existing in the database system can be represented as a set object. For tabular data (e.g. mapping tables, directories) this is straightforward. In the worst case, a set object is defined which consists of a single element only, structured according to the specific needs. The structure is under control of the requesting component.

The description of the *structure* of the elements of a set object is associated with that object and managed by the set-oriented memory manager in a uniform way. Thus no operations of other components (e.g. schema manager) are required and the information needs not to be communicated to functional components separately (e.g. as a part of data flow operations). If set objects are commmunicated between functional components residing at separate processors, it is not necessary to keep the structure information redundantly at both sites. Furthermore, the structure of set objects can be defined dynamically at run time of a data flow program and the information is created and deleted together with the respective set object.

Besides the structure of set objects some properties concerning their behaviour with respect to storage management have to be known. For this purpose we define a number of *attributes* which are associated with each set object that concern issues like memory allocation (contiguous or fragmented), replacement of set objects (even under our assumption of large main memory and data filtering we have to provide this facility at least for very large data objects; then certain objects should be explicitly prevented from being replaced), application of a prefetching strategy when reloading a replaced object (possible if the object is accessed sequentially, otherwise not possible), or representation of the elements (by an explicit representation or by reference to the elements of another set object).

Set objects represent operands and results of suboperations while executing a data flow program. Because of filtering and subsequent set-oriented processing of the data flow program, they normally contain only those data which are actually necessary for processing that operation. In contrast to pages which can be utilized by several concurrent transactions, it is very unlikely that a set object created for a specific transaction can also be used by another one. Thus a set object is always local to a specific transaction (except set objects representing internal data of functional components).

Taking a closer look at the data flow driven execution of a transaction, we observe that set objects are created and manipulated by functional components while processing suboperations of the data flow program. When a suboperation is completed, every set object representing a result is passed along the respective edge of the data flow program to the component executing the next suboperation to be performed on that data object. That component may start executing that operation not before all operands required are available, i.e. all preceding operations have been completed. Thus, a set object can be accessed by at most one functional component at any point in time.

To represent the relation between set objects and functional components, we associate an *object state* with every set object:

- *free*, if it is not currently accessed by a functional component;

- *locked*, while it is being accessed by a functional component.

This is sufficient because data flow programs by definition are free of cycles and thus there is no danger of deadlocks. Consequently, there is no need of a lock table and an associated lock protocol.

As with object attributes, the object state is a part of the description of every set object. Additionally, if a set object is locked, the functional component accessing it is recorded in the description.

4.2   Representation of Set Objects

In order to achieve location transparency and thus a logically global view from functional components to set-oriented memory, set objects must be referenced by logical names. We refer to these logical names as *set identifiers*. The memory manager maps set identifiers to physical addresses. Thus the memory manager is free to move set objects within the memory of a single processors or between processors.

For every set object exists a description of its properties. As it is organized identically for all kinds of set objects, it can be separated from the actual representation of the set object. Thus every set object is represented by a *set descriptor* containing the description and a *set representation* containing the element values. While the set identifier actually refers to the set descriptor, the set descriptor provides the physical addresses of the representation. Consequently, a two-step address mapping results:

$$\text{set identifier} \;\longmapsto\; \text{set descriptor} \;\longmapsto\; \text{set representation}$$

Set Descriptors. As has been discussed, a set descriptor essentially serves two purposes:

- it provides the description of the properties of a set object;
- it provides the addresses of the locations in memory where the elements of a set object are stored.

Thus it can be divided into two components, namely a *header* containing the description, and a *pointer list* containing the addresses of the representation.

Descriptor headers always have the same structure. According to the discussion above, they contain the following information:

- object attributes
- object state
- element structure
- number of elements
- length of pointer list

Some additional information is necessary for the management of objects referring to the representation of other objects and for specialized treatment of different kinds of data (e.g. primary data, index data, schema data, etc.).

Pointer lists have an entry for every memory fragment used for the representation of the object. Each entry includes the base address and the length of the fragment. The length is expressed in the number of set elements the fragment contains. The length of a pointer list depends on the number or fragments allocated to the representation. If for an object memory space has been allocated contiguously, its pointer list consists of a single entry only. An example of a set descriptor is given in Figure 2.

descriptor header	object attributes	
	object state	element structure
	# elements	pointer list length
pointer list	fragment addr 1	fragment length 1
	fragment addr 2	fragment length 2
	fragment addr 3	fragment length 3
	o o o	

Figure 2: A set descriptor

Set Representations. The representation of a set object stores the values of the individual set elements. Elements of the same object have the same internal structure and length. They are stored in a single contiguous memory space or a number of separate fragments. Base addresses and length of the fragments are recorded in the set descriptor. Since all elements of an object have the same length, any element can be accessed by computing its start address from the base address of the fragment and the offset of that element. The offsets of the fields of every element can be derived from the structure information. Figure 3 illustrates the entire concept of organizing set objects

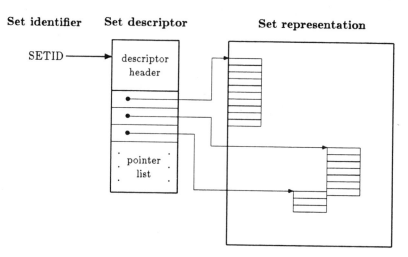

Figure 3: Representation of a set object

Using this technique, sequential access can be realized straightforward. If an object has to be accessed by indexing or hashing, either all of its elements have to be stored contiguously, or an address transformation which has to exploit the element count of the pointer list is necessary.

Sorting of the elements of set objects is not within the responsibility of the memory manager. This has to be done by a functional component since the elements have to be evaluated. However, once a sorted representation of a set object has been created, the memory manager can preserve the order. This is fairly simple as long as set objects are only moved within local memory (e.g. due to garbage collection). When sorted set objects are transmitted between processors, order can only be preserved if a reliable communication mechanism exists, and special provisions are taken when the elements are arranged in the memory of the target processor and the new pointer list is constructed.

4.3   Architecture of the Set-Oriented Memory

Before turning to the functions of the set-oriented memory, we have to consider some aspects of its architecture. These include the questions of whether functional components have a local or global view upon the set-oriented memory and of an appropriate mapping of set objects to memory space.

Logically, functional components can be given the view of a single systemwide set-oriented memory. Alternatively, every component may manage its own local memory. This is independent of a particular physical implementation, which may employ a global shared memory as well as several local memories. It should be noted, however, that a physically global memory tends to be a bottleneck. For this reason, KARDAMOM chooses a solution which is based upon local memory attached to every processor.

The most important aspect of the logical memory organization is that the set-oriented memory should serve as a basis for realizing the flow of data between functional components. Local data of functional components need not be considered in this context. Then, with a logically distributed architecture, every component has to be informed about the location of each of its operands. Operands stored under the control of a remote processor have to be communicated to the own local memory explicitly. Alternatively, results of suboperations can be transmitted to the local memory of the next functional component, which then in turn has to be known.

In contrast, with a global solution, functional components can access memory in a uniform way assuming that the data objects accessed are locally available. Transfer of set objects, if necessary in the case of components being located on different processors, is handled below the interface of set-oriented memory. Thus not only the location of data but also the distribution of functional components across processors remain fully transparent for functional components. Hence, we conclude that the set-oriented memory should be organized in a logically global way.

According to the representation of set objects by set descriptors and set representations, memory is divided into disjoint partitions. One partition each serves for the storage of set descriptors and of set representations. Two more partitions are provided for a page buffer, which is discussed below in more detail, and for internal data of the set-oriented memory manager. Thus, management of each partition can be tailored to the characteristics of the respective data (granularity of memory allocation, garbage collection strategy, etc.).

4.4   Functions of the Set-Oriented Memory Manager

Operations on set objects are divided into operations administrating objects and operations accessing objects. The first group comprises operations like creating and deleting set objects or constructing address information. These operations are realized by the set-oriented memory manager. The second group essentially comprises reading and writing set elements or parts of them. Access operations, however, are performed directly by the functional components operating on the set objects. Theoretically, access operations could be provided by the set-oriented memory manager as well (then set elements would be logically referenced, too). However, as access operations occur very frequently, the step of indirection thus introduced would lead to an increase in runtime which cannot be tolerated. Furthermore, the set-oriented memory manager does not interpret the value of set elements at all, it provides only operations to manage set objects and to access and manipulate their description.

While set representations are accessed directly by physical addresses, the information recorded in set descriptors is available for the administrating operations of the set-oriented memory manager only. These administrating operations again can be subdivided into two classes. Operations of *object management* mainly concern the creation and deletion of set objects. They invoke the appropriate functions of memory management and create the description. Additionally, an operation for retrieving a description is provided.

Functional components must know the physical addresses of set elements for accessing them. They are provided by the pointer lists of set descriptors. Operations of *access management* have to enter the correct information and to make it available to the functional components. Furthermore, they perform state transitions by locking and freeing set objects.

In the following we give a short summary of the operations of the set manager:

Object management:

- *Creation* of a set object includes allocation of the memory space required for the set representation, creation and initialization of the set descriptor, and association of a unique set identifier with that object.

- *Deletion* conversely deletes all components of the set object and releases memory space.

- *Extension* of a set object is required if the initial size has been chosen too small; additional space has to be allocated, and the descriptor has to be updated.

- *Reduction* adjusts the size of a set object, if elements have been removed (due to a selection), or if the size of elements has been reduced (due to a projection).

- *Replication, partitioning,* and *recombination* of set objects support parallel execution of complex operations such as joins.

- *Retrieval* of descriptor information allows functional components to access the description of a set object.

Access management:

- *Requesting* access to a set object includes all operations necessary for direct access of set elements. The requested object is made available in the local memory of the calling component, if necessary by first transmitting it from a remote processor or by reloading it from disk. A valid pointer list is passed to the component. Finally the object is locked. The operation is very similar to the FIX-operation in a conventional database buffer [EfHa84]. However, it is more powerful, as it includes the full communication capability.

- *Releasing* a set object terminates the manipulation of that object. It is unlocked and the pointer list is invalidated. Afterwards, the object is available for moves within local memory or for transmissions between processors, and it can be requested and subsequently accessed by another functional component.

Replacement of data objects, which is an important part of the semantics of the conventional FIX-/UNFIX-operations, can easily be included into the request/release operations. As mentioned above, we assume that main memory is large enough to accomodate all data objects needed for processing a transaction once they have been created there by filtering. However, in certain cases data objects may be too large to be kept there (e.g. in the case of a large join result or if a filter operation yields a whole base relation or a major part of it). But in contrast to a page buffer, set objects cannot simply be written back to the pages of the respective base relation, as they do not directly correspond to pages. Therefore, a replacement mechanism has to be provided, which is independent from base relations and which is itself set-oriented.

4.5   Updating Set Objects

Using filter techniques and set-oriented transaction processing, the problem of performing updates on page-oriented secondary memory arises. In the literature, this issue has been ignored or it is simply stated that update operations are realized using conventional techniques. However, with a strictly set-oriented approach to transaction processing, this problem requires thorough consideration.

Modify and delete operations may contain arbitrary qualifying expressions, hence the actual update operation is preceded by a retrieval operation. Modifications have to be applied to the tuple sets yielded by retrieval, a deletion is defined by the set of tuples to be deleted or by a set of unique identifiers of these tuples. Similarly, tuples to be inserted form a set. Now the problem is that the tuples which have been extracted from the pages by filtering, must be re-inserted into the appropriate pages. Essentially the same is true for insertions and deletions.

A simple solution is to read the pages where modified tuples have to be inserted, to perform the modification, and to write the pages back to disk [Kies83]. However, this has the effect, that every page containing tuples to be modified or to be deleted has to be read twice:

- first it has to be read during the filter operation while determining the set of qualified tuples;

- second it has to be read and transferred into main memory as a whole in order to insert the modified tuples.

Including the final write operation, three I/O-operations per page would be required, which is clearly too inefficient.

Assuming main memory to be sufficiently large, we propose the following procedure:

- filter operations are distinguished whether they are due to pure retrieval operations or to update operations;

- if a filter operation retrieves tuples to be updated, not only the result set is stored in the set-oriented memory, but in the same step the pages containing qualified tuples are completely loaded into a page buffer;

- processing of the transaction affects only the set object, while the pages loaded form a resident part of the respective base relation and are managed separately by the $DBMS_{phys}$ (see section 3.1);

- the result of the update operation being represented as a set object has to be inserted into the pages at earliest after the update operation has been completed and at latest when the pages are to be written back to disk;

- finally the pages can be written to disk.

This way I/O-operations are avoided at the expense of an increased memory demand. However, we can even proceed further in this way: complete base relations or specified parts of them can be kept resident in main memory instead of being loaded only temporarily. A page-oriented representation is not necessarily required for this purpose, but it alleviates propagation of updates. In the extreme, a pure main memory database system can be achieved, where the whole database is resident in main memory.

5 Conclusion

In this paper we have proposed a method for set-oriented main memory management designed for a database machine employing software filtering and data flow control. Compared to the management of pages, this method offers better memory utilization and more efficient communication in a multiprocessor environment, as transactions are processed strictly set-oriented. Furthermore, it supports data flow control by providing tuple sets as units of data flow. We have also considered the update problem in this context: we have proposed a mechanism avoiding unnecessary I/O-operations which can be extended to implement a pure main memory database system. A first version of the proposed mechanisms is currently being implemented within the KARDAMOM-project at FZI Karlsruhe.

Some further issues remain to be covered by a forthcoming companion paper. These include communication between functional components which is needed to transmit set objects according to data flow. Another topic is the choice of an appropriate point in time to map a set-oriented representation of an update result to the respective database pages with respect to synchronization of concurrent transactions. This affects throughput as well as transaction response time.

Bibliography

[Banc83] F. Bancilhon et al.: VERSO: A Relational Backend Database Machine. In: D.K. Hsiao (ed.): Advanced Database Machine Architecture. Prentice-Hall, 1983

[BoDe82] H. Boral, D.J. DeWitt: Applying Data Flow Techniques to Database Machines. IEEE Computer, August 1982, pp. 57–63

[BoDe83]   H. Boral, D.J. DeWitt: Data Base Machines: An Idea Whose
            Time Has Passed? In: H.-O. Leilich, M. Missikoff (ed.): Database
            Machines. Int. Workshop, Munich, Sept. 1983, Springer-Verlag,
            1983

[CFMT86]   J.-P. Cheiney, P. Faudemay, R. Michel, J.-M. Thevenin: A Reli-
            able Parallel Backend Using Multiattribute Clustering and Select-
            Join Operator. Proc. 12th Int. Conf. on Very Large Data Bases,
            Kyoto, August 1986

[DeWi86]   D.J. DeWitt et al.: GAMMA - A High Performance Dataflow
            Database Machine. Proc. 12th Int. Conf. on Very Large Data
            Bases, Kyoto, August 1986

[EfHa84]   W. Effelsberg, T. Härder: Principles of Database Buffer Manage-
            ment. ACM Trans. Database Systems, Vol. 9, No. 4, Dez. 1984,
            pp. 560–595

[EGLT76]   K.P. Eswaran, J.N. Gray, R.A. Lorie, I.L. Traiger: The notions of
            Consistency and Predicate Locks in a Database System. Comm.
            ACM, Vol. 19, No. 11, Nov. 1976

[FKTa86]   S. Fushimi, M. Kitsuregawa, H. Tanaka: An Overview of The Sys-
            tem Software of A Parallel Relational Database Machine GRACE.
            Proc. 12th Int. Conf. on Very Large Data Bases, Kyoto, August
            1986

[Gard83]   G. Gardarin et al.: SABRE: A Relational Database System for
            a Multimicroprocessor Machine. In: D.K. Hsiao (ed.): Advanced
            Database Machine Architecture. Prentice-Hall, 1983

[GRTe84]   R. Gonzalez-Rubio, J. Rohmer, D. Terral: The Schuss Filter:
            A Processor for Nonnumerical Data Processing. Proc. ACM
            SIGARCH Conf., 1984

[HaRe83]   T. Härder, A. Reuter: Principles of Transaction-Oriented Data-
            base Recovery. ACM Computing Surveys, Vol. 15, No. 4, Dez.
            1983, pp. 287–317

[HeHi83]   X. He, M. Higashida et al.: The Implementation of a Multiback-
            end Database System (MDBS): The Design of a Prototype MDBS.
            In: D.K. Hsiao (ed.): Advanced Database Machine Architecture.
            Prentice-Hall, 1983

[JBBa81]   J.R. Jordan, J. Banerjee, R.B. Batman: Precision Locks. Proc.
            ACM-SIGMOD Int. Conf. on Management of Data, 1981

[Kies83]   W. Kiessling: Database Systems for Computers with Intelligent
            Subsystems: Architecture, Algorithms, Optimization. Report
            TUM-I8307, Technical University of Munich, Institute of Com-
            puter Science, August 1983 (in German)

[Schw83]   H. Schweppe et al.: RDBM - A Dedicated Multiprocessor Sys-
            tem for Database Management. In: D.K. Hsiao (ed.): Advanced
            Database Machine Architecture, Prentice-Hall, 1983

Parallel Execution Strategies for Declustered Databases

Setrag Khoshafian
Patrick Valduriez

Microelectronic and Computer Technology Corporation
3500 West Balcones Center Drive
Austin, Texas 78759-6509

Abstract

Data placement and parallel execution strategies are crucial design issues for high performance transaction processing in a parallel database machine. Declustering (horizontal partitioning) is a most promising solution for data placement. We analyze the trade-offs of three alternative execution strategies in the context of declustered databases. Then we focus on the strategy of executing programs at their data repositories which is highly parallel and offers many opportunities for query optimization. Finally, we elaborate on the implications of this strategy on program loading, associative routing, and decentralized concurrency control.

1. Introduction

Efficiency is a major requirement of transaction processing for very large data base applications. The most recent solutions are typically based on parallel architectures as exemplified by multiprocessor database machines (DBM's) [1]. Although many database machines have demonstrated performance enhancements in response time, few have considered throughput improvements. However, high performance in transaction processing requires both throughput *and* response time optimizations.

One of the problems hurting the performance of traditional database management systems is the notorious *I/O bottleneck* [2]. We believe magnetic disks will remain the main type of home repository for large databases. However as disk (magnetic or optic) bandwidth increases at a much lower rate than either processor or RAM bandwidth, technology will accentuate the I/O bottleneck problem.

There are two complementary solutions for solving the I/O bottleneck [3]: (1) increase the I/O bandwidth through parallelism, and (2) minimize the number of I/Os through storing sub-objects with high affinity on the same I/O unit [4]. With a parallel I/O architecture [5] the main issue for (1) is *data placement*. The main issue for (2) is the *storage model*. The storage model is not relevant in this paper. Instead we shall demonstrate how the data placement influences the parallel execution strategies.

Horizontal partioning [6] schemes for enhancing the I/O bottleneck have been proposed and implemented in numerous database machines such as Teradata [7], Gamma [5], Grace [8], and MDBS [9]. In this paper, horizontal partitioning will be called *declustering*. With declustering a set of tuple objects (such as a relation) with a unique key attribute is partitioned either through hashing of range partitioning to a prescribed number of repositories. Declustering is discussed in more detail in Section 3. As for its performance advantages, [10] has shown that declustering improves both response time and throughput. It improves response time through the parallelism incurred in multiple block requests. It improves throughput because "hot" (i.e., frequently accessed) relations are distributed across many repositories, and hence the load balancing is improved.

Besides resolving the I/O bottleneck, there is a potential linear performance enhancement through parallelism if one (or more) processors are associated with each repository. For example, Access Module Processors in Teradata [7], or processors associated with disks in Gamma [5], or Filter Processors in Grace [8], are all capable of performing select operations in parallel. The philosophy here is similar to the "head per track" architecture of the previous decade [11]. These machines have the capability of performing "on the fly" data filtering and hence enhancing the performance through parallelism. However, technology (specifically the infeasibility of incorporating logic on thin–film heads with increased bit densities) made head per track designs obsolete. On the other hand, in the past decade we observed more than an order of magnitude improvement in the cost/performance of (general purpose) microprocessors [12]. This trend is expected to continue. Therefore, we believe the most viable and cost effective multiprocessor for very large database applications is the "shared nothing" architecture [13] in which there are several interconnected nodes each consisting of a RAM, one or more processors, and a disk. This generic architecture is discussed further in Section 2.

Given a declustered data placement strategy, a transaction will be accessing and updating multiple relations on multiple repositories. Typically, transaction accesses will be "associative" or value based: for example, "Retrieve all employees with salary in the range 20K and 50K," or "Retrieve all parts supplied by supplier X." For the former, every repository which stores an employee record with salary in the given range will be involved. The second transaction is more complex and involves a *Join* operation. Repositories storing records of suppliers and/or parts will be involved. As illustrated by these examples, with declustering we must support directories and primitives for sending and routing the data associatively. With more complex queries, several persistent (or base) relations will be involved in the query. Therefore we must also have strategies for decomposing a query into components, as well as strategies for loading, executing, and synchronizing these components pertaining to the same transaction.

So, assuming a declustered data placement strategy and a generic shared nothing architecture, in this paper we discuss design and implementation strategies for executing concurrent transactions in a highly parallel environment. More specifically, we analyze *execution strategies*, which specify how a transaction is decomposed, loaded and executed on the parallel architecture. Three generic types of execution strategies are identified and compared: remote access (RA), program execution at the data repository (ER) and dynamic loading (DL). The ER strategy is highly parallel and exhibits many opportunities for query optimization. We will elaborate on the implications of this strategy on loading, database data traffic, and concurrency control.

The rest of the paper is organized as follows. Section 2 describes the framework of our study: a generic DBM model and an underlying operating system kernel. In Section 3 we discuss declustering in more detail. In Section 4 we analyze the tradeoffs of the three alternative parallel execution strategies. Transaction execution based on ER strategy is further detailed in Section 5, where we present its impact on program loading, associative routing used for sending/receiving the transaction data and transaction synchronization. The synchronization of transactions executed at multiple repositories is achieved through a distributed concurrency control strategy. Finally, Section 6 gives our conclusions and discusses open problems that require further research.

2. Framework

To settle the framework in which this study is done, we present a simplified and generic model of parallel database machine and the functionality of its kernel. The DBM consists of many nodes and an interconnect network as illustrated in Figure 1. Each node consists of one or more processors, a large RAM and a disk.

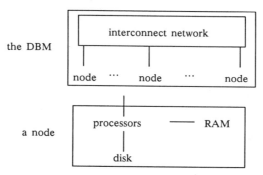

Figure 1: DBM Model

Underlying the DBM is an operating system kernel KEV [14] which, among other things, provides low-level support for task management and communication. A sub-transaction on a node will execute as a task.

A task is a single thread of execution. Tasks are dynamic, i.e., can be created and deleted at any time by a parent task. On each node, there is a special task, called the *node supervisor* (NS), which coordinates with the kernel in "supervising" the node. NS is the first task created at system initialization time and is responsible for creating/destroying other tasks. Also, NS is the "handler" of exceptions and errors : when a problem arises with a task, the kernel "complains" to the NS.

Communication between tasks is done via messages. A message is addressed to a port which consists of the destination node-number, the identifier of the destination task, and a queue number in that task. A sending task is blocked until the kernel can guarantee reliable delivery of the message to the destination node. The advantage of this approach is that there is no copying of messages (which can be large). When a message is sent to a task, the kernel allocates a buffer space in the address space of that task. The message remains in the buffer until the receiving task does a "receive" on the queue of the message. If the receiving task has not yet been created, the message is accepted and given to the NS which will pass it to the task when created.

3. Declustered Data Placement

The persistent database consists of a collection of non-first normal form relations [15, 16, 17]. Each of these relations is stored as an indexed physical file. The elements of each relation are grouped into individual disk blocks having a common range of cluster values. These cluster values are the values of the relation *key* attribute. The blocks are spread, or declustered [10], over a prescribed number of nodes with adjacent nodes containing blocks with adjacent cluster value ranges. This number of nodes is a function of the size and access frequency of the relation. The number of repositories over which a relation is distributed is called the *degree of declustering*. The set of nodes on which a relation is declustered is called the *home* of that relation.

There is a global directory which maps a relation with a predicate onto a set of nodes. The global directory is replicated on each node. Conceptually, the global directory is a two level index with a major clustering on relation name and a minor clustering on some attribute of the relation. Figure 2 provides an example of a global directory. Suppose we want to locate the elements in relation Employee with cluster value 3299. The first level index on set name maps the name Employee onto the cluster value index for relation Employee. Then this second level index further maps the cluster value 3299 onto node j.

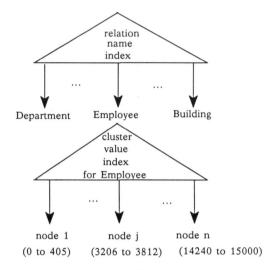

Figure 2: Global Directory Example

There is a local index within each node which maps a relation with a predicate onto a set of storage blocks within the node. Similar to the global index, the local index has two levels with a major clustering on relation name and a minor clustering on some attribute. The minor clustering attribute for the local index is the *same* as that of the global index.

4. Parallel Execution Strategies

Similar to most DBMS architectures, the software architecture of the DBM includes a *conceptual layer* and an *internal layer*. The conceptual model of the DBM is FAD [18]. FAD is a powerful functional language which provides direct support of non–first normal form relations and more general complex objects. FAD is operationally and structurally object oriented [19]. The objects in FAD are built out of atomic (e.g. integer, float etc.), set, and tuple constructors. Persistent set objects of FAD are mapped onto non–first normal form relations in the internal model. This internal model is extended with capabilities to identify program sub–units and communication (*send* and *receive*) primitives for execution in a distributed environment, as well as explicit operations to efficiently access clustered and indexed objects. The mapping from a conceptual to physical objects is one to many. Transaction compilation and execution can be summarized as follows:

(i) A query expressed in FAD is first *compiled* to operate on physical objects. The compiled code consists of FAD program sub–units, with explicit communication between them. The compilation phase also incorporates an *optimizer* whose purpose is to generate an internal query which runs efficiently on the DBM.

(ii) The compiled code is then transformed by a *loader* into one or more *sub-transaction execution units (STU's)*. A STU is a structure containing information and code necessary for executing a sub-transaction on one node. The number of STU's produced depends upon the execution strategies described below. For instance, one strategy (Remote Access) produces exactly *one* STU per transaction. With other strategies, the loader will use the *global directory* to bind the STU's to the *homes* of some relations. Then, the STU's will be sent to the appropriate nodes for execution.

We have identified three characteristic types of execution of a transaction for a declustered database. These are (i) Remote Access (RA), (ii) Execution at Repositories (ER) and (iii) Dynamic Loading (DL). Both (i) and (ii) use static loading. Typically, the algorithms for loading STU's will follow one of these strategies or a hybrid strategy (we shall discuss one such hybrid strategy in the sequel). To simplify the explanation of the strategies, we shall be using relational terminology (instead of FAD) in our examples.

4.1 Remote Access

With the RA strategy, a transaction executes on one node (determined by the loader). When the transaction needs data from another node, it sends a *request* to an *associative data server* (ADC). The approach is very similar to remote procedure calls (RPC) for accessing remote files in a local area network (LAN) [20, 21, 22]. However, there are two main differences between network file servers and ADCs. First, a request to an ADC incorporates a search key (for example an employee number) and *only* the records which have the given key are sent by the server. Secondly, the ADC server also keeps a *trace* of the requests made by the transaction. These traces are used for concurrency control (i.e., to decide whether to abort or commit the transaction). For example, if 2PL (2-phase locking) is used, for read requests the accessed objects or pages will be read-locked until the ADC is told to release the locks. ADC also performs the local updates, providing simple service routines (such as delete a tuple with a given key value, or insert a tuple, etc.) for updating the persistent database on a node. The updates of a transaction should be maintained by the ADC on a per-transaction basis, and propagated to the shared persistent space only after it is determined that the transaction can successfully commit. The locks, workspaces, etc., maintained on a per transaction basis, constitute the trace of the transaction.

The two main advantages of this remote access strategy are the simplicity of the object code generation and the loading. The strategy also has the potential of generating fewer *control* messages. However the number of messages for obtaining the actual data is potentially doubled compared to the other two strategies since each remote access entails *sending* a message (with the data key) to the appropriate node and *receiving* a message which contains the record(s) with the given key. As we shall see, with strategy (2) all that is needed is sending the keys (the program is executed in the nodes of the qualifying records).

Another advantage of the RA scheme is the minimal overhead in transaction initialization. However, this is somewhat misleading since the data servers incur overheads for maintaining the transaction traces.

For the other two strategies we need to *replicate* some of the transaction code in every node which has data which needs to be manipulated by the transaction. RA is optimal in transaction code space since there is exactly *one* copy of the transaction code in the machine. Of course for small transactions and/or with large "cheap" RAM this advantage might become negligible.

Finally, we believe the RA is less amenable to load balancing and its remote access mode of execution is more sequential.

4.2 Execution at Repositories

The ER strategy is at the other extreme. It creates sub–transaction execution units and loads the necessary appropriate sub–transaction code at *all potential* nodes which store relations manipulated by the transaction. Therefore, this strategy will be the most expensive in terms of the transaction initialization and code space. In many cases some nodes will not contain the data that is relevant to a particular transaction execution. Exactly which nodes are relevant is not known until run–time. For example, consider an Employee/Department database, where relation Employee is declustered on EmpNumber and relation Department is declustered on DeptNumber. Furthermore, assume each employee can work in several departments, recorded as a set of DeptNumber in the Employee tuple. Suppose the query is to retrieve all the department names where employee with EmpNumber 10 works. Let us assume that employee 10 works in departments 1, 5, and 7 and each of these departments is stored at a different node. The STU's will be initialized at *all* nodes containing Employee and/or Department tuples. However, at most 4 nodes (the node for employee 10 and the nodes for departments 1, 5 and 7) will be doing "useful" work. The other initializations will be wasted. Furthermore, we need to send messages to terminate *all* the STU's.

This simple example demonstrates the main problem of the ER strategy. However, ER exhibits a tremendous potential in parallelism. First note that *all* STU initializations could be done in parallel. With multicasting, all STU's could be terminated in parallel. Multicasting could also be used in other intermediate phases of ER as well. Operation coordination is one such case. When a FAD operation sends data from the home of one base set to another, the destination nodes should be able to determine when they have received all the data sent (associatively) to them. For example, assume R1 is stored in nodes 1, 2, 3 and R2 in nodes 20, 21, 22, 23. Also assume 1 sends to 20, 21; 2 sends to 21, 22; and 3 sends to 22. Then, in addition to data, each source node sends to an *operation coordinator* (OC) the list of destination nodes to which it sent data. OC then informs each destination node the source nodes from which they should have received data. For node 20 the source node is 1; for node 21 the source nodes are 1 and 2; for node 22 the source nodes are 2 and 3; and for node 23 the node list is nil. Therefore, rather than sending 4 messages, the OC can construct a Source–Destination table and multicast it to all destination nodes.

Besides parallelism in task initialization and completion, ER provides opportunities for parallel executions of STU operations. For example, assuming an Employee/Department database, if a transaction query involves a selection on Employee (for example all employees with salary in a given range and age in a given range) and a selection on Department (for example all departments with a budget in a given range) and a subsequent join on, say, department number of the partial results, then the selections on the Employee and Department relations can proceed in parallel.

ER provides many opportunities for parallel query optimization. In the previous example we mentioned that the selects on relations Employee and Department are done first and *then* the results are joined. This is *one* particular execution scheme. In code generation, the optimizer must consider the following issues: (i) The selectivities of the select operations on Employee and Department should be estimated; (ii) Subsequently, the optimizer should decide if both selects should *precede* the join, or if only one of the selects should be done (and it should decide when) and the second select *after* the join; (iii) In deciding among these cases the optimizer should also decide if the join should be executed at the nodes which store Employee or the nodes which store Department; and (iv) The optimizer should also decide whether execution should proceed in "set mode" or "pipelined mode". In set mode, *all* the elements pertaining to an operation are first materialized and then the set is sent to appropriate nodes. In pipelined mode, records which are generated are immediately sent to the appropriate nodes. The advantage of set mode is a smaller number of messages. The advantage of pipelined mode is more parallelism.

The main point of the previous discussion is that ER opens up the space of potential query execution orderings and strategies, and hence enables the optimizer to choose the "optimal" point in this larger space. The price to pay is complexity.

Note that with RA *all* the transaction code execution is taking place at *one* node and hence the opportunities for query optimization are severely restricted. One could argue that this is an advantage, since it makes the query optimizer much simpler compared to ER or DL.

4.3 Dynamic Loading

As mentioned above, the main problem with ER is the overhead incurred in initializing many STU's, since in many applications, most of these STU's will not be doing *any* useful work. With the DL strategy, STU's will be loaded dynamically *only* as needed. In other words, only the nodes which have the appropriate data will be involved in executing an operation. Other systems [8, 5, 7] also use a similar strategy in some phases of query execution. For example, selecting an Employee tuple through a secondary index select on Employee name on the Teradata machine will involve only two AMPs: the AMP containing the row identifier of the selected name and the AMP storing the Employee tuple with the given name.

A STU is dynamically loaded when the actual values of its inputs are known (after their calculation) and can be sent associatively to the *exact* nodes together with the input data. Hence, every sub-transaction executing as a task on a node will be going useful work. Therefore, the DL strategy distributes the execution of a transaction (still maintaining the policy of executing where the data is), and yet avoids unnecessary initialization and termination overheads.

However, there are two disadvantages of the DL strategy. First, the loading process and the coordination of STU initialization, execution, and termination iare going to be more complex. For example, different pieces of code from many nodes are going to be sent to the same node all pertaining to the same transaction. In this node we must get and discard code and be able to "link" with the existing address space for the given sub-transaction execution.

A second and perhaps more important shortcoming of DL is the fact that it potentially limits parallelism compared to ER. With ER, in the Employee/Department join example, STU's loaded in the nodes storing Employee and Department will all be initialized in parallel. With DL, we first load the STU's at, say, the nodes storing employees (i.e., the home of Employee) and then send the qualifying records with the code for the join to the nodes which store qualifying departments. These have to be initialized subsequently.

In the conclusion we shall discuss another strategy which removes the problems of DL but attempts to maintain some of the advantages of ER.

4.4 Example

To illustrate these three strategies let us take a simple example. Assume relation R_1 is declustered on nodes 1, 2, and 3 and relation R_2 is declustered on nodes 3, 4, and 5. Let the query be $F (\sigma(R_1) \underset{a=b}{\bowtie} R_2)$, where $\sigma(R_1)$ indicates a selection on relation R_1, and $\underset{a=b}{\bowtie}$ indicates a join involving attribute a of R_1 and b of R_2.

Assume the query optimizer has decided to first perform select on R_1, then join the result with R_2 (on specified join attributes a and b) and then apply some operation F (e.g., project) on the result. The compiler/loader will maintain this order of execution.

With the RA strategy, the STU will be loaded at one node, say 1. The task will potentially make "requests" (remote accesses) from nodes 2 and 3 to obtain *all* the qualifying tuples of R_1. Then it will make remote accesses from nodes 3, 4, and 5 (the home of R_2) to obtain all the tuples of R_2 which are join candidates for the selected tuples of R_1 (i.e., $\sigma(R_1)$). After performing the join (in node1), it will apply F on the result.

With the strategy of executing at all repositories (ER) and dynamic loading (DL), the query optimizer must specify (to the compiler/loader) where the join of $\sigma(R_1)$ and R_2 should take place (home of R_1 or home of R_2). Assume, the decision is to have the join executed at the home of R_2 (i.e., nodes 3, 4, and 5). The actual decision depends on the selectivities and will not be discussed here.

With the ER strategy, the loader will load a STU with $\sigma(R_1)$ code in nodes 1, 2, 3, and another STU with code for receiving data from nodes 1, 2, and 3, and joining with R_2 and subsequently applying F in nodes 3, 4, and 5 (i.e., $F(\text{receive} \bowtie R_2)$). The loader will realize node 3 must contain both sub-codes for select, join and project and hence will combine these for node 3. Now the transaction will execute as five tasks on 1, 2, 3, 4, and 5. Note that the select on R_1 will be done in parallel in nodes 1, 2, and 3.

Finally, with DL strategy, a STU will initially be loaded in nodes 1, 2, and 3. After the parallel execution of the select $\sigma(R_1)$, the data for the join as well as the code to perform the join with R_2 and apply F will be sent to *only* those nodes in the set {3, 4, 5} which have potential join values of R_2.

Table I summarizes the advantages and disadvantages of the three strategies. Strategy 2 offers very good performance advantages with little complexity. Strategies hybrid between ER and DL could be better due to less wasted work. Therefore, as a first attempt, we chose to implement strategy ER, keeping in mind future refinements.

5. Transaction Execution with ER

This section presents the implications of ER on transaction execution. We shall describe the impact of ER on sub-transaction code generation and loading, associative routing of data, concurrency control and synchronization. The different components are linked by communication primitive calls which exhibit necessary synchronization of component operations.

5.1. Loading

With ER the internal query generated by the compiler is a sequence of *compiled components*. Each component is associated with a relation and must be executed in the nodes storing the relation (i.e., the home of the relation). Specifically, a compiled component, as illustrated in Figure 5, contains compiled code and header information that indicates the relation name and a symbolic port list. Sends and receives occurring in the compiled code have indexes to the symbolic port list. The header also contains an index for all the sends/re-

	ADVANTAGES	DISADVANTAGES
Remote Access (RA)	• simplicity in code generation and loading • (comparatively) lesser number of control messages • less overhead in initialization of transaction tasks • least amount of transaction code space	• doubling the number of messages for data traffic (and larger data messages) • less amenable to load balancing • complexity in keeping transaction traces until commit time • potentially more sequential
Execution at Repositories (ER)	• optimal parallelism • simplicity and uniformity in transaction task execution • more potential for optimization	• wasteful in runtime initialization and coordination of sub-transactions • wasteful in replicated code space for same sub-transaction execution • more complexity in static loading
Dynamic Loading (DL)	• transaction tasks are initialized only at the nodes of the "useful" data	• complexity in coordinating dynamically loaded transaction tasks • potentially more sequential than (2) but less than (1)

Table I: Comparison of Execution Strategies

ceives occurring in the compiled code. Mapping symbolic ports into physical ones is a run time decision of the loader, since declustered placement can dynamically change for load balancing.

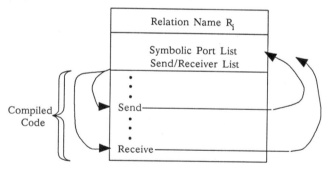

Figure 3: A Compiled Component

The responsibilities of the loader are: (1) to construct the STUs from the compiled components, (2) to allocate physical queue numbers among the STUs (i.e., map symbolic ports into physical ones), (3) to assign operator coordinators, (4) to initiate the creation of a *transaction synchronization controller (TSC)* task for controlling the transaction (see Section 5.3), and (5) to route the STU's to the proper nodes. STU's are sent in messages to the Node Supervisors of the appropriate nodes. In most cases, a STU will be loaded in more than one node. The loader is responsible for the optimum allocation and creation of a single port list for all the components which have to execute at a node.

All of the STU's pertain to the same transaction, therefore the loader includes the same transaction id (to be used as a task id) in each task creation message. The loader also creates an TSC task in one of the nodes that is executing a sub-transaction of that transaction. The message that creates the TSC task contains the information that a TSC task is being created and includes the list of nodes in which the sub-transactions are executing. The structure of a STU is given in Figure 6. The port list is a list of tuples of the form:

```
[Destination Relation Name,
 Source   Relation Name
 Queue Number
 Route Attribute Name]
 Operation Coordinator Node Number]
```

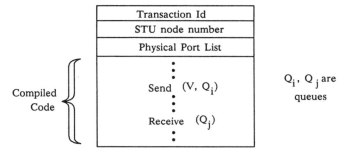

Figure 4: A Sub-transaction Execution Unit (STU)

There will be one tuple in this set for each *send* or *receive* in the STU's compiled code. Queue Number indicates on which task message queue the data is sent/received. The route attribute name is used for sending tuples associatively through the specified attribute.

Therefore, the loader performs the following steps:

(a) *Determine Relation Homes*: For each relation in the header of each of the compiled components, determine the nodes where it is stored.

(b) *Determine STU classes*: In this step, equivalence classes are constructed for the nodes. An equivalence class consists of all of the nodes that will receive the same STU. All of the members of an equivalence class store the same subse of compiled components. It is important to note that the ordering of the components in the STU must be the same as the ordering of the original components because of dataflow dependencies. For each equivalence class, the size of its STU is determined and allocated.

(c) *Bind Queue Numbers to Queue Identifiers* : In each component, replace the Queue ID of each Port List Element with a Physical Queue Number. If a Physical Queue Number has not already been assigned for the Queue ID, one must be allocated. Because of the kernel limitation on the number of queues (currently 30), it is important to reuse queue numbers where possible. The same queue number can be bound to more than one queue identifier as long as the receivers of those queue identifiers do not share any nodes. In other words, ports with destination relations that are stored on disjoint sets of nodes can use the same queue numbers.

(d) *Build STUs*: In this step, the STU's are constructed by copying the compiled code from the components, modifying that code slightly, and creating the Port List for the STU. The copying of components is done in a manner that preserves the ordering of those components as produced by the compiler. The Port List is created by combining the Port Lists of the member components. The *send* and *receive* instructions in the code contain a Port List Index. This is the index of the entry in the Port List that refers to the port on which the operation is performed. These Port List Indexes must be updated to reflect the position of the entry in the new, combined Port List.

(e) *Specify the Operator Coordinators*: For each port (send/receive pair) that is used in the STU's, a node is chosen to serve as the Operator Coordinator (OC). This node will be chosen from the destination home. The node number of the OC is stored in the port list entry of that port. Counters indicating how many times each node has been used as an OC are maintained in order to help distribute responsibilities evenly across the nodes.

(f) *Assign Transaction ID*: In this step, a Transaction ID (TID) is generated for the transaction. This TID must be guaranteed to be unique across the entire system. To accomplish this, the system will maintain a TID Generator on each node.

(g) *Create a TSC Task*: Choose one of the nodes executing the transaction to serve as the transaction synchronization controller (TSC). A TSC task is created by sending a message to the chosen node. The task id of the TSC task is derived by adding a constant to the TID of the transaction. The message that creates the TSC task must include the task id of the TSC and the list of the nodes that are participating in the execution of the transaction. Once constructed, this message is sent to the node supervisor of the chosen node.

(h) *Send the STU's as sub-transaction tasks of the transaction*: Send each STU in a message to the node supervisor that will be executing it. Remember that a single STU may be sent to multiple nodes.

5.2 Associative Routing

By *associative routing* we mean (i) the protocol of sending a key value of a relation (possibly with other data) to a node which stores the desired object of the relation with that key value, (ii) at a coarser granularity, it is the association of a relation name with the list of nodes which store the relation (i.e., the *home* of the relation). Associative routing ensures that objects are sent *only* to the nodes in the destination relation which will require their values; *only* the relevant portions of a relation are sent to any given node in a destination. The association between relations and the nodes which contain subsets of the relation over ranges of key values is stored in the Global Directory. The information needed to perform the sends and the receives are all found in a Port List.

The send instruction format in the compiled code of a STU is of the form:

send (V: [attribute], Destination Relation, Queue)

where V is either a set or a tuple, and Destination Relation is a relation name, and Queue indicates the queue number for the send. The send/receives need coordination. A "receive" will be obtaining data from potentially many nodes. All the data from all the potential senders will be obtained and combined. Thus, we operate in a *set mode* rather than in an object at a time *pipelined mode*. This is a default and simple solution which could be modified to allow associative routing to operate in either mode. The mode would be specified by the optimizer.

5.3 Transaction Synchronization

In [23], an adaptive concurrency control algorithm is proposed and shown to be superior to both pure optimistic or pessimistic schemes. The algorithm starts with a simple certification based scheme. When degradations (due to "hot spots") are detected, the concurrency control algorithm dynamically and selectively adapts itself to finer granularity locking. Here we present a simple concurrency control algorithm based on the certification scheme. This extensible algorithm is the basis of the adaptive strategy. The scheme works as follows. Each STU of a transaction T first performs its updates locally in a private workspace. The concurrency controller keeps track of all the read/write operations of other transactions which could potentially conflict with T. At commit time of transaction T, the concurrency control mechanism simply enforces all transactions conflicting with T to abort. The sub-transactions (corresponding to STU's) of a transaction are coordinated by the Transaction Synchronization Controller (TSC) which applies a two-phase commit protocol [24].

A TSC is a special task executed at one node and each TSC is associated with **one** transaction. A transaction is executed in parallel on multiple nodes. The TSC is responsible for coordinating the commit/recovery process among the participating STUs tasks. Each node can be running multiple TSC's corresponding to different transactions. A TSC is created on the node specified by the loader. The message which requires the creation of the TSC must provide the task id for this TSC as well as the list of node numbers on which the same transaction runs (i.e., the STU's of the transaction). This information is determined at load time.

The main responsibility of the TSC is to apply the two phase commit protocol. Another responsibility of the TSC is to acknowledge abort requests (either from the node supervisor, or from the TSC of another transaction or the node of one of the STUs), and, if the transaction is in a phase where it could be aborted, broadcast the abort request to the component tasks of its transaction.

In the two phase commit protocol, each of the STUs of the transaction computes a *before set,* which is the set of ids for transactions at that node which read a data granule (e.g., a page) the STU is intending to update. The before set thus represents the set of transactions that must comit *before* this transaction commits. Otherwise, the transaction in the before set must be aborted before this transaction commits, in order to guarantee serializability. The TSC sends abort requests to the TSC's of the transactions in the before set. Some of these transactions might be in their commit phase when they receive the abort message and therefore they just acknowledge the request and they commit anyway. Otherwise, if a transaction has not yet committed, the transaction acknowledges the request and sends abort messages to its STU's. We want to emphasize that in either case, the abort request is acknowledged. Finally, there is a special case when the addressee of the abort request has already terminated. The abort message should be sent in such a way that this condition could be detected and then the TSC could simply proceed as if the abort request had been acknowledged. The protocol works as follows:

(1) Read–Write Phase

Each STU writes its updates into a local workspace T. When done with this phase, the component returns an End–Read–Write completion message to TSC. Next it flushes to disk all data pages in workspace and constructs the *Before Set* of transaction T for that particular node. The before set contains the transaction id's of all transactions which are not committed and which have read or written pages which are written by the committing transaction. All pages to update are locked (in an atomic operation so that deadlocks are avoided). After these operations, the Before Set is sent to TSC.

Validation Check:

On receipt of all the before sets for transaction T (from different nodes), the TSC starts the validation phase by doing the union of all the before sets to produce a unique one.

For each transaction T' in the *Before* set of T, the TSC of transaction T' is informed that T' has to abort. After all the acknowledgments from the TSCs of the T's are received, transaction T is declared to be validated. Note that in some cases, a flagged transaction may in fact have been validated. In this case, transaction T can also be validated. But if any transaction sends an abort message to the TSC to terminate T, then T is aborted. When the validation phase is completed, commit messages are sent to all component tasks.

(2) Commit Phase

On receipt of a commit request, each STU commits the updates, releases the locks and allows the waiting STU to proceed. It is important to log these actions, because an node may fail and recover. It is imperative to know how (and whether) to redo a transaction which must be committed. Moreover, restarts have to be idempotent.

6. Conclusion

In this paper, we described three execution strategies for declustered databases in a parallel database machine whose nodes consist of a RAM, a fixed number of processors and a disk. Furthermore, we provided a qualitative analysis of the trade-offs of these strategies. Strategy ER which consists of "executing where the data is" is highly parallel and exhibits many opportunities for query optimization. We further elaborated on the implications of the ER strategy on transaction execution including the functions of loading, associative routing, and concurrency control.

We believe each of the execution strategies will be suitable for certain types of transactions. For example, remote access (RA) will work better for transactions which access a few objects and perform aggregate computations on them. On the other hand, ER will be more efficient for transactions that perform local computations on most of the nodes storing the relations involved in the transaction. The exact identification of the characteristic transaction types for each execution strategy is an interesting research issue. Once these are taxonomized, the next step is to investigate optimization techniques that choose the appropriate execution strategy for a given transaction. However, there is a trade-off, since this general strategy will make the system code and the optimizer more complex.

A simple extension to the robust ER strategy will be to determine statically the nodes which will be involved in a query by examining the select clauses. For example, if the root of a query tree is a selection on Employees with EmpNum in {10,20,30}, then the STU's performing the select need to be loaded only in at most three nodes containing the qualifying Employee tuples. Several existing systems use this strategy. With the relational model, it is rather easy to do this static analysis and selective loading. With FAD it is slightly more complicated but still doable. Another approach under investigation [25] consists in sending the compiled STU codes to the appropriate nodes, but postponing the actual loading until it is decided that the STU *has* to perform some task (i.e., transaction execution manipulates data stored at the node of the STU). Hence when some data arrive for the STU, it gets "activated".

We have mentioned several times the optimization phase of the compiler. One difficult task is the identification of all the parameters to be considered in optimal code generation. As mentioned earlier, although ER opens up the search space of the optimizer, it also has the potential of increasing the complexity of the optimization process.

Finally, future work includes detailed performance analyses of the various execution strategies in order to quantify the qualitative analysis of this paper. Such analyses are difficult because many DBM functions such as loading and transaction synchronization are affected.

Acknowledgements

The authors wish to thank Haran Boral, Carlo Zaniolo, and Marc Smith for many useful comments on this paper.

References

[1]   H. Boral, S. Redfield, Proc. of Int. Conf. on VLDB, Stockholm (August 1985).
[2]   H. Boral, D. DeWitt, Proc. of Int. Workshop on Database Machines, Munich (September 1983).
[3]   H.C. Du, ACM SIGMOD Record, Vol. 14, No. 1 (March 1984).
[4]   C. T. Yu, C. H. Chen, K. Lam, M. K. Siu, ACM Trans. on Database Systems, Vol. 10, No. 2 (June 1985).
[5]   D. DeWitt, G. Graefe, K. Kuma, R. Gerber, M. Heytens, M. Muralikrishna, Proc. of the 12th Int. Conf. on VLDB, Kyoto, August 1986.
[6]   D. Ries and R. Epstein, UCB/ERL Tech. Report M78/22, UC Berkeley, May, 1978.
[7]   Teradata Corporation, C10_0001-02, November 1985.
[8]   S. Fushimi, M. Kitsuregawa, and H. Tanaka, Proc. of the 12th Int. Conf. on VLDB, Kyoto, August 1986.
[9]   D.K. Hsiao et al., in Advanced Database Machine Architecture, D.K. Hsiao (Ed.), Prentice–Hall, 1983.
[10] M. Livny, S. Khoshafian, H. Boral, Proc. of ACM–SIGMETRICS Int. Conf. (May 1987).
[11] D. DeWitt, P. Hawthorn, Proc. of Int. Conf. on VLDB, Cannes (September 1981).
[12] R. Stanley, IBM Journal of Research and Development, Vol. 29, No. 2 (March 1985).
[13] M. Stonebraker, Database Engineering, Vol. 9, No. 1, March 1986.
[14] to appear in proceedings of IWDM, 1987.
[15] G. Jaeschke, H. Schek, Proc. of ACM Sym. on PODS, Los Angeles (March 1982).
[16] F. Bancilhon, S. Khoshafian, Proc. of ACM Symp. on PODS, Boston, (March 1986).
[17] P. Valduriez, S. Khoshafian, G. Copeland, Proc. of Int. Conf. on VLDB, Kyoto (August 1986).
[18] F. Bancilhon, T. Briggs, S. Khoshafian, P. Valduriez, Int. Conf. on VLDB, Brighton, England, 1987.
[19] K.R. Dittrich, Proc. of the Int. Workshop of Object–Oriented Database Systems, September 1986.
[20] G. Andrews and F. Schneider, Computing Surveys, Vol. 15, No. 1, March 1983.
[21] A. Tanenbaum, Englewood Cliffs, N.J.: Prentice–Hall, 1981.
[22] S. Tripathi, Y. Huang, and S. Jajodia, IEEE Transactions, Vol. SE-13, No. 8, August, 1987.
[23] R. Krishnamurthy, H. Boral, G. Copeland, MCC Internal Report DB–159–85, 1985.
[24] B. Lampson, H. Sturgis, Xeros Palo Alto Research Report, Palo Alto, CA (1976).
[25] B. Alexander, G. Copeland, S. Khoshafian, MCC Internal Communication, April, 1987.

III Knowledge Base Machines

A STREAM-ORIENTED APPROACH TO PARALLEL PROCESSING FOR DEDUCTIVE DATABASES

Yasushi KIYOKI, Kazuhiko KATO, Noboru YAMAGUCHI and Takashi MASUDA

Institute of Information Sciences and Electronics
University of Tsukuba
Sakura, Niihari, Ibaraki 305, Japan

ABSTRACT

In this paper we present a parallel processing system for interpreting logical queries in deductive databases. Our system executes basic operations for large data in parallel within the framework of functional computation. By using the demand-driven evaluation as a driving method of functional computation, parallelism is exploited in a limited-resource environment in executing the basic operations.

In order to cope with a great variety of applications and queries, our system implements a flexible environment where new basic operations can be easily defined and integrated.

INTRODUCTION

In recent years, great emphasis has placed on the relationship between relational databases and first-order logical systems [4]. The combination of them has received much attention as a promising approach for implementing knowledge base systems.

The enhancement of the processing performance is one of the key issues in implementing relational or deductive database systems. To enhance the processing performance of relational database operations, many algorithms and architectures have been researched. However, in extending relational database systems to deductive database systems, in addition to relational database operations, other operations for performing high-level queries must be supported. Although non-recursive queries in deductive databases are transformed into the sequence of relational database operations, high level queries which reference recursively defined relations cannot be performed by using only relational database operations. To perform high level queries, several operations must be supported (e.g., [2,5,10]).

We have designed a parallel processing system for performing arbitrary basic operations for large data in the framework of functional programming concepts. The system has been designed on the basis of the following concepts:
(1) New functions or new basic operations can be easily integrated into the parallel processing environment. In order to cope with a great variety of applications and queries, our system implements a flexible environment where new functions can be

475

easily integrated to the system.

(2) Parallelism is exploited under demand-driven control [3,9] in the framework of functional computation [1]. In database applications, *granularity* of data which is transferred by a single demand can be made comparatively larger. Therefore, when compared with the total amount of data transferred by a single demand, the overhead caused by the demand transfer is insignificant. Our system takes advantage of demand-driven evaluation which allows better control of parallelism, more selective evaluation, and a natural way of handling a large amount of data within a limited resource environment. In our system, each function is transformed into the procedural object codes including basic primitives[7]. Each function is allocated to one of the multiple processors, and parallel processing is performed among functions which are allocated to different processors. Furthermore, several functions can be allocated to the same processor. This allocation enables a query to be executed within the limited processor resources. The functions allocated to the same processor are executed in pseudo-parallel under demand-driven control.

(3) General purpose hardware resources are used in implementing the parallel processing environment to enable progress of functions and efficiency of processors, memory and networks to be reflected flexibly.

As an application to our system, we have designed an interpretation model for logical queries. Our approach is based on top-down construction of the rule/goal graph (and/or graph) [10]. In our approach to parallel processing for deductive databases, a rule/goal graph reflecting the structure of the intensional database is constructed dynamically during the interpretation of a query. One of features of our approach is that parallel processing for the rule/goal graph is performed under demand-driven control in the framework of functional computation. Each node of a rule/goal graph represents a function instance, and each arc corresponds to an actual argument or a return value of a function. On the arc, binding environments (variable/value bindings) or tuples are transferred as a stream under demand-driven control.

SYSTEM STRUCTURE

Hierarchy

In our parallel processing system, software hierarchy for creation and execution of functional programs is implemented on the architecture level as shown in Fig. 1.

(1) Functional programming level (FP level)

At the FP level, an environment for functional programming is implemented. Basic operations which will be integrated in the parallel processing system are described as functions. In the case of implementation of a deductive database system, in addition

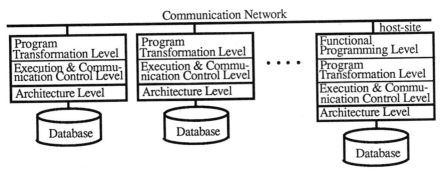

Fig. 1 An overview of the system

to relational database operations, basic operations for interpreting logical queries are added.

(2) Program transformation level (PT level)

To make the FP level programs executed at the architecture level, these programs are transformed into procedural object codes in a unit of a function. The object codes include our proposed basic primitives. This level is implemented at each site independently so as to make processors with different architectures integrated in this system.

(3) Execution & communication control level (ECC level)

At the ECC level, the function instances which are transformed into object codes are actually driven to be executed in parallel or pseudo-parallel at the architecture level. At the ECC level, interpretation of basic primitives is performed and communication between processors is also controlled. This level is also implemented at each site independently.

(4) Architecture level

In our system, general purpose processors and a general network are used as a hardware environment at the architecture level. Our currently being developed experimental system consists of multiple workstations connected to a local area network [8]. In our approach, specialized hardware resources are not used, but general hardware resources are used to enable progress of hardware technology to be reflected to the system as soon as possible. In regard to secondary storages, a disk system connected to each site is independently used one another. Databases are stored over the system. Although the method of distributed allocation of databases is not restricted, it influences the degree of parallelism for accesses to secondary storages.

Parallelism

We discuss that demand-driven evaluation shows attractive advantages in executing the functions which deal with large data. In our system, the following parallelisms inherent in functional computation are exploited.

(1) parallel evaluation for arguments of a function.

To exploit this parallelism, demands are simultaneously issued to the functions which produce actual arguments of the consumer function. Consequently, the independent operations can be executed in parallel.

(2) parallel execution between a function which produces its return value as a stream and a function which consumes the return value as an actual argument in the form of the stream. That is, stream-oriented parallel processing between a function of stream-producer (producer function) and a function of a stream-consumer (consumer function).

To exploit this parallelism in demand-driven evaluation, it is necessary for the producer to begin the computation eagerly before the demand arrives from the consumer. In our approach, parallelism is exploited by *pre-issuing a demand* to the producer function before the consumer function begins computation. When the producer function receives a demand pre-issued by the consumer function, the producer function begins computation. In producing a stream, the producer function does not produce every stream element by a single demand. The producer generates a fixed amount of stream elements by a single demand. This mechanism enables the functional computation to be executed within a limited memory resource environment. In this paper, the fixed amount of stream elements is referred to as granularity. When a producer and consumer functions are allocated to different processors, double buffering mechanism is supported.

PARALLEL PROCESSING FOR QUERIES

In [6], a data-driven model for parallel interpretation of logic programs has been presented. The model is oriented to list processing based on stream manipulation for binding environments. In this model, the eager and lazy evaluations are used to exploit parallelism in a data-driven architecture.

In our interpretation method, three basic operations(AND, R_unify and F_unify) are designed for logical query processing in deductive databases as shown in Fig. 2. These basic operations are defined as functions. As an actual argument, each function receives a set of binding environments from the producer function in the.form of a stream. These binding environments are referred to as "old binding environments." As a return value each function returns a set of binding environments to the consumer function in the form of the stream. These binding environments are referred to as "new binding environments."

Each function is executed exploiting the above mentioned parallelisms, and the production and consumption of a stream is controlled by using demand-driven evaluation.

Basic Operations for Interpretation

(1) AND function

An AND function is created for interpreting a rule clause in the intensional database or a query. It receives the clause body of a Horn clause and old binding environments in the form of a stream, and returns new binding environments as a stream. In the function body, the AND function creates an R_unify or F_unify function instance for each literal of the clause body.

R_unify or F_unify function instances are created corresponding to the sequence of literals in the clause body. This function also creates channels among the AND function itself and those R_unify or F_unify functions to transfer binding environments as a stream.

Each element of a stream is a binding environment representing a binding information of every variable in the clause. The interpretation is proceeded by substituting the binding environment in each R_unify or F_unify function. The important feature of the AND function is that it does not communicate with each R_unify or F_unify function as shown in Fig. 2. As a result, the stream-oriented parallelism is exploited among the AND function itself and the R_unify or F_unify functions created by the AND function. This parallelism is corresponding to the

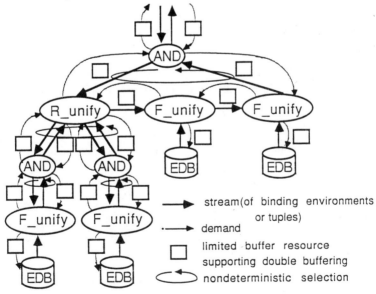

Fig. 2 Interpretation model

AND-parallelism in interpreting logic programs.

The AND function receives the binding environments from the R_unify and/or F_unify functions as a stream, creates the new binding environments and passes them to the consumer function(R_unify), which created this AND function, as a return value of this function.

(2) R_unify function

The R_unify receives a literal of a clause body from the AND function and also receives old binding environments as a stream from the AND, F_unify or another R_unify function. It returns new binding environments to the AND, F_unify or another R_unify function in the form of the stream.

First, in the intensional database, this function detects the rules which have the same predicate name in their head parts as that of the received literal. Then, it creates AND function instances for the rules, and also creates channels to send and receive binding environments to and from each AND function instances. The function passes a clause body of a detected rule to each AND function instance, and then creates intermediate environments by executing unifications between each old binding environment and each head part of the detected rules. Then, the intermediate environments are passed to the corresponding AND function instance as a stream.

A binding environment is a structure consisting of two parts "unify_env" and "rtn_env". The "unify_env" represents a binding information with regard to the variables in a single Horn clause. The "rtn_env" indicates the binding information of each variable appearing in a goal literal and its corresponding variable appearing in the head of the rule clause. For example, when a rule clause

R(X,Z) :- P(X,Y),R(Y,Z)

exists in the intensional database and a goal literal "R(a,X)" is given, the R_unify executes the unification, creates the following binding environments for the rule, and passes it to the AND function instance as a stream element. (Upper case letters are variables and lower ones are constant values.)

unify_env : [[X:a][Z:unbound][Y:unbound]]
rtn_env : [[*:a][X:Z]]

As a result of interpretation for the detected rules, the R_unify function "indeterminately" receives new binding environments from every AND function instance which this R_unify has created, and then merges those streams and returns those new binding environments in the form of a stream.

(3) F_unify function

The F_unify function receives a literal in the clause body from the AND function, also receives old binding environments as a stream from the AND, R_unify or another F_unify function, and returns new binding environments in the form of stream.

The F_unify is a function which unifys old binding environments of the literal with the tuples (fact clauses) of the same relation name (predicate name) as that of the literal. Fact clauses are classified according to predicate names. That is, the fact clauses with the same predicate name are clustered and stored as tuples in a relation in the extensional database. Unlike the tuple-at-a-time approach, the F_unify execrtes unifications for old binding environments and tuples as a set operation under demand-driven control.

This function creates a function (read_relation) to read the corresponding relation with the same name as the literal and also creates a channel to receive sorted tuples of the relation from the read_relation as a stream. Then, it executes set-oriented unification operations between old binding environments and these tuples by using binary search algorithm, produces new binding environments, and returns them to the AND, R_unify or another F_unify function in the form of the stream.

IMPLEMENTATION

The basic primitives for implementing demand-driven evaluation and function application are summarized as shown in Table 1. The basic primitives are implemented at the ECC and architecture levels of each processor. The basic primitives have been presented in [7] in detail. Here, three basic primitives are added in order to support nondeterministic merging of streams which exploits highly parallelism in stream processing. Furthermore, we present the interpreter for query processing in deductive databases in this section.

Table 1 Basic primitives

channel(type,granularity,pid_and_sharing_method)
type: data type of an element of a stream, granularity: an amount of stream elements transferred by a single demand pid_and_sharing_method: identifiers of processors and specifications of "caching" or "recomputation" of stream This primitive creates channel between a producer function instance of a stream and a consumer function instance of it. It returns an identifier of the channel as a return value. The channel corresponds to a buffer which stores elements of a stream.
new(f,pid,parameters,cid)
f: function name, pid: identifier of processor to which the function instance is allocated parameters: arguments(input stream and the other arguments) which are passed to the function cid: identifier of the output channel for the stream returned as a return value from the function instance This primitive creates a function instance specified as "f".
predemand(cid)
cid: idetifier of input channel to which the predemand is preissued This primitive pre-issues a demand eagerly to the producer function of a stream. By this primitive the producer function can begin the computation eagerly.
get(cid)
cid: identifier of input channel from which stream elements are accessed This primitive accesses a stream element in the buffer of input channel. In the case the input channel is set to the single-buffering mode, when the buffer becomes vacant, this primitive issues a demand to the producer function of the stream, then waits until the buffer is refilled with stream elements. In the case of the double buffering mode, when one area of the buffer is vacant, this primitive pre-issues a demmand to the producer function to make the area refilled. Then, it begins to access a stream element in the other erea. Each element is deleted from the buffer once it is accessed by this primitive.

---

put(cid,el)

cid: identifier of output channel to which stream elements are stored,　el: stream element

This primitive stores a stream element　as a part of a return　value of a function　into the　buffer of output channel. When the buffer　is filled with stream elements,　that is,　when the amount of data indicated　as granularity　by the channel primitive is stored,　the execution　of this primitive is suspended　until　a subsequent　demand arrives.

---

select(cid_list)

cid_list: list of identifiers of input and output channels

This primitive is used to merge streams interminately. This　primitive indeterminately　selects　one of the channels specified in cid_list,　and　returns　its channel identifier as a return value. It selects one of input channels in which　the amount of　stream elements corresponding　to the　specified granularity have been stored,　or the output channel in which a demand　has　arrived. This primitive issues　demands　to the　input　channels　to which a demand has not issued yet.

---

send(cid,el)

When another function is called in the function body,　a new function instance　is created by using the primitive "new". This primitive　is used　when a stream element　is passed　to the new function instance. It acts similarly to the primitive "put",　but unlike "put" it does not wait　for the arrival of a demand. It is used in the combination with the primitive "select".

---

receive(cid)

This primitive　is used　to receive a stream element as a return value　from a new function instance created in the function body. It acts similarly to the primitive "get",　but unlike "get" it does not wait for arrival of the stream element. It is used in the combination with the primitive "select".

---

enable(cid)

This primitive is used in the combination of the primitive "select". The channel specified　by "cid" becomes a candidate of choice of the primitive "select".

---

disable(cid)

This primitive is used in the combination with the primitive "select". The channel specified by "cid" is removed from the candidates of choice of the primitive "select".

Implementation of the Interpreter

At the program transformation level, each function (AND, R_unify, F-unify) written as functional programs is compiled into sequential object codes including basic primitives. These functions implement the basic operations presented in the previous section. In the following, the function definitions of the interpreter for logical query processing are presented. The programs abstractly show the transformed object codes of each function using Ada-like notations.

```
type clause is record
      head: literal;
      body: list of literal;
end record;
type environment is list of record
      name: variable name;
      value: variable value including 'UNBOUND';
end record;
type returning_environment is list of record
      name1, name2: variable name;
end record;
type binding_environment is record
      unify_env: environment;
      rtn_env: returning_environment;
end record;
```

```
function AND(env_channel: stream of binding_environment; clause_body: list of literal)
    return new_env_channel: stream of binding_environment
is
    n: integer := number of literals in clause_body;
    intermediate_env_channel(i): i-th (i=0..n) stream of binding_environment;
    selected_channel: stream of binding_environment;
    env, intermediate_env_n, new_env: binding_environment;
    env_channel_exhausted, intermediate_env_n_exhausted: boolean := false;
begin
    for i in 1..n loop
        if clause_body(i) is a predicate of rule then
            if i = 1 then
                intermediate_env_channel(0) := channel(binding_environment, ..);
                -- Create a channel between this AND and a first R-unify.
            end if;
            intermediate_env_channel(i) := channel(binding_environment, ..);
                -- intermediate_env_channel(i) is an identifier of the channel between
                -- the i-th R-unify and the (i+1)-th R- or F- Funify.
            new(R-unify, pid, intermediate_env_channel(i-1), cluase_body(i),
                intermediate_env_channel((i));
        else -- clause_body(i) is a predicate of facts.
            if i = 1 then
                intermediate_env_channel(0) := channel(binding_environment, ..);
                -- Create a channel between this AND and the first F-unify.
            end if;
            intermediate_env_channel(i) := channel(binding_environment, ..);
            new(F-unify, pid, intermediate_env_channel(i-1), cluase_body(i)
                intermediate_env_channel(i));
        end if;
    end loop; -- intermediate_env_channel(n) is an identifier of the channel
              -- between the n-th R- or F-unify and this AND.
    predemand(intermediate_env_channel(n));
    while not env_channel_exhausted loop
        env := get(env_channel);
        if env = EOS then
            env_channel_exhausted = true;
        end if;
        selected_channel := select(intermediate_env_channel(0), intermediate_env_channel(n));
        if selected_channel = intermediate_env_channel(0) then
            send(intermediate_env_channel(0), env);
            -- Send an environment to the first R- or F-unify.
        else -- selected_channel = intermediate_env_channel(n)
            intermediate_env_n := receive(intermediate_env_channel(n));
                -- Receive an environment from the last R- or F-unify.
        new_env := Create a new binding environment by checking unify_env
                        and rtn_env of intermediate_env_n;
            put(new_env_channel, new_env);
    end loop;
    while not intermediate_env_n_exhausted loop
        select(intermediate_env_channel(n));
        intermediate_env_n := receive(intermediate_env_channel(n));
        if intermediate_env_n = EOS then
            intermediate_env_n_exhausted := true;
        endif;
        new_env := Create a new binding environment by checking unify_env
                        and rtn_env of intermediate_env_n;
        put(new_env_channel, new_env);
    end loop;
end AND;
```

```
function R-UNIFY(env_channel: stream of binding_environment; lit: literal)
    return new_env_channel: stream of binding_environment
is
    cl_list: list of clause := clauses unifiable with lit in rule bases (IDB);
    n: integer := number of clauses in cl_list;
    env_to_AND_channel(i), env_from_AND_channel(i):
        i-th (i=1..n) stream of binding_environment;
    env, env_to_AND, env_from_AND: binding_environment;
    selected_channel: stream of binding_environment;
    env_channel_exhausted: boolean := false;
    env_from_AND_channel_exhausted: list (1..n) of boolean := false;
    remainder_EOS_from_AND_channel, remainder_env_to_AND_channel: integer;
    i: integer;
begin
    for i in 1..n loop
        env_to_AND_channel(i) := channel(binding_environment, ..);
        env_from_AND_channel(i) := channel(binding_environment, ..);
        new(AND, pid, env_to_AND_channel(i), cl_list(i).body, env_from_AND_channel(i));
        predemand(env_from_AND_channel(i));
    end loop;
    remainder_EOS_from_AND_channel := n;
        -- remainder_EOS_from_AND_channel indicates the number of channels
        -- from which EOS is not received yet.
    while not env_channel_exhausted loop
        env := get(env_channel);
        if env = EOS then
            env_channel_exhausted := true;
        end if;
        for i in 1..n loop
            enable(env_to_AND_channel(i));
            -- Let each env_to_AND_channel(1..n) be enable to be selected.
        end loop;
        remainder_env_to_AND_channel := n;
            -- remainder_env_to_AND_channel indicates the number of channels
            -- to which env is not sent yet.
        while remainder_env_to_AND_channel > 0 loop
            -- Send env to each env_to_AND_channel(1..n). The sending order is indeterminate.
            selected_channel := select(env_to_AND_channel(1..n), env_from_AND_channel(1..n));
            -- Each env_from_AND_channel(1..n) is initially enabled to be selected.
            if selected_channel is included in env_to_AND_channel(1..n) then
                i := index of selected_channel in env_to_AND_channel(1..n);
                env_to_AND := Creates a binding environment by unifying env and lit with cl_list(i);
                send(env_to_AND_channel(i), env_to_AND);
                disable(env_to_AND_channel(i));
                remainder_env_to_AND_channel := remainder_env_to_AND_channel - 1;
            else
                -- selected_channel is included in env_from_AND_channel(1..n)
                env_from_AND := receive(selected_channel);
                if env_from_AND_channel = EOS then
                    remainder_EOS_from_AND_channel := remainder_EOS_from_AND_channel - 1;
                end if;
                put(new_env_channel, env_from_AND_env);
                    -- Return a new binding environment as a part of the return value
                    -- of this R-unify function.
            end if;
        end loop;
    end loop;
    while remainder_EOS_from_AND_channel > 0 loop
        -- repeat until EOS's are received from all of env_from_AND_channel;
        selected_channel := select(env_from_AND_channel(1..n));
        env_from_AND := receive(selected_channel);
        if env_from_AND = EOS then
            remainder_EOS_from_AND_channel := remainder_EOS_from_AND_channel - 1;
        end if;
        put(new_env_channel, env_from_AND);
            -- Return a new binding environment as a part of the return value of
            -- this R-unify function.
    end loop;
end R-UNIFY;
```

```
function F−UNIFY (env_channel: stream of binding_environment; lit: literal)
   return new_env_channel: stream of binding_environment
is
      env: binding_environment;
      new_envs: page of binding_environment;
      tuple_page_channel: stream of page of tuple;
      tuple_page: page of tuple;
      env_channel_exhausted, tuple_page_channel_exhausted: boolean := false;
begin
      tuple_page_channel := channel(page of tuple, ..);
      new(read_relation, lit, sorting_attribute, tuple_page_channel);
      −− read_relation returns a stream of pages. Each page is sorted on
      −− sorting_attribute. Each page consits of several tuples. The number of
      −− tuples in a page is specified in the primitive channel as granularity.
      predemand(tuple_page_channel);
      while not env_channel_exhausted loop
         env := get(env_channel);
         if env = EOS then
            env_channel_exhausted := true;
         end if;
         while not tuple_page_channel_exhausted loop
            select(tuple_page_channel); −− Wait the arrival of a page produced by read_relation.
            tuple_page := receive(tuple_page_channel);
            if tuple_page = EOS then
               tuple_page_channel_exhausted := true;
            end if;
            new_envs := By set−oriented unification of env with a page of tuples
               (tuple_page) by binary search, creats new binding environments which
               are returned as a return value of this F−unify function;
            for i in (the number of environments created as new_envs) loop
               put(new_env_channel, new_envs(i));
            end loop;
         end loop;
         rewind(tuple_page_channel);
      end loop;
      put(new_env_channel, EOS);
end F−UNIFY;
```

Simulation

We explain recursive query processing using an example. For example, suppose we have the following rule named "Family-friends" in the intensional database. We assume that the relations Parent(P) and Friend(F) are stored as base relations in the extensional databases.

FF(X,Y) :- F(X,Y)

FF(X,Z) :- P(X,Y),FF(Y,Z)

The query is executed as shown in Fig. 3.

To estimate the parallelism, we have constructed a simulator of the interpreter on the Sun-2 workstation [11]. The simulator consists of three simulation modules corresponding to three functions AND, R_unify and F_unify, respectively. In each module, program behavior is simulated faithfully adding the execution time represented by physical parameters. Each physical parameter is corresponding to the execution time of each basic primitive or each main operation. In regard to the basic primitives of stream manipulation, execution times are analyzed in a unit of a binding environment or a tuple. Under demand-driven control, the state transition between the execution state and the suspended state in each module is analyzed, and the dependency between modules is also analyzed. In this simulation, since the actual execution time of the interpreter cannot be measured, we can only recognize the overview of parallel processing for queries. However, physical parameters have been set by using the measurement results of actual execution time of relational database operations in the relational database operation system [8] which we have implemented on the Sun-2 workstation. In the simulation of the example query processing, physical parameters are

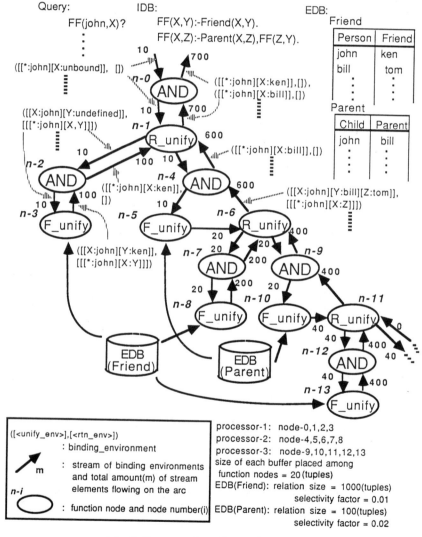

Fig. 3 Interpretation of recursive query

set as follows:

execution time for "get", "put", "send", "receive", "unification", "creation of a new binding environment" and "judgment of rule or fact" : 0.0001 sec.

execution time for "new", "channel": 0.001 sec.

execution time for fetch of a page (corresponding to buffer size(100 tuples, 64 bytes/tuple)) from a disk(EDB): 0.05 sec.

communication time between processors: 16.6 msec/2Kbyte-packet.

Parameters related to a recursive query and its operand relations, and allocation of processors and buffers are summarized in Fig. 3. We consider that in general the dominant operator for performance is the F_unify function because it manipulates large relations. Therefore, three processors are allocated so as to perform different F_unify functions independently.

The time chart in Fig. 4 shows the overview of parallel processing of the recursive query. This time chart shows the overview of processing of the query until three times references to the relation Friend are recursively performed.

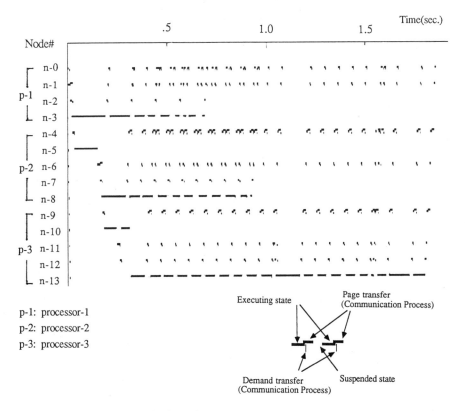

Fig. 4 Time chart

CONCLUSIONS

In this paper, we have presented a stream-oriented approach to parallel processing for executing logical queries. To execute high-level queries which references recursively defined relations in a deductive database, we have presented three basic operations.

In our system, new basic operations can be flexibly defined as functions and easily integrated in the parallel processing environment. By using demand-driven evaluation as a driving method of functional computation, parallelism is exploited within a limited resource environment in executing basic operations.

We have developed the experimental relational database operation system in a local area network [8]. This system has been implemented to execute functional computation in parallel. Currently, by extending the system, we are developing the parallel interpreter for deductive databases.

Acknowledgements

The authors would like to thank Dr. Ryuzo Hasegawa and Dr. Makoto Amamiya for valuable discussions.

References
[1] J. Backus, "Can programming be liberated from the von Neumann style? A functional style and its algebra of programs," Comm. ACM, vol. 21, no. 8, pp. 613-641, Aug. 1978.
[2] F. Bancilhon and R Ramakrishnan, "An amateur's introduction to recursive query processing strategies," in Proc. ACM SIGMOD'86, pp.16-52, 1986.
[3] D. P. Friedman and D. S. Wise, "Aspects of applicative programming for parallel processing," IEEE Trans. Comput., vol. C-27, pp. 289-296, Apr. 1978.
[4] H. Gallaire, J. Minker and J. M. Nicolas, "Logic and databases: a deductive approach," ACM Computing Surveys, vol. 16, no. 2, Jun. 1984.
[5] G. Gardarin and C. Maindreville, "Evaluation of database recursive logic programs as recurrent function series," in Proc. ACM SIGMOD'86, pp. 177-186, 1986.
[6] R. Hasegawa and M. Amamiya, "Parallel execution of logic programs based on dataflow concept," in Proc. 1984 Int. Conf. Fifth Generation Computer Systems, pp. 507-516, 1984.
[7] Y. Kiyoki, K. Kato and T. Masuda, "A relational database machine based on functional programming concepts," in Proc. ACM-IEEE Computer Society Fall Joint Computer Conf., pp. 969-978, 1986.
[8] Y. Kiyoki, K. Kato and T. Masuda, "A stream-oriented approach to distributed query processing in a local area network," in Proc. 1986 ACM SIGSMALL/PC Symp. Small Syst., pp. 146-155, Dec. 1986.
[9] S. R. Vegdahl, "A survey of proposed architectures for the execution of functional languages," IEEE Trans. Comput., vol. C-33, no. 12, pp. 1050-1071, Dec. 1984.
[10] J. D. Ullman, "Implementation of logical query languages for databases," ACM Trans. Database Systems, vol. 10, no. 3, Sept. 1985.
[11] Programmers reference manual for the Sun workstation, Sun Micro System, Inc., Sept. 1986.

DDC: A DEDUCTIVE DATABASE MACHINE

R. Gonzalez-Rubio, J. Rohmer, A. Bradier, B. Bergsten.
BULL SA CENTRE DE RECHERCHE, DSG/CRG/DMIA - PC 58 A 13, B.P. N° 3. 68, Route de Versailles. 78430 Louveciennes. France.

ABSTRACT

This article presents the "Delta Driven Computer" (DDC) project and describes the design decisions made for its first implementation .

DDC is composed of a set interconnected PCM (Processor, Communication Device, Memory) nodes .

DDC is a parallel inference computer. For the first implementation we have studied how to efficiently process a deductive data base.

In this article, special consideration is given to:

- the Virtual Inference Machine (VIM) which is based on a production rule language. The unique operation achieved at this abstract level is "saturation". It is executed with a forward chaining strategy. A special effort has been made to study methods to optimize the execution of VIM programs (Alexander Method);

- the specific execution model DDEM and the data partitioning method which allow us to achieve full parallelism independently in each node of the machine;

- DDCL, the language of the machine, which is a small but powerful language and is oriented toward the execution of operations on relations;

- the internal representation of the data structures and the optimized algorithms which enable us to accelerate the operations on the data base.

This project is under development at the BULL Research Center and is partially supported by ESPRIT-415.

INTRODUCTION.

We present here the "Delta Driven Computer" (DDC), a system that can be specialized to support efficient deductive database processing. This paper reflects the state of this research project at the end of the first quarter of 1987. DDC is a parallel inference multiprocessor computer, currently under development at BULL Research Center. Early papers describe some of our ideas [Gon 85,Gon 86]. An overview of the project is presented in [Gon 87].

As a design methodology, we chose to describe the different levels of languages, from the high level language down to the machine level language, and how to go from one level to the next (such methods are presented in [Boy 78, Dag 84]).

The architecture of DDC can be viewed as a multiprocessor system composed of a set of interconnected PCM nodes , in which there is no need to have a shared memory.

From a conceptual point of view, DDC executes a language based on production rules, called VIM (Virtual Inference Machine). This execution is performed following a forward chaining strategy. Given a set of rules and a set of initial facts, the only mode of operation of the machine is saturation (all conclusions are found).

VIM is an intermediate language; so, in the project, we are studying how to translate from a high level language to this intermediate language. The high level languages which we are considering are declarative ones (i.e. Logic Programming or Functional Programming).

The execution of VIM is possible with the DDEM (Delta Driven Execution Model). In this model the execution is driven by the facts deduced from the rules. We call these "new" facts the Delta. The parallel architecture we propose can support DDEM.

The parallelism of the machine is achieved by distributing the facts among PCM nodes and by firing rules independently in each processor.

The implementation of DDEM is based on operations on relations, so VIM rules are transformed into a DDCL program (Delta Driven Computer Language). DDCL is the level of operation of μSyC (a microprogrammable symbolic coprocessor also being designed at the Bull Research Center).

One goal of this project is to have a running prototype (including both hardware and software) at the end of 1987. We had to make some decisions, and we imposed certain restrictions to implement this prototype. The prototype is mainly oriented toward the execution of logic programs. It must prove that the parallelism handled by the model/machine has an interesting cost/performance rate.

In the second section, we give a general overview of the DDC project, the motivations for its architecture, and the key ideas concerning the different levels of language . The third section presents the architecture, the mapping of DDEM into this architecture and the language DDCL. Lastly, some initial ideas for the first implementation are given along with some conclusions and an outlook on the future work.

A GENERAL OVERVIEW OF DDC.

Motivations.

The basic aim of the DDC project is to design an efficient computer dedicated mainly to symbolic computation, for "large" Artificial Intelligence (AI) applications.

Let us begin by analyzing the situation in the eighties. On one hand, the needs for high efficiency in AI are clear. It is commonly thought that they are from 100 Mlips to 1 Glips (see [Mot 84]).

But to attain this level of performance with only the technological progress offered by Ultra Large Scale Integration is not possible. This is due to the von Neumann model of architecture characterized by its sequential operations. We know that the instruction execution time of a machine is bound by the propagation time of its signals. Then we can predict that a processor's clock period cannot be smaller than 1 ns. Hence, the maximum performanceis lower than one Giga instructions per second [Lun 85]. Thus the only solution is to design parallel architectures.

On the other hand, the requirement of AI machines is to maintain software costs as low as possible. This could be achieved by using a simple high level language where parallelism is hidden for the programmer.

Consequently, a prerequisite to the design of a specialized AI parallel architecture is an execution model well adapted to handle parallelism and symbolic processing.

Another prerequisite is that the architecture must not be dedicated to one particular language. Instead, it must be flexible enough to accommodate a variety of declarative programming styles, including relational and deductive, logic and functional.

Typical applications for this architecture stem from relational databases, deductive databases, expert systems, simulation systems, etc..

An intermediate language approach.

The language levels in DDC are:

- a high level language, issued from logic programming or functional programming. The union of these two programming styles is the subject of many papers, for instance [Fri 84, Sup 84, Vod 84, Dar 85, Bar 86]. Currently we are considering only the logic programming aspect.

- an intermediate language, the key of our approach. This language is based on additive production rules with a forward chaining (saturation) strategy. We call this language VIM.(Some principles of production rule systems are presented in [Ver 77, Wat 78, For 79]).

- to execute the saturation DDEM is provided. This model can be parallelized, as explained below. In fact a VIM program is translated into a DDCL program. DDCL is the DDC machine language and the program is executed following the DDEM.

The optimization of a VIM program is done following an algorithm called the Alexander Method, proposed by J. Rohmer [Roh 85, Roh 86].

We have defined these three levels of language to get a better understanding of how the system works. In the next sub-sections we describe the VIM language, to present how a computation takes place. Then, we examine the Alexander Method to show how a logic program is translated into a VIM program. We also present DDEM, DDCL and the architecture of the machine.

We want to emphasize that what we present in the next sections are just the basic ideas of how to implement DDC, and at the end we consider how the machine might be used.

Virtual Inference Machine VIM.

The design of VIM is based on our previous experience with production systems. [Pug 85]). Basically, this language is composed of production rules [Pug 86], i.e. rules of the form:

$h1 \Rightarrow c1, ... cp$ or $h1, h2 \Rightarrow c1, ... cp$

Where the Hi and Cj are predicates of the form: $p(X1, ..., Xn)$ and where Xi is either an atom (constant) or a variable. This means that functions (or trees) are not visible at this level.

We require that the variables in the conclusions must also appear in the hypotheses.

Note that the restrictions we place on VIM are the same as those of "Datalog", often introduced when studying the domain of deductive databases as in [Gal 78, Ull 85, Sag 86, Ban 86]

This means that if initially there exists a set of facts containing only constants, all the generated facts will also contain only constants.

For implementation reasons, we impose a maximum of two hypotheses in a rule.

The only mode of operation of the machine is the saturation: given a set of rules and a set of initial facts, find all possible conclusions.

The computational model is based on the notion of saturation of a set of rules and a set of facts. This notion corresponds to the generation of the semantic model associated with the logic program made of clauses. This model is in fact the Least Fixed Point of the set of clauses (rules and facts are just clauses in First Order Logic).

Example:
Consider the following rules (with father(Father, Child) and ancestor(Ancestor, Descendant)):
father(X,Y) => ancestor(X,Y)
ancestor(X,Y),ancestor(Y,Z) => ancestor(X,Z)
Consider the set of initial facts:
father(1,2)
father(2,3)
father(3,4)
When a saturation takes place, all the ancestors are deduced.
ancestor(1,2)   ancestor(1,3)
ancestor(2,3)   ancestor(2,4)
ancestor(3,4)   ancestor(1,4)

Saturation stops when no more facts can be deduced. A more formal presentation of the method, including proofs of termination , soundness and completeness can be found in [Ker 87].

In the case of commutative rules, saturation can be executed in parallel. This means that the rules can be fired independently as data are available.

We can describe the DDEM in an informal way at the VIM level. When a rule is applied a fact or a set of facts may be deduced, in our terminology a BΔ (read Black Delta). Only those facts which are not already contained in the database are considered as new ones or in our terminology as a WΔ (read White Delta). This WΔ is inserted in the database, and then the rules can be tried again using just the

WΔ as trigger.

The Alexander Method.

Forward chaining as in VIM exhibits an interesting property of simplicity. But forward chaining has the drawback of computing all possible solutions to all possible predicates included in the set of rules. For instance, if we want to know Jean's descendant, it is useless to start by computing everyone's descendant (by saturating the database) and to select afterward just Jean's descendant.

The Alexander Method is an algorithm to transform a set of VIM rules and a query into a new set of focalized rules. The Alexander Method simulates backward chaining with forward chaining.

The following discussion gives only an informal introduction to the Alexander Method. For a more complete presentation, please see [Roh 86, Ker 87]. (The notion of Supplementary Generalized Magic Sets presented in]Bee 87] is similar to Alexander Method.)

In an informal way the Alexander Method cuts a recursive goal in one problem and in one solution.

For instance, the request ancestor(jean,W) is cut into:

- a new literal: problem_ancestor(jean) which can be interpreted as "The problem of finding the descendants of Jean exists"

- literals such as solution_ancestor(jean,louis) which can be interpreted as "louis is a solution to the problem problem_ancestor(jean)".

To go from backward chaining to forward chaining, we need rules which handle problem_ancestor and solution_ancestor literals. For instance:

problem_ancestor(X),q => r

can be read as "if there is the problem of finding the descendants of X, and q is true, then r is true... "

and   a => solution_ancestor(W,X)   can be read as "if a is true then W is a solution ".

With these intuitive ideas in mind, let us process an example step by step:
Suppose we have the goal ancestor (jean,W) and the rules:
R1:   father(X,Y) => ancestor(X,Y)
R2:   father(X,Y),ancestor(Y,Z) => ancestor(X,Z)
R1 gives:
R1.1:   problem_ancestor(X),father(X,Y) => solution_ancestor(X,Y)
"if there is the problem of finding the descendants of X, and if Y is a son of X, then a solution is Y"
R2 gives:
R2.1:   problem_ancestor(X),father(X,Y),ancestor(Y,Z) =>
                          solution_ancestor(X,Z)
"if there is the problem of finding the descendants of X, and if Y is a son of X, and if Z is a descendant of Y, then a solution is Z"
But this rule contains itself the goal ancestor(Y,Z) and must be transformed. This goal will itself be cut into two pieces, yielding two new rules R2.2 and R 2.3.
R2.2:   problem_ancestor(X),father(X,Y) => problem_ancestor(Y)
"if there is the problem of finding the descendants of X, and if Y is a son of X, then there exists the problem of finding the descendants of Y."
R2.3:   solution_ancestor(Y,Z) => solution_ancestor(X,Z)
"the solutions to the Y problem are also solutions to the X problem".

In fact, rule R2.3 does not respect a restriction of VIM (predefined variables), since X appears in the conclusion and not in the hypotheses. Thus, it is necessary to transmit the information X between rules R2.2 and R2.3. For that purpose, we create a new predicate called continuation. The final version of R2.2 and R2.3 is now:

R2.2':   problem_ancestor(X),father(X,Y)=>
                                    problem_ancestor(Y),continuation(X,Y)
R2.3': solution_ancestor(Y,Z),continuation(X,Y)=>
                                    solution_ancestor(X,Z)

Delta Driven Execution Model DDEM.

DDEM is a model to execute saturation on a VIM set of rules.

Consider the following VIM rule: p,q => r

This rule is first transformed into the two special rules called delta-rules:

WΔp,qc => BΔr   and   WΔq,pc => BΔr

where qc and pc are the current representations of q and p in the database.

When one of the rules is applied, a fact or a set of facts is deduced. In our terminology, what is deduced is called a BΔ, in this example on the predicate r. Among the facts contained in a BΔr, some are already existing in the database: these are called duplicate. In our terminology, a WΔ is what is obtained from a BΔ after the duplicates have been eliminated. So a WΔr contains the set of new facts on r that have been just deduced. Consequently, this WΔr is added to the current representation of r in the database, and then the whole set of rules is tried again using just the WΔr as trigger in rules of the form : WΔr,s => t .

When no more WΔ is produced the logic database is saturated, thus processing is finished.

Two types of process have been specified, the application of rules and the elimination of duplicates.(see figure below). In the case where rules are monotonic and commutative the order of Δ arrivals does not modify the final result. This means that the model is asynchronous and parallelism is implicit.

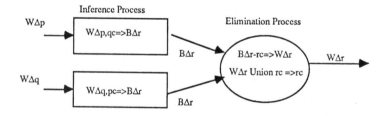

The architecture of DDC.

DDC consists of a set of nodes linked by an interconnection system without shared memory. All nodes are identical, a P-C-M triple: Processor, Communication device and Memory.

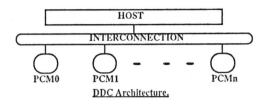

DDC Architecture.

The Processor has two parts: a general purpose microprocessor: Motorola MC68020 and a special purpose custom VLSI chip called μSyC [Cou 87]. The μSyC chip acts as a coprocessor of the MC68020. This means that when a coprocessor code is detected by the MC68020, it "calls" the coprocessor to execute a coprocessor instruction. Each instruction of the coprocessor is a complete relational operation; the entire algorithm is microprogrammed.

The Memory can be divided into three parts: a fast static RAM on the CPU board (without cache), boards with large capacity and a secondary storage.

The Communication Module is responsible for sending and receiving messages to and from the interconnection network.

From VIM to DDCL.

A predicate in the VIM environment corresponds to a relation in the DDCL environment. Thus, fact and tuple are two representations of the same semantic element.

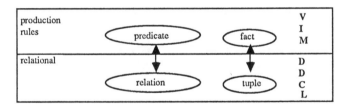

At DDCL level, a delta is a tuple and with each delta is associated a set of primitives that have to be executed on it. The piece of DDCL code that contains this set of primitives is a special entity called an "action", whose identifier is closely related to the delta. An action contains primitives which correspond, at VIM level, to the rules where the associated delta is to be used.

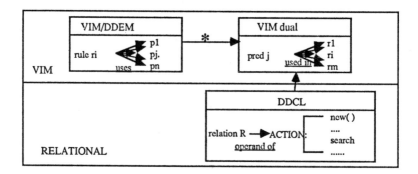

The mapping strategy.

The mapping strategy of DDEM into the DDC architecture is statically determined and dynamically executed. We try to dynamically balance the load in the machine, while minimizing the communications.

So at each moment during a process of saturation we can assume that the facts are distributed among the PCM nodes and all the compiled rules are copied at each node.

A predicate is distributed according to a hash code function applied to the value of one of its arguments. This approach is similar to the notion of buckets introduced in [Bra 84, Kit83] for the representations of relations, where the partitioned buckets represent disjoint subsets of the original relation and provide a natural basis for parallelism (also mentionned in [DeW 87]).

Predicates can be duplicated. If so, the copies are distinguished at compilation time by adding a suffix to the name of the predicate.

The advantage of this mapping is that data are sent toward the only node where they can possibly be used. This improves the locality factor and reduces the rate of communications.

Consider a DDC composed of three nodes, a set of two VIM rules is :
R1:   p(X,Y),q(Y,Z) => r(X,Z)
R2:   p(X,Y),r(X,Z) => p(Y,Z)
and four initial facts:
$$p(aa,bb), q(cc,dd), q(bb,cc), r(aa,cc)$$
These facts must be stored as relations as follows:
At compilation it can be determined that the p relation is used in R1 and R2 but in each one according to different attributes.
So, in the machine, instead of having p , there are two copies: pc.1 and pc.2.
pc.1(X,Y) to be used by R2 distributed according to values of its first argument.
pc.2(X,Y) to be used by R1 distributed according to values of its second argument.
For q there is just qc.1 distributed according to values of its first argument.
For r there is just rc.1.
So if we apply the hash function to values of arguments of the initial facts, we can identify in which processor a tuple will be stored.
$$H(1,p.1(aa,bb)) = H(1,r.1(aa,cc)) = h(aa) = 2$$
$$H(2,p.2(aa,bb)) = H(1,q.1(bb,cc)) = h(bb) = 1$$
$$H(1,q.1(cc,dd)) = h(cc) = 3$$

where H is a function, which takes as arguments: the number of the attribute to which the function should be applied, and a tuple; h is the hash function which takes as argument the value of the selected attribute, and returns the identity of the destination node; and 1,2,3 are the PCM node numbers.

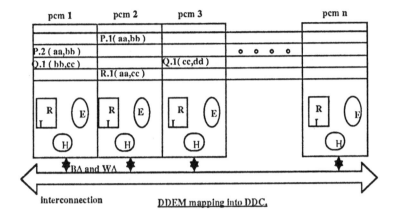

interconnection   DDEM mapping into DDC.

The hash function h is applied to each tuple of a BΔ produced at a given node. Then each tuple is sent to just one processor.

Delta Driven Computer Language DDCL

DDCL is the language of the machine. Its semantical power is the one of µSyC operations.
A DDCL program is structured in several independent modules, each corresponding to the code of an action.

There are four different types of DDCL primitives: primitives for program control, operations on relations, "propagation" operations (communication among processors), and input/ouput primitives.
DDCL consists mainly in operations on relations. Most of these are executed following the principles of filtering by automata presented in [Gon 84], and the join algorithm LA-JOIN presented in [Bra 86].
For example, consider just a join corresponding to the following VIM delta rules (in DDC, the join is done between the flow of deltas which are produced during the saturation and a stored relation):

R11:   WΔp.2(X,Y) , qc.1(Y,Z) => BΔr.1(X,Z)

R12:   WΔq.1(Y,Z) , pc.2(X,Y) => BΔr.1(X,Z)

The current representation of qc.1 will be stored as an automaton in which are represented all the first attributes (resp. the Y). with their pointers to a list of associated second attributes.(resp. the Z). The automaton (the matrix) decides if a tuple of the WΔp.2 can be joined to qc.1 (equality of the Y in the two tuples). If this is the case, the execution of rule R11 produces a BΔ This BΔ contains tuples for r.1 comprising the different values of first attribute of WΔp.2 (resp. the X) and the different values of the second attribute of qc.1.(resp. the Z).

The advantage of this solution is that pattern matching is done very efficiently since the time to retrive an attribute in the automaton (and thus the time to do a join in a node) is directly proportional to the number of characters of this attribute.

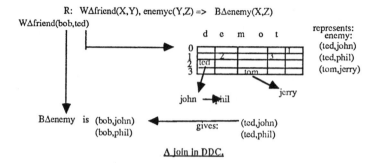

A join in DDC.

Note that with the use of such an automaton, the complexity of LA-JOIN is linear with respect to the size of the two source relations and of the result. Moreover, because the chosen mapping strategy, equi-partitions the facts, for a DDC with N processors, the time required to execute a join is divided by N compared to the time required for the same join on a monoprocessor.

The DDCL primitives are:

- the control primitives for conditions or loops (**if..then..endif**, **with..map..endmap**, **with ..mapfile..endmapfile**);

- the input/output primitives (**file, output**);

- the propagation primitives to create and send a delta to a destination node (**message**). The destination is calculated according to the hash function applied to the attribute values.

- the operations on relations which include:

      - data updating:

           - **add** adds a tuple in the automaton representation of a relation;

           - **new&add** first check if a tuple is in the automaton representation of a relation. If the tuple already exists, **new&add** returns the boolean false, if not, new&add adds the tuple to the representation and returns the boolean true;

      - pattern matching:

           - **search** retrieves part of a tuple in the automaton representation of a relation. Whenever the matching phase succeeds, the final pointer stored in the automaton which points to the list of possible ends of tuples is returned to permit the creation of solution tuples.

Continuing the previous example, the DDCL program to execute rule R would consist in manipulations of the friend and enemy relations:

- add WΔfriend(bob,ted) in the current representation of the relation friend;
- search for "ted" in the automaton of the current representation of the relation enemy and return the pointer to the list "john, phil";
- with the list "john, phil" create and send the messages containing the solution tuples (bob,john) and (bob,phil).

FIRST IMPLEMENTATION.

The first parallel implementation will be done on a BULL SPS7. The configuration chosen for the first prototype has 8 nodes, each comprising a MC68020 working with its local memory (4 Mbytes) using a local bus. The nodes are connected by a SMBUS whose useful transfer rate is 2Mbytes/sec, and communications are made via a global memory. This will probably be too slow. For DDC future implementation improvements we are currently designing a more efficient "DDCBUS" directly linking the local buses of the nodes. One of the processors of the BULL SPS7 acts as a host, the others constitutes the DDC. In this configuration the DDC acts as a coprocessor to execute saturations.

Structure of an executable program:

A program consists of sequential parts and parallel parts grouped in blocks. Each block for the DDC describes a saturation, and contains the set of facts and the set of rules to be saturated. The user must indicate which blocks of the program are parallel, and can be executed by the DDC.

The order of block execution is imposed by the user program and controlled by the host. Serial blocks are executed by the host and calls are made to the DDC whenever a saturation is needed.

The sequential blocks of the user program are compiled into host machine code by the standard compiler for the high level language (C3 in the Fig. below). The parallel blocks are compiled first into VIM (C1), then into DDCL (C2).

The transformation of VIM to DDCL also gives the primitives to execute the loading in DDC, to initialize a saturation and to get results.

CONCLUSIONS.

We have presented in this paper the basis of the design of DDC, an AI parallel machine supporting DDEM, a suitable execution model where rules are executed in parallel with operations on relations.

We described all the levels, from the high level language down to machine level, and how to go from one level to another.

Currently, we are working on the first implementation of DDC. A software version is presently running on a monoprocessor with UNIX processes simulating the DDC processors. We are also studying extensionsto the Alexander Method (lists processing, negation, and aggregates [ker 87']), hardware optimizations to integrate μSyC, DDCL compiler optimizations, possible applications and tests for performance evaluations.

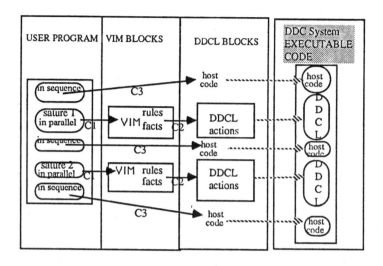

Finally, we would like to thank for their comments: R. Lescoeur, J. M. Kerisit, J. M. Pugin, F. Anceau, and K. R. Apt. Thanks also to D. Bernard, M. Carrel, M. Couprie, L. Gluck, P. Rosier, D. Terral and P Vidil for their work implementing some of the ideas presented here. Thanks to H. Blau for her comments about the redaction of this paper.

<u>**ANNEX 1.**</u>
The following example shows the rules part of a VIM program that permits to deduce from a "father" and an "ancestor" predicate the result which is the set of "ancestors of john".

INPUT "file_father" (X,Y) => ancestor(X,Y).
ancestor(X,Y),ancestor(Y,Z) => ancestor(X,Z).
ancestor("John",X) => OUTPUT "file_solution" (X).

The same program in DDCL looks like:

In the host node.
action *saturation* :
  with open("file_father") mapfile
    message(ancestor,[*1,*2])
    if select([*1="John"]) then
    message(ancestor_1,[*2])
    endif
  endmapfile
endaction

```
action output_1 :
  output "file_solution"
endaction
```

In all the PCM nodes.

```
action ancestor_2 :
  add(ancestor_2,[1])
  with search(ancestor,1) map
    message(ancestor,[*2,*3])
    if select([*2="John"]) then
      message(ancestor_1,[*3])
    endif
  endmap
endaction
```

```
action ancestor :
  if new&add(ancestor,[1,2]) then
    message(ancestor_2,[*2,*1])
    with search(ancestor_2,1) map
      message(ancestor,[*3,*2])
      if select([*3="John"]) then
        message(ancestor_1,[*2])
      endif
    endmap
  endif
endaction
```

```
action ancestor_1 :
  if new&add(ancestor_1,[1]) then
    out(output_1,[*1])
  endif
endaction
```

REFERENCES

[Ban 86]   Bancilhon F., Ramakrishnan R.:"An amateur's introduction to Recursive Query Processing Strategies". Proc. of the ACM SIGACT-SIGMOD Symp. on Princ. of Database Systems 1986.

[Bar 85]   Barbuti R., Bellia M., Levi G., Martelli M.: " LEAF: A Language which Integrates Logic, Equations and Functions. In Logic Programming: Functions, Relations and Equations, D De Groot and G Linstrom, Eds (Prentice Hall 85).

[Bee 87]   Beeri C., Ramakrishan R: "On the power of Magic". ACM PODS 1987.

[Boy 78]   Boyd D.L., Pizzarello A.: "An Introduction to the WELLMADE design methodology". IEEE Trans.Soft.Eng, TSE.4,4 .Jul.1978, pp276-282.

[Bra 84]   Bratbergsengen K.: "Hashing Methods and Relational Algebra Operations". Proceedings of the 1984 Very Large Database Conference. Aug.84.

[Bra 86]   Bradier A.: "LA-JOIN: Un Algorithme de Jonction en Mémoire et sa Mise en Oeuvre sur le Filtre SCHUSS". II èmes Journées Bases de Données Avancées. Giens, Avril. 1986.

[Cou 87]   Couprie M., Garcia J., Marechal T., Terral D.: "µSyC: Coprocesseur Microprogrammable pour les Applications Symboliques". Journées Firftech Systèmes et Télématique. Bases de Données et Intelligence Artificielle. Paris apr.87.

[Dag 84]   Dasgupta S.: "The Design and Description of Computer Architectures".Eds. Wiley-Interscience, 1984.

[Dar 85]   Darlington J., Field A.J., Pull H.: "The Unification of Functional and Logic Languages". In Logic Programming: Functions, Relations and Equations, D De Groot and G Linstrom, Eds Prentice Hall 85).

[DeW 86]   DeWitt D.J., Gerber R.H., Graefe G., Heytens M.L., Kumar K.B., Muralikrishna: " GAMMA- A High Performance Dataflow Database Machine". Computer Sciences Technical report n°635, University of Wisconsin., Mar 1986.

[Fel 79]   Feldman J.A.: "High Level Programming for Distributes Computing". Comm. ACM, vol.22, No.6,1979

[For 79]   Forgy C.L: "On the Efficient Implementation of Production Systems".P.H.D at Carnegie-Mellon University Febr.79.

[Fri 85]   Fribourg L.: "SLOG: A Logic Programming Language Interpreter Based on Clausal Superposition and Rewriting". Proc. 1985 Symp. on Logic Programming (IEEE Comp. Society Press, 1985)

[Gal 78]   Gallaire H., Minker J. (eds.): "Logic and Databases".Plenum, New York 1978.

[Gon 84]   Gonzalez-Rubio R., Rohmer J., Terral D.: "The SCHUSS Filter: A Processor for Non-Numerical Data Processing". 11th Annual International Symposium on Computer Architecture. Ann Arbor. 1984.

[Gon 85]   Gonzalez-Rubio R., Rohmer J.: "From Data Bases to Artificial Intelligence : A Hardward Point of View". Nato Summer School, Les Arcs 1985.

[Gon 86]   Gonzalez-Rubio R., Bradier A., Rohmer J.: "DDC Delta Driven Computer. A Parallel Machine for Symbolic Processing". ESPRIT Summer School on Future Parallel Computers. University of Pisa. June.1986.

[Gon 87]   Gonzalez-Rubio R., Rohmer J., Bradier A.: "An overview of DDC:Delta Driven Computer". Conference on Parallel Architectures and Languages Europe. Eindhoven, Jun.15-19, 1987.

[Ker 87]   Kerisit J.M, Lescoeur R, Rohmer J, Roucairol G: " The Alexander Method an efficient way for handling Deduction on Databases. To appear in Programmers Future General Computers eds.Nivat-Fuchi, North Holland.

[Kit 83]   Kitsuregawa M., Tanaka H., Moto-oka T.: "Application of Hash to Database Machine and its Achitecture", New Generation Computing, vol.1, No.1, 1983.

[Kop 82]   Kopetz H., Lohnert F., "High Level Programming of Distributed Computer Control Systems". Real Time Data 82 Versailles, 1982.

[Lis 79]   Liskov B.: "Primitives for Distribued Computing". Proc. of 7th ACM SIGOPS Symp. on Operating System Principles. 1979.

[Loh 86]   Lohnert F.: "Tutorial on Synchronization and Communication". ESPRIT project 415 Deliverable Working Group on Architectures and Applications Oct.86.

[Lun 85]   Lunstrom S. F., Larsen R. L.: "Computer an Information Technology in the Year 2000- A projection". Computer, September 1985.

[Mot 84]   Moto-oka T., Stone H. S.: "Fifth Generation Computer Systems: A Japanese Project". Computer, March 1984.

[Pug 85]   Pugin J.M.: "BOUM: An Instantiation of the (PS)2 concept". 5èmes Journées Internationales Systèmes Experts. Avignon 1985.

[Pug 86]   Pugin J.M. : "VIM Language". Bull Internal Report 1986.

[Roh 85]   Rohmer J., Lescoeur R. : "The Alexander Method. A technique for the processing of recursive axioms in deductive databases". Bull Internal Report 1985.

[Roh 86]   Rohmer J., Lescoeur R., J. M. Kerisit: "The Alexander Method. A technique for the processing of recursive axioms in deductive databases". New Generation Computing, 4. 1986.

[Sag 86]   Sagiv Y.: "Optimizing Datalog Programs". Stanford University 1986.

[SUP 84]   SUPER "First annual report" Syracuse University. Dec 84.

[Ull 85]   Ullman J.D.: "Implementation of Logical Query Languages for Databases". ACM Trans. on Database System 10(3) p289..321 Sept.85.

[Ver 77]   Vere S.A.: "Relational Production Systems". Artificial Intelligence 8(Febr.77) p47.68.

[Vod 84]   Voda P., Yu B.: "RF-Maple: a Logic Programming Language with Functions , Types and Concurrency". In FGCS'84 (ICOT, 1984)

[Wat 78]   Waterman D.A, Hayes-Roth F.: "An Overview of Pattern-Directed Inference Systems". Pattern Directed Inference Systems, D.A Waterman and F.Hayes-Roth. Ed.,Academic Press, New York, 1978.

AN INFERENCE MODEL AND A TREE-STRUCTURED MULTICOMPUTER SYSTEM FOR LARGE DATA-INTENSIVE LOGIC-BASES

GHASSAN Z. QADAH

Department of Electrical Engineering and Computer Science, Northwestern University, Evanston, IL 60201, USA.

Abstract. This paper presents an inference model suitable for data-intensive logic-bases. Such a model is well suited for parallel processing and does not involve any redundant data processing. The implementation of such a model on a tree-structured multicomputer system is also presented. Such a structure is very suitable for the implementation of the proposed model since the basic operations encountered in such a model can be effectively supported by the tree structure.

INTRODUCTION

A logic-base is a set of horn clauses (facts and rules) that express knowledge about a collection of objects and the relationships which exist between these objects[1]. Conceptually, a logic-base can be partitioned into two parts, the extensional database (EDB) and the intensional database(IDB)[2]. While EDB stores the facts of the logic-base, IDB, on the other hand, stores its rules. All of the facts with the same predicate symbol is stored as one relation and such a predicate is an extensional predicate. On the other hand, all of the rules with the same head predicate symbol is grouped together and referred to as a virtual relation and such a predicate is an intensional predicate. The data-intensive logic-base systems have two distinguishing characteristics, namely, it has a very large fact base(and some what moderate size rule base) and whenever such a system is invoked by a query, it is expected to respond with all of the possible solutions to that query rather than only one solution as in the AI-oriented logic processing systems[3]. Deductive databases [2] and data-intensive expert systems are good examples of the data-intensive logic-base systems.

The traditional implementation of data-intensive logic-base systems [4,5] associates a relational database management system(RDBMS)[6] and the inference procedure of Prolog[7], to EDB and IDB, respectively. The RDBMS and EDB, on one hand, and Prolog and IDB, on the other hand, form two processes that run either concurrent to each other or in a master/slave fashion on a general purpose computer. When Prolog encounters an extensional predicate (subgoal), a request is send to RDBMS to search the corresponding relation for tuples that satisfy the instantiated predicate. RDBMS returns, in turn, all of the tuples found during that search. Since Prolog needs only one tuple to continue its search for a solution, the rest of the returned tuples have to be saved for future use by Prolog upon backtracking to find additional solutions. This implementation is elegant since it couples two well developed technologies, the relational database and Prolog to construct the logic management system. Unfortunately, however, such coupling has resulted in slow and inefficient logic systems. The inefficiency is attributed to the fact that a large amount of storage is needed in Prolog to buffer the sets of tuples generated from searching the base relations. Low speed is attributed to the fact that Prolog uses the backtracking mechanism to generate all of the solutions for a query. To illustrate this point consider the rule[1] "p(X,Y):-q(X,W),s(W,Z),t(Z,Y)," where the extensions of the predicates q, s and t are, respectively, the relations Q, S, and T of EDB. In general, finding all of the solutions to the query "?p(X,Y)" is equivalent to finding the join of the relations Q(X,W), S(W,Z) and T(Z,Y). The backtracking mechanism of Prolog uses the nested-loops join algorithm to perform such a join. Such algorithm performs well when one or few solutions are needed, however, when all solutions are needed, the nested-loop join algorithm has bad performance and other much better algorithms can be used [8,9].

To overcome the drawbacks of the traditional implementation, the inference procedure in such an implementation has to be modified for

---

[1] In this paper, we use the syntax of Prolog.

working with sets of values rather than one value. In addition, the backtracking mechanism must be replaced with more efficient methods for performing the join operation. The procedures designed to follow these guidelines are referred to as set-oriented inference procedures. Basically, two approaches to design such procedures have been followed , namely, the compiled approach[10] and the interpretive approach[11]. In the compiled approach, all of the intensional predicates of a given query are first resolved using the rules in IDB. The processing of the query is then continued by searching EDB to resolve the extensional predicates and construct the solution set. In the interpretive approach, on the other hand, the deduction steps and the search of EDB are interleaved.

In this paper, we propose a set-oriented inference model suitable for data-intensive logic systems. Such a model is interpretive and involves no redundant data processing. The implementation of such a model on a tree-structured multicomputer system is also presented.

A SET-ORIENTED INFERENCE MODEL

The proposed inference model is a modified version of that of Prolog. It adopts the depth-first search strategy of Prolog, but works with sets of values at a time rather than one value as in classical Prolog. That is, the proposed inference mechanism unfolds the AND/OR tree of a given query in a depth-first fashion until a leaf node (extensional predicate or subgoal) is encountered. The subgoal is, then, completely reduced using the corresponding relation of EDB. The reduction process produces a set of solutions to the uninstantiated variables in the reduced subgoal. Such a set is then passed on to the subgoal that will be reduced next. The solution set is used to instantiate some of the variables in the subgoal and the reduction of such subgoal is performed. The resulting solution set is combined with the old one and passed on to the next subgoal. Such a process continues until all of the nodes in the AND/OR tree are reduced. The various data structures and operations that are needed to support the inference mechanism are presented next.

Elements of the Model

To support the set-oriented depth-first search and the reduction process of the inference mechanism, two types of data structures are needed, namely, a set of relations[12] and a stack, together with the operations that manipulate these structures. These elements are presented next.

The Relations and the Relational Algebra Operations. A relation [12] is a mathematical structure defined on a fixed number of attributes and contains an arbitrary number of unique tuples(no duplicate tuples may exist in a relation). A relation can be normalized or non-normalized. A normalized relation is characterized by non-decomposit (atomic) attributes and can be represented, therefore, as a two-dimensional table in which the attributes are the columns and the tuples are the rows. A normalized relation can be used to store the instantiation and partial solution sets passed between the nodes of the AND/OR tree if the data types of the arguments within any literal of the logic base is restricted to type "constant" or type "variable"(type structure is not allowed). Otherwise, non-normalized relations are needed to store the value sets. In this paper, we restrict our logic bases such that the instantiation sets can be stored in normalized relations(tables). In such a case, the instantiated variables correspond to the attributes (columns) of the relation(table) and the sequences of values which represent the instantiations to these variables are the tuples(rows) of the relation.

During the processing of the AND/OR tree of a given query, the proposed inference mechanism makes use of a relation called the current relation(RC). RC is used to carry the instantiations and the partial solutions that are passed from one node to another during such processing. As RC moves between the nodes of an AND/OR tree, it gets modified by interacting with these nodes or with other relations, the extensional relations for example. These modifications are equivalent to performing the relational algebra operations[13], selection, equi-join(or simply join) and semi-join, projection and the union operations, on RC and/or the other relations.

The Control Stack. The control stack saves the control information needed to implement the depth-first search of the query's AND/OR tree. During the search of this tree, the stack saves the "And" and "Or" nodes along the current active search path. Together with the non-leaf or-nodes, some other information needed to successfully evaluate these nodes are saved.

Dynamics of the Model

The processing of queries using the proposed inference model is presented here through the following example: consider the processing of the query "?p(a,Y)" against the following simple non-recursive logic-base:

$$p(X,Y) :- q(X,W), s(W,Z), t(Z,Y) \qquad (1)$$
$$t(Z,Y) :- c(Z,Y,Y1) \qquad (2)$$
$$t(Z,Y) :- d(Z,Y) \qquad (3)$$

where q, s, c and d are extensional predicates. Their extensions are, respectively, the relations Q, S, C, and D. Figure 1 presents the state of the control stack as well as the corresponding unfolded portion of the tree at the various points of the query execution. The inference mechanism, in response to "?p(a,Y)", initializes first an instantiation relation for p(X,Y), namely, $RI_p[X]$, and stores in it the instantiations of the variable X, the constant a. p(X,Y) is, then, "pushed" on the stack as an or-node[2], together with a pointer to $RI_p[X]$. This is depicted in step 1 of Figure 1. The processing continues by "popping" the top of the stack, the node "p(X,Y)", and finds out that it is an or-node. The inference mechanism searches the rule base for a rule that unifies with such a node. Rule 1 is found. A relation, called the current relation RC is initialized and a copy of $RI_p[X]$ is placed into it. The or-node "p(X,Y)" is again pushed on the stack. The head of the unifying rule is pushed on the stack as an and-node. Each of the literals in the body of the rule is pushed on the stack as an or-node.[3] These actions are depicted in step 2.

---

[2] If the query is a conjuction of literals, then, each of these literals is pushed on the stack as an or-node.
[3] Some heuristics can be used, at this point of execution, to determine the order in which the literals are pushed on the stack.

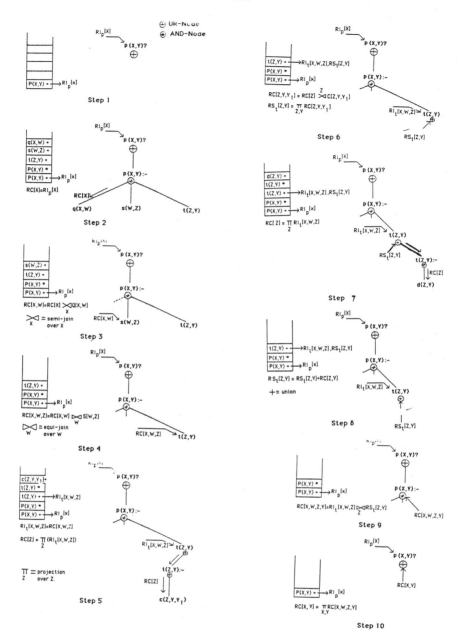

Figure 1. The Evaluation of the AND/OR Tree for the query "p(a,Y)?."

The inference mechanism continues by popping the current top of the stack, namely, the or-node $q(X,W)$. The search of the rule base for a rule that unifies with such a node fails and, therefore, $q(X,W)$ is an extensional predicate. The corresponding extensional relation $Q[X,W]$ is, then, joined with the current relation $RC[X]$ to form the new current relation $RC[X,W]$. This is depicted in step 3. Step 4 shows the sequence of events performed to reduce the new top of the stack, the or-node $s(W,Z)$.

Popping the current top of the stack, namely, the or-node $t(Z,Y)$, and searching the logic base for a rule that unifies with such a node, yields rule 2. The node "$t(Z,Y)$" is pushed back on the stack as an or-node. In addition, $RC[X,W,Z]$ is copied to the relation $RI_t[X,W,Z]$ and a pointer to RI_t is saved together with the or-node t on the stack. The head and body of rule 2 is pushed on the stack. A new current relation $RC[Z]$ is initialized to the projection of the instantiation relation $RI_t[X,W,Z]$ on the variable Z. This sequence of actions is depicted in step 5.

Step 6 depicts the processing of the stack two top nodes, the or-node $c(Z,Y,Y1)$ and the and-node $t(Z,Y)$. In step 7 and 8, the left subtree of the or-node $t(Z,Y)$ is unfolded and, then, reduced, respectively. Step 9 depicts the complete reduction of the or-node $t(Z,Y)$ resulting into the new current relation $RC[X,W,Z,Y]$. In step 10 the processing of the and-node $p(X,Y)$ results in projecting $RC[X,W,Z,Y]$ on the variables X and Y to yield the current relation $RC[X,Y]$. This relation carries all of the valid solutions to the and-node $p(X,Y)$. Finally, the or-node $p(X,Y)$ is reduced and the projection of the current relation $RC[X,Y]$ over the variable Y, is returned to the user as the solution set to the query "$?p(a,Y).$"

The inference model, presented above, has two important features, namely, it uses the depth-first search strategy and it is set-oriented. The fact that the inference mechanism is depth-first has permitted us to find for it an elegant stack-based implementation. In addition, the maximum number of temporary relations that has to be saved and maintained during the processing of an AND/OR tree is proportional to the number of or-nodes in a path that links the root of the AND/OR tree with the deepest leaf-node in the tree. Thus, the number of relations is linear with respect to the number of levels in the AND/OR tree. A substantial saving in storage cost relative to the other search methods(breadth-first search method for example). The fact that the proposed inference mechanism is set-oriented has replaced backtracking with much better techniques to solve the subgoals within the body of a rule. Furthermore, the amount of control information needed to be saved on the control stack is substantially reduced in comparison with those needed to control the execution of Prolog programs. One must notice, however, that the proposed inference model does not totally eliminate backtracking. Still some form of backtracking, a set-oriented backtracking, is used to find and combine all of the solution sets that are generated from searching the various paths that descend from a given non-leaf or-node(subgoal).

In [13], we have implemented and evaluated the performance of the proposed inference mechanism. An interpreter for such mechanism has been developed by modifying an already existing Prolog interpreter. The two interpreters ran on a single-processor computer which stores a relatively small, main-memory-resident logic base(program). We benshmareked the two interpreters with queries that have narrow and deep, wide and shallow and full binary AND/OR proof trees. In all of these cases and even for a small number of facts, the set-oriented inference mechanism has been found to be many times faster than the traditional one.

THE TREE-STRUCTURED MULTICOMPUTER

The Hardware Organization

The relational algebra operations generated interpretively by the inference mechanism in response to a user query can be implemented using the more primitive search and sort operations[8]. Within the context of very large extensional bases, a tree-interconnected multicomputer implements both of these operations efficiently. Such a system consists of a number of processing units organized into a binary tree. The nodes of the tree represent the processing units and the branches represent the communication links between these units. The nodes in the tree intercommunicate by passing packets of information. The extensional (fact) relations are uniformly distributed between the nodes of the tree. In addition to its share from the extensional relations, the root node stores the temporary relations generated during the processing of the AND/OR tree. The root node is implemented as a powerful multiprogramed mini/microcomputer with its own long term high capacity secondary storage.

The rest of the processing nodes in the tree are implemented as moderate size computers, each of which consists of a processor and two types of memory, namely, a high speed random access memory(RAM) and a moderate size disk-like secondary storage. A node stores its portion from the extensional relations together with some auxiliary structures that provide fast accesses to those relations. A node in the tree implements five basic operations, namely, search, sort, broadcast, split and merge. The operation "search" finds all of the tuples in a node which satisfy a certain criteria.

The operation "sort" sorts a collection of tuples within a node based on one or more fields within these tuples. A tree node implements two variations of the sort operation, namely, sort with duplicates removal(sort-With) and sort without duplicates removal(sort-without).

The "broadcast" operation within a node replicates the packet of information received from the node's parent, keep one copy to itself and sends one copy to each of the node's two immediate children. On the other hand, the "split" operation partitions a packet (normally contains a set of tuples) received form the node's parent into three subsets, the node retains one of these subsets, and each of the other two subsets is send to one of the node's children. The "merge" operation within a node takes three packets, each containing a set of sorted tuples, one form the node itself and the other two from the node's two children, and produces one sorted set of tuples. This set of tuples is, then, forwarded to the node's parent. Similar to the sort operation, the merge can be with or without duplicates removal.

The interconnection of the processing units in the form of a binary tree and the implementation of the above operations in each of these units have resulted into a fast parallel machine for performing the searching and sorting of very large relations, the two most basic operations in implementing the relational algebra operations. In implementing the search operation, such a machine distributes, not only the processing part of such an operation, but also the I/O part. This is very important in the context of very large relations since several studies have shown that an I/O bottleneck do exist in the machines which centralize the I/O part of the search operation[14].

Using the sort and merge capabilities of each node in the tree-structured multicomputer, the tuples of an extensional relation or the tuples which result from the parallel search of an extensional relation can be sorted on one or more fields while moving them upward towards the root. Such a sort is referred to as the up-sort. Using the split, sort and merge capabilities of each node in the tree, another type of sorting, down-sort, can be performed. Using such an operation, a temporary relation stored in the root node gets sorted. When executing the down-sort operation, the referenced relation is read into the main memory of the root node. If the relation fits in such memory, then, it is sorted in the root node. Otherwise, the tuples of the relation which can not find space in the root's memory are split (using the split operation in the root) into two sets, each of which is send to one of the root's children. The splitting operation continues until all of the tuples in the relation find enough main memory space in the nodes of a certain level of the tree, or the tuples reach the leaf nodes. The various sets of tuples are, then, sorted, in parallel, in the nodes of the tree. The sorted sets, then, form one sorted set at the root as they are successively merged while moving upwards towards the root node.

Performing the Relational Algebra operations

The execution of the relational algebra operations on the tree-structured multicomputer is performed in the root node, possibly in cooperation with the rest of the nodes in the tree. Executing a selection operation which reference a temporary relation involves invoking the search operation in the root node to find those tuples from the temporary relation which satisfy the selection criteria. On the other hand, the execution of the selection operation referencing an extensional relation involves the broadcast, by the root node, of the search operation together with the selection criteria to all of the processing nodes. The processing nodes, then, search, in parallel, for those tuples in the nodes which satisfy the broadcast search criteria.

The projection of a temporary relation over one or more attributes is performed in the root node by first eliminating the unwanted attributes from the referenced relation. If the result set of tuples are sorted, then, the duplicate tuples are removed by the root node using a linear scan of the tuples in the set. If the result set is not sorted, then, it is first sorted using the down-sort technique presented above. Then, the duplicate tuples are removed by the root as the sorted tuples arrive at the root node. The execution of the projection operation referencing an extensional relation is performed by broadcasting the sequence of operations, " search, sort-with and merge-with," together with some appropriate arguments to all of the processing nodes in the tree. In parallel, each of these nodes executes such sequence of operations. In response to the search operation, a processing node accesses its own portion of the relation to be projected and removes from it the unwanted attributes. In response to the sort-with operation, the set of tuples resulted from the search operation is sorted and the duplicate tuples are removed. During the execution of the merge-with operation the sets of the sorted tuples travel upward towards the root of the tree. The execution of the merge-with operation in a processing node results in merging the node's own set of tuples together with the two sets of tuples forwarded from the node's two immediate children. During such a merge any duplicate tuples are removed. The tuples of the projected relation finally arrive at the root of the tree as two sets of sorted tuples. The root node, then, performs its own merge-with operation on its own set of tuples and the incoming ones to produce the duplicate-free projected relation.

Within the context of the proposed inference model, the semi-join operation reference normally a temporary relation stored in the root node and an extensional relation. The execution of the semi-join operation on one or more attributes of the two relations is carried out by first obtaining the values of these attributes from the temporary relation and then broadcast them together with a search operation to all of the processing nodes in the tree. The processing nodes, in parallel, find all of the tuples, in the extensional relation, with join attribute(s) values that match the broadcast ones. The result sets of tuples are, then, sorted and send upward to the root node. On its way to the root, the sets of sorted tuples are merged into a totally sorted relation at the root. The (equi-)join between a temporary relation and an extensional one is performed by first executing a semi-join operation. The result relation arriving at the root is then joined with the temporary relation. If the temporary relation is sorted on the join attribute(s) then the root node performs the join using a simple merge operation. If the temporary relation is not sorted then it is first sorted using the down-sort technique. The join of the two sorted relations, then, follows in the root node.

The union operation of two relations is executed in the root node whenever both of these relations are sorted using the merge-with operation. If one or both of the relations are not sorted, then, they are first sorted using the down sort technique, then, the root node union the two sorted sets of tuples as before.

IMPLEMENTING THE INFERENCE MODEL ON THE TREE-STRUCTURED MULTICOMPUTER

The inference mechanism presented in section 2 can be implemented using two processes, the inference and data-management processes. These processes run concurrent to each others in the root node of the tree multicomputer and exchange information through message passing. The inference process interfaces the user to the system, stores, in its virtual space, the rule base, implements the control stack, performs the query optimization and performs the inference steps. In response to a query, the inference process generates a stream of high level operations, mostly of the relational algebra operations type. These operations are send to the data management process for execution. The data process, on the other hand, is responsible for storing and managing the temporary and the extensional relations and supervises the processing of the operations received from the inference process.

The inference process executes the query "p(a,Y)?"(refer to step 1 of Figure 2) by pushing the literal p(X,Y) on the control stack. A request to create a temporary relation and name it RI_p is send to the data management process. The set of instantiations ({a}) to the query is also send to the data process and is stored in the relation RI_p. In step 2, the inference process sends the data process a request to create the temporary relation RC and store in it a copy of the relation RI_p. In step 3, the inference process issues to the data process a request to perform the semi-join of RC and the extensional relation Q based on the shared attribute X and store the result in RC. In addition, a request to sort the new RC on the variable W is send to the data process. The data process performs the semi-join using the algorithm presented in section 3.2. The tuples of the result relation are sorted using the tree structure while these tuples are moved upwards to be stored at the root. The generation of high level operations by the inference process continues until the AND/OR tree is completely reduced(control stack is empty). At this point, the inference process requests the tuples of the projected RC from the data process. When the inference process gets these tuples, it hands them over to the user.

CONCLUDING REMARKS

In this paper, an inference model suitable for supporting the processing of data-intensive logic bases is presented. Such a model is set-oriented and uses the depth-first search to evaluate the AND/OR trees of logic queries. The fact that the inference mechanism is depth-first has permitted us to find an elegant stack-based implementation for it. In addition, the maximum number of relations that has to be saved during the processing of an AND/OR tree is at most linear with respect to the number of levels in that tree. We have also presented a tree-structured multicomputer system to support the various relational algebra operations that are generated by the inference mechanism during the processing of an AND/OR tree.

In implementing the proposed inference model, we have centralized the storage and the processing of the temporary relations into the root node of the tree multicomputer. We intend to investigate the effect of distributing such relations and their processing among all of the nodes in the tree. In addition, the stack-based implementation of some types of recursive queries is another research direction we intend to follow.

References

[1] Genersereth, M. R. and Ginsberg, M. L., "Logic Programming." CACM, Vol. 28, No. 9., 1985, pp. 933-941.

[2] Gallaire, H., Miker, J. and Nicolas, J. M., "Logic and Databases: A Deductive Approach." Computing Surveys, Vol. 16, No. 2(June 1984), pp. 153-185.

[3] Qadah, G. Z. and Nussbaum, M., "Logic Machines: A Survey." Proceedings of NCC, AFIPS Press, 1987, pp. 265-278.

[4] Boas, H., Boas P. and Doedens, C., "Extending a Relational Database with Logic Programming Facilities." Document No. TR 13.195. IBM INS Development Center, The Netherlands, November 1984.

[5] Chang C. L. and Walker, A., "PROSQL: A PROLOG Programming Interface with SQL/DS." Proc. of the First International Workshop on Expert Database systems, pp. 378-396, 1984.

[6] Kim, W., "Relational Database Systems." Computing Surveys, Vol. 11, No. 3, September 1979.

[7] Clocksin, W. F. and Mellish, C. S., "Programming in Prolog." Spriger-Verlag, 1984.

[8] Bitton, D., et al., "Parallel Algorithms for the Execution of Relational Database Operations." TODS, Vol. 8, No. 3(September 1983), pp. 324-353.

[9] Qadah, G. Z.,"The Equi-Join Operation on a Multiprocessor Database Machine: Algorithms and the Evaluation of their Performance." Proceedings of the fourth IWDM, 1985.

[10] Reiter, R., "Deductive Question-Answering on Relational Databases." In Logic and Databases(H. Gallaire and J. Minker, Eds.), Plenum Press, 1978.

[11] Minker, J., "Search Strategy and Selection Function for an Inferential Relational Systems." TODS, Vol. 3(1978), No. 1.

[12] Codd, E. F., "A Relational Model for Large Shared Data Banks." CACM, Vol. 13, No. 6(June, 1970), pp. 377-387.

[13] Nussbaum, M. and Qadah, G. Z., "An Inference Mechanism for Large Knowledge-Based Systems." Technical Report # 86/3, Institute for Integrated Systems, ETHZ, Switzerland, December 1986.

[14] Boral, H. and Dewitt, D. J., "Database Machines: An Idea Whose Time has Passed? A Critique of the Future of Database Machines." Proceedings of the third IWDM, 1983, pp. 166-187.

A SHARED MEMORY ARCHITECTURE FOR MANJI PRODUCTION SYSTEM MACHINE

J. MIYAZAKI, H. AMANO, K. TAKEDA, H. AISO

Department of Electrical Engineering Keio University
3-14-1 Hiyoshi, Yokohama 223 Japan

Abstract

In this paper, an architecture for the parallel execution of production systems called MANJI is described. MANJI is a MIMD type system and consists of tens of powerful processing units (PUs). All the PUs have special shared memory, VMRM (Virtual Multiple Readout Memory). VMRM supports a large virtual logical space which allows the reading of data simultaneously with minimal copies of data and conflicts on the bus. This system also provides a mechanism for effective message multicast. OPS5 is adopted as the specification language for MANJI. OPS5 is compiled into a data flow graph (M-RETE network), and this network is divided and mapped to each PU statically. According to this network, PUs matches the production rules in parallel and communicate with other PUs through VMRM if necessary. The performance of MANJI is evaluated under several programs.

1 INTRODUCTION

Production systems are widely used for implementing expert systems, because description, addition, or even the entire rewriting of rules is easy. To produce expert systems, rapid prototyping is important. However once the rule set becomes concrete, ease of rapid prototyping spoils the execution speed of production systems[AG]. Most existing expert systems do not change their rule set during their execution, because the management of the rule set becomes difficult when dynamic adding / deleting of rules is employed.

Parallel execution is one of the approaches for speeding up production systems[For80]. There are two main approaches for speeding up production systems in parallel:

(1) Fine grain approach: This approach employs thousands of relatively small processors with relatively small local memories. The DADO project [SJS82] falls into this group.

(2) Coarse grain approach: This approach employs tens of powerful computers with large local and shared memories. The PSM project [AGW86] and our MANJI [JMA87] are in this group.

We have adopted OPS5 as the specification language because it is one of the most successful production systems, and many application programs have been implemented. Forgy and Gupta have found that if an RETE network is used for matching, the degree

517

of inherent parallelism of OPS5 is in *tens* rather than thousands. We compile OPS5 into a data flow graph based on the RETE network [Gup86]. Thus, the coarse grain approach is suitable for our objective. The fine grain approach is advantageous if there are thousands of changes in the working memory (WM) simultaneously. However, OPS5 does not support this feature, and the inherent parallelism of OPS5 is not large enough for the fine grain approach.

The PSM project adopts a simple shared memory architecture. However when very fast processing units are adopted, bus congestion becomes the main problem. In our approach, we adopted a special shared memory architecture which is suitable for parallel execution of production systems and reduces the bus congestion.

1.1 The M-RETE Network and Token Passing

The RETE network is a kind of data flow graph, and its purpose is the effective searching and matching for sequential OPS5 [For82]. We modified the RETE network so it can execute in parallel, and this network is called the M-RETE network. The network is obtained by compiling the condition part of each rule. Figure 1.1 shows an example of the M-RETE network. Figure 1.1 corresponds to the condition part of the following 2 rules:

$$(p\ rule1\ (c1\ \hat{}attr1\ 10)\ --> \ (remove\ 1))$$
$$(p\ rule2\ (c1\ \hat{}attr2\ <x>)\ (c2\ \hat{}attr1\ <x>)\ --> \ (modify\ 2\ \hat{}attr1\ 20))$$

The M-RETE network consists of three kinds of nodes: test nodes, L-two-input nodes, and terminal nodes.

A test node tests whether or not the current token matches a constant in the working memory elements. The test involves string matching, numerical equality, and the greater or smaller than relation.

L-two-input nodes have memories at their right and left inputs and store tokens which reach these nodes. Thus the network is able to memorize the state of the previous match phase. After a token has arrived, L-two-input nodes compare tokens stored in its left input memory with tokens stored in its right input memory. If an L-two-input node finds a pair of tokens that can be matched, it makes a larger token and passes it to the successor nodes.

If a terminal node is activated, the production rule instances corresponding to this node are added to / deleted from the conflict set.

The network is folded over test nodes to prevent redundant searching. Therefore, test nodes can have multiple successors.

A token consists of the information about a change in WM. The following are example of tokens:

$$(+\ C1\ \hat{}attr1\ 10) \qquad (-\ C2\ \hat{}attr2\ 15)$$

The first token indicates the adding of the class C1 attribute 10 to WM, the second indicates the deleting class C2 attribute 15 from the working memory. If the first token is sent to in the network in Figure 1.1, this token will activate the *rule1* terminal node and is stored in the L-two-input-node which is connected to the *rule2* terminal node.

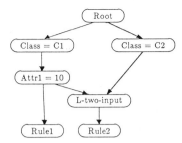

Figure 1.1 M-RETE network

2   DESIGN CONCEPT FOR MANJI

In this section, the design concept for MANJI is described. The concept is divided into two levels: the algorithm level and architecture level.

2.1   Overview of The Algorithm

There are three methods for mapping the nodes of the M-RETE network into each PU:

1. Map every node dynamically according to a scheduler. This is employed by the PSM project.

2. Map every node statically into each PU. This is employed by the Fine-grain RETE algorithm in the DADO project[Sto84].

3. Map every node statically into each PU, and within each PU, nodes are evaluated dynamically in the order of token arrival. This is the method adopted in MANJI.

Most of the typical expert systems do not change their rule sets after debugging, and after compilation the M-RETE network does not changed at all. Thus we can realize the data dependency between nodes statically at compile time. We map each node into each PU to obtain the highest parallelism possible. Because of the degree of inherent parallelism of OPS5 under the RETE network, tens of parallel processors are enough. In MANJI, the rule set is compiled into one large M-RETE network at the first stage, and this network is divided into several nodes. The data dependency among these nodes is statically analyzed, and each node is mapped in such a way as to obtain the highest parallelism possible and executed dynamically by the order of token arrival. The details of the mapping of the M-RETE network are described in section 4.

2.2   Overview of The Architecture

To make the best use of a relatively small degree of parallelism, an MIMD (Multiple Instruction stream Multiple Data stream) type machine with tens of powerful PUs is advantageous for our approach. Recent developments in 32 bit general purpose micro-processors enable us to use powerful processors economically. We have designed MANJI as an MIMD machine using such microprocessors. The most important problem of such a parallel machine is how to connect these microprocessors. To adapt the characteristics of parallel algorithms described above, the communication mechanism for MANJI should provide the following features:

1. Two kinds of communication are needed for MANJI. One is for WM and the other is for sending tokens in the M-RETE network. Since characteristics of these two kinds of communication are different, a communication mechanism of MANJI should support both of them.

2. Since the size of WM and the M-RETE network can be enlarged, the size of the shared storage must be large.

3. Communication mechanisms should provide enough performance to avoid bottle-necking, and they also should be economical.

Since each node of the M-RETE network is assigned to processors statically, the relationship between data in WM shared by processors is decided at compile time. A processor also recognize to which processor it should send tokens to in the M-RETE network. To take advantages this feature, we propose a shared memory system named "Virtual Multiple Readout Memory" for MANJI. This system supports high performance communication for both WM and token passing in the M-RETE network with minimal copies of data and conflicts on the bus.

3 VIRTUAL MULTIPLE READOUT MEMORY

3.1 The Basic Concept of Virtual Multiple Readout Memory

An interleaved memory connected with a switching network, like the Omega-network is a structure widely used in recent parallel machines [DG83][AGo83][GFP]. However, these networks are expensive even if VLSI technology is utilized. Another method for reducing bus conflicts without a switching network is using multi-port memory. Since the amount of reading from WM or the M-RETE network is far larger than the amount of writing, this approach is advantageous for a production system. Virtual Multiple Readout Memory (VMRM) is a kind of multi-port shared memory system suited for production systems.

There are two major methods for constructing a multi-port memory system for a parallel machine. One is by utilizing a specially designed memory chip [Cha], and the other is by providing all PUs with the same copy of data [TN80]. Since the former method is designed for small size (3 to 10) processors, the latter method is advantageous for MANJI.

This method is called Multiple Readout Memory or MRM. In MRM, each PU has its own communication memory and controller (Figure 3.1). These communication memories are interconnected with each other via a bus. Data written into the communication memory from the attached PU is also written into the same location in all communication memory through the bus. When reading data from MRM, a PU reads from its adjacent communication memory, and all PUs can access the given address independently or simultaneously. There is no reading collision. When writing data, a high speed arbiter selects one PU. Basic functions for synchronization among PUs (eg. Test&Set) are provided by the controller.

MRM provides a high communication capacity with only a simple bus. However, the following problems still remain:

(1) To store full data copies, the total amount of memory becomes great. The cost becomes great even if recent economical CMOS RAM is utilized.

(2) Usually a PU does not access all the data of shared memory. However, the PU is forbidden to access MRM while data is being written, even if the data is not necessary for the PU.

If each PU can recognize at the compile and mapping time which shared data must be accessed, it is sufficient that each PU saves only the shared data which the PU must access. Figure 3.2 shows the basic concept of Virtual Multiple Readout Memory (VMRM). In this memory, the logical space of shared memory is divided into a certain page size, and each PU provides its page table. When data is written into a shared memory space, the page table is referred to and the inner address is obtained to save the data in its communication memory. If the page is unnecessary for the PU, a special value (all-1 in this case) is obtained from the table, and the data is discarded. The contents of the page table are decided at compile time, and provided at the beginning of parallel computation. This method provides the following advantages:

(1) A PU can read data from its own communication memory while another PU is writing data into a page which is unnecessary for the reading PU. Reading does not conflict with the writing into an unnecessary page.

(2) There is no actual memory for the entire global logical address, and the communication memory can usually be small because only pages necessary for a PU is stored in it.

VMRM is designed based on this concept. To adapt it to production systems, we introduce different types of pages each of which provide special functions.

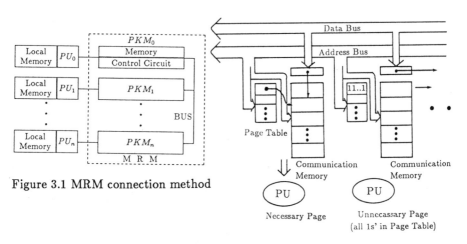

Figure 3.1 MRM connection method

Figure 3.2 Concept of VMRM

3.2 Separation of Shared Memory Area

In many applications, shared memory is used for two purposes. One purpose is synchronization of processes using Test&Set, Semaphores, or other synchronization functions. For this purpose, a hardware controller for managing synchronization is necessary. Another purpose is transferring information from one process to other processes by accessing the shared data.

In most application programs, the amount of shared memory used for the latter purpose is far larger than that for the former. In particular in production systems, writing requests into WM are issued only in the Act phase. Therefore, few words of shared memory are needed for synchronization, and most of the area is used only for simple writing or reading. Hardware synchronization mechanisms are not necessary for such simple writing or reading. Therefore, such an area can be located in the local memory, which can be enlarged easily by using economical dynamic RAM chips.

We divide shared memory into the synchronization area and the data communication area. Logically, all pages are used either for synchronization or data communication. Physically, a certain amount of memory with a controller is provided in the communication manager. Pages for synchronization are assigned to this memory, and pages for data communication are located in a large space local memory (Figure 3.3).

When data is written into a synchronization page, the synchronization mechanism in the communication manager is activated. On the other hand, data which is written into a data communication page is transferred into the local memory through a queue using a DMA (Direct Memory Access) mechanism. As mentioned above, data written into unnecessary pages is discarded. If the amount of the synchronization area becomes great, a swapping mechanism between the communication memory and the local memory is necessary. However, for WM, the size of communication memory is not so large and such a mechanism is not needed. Using this method, a large shared memory is supported for WM with minimal hardware.

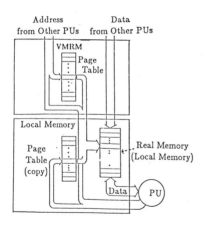
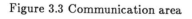

Figure 3.3 Communication area

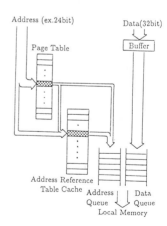

Figure 3.4 Token passing page

3.3 Communication Mechanism for Token Passing

WM is efficiently supported using the above described VMRM. However, in order to share the M-RETE network when using a static mapping method, a shared memory system is not suitable. In a static mapping method, each processor performs tasks corresponding to nodes of the M-RETE network. Since tokens are transferred among nodes in the match phase, small sized packets need to be exchanged among processors. Therefore, we support special pages for token passing in VMRM. This area is called the token passing page and is illustrated in Figure 3.4. The difference between this page and the data communication page of VMRM are the following:

(1) In this area, another address table is referred to by the address from the page table when data is written into (Figure 3.4). An entry of the address table corresponds to the size of one token.

(2) The local address obtained from the page table and tokens are pushed into two sets of queues. The processor recognizes data arrival by checking these queues.

Using this mechanism, this area of VMRM can be regarded as a message multicast mechanism rather than shared memory. One shared address can be assigned to a link in the M-RETE network. A processor can send a message to multiple processors through a link by writing into a logical address of this area. Since there are high fanout test nodes in the M-RETE network, a token is often sent to multiple nodes in the match phase. Because of this characteristic, a processor is needed for sending messages to multiple processors at the same time, and this mechanism works effectively.

3.4 Details of The Communication Mechanism in MANJI

Figure 3.5 illustrates a communication mechanism in MANJI. Each PU provides a large local dynamic RAM and Communication Manager. From a user point of view, the communication mechanism in MANJI is a simple shared memory which is divided by a certain page size. There are five kinds of page in this system. The function of a page is decided by 3 bit tags in the Page Table. Note that the function of a page is decided by each processor independently.

(1) Data communication page: Data written onto this page is stored in the local memory. This page is used for shared memory without synchronization, like WM.

(2) Synchronization page: Data written onto this page is stored in a high speed memory in the Communication Manager. Test&Set, Semaphore and other functions for synchronization can be performed using the hardware controller.

(3) Token passing page: When data is written onto this page, the Address Table is accessed. Local address and data which are pushed into queues, also work to perform message multicasting. This page is used for token passing in the M-RETE network.

(4) Unnecessary page: When data is written onto this page, it is discarded.

(5) Private page: This page is private for each PU. Accessing of this page never influences the communication mechanism. Instructions are stored in this page.

To cope with the larger size of the M-RETE network, the Address Table for the token passing page needs to be enlarged in future. In this case, the Address Table should be located in local memory and the table in the Communication Manager is used as a kind of cache. If a data is written onto a token passing page which provides no corresponding table in the Address Table in the Communication Manager, the whole system is locked and the table is swapped from local memory into the table in the Communication Manager.

Since such a staging of the table degrades performance, the size of a page and the swapping strategy must be carefully decided.

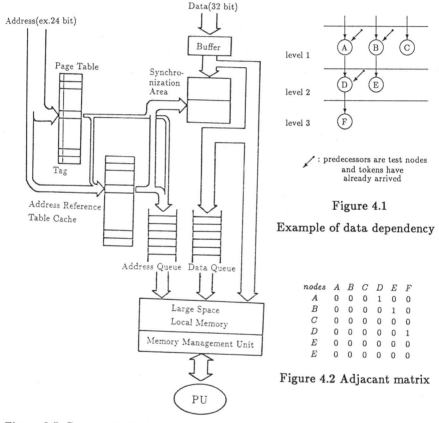

Data(32 bit)

Address(ex.24 bit)

Buffer

Page Table

Synchro-
nization
Area

Tag

Address Reference
Table Cache

Address Queue Data Queue

Large Space
Local Memory

Memory Management Unit

PU

Figure 3.5 Communication mechanism in MANJI

level 1

level 2

level 3

↗ : predecessors are test nodes
and tokens have
already arrived

Figure 4.1

Example of data dependency

nodes	A	B	C	D	E	F
A	0	0	0	1	0	0
B	0	0	0	0	1	0
C	0	0	0	0	0	0
D	0	0	0	0	0	1
E	0	0	0	0	0	0
E	0	0	0	0	0	0

Figure 4.2 Adjacant matrix

4 MAPPING THE M-RETE NETWORK

In our approach, the M-RETE network is divided and mapped into each PU statically. We have two choices for dividing the M-RETE network:

(1) Dividing at the rule level: Rules are divided into small groups before compiling. If we divide the similar rules into different groups, distribute each group into a different PU, and compile each group independently, we can obtain a divided network. Rules which are similar can be matched in parallel.

(2) **Dividing at the node level:** All the rules are compiled into one M-RETE network, and we divide the network in such a way as to extract as high a degree of parallelism as possible.

When we divide the network at level (1), the load balancing of the PUs is low. If only one rule is affected by updating WM in the Act phase, the whole network for this rule is in one PU, and thus matching is processed only by this PU. Thus we have chosen the division at level (2).

First we compile the OPS5 program into one large M-RETE network, and then divide the network into node units. We then analyze the data dependency among nodes, and map each node into each PU statically.

From our experience in the first version simulator of MANJI on the $(SM)^2 - II$ general purpose multi processor[HAm85], the ratio of processing time for a test node to an L-two-input node is about 1 : 20. In the M-RETE network, test nodes appear in the early stage of the network, and L-two-input nodes and terminal nodes appear in the latter stage of the network. Thus the processes for test nodes do not dominate the whole execution, but they are processed at the very first stage of the match phase, and after this stage the processes for L-two-input nodes begin. There exist a few test nodes which have very high fanout (e.g. Nodes which test class names or attributes). For these nodes, in MANJI multicasting is supported by hardware (VMRM). To avoid load unbalance, high fanout test nodes should be mapped into different PUs. The processes for L-two-input nodes dominate the rest of the execution, and thus the data dependency among L-two-input nodes and terminal nodes should be analyzed.

4.1 Mapping Algorithm for The M-RETE Network

The mapping algorithm for the M-RETE network utilizes the characteristics of the M-RETE network which are described in the previous section.

1. Search high fanout test nodes and map these nodes into different PUs.

2. Map the other test nodes into PUs at random.

3. Make an adjacent matrix consisting of L-two-input nodes and Terminal nodes.

   (a) Analyze data dependency among L-two-input nodes and Terminal nodes.

   (b) Map the same level nodes into different PUs as possible.

An example of Step 3 is shown in figure 4.1. In figure 4.1, node A, B, and C are L-two-input nodes, and at least one of the predecessor is a test node. The tokens have already arrived through VMRM. Node C, D, and E are Terminal nodes. Figure 4.2 shows the adjacent matrix for Figure 4.1. In this matrix, the arc from node A to node D is represented by 1 in element (0,4). Using this matrix, data dependency levels among nodes can be analyzed. In Figure 4.1, Node A, B, and C are in level 1, D and E are in level 2, and node F is in level 3. In Step 3, A, B, and C are mapped into different PUs, and D and E are also mapped into different PUs. Nodes in level 1 and nodes in level 2 can be mapped into the same PU. because nodes in level 2 are processed after nodes in level 1.

A precise analysis should include test nodes, but because of the ratio of processing time for test nodes to that of L-two-input nodes, before processes for L-two-input nodes begin, most of the processes for test nodes have been finished. Thus an analysis including only L-two-input nodes and terminal nodes is sufficient. Generally, precise analysis of data dependency is an NP-complete problem, but our analysis is not a burden at compilation. We evaluate our mapping algorithm in section 6. Within each PU, nodes are executed dynamically according to data arrival. In the next section, we describe the execution of nodes in each PU.

5 PARALLEL EXECUTION AND VMRM

In this section several points for implementation are described. First, the execution algorithm is shown. Next our interpretation of the links of the M-RETE network and tokens to VMRM is described.

5.1 The Parallel Execution Algorithm

After mapping nodes to each PU, the M-RETE network is ready to be executed in parallel. Within a PU, the nodes are executed dynamically according to data arrival. There is a process scheduler in each PU, and the process priorities are:

test process > L-two-input process > terminal process

As described in section 4, the ratio of execution time for the test process to that of two-input process shows that the test process has priority over the L-two-input process. Because terminal processes must synchronize at the conflict resolution phase the L-two-input process has priority over the terminal process.

The abstract algorithm for parallel execution is the following:

1. Initialize: Load the node interpreter into each PU. Distribute units of the M-RETE network to each PU. Set initial WM elements and generate tokens.

2. Repeat until no rule is activated.

   2.1 Match: Multicast tokens from the root in a pipeline manner.
      a. **for each** token **each** node **do**
      b. **case** (node is a test node), test tokens. If test is true, multicast tokens to successors, else delete tokens.
      c. **case** (the node is an L-two-input node), examine whether both sides of the inputs are reached. **If** both are reached, compare tokens in the left input memory with those in the right input memory. **If** one of the inputs is not reached, process switching occurs.
      d. **case** (the node is a terminal node), the rule instance associated with this node is added to / delete from the conflict set.
      e. process switching occurs.
      f. **end for**

4. Conflict resolution: One of the rule instances is selected in the conflict set.

5. Act: the action part of the selected rule is executed. WM is updated. Tokens which correspond to changes in WM are generated for the next match.

6. **End Repeat.**

5.2 Interpreting The M-RETE Network Using VMRM

First the links in the M-RETE network must be assigned to one linear address of the token passing pages. Thus numbering is needed for these links. To reduce the number of page faults, links in the M-RETE network are assigned to the address of VMRM as follows:

(1) test nodes with high fanout must be assigned from the first page of VMRM. These pages remain permanently in VMRM during the execution.

(2) The nodes in a PU which have unassigned input after step 1 are numbered and assigned to the VMRM address.

A node interpreter is loaded into each PU. It interprets nodes and searches the Arrival Detect Queue in order to receive tokens from other PUs. A kind of process switching mechanism to perform data driven operations is necessary. Node interpretation is suspended when the node needs a token from other PUs and the token has not arrived yet. In this case, process switching occurs, and another node starts to be interpreted. When there is no node to be interpreted, the interpreter searches the Arrival Detect Queue. At that time, if a token from another PU exists, the suspended node needing the token which has arrived starts to be interpreted again.

6 PERFORMANCE EVALUATION OF MANJI

In this section, first, the effect of the static allocation method is confirmed. Then, the performance of MANJI is evaluated using a simulator under realistic conditions. The following four example programs are used in this section:

(1) HANG-A expert system: number of rules = 80 This is the trouble shooting expert system for the hardware of $(SM)^2 - II$ general purpose multiprocessor system.

(2) Arizuka expert system: number of rules = 1036 This is the expert system for making input file for a queuing simulator.

(3) Wine advisor: number of rules = 67 This is a wine advisor program for various types of meals.

(4) Monkey and banana program: number of rules = 20 Monkey and banana planning program.

6.1 Effect of The Static Allocation Method

To evaluate our static mapping algorithm, we made an algorithm evaluator for parallel execution using MANJI. We compare these three algorithm.

(1) Our mapping Algorithm: This algorithm was described in section 4.

(2) Dynamic scheduling: This scheduling simply allocates nodes to idle PUs.

(3) Random Mapping: Nodes are mapped statically into each PU at random.

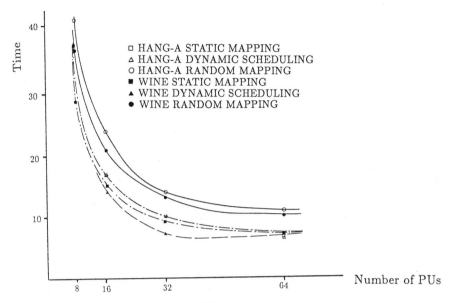

Figure 6.1 Effect of static mapping

Figure 6.1 shows the simulation results. Table 6.1 shows the number of nodes in each program.

The number of nodes	HANG-A	Wine advisor	Monkey and banana
Test nodes	120	77	23
L-two-input nodes	185	149	28
Terminal nodes	80	67	20
Performance degradation	12.8%	8.6%	—

Table 6.1

In Figure 6.1, there is no difference between our static mapping and the dynamic scheduling. Random mapping takes about 140 % more time. According to this result, our mapping is as good as dynamic scheduling which is adopted in PSM, and static mapping is reasonably powerful for the parallel execution of the M-RETE network.

6.2 Evaluation of Architecture

To evaluate the performance of MANJI exactly, we constructed a simulator which consists of the following three parts:

(1) M-RETE network node interpretor and tracer

(2) Mapper

(3) Processor simulator

The M-RETE network node interpretor interprets the example programs under the parallel algorithm described in section 5, and records the state of nodes and tokens. The Mapper assigned M-RETE nodes to processors using algorithms described in section 4. The processor simulator simulates exactly the processor and bus status based on informations from the M-RETE network tracer and Mapper. Using this method, an evaluation of MANJI can be made which includes the loss of process switching. We set the bus cycle time at the unit time, and assume the following values:

Time for interpreting a L-two-input node	: 100
Time for interpreting a constant atom equation test node	: 6
Time for interpreting a constant number equation test node	: 18

These values are decided from the speed in the M-RETE network interpreter.

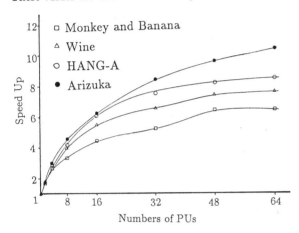

Figure 6.2 Speedup ratio

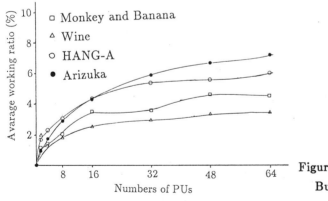

Figure 6.3
Bus occupying ratio

6.2.1 Performance of MANJI

Figure 6.2 shows the relationship between the number of PUs and the speedup ratio. In small problems, the performance gain is not very high if the number of PUs is over 32. In these cases, the loss of performance is mainly caused by insufficient parallelism in programs. If the example program is large enough like the Arizuka expert system, the performance of MANJI with 64 PUs is close to 10 times higher than that of a single PU. Figure 6.3 shows the relationship between the number of PUs and the bus occupying ratio. The bus is occupied only 8%, even if the number of PU is 64. Figure 6.4 shows a trace of the number of PUs which issue the writing requests. There are 5 peaks in this figure, and these peaks are caused by multicast from test nodes for 5 tokens. This shows the pipeline effect of tokens.

Although figure 6.4 shows the typical congested case in Arizuka expert system, the maximum number of writing request is 4. In MANJI, writing requests among nodes which are mapped into the same PU, are not issued to the bus. Moreover in VMRM, a processor can send a message to multiple processors through one link in the M-RETE network by writing only *one* global logical address. Therefore, the congestion on the bus is minimized. From these results, it appears that the capacity of the bus still has a margin, and VMRM provides enough performance. It is possible to connect larger number of PUs to cope with larger problems.

This result is not very high compared with the performance of PSM [AGW86]. However, the architecture of MANJI dose not provide a hardware scheduler, which will bottleneck the system. Since VMRM provides excess performance, MANJI is suitable for larger problems with a larger number of PUs.

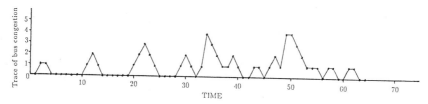

Figure 6.4 Writing requests

7 CONCLUSION

In this paper, MANJI, an architecture for the parallel execution of production systems, and its mapping algorithm have been presented and evaluated. According to the evaluation, VMRM in MANJI effectively supports a large amount of shared data and a token passing mechanism without bus congestion. The static mapping algorithm for nodes in the M-RETE network is not a burden at compile time, and is effective enough when compared to dynamic scheduling.

8 ACKNOWLEDGEMENTS

The authors are grateful to Toshiba corporation, especially Naomichi Sueda and Toshikazu Tanaka, for allowing us to analyze their large expert system. And the authors are grateful to Masahiro Nakazawa, for his advice in implementing the network compiler for the M-RETE network. Mr. Nakazawa is now a software specialist at Nihon Digital Equipment Corporation.

531

References

[AG]   C. L. Forgy A. Gupta. *Measurements on production systems.* Technical Report CMU-CS-83-167, Carnegie-Mellon University.

[AGo83]   A.Gottlieb. et al. The NYU ultracomputer-designing an MIMD shared memory parallel computer. *IEEE Trans. on Computers*, vol. C-32(No.2):pp.175–189, Feb. 1983.

[AGW86]   A. Newell A. Gupta, C. L. Forgy and R. Wedig. Parallel algorithm for rule-based systems. In *Proc. of 13TH Annual International Symposium on Computer Architecture*, 1986.

[Cha]   S.S.L. Chang. Multiple-read single-write memory and its applications. *IEEE. Trans. on Computers*, vol C-29(No.8):pp.689–694.

[DG83]   D. Gajski. et al. Cedar-a large scale multiprocessor. In *Proc. of the International Conference on Parallel Processing*, pages pp.524–529, Aug. 1983.

[For80]   C. L. Forgy. *Notes on production systems and Illiac IV.* Technical Report CMU-CS-80-130, Carnegie-Mellon University, 1980.

[For81]   C. L. Forgy. *OPS5 User's Mannual.* Technical Report CMU-CS-81-135, Carnegie-Mellon University, 1981.

[For82]   C. L. Forgy. Rete: a fast algorithm for the many pattern/many object pattern match problem. *Artifitial Intelligence*, September 1982.

[GFP]   G.F.Pfister. et al. The IBM research parallel processor prototype (rp3): introduction and architecture. In *Proc. of the International Conference on Parallel Processing*, pages pp.764–771, Aug.

[Gup86]   A. Gupta. *Parallelism in Producion Systems.* Technical Report CMU-CS-86-122, Carnegie-Mellon University, 1986.

[HAm83]   H.Amano. et al. $(SM)^2$: Sparse Matrix Solving Machine. In *Proc. of 10TH annual International Symposium on Computer Architecture*, June 1983.

[HAm85]   H.Amano. et al. $(SM)^2 - II$:the new version of the Sparse Matrix Solving Machine. In *Proc. of 12th Annual International Symposium on Computer Architecture*, June 1985.

[JMA87]   H. Amano J. Miyazaki and H. Aiso. Manji: an architecture for production systems. In *Hawaiian International Conference on System Sciences*, January 1987.

[PSRO85] J. McDermott A. Newell P. S. Rosenbloom, J. E. Laird and E. Orciuch. *R1-Soar: Experiment in Knowledge Intensive Programming in a Problem-Solving Architecture.* Technical Report CMU-CS-85-110, Carnigie-Mellon University, 1985.

[SJS82]   R. C. Mills S. J. Stolfo. Dado: a tree-structured machine architecture for production systems. In *AAAI*, 1982.

[Sto84]   S. J. Stolfo. Five parallel algorithms for production system execution on the Dado machine. In *AAAI*, Aug. 1984.

[TN80]   T. Nakagawa. et al. A multi-microcomputer approach to discrete system simulation. In *CompCon80 Spring*, Feb. 1980.

[YKa82]   Y.Kaneda. et al. The O(n) Time computing method of n linear simultaneous equations on the matrix broadcast-memory connected array processor system. In *IFIP 24.2*, pages pp 350–355, 1982.

A REAL-TIME PRODUCTION SYSTEM ARCHITECTURE USING 3-D VLSI TECHNOLOGY

Satoshi FUJITA, Reiji AIBARA, and Tadashi AE

Electrical Engineering, Faculty of Engineering,
Hiroshima University
Saijo, Higashi-Hiroshima, 724 Japan

INTRODUCTION

Production systems are a special class of expert systems which are strictly data driven, and a mechanism which is most frequently applied to actual systems [1][2].   Since it possesses attractive properties such as the ease of description, it might be applied for the real-time software if sufficiently fast execution time is obtainable [3].

They, however, have a serious problem essential for inference systems, that is, it might cause the combinatorial explosion due to the nondeterminism.   The adequate selection of conflict resolution strategy, therefore, becomes to be an essential problem for real-time production systems, in particular [3].   In practical systems, e.g., OPS5 [4] provides conflict resolution strategy MEA and LEX, while OPS83 [5] permits user to describe his own strategy.   Although they offer us sufficient performance in practice, to accomplish the real-time processing and to describe a problem-oriented strategy always compel users to be skillful with problems to be solved.

On the other hand, for supporting of the real-time processing in production systems, to save the time (i.e., the cost) for matching is also indispensable, since it usually spends much of time in the series of phases of the processing, namely,

> the conflict resolution phase,
> the action phase, and
> the matching phase.

Forgy has concentrated on this point, in particular, and proposed an efficient pattern matching algorithm Rete [4] which is a typical state-saving method [6] to reduce the cost for matching.   Rete algorithm, however, spends much of time for state modification caused by the deletion of working memory elements (in short, WME) from the working memory (in short, WM), though it could save the matching cost by keeping the history of matching in a specific data-structure (they call it Rete network).

The cost for matching is also reducible by applying the multi-processor architecture. DADO2 implemented by Stolfo, et al. [7] is a tree-structured massively parallel multiprocessor architecture with 1023 components. It applies a parallel search method in the multiple single-instruction and multi-data stream scheme to shorten the time for matching. The architecture, therefore, is quite adequate to a special class of problems, namely, almost decomposable searching problems such as the membership problem [8].

On the other hand, Aiso, et al. have proposed MANJI, which is a bus-connected multiprocessor architecture with rather few number of processors [9]. It could provide a good cost/performance in point of the efficient execution of Rete algorithm, whose parallelism is at most dozens as is pointed out by Gupta, et al [6]. Nevertheless, it does not resolve the problem as before that the algorithm is not very efficient if the modification of WM happens frequently.

In this paper, we propose an architecture **ISAC** (an Integrated production System Architecture with inference Control), which is a multiprocessor architecture for real-time production systems. ISAC explicitly introduces the concept of "state" for inference to reduce the combinatorial explosion [3]. Furthermore, it assumes that three-dimensional integrated circuits (in short, 3-D IC) technology [10][11] has to be established in the near future, namely, it adopts the 3-D IC technology to provide a fast matching mechanism which would resolve the above problem.

In the following, we overview the basic concept of ISAC, namely, the concept of state control. Next, we describe a fast pattern match mechanism which could reduce the cost for matching in production systems. The practical use of the proposed method is estimated in the last section.

STATE-CONTROLLED INFERENCE IN ISAC

Production systems essentially possess the nondeterminism which should cause the combinatorial explosion. To avoid this, several conflict resolution strategy have already been proposed and actually implemented [5][12]. ISAC explicitly introduces the concept of "state" which assists the conflict resolution, and could be reflected to the architecture for real-time production systems.

Suppose the following production rule to be;

$$\langle X \rangle \rightarrow \langle Y \rangle,$$

which means that if the condition X is satisfied, it causes the action Y according to the firing of the rule.   In ISAC, we can explicitly append the "state" to rules as follows;

$$\langle X,S \rangle \rightarrow \langle Y,S' \rangle,$$

which means that X is applied on the state S, and the firing also causes the state transition from S to S', namely, the inference is controlled by the state.   This situation is similar to that of the scheduler in the real-time operating system, which treats the collection of status on each task as a state, and inputs them as if it was a state-controlled machine.   Note that the rule $\langle X \rangle \rightarrow \langle Y \rangle$ means $\langle X,S \rangle \rightarrow \langle Y,S \rangle$ as a default, i.e., it means the rule, on which the state is not changed by the firing.

Consequently, we use the following representation;

$$\langle X_1, S_1 \rangle \rightarrow \langle Y_1,S_1' \rangle$$
$$\langle X_2, S_2 \rangle \rightarrow \langle Y_2,S_2' \rangle$$
$$\cdots\cdots\cdots$$
$$\langle X_k, S_k \rangle \rightarrow \langle Y_k,S_k' \rangle,$$

where state control is performed **deterministic,** though the drive of conditions X_i (i=1,2,...,) by other rules or external events might be happened **nondeterministic.**

FAST PATTERN MATCHING IN ISAC

Interest of many reseachers are focused on the fast match phase realization as well as the conflict resolution problems.   ISAC provides a fast pattern match mechanism assuming a special purpose hardware, namely, the processor with three-dimensional integrated circuits (in short, 3-D IC) technology.

Optically-connected three-dimensional common memory

3-D IC is a new device fabrication technology which is expected to realize not only a high-integrated, but also a high-functional semiconductor chip [11].   Although many researches on 3-D IC is actively attempted, most of them is device-oriented, and therefore, the architectural proposal on the 3-D IC is seriously required.

From this point of view, we have already proposed an idea of three-dimensional common memory (in short, 3-D common memory), which is an application of the broad inter-layer bandwidth of the 3-D VLSI [11]. In particular, the **optically-connected 3-D common memory** chip, in which each layer is connected optically to each other, is under development at the Integrated Circuit System Research Center of Hiroshima university, which is already in the design stage. The optical inter-layer connection in 3-D IC is expected to bring us not only high integration of layers, but also high yield on the fabrication stage because it requires no vertical wiring essentially. Furthermore, it can be used as a multi-read and multi-write memory, since any processor connected to each layer can independently access its own memory-cells.

The figure 1 (a) illustrates the principle of the optically-connected 3-D common memory. Each of arrayed memory-cells on each layer has two pairs of light emitting diode (in short, LED) and photo diode (in short, PD), where every light emission is externally controlled by the light emission controller as is shown in the figure 1 (b).

Assume that a data is written on a memory-cell at j-th address on the i-th layer (the figure 1 (a)). It is optically propagated and written on memory-cells at the same address on adjacent two layers (the (i+1)-th and the (i-1)-th layers), which is indicated by the arrow (1) in the figure 1 (a). The propagated and written data also propagates to its adjacent layers (the (i+2) -th, the i-th, and the (i-2)-th

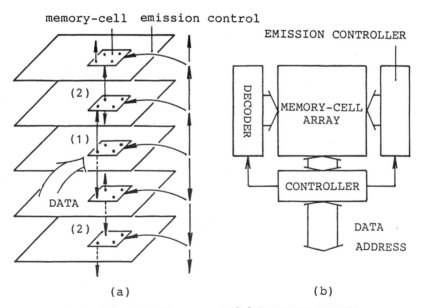

memory-cell emission control

EMISSION CONTROLLER

(2)

(1)

DATA

(2)

(a)

DECODER

MEMORY-CELL ARRAY

CONTROLLER

DATA

ADDRESS

(b)

Fig.1 The optically-connected 3-D common memory.
(a) The principle, and (b) the top view.

536

layers, which is indicated by the arrow (2) in the figure 1 (a)), since the signal for the light emission control is similarly propagated. By repeating similar propagation, contents of all memory-cells at j-th address can be kept identical. Note that the signal for emission control has to be turned off when a constant time is passed away from the turned-on time, to terminate the emission.

State memory

The figure 2 illustrates the block diagram of the inference engine in ISAC, which is composed of a controller, a production-memory (in short, PM), and m state-memories (in short, SM) with private m controllers (in short, CR).

The controller (not CR) repeats the series of operations similar to conventional production systems, that is, the conflict resolution, the action, and the matching phases, until the final results can be obtained. While the former two phases are executed on the controller by itself according to the state-controlled scheme as mentioned in

(other processors, database)

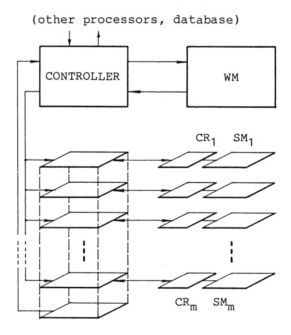

PRODUCTION MEMORY   STATE MEMORIES
((m+1) layers)

Fig.2 The matching mechanism in ISAC.

previous sections, the matching phase is performed on PM and SM, namely, we use them as an attached processor for pattern matching.   In
order to change the **state** of SM and to find the adequate productions,
the controller transfers the appended or removed WME after every modification of WM. (Note that WM and SM are margable.)

SM is composed of m memories denoted by SM_i (i=1,2,...,m), which
is separated due to the class (which is determined at the compile time)
of WME to be stored.   In order to fasten the access time, each SM_i is
structured by content addressable memory (in short, CAM) [14].

Each CR_i (i=1,2,...,m) has a queue which is long enough, and
performs the operation as in the producer-consumer fashion through the
queue.   From the view of PM, each CR_i performs the operation on SM_i,
in the following two modes.

(1) reference   input : key data (from PM)
                output: corresponding data (or, existence)
(2) write-in   input : data (from controller)
   (or delete) output: existence of the data

Production memory

The production memory (in short, PM) is structured by the optically-connected 3-D common memory.   The i-th layer of PM is connected
to SM_i (i=1,2,...,m), namely, the number of layers is the same as the
number of state-memories.

Suppose the following two productions to be;

```
(p    p1(C1 ^attr1<x> ^attr2<y> ^attr3 12)
        (C2 ^attr1<y> ^attr2<z>)
        (C3 ^attr1<x> ^attr2<z> ^attr3 10)
    → (remove 2)),                              and

(p    p2(C1 ^attr1<x> ^attr2<y> ^attr3 12)
        (C4 ^attr1<x> ^attr2 11)
    → (modify 1 ^attr3 10)).
```

Productions are stored in PM as shown in the figure 3, where each
row is corresponding to each layer of 3-D IC, and arrows between two
rows mean the shared data by different clauses in the same production.
The sharing of data is physically realized by the inter-layer connection allowed only for the same address, and therefore, it requires a

```
        p1            p2    ....              p1            p2  ....

C1:  (x,y,12)    (x,y,12)        C1:  (x,y,   12)(x,  y,  12)

C2:  (y,z)                       C2:  (   y,z)

C3:  (x,z,10)                    C3:  (x,   z,10)

C4:              (x,11)          C4:              (x,     11)

RHS:(remove 2)(modify 1 ...)   RHS:(remove 2)(modify 1 ...)

          (a)                              (b)
```

Fig.3   The data allocation in PM.
a) The stored data, and b) an optimal allocation.

little tactics such as the adequate allocation of variables at the compile time.

The deletion of WME from the SM_i is terminated in a constant time, since state-memories is classified by the class of stored WME, and is structured by CAM.   We, therefore, next mention the addition of WME and the searching of productions to be fired (the figure 4).   Suppose that the WME

(C1 ^attr1 10 ^attr2 2 ^attr3 12)

is appended to the working memory as a result of the previous firing.

It is firstly send to CR_1 through the first layer of the PM, since the class of appended WME is the "first" (the figure 4(a)).   The value of the WME is simultaneously broadcasted to productions on the first layer of PM which has the clause of the same class. CR_1 judges that whether or not there exists the same WME on SM_1 in a constant time using CAM mechanism, and reply the result to the centralized controller through PM.   If there exists, it terminates the state modification, and if not (the figure 4(b)), CR_1 writes the WME on SM_1 and starts the searching of productions which becomes available (i.e., be able to fire) by the appending of the WME, according to the following procedure.

PM transfers the actual value of variables which is determined by the appended WME, to the corresponding clauses in other productions (the figure 4(c)).   In this example, x=1 is sent to the C2 (in p1) and

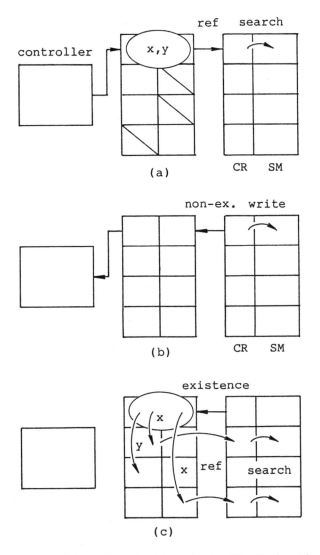

Fig.4 The searching of productions to be fired. (continued)

the C4 (in p2), and y=2 is sent to the C3 (in p1).   If all value of
variables in a clause (suppose that its class is i) are determined, the
CR_i reads out the clause in PM and transfer it to SM_i in order to judge
whether or not there exist the **same** WME on it.   If there are no such
clauses, remained clauses are evaluated in a specific priority, namely,
for the first clause (suppose that its class is j), the CR_j refers to
SM_j that whether or not there exist **corresponding** WMEs on it, and reads
out them sequentially, where the correspondence means that it is

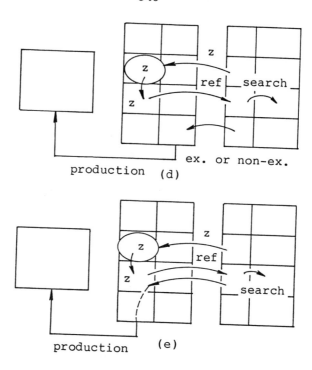

production   (d)

production   (e)

Fig.4   The searching of productions to be fired.

matched except for variables. The read data are transfered to the next clause (i.e., the layer) sequentially and similarly evaluated, namely, the evaluation of AND-parallelism might be performed in a pipelined fashion (the figure 4(d)(e)).

The proposed scheme also supports the parallel evaluation of different productions (i.e., OR-parallelism) using broad inter-layer bandwidth of PM, which essentially can be evaluated in parallel. In other words, PM is a kind of communication channels with broad bandwidth, to execute **streamed** evaluation of AND-parallelism **in parallel.** The order of evaluation is determined in static at the compile time, which might be in accordance with that of Rete algorithm [4].

ESTIMATION

In this section, we estimate the memory size of PM and SM to suggest the practical use of the proposed method.

The figure 5 shows a memory-cell circuit of the optically-connected 3-D common memory. Since two photo diode (PD_1, PD_2) are applied instead of two load transistors, optical and direct data writing to the memory-cell is available. Furthermore, since the light emission is externally controlled by a control line, the size of memory-cell can be quite small, i.e., it includes only eleven active elements per memory-cell.   It is remarkable that the number is twice of that for usual static RAM (with six transistors).

Suppose that the size of LED and PD are both 5 μm x 5 μm, and that gate length is 1 μm in the Mead and Conway design rule [15]. The total memory-cell size, at this time, is approximately 1000 μm^2, which means that it would realize 1 kbit/layer if the total memory area is 1 mm^2. The similar estimation is applicable to SM_i whose memory-cell circuit is illustrated in the figure 6.   By applying the same design rule, it causes 2 kbit/layer if the total memory area is 1 mm^2.

Above estimation means that, in the present technology, the proposed device architecture would be available if the number of productions are rather small (e.g., dozens), which should restrict the class of problems to be solved.   Nevertheless, it is suited to the multiprocessor environment in ISAC, on which the WM is separated for the parallel search [15], that the number of WME on one WM has to be rather

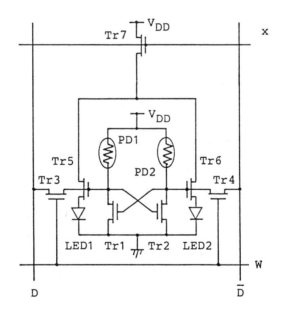

```
x   ; emission control line
w _ ; word line
D,D̄ ; data lines
```

Fig.5 A memory-cell of the optically-connected 3-D common memory.

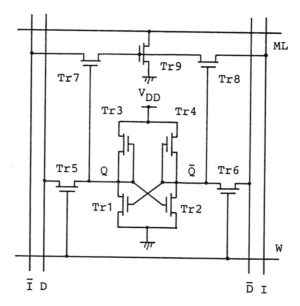

w _; word line
D,D̲; data lines
I,I̲; reference data lines
ML ; output line (wired or)

Fig.6 A memory-cell of the content addressable memory.

small.   To establish the validity of the proposed scheme, the waste of
PM due to the appropriate variable allocation, and the optimum scheduling of SM must be resolved and estimated, which is a problem in the
next step.

REMARKS

In this paper, a new architecture ISAC for real-time production
systems is proposed.   In particular, we concentrate on the conflict
resolution strategy and the fast matching phase realization, namely,
the concept of state-controlled inference and an idea of the fast
matching device architecture with 3-D IC technology is provided.

ISAC prototype is under development in our research group, which
does not include the support of 3-D IC technology. It might take us
several more years to fabricate the first optically-connected 3-D
common memory chip, however, it is surely expected to break the limitation of the conventional architecture with two-dimensional semiconductor chips.

For the future, we would continue the performance estimation of the proposed device architecture previous to the fabrication, in the actual application field. Furthermore, the effect of inference control should be evaluated on the prototype multiprocessor.

ACKNOWLEDGEMENTS

The authors wish to express their thanks to research staffs of Integrated Circuit System Research Center of Hiroshima University, especially, Professors M. Hirose and M. Yamanishi for their helpful advices on the device fabrication technology.

REFERENCES

1. Lehr, T.F. Carnegie-Mellon University, CMU-CS-85-126 (May 1985).
2. Kobayashi, S. IPS Japan, Vol.26, No.12, pp.1487-1496 (Dec. 1985), in Japanese.
3. Ae, T. and Aibara, R. IEICE Japan, Report SIG Computer System, CPSY 87-01 (June 1987), in Japanese.
4. Forgy, C.L. Artificial Intelligence, Vol.19, pp.17-37 (1982).
5. Forgy, C.L. tech. report, Production Systems Technology (1985).
6. Gupta, A., Forgy, C.L., Newell, A. and Wedig, R. Proc. 13th Annual Int'l Symp. Computer Architecture, IEEE/ACM, pp.10-19 (June 1986).
7. Stolfo, S.J. IEEE Computer, 20, 1, pp.75-83 (Jan.1987).
8. Bentley, J.L. Information Processing Letters, 8, 5, pp.244-251 (June 1979).
9. Miyazaki, J., Amano, H., Takeda, K. and Aiso, H. Proc. 1987 IPS Japan National Meeting, 7P-4, pp.207-208 (Mar. 1987), in Japanese.
10. Kurokawa, K., and Aiso, H. IPS Japan, 27, 7, pp.718-729 (July 1986), in Japanese.
11. Aibara, R. Doctoral Dissertation, Hiroshima university (1986).
12. Tano, S., Masui, S. and Funabashi, M. Proc. 1986 IPS Japan National Meeting, 5M-7, pp.1515-1516 (Mar. 1986), in Japanese.
13. Ogura, T. and Yamada, S. IPS Japan, Vol.27, No.6, pp.593-600 (June 1986), in Japanese.
14. Mead, C. and Conway, L. Addison Wesley (1980).
15. Aibara, R., Fujita, S. and Ae, T. Proc. 1987 IPS Japan National Meeting (Sep. 1987), to be published in Japanese.

ARCHITECTURAL EVALUATION OF A SEMANTIC NETWORK MACHINE

Tatsumi FURUYA, Tetsuya HIGUCHI, Hiroyuki KUSUMOTO,
Ken'ichi HANDA, and Akio KOKUBU
Electrotechnical Laboratory
1-1-4 Umezono, Sakura-mura, Niihari-gun, Ibaraki 305, Japan

ABSTRACT

This paper describes the architecture of the semantic network machine IXM and simulation results on its performance. IXM consists of an associative network with a large number of processing elements connected to it. Each processing element has two associative memories in order to take advantage of the possibility of parallel execution of basic operations in semantic network: association, set operation, and marker propagation. The associative network is a functional network whose node processor has also an associative memory for parallel marker propagation. Execution time of IXM does not necessarily depend on the size of semantic network because the basic operations of IXM can be executed in parallel.

INTRODUCTION

Semantic network is one of the typical knowledge representation schemes for declarative knowledge. Special purpose computers which utilize the parallelism in semantic network have been proposed [1-3] , because computers with the Von Neumann architecture are unlikely to be candidates for processing large semantic network at a high speed. Those are focused on the declarative knowledge processing and are not intended to process procedural knowledge which is important to describe practical applications flexibly with semantic network.

A knowledge processing system based on semantic network described is named IX (pronounced [iks]) and provides:

544

IXL - a semantic network language for knowledge representation, which can describe both declarative and procedural knowledge [4].

IXM - a parallel semantic network machine which is designed to process both declarative knowledge and procedural knowledge represented in IXL [5-6].

IXG - a graphical user interface which gives a comfortable environment of semantic network construction.

Marker propagation, set operation, and association are basic operations for a query processing in semantic network. IXM is designed to utilize the parallelism of those basic operations. IXM consists of a number of processing elements and an associative network which connects among the processing elements. Each processing element includes two associative memories which are intended to process the basic operations in parallel.

A feature of IXM is in assigning multiple nodes of semantic network to an associative memory of a processing element rather than assigning a single node to a register of a simple processing element. A semantic network is partitioned into sub-semantic networks and each sub-semantic network is stored in one of the associative memories in each processing element. Association and set operation are executed in parallel using the associative memory in each processing element. The other associative memory in a processing element is used to implement a marker driven model which enables the MIMD control of processing elements.

An associative network is used for parallel marker propagation. The network consists of a number of network processors which are connected in a pyramid shape. An associative memory is also used in a network processor to support parallel marker propagation.

Section 2 describes semantic network and IXL. Section 3 outlines IXM architecture, and shows the execution mechanism. Section 4 describes simulation results of IXM performance.

SEMANTIC NETWORK AND IXL

Semantic network is a well known knowledge representation scheme. Knowledge is represented with nodes and links in a form of network. A node represents a unique concept and a link represents a relationship between two concepts. An important characteristic of semantic network is an inheritance of concept. Properties of super-class are inherited by sub-class along links (e.g. *is_a* links). Figure 1 shows an example of a semantic network representation. The address of *computer_ division* is inherited by every section along the *is_a* links.

There are two basic phases in the knowledge processing system based on semantic network : (1) construction of semantic network, (2) information retrieval from semantic network. IXL is a semantic network language which supports those two phases efficiently. IXL provides two command groups. The first group is used for construction of semantic network. The second group is for queries. Semantic network construction commands have three arguments. The first argument is a link name which connects two nodes. The second and third arguments are node names which are connected each other by the first argument. For example, IXL command *link(is_a, animal, dog)* constructs a relation *is_a* between *animal* and *dog*.

In addition to the classical scheme of semantic network, IXL has the following features to support flexible knowledge representation.

(1) A link except system-support links can be described by semantic network. System-support links (*is_a*, *instance_of*, etc.) and user-defined links can be used for constructing a semantic network. A user-defined link is broken down by the system in the form of nodes and system-support links.

(2) A procedural knowledge is described as a clause of logic programming, and is linked to a node by a rule link. The rule *superior* in Figure 1 is an example of that. A procedural knowledge can be translated into a sequence of IXL commands. This means that the declarative knowledge and the procedural knowledge are represented uniformly in IXL commands. Therefore, we can expect that a dedicated machine designed for IXL will process both declarative and procedural knowledge efficiently.

A user who wants to retrieve information from semantic network issues an IXL command for a query. Query commands have the same three arguments as construction commands. If any arguments are not explicitly specified, IXL searches nodes which match the argument. For example, an IXL command *prop(address, X, hardware_section)* searches the address of *hardware_section* (see Figure 1) where the X is a variable argument to be searched. *Tokyo_Japan* is bound to X. In this example, the inheritance hierarchy along *is_a* is traversed.

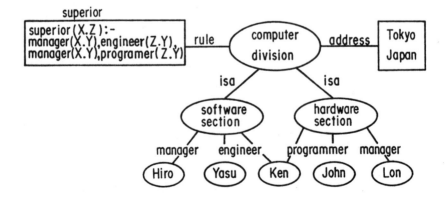

Figure 1. An example of semantic network

A search mechanism which traverses the inheritance hierarchy in semantic network, namely the implementation of IXL query commands is the most important function in IXL. Answer nodes can be searched by the use of marker information and the following four operations : (1) association, (2) set operation, (3) marker propagation, and (4) arithmetic operation. Marker is a one bit information which is transmitted along link(s) of semantic network. Marker can be stored in node(s).

A query that searches for a person who belongs to both *software_section* and *hardware_section* in Figure 1 is processed as follows : First, associate (search) the *hardware_section* and the *software_section* , then set marker No.1 and No.2, respectively. Markers are sent from the *hardware_section* and the *software_section* along the downward links (*manager*, *engineer*, and *programmer*). Marker No.1 is sent to all the members of *hardware_section* and marker No.2 is sent from the *software_section*. The marker bit No.1 and No.2 are ANDed to obtain an answer. *Ken* is the answer. This is a typical search sequence.

Arithmetic expression can be used for procedural knowledge description in IXL. Arithmetic operation is provided for that processing in IXM.

It would require a large amount of execution time, if we program those basic operations on a conventional machine. The association and the set operations have to examine every node one by one, and the marker propagation has to traverse links step by step. Therefore, we need a dedicated machine where the association, set operation, and marker propagation can be executed in parallel.

IXM ARCHITECTURE

Overall Structure

IXM is designed to process the knowledge which is written in IXL efficiently. The basic idea of IXM is to realize a highly parallel execution of the four basic operations (association, set operation, marker propagation, and arithmetic operation). IXM operates under the control of a host computer. IXM consists of an associative network and processing elements (PEs) as shown in Figure 2.

The associative network consists of connection pathes and network processors at each node of the network. One network processor at the bottom layer of the pyramid-shaped network connects four PEs. Each upper network processor is connected to four lower network processors. In addition, a network processor is connected to four adjacent network processors of the same layer. A network processor includes message routing logic and an associative memory to exploit the concurrency in marker propagation.

A PE includes an ALU and two associative memories. The ALU is used for the arithmetic operations for procedural knowledge processing. The first associative memory (called SNAM) is for the storage and the processing of semantic network. Association and set operations are executed in parallel using the function of the associative memory. A large semantic network is partitioned into sub-semantic networks and each sub-semantic network is stored in SNAM. One triple of semantic network (source node, link, destination node) is stored in one word of SNAM. Namely, multiple nodes are stored in SNAM in one PE.

The second associative memory (called IRAM) is to store the IXL command interpreter. The interpreter is written in IXM machine instructions which are executed in non-deterministically depending on the arrival of markers. IRAM searches executable IXM machine instructions.

The associative network is a functional network designed for parallel marker propagation. Network processors are connected in the shape of pyramid. The connection pathes between the PEs on the same layer of the network are not used in the first version of the IXM for the implementation convenience. The network treats the following three types of packet communication.

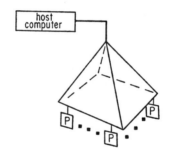

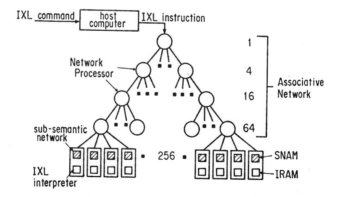

Figure 2. System organization

(1) Host-to-PE: Broadcast of an IXM command.

(2) PE-to-PE : Marker, value, and node identifier are transferred from PE to PE.

(3) PE-to-Host : Collection of computational results.

This network provides a special mechanism for parallel marker propagation. An associative memory is included in each network processor for this mechanism. This is shown in later section.

Execution Mechanism

The interface between the IXM and its user is IXL commands. User inputs an IXL command into the host computer to construct or search the semantic network. The host computer accepts the IXL command and broadcasts it to each PE via the pyramid-shaped network, as shown in Figure 2. The IXL command is input into the IXM one at a time from the host computer. Next IXL command is accepted after the end of previous IXL command.

All the PEs interpret the same IXL command in parallel because each PE stores the same IXL command interpreter. Each PE applies the IXL command to the sub-semantic network stored in each PE's SNAM. Once an IXL command is arrived at a PE, each PE interprets the command independently. That is, the IXM works under an MIMD control. The IXL command interpreter is a collection of IXM instructions. IXM instruction is executed non-deterministically depending on the arrival of marker.

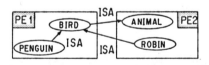

IDF (21 bit)	DSF (21bit)	LN (4b)	MBF(18b)
BIRD	PE2(1) ANIMAL	ISA	|·|
BIRD	PE1(4) PENGUIN	RISA	|·|
BIRD	PE2(2) ROBIN	RISA	|·|
PENGUIN	PE1(1) BIRD	ISA	|·|
SNAM1 (PE1)			

ANIMAL	PE1(1) BIRD	RISA	|·|
ROBIN	PE1(1) BIRD	ISA	|·|
SNAM2(PE2)			

LEGEND IDF: identifier field   LN: link name
DSF: destination field   -> PE No.(displacement)
MBF: marker bit field   RISA: reverse isa

Figure 3. SNAM organization and the partition of semantic network

It is necessary to know how a semantic network is stored in SNAM in order to understand the IXM instruction execution. Figure 3 shows the organization of SNAM and how the partitioned semantic networks are stored in SNAMs. The semantic network in the Figure 3 is partitioned into two sub-networks and stored separately in two SNAMs. One word consists of four fields: the identifier field (21 bits) , the destination field (21 bits), the link name field (4 bits), and the marker bit field (18 bits).

An SNAM word represents a link and the node which is connected to the link. The identifier field and the destination field are used to identify nodes. A node name is converted to a node identifier and stored in the identifier field. A link occupies two SNAM words to enable the marker propagation for both direction. The link name field indicates a system-support link such as *is_a* and *instance_of.* A user-defined link is described with nodes and system-support links. A triple (link,node1,node2) whose link is a user-defined link is translated to some triples whose link is a system-support link and stored in SNAM. The marker bit field contains 18 marker bits (numbered from 0 to 17). Each marker bit holds the result (marker) of the basic operations such as association and set operations.

There are three basic instructions (association, set operation, and marker propagation) in IXM instruction set. The association instruction sets a marker bit of a node whose name is specified in the instruction. Association of the identifier field (node name) is executed by the associative memory in parallel when a IXL command is accepted. The set operation can be executed by the associative memory, as markers are set in the marker field. Set operation (i.e. intersection) corresponds to find a word whose two marker bits are set. Set operation finds every nodes in parallel by SNAM. Set operation starts its execution when any marker bit is set. The marker propagation instruction is executed when a marker arrives to a node. The marker is passed to its destination.

For example, a query " What is a bird ? " to the Figure 3 is processed as follows. IXL command for the query is *ISA(bird,X)* and this command is interpreted by the next three IXM instructions.

associate(bird,1)   : associates *bird* node and set its marker bit No.1.
marker_propagation(1,isa,2) : when marker No.1 is arrived, send marker No.2
                                  along *is_a* link.
report(2)   : when marker No.2 is arrived, report it to the host computer.

These instructions are stored in every IRAM. IXL instruction is to be executable, when a marker which is specified in an argument of the IXL instruction is arrived at any node in PE. Thus, IXL instruction is called marker driven. When the IXL command is broadcast *association* instruction is activated. The *association* instruction sets the marker bit No.1 of *bird.* If a marker bit No.1 is set, *marker_propagation* instruction in

PE1 is activated. The *marker_propagation* instruction sends a marker No.2 along *is_a* link. Arrival of marker No.2 to *animal* activates *report* instruction of PE2. The *report* instruction returns an answer to the host computer.

Node of Equivalence

Markers are propagated through the associative network in parallel. It seems to be very effective in speeding up large semantic network processing. One problem in implementing marker propagation is a propagation from a node with many fanout nodes. Since such a node would have to repeat propagations as many times as the number of the links connected to it and would become a bottleneck in marker propagation. Nodes with hundreds of links appear frequently in semantic network applications because semantic networks are useful to represent taxonomical knowledge.

The authors introduced the idea of *nodes of equivalence* in order to solve this problem and exploit the concurrency in marker propagation. The idea is to partition the bottleneck node into nodes with a smaller number of connecting links and to distribute them among the PEs. A partitioned node is called a *node of equivalence*. For example, the student node in Figure 4 (a) is the bottleneck of marker propagation, because it must repeat propagations 26 times. Therefore, the student node is divided, for example in this case, into three *nodes of equivalence* as shown in Figure 4 (b). If the bottleneck node is partitioned into N *nodes of equivalence*, the parallelism increases N times.

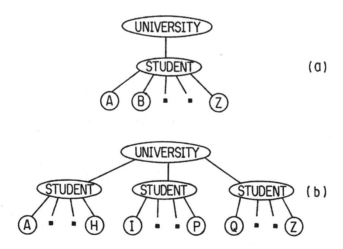

Figure 4. The nodes of equivalence

If a message is sent to one of the *nodes of equivalence*, the message has to be duplicated and sent to the other *nodes of equivalence*. For example, the hatched PEs in Figure 5 (i.e. B,C,D) contain the *nodes of equivalence*. If a message comes from the A and the destination is the B, the message is duplicated and sent to the C and the D by the network processors of the associative network.

Marker for the *node of equivalence* is duplicated in the network processor. An associative memory is used with a network processor to identify whether the marker is for a *node of equivalence* or not. Destination of marker is checked by the associative memory.

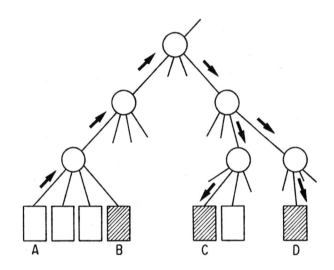

Figure 5. Message transfer using nodes of equivalence

PERFORMANCE STUDY

We discuss the performance of IXM based on some simulation results. We developed a simulator which simulates IXM at a register transfer level. The assumptions of IXM architecture are; the machine cycle of PE is 100 ns, the average access time of associative memory is 300 ns, the communication path is 64 bit width and its transfer rate is 100 ns. Knowledge bases written in IXL can be processed by the simulator. Our benchmark results is from a French wine knowledge base of three different sizes. Response time of queries, network contention, and semantic network allocation are studied.

The first study is a comparison of execution time of semantic network processing on IXM (with 128PEs) with that of a conventional computer (Micro VAX II). We have the IXL processor written in Prolog on Micro VAX II. Table 1 is the execution time of two queries to three knowledge bases of different sizes.

The query (1) asks the knowledge base whether a particular fact holds or not. In our example, an IXL command which asks whether the Chablis wine is rated as two-starred or not is issued. As shown in Table 1, a user can get an answer (yes or no) in about two second, although the execution time depends on where the fact is located in the knowledge base. The query (2) asks the knowledge base all the solutions of the query. An IXL command which asks to reply all the wines rated as two-starred is issued.

The execution time of this type of query increases abruptly as the size of knowledge base grows larger. A user have to wait fifteen minutes for the query to the knowledge base of 4500 links. This is because of the explosion of the search space. The result will show the same tendency as in Table 1, even if the IXL processor is implemented not in Prolog but in Lisp. On the other hand, as shown in Table 2, the result of IXM machine simulation shows that the total of IXM machine cycles required for query (2) does not increase abruptly as the the size of knowledge base grows. This is because IXM machine can find all the solutions in parallel by associative memory.

A semantic network is divided into many sub-semantic network and each sub-semantic network is stored in a PE. It is easy to understand that the allocation methods

Table 1. Execution time of the knowledge base (KB) search by IXL language processor on Micro VAX II

KB size	1600 links	3300 links	4500 links
query 1	66 - 600 msec.	66 - 1183 msec.	66 - 1633 msec
query 2	2.1 min.	8.7 min.	14.6 min.

Table 2. Execution time of IXM (micro sec.)

KB size	1600 links	3300 links	4500 links
query 1	156	211	240
query 2	245	276	356

Table 3. Effect of allocation methods : execution time (micro sec.)

	random allocation	width oriented allocation	depth oriented allocation
French wine KB	201	105	152
Tree with large funout	105	344	918

make effects on the performance. Table 3 shows the effect of allocation methods in cese of 128 PEs. Two semantic network and three allocation methods are studied. The first semantic network is the French wine knowledge base with 4500 links. The second one is a tree structured semantic network which has large fanout nodes. The first allocation method called *random* makes sub-semantic networks without consideration about the semantic network structure. The second allocation method called *width oriented* distributes equivalence nodes to different PEs as many as possible. The third allocation method called *depth oriented* does not use *node of equivalence* as possible. The difference between the width oriented and the depth oriented shows the effect of equivalence node. However, in general, the effects of allocation method largely depend on the structure of semantic network and queries to the network.

The associative network design will effect on the performance of IXM. As the parallelism of association and set operation is implemented perfectly by associative memories, the associative network is only one element which may limit the parallelism of semantic network processing. Figure 6 shows execution time of a query (2) for French wine knowledge base with 4500 links. The two curves in the Figure 6 shows the performance of two different associative network structures : binary tree, and quadruple tree.

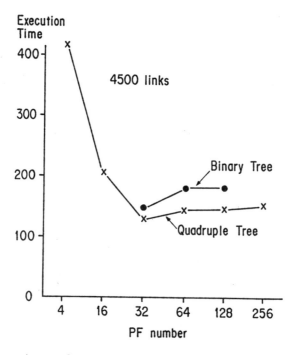

Figure 6. Effect of network contention

The results show the effect of contention of the associative network. When PE number is small, markers from PEs frequently conflict at the network. The descent part of the curve means the performance degradation by network contention. This means that we do not necessarily need so many PEs even in case of 4500 links. If a knowledge base size grows, large associative network (with large number of PEs) will be necessary to avoid network contention.

CONCLUSION

The semantic network described in IXL is a extended version of classical semantic network. Users can describe not only declarative knowledge but also procedural knowledge with IXL. IXM is a massively parallel architecture machine which is designed to process semantic network. IXM executes IXL commands efficiently.

We utilize associative memories to exploit the parallelism in semantic network processing. The associative memories in IXM are used for three purposes. The first is the utilization of parallel structure in association and set operation. The second is for parallel marker propagation. The third is the exploitation of the parallelism in IXL interpreter.

The simulation result shows that execution time of IXM does not so related to semantic network size compared with conventional machine. Fully parallel execution of association and set operation on SNAM contributes to this results. The simulation result about the network contention shows that parallelism of marker propagation is not so high compared with that of association and set operation in the case of French wine knowledge base. Though association and set operation are applied on every node, markers flow on a limited area of semantic network. This shows that our associative memory approach is reasonable.

In order to apply IXM to large knowledge based systems, it is important to develop an optimizing allocator which partitions a large semantic network and allocates each sub-semantic network onto a PE. Simulation result shows throughput of IXM is greatly influenced according to the allocation algorithms. An allocation method which utilizes the *node of equivalence* makes good effect on the performance. In designing optimizing allocator, analysis of communication will be necessary. This is our open problem.

We completed the work on the first version of IXL written in Prolog . Some knowledge bases were written in IXL. Now, we are building the IXM prototype with 32 PEs. The PE and the network processor of the prototype consist of Transputer and associative memory chips.

References

[1] S.E.Fahlman, "Design sketch for a million NETL machine", Proc. of First Annual National Conf. on AI, 1980.

[2] G.E.Hillis, " The connection machine", MIT Press, 1985.

[3] D.I.Moldovan and Yu-Wen Tung, ""Semantic Network Array Processor", Univ. of Southern California, Tech. Rep. PPP-84-2,1984.

[4] K.Handa, T.Higuchi, A.Kokubu and T.Furuya, "Flexible Semantic Network for knowledge Representation", to appear in Journal of Information Processing Society of Japan.

[5] T.Higuchi,K.Handa,T.Furuya and A.Kokubu, "A Semantic Network Language Machine", Proc. of EUROMICRO, 1985.

[6] T.Higuchi, T.Furuya, H.Kusumoto, K.Handa, A.Kokubu , "The IX Super Computer for Knowledge Based System", FJCC,1986.

AN ARCHITECTURE FOR VERY LARGE RULE BASES BASED ON SURROGATE FILES[1]

DONGHOON SHIN
P. BRUCE BERRA

Syracuse University, Syracuse, New York 13244-1240, USA

ABSTRACT

To support a large set of rule bases as well as ground facts, we propose an efficient retrieval method by transforming heads of clauses and facts into Concatenated Code Words (CCW) to form a surrogate file. By adopting the 'mode' declarations used in PARLOG, the heads of clauses can be represented by function-free terms, and then are transformed to CCW to be used as an index to gain access to the actual database. A simplified unification operation on surrogate files can be efficiently implemented by means of a specialized associative processor due to the uniform structure of surrogate files.

1

This work was supported by the Air Force Systems Command, Rome Air Development Center at Griffiss Air Force Base in New York, and the Air Force Office of Scientific Research at Bolling AFB in Washington DC under Contract No. F30602-85-C-0008. This contract supports the Northeast Artificial Intelligence Consortium (NAIC).

557

INTRODUCTION

Future computer systems will be expected to provide highly efficient management of large shared knowledge bases for knowledge-directed applications such as expert systems. Previous knowledge base systems such as ILEX (1) and DELTA (2) have the dual structure consisting of an inference engine and a knowledge base. These have attempted to combine a relational database system to manage the knowledge base with a logic programming system to serve as the inference engine. For efficient management of a large database, the Extensional Database (EDB) is separated from Intensional Database (IDB). Though this approach has exhibited a great deal of efficiency for handling a large set of facts (EDB), it may not be suited to applications supporting large rule bases (IDB) which heretofore have been assumed to be small enough to reside in the main memory. It has also been observed that most inefficiencies stem from the interface between these two very different systems.

On the other hand, in some recently proposed systems, there is no distinction between the IDB and EDB. That is, both facts and rules are managed and stored uniformly. A machine that uses the idea of database retrieval based on the unification operation is the Sabbatel's Prolog database machine (3). It can search desired data form secondary storages by the "on the fly" execution of unification. Sabbatel proposed the Prolog's top-down evaluation strategy with AND/OR parallelism and set-oriented processing to reduce the number of accesses to secondary storage. Recently, Yokota and Itoh proposed the "Relational Knowledge Base Model" to provide a machine with a uniform representation of the knowledge base (4). Unlike the relational database model that consists of only ground instances, this model can accommodate variables and complex structured terms. In this case, the exact match of database operations should be extended to unification due to the variables and structured terms that can appear in the knowledge base. However, the processing load required for such an operation on a large knowledge base stored in secondary storage is expected to be enormous. Furthermore, this approach can be inefficient because of the 'top-down' query evaluation strategy, especially when a large set of ground facts are involved.

Presented in this paper are techniques for managing a very large knowledge base to support diverse requirements for applications of logic programming systems based on surrogate files (5) and associative processors. We also propose an integrated knowledge base machine architecture that can effectively support very large sets of rules as well as facts in the context of logic programming environment.

The rest of this paper consists of the following; in the next section we give some basic definitions followed by restricted representations of clause heads to be used to form a surrogate file. Then we present the basic method of constructing a surrogate file for rules and facts, and describe the basic idea for unification on a surrogate file and an associative processor to realize it. This leads to the basic architecture of the proposed knowledge base machine and its parallel processing model, together with an example. Finally, we present some conclusions and suggestions for future work.

PRELIMINARIES

Conery (6) has classified the inherent parallelism in logic programming systems into three major categories: AND-Parallelism, OR-Parallelism and Low-level Parallelism. Our major concern here is a special case of OR-parallelism called search parallelism which has been defined as a parallel distributed search to find every clause with a head that unifies with the selected goal. Since a search performed by integrated knowledge base machines should be based on unification rather than equality, it is well known that an efficient implementation of unification is the central issue in logic based systems. Several processors dedicated to the unification operation have been proposed in recent years to accelerate this most time-consuming operation in logic programming evaluation (7)(8)(9).

Informally, the main purpose of unification is to make two or more terms identical by proper and the most general substitutions for logical variables in the terms. A term is defined as follows (10):

(1) A variable is a term denoted by a capital letter such as X,Y,Z,...

(2) A constant is a term denoted by a lower case letter such as a,b,..

(3) If f is an n-ary function and $t_1,..,t_n$ are terms, then $f(t_1,..,t_n)$ is a term.

Ever since Robinson introduced the basic algorithm of the unification operation for the resolution principle (11), more efficient algorithms have been proposed and the complexity of the unification operation has been analyzed by many researchers (12)(13). Among them, two algorithms (14)(15) are claimed to be linear. These algorithms are based on a complex data structure called Directed Acyclic Graph (DAG). Also, Morita proposed a linear representation of a term suited to stream processing of unification (16). The DAG and linear representations of a term are shown in Fig. 1 (a) and (b) respectively.

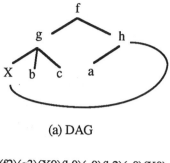

(a) DAG

(f2)(g3)(X0)(b0)(c0)(h2)(a0)(X0)

(b) Charcter String

Fig.1 The Representations of a Ter m(f(g(X,b,c), h(a,X))

Our major concern in implementing unification for very large rule bases in secondary storage, is finding all potential candidate clauses within a small amount of time so that we can deal with real time applications. Since the full unification on such data will require a heavy processing load, our goal may not be achieved without restricting unification. Furthermore, the results of (12) indicate that, since unification is inherently sequential, even parallel evaluation of a unification algorithm may not offer a considerable speed-up over a sequential one.

The major processing load stems from 'occur checks' to prevent the unification from entering an infinite loop. That is, when testing if a variable X unifies with a structured term **t**, a check should be done whether X occurs in **t** (i.e. {X/f(X)}). We can eliminate these requirements by adopting mode declarations to construct a 'standard form' of clauses as in PARLOG (17) where the structured arguments appearing in clause heads can be transferred to the bodies of clauses.

A PARLOG program that possesses a single solution consists of a sequence of guarded Horn clauses. A guarded Horn clause of PARLOG has the form

A:-$G_1,G_2,...G_m$:$B_1,B_2,...,B_n$.

m,n$\geq$0

If m=0 then the commit operator can be omitted. A candidate clause of PARLOG is one which succeeds in all input matching with the call (subquery) and whose guard literals ($G_1,G_2,...,G_m$) are proven to be true.

PARLOG exploits "mode" declarations for the clauses in the single solution relation to avoid the requirement of full unification, and to control process synchronization (17). A mode declaration for a predicate can constrain the unification between a goal and a clause (head) in a program. Mode declaration is of the form

mode $R(m_1, m_2, ..., m_k)$

where R is a predicate name and each m_i is either '?' or '^'.

An argument annotated with a '?' in the mode declaration for a predicate can only be used for input matching against the corresponding argument of a call. That is, the unification between a call and the head of the clause is successful only if the corresponding argument in the call is instantiated (i.e. not a variable). Otherwise the evaluation suspends. On the other hand, an argument annotated with a '^' must be used for output matching against a variable of the corresponding position of a call. In other words, the corresponding argument of a call should be an uninstantiated variable on unification. If the argument is not an uninstantiated variable, the unification fails.

The mode declaration is used to determine the 'standard form' of clauses at the first stage of compilation. In the standard form, all complex terms appearing in the heads of clauses can be represented as pure variables, and all input and output matching between a call and the heads of clauses are translated to explicit unification primitives instead of general unification.

Consider, for example, a simple PARLOG program

mode member(?,?).

member(H,[H|T]).

member(H,[X|T]) :- ~H=X : member(H,T).

where ':' is the commit operator and ~H=X is a guard.

This program can be mapped into the standard form

member(H,Y) :- [X|T]<=Y,H=X:.

member(H,Y) :-[X|T]<=Y,~H=X: member(H,T).

The term [X|T] that was in the second argument position of the second clause head appears as [X|T]<=Y because it has the mode '?'. Here '<=' is the one way unification primitive that can only bind variables in its left argument([X|T]). This implies that this term can only be used for input matching against the given argument Y of the call. The repeated use of the term H in the head of the first clause is detected as an implicit test because both terms have the mode '?'. Thus the term [H|T] is changed to [X|T] (here X is an arbitrary variable) and an explicit test unification primitive '=' is added in the guard. In order to change a non-variable term with the mode '^' to the standard form, the assignment unification primitive ':=' should be used in the body. The unification primitives of PARLOG are described in (17). Maluszynski and Komorowski (18) have also discussed the use of mode to constrain full unification.

Consequently, the structured arguments (e.g. [H|T]) in the clause head can be transferred to the guard or body of a clause as shown in the above examples.

SURROGATE FILES

Surrogate files are constructed by hashing transformation of terms. The principal techniques that we have considered for the construction of the surrogate file for very large ground facts in the logic programming framework include concatenate code words (CCW), superimposed code words (SCW), combinations of CCW and SCW, and transformed inverted list (TIL). But, we will use CCW to illustrate how the surrogate file technique can be extended to very large rule bases. The reader may refer to Berra (5) to see the construction of SCW and TIL for ground facts. Some simulation results about the size of surrogate files are also presented in (5). See Ramamohanarao (19) for the SCW representation of general terms containing variables and structured terms as arguments.

Suppose we have a fact called parent(timothy,johnson). We would first hash the individual values of each argument,

H(timothy)   H(johnson)

| |

010111111   010110000

concatenate them, and then attach a unique identifier to obtain the CCW

010111111 | 010110000 | uid

where the vertical line shows the boundaries.

The same unique identifier would also be added to the actual fact itself so that a CCW can be used as an entry for each fact via the unique identifier.

This technique has been used for partial match retrieval on large set of facts with varying degrees and cardinalities. In retrieving facts, we assume that the facts are stored in such a way that one first accesses the relation and then a particular tuple using a unique identifier. Thus, we do not need to transform the predicate name (e.g. parent) for the facts. We obtain the unique identifier from processing the surrogate file, and the name of the relation from the given query. Thus, the storage structure for the facts themselves would be very simple and the desired facts can be retrieved in at most two disk accesses.

Most relational operations such as selection and join, which are required for the bottom-up query processing in logic-oriented database systems, can be performed on the surrogate file rather than on the actual database. This makes relational operations much faster and increases the system's performance when a large volume of ground facts exist.

In a CCW representation of a clause head containing variables, we do not consider structured terms and assume that the clause head contains pure variables and constants as arguments based on the transformation technique by adopting the mode declaration.

Variables should be distinguished from constants. This can be done by setting the msb (most significant bit) of the CCW to ' 1 '. Unlike facts, there are only a small number of rules that define a predicate, i.e. rules with the same head. Thus, we need to transform the predicate name as well as arguments.

Suppose we have rules for 'ancestor',

ancestor(X,Y):-parent(X,Z),ancestor(Z,Y).

ancestor(X,Y):-parent(X,Y).

We hash the predicate name and arguments by the same hashing function used in CCW for facts. The number of arguments is also concatenated to the hashed value of predicate name.

H(ancestor)	2 (No. of Arg.)	H(X)	H(Y)
011100000	0010	100100111	100101001.

The CCW representations for the two rules would be the same except for the uid's to be attached to them.

0111000000010 | 100100111 | 100101001 | uid_1
0111000000010 | 100100111 | 100101001 | uid_2

Thus, a surrogate file can be used to find the corresponding bodies of clauses with which a goal can unify via uid's.

This method guarantees retrieval of all desired terms (clause heads or facts) although, due to possible collisions resulting from the hashing method some undesired terms may be retrieved. A longer word length for the CCW can minimize such collisions, and post retrieval comparisons can be used to eliminate unwanted terms.

In the next section, we describe how one might perform unification on a surrogate file by proposing a special associative memory for bidirectional don't care matches.

UNIFICATION ON SURROGATE FILES

In this section, we present the basic idea of unification on a surrogate file using an associative processor. We have shown in section 2 how to transfer the complex structured arguments in the head of a clause to its body. For simplicity, we assume that the query contains only pure variables and constants. Thus, the Query Code Word (QCW) can be encoded by the same technique as described in section 3.

First, for all constants in a QCW, the corresponding arguments of the CCW must be either the same constant or a variable in order for the terms to be unifiable (Input matching condition).

In the input matching step, we regard all variables as "don't care match" indicators. Unlike usual "don't care" matches, however, we need bidirectional don't care matches because the data residing in associative memory, as well as the QCW, may also contain variables. Since general associative memories do not provide this capability, a special associative memory is required. We designed an enhanced associative memory for bidirectional don't care matches, as shown in Fig. 2. Since by assumption only variables and constants appear in a QCW, input matching among a QCW and a number of CCW's, each representing a head of a clause, can be performed in $O(1)$ time [2] (i.e. constant time).

By input matching, most unqualified terms can be pruned. After input matching, we assume that the qualified terms (heads) are read one by one for further processing. Thus post processing will be required for only a relatively small number of terms, namely the qualified terms.

Obviously, the above condition is not sufficient. Consider, for example, two terms of the form $q(a,X,b)$ and $q(Y,a,Y)$. Though they satisfy the condition, they

---

[2]

To process a QCW with a longer word length than that of the associative memory's, the QCW should be split into parts and the unification performed on the parts in sequence. Since the unification for the QCW has to be performed in parts, the variable bindings along with the content of match registers resulting form that unification should be stored for the next unification. For simplicity, we assume that the word size of a QCW is always shorter than that of the associative memory.

are not unifiable. We need post processing for the shared variables that appear in arguments of qualified CCW's. If the same variable appears in arguments of a CCW, they should be bound to the same constant or variable (Input matching consistency).

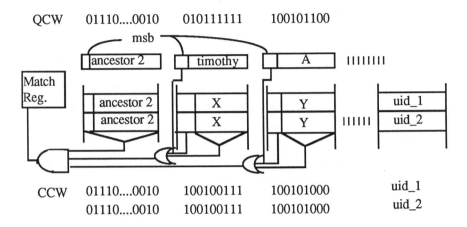

Fig. 2   An Associative Memory for CCW

The prime objective of unification is to find proper bindings for variables. After input matching and consistency checking are performed, the variables of qualified terms (CCW's) are substituted by the constants obtained from input matching. The reverse operation is required to bind variables in QCW. If these terms are unifiable, then the similar condition as the input matching condition will be satisfied. That is, for all constants in a qualified CCW, the corresponding arguments of QCW should be either the same constants or variables (Output matching condition).

Finally, a consistency check for the variables in the QCW needs to be performed. That is, if the same variables appear in the arguments of the QCW, they should be bound to the same constant or variable (Output matching consistency).

The unification method always works with the function-free terms. In the next section, the overall architecture and a processing model, as an example of parallel evaluation of logic programs, are described.

THE KNOWLEDGE BASE MACHINE ARCHITECTURE

The knowledge base machine architecture for surrogate file processing consists of four major components (Fig. 3):

1) A control processing element
   (Control Processor(CP) + Main Memory),
2) A database manager,
3) A high speed shared memory and
4) Several surrogate file processors (SFPs).

The CP can be a general purpose high performance processor. The main memory can be viewed as a local memory of the CP. In the logic programming framework, the CP performs the resolution (variable substitution) and accesses the actual KB. In our logic programming framework, we assume that the clause heads and facts are stored across distributed surrogate files under SFPs. The clause bodies, on the other hand, are contained in the database which is controlled by the control processor.

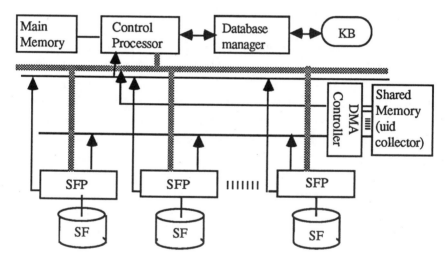

Fig. 3 Proposed Knowledge Base Machine Architecture

Our system can be viewed as a shared-memory system which is a tightly coupled multiprocessor that provide all SFPs equal access privileges to the shared common memory. Because of the tight coupling between processors and memories, this system can exhibit high performance. As can be seen in Fig. 3, SFPs do not need to communicate with each other. That is, the unification operation is local to each SFP, the CP does not access the local memories of the unification processors, and a SFP is not allowed to access the main memory. All the communications required between the CP and SFPs are performed by accessing shared memory. The contents of shared memory, once written by a SFP as a result of a successful unification, are not changed until a new initial goal is to be executed. Since the data in the shared memory is always valid, whenever the shared memory gets new data from a surrogate file processor, the CP can read the data. The maximum performance is achieved when the CP does not have any idle time.

As shown in Fig. 4, to prevent possible contention problems, we propose to use high speed shared memory and to give the CP a higher priority in accessing (read) the memory than the SFPs (write).

Since our architecture incorporates several SFPs for unification, OR-parallelism can effectively be exploited in top-down evaluation of a query. AND-parallelism, however, may not give us a considerable speed-up due to the binding conflicts among shared variables. Consequently, an OR-parallel/AND-sequential processing model with breadth-first search strategy is currently considered. Due to its breadth first search nature, the resulting model is in some respects similar to the LPS algorithm of DADO (20).

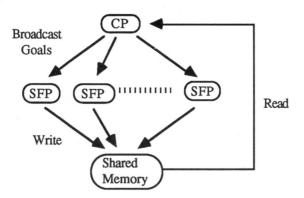

Fig. 4 The Sequence of Data Paths in Run Time

The CP broadcasts the initial goal to each SFP, where the surrogate file is managed and unification is performed. A processor that succeeds in a unification, accesses the shared memory to write the variable bindings and uid. The uid can be used by the CP to identify the corresponding body portion of a qualified head. The control processor resolves the body literals with the bindings and broadcasts the subgoals one at a time. The flow chart of this method is presented in Fig. 5.

For example, to evaluate the goal :-? ancestor(timothy,X), the control processor broadcasts it to each SFP. Each SFP tests to see if an ancestor(timothy,A) can be unified with any header it contains by transforming the goal to a QCW. There will be two matches in our example, the one from ancestor(X_1,Y_1):-parent(X_1,Y_1) and another from   ancestor(X_2,Y_2):-parent(X_2,Z_2), ancestor(Z_2,Y_2).

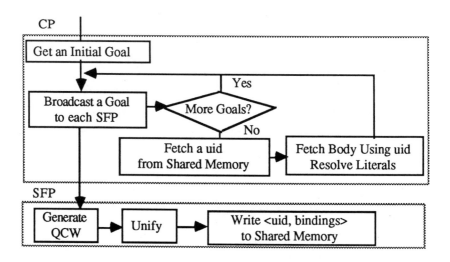

Fig. 5   Logic Programming Evaluation based on Surrogate Files

Assume that the uid of the first clause is 'uid_1' and the one corresponding to the second clause is 'uid_2'. The control processor reads the shared memory to get the corresponding uids and variable bindings resulting from a successful unification. In our example, the contents of shared memory that can be accessed by the CP after broadcasting the initial goal would be either <{X_1/timothy, Y_1/A}, uid_1> or <{X_2/timothy, Y_2/A}, uid_2>. We do not care which clause succeeded first. A portion of the body corresponding to either uid_1 (i.e. parent(X_1,Y_1)) or uid_2 (i.e. parent(X_2,Z_2), ancestor(Z_2,Y_2)) is accessed from actual database via uid's, and the corresponding body is resolved by the bindings. That is, the variables which appeared in the body portion are substituted by obtaining them from shared memory. If the second clause is unified before the first one, the CP creates two AND processes of parent(timothy,Z_2) and ancestor(Z_2,A). Then the goal, parent(timothy,Z_2), is broadcast first.

In our processing model, if the SFP is efficient enough to make the control processor busy, the time required for unification is negligible. Hence a considerable amount of speed up can be gained in accessing secondary storages. The overall architecture is designed to exploit the advantages of both shared and private memory systems based on the top level algorithm described in Fig. 5.

CONCLUSION AND FUTURE WORK

We described surrogate file structures and a processing method that one might use to evaluate goals in top-down fashion when a large number of rules exist. When a large volume of facts are involved, the top-down query processing may be inefficient (21). In this case, a set-oriented, bottom-up query processing is more desirable than the top-down, tuple based one. Since the surrogate file technique has been originally designed for ground instances of facts, they can be effectively used for the bottom-up, set-oriented query processing in the framework of logic-oriented database systems. In addition, by separating the bodies (the actual codes for operations) from heads (an entry point for the procedure call), the surrogate file processing technique could support multiple knowledge representation schemes as well as conventional procedure- based, compiled languages.

We are currently approaching an efficient implementation of a knowledge base system in two ways. The first is to develop special hardware to process surrogate files; these files can allow efficient access to the knowledge base residing in secondary storages. The second is to consider optical techniques that can potentially increase data rates by orders of magnitude and thus speed access to the knowledge bases. This paper presented one of the first approaches.

REFERENCES

1. Li, D.   A Prolog Database System, Research Studies Press, London,1984.
2. Murakami, K. et al.   IEEE Computer, pp. 76- 92, June 1985
3. Sabbatel, G. B.   et al. Proc. of the Second Int. Logic Programming Conference, pp. 207-217, 1984
4. Yokota, H. and Itoh, H. Proc. of the 13th Int. Symp. on Computer Architectures, pp. 2-9, 1986
5. Berra, P. B. , Chung, S. M. and Hachem, N. I. IEEE Computer, pp. 25-32, March 1987
6. Conery, J. S. , Parallel Execution of Logic programs, Kluwer Academic Publishers, Boston, 1987
7. Woo, N. S.   Micro 18 Proceedings, pp. 89-98, 1985
8. Shobatake, Y. and Aiso H. Proc. of 13th Int. Symp. on Computer Architectures, pp.140-148, 1986
9. Stormon, C. D. CASE Center TR 8611, Syracuse University, October 1986
10. Lloyd, J. W. Foundations of Logic Programming, Springer-Verlag, 1984
11. Robinson, J. A. J. of the ACM, Vol.12, pp. 23-44 , 1965
12. Dwork, C., Kanellakis, P. and Mitchell, J. Journal of Logic Programming, Vol. 1, pp. 35-50, 1984
13. Vitter, J. S. and Simons, R. A. IEEE Transactions on Computers, Vol. C-35, No. 5, pp. 403 -418, 1986
14. Paterson M. S. and Wegman, M. N. Journal of Computer and System Sciences 16, pp. 158-167, 1978
15. Martelli, A. and Montanari, U. ACM Transactions on Programming Languages and Systems, Vol.4, No.2, pp. 258-282, April 1982
16. Morita, Y., Yokota, H. and Itoh, H. 12th VLDB, pp. 52-59, August 1986
17. Clark, K. and Gregory, S. ACM Transactions on Programming Languages and Systems, Vol.8, No.1, pp. 1-49, January 1986
18. Maluszynski, J. and Komorowski, H. J. Proc. of Second Int. Symp. on Logic Programming, pp. 78-86, 1985
19. Ramamohanarao, K. and Shepherd, J. Proc. of the Third Int. Conf. on Logic Programming, pp. 569-576, July 1986
20. Lowry, A., Taylor, S. and Stolfo, S. Proc. of the Int. Conf. on Fifth Generation Computer Systems, pp. 436-448, 1984
21. Kifer, M. and Lozinskii, E. Proc. of Third Data Engineering, pp. 375-385, 1987

A Superimposed Code Scheme for Deductive Databases

Mitsunori Wada[†], Yukihiro Morita[‡], Haruaki Yamazaki[†], Shouji Yamashita[†], Nobuyoshi Miyazaki[†] and Hidenori Itoh[‡]

[†] Oki Electric Industry Co., Ltd., Tokyo, Japan
[‡] Institute for New Generation Computer Technology, Tokyo, Japan

ABSTRACT

An experimental distributed knowledge base system, KBMS PHI, is being developed as a part of the knowledge base research in the Fifth Generation Computer Systems project. A query expressed in Horn clause form is combined with related rules and compiled to relational operations to realize efficient processing in PHI.

A superimposed code scheme is being developed to speed up the processing. This paper describes the superimposed code scheme for compiled relational operations and analyzes its performance. An extension of the scheme for the processing of terms and rules is also discussed.

INTRODUCTION

The management of large shared knowledge bases is one of the most important research topics in realizing knowledge information processing systems. An experimental distributed knowledge base system, KBMS PHI, is being developed as part of knowledge base research in the Fifth Generation Computer Systems (FGCS) project. Two principal knowledge base models, the combined model and the integrated model, are being investigated in the FGCS project[1]. PHI is based on a variation of the combined model which is essentially a deductive database system. Horn clause queries are combined with related rules in the intensional database (IDB) and compiled to relational operations for the processing the extensional database (EDB) to utilize the database technology effectively. A superimposed code scheme is being investigated to support relational operations as well as the processing of rules. The major topic of this paper is the use of superimposed codes for relational operations in deductive database systems. The extension of the method for terms and rules is also briefly discussed.

KBMS PHI

KBMS PHI physically consists of a number of personal sequential inference machines (PSIs) linked by the ICOT LAN. The PSI is a personal computer system developed by ICOT that executes a logic programming language[2]. The ICOT LAN is an ethernet like local area network whose broadcast communication capacity reduces the communication overhead[3]. Some PSIs act as knowledge base machines which serve the requests from other PSIs used as host computers on which user programs run. This configuration represents one of the approximate models of the combination of the inference machine and the knowledge base machine for the FGCS. PSIs which have the role of knowledge base machines are called PHi machines in this paper.

Logical Configuration of PHI

KBMS PHI logically consists of global knowledge base managers and local knowledge base managers, as shown in Figure 1. One global knowledge base manager is dynamically assigned as a coordinator for each user program that accesses the knowledge bases. Local knowledge base managers that manage the related knowledge bases cooperate to answer requests from the user program. This configuration is a distributed and extended version of the model proposed in [4]. The major features of the previous model are as follows.

(1) A relational database management system (RDBMS) manages the EDB. The use of set oriented relational operations for large knowledge bases is essential to improve the overall performance.

(2) The Horn clause interface is used between the logic programs and the extended RDBMS. The extension is for recursive queries.

The first feature represented the commonly accepted view of the relationship between the inference and the relational databases when ICOT was inaugurated[5]. The second is the major issue of this proposal.

The model was extended for PHI to include the following additions.

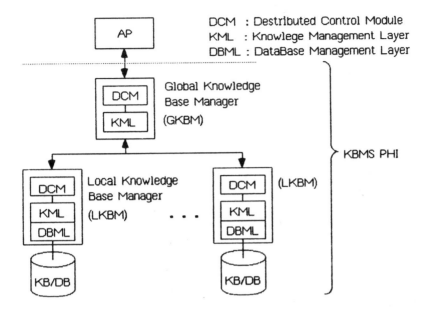

Figure 1   Logical Configuration of KBMS PHI

(3) The extended part is separated from the RDBMS as a knowledge management layer to broaden the scope of IDB management.

(4) A distributed control module has been added to cope with the distributed environment.

Thus, the kernel of KBMS PHI is a distributed deductive database system.

Query Processing in KBMS PHI

Query processing strategy in KBMS PHI was investigated by dividing the problem into two sub-problems: query processing of the distributed relational database and query processing of the deductive database. An integrated strategy is being developed based on strategies for these sub-problems. Query processing of the deductive database is summarized in this section.

The size of the IDB is assumed to be relatively small compared to the size of the EDB. The relational database operation is an attractive alternative in such a case to realize the deductive inference based on the well known one-to-one correspondence between a fact of the logic program and a tuple of a relation. A query is first combined with related rules in the

IDB. The resultant rule set can be regarded as a Horn clause query. A Horn clause query without functions (structures) can be easily compiled to a relational query if there are no recursive expressions in it. Thus, the central issue of query processing is how to deal with recursion. There have been many strategies proposed for recursive query processing. They can be classified based on their main characteristics, i.e. interpretation versus compilation and top down versus bottom up[6]. The compiled approach enables techniques developed in the database field to be applied in order to improve performance. Therefore, a strategy based on the compiled and bottom up approach was proposed for PHI[7]. It uses a procedure called Horn clause transformation to simplify queries for bottom up processing. Part of this strategy was implemented to study the behavior[8].

It is easy to process simple queries efficiently using the bottom up approach[7]. However, some kind of the binding (condition) propagation mechanism is necessary to improve the performance of a bottom up strategy for complex queries. The principle of restricted least fixed points that reduces the size of virtual relations was proposed for this purpose[9]. It introduce a rule set called restrictor rules, which are similar to the magic sets summarized in [6]. With this improvement, most queries including "not" predicates, and mutual recursions, can be processed effectively by relational operations in PHI.

Application of Superimposed Codes in KBMS PHI

The query processing of PHI consists of two phases. The first is the processing of the IDB related to the query. This phase includes the extraction of related rules from the IDB and the compilation of the query. The second phase is the execution of the compiled relational operations on the EDB to compute the answer. The system is being designed and implemented on PSIs, and part of it, the database management layer (RDBMS), is currently operational. The hardware support of the processing is also being investigated to improve the performance.

The use of superimposed codes possibly provides a unified approach to realize the efficient processing of deductive databases that consist of the IDB and the EDB. Therefore, a superimposed code scheme is being investigated as an alternative way of realizing the deductive database processing. Relational operations that frequently appear in compiled queries are selections, joins, set operations and set comparisons. The frequent use of set operations and set comparisons is the major difference between deductive and relational databases. The use of superimposed codes in these operations is an effective way of improving the performance of the overall processing. PHI was designed under the assumption that the size of the EDB would be much larger than that of the IDB. Therefore, processing of these relational operations is more critical than IDB processing. An experimental knowledge base engine (KBE) is being designed based on a superimposed code scheme to process relational operations. The KBE is hardware attached to the PSI. The logical structure of the KBE is shown in Figure 2. The accelerator is simple dedicated hardware to process indices that consist of superimposed codes. The method to be used in the KBE is discussed in the following sections.

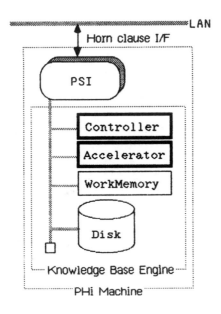

Figure 2 Knowledge Base Engine

RETRIEVAL USING A SUPERIMPOSED CODE

This section explains how to make an index, demonstrates retrieval with it, and discusses the optimum index parameters.

Index Creation

To retrieve large amounts of text data, a method using the superimposed code was proposed[10]. This method assigns index records with superimposed code words (SCWs) to a record file that has multiple key words. This method provides powerful partial match retrieval.

For quick tuple retrieval, an index with SCWs is introduced. An index value is derived as follows:

Suppose a relation, R, consists of N tuples; $R = \{T_1, T_2, \ldots, T_N\}$. The relation, R, has r^R key attributes. To compute an index value, a hashing function is defined to map attribute values to codes called binary code words (BCWs) according to data type. For a given tuple, T_i, the index value is produced as follows:

(1) The value of each key's attributes of T_i is transformed to the BCW.

(2) All BCWs derived are ORed together.

The result of the OR operation is a SCW, an index of T_i. The index table of R is produced by pairing index values and a pointer to the corresponding tuple for all tuples of R. Figure 3 is an example of the index table.

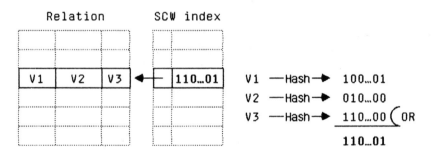

Figure 3   Index Creation

Retrieval Using an Index

As explained above   an index table is used for retrieval. In retrieval query q, r^q key attribute values are specified as a retrieval condition. The first phase, PHASE1, extracts candidate tuples that satisfy the retrieval condition comparing index values with a binary value, called a query mask. PHASE2 examines the contents of each candidate to extract the tuples satisfying the retrieval condition.

In more detail, query mask Q is computed from the set, Sq, of attribute values specified in the retrieval condition, analogous to the way in which an index value is derived. First, the hashing function maps each element in Sq into a BCW. The query mask is derived from ORing together the r^q BCWs.

If Q and any index value, S_i, do not satisfy equation 1, the tuple corresponding to the index record dose not satisfy the query.

$$Q \wedge S_i = Q \ldots\ldots (1)$$

As a result of PHASE1, a collection, C, of tuples whose index value, S_i, satisfies equation 1 is extracted. PHASE2 examines C so that the tuples which satisfy the retrieval condition can be picked up.

Set operations and set comparisons are frequently executed in PHI, as discussed in previous sections. Each tuple in a relation should be compared to every tuple in another relation in these operations. This tuple-wise comparison is very time consuming. The comparison time is $O(M \times N)$ for relations having M and N tuples.

It is difficult to use index methods such as B^+ or a hash table to reduce the processing time of these operations. The SCW index can reduce the time for these operations. First, relations are divided into tuple groups based on their index values. Next, each group of a relation is paired with a group of another relation that has the same index value. Then, comparisons can be made within these paired groups. The comparison time can be greatly reduced by pairing groups. The time for grouping and pairing is in the linear order of the size of relations. The details of these operations are discussed in [11].

Design of Index Parameters

An index value is assumed to have uniform distribution. Then $p(drops)$ is defined by equation 2:

$$p(drops) = (\text{ the number of } C \text{ elements } / \text{ the number of all tuples in } R \text{ })$$

$$= \sum_{x=0}^{b} \phi(b,k,r^q,x) \; p(b,k,r^R,x) \tag{2}$$

$$\phi(b,k,r^q,x) = (-1)^x {}_bC_i \sum_{i=0}^{x} (-1)^i {}_xC_i \left(\frac{{}_iC_k}{{}_bC_k} \right)^{r^q}$$

$$p(b,k,r^R,x) = \sum_{i=0}^{x} (-1)^i {}_xC_i \left(\frac{{}_{b-i}C_k}{{}_bC_k} \right)^{r^R}$$

$p(drops)$ can be computed using parameters b, k, r^R, r^q[10], where r^R is the number of key attributes in the relation, r^q is key attributes specified at retrieval condition, b is the length of BCW and k is the weight of BCW (number of '1' in BCW). b and k are parameters that specify the nature of the index. This section discusses the optimal value of k.

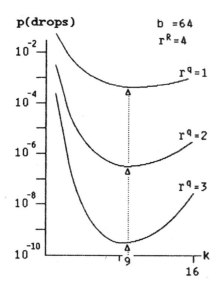

Figure 4 Transition of Selectivity (1)

As shown in Figure 4, when b and r^R are fixed, the transition of $p(drops)$ according to k's value is examined. The results is that the more r^q increases, the more $p(drops)$ decreases. Hence, the more key attributes specified in the query, the fewer tuples satisfy the query. The number of tuples satisfying the query is maximal when $r^q = 1$. Thus, the optimization of value k is the most important design criterion. As can be seen in Figure 4, this optimal value of k does not change in other curves.

Next, as shown in Figure 5, the transition of $p(drops)$ in the case of $r^q = 1$ according to k's value when b is fixed is examined. The result is that $p(drops)$ increases in proportion to r^R. Hence, if the number of key attributes in the relation increases, the number of tuples which do not satisfy queries is expected to increase.

Next, the value of b is set in proportion to r^R. Figure 6 illustrates the transition of $p(drops)$ in the case of $b = r^R \times 16, 24, 32$ and $r^R = 2, 8$. The value of k that minimizes $p(drops)$ is in this range. It is clear that if r^q is a constant, then the transition is very small, within

$$\frac{1}{2} \times \left(\frac{b}{r^R} \right) \leqq k \leqq \frac{2}{3} \times \left(\frac{b}{r^R} \right).$$

Therefore, k should be set in this range.

ESTIMATED PROCESSING TIME

This section estimates the cost of retrieval processing with SCWs, and compares it with the costs using the hashing table or B$^+$tree. The retrieval operation is the operation executed most often. The relational algebraic

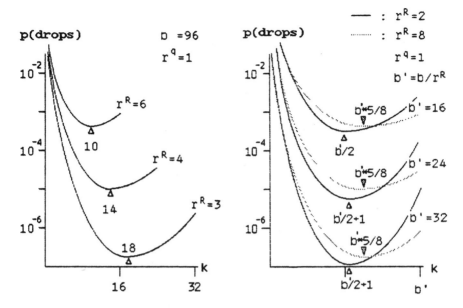

Figure 5 Transition of Selectivity (2)   **Figure 6 Transition of Selectivity (3)**

command sequence is optimized by the selection-first strategy in the PHi machine. Therefore, the execution cost of retrieval command affects the entire execution cost of the PHi machine.

Here, a retrieval is executed to select all tuples satisfying a retrieval condition, and in the condition, some attribute values are specified and ANDed. When a retrieval command is applied to a relation that has a hashing table or B^+ tree index of key attributes, it is applied in two phases as in the SCW method. The first phase, PHASE1, selects tuples that match one key value specified in the retrieval condition, called candidate tuples. The second phase, PHASE2, tests the candidates and determines tuples satisfying the retrieval condition completely.

Comparison Time

This section estimates the comparison time to select candidate tuples, and evaluates the effect on retrieval. All index records must be tested in the SCW method regardless of the number of tuples in a relation.

When retrieval is performed for an N tuple relation, PHASE1 should test index records N times. The number of comparison steps to select all candidates is N. When retrieval is performed for a relation that has hashing tables, only one access after hashing is required to select all candidates. One comparison step is required to select all candidates. For the B^+ tree, the number of comparison steps to select all candidates is $(\text{Constant} \times \log_B N)$ B:number of branches.

Therefore, the number of comparison steps of each method is estimated.

1) SCW index method   : N

2) Hashing table method: 1

3) B^+ tree index method : $\text{Constant} \times \log_B N$

Obviously, the SCW method gives the largest number of steps. The following values are assumed to estimate the order of comparison time.

Parameters

Number of tuples (N)   : 2^{16}

Frequency of comparing one index value (f) : $1 \sim 10$

Comparison time   : $10 \sim 10^2$ nsec

Here, f is set to be 1 to 10, since the limitations of the register size of the accelerator mean that index values must sometimes be compared several times. The order of each method is:

$O(\text{SCW index method})$ $= 10^{-1} \sim 10$ msec

$O(\text{Hash table method})$ $= 10 \sim 10^3$ nsec

$O(B^+\text{tree index method})$ $= 10^{-1} \sim 10$ µsec

The total comparison time with the hashing table or B^+ tree is negligible compared to the disk access time, which is in the order of milliseconds. Because total comparison time with the SCW index is greater than in other methods, an accelerator is being designed to realize high-speed index processing in the KBE.

Estimated Disk Access Time

This section estimates the time to read candidate tuples from disk hardware in PHASE2. The following parameters are used:

s : Average seek time (msec)

r : Rotational latency (msec)

d : Disk transfer time (msec/byte)

P : Page size (bytes)

N : Number of tuples in a relation

n : Number of tuples satisfying a query

In the SCW method, when $p(drops) \ll 1$, the same number of pages as candidate tuples will be read. Candidate reading time T_{tuple} for disk access is estimated as follows:

$$T_{tuple} = N \times p(drops) \times (s + r + P/d)$$

In this expression, $N \times p(drops) = N_d$ is the expected number of candidates in PHASE1.

Figure 7 shows the disk read time. In this figure, the axis of the abscissa is the rate of n to N_d. Here, the following values are estimated:

1) Disk

$\qquad s + r = 25$ msec

$\qquad d \quad = 1$ Kbytes/msec

$\qquad P \quad = 4$ Kbytes

2) Number of tuples in a relation : 2^{16}

3) Index value length : 16, 24, or 32 bits per attribute

For $b/r^R = 24, 32, \ldots$, the disk access time to read candidates is represented by curve L_0. For $b/r^R = 16$ and $r^q = 1$, disk access time is constant up to a certain point as shown in L_1 and L_2. For $r^q \geq 2$, disk read time is represented by curve L_0.

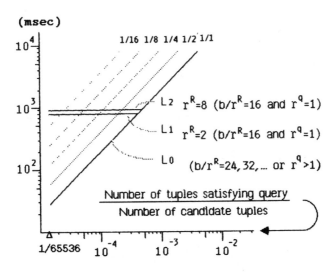

Figure 7   disk access time

When tuples are retrieved with the hashing table or the B^+tree index, candidate tuples are selected by using them for a single attribute. Next, the candidates are tested to see whether they satisfy the query. Candidate hit ration $P(HIT)$ is defined as follows:

$P(HIT) = (Number\ of\ tuples\ satisfying\ query\ /Number\ of\ candidate\ tuples\ )$.

With $P(HIT)$, the expected reading time, T_{tuple}, for candidates can be calculated as follows:

$$T_{tuple} = n \times (s + r + P/d) / P(HIT).$$

According to this expression, Figure 7 explains the disk access time for $P(HIT) = 1/1, 1/2, 1/4, 1/8, 1/16$.

In the SCW method, for $r^q \geq 2$ the disk access time follows L_0. In other methods, $P(HIT)$ is expected to decrease as r^q increases. If the number of the tuples satisfying a query exceeds a certain threshold, then the SCW method is better than the other methods in terms of disk access time to read candidates. As $P(HIT)$ decreases, the threshold value decreases. In other words, the performance of retrieval using the SCW method is expected to be better than other methods as the number of key attributes specified in the retrieval condition increases.

EXTENDING THE SUPERIMPOSED CODE SCHEME FOR TERMS AND RULES

PHI deals with not only the EDB but also the IDB. Therefore, a fast retrieve mechanism for rules is necessary if the size of the IDB becomes large. Another problem is processing structures in the IDB and EDB. These two problems can be handled by the superimposed code scheme for terms.

The main problem in processing terms is expressing variables and composite terms by superimposed codes. A scheme called the structural superimposed code word (SSCW) method is being investigated.

First, a term is represented by a tree. If the term is an atom or a variable, it is represented by a simple tree that consists of only a root node. If the term is composite, the functor of the term is represented by the root and its arguments become its children. If some arguments are again composite, they are represented by subtrees. The hashing function for the BCW is decided under the following conditions.

(1) Each functor, atom, or variable that is a component of a term is mapped to a BCW shorter than the intended SSCW.

(2) Variables are mapped to the codes whose components are all '1' for indices of terms in the IDB or the EDB. They are mapped to all '0' for query masks.

(3) The range of the BCW for a parent node covers those of its children.

An SSCW for a term is computed by superimposing BCWs of its components according to its structure, as shown in Figure 8. If a term, t_1, is unifiable with another term t_2, then the index value (SSCW), S, for t_1 and the query mask, Q, for t_2 satisfy equation 1 in the previous section.

There have been several indexing schemes proposed for terms and rules [12] to [15]. The relationship of these methods are briefly analyzed in [16] and [17], and it is shown that the selectivity of the SSCW scheme is better than that of methods discussed in [12] and [13].

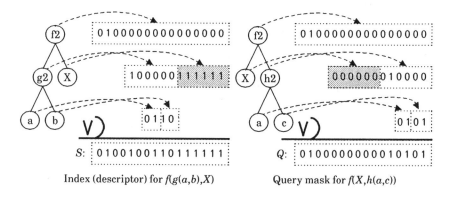

Figure 8 Example of SSCW

CONCLUSIONS

This paper described a superimposed code scheme planned to be used in KBMS PHI. PHI compiles a deductive query to relational operations to effectively process the query. The superimposed code scheme is used for indices of the EDB, i.e. the relations, to improve the performance of the execution of the compiled query. The advantages and disadvantages of the scheme were analyzed. The scheme is expected to be more effective than other methods if the number of key attributes specified in the retrieval condition is larger than one. This scheme is also very effective for the set operations and comparisons frequently used in deductive database processing. An experimental knowledge base engine is being designed based on this scheme.

The extension of the scheme for the processing of the IDB, i.e. rules, were also briefly discussed. The superimposed code scheme is suitable for a parallel architecture because it is structurally simple. The investigation of the parallel architecture is considered to be one of the directions of future research.

REFERENCES

[1] Itoh, H., Research and Development on Knowledge Base Systems at ICOT, *Proc. of 12th VLDB*, pp.437-445, 1986
[2] Uchida, S. and Yokoi, T., Sequential Inference Machine: SIM, *Proc. of FGCS*, pp.58-69, Tokyo 1984
[3] Taguchi et al., INI: Internal Network on the ICOT Programming Laboratory and Its Future, *ICCC*, Sydney, Australia, Oct. 1984
[4] Miyazaki, N., A Data Sublanguage Approach to Interfacing Predicate Logic Languages and Relational Databases, ICOT Technical Memorandum, 1982
[5] Fuchi, K., Aiming for Knowledge Information Processing Systems, *Proc. of FGCS*, p.2-15 to p.2-28, Tokyo, 1981
[6] Bancilhon, F. and Ramakrishnan R., An Amateur's Introduction to Recursive Query Processing Strategies, *SIGMOD '86 Proc.*, pp.16-52, 1986
[7] Miyazaki, N., Yokota, H. and Itoh, H., Compiling Horn Clause Queries in Deductive Databases: A Horn Clause Transformation Approach, ICOT Technical Report, 1986
[8] Abiru, Y., Haniuda, H., Miyazaki N. and Morita, Y., KBMS PHI: An Experimental Deductive Database System PHI/K^2, *Proc. 34th Annual Convention IPS Japan*, pp.1491-1492, 1987 (in Japanese)
[9] Miyazaki, N. and Itoh, H., Restricted Least Fixed Points and Recursive Query Processing Strategies, ICOT Technical Report,1987
[10] Roberts, C.S., Partial-Match Retrieval via Method of Superimposed Codes, *Proc. of IEEE*, 67(12), pp.1624-1642, 1979
[11] Wada, M., et al., KBMS PHI: Superimposed Codes for Relational Algebra Operations, *Proc. 34th Annual Convention IPS Japan*, 3K-7, pp.1489-1490, 1987, (in Japanese)
[12] Wise, M. J., and Powers, D. M. W., Indexing PROLOG Clauses via Superimposed Code Words and Field Encoded Words, *Proc. IEEE Conf. Logic Programming*, Atlantic City, NJ, January 1984, pp.203-210.
[13] Morita, Y., et al., Retrieval-By-Unification Operation on a Relational Knowledge Base, *Proc. of the 12th VLDB*, 1986
[14] Ramamohanarao, K., and Shepherd J., Answering Queries in Deductive Database Systems, *Logic Programming: Proc. Fourth Int'l Conf.* Vol.2, pp.1014-1033, 1987
[15] Berra, P.B. et al., Computer Architecture for a Surrogate File to a Very Large Data/Knowledge Bases, *IEEE COMPUTER*, March 1987
[16] Morita, Y., Wada, M. and Itoh, H., Structure Retrieval via the Method of Superimposed Codes., *Proc. 33rd Annual Convention IPS Japan*, 6L-8, 1986, (in Japanese)
[17] Morita, Y., et al., A Knowledge Base Machine with an MPPM (3) - An Indexing Scheme for Terms -, *Proc. 35th Annual Convention IPS Japan*, 2C-7, 1987, (in Japanese), (to appear)

A SIMULATION STUDY OF A KNOWLEDGE BASE MACHINE ARCHITECTURE

Hiroshi SAKAI, Shigeki SHIBAYAMA

Toshiba R & D Center, Komukai-Toshiba-cho, Saiwai-ku, Kawasaki, 210, Japan

Hidetoshi MONOI, Yukihiro MORITA, Hidenori ITOH

ICOT Research Center, Mita-Kokusai-Build., Mita,Minato-ku, 108, Tokyo, Japan

ABSTRACT

As part of Japan's Fifth Generation Computer Project for the development of a knowledge base machine (KBM), an advanced database machine incorporating a new data model and hardware architecture is proposed. For the data model, an extension of the ordinary relational model is used. In this model, a term which may contain variables is allowed as an attribute value and operations over relations concerning unifiability between terms are defined. For the hardware architecture, unification engines handle unification operations over relations in parallel, and a multiport page-memory reduces the bottleneck between primary and secondary storage.

An estimation of the system performance is made by simulating the system. A precise model of the hardware architecture and control strategies were implemented. A control strategy in which a join operation is divided into small ones according to the sizes of the relations and the number of engines is proposed and found to be useful for this hardware architecture in that it saves processing time and memory usage.

FRAMEWORK OF OUR KBM RESEARCH PROJECT

Research Objectives

We have conducted research on constructing a knowledge base machine (KBM) within Japan's Fifth Generation Computer Project. The term KBM means a database machine with advanced functions for knowledge. In an intermediate project lasting four years, we aim to develop a prototype KBM which provides a common knowledge base for inference machines.

Design Philosophy of the KBM Functions

We developed the relational database machine, Delta, as the first step of our research [Kakuta 85], [Sakai 86]. Through the experience, we have arrived at the following conclusion: while a database system is needed, an ordinary relational model is not sufficient; data structures such as list and term which appear in Prolog programs cannot be represented efficiently. So we adopted an extension of the ordinary relational model [Morita 86], [Yokota 86]. In this model, a term having variables is allowed as an attribute

585

value. The scope of a variable is within the tuple, as in a Horn clause. Operations over relations concerning unifiability and/or generality of terms are defined. Figure 1 shows sample relations and operation. The operation is called a unification join (U-join). This model allows not only nested relations but also a kind of inference. A similar model and a knowledge base mechanism different from ours are reported by Ohmori [Ohmori 86].

R	R_a	R_b		S	S_a	S_b
	X	f(X, a)			g(X, b)	f(X, b)
	h(X, X)	g(a, Y)			g(X, c)	g(X, d)
	f(a, b)	g(b, c)				

$$T \leftarrow R \, _{R_b} \!\!\stackrel{\times}{\bowtie}\, _{S_a} S$$

T	R_a'	R_b'	S_a'	S_b'
	h(X, X)	g(a, b)	g(a, b)	f(a, b)
	h(X, X)	g(a, c)	g(a, c)	g(a, d)
	f(a, b)	g(b, c)	g(b, c)	g(b, d)

Figure 1   Example of relations and an operation

Design Philosophy of the System Architecture

Through the experience with Delta, we found that it is useful (1) to use multiple special-purpose processors to cope with heavy operations like U-join in parallel, and (2) to use a large disk cache to reduce the bottleneck between primary and secondary storage. To achieve the first goal, a unification engine (UE) was designed [Morita 86]. To achieve the second, a multiport page-memory (MPPM) [Tanaka 84] was adopted. This is a kind of multiport memory without any contention although its accessible unit is limited to a page, not a word.

Figure 2 gives an overview of the system architecture. It contains disk devices which store permanent relations, an MPPM which behaves as a disk cache shared by the disk devices and UEs, UEs which process operations on relations within the MPPM, and a processor which controls the whole system.

Overview of the Simulation Study

Before undertaking the actual implementation, we simulated our KBM architecture to estimate the system performance. A precise model of the UE was required since it significantly affects the execution time, so we made a simulation study on design alternatives of the UE first [Morita 87]. Like other kinds of parallel processing, the question of control was also important. We adopted alternative control strategies and compared them in the simulation study.

Unification Engines

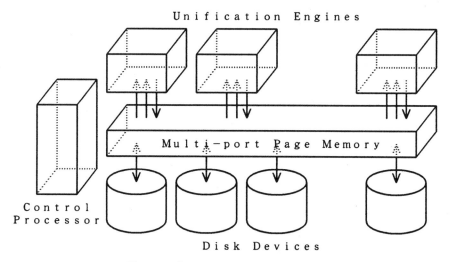

Multi-port Page Memory

Control Processor

Disk Devices

Figure 2 System configuration of a KBM

KBM MODEL

System Architecture

In the simulation study, we adopted the system architecture illustrated in figure 2 except for disk devices. Therefore, we assumed that relevant relations are always staged in the MPPM; it is the best case of system performance.

The MPPM is a shared memory with multiple ports. It allows constant data transfer rate for each port. The rate is assumed to be 20 Mbytes/sec so that it is equal to the processing speed of the UE. The MPPM stores relations on a page basis. The term "page" has two meanings. One is a unit of size of data access which causes a time delay. It depends on the hardware implementation and is called the track size. It is assumed to be 512bytes. The other is a unit of size of storage that must be a multiple of the track size. It is determined by the management software of the system. We compare the cases of 0.5, 1, 2, 4, 8, 16, 32, 64 Kbyte pages in the simulation study.

The UE can process a U-join operation between pages of a relation within the MPPM and pages of another, and output resultant tuples into the MPPM in a page scheme. Each UE is connected to the MPPM through three ports, two of which are used to input tuples of two relations simultaneously and the other to output the resultant tuples. Figure 3 shows its configuration. Here, the pair generator, receiving arranged sequences of input tuples from the sorters, produces pairs of tuples which is possibly unifiable. The unification unit checks the unifiability of each pair and outputs the resulting tuples. The

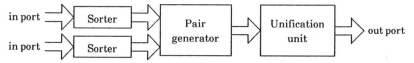

Figure 3 Internal configuration of UE

amount of pages that can be processed by a UE at one time is limited to the size of its buffer memory. The number of tuples that can be processed is also limited by the sorter.

A tuple is represented as a sequence of four-byte words, each of which stands for a component of a term (atom, functor, variable). Every unit of a UE is designed to process the word within a certain period, assumed to be 200 nsec. At the beginning of a period, a unit receives a word (if any) from the adjacent unit, and sends the resultant word at the end of that period.

The control processor manages all the resources in the system. The overhead time is ignored. The important specifications are summarized below.

MPPM	Track Size	0.5 Kbytes (access delay 0.0256 msec)
	Logical Page Size	0.5, 1, 2, 4, 8, 16, 32, 64 Kbytes
	Data Transfer Rate	20 Mbyte/sec for each port
UE	Number of UEs	1 to 32
	Processing Speed	200 nsec per four-byte word
	Number of I/O Ports	3 (2 for input and 1 for output)
	Buffer Size	4, 8, 16, 32, 64 Kbytes
Control Processor	control overhead	None

Input Resolution in the System

In the simulation study, we focus on input resolution for the following reasons.

(a) It is suitable for studying the system behavior since input resolution is realized by the repetition of U-joins.

(b) It is a typical operation that an ordinary relational database is not able to handle.

Representation of Definite Clauses and a Goal Clause.   Definite clauses are stored in a relation with two attributes. One stores the head of a definite clause and the other stores its body. Both attributes are stored in list form, with the same variable attached as the last component. The relation is called a permanent relation (PR)

A goal clause is stored in another relation with two attributes. One stores the expected form of the goal and the other stores the original goal clause in list form, with '*nil*' attached as the last component. The relation with a goal clause is called a temporary relation (TR). Figure 4 illustrates an example of a PR and TRs.

PR	Head	Body
	[ancestor(X, Y)|L]	[father(X, Z),ancestor(Z,Y))|L]
TR_0	Answer	Resolvent
	X	[ancestor(tom, X)]
TR_1	Answer	Resolvent
	X	[father(tom, Z), ancestor(Z, X)]

Figure 4   Knowledge representation for input resolution

Realizing Input Resolution. In the system, a U-join operation between the first attribute of the PR and the second attribute of the TR makes one step of input resolution and generates tuples which contain resolvents in the second attribute.

If TR_0 is the relation which contains the original goal clause, then a U-join between the PR and TR_0 generates a relation with new resolvents, TR_1. In general, a U-join between the PR and TR_n generates a relation, TR_{n+1}.

If the value of the second attribute of a tuple in TR_n is equal to 'nil', this indicates that the original goal clause becomes a sequence of ground clauses and that the value of the first attribute is the answer. A restrict operation is used to pick up these tuples. The input resolution ends when the U-join operation generates no more tuples.

Basic Considerations for Parallel Processing of U-join

Let us consider a U-join operation between relations R and S. If R_1 to R_m are the partitions of relation R, and S_1 to S_n are those of relation S, then the equation (1) holds. A U-join operation can be executed in parallel by assigning the indivisual $R_i \bowtie S_j$ to UEs.

$$R \bowtie S = \bigcup_{i=1}^{m} \bigcup_{j=1}^{n} R_i \bowtie S_j \tag{1}$$

Let F(r, s, t) be the execution time for a UE to execute a U-join operation between a part of relation R and that of relation S. Here, parameters r and s are the size of the portions and parameter t is the size of the result. Then as a first approximation, F(r, s, t) can be given by formula (2).

$$F(r, s, t) = a^*(r+s) + b^*t + c^*r^*s \tag{2}$$

Here, parameters a and b are almost independent from the characteristics of the relations. However, parameter c depends on how many tuple pairs generated by the pair generator of the UE are actually unifiable. Parameter c is called the antiselectivity ratio.

Basic inequation (3) holds, which shows that partitioning a U-join operation takes time unless the number of UEs increases.

$$F(r_1+r_2, s, t_1+t_2) < F(r_1, s, t_1) + F(r_2, s, t_2) \tag{3}$$

Now let us consider the execution time of the U-join operation between R and S relations in parallel. This is given by E in the inequations in (4), where

r_i = size of R_i r = summation of r_i
s_j = size of S_j s = summation of s_i
t_{ij} = size of the result of R_i S_j t = summation of t_{ij}
k = number of UEs

$$E \geq \sum_{i=1}^{m} \sum_{j=1}^{n} F(r_i, s, t_{ij})/k \tag{4a}$$

The equation holds when all UEs work continuously.

$$= (a^*(m^*r+n^*s) + b^*t + c^*r^*s)/k \tag{4b}$$

$$\geq (2a\sqrt{m^*n^*r^*s} + b^*t + c^*r^*s)/k \tag{4c}$$

The equation holds when $m^*r = n^*s$.

$$\geq 2\,a\sqrt{r^*s}\,/\,\sqrt{k} + (b^*t + c^*r^*s)\,/\,k \qquad\qquad (4d)$$

The equation holds when $m^*n = k$.

For inequation (4d), note that the product of m and n must be greater than k in order to use all the UEs. These inequations tell us the following facts.

(a) To minimize the execution time, m should be $\sqrt{k^*s\,/\,r}$ and n be $\sqrt{k^*r\,/\,s}$.

(b) To make all UEs work continuously, it seems reasonable to make all r_i equal and all s_j equal.

(c) (a) and (b) suggest that all r_i and s_j should be made equal to $\sqrt{r^*s\,/\,k}$.

Fact (c) suggests that relations should be partitioned according to their size and the number of UEs. Therefore, we adopt what we call the MP (Multiple Pages at a time) method. In the MP method, the page size is set relatively small and a U-join request between multiple pages of a relation and multiple pages of another relation is assigned to a UE. In the simulation study, we compare it with what we call the SP (Single Page at a time) method. Following the SP method, each join request is limited to between single page of a relation and single page of another. The simulation study found that the MP method is almost always better than the SP method.

Control Model for Parallel Execution of Input Resolution

Parallel Execution of an Input Resolution. During input resolution, the control processor of the system does the following jobs many times: generating U-join requests between parts of the PR and TR, assigning these requests to UEs, attaching the resulting pages to the TR, releasing a page of the TR when all the requests concerning it are completed. Therefore, the pages within the TR vary as input resolution progresses.

The control model based on the SP method, as illustrated in figure 5, does not contain significant alternative choices because the generation of U-join requests does not contain any time-dependent factors. On the other hand, the control model based on the MP method contains alternatives since the request generation depends on two time-dependent factors: the size of the TR and the number of UEs. In the control model illustrated in figure 6, output pages are first stored in a page pool. The control processor is able to generate U-join requests between the pages within the pool and PR whenever it wants to. The requests are stored in the request queue before being assigned to a UE. The remainder of this section introduces two parameters which describe the freedom within the MP method.

Partitioning Factor. In the course of input resolution, the activation of UEs is not necessarily synchronized. Therefore, in generating U-join requests between the PR and TR, there is room to consider how many UEs are available at the moment, in other words, how many requests should be generated.

If $UEfree$ is the number of currently free UEs and $UEtotal$ is the number of UEs in the system, it seems reasonable to choose the number of requests from $UEfree$ to $UEtotal$. Therefore, a parameter 'p' is introduced so that the number of requests is calculated by the formula, max$(UEfree, p \times UEtotal)$. This parameter is called the partitioning factor.

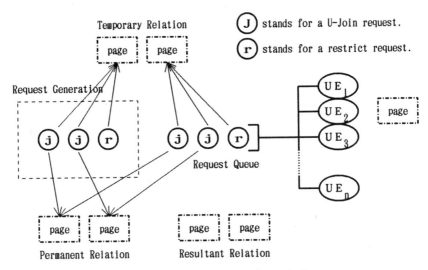

Figure 5   Control model based on the SP method

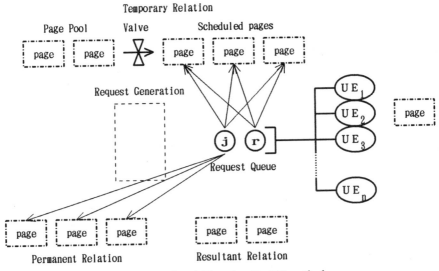

Figure 6   Control model based on the MP method

Waiting Ratio.   If the system postpones generating U-join requests, the page pool may contain more pages. This leads to higher performance unless the working-ratio of UEs decreases, because the accumulated contents of the TR during input resolution do not vary whatever control strategy is adopted. It is possibly better that the system postpones generating requests until a certain number of UEs become free. In the simulation study, a parameter 'wt' is introduced so that the system postpones the request generation until $UEfree$ becomes greater than or equal to $wt*UEtotal$. This parameter is called the waiting-ratio.

SIMULATION METHODOLOGY
Simulator Overview

The simulator is an ordinary single task program which runs on a conventional computer. It has a module which simulates the activity of a UE at the register transfer level and a scheduling module which reflects parallel processing based on the control model described above. The simulator is executed every time the parameters within the KBM model are modified. This gives reliable results except that the KBM model does not account for the overhead time due to the control processor.

Measures for Evaluation

To compare alternatives within the KBM model, the measures listed below are selected:

(a) Execution Time (Et)

This is the time elapsed in executing an input resolution in parallel.

(b) Page Loading Factor (Ld)

This is an average over output pages which shows how much the pages are loaded with resultant tuples.

(c) Performance Stability (Ps)

This shows to what extent the system exhibits stable performance over variance of the tuple size or other system parameters.

Sample Problems Used in the Simulation Study

Ancestor Problem.   Finding all the ancestors of a certain person in a collection of parent-child relationships is a typical problem for deductive databases. A computer-generated family tree based on a simple model of human life cycle is used. The PR consists of 1800 relationships among persons and several related rules. Since the pair generator does not generate any non-unifiable pair, the antiselectivity ratio is 0.

Eight-queen Problem.   The eight-queen problem is also frequently used to evaluate the performance of inference machines. In the simulation study, we use not an ordinary set of rules but a set of nine complicated rules, each of which has twenty-five variables and does not require any arithmetic operations. Since each tuple has a similar form, the pair generator generates almost all tuple combinations. Less than one seventh of these are exactly unifiable. Therefore, the antiselectivity ratio is large.

The differences between the sample problems are listed in figure 7.

	Ancestor	8-queen
Tuple Size of TR	44 - 60 bytes	188 - 220 bytes
PR size	64 Kbytes	2 Kbytes
TR size (accumulated)	36 Kbytes	386 Kbytes
No. of inference steps	16	10
Antiselectivity ratio	0	Large

Figure 7   Comparison of the sample problem

RESULTS AND DISCUSSION
SP method versus MP method

Here, the SP and MP method are compared. For the parameters of the MP method, the partitioning factor is 1 and the waiting ratio is $1 / UEtotal$.

Ancestor Problem. Figure 8 shows the relationship between $UEtotal$ and the execution time. For the SP method it shows that:

(s1) If the page size is small, the execution time becomes large when $UEtotal$ is small. This is because too many small U-join requests are generated.

(s2) If the page size is large, the execution time does not decrease when $UEtotal$ increases. This is because the number of requests generated during the input resolution remains so small that the working-ratio of UEs becomes low.

For the MP method, it shows that:

(m1) The page size does not affect the execution time much.

As a whole, the figure shows that the MP method is superior to the SP method for measures (Et) and (Ps).

Figure 9 shows the relationship between $UEtotal$ and the page loading factor. For the SP method, it shows that:

(s3) The page loading factor is law and does not depend on the number of UEs.

For the MP method, it shows that:

(m3) The page loading factor becomes lower when the number of UEs increases, because each U-join request, partitioned into smaller pieces, generates smaller number of resultant tuples.

(m4) The page loading factor at a certain number of UEs decreases, when the page size grows, because a small page size means that the unit of space for holding resultant tuples is also small.

As a whole, the figure shows that the MP method is superior to the SP method for measures (Ld) and (Ps).

Eight-queen Problem. Figure 10 and 11 show the results. They also show that the MP method is superior to the SP method, but the degree of superiority is small.

(s5) Unlike the ancestor problem, even when the number of UEs is small, the execution time in the SP method does not increase much. This is chiefly because both sides of inequation (3) become almost the same value since the antiselectivity ratio is large.

(s6) The page loading factor in the SP method becomes larger than in the ancestor problem, because the eight-queen problem generates a large number of resultant tuples compared with the ancestor problem.

For the MP method, figure 11 shows that:

(m6) Unlike the ancestor problem, a small page size does not always mean a high page loading factor. This is because the tuple size is close to the page size; i.e., 512 byte page can hold only two tuples and about 20 percent of the page size remains unused.

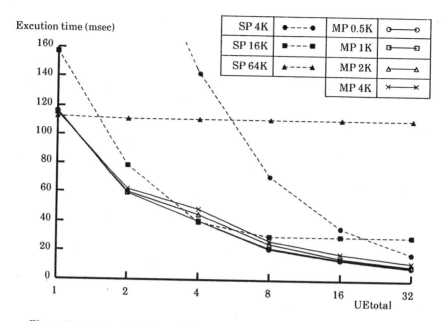

Figure 8　Relationship between *UEtotal* and execution time (Ancestor problem)

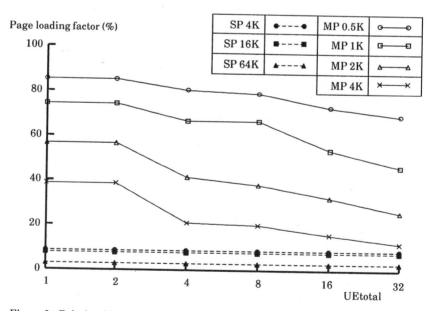

Figure 9　Relationship between *UEtotal* and page loading factor (Ancestor problem)

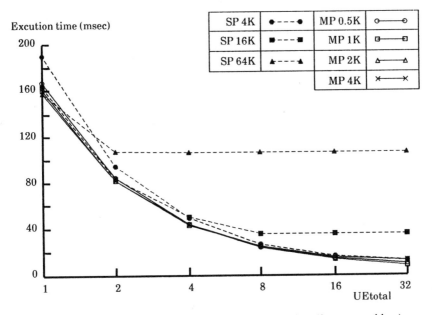

Figure 10   Relationship between *UEtotal* and execution time (8-queen problem)

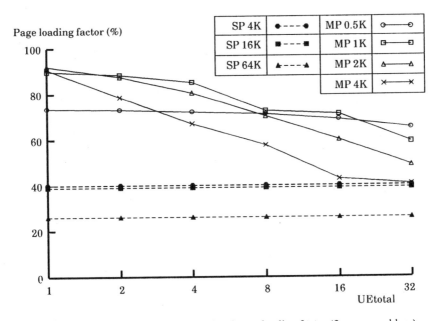

Figure 11   Relationship between *UEtotal* and page loading factor (8-queen problem)

Details of the MP Method

Effects of the Partitioning Factor. The partitioning factor determines the number of U-join requests generated at one time. If the parameter is 0, the system tries to generate as many requests as *UEfree*. If it is 1, the system tries to generate as many requests as *UEtotal*.

When the parameter is 0, the system performance is not stable. This is because it sometimes occurs that only a small number of UEs are processing U-join requests for a long time and the other UEs are just idling.

Further simulation study found that the system shows good and stable performance for both problems when the parameter is between 0.8 and 1.0.

Effects of the Waiting Ratio. The waiting ratio is used to trigger the generation of new U-join requests. This section discusses the effects of this parameter when the partitioning factor is equal to 1.

If the waiting ratio is low, the system generates new U-join requests as soon as a small number of UEs become free. Therefore, the working-ratio of UEs becomes larger than that when the waiting ratio is high. However, the system has to generate U-join requests more times since each request generation consumes a smaller part of the TR.

For the eight-queen problem, the performance when the waiting ratio is $1/UEtotal$ is 10% to 20% better than that when the waiting ratio is 1. This is because the PR size is very small and the antiselectivity ratio is large. Therefore, increase in the frequency of request generation is of little importance.

For the ancestor problem, if *UEtotal* is less than a certain threshold, the waiting ratio should be 1. This is because the PR size is large and the antiselectivity ratio is 0. However, if the *UEtotal* exceeds the threshold, the waiting ratio should be $1/UEtotal$, because the high working-ratio of UEs becomes more important.

Relationship between UEtotal and System Performance. Figure 12 shows the relationship between *UEtotal* and performance of both problems. Here the partitioning factor is 1, the waiting ratio is $1/UEtotal$, and the page size is 0.5Kbyte. The figure shows

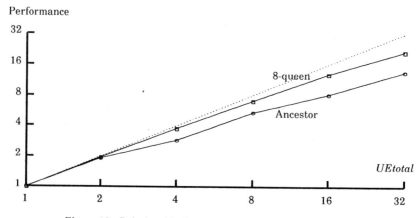

Figure 12 Relationship between UEtotal and Performance

that the performance improvement of the ancestor problem is smaller than that of the eight-queen problem.

This is because:

(1) In the ancestor problem, the low antiselectivity ratio (= 0) causes higher costs of partitioning of a U-join operation than in the eight-queen problem.

(2) In the ancestor problem, the PR size is large. Therefore, the increase in the frequency of request generation obstructs the performance improvement more than in the eight-queen problem.

Discussions on KBM Architecture

Use of MPPM. This section discusses how much of the potential data transfer capability of the MPPM is used during input resolution. A new measure, port utilization ratio, is introduced and defined as follows:

$$\frac{the\ actual\ size\ of\ transferred\ data\ through\ a\ port}{the\ execution\ time\ *\ data\ transfer\ capability\ of\ a\ port}$$

Figure 13 summarizes the port utilization ratio in both problems.

The figure shows that although the port utilization ratio of a certain port varies widely, the average over three ports of a UE is stable. The port utilization ratio seems rather low. However, simulation shows that the port utilization ratio becomes about 45% in the ancestor problem and about 30% in the eight-queen problem by assigning only one port to each UE. In this case, the performance will degrade 5% to 30%, assuming that *UEtotal* is equal and that the MPPM has only one third of the ports as in the current architecture model.

Towards Processing a Large Number of Definite Clauses. Since a knowledge base machine is expected to have enough power for problems with a large number of definite clauses, it is hoped that the system performance does not depend much on the number of definite clauses. From this point of view, though such a system with the MPPM shared among processors and disk devices seems to have a potential capability, it has a problem in that the execution time is proportional to the number of definite clauses. It comes from the fact that each U-join operation causes the transfer of all the relevant definite clauses from the MPPM to the UE. We think that a clustering method on terms may reduce the amount of data transfer.

	Ancestor	8-queen
Port for PR	4 % - 18 %	16 % - 23 %
Port for TR	36 % - 45 %	1 % - 14 %
Port for output	0.7 % - 2 %	7 % - 12 %
Average	16 % - 18 %	11 % - 13 %
When only one port per a UE	36% - 49 %	25 % - 35 %

Figure 13   Port Utilization Ratio of the MPPM

CONCLUSIONS

A simulation study of a knowledge base machine architecture and its control strategies was reported. For the control strategy, the MP method was proposed and found to be superior to the SP method for both the execution time and the page loading factor.

For hardware architecture, although the simulation showed that the potential data transfer capability of the MPPM is not fully used, it can be resolved by assigning only one port to each UE. We are currently conducting research into clustering methods on terms in order to improve the performance when the amount of definite clauses becomes large.

ACKNOWLEDGEMENT

We express thanks to Mr. Kazuhide Iwata for fruitful discussions.

REFERENCES

[Boral 82] Boral, H., et al., Implementation of the Database Machine DIRECT, *IEEE Transactions on Software Engineering*, Vol. SE-8, No. 6, 1982.

[Kakuta 85] Kakuta, T., et al.: The Design and Implementation of Relational Database Machine Delta, *Proceedings of the Fourth International Workshop on Database Machines*, pp.13-34, 1985.

[Morita 86] Morita, H., et al.: Retrieval by Unification Operation on a Relational Knowledge Base, *Proceedings of the 12th International Conference on VLDB*, 1986.

[Morita 87] Morita, H., et al.: Performance Evaluation of a Unification Engine for a Knowledge Base Machine, *ICOT TR-204*, 1987.

[Sakai 84] Sakai, H., et al.: Design and Implementation of the Relational Database Engine, *Proceedings of the International Conference on Fifth Generation Computer Systems*, pp.419-427, 1986.

[Sakai 86] Sakai, H., et al.: Development of Delta as a First Step to a Knowledge Base Machine, *Database Machines Modern Trends and Applications*, NATO ASI Series F, Vol 24, 1986.

[Shibayama 85] Shibayama, S., et al.: A Knowledge Base Architecture and its Experimental Hardware, *Proceedings of IFIP TC-10 Working Conference on Fifth Generation Computer Architectures* 1985.

[Ohmori 86] Ohmori, T., et al.: An Optimization in Unifiable Pattern Search.

[Tanaka 84] Tanaka, Y.: A Multiport Page-Memory Architecture and A Multiport Disk-cache System, *New Generation Computing*, Vol.2,no.3, pp.241-260, 1984.

[Yokota 86] Yokota, H., et al.: A Model and an Architecture for a Relational Knowledge Base, *Proceedings of the International Symposium on Computer Architecture*, 1986.

IMPLEMENTING PARALLEL PROLOG SYSTEM ON MULTIPROCESSOR SYSTEM PARK

H. MATSUDA[*], M. KOHATA[**], T. MASUO[***], Y. KANEDA[*], S. MAEKAWA[*]

[*]   Department of Systems Engineering, Faculty of Engineering, Kobe University
[**] Department of Electronic Engineering, Faculty of Engineering, Okayama University of Science
[***] Electrical Communications Laboratories, Nippon Telegraph and Telephone Corporation

ABSTRACT

A parallel Prolog "PARK-Prolog" is now running on a multiprocessor system PARK designed by the authors. The processor element of PARK is 16-bit microprocessor 68000. This paper focuses the implementation of PARK-Prolog. An instruction set for compiling a program in PARK-Prolog is presented. The set is based on Warren Abstract Machine and extended for parallel execution. The execution speed at 8 Queen in PARK-Prolog is more than DEC-10 Prolog and Quintus Prolog.

INTRODUCTION

Many studies for exploiting parallelism in logic programs have appeared in the past several years. Several cases of the implementation are reported, but the execution speed is not enough to compare with the sequential execution by dedicated machine for logic programming. This paper describes how the speed is increased in parallel execution. For achieving this, two conditions must be satisfied. First, the speed must be increased in sequential execution on each processor elements. Second, the overhead in parallel execution, such as synchronization and communication overhead in inter-process communication, must be decreased. The scheme for parallel execution must be decided in consideration of the two factors. This paper presents the implementation of a parallel Prolog, named PARK-Prolog, on multiprocessor system PARK (PARallel processing system of Kobe university) designed by authors. The design

599

characteristics of PARK-Prolog are described as follows:

(1) A process is regarded as a sequential execution of program to utilize the techniques for accelerating the execution, such as compiling, indexing, TRO, etc.

(2) Inter-process communication are performed not on variables shared into processes but on channels supported with builtin predicates for decreasing interactions among processes. The variable binding environments of all processes are independent for each other.

STRUCTURE OF PARK

Overall Structure

Fig. 1 shows the structure of PARK. PARK is tight coupled multiprocessor system with a common bus. PARK consists of two types of processor. The first is called "host" and performs input/output operations and the second is called "slave" and executes Prolog

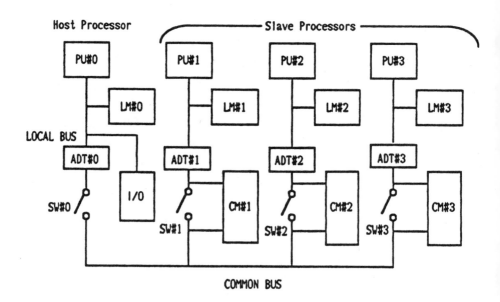

PU: processing unit (68000, 8MHz), LM: local memory
(host 256KB, slave 128KB), CM: common memory (512KB),
ADT: address translation unit, SW: bus switch

Fig. 1. Hardware structure of PARK.

program. The numbers of them are one as the host and three as the slave in the current prototype, and it can be extended up to 16 (1 host and 15 slaves) on the design. Each processor is composed of PU (16-bit microprocessor Motorola 68000), LM (local memory), ADT (address translation unit), and SW (bus switch with controller). Each slave processor has CM (a bank of common memory). A broadcast function to all the CMs is provided for inter-processor communication.

Common Memory

A bus-coupled system can be easily constructed and operated since the structure of the system is simple. However, the idle time arises when a contention on the bus occurs. To minimizes the bus contention, the common memory is divided into several banks and attached to each slave processors. Each slave processor can access its own memory bank without bus contentions. Each bank is allocated to its respective address space (see Fig. 2). A broadcast function can be performed to write data to a broadcast area. The data is simultaneously written to

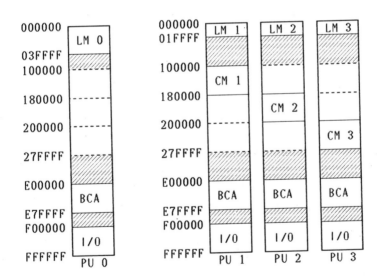

LM: Local Memory
CM: Common Memory
BCA: BroadCast Area
I/O: Areas for memory mapped I/O

Fig. 2. Memory map of PARK.

all banks of common memory. The broadcast function is useful for updating data shared in all processors and it significantly reduces the traffics on the bus.

Address Translation

PARK has one level address translation function. Translation is performed per page (8KB) unit. A page of data in the common memory can be mapped to any address in the 16-Mega Byte address space of the 68000 microprocessor. Mapping is performed separately for writing and reading. Thus, a function of writing protection can be easily applied. Address translation is accomplished within 1 CPU clock (125ns) using a high speed static RAM as the table.

PARALLEL PROCESSING METHOD

Process

We use the concept of "process" to describe a parallel processing method in PARK-Prolog. In this paper, a process is not a goal in the clause of a Prolog program but a sequence of execution of the program. Variable binding environments are held separately for each process (multi-environment). In case of creation of a new process and sending data to the other process, values of variables are copied and sending them to the process. If the value of the variable is undefined, the data means "undefined" is sent. Communication between processes are performed through a channel. Unlike the channel of Occam (2) or the "event" of Delta-Prolog (3), the channel of PARK-Prolog is created dynamically during execution. In addition, PARK permits sending data from several processes through one channel (non-deterministic merge in one channel). Receiving data from the channel is limited to one process. The method of the PARK-Prolog parallel processing system differs from the method of GHC (4) as described below.

The granularity of parallel execution of PARK-Prolog is larger than that of GHC, which has the goal literal as its process. This is because the physical granularity of PARK is big i.e. the ratio occupied by one processor element in relation to the entire system is big. Variable binding environments differ greatly between single-environment GHC and multi-environment PARK-Prolog. GHC accomplishes communications between processors by updating and referencing shared variables. PARK performs communication by means of special built-in predicates (sending and receiving through channel). Stream communications using differential lists are easy with GHC but difficult with PARK-Prolog. On the other hand, PARK-Prolog easily merges streams (one channel can be used for sending data from several processes) and occupies less memory area since communication data can be overwritten on channels after the communication and TRO (tail recursion optimization) and garbage collection on global stack can be performed locally for each process without referencing other process environments. The paging function in address translation can be used to control multi-environment.

Notation

In PARK-Prolog two binary operators, sequential AND ',' and sequential OR ';', are used for describing sequential execution. The following notation is used for describing parallel execution.

(1) Creating Processes

Goal1 // Goal2

fork (Goal)

'//' is used as a binary operator for joining a goal to another goal and creates two processes executing Goal1 and Goal2. This operator is syntactically a parallel AND but does not establish a logical AND relation: execution of one goal may continue unaffected even if execution of the other has failed. Also, even if both of the goals use shared variables, only the values of the variables are copied and the variables become independent after process creation. It is necessary to maintain consistency in the values of these variables by means of using inter-process communications to explicitly indicate in programs. "fork" is a builtin predicate creating a process that executes the goal given as an argument.

(2) Making channel / Removing channel

mkchan([ChannelList])

rmchan([ChannelList])

These are built-in predicates for making and removing channels for inter-process communications. "mkchan" creates the channels corresponding to the variables in the list and channel pointers are substituted into each variable. "rmchan" removes the channels corresponding to the pointers in the list.

(3) Sending data

Channel ! Data (Synchronized)

Channel !! Data (Unsynchronized)

These are builtin predicates for sending data through channel. Sending data is carried out by one of two methods: the first is "synchronized" by which execution is suspended unless the data is received, and the second is "unsynchronized" by which execution continues regardless of channel status. With synchronized method, the pointer to the sending process is written into channel along with data sent.

(4) Receiving data

Channel ? Pattern

This is a builtin predicate for receiving data from channels. Receiving is suspended if sending has not already been initiated. Receiving is performed by means of unification of sent data and the pattern. Substitution of values into variables during unification is performed in only one direction, from sending to receiving. If unification fails, backtracking is occurred as failure to execute this predicate. After unification, the receiving process searches for presence of pointer to the sending process. If it is present, the execution of the sending process is resumed.

PARK-PROLOG

Instruction Set

PARK-Prolog programs are compiled with two phases. Programs are finally compiled down to the machine language of 68000 microprocessor but are first compiled into intermediate codes. The intermediate code is based on an instruction set described below.

The instructions are defined as macro commands on 68000 assembler. Compiling from intermediate code to machine language is achieved by simply expanding macro commands.

The instruction set includes respective instructions for sequential execution. They are based on the set of WAM (Warren Abstract Machine) (5). In the WAM, type checking, dereferencing, and trail processing are carried out within instructions. As the method in (6), we separate these operations from the instructions and established as new instructions. In addition, the "get/unify" commands that changed operation by means of "mode bit" are established as independent instructions for read and write modes respectively. Data type is declared within mode declarations in addition to input and output mode declaration of goal argument. Some instructions are specially provided for each type (undefined variable, reference, nil, atom, integer, list, structure). As shown in paper (6) a "notrail" declaration is used to eliminate trail processing and increase speed of execution in deterministic program. PARK-Prolog proceeds a step further and provides a "nocheck" declaration that eliminates both dereferencing and trail processing. When the value of a goal argument is reference (or when the goal argument is declared as an output variable by mode declaration), it is assumed that the value of the argument is a pointer to a value cell of undefined variable. In such a case, dereferencing is not necessary. In addition, on backtraking, even if "undo" is not performed, the value of the variable is assumed as "undefined" and the substitution to the variables can be performed. So, trail processing can be omitted.

Fig. 3 shows a deterministic append program, performing mode declarations and "nocheck" declarations, and an example of its compiled codes. In Fig. 3 (b) and (c), all numeral operands of instructions indicate the number of corresponding temporary variables. Among the temporary variables, numbers 0, 1 and 2 are used as goal arguments. The operands of a "case_type" instruction are as follows: the first is a temporary variable number, the rests are labels to jump if the type of variable is reference to except undefined variable, undefined variable, nil, atom, integer, list, and structure respectively. The label only exists where there exists corresponding mode declaration. Types consisting of empty column are not checked. An error occurs in case in which variable type does not match any of the types indicated by the mode declaration. For this reason, all types possible for goal arguments must be written in mode declarations regardless of types of head argument of clause. When a type indicated by mode declaration cannot match all types of head argument of the clause, the label of "case_type" becomes "fail" (corresponding to the address of backtracking routine). If the mode declaration is omitted, it is assumed that all argument are declared as all possible combinations of input, output, and type descriptions.

Although the "notrail" declaration cannot be used in clauses

```
mode append(in(nil,list),in(nil,list),out(nil,list)).
append([],Y,Y).
append([V|X],Y,[V|Z]) :- append(X,Y,Z).
```

(a) Program of deterministic append

| ```
app@3:
 case_type 0,app@3_0,,
          app@3_1,,,app@3_2
app@3_0:
  deref       0
  execute    app@3
app@3_1:
  trail_check  2
  get_x_val_w  1,2
  proceed
app@3_2:
  get_list_r     0
  unify_x_var_r  3
  unify_x_var_r  0
  trail_check    2
  get_list_w     2
  unify_x_val_w  3
  unify_x_var_w  2
  execute       app@3
``` | ```
app@3:
 case_type 0,,,app@3_0,,,
              app@3_1
app@3_0:
  get_x_val_w   1,2
  proceed
app@3_1:
  get_list_r     0
  unify_x_var_r 3
  unify_x_var_r 0
  get_list_w     2
  unify_x_val_w 3
  unify_x_var_w 2
  execute        app@3
``` |
| (b) Without declaration | (c) With nocheck declaration |

Fig. 3. Compiled codes (deterministic append).

called from goals executed with non-deterministic, the "nocheck" declaration can be used even in programs (such as 8 Queen program) that are executed with non-deterministic, as long as the previously mentioned assumption holds true. Generally, it is difficult to judge whether the "nocheck" declaration can be used or not. The assumption no longer holds true if undefined variables are unified with each other (for example, unification of two different undefined variables within the goal argument). Dynamic analysis during execution is necessary to determine whether the "nocheck" declaration can be used or not.

The instructions for parallel execution consist of process creation / control instructions and inter-process communications

transmission / reception instructions.   The information for   creation
of process and the data for interprocess communication are temporarily
stored in MSB (message buffer). The value cells of undefined variables
and the element cells of list or structure are temporarily copied to
MSB, and then copied into global stack of reception process after
inter-process communication.

Fig. 4 shows examples of compilation of built-in predicates of
process creation and inter-process communication. ("C" and "X" in
Fig. 4 indicate numbers of temporary variables expressing variables
"C" and "X".)

Process Implementation

Table 1 shows the various areas composing processes.   The process

Creation of process fork(p(a))		Sending (Syncronized) C!a	
allocate_MSB	2	allocate_MSB	1
put_entry_MSB	p@1,0	put_atom_MSB	a,0
put_atom_MSB	a,1	lock_chan	C
fork		resume_receiver	C
		put_message_MSB	C
		suspend_sender	C
		unlock_chan	C
		switch	

Sending (Unsyncronized) C!!a		Receiving C?X	
allocate_MSB	1	lock_chan	C
put_atom_MSB	a,0	check_message	C,L1
lock_chan	C	suspend_receiver	C
resume_receiver	C	unlock_chan	C
put_message_MSB	C	switch	
unlock_chan	C	lock_chan	C
		L1: get_message_MSB	C
		get_x_var_MSB	X,C
		resume_sender	C
		deallocate_MSB	
		unlock_chan	C

Fig. 4. Compiled codes (builtin predicates for parallel execution).

Table 1. Areas composing process.

	Memory allocation	Contents
P C B	Common memory (Broadcast area)	State of process, Address of PWB
P W B	Local memory	Saved values of register, Temporary variables Pointer to other areas, Stack for subroutine
E N V	Common memory	Local variables Choice point
C O D E	Local memory	Object code
C H A N	Common memory (Broadcast Area)	Channel
M S B	Common memory (Broadcast Area)	Message Buffer

PCB: Process Control Block, PWB: Process Working Block
ENV: Environment, CHAN: Channel, MSB: Message Buffer

control block (PCB) is central and other areas are referenced from PCB through the process working block (PWB). Data (semaphores for mutual exclusion, links to other PCBs, status, allocated processor number) that must be referenced from other processes for monitoring the process is put into the PCB and other all data is put into local memory PWB, reducing referencing time.

Process monitoring is carried out by monitor. The monitor provides such capabilities as creation and termination of processes, suspension and resumption to control the process and scheduling. The monitor determines process status and arranges the PCBs into free list, scheduled list and ready list accordingly. Scheduled and ready lists are circulating lists and construct queues in which processes are lined up in order or arrival (see Fig. 5). A running process is directly pointed by the register of the 68000 slave processor. Processes of which execution has been suspended in synchronized transmission are pointed from the MSB. When several processes simultaneously transmit data through one channel, a chain can be made linking their respective MSBs. When execution has been suspended in reception, the PCB for that process is directly pointed from the

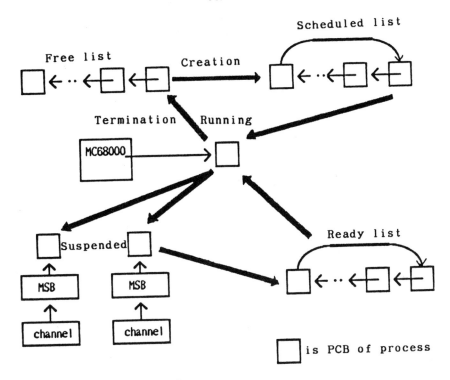

Fig. 5. State transition of process.

channel.

A new process is allocated to the slave processor by the monitor on creation of the process. The monitor and the three lists shown in Fig. 5 exist as many as the number of slave processors. Process scheduling is carried out locally on each slave processor, and with priority given to processes ready for execution. Processes on the ready list are executed first. When ready list is empty, a process to be executed is selected from the scheduled list. Since processes ready for execution are usually terminated first, this method reduces the load on processor during execution and the number of processes assigned.

PERFORMANCE EVALUATION

Table 2 shows the execution times in sequential execution by a single processor element. APPEND-100 means appending of list of 100 elements, and REV-30 means reversing of list of 30 elements. The

Table 2. Execution times in sequential execution.

programs	nocheck	notrail	check
APPEND-100	5.45	6.26	7.87
REV-30	28.3	32.2	39.6

(unit is millisecond)

columns "nocheck", "notrail", and "check" means execution with nocheck declaration, with notrail execution, and with no declaraion. In the cases of "nocheck" in sequential execution, the speed of PARK-Prolog on a single processor is about 18 kilo LIPS.

Table 3 shows the execution times of 8-Queen-All (searching for all solutions of 8 queens). In Table 3, "syncronized" means all inter-process communications are performed by syncronized method, "unsyncronized" means by unsyncronized method. For parallel execution, measurements were made by means of an 8-Queen-All program rewritten for parallel execution. The program is shown in Fig. 6. Fig. 6 shows a program of N queens, called by means of goal queen(8,N). (Number of solutions is entered at variable N.) The 8-Queen problem was divided into eight processes for parallel execution. Inter-process communications were used for counting the number of solutions and detecting end of all of the process. When we measured the time to execute the program, builtin predicates "write" and "nl" were omitted.

Table 3. Execution times of 8 Queen problem.

communication	parallel execution No. of processors			sequential execution
	1	2	3	
Syncronized	3009	1645	1298	2930
Unsyncronized	2989	1501	1137	

(unit is millisecond)

In Table 3, the speed in unsynchronized communication is better than that in synchronized communication. We think the difference is result of overhead from synchronization. Execution with unsynchronized communications and by three processors is 2.6 times faster than that by one processor.

As the processor element of PARK is general-purpose microprocessor, we compare the execution times of PARK-Prolog with execution times of Prolog system on general-purpose machine, DEC-10 Prolog compiler on DEC SYSTEM-2060 and Quintus Prolog on VAX-11/785.

```
nocheck.

mode queen(in(int),out(int)).
queen(N,S) :-
  qlist(N,L), mkchan([C]), fork(q1(L,C)), qa(N,C,S,0).

mode qlist(in(int),out(nil,list))
qlist(0,[]) :- !.
qlist(N,[N|L]) :- N1 is N-1, qlist(N1,L).

mode qa(in(int),recv(atom),out(int),in(int)).
qa(0,C,S,S) :- !, rmchan([C]), write(S), nl.
qa(N,C,S,S1) :- C?A, qa1(N,C,S,S1,A).

mode qa1(in(int),recv(atom)),out(int),in(int),in(int)).
qa1(N,C,S,S1,end) :- !, N1 is N-1, qa(N1,C,S,S1).
qa1(N,C,S,S1,sol) :- S2 is S1+1, qa(N,C,S,S2).

mode q1(in(nil,list),send(atom)).
q1(L,C) :- select(L,U,V), fork(q2(V,[U],C)), fail.
q1(_,_).

mode q2(in(nil,list),in(list),send(atom)).
q2(X,Y,C) :- q3(X,Y,Q), write(Q), nl, C!sol, fail.
q2(_,_,C) :- C!end.

mode q3(in(nil,list),in(list),out(nil,list)).
q3([],Y,Y) :- !.
q3(X,Y,Q) :- select(X,U,V), safe(U,Y,1), q3(V,[U|Y],Q).

mode select(in(nil,list),out(int),out(nil,list)).
select([U|V],U,V).
select([X1|X2],U,[X1|V]) :- select(X2,U,V).

mode(in(int),in(nil,list),in(int)).
safe(_,[],_).
safe(U,[P|Q],N) :-
  U =/= P+N, U =/= P-N, M is N+1, safe(U,Q,M).
```

Fig. 6. Program of N Queen.

The times are 1624 milliseconds in DEC-10 Prolog (7) and 3660 milliseconds in Quintus Prolog. The speed of PARK-Prolog is more than those of the Prolog systems.

CONCLUSION

This paper described and evaluated the performance of the PARK-Prolog system implemented on PARK multi-processor system. In PARK-Prolog, a process is regarded as a sequential execution of programs and the function of inter-process communication is provided as builtin predicates.

The performance of PARK-Prolog is 18 kilo LIPS at "append" program in sequential execution by one processor. The performance at "8-Queen-all" program in parallel execution by 3 processors is 2.6 times more than that by one processor. The speed is more than that of DEC-10 Prolog compiler on DEC SYSTEM-2060, and Quintus Prolog on VAX-11/785. The results are significant in consideration that the system was developed on 68000 microprocessor with 8MHz clock.

REFERENCES

1. Matsuda,H., Kohata,M., Masuo,T., Kaneda,Y. and Maekawa,S., LNCS 221, Springer-Verlag, 1986, pp. 35-43.
2. Occam Programming Manual, Prentice Hall 1984.
3. Pereira,L.M. and Nasr,R., Proc. FGCS'84, ICOT, 1984, pp. 283-291.
4. Ueda,K., LNCS 221, Springer-Verlag, 1986, pp. 168-179
5. Warren,D.H.D., SRI Technical Note 309, 1983.
6. Komatsu,H., Tamura,N., Asakawa,Y., and Kurokawa,T., Proc. LPC'86, ICOT, Tokyo, 1986, pp. 143-149.
7. Okuno,H., WG-SYM 33-4, IPS Japan, 1985.

SEARCH STRATEGY FOR PROLOG DATA BASES

G. BERGER SABBATEL, W. DANG

TIM3-IMAG/INPG, 46 Avenue Félix Viallet - 38031 GRENOBLE CEDEX

ABSTRACT

The paper presents a search strategy suitable for accessing Pro-log data bases stored in secondary memory. This strategy is based on a pipelined processing of sets of environments through the literals of a clause, and exploits the ability of unifying sets of goals with a data stream read from a disk. It is intended for implementation on OPALE, a distributed architecture for knowledge base management.

INTRODUCTION

Direct access to Prolog clauses stored in secondary memory is an approach of deductive databases, opposed to interfacing Prolog with relational databases [1,2]. However, the sequential depth first search strategy of Prolog is likely to provide poor performances, when the data base resides in secondary memory. On the other hand, the second approach involves an additional level in the access to the data, hence more complex systems, and a loss of expressive power.

The main problem for the direct use of Prolog for data bases is then the definition of a suitable search strategy, considering the specificities of disk accesses. This problem has been studied in the Opale project [3] which aims at designing a data base machine oriented toward the direct use of Prolog.

BACKGROUND

The Opale machine is depicted in figure 1:

The control processors communicate with the outside world (local network), and manage the machine. The disks are connected through disk processors, which manage them, and can execute the unification

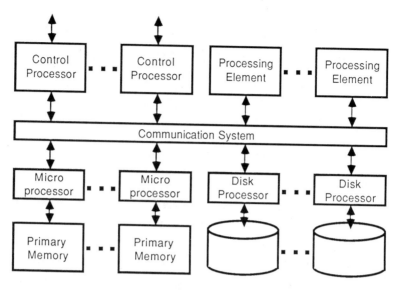

Figure 1.

on data streams read from the disk. The primary memories are used for storing temporary results and executing intelligent accesses to them. The processing elements execute the sequencing of the operations.

The unification of sets of goals (not only individual goals) with clause headers read from the disk can be executed "on the fly" [4]. Our solution is based on a decomposition of the unification in two operations:

The preunification: it is a unification in which the substitutions generated are not immediately processed. Hence, if several occurrences of a variable occur in one term, inconsistent substitutions can be generated.

The association: it checks the consistency of the substitutions generated on multiple occurrence of a same variable, and associates the substitutions with the corresponding goals.

The preunification can be executed by a set of VLSI operators, and the association can be executed by software on conventional processor (MC 680X0). The efficiency of the algorithms has been verified with software simulation and evaluation of Prolog programs.

SEARCH STRATEGY

When accessing clauses in secondary memory, a good strategy would be to find every clause whose header unify with a given set of goals, in a disk block (track). A solution is to bufferize the selected clauses and process them in the classical order. An alternative is to adapt the search strategy, even if this changes the semantic of the programs: for instance, a reasonable assumption for data base should be to consider the order of results as non meaningful.

Several alternatives to depth first strategy has been proposed [5]. They are generally related to parallel interpretation of logic programs rather than access to data bases:

AND-parallelism: parallel evaluation of the literals in a clause. This parallelism is unadapted to data bases, as each literal can produce a high volume of partial results which must therefore be joined.

OR-parallelism: parallel evaluation of the alternatives of the clauses. Another related level of parallelism is the induced AND-parallelism, i.e. the parallel processing of the results returned by literals.

Other approaches may be found in [6], and [7].

Set oriented approach

In our approach, the verification of a clause is considered as a pipe-line operating on sets of solutions, each literal receiving results (environments) from the previous one, and sending its results to the next one. The last literal in a clause returns its results to the caller of the clause.

The Figure 2 depicts the processing of the clause:
c(X,Y) :- 11(X,Z), 12(Z,Y).

The processing is distributed between 3 types of processes:

AND-processes: they are attached to every literal in the body of the clauses. They receive environments produced by the previous literal, apply the substitutions to the literal to produce new goals, and activate SEARCH-processes to verify every goals. For the first literal in the body of a clause (11(X,Z) in the example above), there is only one environment, produced by the unification of the clause header with the literal which called the clause.

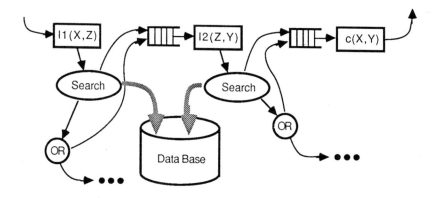

Figure 2.

SEARCH-processes: they receives the goals transmitted by the AND-processes, and search the clauses whose headers unify with a goal. They apply indexing to get the address of the disk tracks which must be searched, send filtering requests to the corresponding disk processors, and collect the substitutions produced by the unifications. When non atomic clauses are generated, OR-processes are created to verify them. For atomic clauses, the substitutions are sent to the next process in the pipe-line.

OR-processes: they create a new set of AND-processes to verify the clause. They collect the solutions and send them to the next process in the pipe-line.

Three kinds of parallelism are exploited in our approach: the OR-parallelism in the processing of non atomic clauses, the parallel processing of different partial solutions applied to different literals (pipe-lining), and the parallel search of clause headers which unify with goals (search on several disk units, or search of several goals in a single disk access on a disk unit, using our unification operator).

The role of SEARCH-processes is to allow parallel searches. Filtering requests are generated by the SEARCH-processes and sent to disk processors to be executed. The disk accesses are usually delayed, due to disk latency and wait queues, so that several filtering requests can be processed in a single access: this is the case when the requests are generated for example by a same AND-process processing the solutions of a previous disk access. Furthermore, the execution of disk accesses can be reordered to improve efficiency. In fact, the real sequencing of the operations is determined by the disk accesses, so that this solution can be considered as "disk driven".

Example

A more complete example will help describing the search strategy. Lets consider the following program:

```
p(X,Y,Z) :- l1(X,Y), l2(Y,Z).
l1(a,b).     l1(b,c).
l2(b,d).
l2(c,X) :- l4(X), l5(X).
l2(c,X) :- l6(X).
l4(b).       l4(a).
l5(a).
l6(b).
```

Now lets consider the query: p(X,Y,Z). The network of processes which solves this program is depicted in figure 3. In this figure, we show the sets of solutions transmitted among the processes. For the AND-processes, we give the literal processed, for the search processes, we give the corresponding goal, and for the OR-processes, we only put an arrow toward the first AND-process.

The top level process corresponds to the goal p(X,Y,Z). The single clause which defines p give rise to an OR-process for its resolution. At this point, the (single) environment is empty, as there is no substitution. The OR-process creates two AND-processes for the resolution of the literals l1(X,Y) and l2(Y,Z).

The AND-process l1(X,Y) receives a single empty environment, and so generates a single goal l1(X,Y), and creates the corresponding search process. This one finds (through filtering) two solutions, with the environments {X=a,Y=b} and {X=b,Y=c}. These solutions are transmitted to the next AND-process (l2(Y,Z)).

The AND-process l2(Y,Z) applies the substitutions to the literal, and creates two search-processes corresponding to the goals l2(b,Z), and l2(c,Z). The first one finds a single atomic clause which

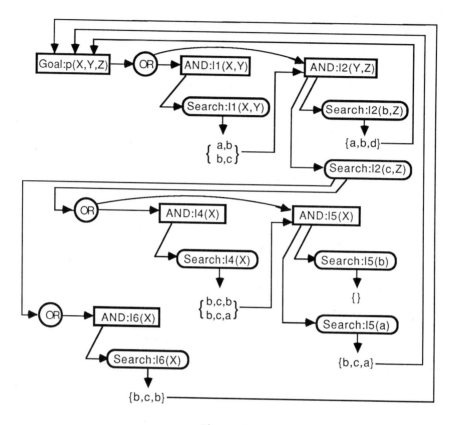

Figure 3.

verifies the goal, and returns a solution: {X=a,Y=b,Z=d}. The second one finds two non atomic clauses and creates two OR-processes (O1 and O2).

The OR-process O1 creates two AND-processes, A1 and A2, and sends the environment {X=b,Y=c} to A1. This one finds two solutions, sends them to the AND-process A2, which creates two search-processes, S1 and S2. S1 finds no solution. S2 finds a single solution {X=b,Y=c,Z=a} which is returned to the top-level process.

The OR-process O2 creates one AND-process, and send the environment {X=b,Y=c} to him. This one creates a search-process which returns the last solution: {X=b,Y=c,Z=b}.

Algorithms

We will give here an informal presentation of the algorithms. We assume that the communication primitives are:

receive(<data>): receive data on an entry port, each process has a single entry ports on which messages can be sent by multiple processes. The messages are managed in a FIFO basis.

send(<process-id>,<data>): send data to a given process.

create(<process>): create a son process, transmitting parameters to him, and return the process identifier.

wait: wait for the termination of the son processes. Every process must wait for the end of its son processes, so that the end of solutions streams can be detected.

Other primitives are:

index(<goal>): invoke the indexing mechanism of the data base, and return the disk addresses where the data must be searched for.

filter(<goal>,<disk address>): create a filtering process, which searches for clauses whose header unify with the goal in the disk track(s) specified, send the resulting substitutions and the body of non atomic clauses, and sends END when the filtering is completed. The filtering process can be distributed on several disk processors.

apply(<environment>,<literal>): apply the substitutions in the environment to the variables in the literal, and return the resulting term (goal).

compose(<environment>,<environment>): merge two environments, applying substitutions when required.

```
AND-process(L);           /*  L = the literal  */
begin
   receive(NP);           /*  number of next process  */
   receive(ENV);          /*  first environment  */
   while (ENV != END);
   begin   /* apply substitutions and start search process  */
      GOAL = apply(ENV,L);
      create(SEARCH_process(GOAL,NP,ENV));
      receive(ENV);       /*  next environment  */
   end;
   wait; send(NP,END);    /*  signal end to next process  */
```

```
end.
SEARCH-process(GOAL,NP,ENV);
begin
    filter(GOAL,index(GOAL));  /*  spawn a filtering process  */
    /*  S = substitutions generated by unification
        B = body of the clause  */
    receive({S,B}); /*  receive first solution of filter */
    while (S != END)
    begin
       NEW_ENV = compose(ENV,S);
       if (B = empty) then send(NP,NEW_ENV);
       else create(OR-process(NP,NEW_ENV,B));
          receive({S,B});   /*  receive another solution  */
    end;
    wait;                             /*  wait for the end of OR-processes  */
end.
OR-process(NP,ENV,B);
begin
    /*  the body (B) of a clause is represented
         as an array of literals B[I].  */
    NB = number of literals in B;
    for I = 1 to NB do NPROC[I] = create(AND-process(B[I]));
    for I = 1 to NB - 1 do send(NPROC[I],NPROC[I+1]);
    send(NPROC[NB] , NP);
    send(NPROC[1],ENV); /*  send environment to first process  */
    send(NPROC[1],END); /*  last environment  */
    wait;                     /*  wait for termination of the AND-processes  */
end .
```

Optimizations

In the resolution of a clause, some substitutions can be discarded if they are unuseful in the sequel (in a non structure sharing
scheme [8]). Lets consider the following example:

$c(X,Y,Z) :- l1(V,U,Z), l2(X,V,Z), l3(X,Y).$

The variable U is only used in l1, and should be discarded as
soon as it has been verified. V and Z are not used after l2. A
static analysis of the clause can determine, for every literal, if

every variable is to be transmitted to the next literal, or discarded. The variables can be classified in 6 classes:

Main (M): the variable is free and will be used in the sequel of the operation. The literal is the producer of the substitutions for this variable, and the substitutions must be passed to the next literal.

Anonymous (A): the variable is used only once, so the substitutions will not be used, and can be discarded.

Immediate (I): the variable has been bound by the unification of the clause header with the calling predicate. The substitution is applied during the initialization of the AND-processes, and is not further carried in the environments.

Filtered (F): the variable is bound by a previous literal, and will be used in the sequel of the evaluation. The substitution must be sent to the next process.

Temporary (T): the variable is bound but will not be used in the sequel of the evaluation. The substitutions are discarded after the verification of the literal.

To copy (C): the variable is not used by the literal, but must be sent to the next literal.

In the example above, for the request "c(term,X1,X2)" the types of the variables for every literal in the clause are the following:

Predicate	V	U	X	Y	Z
l1	M	A	-	-	M
l2	T	-	I	-	F
l3	-	-	I	M	C

Discussion

This strategy is intended for data base access, with limited complexity of the clauses, and no side effects. A problem which is not considered is the possible use of the cut operator: this one results in a partitioning of the demonstration, which should be taken into account by our scheme. However, we consider than more suitable operators can be found for knowledge bases, which can avoid the use of cut, and are easier to process: find the first solution of a goal, negation operator, if-then-else...

Our scheme does not either consider the recursivities. The strategy is expected to perform correctly when recursivities are present in the rules, but probably non optimally. A minimal enhancement should be to bring recursive rules in primary memory: then, the set oriented approach, and the possibility of unifying multiple goals can provide acceptable performances. It is also possible to adopt particular algorithms for the resolution of such rules.

IMPLEMENTATION

An experimentation of the strategy was carried out in Occam: this language is based on CSP [9], and developed by INMOS [10]; it provides tools for specifying parallel communicating processes. However, its communication model implied some modifications of our model, as processes can communicate only with their son or father.

The processes tree

As described in the previous section, an execution of a Prolog program can be modelized by a process tree. The nodes in the tree are OR-processes, AND-processes and SEARCH-processes. The OR-processes only create a set of AND-processes, and wait for their termination, hence, the information that must be stored in the process tree is reduced to the AND-processes nodes. The previous example gives rise to the Process-tree depicted in figure 4.

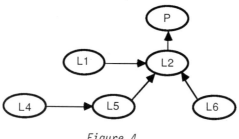

Figure 4.

The information which must be stored for every node are:
- The name of the process,
- The skeleton of the predicate,
- The number of son processes,
- The name of successor process (next process in the data stream)

- State informations: data base name, type, success/fail, etc...
- Received environments.

Subtrees of a node are appended during the evaluation: the OR-processes append a node for every predicate in the body of a clause. For the first predicate in the body, the substitutions in the environment generated by the unification are written in the Process-tree, then, goals are constructed by applying them to skeletons.

The dispatching algorithm

The dispatching algorithm is depicted in figure 5.

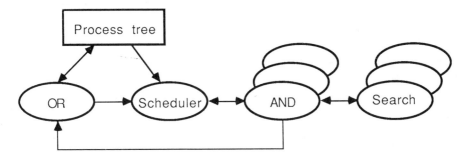

Figure 5.

The data base is assumed to be stored on several disk units, which allows concurrent accesses by SEARCH-processes. The Process-tree is stored in the memory units which can execute associative searches. The OR-processes, AND-processes, SEARCH-processes and Scheduler-processes are allocated respectively to OR-processors, AND-processors, SEARCH-processors and Scheduler-processor. The SEARCH-processes will also trigger operations on the disk processors and memory units to execute indexing and filtering.

In the initial stage, the Scheduler-processor takes user's query as skeleton and sends it to one AND-processor with an empty environment. This AND-processor creates a SEARCH-process and transmits the goal to it. The results of the search are returned back to the AND-processor, and the solutions are transmitted to an OR-processor.

The OR-processor tests the data received from the AND-processors. If the clause get from the disk is an axiom, it appends the environment to the Process_tree and signals this to the Scheduler-processor.

Otherwise, it creates new AND-processes by appending new nodes in the Process_tree, and informs the Scheduler-processor.

When the Scheduler-processor is informed that an AND-process is ready to be evaluated, it analyses the successor nodes of the ready process: all nodes which can be arranged in a pipelined evaluation are written in an entry of a buffer called Ready-pool.

The processors allocation is executed according to the number of available physical processors and the number of AND-processes in the Ready_pool. These AND-processes are allocated to a set of AND-processors. The environments generated by an AND-process are transmitted directly to its successor, which start its evaluation after receiving a set of environments.

The Process-tree may be stored in several memory modules, which allows multiple accesses. There may also be multiple Scheduler-processors and OR-processors when necessary. The overall system can be configured dynamicaly according to the distribution of the load.

Results of the experimentation

The first result of the experimentation was a validation of the strategy. Due to limitations in early versions of OCCAM, it was difficult to get precise evaluations of number of processes and CPU time. Some results have been obtained by running examples with one OR-processor, one Scheduler-processor and a maximum of six AND-processors and SEARCH-processes.

example

We consider a logic data base composed of three facts bases and two rules bases as following:

```
person(name,sex,age). ...
father(father_name,child_name). ...
mother(mother_name,child_name). ...
parent(X,Y) :- father(X,Y).
parent(X,Y) :- mother(X,Y).
sister(X,Y) :- parent(P,X), parent(P,Y), person(X,female,_).
```

These informations are stored in several files simulating disk tracks.

The query ":- sister(X,Y),print(X,Y)." was run and returned 17 solutions. The following table gives the simulation results.

Number of processors	2	4	6
Execution time (*)	133	87	62
Number of AND nodes	52	52	52
Work space for Process-Tree (K Bytes)	5.7	3.6	3

(*) *The unit of time is the mean execution time of a SEARCH-process.*

52 AND-processes and 98 SEARCH-processes were created. For 2, 4 and 6 AND-processors and SEARCH-processors, the execution time is in inverse ratio to the number of processors, as can be expected. Of interest is also the save of working space in the Process-tree, as the pipeline scheme avoids to bufferize the environments and recopy them after the activation of a process.

For large data bases, the amount of partial solutions can be important. When the size of the process tree grows too large, a solution is to swap parts of it in secondary memory. However, as has been shown in the previous section, sufficient processing power considerably reduce the size of the process tree, and hence, the need for swapping it.

CONCLUSION

The experimentation proves that our strategy is an efficient alternative to depth first strategy for data base processing, allowing OR-parallelism, SEARCH-parallelism, and pipe-lining of AND-processes.

A limited implementation of the strategy has also been inserted in a Prolog interpreter, using our unification algorithm. It allows the access to fact bases, which does not include non atomic clauses (i.e. we did not implement the OR-processes), but allow the pipelining of literals. This implementation is significantly faster (in terms of CPU time as well as response time) than the classical depth first strategy, when the number of solutions is high.

The next steps will be the complete implementation of the strategy (including rules processing) on a multiprocessor machine, and the VLSI implementation of the unification algorithm.

References
1. H Gallaire, Impacts of logic on data bases , *VLDB 81*, , 1981.
2. J Minker, An experimental relationnal data base system based on logic, in *Logic Programming*, Clark and Taernlund (ed.), Academic Press, 1982.
3. G Berger-Sabbatel, J C Ianeselli and G T Nguyen, A PROLOG Data base machine, in *Data base machines*, Springer Verlag, Sep. 1983.
4. G Berger-Sabbatel, W Dang, J C Ianeselli and G T Nguyen, Unification for a Prolog data base machine, *2nd Int. Logic programming Conf*, Uppsala, July 1984.
5. J S Conery and D F Kibler, Parallel interpretation of logic programs, *ACM Conf on functionnal prog. lan. and comp. arch*, Portsmouth, Oct. 1981.
6. N Tamura and Y Kaneda, Implementing parallel Prolog on a multiprocessor machine, *Int. Symp. on logic programming*, Atlantic City, Feb. 1984, 42-48.
7. G Lindstrom and P Panangaden, Stream-based execution of logic programs, *Int. Conf. on Logic Programming*, Atlantic City, Feb. 1984.
8. C S Mellish, An alternative to structure sharing in the implementation of a PROLOG interpreter, in *Logic Programming*, Clark and Taernlund (ed.), Academic Press, 1982.
9. C A R Hoare, Communicating sequential processes, *Comm. ACM 21*, 8 (1978), .
10. P Wilson, Occam architecture bases system design, *Computer design*, , Nov. 1983.

THE UNIFICATION PROCESSOR
BY PIPELINE METHOD

M. TANABE, H. AISO

Department of Electrical Engineering
Keio University
3-14-1 Hiyoshi, Yokohama 223 Japan

Abstract

Unification is one of the most important processes in Prolog systems. In this paper, We propose a dedicated hardware unifier consisting of four stages of pipelined processors, which find variable bindings known as 'mgu'. To achieve pipelining, terms are expressed especially by a sequence of symbols with their arities. To enhance its performance, only terms which are bound by variables are managed within this unifier, and the structure sharing method is also adopted to prevent the occurrence of redundancy of variables. Moreover 'occur-check', which is known to be a heavy load on software systems, is easily performed during unification.

1 INTRODUCTION

Unification, one of the most important operations in Prolog systems, is based on the *resolution principle* of the first-order predicate logic[1]. The implementation of unification has had a great effect on the organization and the performance of Prolog systems. There have been many proposals for the efficient implementation of unification. These includes algorithms using effective data structures suitable for unification[2,3], the theoretical analysis of parallel unification[4], an implementation for reducing the amount of memory space using structure sharing[5,6,7], efficient implementation using structure copy[7,8], and so on. In the research on Prolog machines proposed in [9-11], there have been many proposals of unification processors[12-15] because its implementation is one of the most important subjects and has a great effect on their micro-codes and stack structures.

In the Prolog systems, only information about binding variables, known as 'mgu', is necessary. Here, we examine the parallelism of unification and suggest an algorithm of unification that suits it. In accordance with these results, we propose a dedicated hardware unifier which consists of four stages of pipelined processors.

2 DEFINITION

2.1 The Expression "Terms"

First, the expression "term", which is treated in this paper, is defined here.

1. symbols: There are two classes of symbols: the variable class and the function class. Symbols which belong to the variable class are called variables. Symbols which belong to the function class are called functors. Each functor has its arity, which indicates the number of its arguments. The arity of a variable is treated as 0. In this paper, we express functors using lower case letters and variables using upper case letters.

2. terms: All terms are constructed with the following recursive rules:

   (a) Every variable is a term.

   (b) Every functor whose arity is 0 is a term.

   (c) if t_1, t_2, t_3, ..., t_n are terms and f is a functor whose arity is n,
   then f (t_1, t_2, t_3, ..., t_n) is a term,
   and t_i ($i = 1$, ..., n) are called subterms of this term.

A term and its arity have the following relationship. Assume that the number of symbols in an arbitrary term is S_a, and the total number of the arities of the symbols which make up the term is A_a, then $S_a = A_a + 1$.

We check the last subterm using this property. That is, if $S_a = A_a + 1$ is satisfied by one symbol, it is the last subterm in a term. Here, checking the last subterm in this manner is called an 'arity check'.

2.2 Substitution

A substitution is expressed as follows:
$$\{t_1 \ / \ V_1 \ , \ t_2 \ / \ v_2 \ , \ ... \ , \ t_n \ / \ V_n \ \}$$
where t_i are terms and V_i are variables. In each pair $\{t_i \ / \ V_i\}$, V_i is not a subterm in t_i for $i,j = 1$, 2, ..., n and $i \neq j$, $V_i \neq V_j$. If V_i is a subterm of t_i in $\{t_i \ / \ V_i\}$, the substitution is repeated forever. Checking for this infinite repetition is called an 'occur-check'. Each pair $\{t_i \ / \ V_i\}$ is read "V_i is bound by t_i". We will use Greek letters to represent substitutions. Given the term t and the substitution θ, $t\theta$ expresses a form which is made by replacing all V_i in θ appearing in t by t_i. This $t\theta$ is called an 'instance' of a term.

Let
$$\theta = \{t_1 \ / \ X_1, t_2 \ / \ X_2 \ , ..., t_n \ / \ X_n\}$$
and

$\lambda = \{u_1 \ / \ Y_1, \ u_2 \ / \ Y_2, \ ..., \ u_m \ / \ Y_m \ / \ Y_m\}$

be two substitutions. Then the composition of θ and λ is the substitution, written $\theta^*\lambda$, that is obtained from the set

$\{t_1 \ \lambda \ / \ X_1 \ , t_2 \ \lambda \ / \ X_2 \ ,..., \ t_n \ \lambda \ / \ X_n, u_1 \ / \ Y_1 \ ,.., u_m \ / \ Y_m\}$

by deleting any element $\{u_i \ / \ Y_i\}$, such that Y_i belongs to $\{X_1 \ ,.., \ X_n\}$ and any element $\{t_i\lambda/X_i\}$ such that $t_i\lambda$ is X_i.

2.3   Unification

If there exists a substitution θ such that $t\theta = s\theta$, where t and s are terms, then these terms t and s are called unifiable, and such a θ is said to be a unifier. Also, we say that the unifier θ unifies terms t and s. A unifier θ for a pair (t, s) of terms is an 'mgu' (most general unifier) if and only if for each unifier σ for the pair, there is a substitution λ such that $\sigma = \theta^*\lambda$. The unification problem consists of deciding whether the pair (t, s) is unifiable or not, and if this pair is unifiable, finding the mgu θ.

2.4   Unification Algorithm

The disagreement set W_k of the pair of terms in W is obtained by comparing their subterms in corresponding positions and placing them in W_K if any of the symbols differ. The set of these respective subterms is the disagreement set of W.

In this unification processor proposed in this paper, we adopt the following algorithm.

step 1 :   Set $k = 0$, $W_k = W\{$ initial pair of terms $\}$, $\theta_k = \{$empty substitution$\}$

step 2-1:   Find the disagreement set by comparing terms from left to right. This process is repeated until the end of the longer term. If a disagreement set is a pair of functors, then stop unification in failure. If not, select $\{t_k \ / \ V_k\}$.

step 2-2:   Let $\theta_{k+1} = \theta_k\{t_k \ / \ V_k\}$. If there is a contradiction, the terms are not unifiable.

step 3 :   If step 2-1 and 2-2 are terminated, we regard θ_{k+1} as the mgu.

step 4 :   Do occur-check

In this algorithm, step 2-1 and step 2-2 can be executed in the pipeline manner.

3   UNIFICATION PROCESSOR

3.1   The Basic Concept of The Unification Processor

The unification processor is designed based on the following three concepts.

1. Separation of the checking of functors and the checking of the inconsistency of terms:

   Failures of unification fall into the following two categories. One is caused by a difference of functors and the other is caused by inconsistencies in binding variables to terms. A difference of functors can be detected in the earlier stage of the process by checking pairs of functors or arities. However, in the latter case it cannot be judged whether the terms are unifiable or not until all subterms have been checked. Therefore, checking for an inconsistency in terms and checking a difference of functors should be performed independently by different processors.

2. Unification of terms is regarded as finding the 'mgu':

   A Prolog machine consists of the unification processor and a control processor which manages environments. The unification processor receives a pair of terms to unify from the control processor. Since information about the pair of terms is still held in the control processor, the unification processor is only needed to keep terms bound to variables (mgu). The unification processor is designed to return whether or not a pair of terms is unifiable and the 'mgu'.

3. Processes are performed by the pipeline method:

   Stages of unification are performed in dedicated processors. To enhance the performance, these processors work in a pipeline manner.

3.2   Outline of The Unification Processor

A diagram of the unification processor is shown in Fig-1. It consists of the following four kinds of processors:

    STBV (Select Term Binding Variable processor)

    AVTC (Assign variable to **CTBV**)

    CCTBV (Control **CTBV**)

    CTBV (Charge Term Binding Variable)

    STBV selects terms bound to variables. This function corresponds to step 2 of our unification algorithm mentioned above.

    CTBVs (i.e. Charge Term Binding Variable) manage the terms bound to variables. Every **CTBV** has a local memory to contain the term. One is allocated to each variable.

    First, a pair of the terms are transferred to the **STBV**. The **STBV** checks whether the terms are functors or not. If both of them are functors, the **STBV** compares them.

    The **AVTC** manages a table of variables and key numbers for the **CTBV**. A key number for the **CTBV** is referred to from variables in the **AVTC**, and transferred with terms to the **CTBV**. This key number is called the **CTBV-number** (indicated by a * sign in Fig.1-7). Consistency checks are performed by the **CTBV** and **CCTBV**.

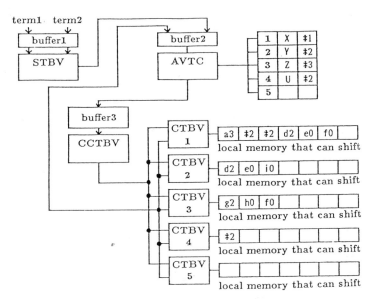

Fig.1 Diagram of the system of the pipeline Unification Processor

CTBV-numbers are returned to the **AVTC**, if necessary. These processors all work using the pipeline method.

The process performed in the **STBV** corresponds to step 2-1 in the unification algorithm, that is, detecting the disagreement set between terms.

Step 2-2 (consistency checks) is performed in the **CTBVs**. If a variable has not been bound to any term, a consistency check is not necessary. The variable is written directly into the local memory of the **CTBV**. On the other hand, if the variable has already been bound, a consistency check is needed. To accomplish this, a comparison of the pointers for the variable is performed. Note that the number of the **CTBV** equals that of the variables, and both can be identified by the **CTBV-number**.

CCTBV controls all these **CTBVs**, and the **AVTC** manages the mapping of variables into **CTBVs**. The **AVTC** has a table that manages variables and their **CTBV**, which is called the **AVTC-table**.

3.3 The Work of The STBV

In this unification processor, terms are expressed by a line of symbols and the arity of each symbol[15]. A pair of terms to be unified are inputed at the same time. Symbols of the terms to be unified are read from one or the both of the dual inputs. This processor compares a pair of terms and sends variables and the terms which bound those variables to the **AVTC** through the pipeline. The purpose of **STBV** is to find quickly pairs of terms which obviously cannot be unified, that is, the term which has different functors or arities. If both terms to be compared are ground terms (i.e. no bound variable inside), the whole unification ends only within the **STBV**. **STBV** works in the following three cases (Fig.2).

Case 1: Comparison of a pair of functors

Compare a pair of symbols or arities with each other. If they are the same, both terms are shifted, otherwise, the unification ends in failure.

Case 2: Comparison of the functor with the variable

This corresponds to the case in which functors are bound to a variable. The **STBV** sends the variable and functor to the **AVTC**, and performs the 'arity-check' in order to find the end of the term. Until the 'arity-check' is satisfied, the **STBV** receives symbols from the input for the functor. After the 'arity-check', the **STBV** sends the symbols to the **AVTC**. Then if the symbols to be sent are variables, they are treated in the same way as a functor. And if the 'arity-check' is satisfied, that is the symbol is the last one in the each term, then a pair of symbols will be shifted. Meanwhile, the next comparison starts.

Case 3: Comparison of a pair of variables

The **STBV** sends a pair of variables to the **AVTC**, shifts both symbols in, and performs the next comparison.

In addition the **STBV** sends the **AVTC** the information for identifying Case 2 (indicated by a + sign in Fig.2) and Case 3 (indicated by a - sign). Here, we call a variable and a term bound to it a series of symbols.

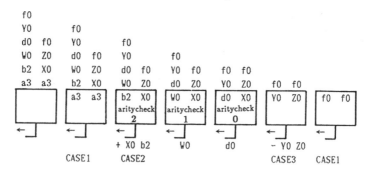

Fig.2 Example of STBV execution

3.4   The Work of the AVTC

AVTC manages the variable's name in a series of symbols which is received from the STBV, and the **CTBV-number** to be assigned to it. This processor has an **AVTC-**

table which stores the variable's name and the **CTBV-number** to be assigned to it. Since this is a kind of CAM, we can know the **CTBV-number** from the variable's name. This processor's action is as follows (Fig.3).

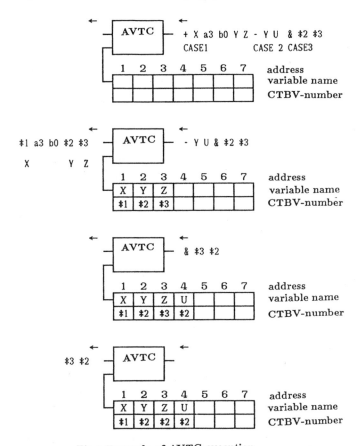

Fig.3 Example of AVTC execution

Case 1: Binding information for assigning a term to a variable

All the **CTBV-numbers** assigned to variables by the **AVTC** are entered in the **AVTC-table**. If the variable is already entered, the **CTBV-number** is returned. **AVTC** sends the **CTBV-number**, not the variable's name, and does nothing to the functor.

Case 2: Binding information for assigning a variable to another variable

The **AVTC** enters a pair of variables and returns the **CTBV-number**. In this case the pair of variables is the same, therefore, the **AVTC** rewrites the smaller **CTBV-number** into the lager **CTBV-number(s)** in the **AVTC-table**.

Case 3: Binding information for assigning a **CTBV-number** to another **CTBV-number**

In this case bound information is sent from the **CTBV** to buffer 2 (Fig.1). The **AVTC** rewrites all smaller **CTBV-number** into a lager **CTBV-number(s)**.

3.5   The Work of The CTBV and The CCTBV

A **CTBV** stores a term to substitute into the proper variables in its local memory, and checks for inconsistency in the substitution. after the unification has succeeded, the 'mgu' will be stored in the local memory of the **CTBV**. A series of symbols, of which the head is the **CTBV-number** and the remainder a term to bind the variable, come in from the **AVTC** through the pipeline. When the **CCTBV** receives the head **CTBV-number** in a series of symbols, it invokes the **CTBV** which corresponds to this head number, and send it the term to be bound to the variable. The **CTBV** will do an 'arity-check', and when the **CTBV** receives the last symbol in the term, the **CTBV** sends the end signal of a term to the **CCTBV**. Each **CTBV** invokes the other **CTBVs** recursively. Looking at the computation in **CTBVs** in certain time slice, relationships among four kinds of **CTBVs** can be defined : sender-**CTBV**, current-**CTBV**, parent-

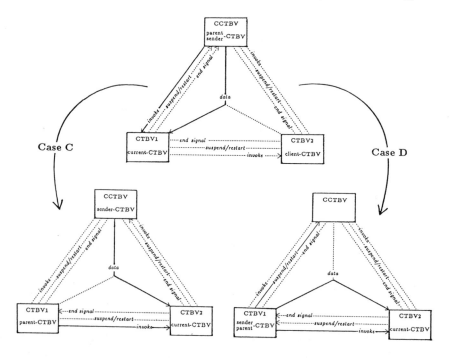

Fig.4 Relationships between CTBV

CTBV and client-CTBV (Fig.4).

The sender-CTBV sends data to the current-CTBV, the current-CTBV processes the data from its sender, the parent-CTBV activates the current-CTBV, and the client-CTBV will be activated by the current-CTBV in the near future. By using the notations mentioned above, the five kinds of actions for the current-CTBV are expressed as follows:

Case 1: There is no entry in the local memory

The current-CTBV does the arity-check of the term which has been received from the sender-CCTBV and writes it to the local memory. After the arity-check is satisfied, i.e. the last symbol has been received, the current-CTBV sends the end signal of the term to the parent-CCTBV. As shown in Fig.5:

a. Receive a2 and do the arity-check and write it into the local memory.

b. Do the same to **CTBV-number** *2.

c. Repeat b in the same way.

d. Receive f0, finish the 'arity-check', and tell the parent-CCTBV that the last symbol has been received.

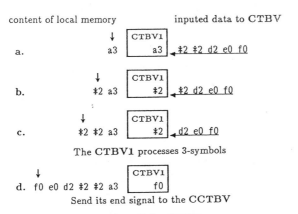

Fig.5 Example of the action of the CTBV
when the memory is not registered

Case2: There are some entries in the local memory

This case is divided into the following four cases according to the different kinds of symbols as shown in Fig.6:

Case A: Both symbols are functors

Compare the functor with the arity and if both functors are the same, go to the next step, otherwise the unification fails.

Case B: Both symbols are **CTBV-numbers**

If these symbols are different, give their **CTBV-numbers** to the **AVTC** and write the smaller one into the local memory.

Case C: The local memory is a **CTBV-number** and the input is a functor

Invoke the **CTBV-number's CTBV** and wait until receiving the end signal from this client-**CTBV**.

Case D: The local memory is a functor and the input is a **CTBV-number**

Suspend the sender-**CTBV** through which the data is passed. Invoke the inputed **CTBV-number's CTBV** and this **CTBV** becomes the client. Send the subterm in the local memory of the current-**CTBV** to the client-**CTBV**. When the end signal comes from the client-**CTBV**, write the **CTBV-number** into the local memory of the current-**CTBV**, then restart the suspended sender-**CTBV**.

In all the above case, in the current-**CTBV** the 'arity-check' is satisfied by the symbol, and its end signal is sent to the parent-**CTBV**. After the **CCTBV** receive the end signal, it processes the next series of symbol.

content of local memory   inputed data to CTBV

        ↓ | CTBV1 |

Case A: f0 e0 d2 ‡2 ‡2 a3 | a3   a3 | ← ‡4 d2 e0 f0 ‡2

        ↓ | CTBV1 | Send AVTC 2-symbols, ‡2 ‡4

Case B: f0 e0 d2 ‡2 ‡2 a3 | ‡2   ‡4 | ← d2 e0 f0 ‡2

        ↓ | CTBV1 | Wait

Case C: f0 e0 d2 ‡2 ‡2 a3 | ‡2   d2 | ← e0 f0 ‡2

The **CCTBV** sends 3-symbols and the **CTBV2** processes them respectively

           | CTBV1 | Suspend CCTBV

Case D: f0 e0 d2 ‡2 ‡2 a3 | b0   ‡2 |

The **CTBV1** sends 3-symbols and the **CTBV2** processes them respectively

The **CTBV2** sends its end signal to the **CTBV1**

        ↓ | CTBV1 |

End: ‡2 ‡2 ‡2 a3 | b0 |

Send its end signal to the **CCTBV**

Fig.6 Example of the action of the CTBV when the memory is registered

3.6   Output of 'mgu' and Occur-check

After all of the processors (**STBV**, **AVTC**, **CTBV** and **CCTBV**) have ended, 'mgu' is created in the local memory of the **CTBV**. Then the unification processor will output this 'mgu'. When the control processor receives the signal for termination from the unification processor, the control processor sets its mode into the output-mode and sends variables to the **AVTC** if necessary. Then the **AVTC** picks up the **CTBV-number** and sends it to the **CCTBV**. The **CCTBV** invokes the corresponding **CTBV** which then sends the content of the local memory to the bus. Here, if there is any **CTBV-number** in the memory, the **CTBV** invokes the corresponding **CTBV** and waits until its end signal comes. If there is nothing in the local memory of the invoked **CTBV**, its own **CTBV-number** will be sent as an output.

In the case that the waiting **CTBV** is invoked by the other current-**CTBV**, it means there is *at least the re-substitution of a variable*, i.e. a unification has been failed by 'occur-check'. At this time the **CTBV** sends a message to the control processor to inform it of the failure (Fig.7).

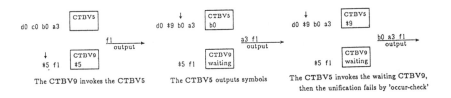

Fig.7 Example of 'occur-check'

4   FEATURES OF THIS UNIFICATION PROCESSOR

In the simulation of this unification processor, the following results were attained. Assume the total number of symbols in both terms to be unified is n. This unification processor's hardware cost is $O(n^2)$, and its computation complexity is $O(n^2)$. The computation is complicated by the fact that a current-**CTBV** must send its subterm to its client-**CTBV** when the input of the current-**CTBV** is the client **CTBV-number**, and while it is being sent the sender-**CTBV** must be suspended (case D in case 2 mentioned in the section 3.5). In order to eliminate this problem, we reorder the subterms with the control processor to suit the unification processor when loading a pair of terms. This gives a higher degree of sophistication to the complexity of computation, $O(n)$. Concerning hardware cost, this system adopts 'data-sharing', so that the cost will be $O(n)$ if a way can be found to make the **CTBV**'s local memory into virtual memory.

5   CONCLUSION AND FUTURE WORK

In this paper, we proposed a unification processor using a pipeline method. We regard unifying a pair of terms as finding the 'mgu' in order to decrease redundant information that is in the control processor. We divide the unification into two stages because there are two cases of unification failure.

We designed a unification processor based on the above ideas. As to future work, we will study a control processor that provides an input/output function and backtracking of the environment. Moreover, we will also study the implementation of the Prolog machine using the unification processor presented in this paper.

6 ACKNOWLEDGEMENTS

The authors gratefully acknowledge the advice and guidance of Dr. Hideharu Amano, and Dr. Rong Yang, Dept. of E.E., Keio Univ.. The authors would also like to thank Jun Miyazaki, Yasuro Shobatake, Hideo Tamura and Kunihito Matsumura, students of Aiso Lab.,Dept. of E.E., Keio Univ., for many interesting hours of discussion. The authors are also grateful to Kenichi Nakanishi, Hiroshi Shinkai, Kenji Ogura.

References

[1] J.A.Robinson, "A Machine-Oriented Logic Based on the Resolution Principle," J. of ACM, Vol.12, No.1, Jan., 1986, pp.23–41.

[2] M.S.Paterson, M.N.Wegman, "Linear Unification," J. of Computer and Systems, Vol.4, No.2, pp.258-282, Apr., 1982.

[3] A.Martelli, U.Montanari, "An Efficient Unification Algorithm," ACM Trans. on Programming Languages and Systems, Vol.4, No.2, pp.258-282, Apr., 1982.

[4] H,Yasuura, "On Parallel Computational Complexity of Unification," in Proc. of Inter. Conf. on FGCS'84, pp.235-243, Nov., 1984.

[5] R.S.Boyer, J.S.Moore, "The Sharing of Structure in Theorem-proving Programs," Machine Intelligence, Vol.7, Edinburgh U.P., 1972.

[6] D.H.D.Warren, "IMPLEMENTATION PROLOG - compiling predicate logic programs," D.A.I. Research Report No.39, 1977.

[7] M.Bruynooghe, "The Memory Management of PROLOG Implementations," LOGIC PROGRAMMING,pp.83-98,Academic Press, 1982.

[8] C.S.Mellish, "An Alternative to Structure Sharing in the Implementation of a PROLOG Interpreter," LOGIC PROGRAMMING, pp.99-106,Academic Press, 1982.

[9] K.Taki, M.Yokota,et. al., "Hardware Design and Implementation of the Personal Sequential Inference Machine(PSI)," in Proc. of Inter. Conf. on FGCS'84, pp.542-550, Nov., 1984.

[10] N.Tamura, K.Wada et. al., "Sequential Prolog Machine PEK," in Proc. of Inter. Conf. on FGCS'84, pp.542-550, Now.,1984.

[11] E.Tick,D.H.D.Warren, "Towards Pipelined Prolog Processor," in Proc. on 1st Inter. Sym. on Logic Programming, pp.29-40, Feb., 1984.

[12] M.Yuhara, H.Koike, H.Tanaka, T.Moto-oka, " A Unify Processor Pilot Machine for Pie," in Proc. of the Logic Programming Conf.'84, ICOT, Mar, 1984.

[13] N.S.Woo, "A Hardware Unification : Design and Analysis," in Proc. of 12th Inter. Sym, on COMPUTER ARCHITECTURE, pp.198-205, June, 1985.

[14] M.Carlsson, "A Microcoded Unifier for Lisp Machine Prolog," in Proc. of 2nd Sym. on Logic Programming, pp.162-171, July, 1985.

[15] M.Shobatake, H.Aiso, "A UNIFICATION PROCESSOR BASED ON A UNI-FORMLY STRUCTURED CELLULAR HARDWARE," Proc. of the 13th Inter. Sym. on Comp. Arch., June 1986.

[16] C.Chang, R.C.Lee, "Symbolic Logic and Mechanical Theorem Proving," Academic Press,1973.

KNOWLEDGE-BASED SYSTEM FOR CONCEPTUAL SCHEMA CONVERSION ON A MULTI-MODEL DATABASE MACHINE

Esen Ozkarahan

Department of Computer Science, Arizona State University, Tempe, Arizona, 85287

Aime Bayle

Large Computer Product Division, Honeywell Bull, Phoenix, Arizona, 85066

ABSTRACT

The design of a "good" conceptual schema for a multi-model database machine or application is often the object of an iterative process that is performed usually manually and in an ad-hoc manner. With the advent of knowledge-based systems and rule-based programming, it has become feasible to encapsulate a substantial amount of the database administrator's knowledge into a system capable of performing normalization operations and making database design decisions. The interactive knowledge-based system described in this paper attempts to automatize the normalization process of a E/R conceptual schema and to produce an equivalent "better" normalized schema. The ultimate goal is to produce a "proper" conceptual schema i.e. a conceptual schema that yields lossless, dependency-preserving and normalized external schemas.

INTRODUCTION

During the past sixteen years since Codd has introduced the relational data model, major advances have taken place in the theory and design of relational databases. A comprehensive normalization theory has emerged of significant value to the database designers [5, 7, 13, 14, 18]. Elimination of data redundancy and avoidance of data manipulation anomalies are some of the well-known benefits of that theory [13, 14, 18]. Although concepts like "functional dependencies" and "normal forms" have become fairly widespread and have been used in the design of some practical databases, the use of normalization theory algorithms and techniques remains largely manual and minimal. With the advent of knowledge-based system and rule-based programming, it has become feasible to encapsulate that vast body of knowledge into a system capable of performing normalization operations and making database design decisions. This paper describes the application of artificial intelligence techniques and knowledge engineering methodology to the development of an interactive knowledge-based system capable to assist the database administrator in the performance of his/her task. The database administrator is considered in this approach as the domain expert and his/her valuable knowledge is codified in terms of production rules. The need to transform a schema into a "better" but "equivalent" schema has been recognized by many researchers and thoroughly analyzed by Tsichritzis and Lochovsky [16]. This paper focuses on the important task of schema design and the algorithmic and heuristic transformations required to refine it and make it better. The construction of a system capable to perform the database administrator's schema design functions is a complex task well-suited to the knowledge-based system technology. The difficulties and technical issues encountered are reported and analyzed. This system resembles an expert system but does not possess all the features (e.g. explanation facility) usually encountered in one.

MULTI-MODEL DATABASE MACHINES

A database machine system capable of supporting all of the generally accepted data models within a common framework is referred to as a multi-model database machine. The question as to how one supports a multi-model environment with a database machine can be answered in various ways. One straightforward approach is to build one database machine per data model, structure the data for each model (hence replicate the database), and provide data and language transformations among the database machines. We will refer to this approach as the "machine-per-model" scheme. This would imply that for n data models, hence n database machines, we must support n2 transformation schemes for the data and operations. Not only the theoretical difficulties involved in such an approach, but the inconsistency resulting due to updates over incompatible data files would create problems of semantics and lack cost effectiveness.

A sensible alternative to providing multi-model support within a common framework, both in logical and physical terms, is to use the ANSI/SPARC generalized DBMS (GDBMS) architecture [16]. Figure 1 depicts this architecture. As can be seen in Figure 1, all data models and/or views at the external schema level, which is the user interface, are supported within a common framework. This is because the enterprise schema is created at the conceptual schema interface from which all the data models of the external schema are generated. This can be noticed from the upwardly directed arrows. The user queries executed by the application programs at the external schemas are translated into the conceptual schema level (downward going arrows) which in turn maps them onto the physical database via the internal schema interface. The physical database is stored once and common for all the data models. By simply building the levels below the conceptual schema level into a database machine we can accomplish a database machine supported multi-model environment which would not possess the difficulties of the model-per-machine scheme described earlier.

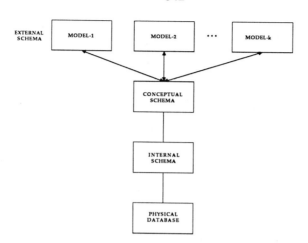

Figure 1: ANSI/SPARC GDBMS Architecture

One important issue remains to be discussed is the structure of the lower level of the GDBMS architecture and its support by the database machine. All data models can be structurally generalized into a graph whose nodes represent sets (i.e, record-types, relations, point sets) and arcs correspond to links (i.e., relationships supported by explicit pointers or content associations). In addition to this graph structure we must provide a universal data language [2] whose capabilities include relational completeness, recursion (for transitive closure, fixed point operators), aggregates, and updates.

In RAPGDBMS project we have come up with a multi-model architecture which is compatible with the ANSI/SPARC GDBMS and utilizes the extended version of the Entity Relationship model as the conceptual schema. At the lower level, RAP tabular structures and the RAP language provide the necessary support for the general data model inclusive of the universal language features. The RAPGDBMS architecture is shown in Figure 2.

Our present paper focuses on the important issue of schema design in the RAPGDBMS multi-model environment. The schema design in this environment entails the task of providing a "proper" conceptual schema design. A proper conceptual schema design is one that yields legal external schemas upon transformation from the conceptual schema into each of the external schemas. Because in RAPGDBMS all of the non-relational models are set-oriented structures created in a one-to-one mapping from the conceptual model, they are equivalent to the relational interface. Therefore, our problem reduces to one of providing a legal relational schema from the conceptual schema. By "legal" relational schema we imply the desirable features of a lossless, dependency-preserving, and normalized schema. The interactive knowledge-based design system we will be describing in the remainder of this article aims at providing such legal schema transformation. In the interactive design provided by this system, a legal schema is the end product, however, it is often the case that this design process ends up in a feedback for the conceptual schema definition process. In this feedback the conceptual schema is refined until it becomes proper, in other words a conceptual schema yielding a legal relational schema when transformed to external schemas.

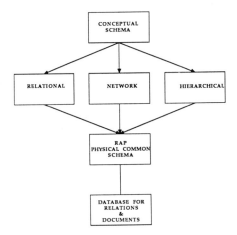

Figure 2: RAP Generalized Database Management System Architecture

THE RAPGDBMS ENVIRONMENT

The RAPGDBMS system is operational under UNIX on a VAX 11/780 system at the Arizona State University. Its architecture is ANSI/SPARC-like and can be represented by the architecture shown in Figure 2. The Entity/Relationship (E/R) model is used at the conceptual level to define the entities, their relationships, and the mapping properties of these relationships. Relationships can be unary or k-ary (k >= 2), weak or strong, 1-to-1, 1-to-n or m-to-n. The E/R model in RAPGDBMS has been extended with proper Data Definition Language (DDL) (refer to the appendix A for an example) to incorporate the following features:

a) Higher-level abstractions such as aggregations and generalizations

b) Mapping constraints such as functional, total

c) Roles of attributes (i.e. a unary relationship)

d) Types and value ranges for domains

f) Integrated support of unformatted document entities.

The RAP GDBMS system contains a very comprehensive set of integrated facilities:

1) data definition language (DDL) to express the E/R model conceptual schema

2) DDL interpreter

3) interactive manipulation commands for the conceptual schema and database; these commands can operate standalone or be embedded in a host language (which is the C language in the existing implementation)

4) transformation function to convert the conceptual schema to the logical data models of the external schema (relational, hierarchical and network) which in turn is mapped into RAP tabular forms (or RAP relations)

5) insertion or deletion of the view table

6) assertion or removal of integrity constraints

7) multilevel database access privilege grant and revoke capabilities

8) a report builder of the display information stored in the data dictionary.

In addition, the RAPGDBMS system is presently being extended to support object-oriented management by associating procedures with relations. The word "object" is usually used to describe an entity that encapsulates some data and the allowable operations on it. In the extension under development, a relational attribute can be defined as an abstract data type "procedure". The RAPGDBMS allows the programmer to introduce the procedure types for attributes and define the details of the operations on these new procedure types through the C host language interface. The definition of a new data type is specified in a Data Description Language statement and this data type is available in the Data Query Language by writing the procedure name. The capability of interfacing the C host language at the operational interface of the external schema also provides us the capability of using C-PROLOG environment coexistently with RAPGDBMS. In this way both environments can be used within the C host program accessing and manipulating the common data in the database. In this way we are capable of using attributes, relationships and entities of type inference by linking the data manipulation functions of RAPGDBMS with the rule capability of C-PROLOG.

OVERVIEW OF THE NORMALIZATION KNOWLEDGE-BASED SYSTEM

The goal of the normalization knowledge-based system is to normalize the RAPGDBMS E/R conceptual schema supplied by the user and to produce a detailed report of the normalization process. The system is intended to assist the database administrator in the design of his/her RAPGDBMS database. The system is interactive and requires the following information from the terminal user:

- the pathname of the file containing the GDBMS E/R conceptual schema data description language

- the functional dependencies applicable to the user's application (FDs)

- the applicable multivalued dependencies (MVDs).

645

The system produces two types of outputs:

- a detailed normalization report
- a file containing the normalized GDBMS conceptual schema data description language.

The normalization theory is applied to the RAPGDBMS E/R conceptual schema by viewing the entities and relationships in their tabular form that can be interpreted as the "pseudo-relational" forms. The processing performed by the knowledge-based system consists of three phases:

- the input transformation phase
- the normalization phase
- the output transformation phase.

Figure 3 illustrates the decomposition of the processing into the three phases.

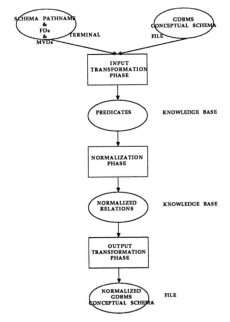

Figure 3: Processing decomposition in three phases

The following functions are performed during the input transformation phase:

- read the RAPGDBMS conceptual schema DDL file pathname, the functional dependencies (FDs) and multivalued dependencies (MVDs)
- record each functional dependency in the knowledge base as a predicate of the following form:

    infd([lhs],[rhs])

where [lhs] and [rhs] are the lists of the left-hand side and right-handside attributes, respectively, of the functional dependency.

- record each multivalued dependency in the knowledge base as a predicate of the following form:

    inmvd([lhs],[rhs])

where [lhs] and [rhs] are the lists of left-hand side and right-hand side attributes, respectively, of the multivalued dependency

- parse the RAPGDBMS conceptual schema
- save all "domain" information in terms of predicates
- extract all the relations from the 'entity', 'relationship', 'generic', 'aggregate' and 'document' conceptual schema statements and represent the corresponding information in terms of predicates
- save the generated predicates in the knowledge base.

The following functions are performed during the normalization phase for each relation (table) present in the conceptual schema:

- select a relation from the conceptual schema
- project the FDs onto the selected relation
- from the set of attributes in the selected relation and the projected dependencies synthesize some new relations in third normal form using the Bernstein algorithm [6]; the set of those synthesized relations which are equivalent to the relation initially selected from the conceptual schema will be considered as the decomposition of that relation into third normal form
- test for losslessness using Loizou and Thanish's algorithm [11]
- make the relation lossless, if necessary, by adding the "key" relation
- determine all the keys using Lucchesi and Osborne's algorithm [12]
- test if the relation is in Boyce-Codd normal form
- transform the relation into Boyce-Codd normal form, if necessary, using Tsou and Fischer's algorithm [17]
- test if the relation is in fourth normal form
- transform the relation into fourth normal form, if necessary, by splitting the multivalued dependencies
- project the functional dependencies on the synthesized relations and find all their keys.

Figures 4 and 5 depict the decomposition into third normal form and fourth normal form respectively. The following functions are performed during the output transformation phase:

- create the output file, if necessary, and open it in output mode
- generate the "domain" statements from the saved predicates

- generate the normalized "entity" statements from the normalized e-type relation predicates
- generate the normalized "relationship" statements from the normalized r-type relation predicates
- generate the normalized "document" statements from the normalized d-type relation predicates
- generate the normalized "generic" statements from the normalized g-type relation predicates
- generate the normalized "aggregate" statements from the normalized a-type relation predicates
- close the output file.

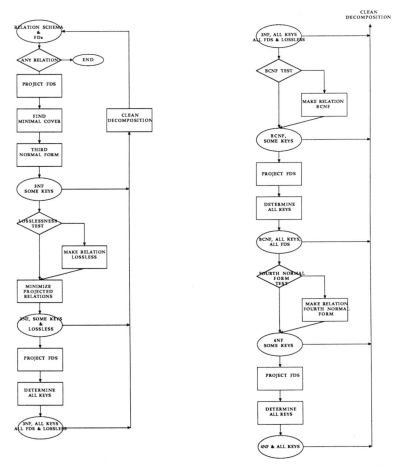

Figure 4: Decomposition into third normal form   Figure 5: Decomposition into bcnf and fourth normal form

ARCHITECTURAL ORGANIZATION

Figure 6 shows an overview of the architecture of this system. The **Executive** controls the scheduling and execution of the functional components. The functional components are either input/output processors or normalization processors. The input/ouput processors are responsible for dialoging with the user at the terminal (**Dialogue**), producing the normalization report (**Report**), reading in and parsing the user-supplied schema (**Parse**) and formatting the normalized schema (**Build**). Each normalization processor is specialized and expert in performing a certain normalization function. Each normalization processor takes its input from the knowledge-base and stores its output in it. All processors communicate and cooperate via the knowledge base. In this sense, this architecture is similar to the blackboard architecture used by other knowledge-based systems. The knowledge base plays a central role in the overall organization of the system. The knowledge base is the repository of both the static normalization knowledge and the dynamic state of the normalization process.

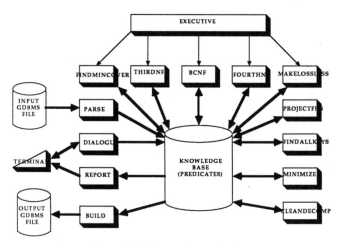

Figure 6: Architectural organization

Each of these functional components are introduced next:

Executive: responsible for the overall sequencing of the operations: input operations, normalization operations and output operations.

Knowledge Base: contains all the rules and facts used by the system. The rules are fixed (since the system does not learn) and encapsulate the normalization theory knowledge. The facts dynamically vary in time and represent the state of the conceptual schema normalization processing at each stage.

Dialogue: consists of the set of rules required to interactively communicate with the user at the terminal.

Report: responsible for preparing the normalization report.

Build: builds the normalized conceptual schema from the predicates that have been created in the knowledge base.

Findmincover: finds a minimal i.e. nonredundant cover of the functional dependencies applicable to a relation.

Thirdnf: synthesizes a relation into third normal form using Bernstein's algorithm.

Bcnf: decomposes a third-normal-form relation into Boyce-Codd normal form.

Fourthnf: decomposes a Boyce-Codd-normal-form relation into fourth normal form by splitting the multivalued dependencies, if necessary.

IMPLEMENTATION

This knowledge-based system is entirely coded in PROLOG and was developed on the VAX/Unix system using the C-PROLOG interpreter that is based on the original design of the DECsystem-10/20 PROLOG developed by David Warren, Fernando Pereira, Lawrence Byrd and Luis Pereira. The use of the PROLOG language for building the system is fundamental to the chosen approach. PROLOG makes possible a unified and integrated description of data structures ("facts") and algorithms ("rules"), where the algorithms are produced and added incrementally to the system as small "chunks" of knowledge. Existing rules can easily be refined, expanded or perfected. Therefore, the system implementation is very modular. Besides, the PROLOG code is quite concise and compact. Finally, the use of PROLOG facilitates the interactive development and testing of the system. At each step it is possible to interactively check the correct behavior of one or more rules.

KNOWLEDGE REPRESENTATION

Fundamental to the PROLOG-based approach is the use of predicates to represent the knowledge of the world. Predicates are used to represent relation schemas, functional and multivalued dependencies, relation keys, facts about relation decompositions and facts related to the various RAPGDBMS conceptual schema DDL statements: "domain", "entity", "relationship", "document", "aggregate" and "generic". For example, when a "relationship" statement is parsed, the information it contains is expressed by the following assertions:

```
relation_rel(rn,tn,rwi).
relation_entity(rn,en,ro,ewi,map,fun).
relation_attr(rn,an).
attr_domain(an,dn).
```

The argument "rn" is the relationship name; "tn" is the number of estimated tuples i.e. occurrences expected for that relationship; "rwi" is an indicator specifying whether or not the relationship is weak; "en" is the name of an entity in the relationship "rn"; "ewi" indicates whether the entity is weak i.e. optional; "map" specifies if the entity mapping is 1-to-1, 1-to-n or m-to-n; "fun" indicates whether the functionality is partial or total; "an" is the name of a relationship attribute; "dn" is the name of the domain associated with the attribute "an".

HEURISTICS AND NORMALIZATION ALGORITHMS

The normalization knowledge-based system attempts to find for each given schema relation a decomposition that satisfies the following heuristic rules:
- the decomposition should preserve functional dependencies
- the decomposition should prevent loss of information
- the decomposition should minimize the number of decomposed normalized subrelations
- the decomposition should contain the smallest number of attributes common to two or more normalized subrelations.

These heuristic rules enable the knowledge-based system to eliminate unworthy decompositions, to select at each step the best candidate decomposition and to cope with the combinatorial explosion resulting from the decomposition of relations into normalized subrelations.

It is well known that "knowledge is power" [8]. Knowledge is the key factor in the performance of any knowledge-based system. Therefore, we have encapsulated in the system knowledge base as much database management knowledge and normalization theory as possible. In particular, the knowledge base contains rules that correspond to the procedural knowledge of the following normalization algorithms:
- algorithm to determine the closure of a set of attributes
- algorithm to eliminate extraneous attributes
- algorithm to eliminate redundant functional dependencies
- algorithm to project functional dependencies
- algorithm to find a minimal key (i.e. a key from a superkey)
- algorithm to find one key
- algorithm to find all keys
- algorithm to synthesize a third normal form relation (Bernstein's algorithm)
- algorithm to decompose into Boyce-Codd normal form
- algorithm to decompose into fourth normal form
- algorithm to test for decomposition losslessness
- algorithm to make a relation decomposition lossless.

Algorithm to determine the closure of a set of attributes

The closure of a set of attributes X with respect to a set F of functional dependencies is the set of all the attributes Y such that X --> Y can be deduced by Armstrong's axioms of reflexity, augmentation and transitivity [3, 7, 10, 13, 14, 18]. This set can be built by an iterative algorithm [15] or by a recursive one [7]. This well-known algorithm can be specified as follows:

Algorithm Closure(REL, X, F)

1. Select one of the functional dependencies L --> R applicable to the relation REL;

2. F' = F - { L --> R};

3. If L is contained by X and R is not contained by X, let W = X U R and compute Z = Closure (REL, W, F');

4. If L is not contained by X or R is contained by X, compute Z = Closure (REL, W, F');

5. return Z;

6. end.

Algorithm to eliminate extraneous attributes

An attribute A is extraneous if it can be eliminated from the left hand side L of a functional dependency L --> R so that the new dependency (L - {A}) --> R holds. The basic algorithm "Elim_Extattr" is again recursive and progressively eliminates attributes from the left hand side L of the functional dependency until no further elimination is possible.

Algorithm Elim_Extattr (REL, L, R, NEWL)

1. Select an attribute A from L;

2. Z = L - {A};

3. If Z is not empty then do

4. Compute ZCLOSURE = Closure (REL, Z, F);

5.   If R is contained by ZCLOSURE, compute Elim_Extattr(REL,Z,R,NEWL);

6.   end;

7. If Z is empty then do

8.   NEWL = L;

9.   return NEWL;

10.   end;

11. end.

Algorithm to eliminate redundant functional dependencies

One way to determine whether a functional dependency L --> R is redundant or not is to eliminate it from the input set F of functional dependencies and to compute the closure of · the left hand side L with respect to the set F - {L - R} of functional dependencies. If the right hand side R of the functional dependency is contained in this closure, then the dependency can be inferred from the smaller set F'; hence, it is redundant and can be eliminated.

Algorithm Elim_rfd (REL, F, NEWF)

1. Select a functional dependency L --> R from F;

2. F' = F - {L --> R};

3. Compute Z = Closure (REL,L, F');

4. If R is not contained by Z then do

5.   L --> R is not redundant;

6.   NEWF = NEWF U {L --> R};

7.   end;

8. If R is contained by Z then "L --> R is redundant";

9. Compute Elim_rfd (REL, F', NEWF);

10. end.

Algorithm to project functional dependencies

Given a set of functional dependencies, it is sometimes necessary to determine the subset of those dependencies that are applicable to a given relation R. Thus, the original functional dependencies must be projected over the set of attributes constituting the schema of the relation R. This projection is not trivial, and known methods have an exponential complexity [18]. To perform the projection of functional dependencies, we use an algorithm developed by Gottlob in [9] that builds a cover for the dependencies holding on R by iniatially copying all the original dependencies, and then progressively eliminating from them the attributes that do not appear in the relation R. This algorithm is used in two particular circumstances, first, to project all the global input dependencies on each relation and, secondly, once a third-normal-form decomposition has been performed, to determine the functional dependencies applicable to each synthesized subrelations.

Algorithm to find a minimal key

There exists an algorithm developped by Lucchesi and Osborne [12] for finding the minimal key of a relation, given its schema S, the set of functional dependencies F holding for it and a superkey K. The algorithm can be expressed as follows:

Algorithm Find_Minimal_Key (S, F, K)

1. Let K' be the set of attributes obtained from K by eliminating one attribute.

2. Compute the closure of K' for the set of functional dependencies F using the algorithm to compute the closure of a set of attributes, previously described

3. If the closure of K' is not equal to the complete schema S, K is a key of the relation

4. If the closure of K' is equal to the complete schema S, make K equal to K' and go to step 1.

5. end.

Algorithm to find one key

Given the algorithm to find a key from a given superkey, described above, Lucchesi and Osborne [12] uses it to find one key for a relation by applying to the complete schema S, which is by definition a superkey for the relation. Therefore, given the Find_Minimal_Key algorithm, the algorithm to find one key is trivially simple.

Algorithm Find_One_Key (S, F)

1. Find_Minimal_Key(S, F, S);

2. end.

Algorithm to find all keys

In [12], Lucchesi and Osborne use the Find_Minimal_Key algorithm to develop an algorithm capable of finding all the keys of a given relation given its schema S and the set F of functional dependencies holding for it. The algorithm Find_All_Keys can be specified as follows:

Algorithm Find_All_Keys(S,F)

1. K_set = {Find_One_Key (S,F)};

2. For each K in K_set do

3.   For each functional dependency L --> R in F do

4.   Z = L U (K - R);

5.   test = true;

6.   For each J in K_set do

7.   If Z includes J then test = false;

8.   If test then K_set = K_set U {Find_Minimal_Key (S, F, Z)}

9.   end;

10. end;

11. return K_set;

12. end.

Algorithm to synthesize a third normal form relation

In database management articles and textbooks, the normalization of a relation into normal form follows the presentation of the normalization into first and second normal forms. It is very often treated in a non-algorithmic way, requiring the reader to recognize a certain pattern from the examples that are provided [15]. However, this approach is unnecessarily complex since there exists a very good algorithm, invented by Bernstein [6], that allows to build a third-normal-form relation directly. This algorithm basically consists of five steps:

1. Find a minimal cover H of the input functional dependencies without extraneous attributes;

2. Partition the set of dependencies H into groups Hi such that all dependencies in each

group have identical left sides;

3. Merge two groups Hi and Hj with left sides X and Y, respectively, when the dependencies X --> Y and Y --> X hold; X and Y are called equivalent keys;

4. Build a particular cover of H that includes all dependencies X --> Y, where X and Y are equivalent keys, such that all other dependencies are nonredundant;

5. Construct the synthesized relations;

6. end.

Algorithm to test if a relation is in Boyce-Codd normal form

A relation R is in Boyce-Codd normal form if all the left sides of the functional dependencies contain a key of R. Therefore, the relation R is not in Boyce-Codd normal form if there exits one functional dependency holding for R whose left side is not a key. This can be tested by computing the closure of the left side and comparing it with the relation schema of R. Hence, the algorithm to determine a Boyce-Codd normal form relation can be expressed as follows.

Algorithm Test_Bcnf (REL, F)

1. test = true;

2. For each functional dependency L --> R in F do

3.   Compute closure (REL, L, LCLOSURE);

4.   If LCLOSURE ^= schema(REL) then test = false;

5.   end;

6. return test;

7. end.

Algorithm to decompose into Boyce-Codd normal form

The Tsou and Fischer algorithm [17] is used to decompose a relation which is not in Boyce-Codd normal form into some new relations which are in Boyce-Codd normal form by construction. The Tsou and Fischer algorithm is based on a pair of conditions sufficient for a relation R to be in Boyce-Codd normal form:

1. If the schema of a relation R has only two attributes, then R is in Boyce-Codd normal form

2. If the schema of a relation R has more than two attributes, then R is in Boyce-Codd normal form if, for any pair of distinct attributes X and Y of R, attribute X does not belong to the closure of schema(REL) - {X,Y}.

The Tsou and Fischer algorithm uses repeated applications of the test above to reduce subsets of the relation schema. When the test succeeds, a subrelation in Boyce-Codd normal form has been synthesized.

Algorithm to decompose into fourth normal form

In practical terms, a relation is in fourth normal form if it is in Boyce-Codd normal form and has at most one multi-valued dependency (MVD) that is not also a functional dependency. Therefore, the algorithm to decompose a relation in Boyce-Codd normal form into fourth normal form consists of splitting any relation in Boyce-Codd normal form that contains two or more MVDs.

Algorithm Make_4nf(REL, M)

1. If the relation REL in Boyce-Codd normal form contains 0 or 1 multivalued dependency
      (MVD), the relation REL is in fourth normal form;
2. If the relation REL contains two or more MVDs then do
3.   Select one MVD $X ->> Y$ from the set M of MVDs;
4.   Partition REL into two relations (X, Y) and $REL' = M - \{X ->> Y\}$;
5. $M' = M - \{X ->> Y\}$;
6.   Compute Make_4nf(REL', M');
7.   end;
8. end.

Algorithm to test for decomposition losslessness

Given a set F of functional dependencies, the decomposition of one relation REL into several component relations RELi is lossless if it is possible to reconstruct the original relation REL by equijoining the component relations RELi over the common attributes. A tableau-based algorithm due to Aho, Beeri and Ullman [1] is widely used to perform this test. More recently, Loizou and Thanish have proposed another algorithm based on closures to test for losslessness of relation decomposition. A decomposition is lossless if and only if the closure schema of one of the component relations is equal to the schema of the original relation.

Algorithm Test_Lossless ({RELi}, REL, F)

1. test = false;
2. For each RELi relation do
3.   Z = Closure(RELi, schema(RELi),F)
4.   If Z = schema(REL) then do
5.   test = true;
6.   return test;
7.   end;
8.   end;
9. return test;
10. end.

<u>Algorithm to make decomposition lossless</u>

Given a set F of functional dependencies, the application of the losslessness test to the decomposition of a relation REL into several component relations RELi may fail. In order to make the decomposition lossless, the following well-known algorithm [10, 14, 18] is applied.

Algorithm Make_Lossless ({RELi}, REL, F)

1. K = Find_One_Key(schema(REL), F);

2. Add relation REL_KEY with the schema K to the set of relations {RELi};

3. end.

The knowledge-base rules corresponding to the algorithms described above could not be included here due to space limitations. However, they are contained in our detailed technical report [4].

DIFFICULTIES AND ISSUES

The implementation of this knowledge-based system prototype to normalize the schemas of real-world databases has made apparent some difficulties, which are:

1) the projection of the user-input global dependencies onto the schema relations is a time-consuming operation of exponential complexity

2) some high-level constructs of the extended E/R schema such as generalization are difficult to generate.

3) the management of the combinatorial explosion resulting from the decomposition of relations into normalized subrelations becomes complex and expensive as the number of relations in the schema increases.

The problem associated with the projection of functional dependencies onto individual schema relations appears to be of an intrinsic nature since all known methods of projection have an exponential complexity [18]. This problem could be avoided if one accepts to compromise the convenience and simplicity of the user's interface. The user could be asked to supply the functional dependencies applicable to each individual schema relation separately. This would cause a certain amount of redundant input since functional dependencies are typically applicable to several relations.

The generation of the high-level constructs of the extended E/R schema such as generalization and aggregation requires both additional semantic knowledge and some additional heuristic rules. Schema relations, functional dependencies and multivalued dependencies are not sufficient inputs to be able to generate those high-level constructs. The implemented system fell short of its goals and was not able to systematically and correctly generate the schema DDL statements required for the generic and aggregate entities. A certain interaction exists between high-level data abstraction and normalization and the interrelationship of those two concepts deserves further study.

The combinatorial explosion resulting from the recursive decomposition of relations into normalized subrelations could be more effectively managed by using better structures to keep track of the relationships between relations and subrelations as well as more powerful and flexible backtracking techniques when the exploration of a certain path is abandoned and another path is attempted.

A simple knowledge-base driven RAPGDBMS conceptual design scenario is presented in the appendix B. The interactive session starts with a dialogue with the user who provides the name of the file containing the E/R RAPGDBMS conceptual schema, the functional and multivalued dependencies. The session continues with the schema normalization processing and outputs the normalization report.

CONCLUSIONS

The knowledge-based system described in this paper attempts to entirely automatize the normalization process of a real-word database schema and to produce an equivalent "better" normalized schema within the framework of a multi-layered GDBMS architecture. The implemented system prototype has demonstrated the feasibility of the approach for small databases with simple schemas i.e. schemas with no high-level constructs. For more complex schemas such as extended E/R schemas with generalization and aggregation high-level constructs, the project made apparent the need for the user to provide more domain-specific semantic knowledge beyond relation attributes, functional and multivalued dependencies. The technical difficulties related to the interaction between high-level abstraction and normalization, the projection of global functional dependencies and the management of the combinatorial explosion of decomposed relations have been analyzed.

The project has also proved that the multi-model RAPGDBMS architecture which is compatible with the ANSI/SPARC GDBMS and utilizes the extended Entity Relationship model as the conceptual schema constitutes a valid approach to providing multi-model support for database machines . The design of a refined conceptual schema that is proper and yields legal i.e. lossless, dependency-preserving and normalized relational schemas of the highest form possible makes the interactive knowledge-based system a valuable tool to the database administrator in the performance of his/her task.

REFERENCES

1. Aho, A. V., Beeri, C., and Ullman, J. D.
   The theory of joins in relational databases, *ACM Transactions on Database Systems*, 4, 3 (September 1979), 297 - 314.
2. Aho, A. V., Ullman, J.D.

Universality of Data Retrieval Languages, *Proceedings of ACM Symposium on Principles of Programming Languages*, 1979, 110 - 120.

3. Armstrong, W. W.
    Dependency structures of database relations, *Information Processing*, North-Holland, Amsterdam, 1974, 580-583.

4. Bayle, A., Ozkarahan, E.
    A Knowledge-based system for relational normalization of RAPGDBMS conceptual schemas, *Technical Report TR87-001*, Department of Computer Science, Arizona State University, Tempe, January 16, 1987.

5. Beeri, C., Bernstein, P. A., and Goodman, N.
    A sophisticate's introduction to database normalization theory. In *Proceedings of the 4th International Conference on Very Large Data Bases* (West Berlin), 1978, 113 - 124.

6. Bernstein, P. A.
    Synthesizing third-normal-form relations from functional dependencies. *ACM Transaction on Database Systems* 1, 4 (Dec. 1976) 277 - 298.

7. Ceri S., and Gottlob C.
    Normalization of relations. *Communications of the ACM*, June 1986, Vol. 29, Number 6.

8. Feigenbaum, E. A. and McCorduck, P.
    The Fifth Generation - Artificial Intelligence and Japan's Computer Challenge to the World, Addison-Wesley Publishing Company, 1983.

9. Gottlob, G.
    Computing covers for embedded functional dependencies, *Internal Report 86-006*, Dipartimento di Elettronica, Politecnico di Milano, Italy.

10. Hawryszkiewycz, I. T.
    Database Analysis and Design, Science Research Associates, Inc., 1984.

11. Loizou, G., and Thanish, P.
    Testing a dependency-preserving decomposition for losslessness. *Information Systems, 8, 1.*

12. Lucchesi, C. L., and Osborn, S. L.
    Candidate keys for relations, *Journal Computer System Science 17, 2* (Oct. 1978).

13. Maier, D.
    The Theory of Relational Databases, Computer Science Press, 1983.

14. Ozkarahan, E.
    Database Machines and Database Management, Prentice- Hall, 1986.

15. Salzberg, B.
    Third normal form made easy, *SIGMOD RECORD*, Vol. 15, Number 4, (December 1986).

16. Tsichritzis, D. C., and Lochovsky, F. H.
    Data Models, Prentice-Hall, 1982.

17. Tsou, D. M., and Fischer, P. C.
    Decomposition of a relation scheme into Boyce-Codd normal form, *ACM-SIGACT 14, 3* .

18. Ullman, J. D.
    Principles of Database Systems, second edition, Computer Science Press, Rockville, Md., 1982.

Appendix A: RAPGDBMS Extended E/R Model Data Definition Language

```
            /* domain definition */
domain lname                literal(30);
domain empno                integer(5) (1:80000);

    . . .
            /* entity definition */
entity library(30) (*libcode, libname:lname, phone, mailstat);
entity division(30) (*divcode, divname:lname, divphone:phone);
```

. . .

/* generic entity definition */
generic document(50000) (book, manual, report; *lcode, price);

. . .

/* aggregate entity relationship */
aggregate task implement;

. . .

/* relationship definition */
relationship employ(80000) (division:one, employee:n:total; hiredate:date);
relationship implement(80000) (employee:m:total, product:n);

. . .

Appendix B: Example of an interactive design session

```
% cprolog
C-Prolog version 1.5
| ?- [norma].
norma consulted 42648 bytes 11.8167 sec.

yes
| ?- go.

GDBMS E/R schema file pathname? schema.file

Functional Dependencies (FDs)?
|: product_no, part_name --> part_no.

|: part_no --> product_no.

|: supplier_no --> supplier_name.

|: supplier_no, supplier_name --> address.

|: supplier_name --> supplier_no.

|: supplier_name --> address.

|: .

Multivalued Dependencies (MVDs)?
|: .

**********************************************************
        START NORMALIZATION PROCESSING OF RELATION: sell
**********************************************************
        Projected functional dependencies:
        [product_no, part_name]-->[part_no]
        [part_no]-->[product_no]
        [supplier_no]-->[supplier_name]
        [supplier_no, supplier_name]-->[address]
        [supplier_name]-->[supplier_no]
        [supplier_name]-->[address]

STEP1: Decomposition of  sell into third normal form:
        Making the cover of sell nonredundant.

        Elimination of extraneous attributes from the cover of sell:
        dependency [supplier_no, supplier_name]-->[address]
        new left hand side = [supplier_name]
        * all extraneous attributes eliminated.

        Elimination of redundant functional dependencies from
        the cover of: sell:
        redundant fd [supplier_name]-->[address] eliminated.
        * all redundant functional dependencies eliminated.

STEP2: Decomposition of  sell into third normal form:
        Partitioning the cover into groups
        group based on LHS: [supplier_name]
```

An Algebraic Deductive Database Managing a Mass of Rule Clauses

Tadashi OHMORI and Hidehiko TANAKA
University Of Tokyo, Information Engineering Course

Abstract

This paper proposes a deductive database which manages a mass of rule-clauses in a disk as well as many fact-clauses in a disk. For this purpose, we propose a variant of relational algebra, *Relational Algebra extended with Unification* (RAU). Our original point consists in query-processing by RAU in this DBMS. This paper describes a compilation of a query to a RAU's expression, optimization strategies for it, and an algorithm for a heavy RAU-operator.

1 Introduction

Conventional deductive databases concentrate on fast retrieval of many fact-clauses in a disk through a few rule-clauses in a main memory [KHT86,Boc86,YSI86].

Practical applications, however, will need a DBMS which manages a mass of rule-clauses stored in a disk as well as many fact-clauses in a disk.

This paper proposes such a deductive database. This DBMS, which we call a *rule-DBMS*, must retrieve rule-clauses fast from a disk, execute them fast, and retrieve fact-clauses fast from a disk.

Our approach is simple; A mass of rule-clauses are managed as a set called a *meta-relation*. Each query to a rule-DBMS is described as a tree form of set-operators defined on meta-relations.

Those set-operators, which we call *RAU*, are a variant of relational algebra for dealing with unification. *RBU-operations* in [YI86] is the first that extends relational algebra for unification. Our RAU is, however, aimed at a faster query-processing in a large scale rule-DBMS.

The rest of the paper is organized as follows; Section 2 illustrates a large database of rule-clauses, and describes requirements for a rule-DBMS. Section 3 gives our basic ideas and defines RAU. Section 4 describes a compilation of queries to RAU-expressions and optimization strategies for them. Section 5 gives an algorithm for one heavy RAU-operator. Lastly, Section 6 discusses open problems.

2 Rule-DBMS

2.1 Preparations

Deductive databases in this paper allow functor symbols as in [Zan85]. A rule-clause is abbreviated as a *rule* and a fact-clause as a *fact*. We use usual notations in PROLOG. We restrict each rule to a non-recursive view definition. Hence it can be compiled

```
% store(Media,Type,Data):- Cond.
 10⁴ ⎧ store( imagedb(T), image(sub1,A), D ):- q1(T,A,D).
      ⎨ store( textdb(sub2(T)),
rules ⎩ :               text(f(b,F),A) , D ):- q2(T,F,A,D).

% key(Type,Keyword,User):- Cond.
 10⁴ ⎧ key( text(F,h(A,b)), K, japan(ic,X) ):- p1(F,A,K,X).
      ⎨ key( image(S,g(A)), story(K),
rules ⎩ :            japan(pie,tokyo(X)) ):- p2(S,A,K,X).

% query
q(T,D):- ruledb(kb1, key(T, story(aaa), japan(P,X)), C1),
         ruledb(kb2, store(M, T, D), C2 ),
         demo( to, (C1,C2) ).
```

Figure 1: an example of rule database

into an expression of a modified relational algebra such as ERA in [Zan85]. Recursive views are discussed later in Section 6.

In general, deductive databases have two databases; a database of facts (factDB) and the other one of rules (ruleDB). We assume that those two databases are so large that both of them are stored in a disk. Let's call this DBMS a *rule-DBMS*. A factDB is managed by a relational database system; facts with a common predicate are regarded as tuples of a usual relation.

We use two meta-predicates ruledb and demo in [Bow81] for managing a ruleDB. ruledb(KB, Head, Body) says "a knowledgebase KB knows a rule Head:-Body ". demo(T,Goal) says " a theory T proves Goal ". In this paper, we say that a head-predicate of a given rule is the rule's *kind*, and the rule *belongs to* or *expresses* its kind. e.g. p(a,X):-q(X). and p(f(X),b):-r(X). belong to one common *kind* p.

2.2 Large rule database

In practical applications, two cases enlarge a ruleDB; either there are many *kinds* of rules, or many rules belong to one *kind*.

The latter case corresponds to "many different implementations for a common interface". In an object oriented paradigm, it is the case that a superclass C requires a common interface p and allows each subclass of C to implement p independently. With 10^4 subclasses, 10^4 rules belong to a kind p. We expect this large scalability will arise naturally when developing a database of "a mass of heterogeneous data with common interfaces". Possibly, each rule may be implemented by a simple relational algebra program such as a single selection or at most one large size join.

Figure 1 is an example of the latter case. store(Media, Type, Data) is a common interface of a class Media. It says "a Data with a Type is stored in a Media.". In Figure 1, subclasses and attributes' values in Media, User... are expressed by compound terms. e.g. User has a structure of *nation(group, city(id))*.

Suppose that each rule expressing store operates different relations differently, depending on a subclass of Media (e.g. image-database subtype1,...), and a Type of Data (image, text, format,..). Then, with 10^2 subclasses of Media and 10^2 Types of Data, 10^4 rules express the kind store.

In the same way, key(Type, Keyword, User) is a common interface of a class Type of data. It says "a Type of data is indexed with a Keyword by a User.". Depending on 10^2 Types of data and 10^2 properties of a User, 10^4 different rules belong to key.

Most of queries are issued via only those common interfaces regardless of different implementations. e.g. a query $Q1$ is given as follows; "q(T,D):- key(T, story(aaa), japan(P,X)), store(M, T, D).".

Assume that only 100 combinations of rules expressing "key and store" are necessary for this query $Q1$, though the ruleDB has 10^4 rules for either "key" or "store". Then, we should decide those combinations of rules at first before executing rules, in order to restrict rules and reduce useless facts-retrieval.

The above situation will often happen when we have a mass of heterogeneous data with a few common interfaces. Because more constraints will arise in this case. e.g. *this subclass of media stores only this type of data by this group of users.* The query in Figure 1 describes those above operations of $Q1$ by meta-predicates. In the query, "to" is a object-theory in [Bow81]. "(C1,C2)" refers to "C1 and C2". The query retrieves applicable combinations of rules at first, and execute them.

2.3   Requirements

It needs two points for fast execution of the query in Figure 1.

(a) fast retrieval of necessary combinations of rules. It is important especially when many rules belong to one kind. We think this function is the most important for a large ruleDB. (b) to avoid random accesses to a ruleDB in a disk when executing rules; e.g. Executing a rule p:-q. calls another rule q:-r, which may be stored in another page of a disk.

A limited solution of (b) is a partial compilation; transformation of each rule to simpler ones which operate a factDB directly [Miy86]. e.g. a rule p:-q. is transformed into 100 rules p:- r_1 , ... p:- r_{100} if we have q:- r_i (i = 1,...100). (Possibly each r_i may be a relational algebra program for the factDB.) This transformation makes more rules belong to one kind as shown above. Thus the requirement (a) gets more fundamental for a fast query-processing in a large scale rule-DBMS. Note that (a) and (b) are caused only because a ruleDB is so large.

Other requirements arise from a fast retrieval of facts through executing rules. (c) to select an appropriate evaluation-strategy or capture rule [Ull85] for reducing irrelevant facts. (d) common subexpression sharing [Sel86]. These two are also inherent problems for conventional deductive databases.

2.4   Conventional studies

Conventional deductive databases are based on a topdown or bottom-up approach [Ull85]. Recently, both prepare a graph of given rules in advance. In orthodox studies based on the topdown approach, a given query is transformed into a relational algebra program so-called *plan* and executed in a relational database [Boc86,YSI86], [Rei78,GM78]. Studies based on bottom-up pick up a partition of graph-of-rules corresponding to a given query, optimize the graph, and execute it by a relational algebra engine [KHT86,Zan85] or a data-flow framework [KL86,Gel86].

Both conventional studies are naive in terms of the requirement (a) only because they don't assume a large ruleDB. They process (a) by *one rule at a time* and don't process this large scalability efficiently.

In topdown-based ones, plans are generated by *selecting one rule at a time*. In bottom-up based ones, the picked-up graph is *optimized by one rule at a time* before/during execution. Therefore in the example of Section 2.3, it takes 10^8 processing to decide only 100 applicable combinations of rules for the query.

On the other hand, conventional studies satisfy the requirements (c), (d) to some extent. Hence it is hopeful to develop dexterous mechanisms for (a) which is consistent with conventional techniques for (c), (d).

3 Algebraic approach

3.1 Basic ideas

We propose an *algebraic* approach for a large rule-DBMS as follows;

At first, we compile in advance each rule into simpler rules which operate the factDB directly. They can be expressed by a variant of relational algebra such as ERA. The variant must be able to deal with functor symbols.

Second, we make a set of rules expressing one common kind. In Figure 2, $R[A, B, C]$ or $T[A, D]$ is a set of rules "$r(A,B):- C.$" or "$t(A):- D.$" respectively. We call these sets of rules *meta-relations*. e.g. In the figure, the scheme $T[A, D]$ of a meta-relation T is depicted over a horizontal bar, and a tuple $(X, q(X))$ is under it. Corresponding to the interpretation of the scheme $T[A, D]$, this tuple refers to a rule "$t(X):- q(X)$". In a large ruleDB, each meta-relation will have many tuples; e.g. 10^4 tuples.

Third, we prepare four set-operators $\bowtie, \sigma, I, \pi$ on those sets as follows; Their examples are in Figure 2. (R, T are meta-relations and $A, B, C, D, \ldots$ are attribute-names.)

- $R \overset{u}{\bowtie} T$ with a scheme $[A, B, C, D]$ is a set of rules "$q(A,B):- C,D.$". These rules are defined by "$q(A,B):- r(A,B),t(A).$". It expresses "r and t".

- $\sigma_{A \overset{u}{=} f(X)} T[A, D]$ with a scheme $[A, D]$ retrieves a set of rules "$q(A) :- D.$". This kind "q" is defined by "$q(A):-t(A),A \overset{u}{=} f(X).$". It expresses t whose value in the attribute T[A] is restricted to be unified with "$f(X)$".

- $I_D T[A, D]$ is a set of facts satisfying a rule expressing t.

- $\pi_{[A,C]} R[A, B, C]$ with a scheme $[A, C]$ is a set of rules "$q(A):- C.$" defined by "$q(A):- r(A, B).$". Those rules express r which is restricted to the attribute $R[A]$ excluding $R[B]$.

These operators are called *Relational Algebra extended with Unification* (RAU).

Fourth, we express queries to a rule-DBMS as tree forms of those operators. e.g. Let a query Q be "retrieve a set of facts satisfying both a rule expressing r restricted by F1 and a rule expressing t restricted by F2." It is expressed as follows; $Q = \pi I [(\sigma_{F1} R) \overset{u}{\bowtie} (\sigma_{F2} T)]$. This query-tree describes what rules to be retrieved and when to execute them.

R[A,B,C] : a set of rules r(A,B):- C.   T [A, D] : a set of rules t(A):-D.

(R,T : meta-relations.   A, B, C, D : attribute)

this tuple is   R [A   B   C]   this tuple is   T [A   D]
"r(f(X),a):- p(X)" ↖ f(X) a   p(X)   "t(X):- q(X)." ↘ X   q(X)

- projection

$$\pi_{[A,C]} R = \frac{[A \quad C]}{f(X) \quad p(X)}$$

- selection

$$\sigma_{A \overset{u}{=} f(X)} T = \frac{[A \qquad D \;]}{f(X) \quad q(f(X))}$$

- $\overset{u}{\bowtie}$

$$R \overset{u}{\bowtie} T = \frac{[A \quad B \quad C \qquad D \;]}{f(X) \quad a \quad p(X) \quad q(f(X))}$$

- instantiation

$$I_D T = \frac{[A \quad D]}{a \quad q(a)} \quad \begin{array}{l} \text{where} \\ q(a) \text{ is true.} \end{array}$$

Figure 2: an example of meta-relations

Fifth, after optimizing the query-tree, we execute each operator, especially $\overset{u}{\bowtie}$ and I-operator by a fast set-operation algorithm. Note that I-operator execute a set of (modified) relational algebra programs on the factDB. We execute I-operator by a relational database system, after global query optimizations such as common subexpression sharings. □

Our approach satisfies the requirements (a), (b), and partly (c) and (d) in Section 2; (a) is satisfied by fast executions of RAU-operators, especially $\overset{u}{\bowtie}$ operator as described later in Section 5. So is (b) by exhaustive compilations. (c) is satisfied at a "macro level". i.e. a query including I-operator is transformed as follows; $I(R \overset{u}{\bowtie} T)$ = $I((IR) \overset{u}{\bowtie} T) = IR \overset{u}{\bowtie} IT$. They correspond to topdown, sideway, and bottom-up strategies at a "macro level" respectively.

(c) at a "micro level" refers to changes of strategies in executing each compiled form of rules. This function and (d) should be supported when implementing I-operator. Apparently I-operator is a function of conventional deductive databases.

Till Section 6, we concentrate on the requirement (a) in our approach.

3.2   Meta-relation

This section defines a *meta-relation* by using a meta-theory [Bow81].

Definition 1 Let $p(\text{arg}1,.., \text{arg}n)$ be a predicate in a meta-theory T_m wrt an object-theory T_o. A *meta-relation* $rel(p)$ is defined as follows.

- A scheme of $rel(p)$ is $[\text{arg}1,\ldots,\text{arg}n]$, where each $\text{arg}i$ is an attribute. A domain of each attribute is a set of compound terms of T_m.

- A tuple satisfying the scheme is a function from each attribute to each domain in the scheme.

- A meta-relation $rel(p)$ is a set of non-redundant tuples satisfying its scheme.

(A1, A2, B1, B2 : attribute)

- synthesizing $S_{[\ f(A1,A2),\ c]}\begin{bmatrix} \underline{A1\quad A2} \\ g(X)\quad a \end{bmatrix} = \begin{array}{c} \underline{[\ B1\quad B2\ ]} \\ f(g(X),a)\quad c \end{array}$

- parsing $P_{[\ f(A1,A2),\ c]}\begin{bmatrix} \underline{[\ B1\quad B2]} \\ f(g(X),a)\quad c \end{bmatrix} = \begin{array}{c} \underline{[\ A1\quad A2]} \\ g(X)\quad a \end{array}$

- rho-operator

  $\rho_{[\ f(B1),\ c]}\begin{bmatrix} \underline{[\ A1\quad A2\ ]} \\ f(g(Y))\quad c \end{bmatrix} = \begin{array}{c} \underline{[B1]} \\ g(Y) \end{array}$

- Conditional difference

$$\begin{array}{c} \underline{[\ A1\quad A2\ ]} \\ X\quad f(X) \\ h(X)\quad a \end{array} \ -\ \begin{array}{c} \underline{[\ A1\ ]} \\ A1\quad g(X) \end{array} = \begin{array}{c} \underline{[\ A1\quad A2\ ]} \\ h(X)\quad a \end{array}$$

Figure 3: an example of RAU-operators

Tuples t_1 and t_2 are redundant if $\exists \theta$: substitution; $t_1 = t_2\theta$. The scope of any variable symbol in each tuple is restricted within that tuple. Every tuple $[a_1,\ldots,a_n]$ in $rel(p)$ is mapped into $p(a_1,\ldots,a_n)$; an atomic formula of T_m. This mapping [tuple $\rightarrow$ wff] is defined by each meta-relation's scheme. □

Our meta-relation is almost the same as a *term-relation* in [YI86] except introducing a meta-theory. In Figure 2, a meta-relation $R[A,B,C]$ corresponds to a meta-predicate $R(A,B,C)$, which asserts that "there is an object-level wff $r(A,B)$:- C." It is a set of object-level rules belonging to one common kind r.

In the rest of the paper, attributes are referred to by their names or positionID; e.g. an attribute B of $R[A,B,C]$ is referred to by $R[B]$, or $R[2]$, or only 2 if trivial.

Definition 2 given a tuple t and a meta-relation R,

- $t \in R \overset{\text{def}}{=} \exists t_1, \exists \theta_0 ; t = t_1\theta_0$, where
  θ_0 is a renaming substitution, and t_1 is a tuple and an element of R.

- $t \in_w R \overset{\text{def}}{=} \exists t_1 :$ tuple, $\exists \theta :$ substitution $; t_1 \in R$ and $t = t_1\theta$. □

e.g. In Figure 2, $t_1 = [\ f(Y),\ a,\ p(Y)] \in R$. $t_2 = [\ f(c),\ a,\ p(c)] \in_w R$, but $\notin R$. $t[i]$ is the i-th element of a tuple t; $t_1[3] = p(Y)$.

3.3 RAU operators

RAU-operators are defined below. (M, N, R refer to meta-relations. θ refers to a substitution. "$\overset{u}{=}$" refers to "be unified with". As logical connectives , {and, or, not, imply, equivalent} are expressed by { $\wedge$, $\vee$, $\neg$, $\rightarrow$, $\equiv$}.) Figure 2 and 3 gives their examples.

Definition 3 The following operators are called *Relational Algebra extended with Unification* (RAU).

- $\langle$ union $\rangle$ $M \cup N$ — same as that in relational algebra [Ull82], where the scheme of M is the same as that of N.

- $\langle$ cartesian product $\rangle$ $M \times N$ — same as that in relational algebra. M and N share no common variable because of the scope restriction of their variables.

- $\langle$ selection $\rangle$ $\sigma_{F(t)} M[A_1, \ldots, A_n] \stackrel{\text{def}}{=} \{\, t \mid t \in_w M \text{ and } F(t)\,\}$,
  where $F(t)$ is $\wedge_{i=1}^{n}(t[i] \stackrel{u}{=} C_i)$, abbreviated as $[A_1, \ldots, A_n] \stackrel{u}{=} [C_1, \ldots, C_n]$. C_i is a compound term allowing $t[j]$ $(i \neq j)$ as a variable symbol. The scope of variables in C_i is restricted within $F(t)$. e.g. $F(t)$ is $t[1] \stackrel{u}{=} f(t[2], X)$. (abbreviated as $A_1 \stackrel{u}{=} f(A_2, X)$).

- $\langle$ synthesizing $\rangle$ $S_{scheme}(M[A_1, \ldots, A_n]) \stackrel{\text{def}}{=} R[B_1, \ldots, B_m] =$
  $\{t \mid \exists t_1; t_1 \in M, \text{ and } t = scheme(t_1)\}$,
  where $scheme = [B_1, \ldots, B_m]$, each B_i is a compound term. Its variable symbols must be $A_1, \ldots, A_n$. $scheme(t)$ is a compound term gained from $scheme$ by substituting $t[i]$ for A_i respectively.

- $\langle$ parsing $\rangle$ $P_{scheme}(R[B_1, \ldots, B_m]) \stackrel{\text{def}}{=} M[A_1, \ldots, A_n] =$
  $\{t \mid \exists t_1; t_1 \in R, \text{ and } t_1 = scheme(t)\}$,
  where $scheme$ is the same as that in S-operator. $A_1, \ldots, A_n$ are those appeared in $scheme$.

- $\langle$ instantiation $\rangle$ $I_{cond} M[A_1, \ldots, A_n] \stackrel{\text{def}}{=} R[A_1, \ldots, A_n]$
  $= \{\, t \mid \exists t_1, \exists \theta; t_1 \in M \text{ ,and } demo(T_o, cond(t_1)\theta) \text{ ,and } t = t_1\theta.\}$,
  such that $cond$ is a propositional wff whose propositional variables are $A_1, \ldots,$ A_n. e.g. $A_1 \wedge A_2$. T_o is an object-theory in Definition 1. $cond(t_1)$ is a wff gained from $cond$ by substituting $t_1[i]$ for A_i respectively.

- $\langle$ conditional difference $\rangle$
  $M[A_1, \ldots, A_n] -_{Alist} N[A_1, \ldots, A_m] \stackrel{\text{def}}{=} R[A_1, \ldots, A_n]$
  $= \{\, t \mid t \in M \text{ and } \forall s(s \in N \rightarrow \neg(t[Alist] \stackrel{u}{=} s[Alist]))\}$,
  where $Alist$ is a subset of $\{A_1, \ldots, A_n\}$.

Furthermore, abbreviations are defined.

- $\langle$ projection $\rangle$ $\pi_{Alist} M[A_1, \ldots, A_n] \stackrel{\text{def}}{=} S_{Alist} M$,
  where $Alist$ is a subset of $\{A_1, \ldots, A_n\}$.

- $\langle$ natural join extended with unification — $\bowtie$ $\rangle$
  $M[A, C] \overset{u}{\bowtie} N[B, C] \stackrel{\text{def}}{=} R[A, B, C] = \pi_{[A,B,C]} \sigma_{M[C] \stackrel{u}{=} N[C]} (M \times N)$.
  C is a list of common attributes of M and N.

- $\langle$ rho-operator $\rangle$
  $\rho_{TERM} M[A_1, \ldots, A_n] \stackrel{\text{def}}{=} \pi_{Vlist} P_{TERM} \sigma_{[A_1, \ldots, A_n] \stackrel{u}{=} TERM} M[A_1, \ldots, A_n]$,
  where $TERM$ be a list of compound terms. $Vlist$ is a list of distint variable symbols in $TERM$.

$\square$

RAU-operators defined above can express those four operations in Section 3.1.

Let's make a meta-relation $ruledb[K, H, B]$ by a meta predicate $\texttt{ruledb(KB, Head, Body)}$. Then the query in Figure 1 is described as a query tree $Q[T, D]$ as follows;

$$Q = \pi_{[T,D]} \, I_{B1 \wedge B2}(\rho \, _{TERM1} \, ruledb[K, H, B1] \bowtie \rho \, _{TERM2} \, ruledb[K, H, B2]) \quad (1)$$

such that $TERM1 = [kb1, key(T, story(aaa), japan(P, X)), B1]$ and
$TERM2 = [kb2, store(M, T, D), B2]$.

Among RAU-operators, I-operator is definitely unique to our RAU. S,P and ρ are almost the same as *combine, extended projection*, and *extended select/project* operators in ERA [Zan85] respectively. Hence compiled forms of rules are expressed by our RAU without unification. σ and $\bowtie$-operator are the same as *unification-restriction* and *unification-join* in RBU [MYNI86].

Our original points consist in the query-processing itself by RAU for a rule-DBMS; i.e. a RAU query tree is a PROLOG meta-interpreter with exhaustive compilation of rules to relational algebra programs. It expresses what combination of rules to be retrieved, when to execute them, and calls execution of relational algebra query trees to a factDB. We accelerate this processing by fast executions of RAU-operators after optimizing the query-tree.

4 Query processing by RAU

4.1 Compilation of query

A query "$q(D_1, \ldots, D_n)$:- $demo(kb_i, r_i(LIST_i))$." is given, where $LIST_i$ is a list of compound terms. If $LIST_i$ is $[f(X), a, X]$, $r1(LIST_i)$ refers to $r1(f(X), a, X)$. r_i is a name of either base relation or derived one in deductive databases. $D_1, \ldots, D_n$ are distinct variable symbols in $LIST_i$. kb_i is a subset of an object-theory.

Then this query is compiled to a RAU query-tree as follows;

$$R_i[D_1, \ldots, D_n] = \pi_{[D_1, \ldots, D_n]} \, I_B \, \rho_{[kb_i, \, r_i(LISTi), B]} ruledb[K, H, B]$$

Note that R_i is ground because a base/derived relation r_i should be so. Apparently, the following theorem holds.

Theorem 1 A query "$q1(C_1, \ldots, C_m) : -w(D_1, \ldots, D_n)$" is given such that $C_1, \ldots, C_m$ is a subset of $D_1, \ldots, D_n$. Then, it is compiled into a RAU query tree if
    1. $w(D_1, \ldots, D_n)$ is a wff composed by $\{ \wedge, \neg, \exists \}$ of $demo(kb_i, r_i(LIST_i))$.
and
    2. Let $R_i[V_1, \ldots, V_k]$ be a meta-relation expressing a query
"$pi(V_1, \ldots, V_k) : -demo(kb_i, r_i(LIST_i))$." such that $V_1, \ldots V_k$ are variable symbols in $LISTi$. Then, $q1$ is a safe relational calculus expression by substituting a relational predicate $R_i(V_1, \ldots, V_k)$ for $demo(kb_i, r_i(LIST_i))$ in w respectively.

$\square$

e.g. a query "$q(T, D) : - demo(kb1, key(LIST1)), demo(kb2, store(LIST2))$." is given such that $LIST1 = [T, story(aaa), japan(P, X)]$ and $LIST2 = [M, T, D]$. This query is another form of that in Figure 1.

    "$q(T, P, X) : -demo(kb1, key(LIST1))$" is compiled to R_1, and
    "$q(M, T, D) : - demo(kb2, store(LIST2))$" is compiled to R_2 respectively as follows;

$$R_1[T, P, X] = \pi_{[T,P,X]} I_B \, \rho_{[kb1, \, key(LIST1), B]} \, ruledb[K, H, B]. \tag{2}$$

$$R_2[M, T, D] = \pi_{[M,T,D]} I_B \, \rho_{[kb2, \, store(LIST2), B]} \, ruledb[K, H, B]. \tag{3}$$

Apparently the given query $q(T, D)$ is a safe relational calculus expression "$q(T, D) : - R_1(T, P, X), R_2(M, T, D).$ " . It is because R_1, R_2 are ground. The query is compiled into a relational algebra expression

$$Q[T, D] = \pi_{[T,D]} (R_1[T, P, X] \bowtie R_2[M, T, D]) \tag{4}$$

($\bowtie$ is the same as usual join operation if it is restricted to a set of ground terms.) Q is just a RAU-expression if substituting (2), (3) for R_1, R_2 in (4).

This compilation generates a RAU-query tree having the following outline.

$$Q = IT_1 \bowtie \ldots \bowtie IT_i -_{c1} IR_1 -_{c2} \ldots -_{cn} IR_n$$

Their evaluation strategies are fixed but changed by commutative laws in the next section.

4.2 Commutative laws of RAU-operators

A given RAU-query tree is optimized by commutative laws for RAU-operators. Each law takes the form of $expression1 =_w expression2$. "$=_w$" is defined as follows;

Definition 4 Given meta-relations M and N,

- $M \subseteq_w N \stackrel{\text{def}}{=} \forall t \in M; t \in_w N.$
- $M =_w N \stackrel{\text{def}}{=} M \subseteq_w N$ and $N \subseteq_w M.$

□

By Definition 1 , any meta-relation M expresses a wff $L(M)$; a conjunction of a universal closured wff mapped from each tuple in M. If meta-relations M and N have a common scheme and mapping [tuple → wff], $M =_w N$ implies $L(M) \equiv L(N)$.

Commutative laws hold as follows [Ohm87]; (M, N, R are meta-relations. 1,2,... and a, b, c are attributeID).

1. $\sigma_{p1 \wedge p2}(M \times N) =_w \sigma_{p1 \wedge p2}(\sigma_{p1} M \times \sigma_{p2} N),$
   where $p1$ (or $p2$) is a selection-predicate about only attributes in M (or N). e.g.

   $$\sigma_{1 \stackrel{u}{=} f(X) \wedge 2 \stackrel{u}{=} g(X)}(M[1] \times N[2]) =_w \sigma_{1 \stackrel{u}{=} f(X) \wedge 2 \stackrel{u}{=} g(X)}(\sigma_{1 \stackrel{u}{=} f(X)} M[1] \times \sigma_{2 \stackrel{u}{=} g(X)} N[2]).$$

2. $S_{[p1, p2]}(M \times N) =_w S_{p1} M \times S_{p2} N,$
   where $p1$ (or $p2$) is a scheme consisting of only attributes in M (or N). e.g.

   $$S_{[f(1,2), g(3)]}(M[1, 2] \times N[3, 4]) =_w S_{[f(1,2)]} M[1, 2] \times S_{[g(3)]} N[3, 4].$$

3. $(M \bowtie N) \bowtie R =_w M \bowtie (N \bowtie R).$

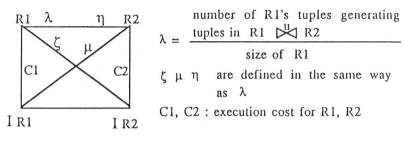

number of R1's tuples generating

$$\lambda \simeq \frac{\text{tuples in R1} \bowtie^u \text{R2}}{\text{size of R1}}$$

ζ μ η are defined in the same way as λ

C1, C2 : execution cost for R1, R2

Figure 4: a query graph for $IR_1 \bowtie^u IR_2$

4. $\sigma_p I_2 M[1,2] =_w I_2 \sigma_p M[1,2]$,
   p is a selection predicate only about $M[1]$.

5. $\pi_1 I_3 M[1,2,3] =_w \pi_1 I_3 \pi_{1,3} M[1,2,3]$.

6. $I_{a \wedge b} (M[a,c] \bowtie^u N[b,c]) =_w I_b ((I_a M[a,c]) \bowtie^u N[b,c]) =_w I_a M[a,c] \bowtie^u I_b N[b,c]$.

7. $I_b M[a,b] -_a I_c N[a,c] =_w I_b M[a,b] -_a I_c ((\pi_a I_b M[a,b]) \bowtie^u N[a,c])$,
   where $\pi_a I_b M$ must be ground.

4.3 Optimization strategies

The above laws $1 \sim 3$ enable the same optimization strategies as those in PSJ query class in a relational database [Ull82]. The laws 4 and 5 restrict rules before execution; they reduce search-space when users give constraints interactively.

$$\text{e.g. } \pi_Y I [p(X,Y) : -RAP] = \pi_Y I [q(Y) : -\exists X (RAP)].$$

This $\exists X$ is π operator to relational algebra programs RAP.

The law 6 assures changing evaluation strategies for a query

$$q : - \wedge_{i=1}^{n} demo(kb_i, r_i(LIST_i)).$$

It is compiled into an expression $E = IR_1 \bowtie \ldots \bowtie IR_n$ (ρ, π are omitted.) . Each meta-relation R_i is a set of restricted rules expressing a kind "r_i". Each rule in R_i is a necessary one for evaluating $demo(kb_i, r_i(LIST_i))$. E is optimized by changing I-operator's places and $\bowtie$'s sequence in it based on a "query graph".

Figure 4 illustrates a "query graph" for "$IR_1 \bowtie IR_2$". Each edge (n_1, n_2) except (R_i, IR_i) expresses a RAU-expression $n_1 \bowtie n_2$. Parameters on the edge is a success-ratio in unification. An edge (R_i, IR_i) is a RAU-expression IR_i. A parameter on the edge is the cost of I-operators to R_i. Suppose that, when one edge in the query graph is marked, a RAU-expression corresponding to the edge is executed and the sum of execution-cost is incremented. Then , an optimization of I-operator and $\bowtie$ sequence is a problem to search the least-cost *terminated* sequence of edge-marking in the query graph.

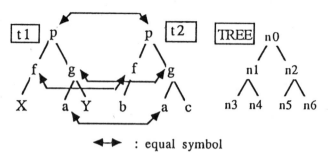

➤⬅ : equal symbol

Figure 5: an example for unifiable atomic formulae

e.g. In Figure 4, a sequence $\langle (R_2, IR_2), (R_1, IR_2), (R_1, IR_1) \rangle$ corresponds to a RAU-expression $I(R_1 \bowtie (IR_2))$. This sequence is called *terminated* because it executes all necessary operations for computing all tuples in $IR_1 \bowtie IR_2$.

This optimization-problem is NP-complete. We use a little modified version of Nearest Neighbourhood strategy for the optimization [Ohm87]. e.g. The query-tree (4) in Section 4.1 is transformed to the query-tree (1) in Section 3.3 by the laws 5, 6 and other trivial laws about π and $\bowtie$.

Lastly, the law 7 corresponds to *Negation as Failure* [Llo84].

5 An algorithm for a RAU-operator

Among RAU-operators, σ, S can be executed by a filtering processor. The heaviest operators are $\bowtie$ and I-operator. This section proposes an algorithm for $A \bowtie B$ such that A, B : metarelations. I-operator is discussed in the next section.

For simplicity, we assume that both A and B consist of one attribute. Moreover, they are sets of atomic formulae with one common $\langle predicate/arity \rangle$.

e.g. $A = \{ p(f(X), g(a, Y)), \ p(a, h(X)) \}$, $B = \{ p(X, h(a)), \ p(f(b), g(a, c)) \}$. Then, $A \bowtie B = \{ p(f(b), g(a, c)), \ p(a, h(a)) \}$. □

Our algorithm's strategy is explained at first.

(STRATEGY) Tuple t_1, t_2 are given. They are atomic formulae having a common predicate. Depending on the predicate's arity, we make a tree-structure **TREE** which has nodes $\{ n_i \}_{(i=1,...)}$. Figure 5 illustrates a **TREE** when the arity is 2. Next, we parse t_1 and t_2 based on the structure of **TREE** as in Figure 5. Let S_1, S_2 be respectively the symbols of the parsed tuples t_1 , t_2 on the node n_i of **TREE**. Then, the following assertion holds; (*) *if t_1 and t_2 are unifiable and neither S_1 nor S_2 is a variable symbol, then S_1 must be equal to S_2.*

Our algorithm filters out pairs of non-unifiable tuples by this assertion (*). Figure 6 is an example of the algorithm.

[$\bowtie$ algorithm]

step0 Set up a tree-structure **TREE** having nodes $\{ n_i \}(i = 1, ...)$.

step1 For each tuple $t \in A$ or B, parse t on **TREE** into a sequence of symbols $\{ S_i \}(i = 1, ...)$. Each S_i corresponds to a node n_i of **TREE**.

step0	(t1, t2 : tuples. A,B: meta-relations)

$$t1 = p(f(X),g(a,Y)) \in A \qquad t2 = P(f(b),g(a,c)) \in B$$

(TREE is that in Figure 5)

step1	divide A, B to buckets by hash-vector.

H(Ai), H(Bj) : hash-vector of bucket Ai,Bj.

$$\qquad n0 \quad n1 \quad n2 \quad n3 \quad n4 \quad n5 \quad n6$$

t1 ∈ Ai : H(Ai) = [h(p) , h(f) , h(g) , 0 , 0 , h(a) , 0]

t2 ∈ Bj : H(Bj) = [h(p) , h(f) , h(g) , h(b),0, h(a), h(c)]

step2	○ ○ ○ ✕ ✕ ○ ✕

N = [n0, n1, n2 , n5] for bucket combination (Ai ,Bj).

make a sort-key for each tuple on N, and sort

Ai ∋ t1 : sort-key= | p f g a | — unification-try in

Bj ∋ t2 : sort-key= | p f g a | — the sorted stream.

Figure 6: an example of a ⋈-algorithm

Compute a vector-formed hash value $H(t) = [h(S_0), h(S_1), \ldots]$ for each tuple t where $h(\langle \text{variable} \rangle) = 0$, $h(\langle \text{non} - \text{variable} \rangle) \neq 0$, $h(S_i) = 0$ if S_i does not exist. This H is called "hash-vector" of a tuple t.

Cluster A, B into buckets $\{A_i\}_{(i=1,\ldots)}$, $\{B_i\}_{(i=1,\ldots)}$ by each tuple's hash-vector H.

step2 For all bucket-combination (A_i, B_j), let $H(A_i) = [p_1, \ldots, p_n]$ and $H(B_j) = [q_1, \ldots, q_n]$ be the hash-vectors of the bucket A_i, B_j respectively.

If there is some k such that $p_k \neq 0$, $q_k \neq 0$, and $p_k \neq q_k$, then there is no pair of unifiable tuples in (A_i, B_j) by the assertion (*).

If not, make $\mathbf{N} = \{n_k, \ldots\}$ of nodes in **TREE** such that $p_k = q_k \neq 0$ as in Figure 6. Mergesort all tuples in $A_i \cup B_j$. Each tuple's sort-key is a sub-sequence $[S_{k1}, S_{k2}, \ldots]$ of the tuple's parsed symbols such that each S_{ki} corresponds to n_{ki} in $\mathbf{N}$. Try a unification of each pair of tuples (t_1, t_2) in the sorted stream where t_1 and t_2 have a equal sort-key.

□

TREE in step0 should consist of those nodes $\{n_i\}$ such that the symbol S_i of parsed tuples on n_i become non-variable symbols frequently over operand relations. Probably, those nodes generate many tuples in each relation because they take many different constant values. In **Step2**, the sort-key consists of those "tuple-generating" nodes, and filters out many pairs of non-unifiable tuples in $A_i \cup B_j$.

If **TREE** includes a node which tends to become variable symbols, sorting in

step2 will not reduce unification-load. Therefore, it is important to set up an appropriate **TREE** in **step0**. For this purpose, we use statistic informations about distributions of tuples' values in meta-relations [Ohm87].

6   Discussion

This paper has proposed a deductive database by *Relational Algebra extended with Unification* (RAU) for managing both a mass of rules and many facts in a disk. We have given a compilation of query to a RAU query-tree, optimization for it, and an algorithm for a RAU-operator ⋈̈.

In a RAU query-tree, retrieval of rules is accelerated by fast set-operation algorithms for RAU-operators, especially ⋈̈. Retrieval of facts is a role of I-operator, including common subexpression sharing. In our experimental system, each rule is a simple relational algebra program such as a single selection or at most one large size join. I-operator is executed by usual relational algebra algorithms with naive common subexpression sharings.

Our approach has several open problems as follows;

1. implementation of I-operator by conventional deductive databases. In conventional fields, our RAU accelerates optimizing a "graph-of-rules" before/ during facts-retrieval. We think our system and conventional ones are supplements to each other.

2. recursive predicate. A recursive system is a strongly connected component in a "graph-of-rules" [CGL86]. It should be treated as a non-decomposable unit. Because our approach only needs a unit of compiled relational algebra program, current trends in this field are consistent with ours.

3. random access to a ruleDB. In general, each rule is transformed into simpler ones, but they don't always operate a factDB directly. In this case, a solution is a virtual memory for PROLOG machines though it may be difficult. A trivial one is a main-memory database.

Lastly, we must tell the difference between our RAU and *RBU* in [MYNI86]; *RBU* describes SLD-resolution in [Llo84] on a database machine. On the other hand, our DBMS processes both a large ruleDB and a large factDB through a common paradigm. i.e. RAU query-trees for the ruleDB and relational algebra query-trees for the factDB.

References

[Boc86]   J. Bocca.   On the Evaluation Strategy of EDUCE.   In *Proc. of ACM-SIGMOD International Conference on Management of Data '86*, pages 368–378, 1986.

[Bow81]   K. Bowen. *AMALGAMATING LANGUAGE AND METALANGUAGE IN LOGIC PROGRAMMING*. Technical Report, Syracuse University, June 1981.

[CGL86]   S. Ceri, G. Gottlob, and L. Lavazza. Translation and optimization of logic queries: the algebraic approach. In *Proc. of the 12th Conference on Very Large Data Base*, pages 395–402, 1986.

[Gel86]   A.V. Gelder. A Message Passing Framework for Logical Query Evaluation. In *Proc. of ACM-SIGMOD International Conference on Management of Data '86*, pages 155–165, 1986.

[GM78]   H. Gallaire and J. Minker, editors. *LOGIC AND DATABASES*. Plenum press, 1978.

[KHT86]   C. Kellog, A.O'. Hare, and L. Travis. Optimizing the Rule-Data Interface in a KBMS. In *Proc. of the 12th Conference on Very Large Data Base*, pages 42–51, 1986.

[KL86]   M. Kifer and E.L. Lozinskii. A Framework for an Efficient Implementation of Deductive Databases. In *Proc. of the 6th Advanced Database Symposium*, pages 109–116, Information Processing Society of Japan, 1986.

[Llo84]   J. Lloyd. *Foundations of Logic Programming*. Springer-Verlag, 1984.

[Miy86]   N. Miyazaki. *Compiling Horn Clause Queries in Deductive Databases: A Horn Clause Transformation Approach*. Technical Report 183, ICOT, 1986.

[MYNI86]   Y. Morita, H. Yokota, K. Nishida, and I. Itoh. Retrieval-By-Unification Operation in a Relational Knowledge Base. In *Proc. of the 12th Conference on Very Large Data Base*, pages 52–59, 1986.

[Ohm87]   T. Ohmori. *An Algebraic Approach to Deductive Database system for managing a large amount of procedural knowledge*. Master's thesis, The University of Tokyo, 1987.

[Rei78]   R. Reiter. Deductive Question-Answering on Relational Data Bases. In [GM78], pages 149–177, 1978.

[Sel86]   T.K. Sellis. GROBAL QUERY OPTIMIZATION. In *Proc. of ACM-SIGMOD International Conference on Management of Data '86*, pages 191–205, 1986.

[Ull82]   J. Ullman. *Principles of Data Base Systems*. Computer Science Press, 1982.

[Ull85]   J. Ullman. Implementation of Logical Query Languages for Databases. *ACM Transaction on Database Systems*, vol.10(No.3):pp.289–321, 1985.

[YI86]   H. Yokota and H. Itoh. A Model and an Architecture for a Relational Knowledge Base. In *Proc. of the 13th International Symposium on Computer Architecture*, pages 2–9, 1986.

[YSI86]   H. Yokota, K. Sakai, and H. Itoh. Deductive Database System based on Unit Resolution. In *Proc. of the 2nd International Conference on Data Engineering*, 1986.

[Zan85]   C. Zaniolo. The Representation and Deductive Retrieval of Complex Objects. In *Proc. of the 11th Conference on Very Large Data Base*, pages 458–469, 1985.

AN APPROACH FOR
CUSTOMIZING SERVICES OF DATABASE MACHINES

Sadayuki HIKITA, Suguru KAWAKAMI, Akifumi SAKAMOTO
and Yutaka MATSUSHITA

Oki Electric Industry Co., Ltd.
Warabi-shi,Saitama, 335, Japan

ABSTRACT

Design and implementation of a database machine to reduce communication overhead are described in this paper. Database machines have improved the performance of database management. However, from the point of view of practical usage, total performance should be improved as well as database management itself. Communication overhead between a host computer and a database machine is one of the major problems of total performance in application systems.

In order to resolve this problem, the interface concept of a database machine is analyzed and the concept of customization of its interface is introduced. Then, functions required for that purpose and a virtual machine approach for its implementation are also explained.

1. INTRODUCTION

Commercial database machines have been supplied since the beginning of 1980s [SHEM84][ELEC84][EPST80][HIKI85] and it can be said that they are at the stage of practical usage. However, field experiences of database machines show various performance problems. One of the major problems is the communication bottleneck between a host computer and a database machine.

Of course, relational data model helps database machine to reduce the communication overhead because relational data model provide higher level data manipulations than network data model or hierarchical one [HIKI81][CANA74]. But relational database machines still require interaction. Furthermore, advanced applications such as knowledge based ones, decision support systems, or semantic database systems need much more interaction between a host computer and a database machine [TSUR84].

This paper discusses an approach to resolve the communication overhead problem from the viewpoint of database machines. In chapter 2, the interaction problem between a host computer and a database machine is analyzed. In chapter 3, customization of interface is introduced and required primitives are explained and discussed. Then the virtual machine approach is described. In chapter 4, the design of the database machine (V-FREND) which provides flexible interface is explained.

674

Then, the effect of this method is evaluated using an example.

2. PROBLEMS OF DATABASE MACHINES

2.1 Communication overhead

According to the benchmark tests [BITT83], database machines are effective to improve the performance of database management. However, the performance must be evaluated in not only database management itself but also in total processing. In order to show the communication overhead, processing time is analyzed using database machine FREND[HIKI85]. A host computer and FREND are connected to LAN through LAN-adapter. A request to fetch one tuple is sent from a host computer to FREND and a tuple is returned back to a host computer from FREND. Fig.1 shows time ratio among processing time of FREND and a host, LAN protocol overhead, and data transmission time to/from LAN-adapter. Data transmission time could be reduced almost zero by widening the band-width. While, LAN protocol overhead could not be reduced to zero. This is because the number of interaction can not be reduced even though band-width of LAN is to be maximized.

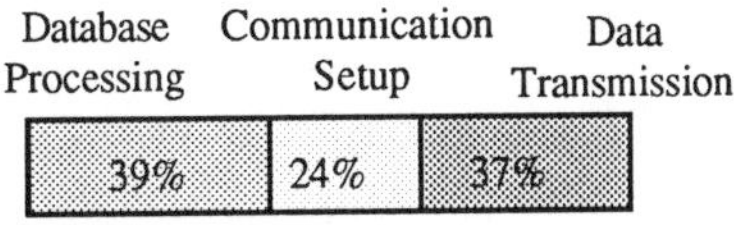

Database Processing	Communication Setup	Data Transmission
39%	24%	37%

Environment
  relation
   tuple length: 1000 byte
   cardinality 10000
  hardware
   LAN:10 Mbps
   database machine: FREND

Fig.1 Processing Time Ratio

As the result of above discussion, both the volume and the number of interaction should be reduced in order to enhance the total performance of a system.

2.2 Interface types of database machines

Here, the word 'interface' is used for functions which database machines provide for host computers, while the word 'primitive' for functions which are provided as instructions of database machines. The ability of interface of database machines is classified into following three types.

Type 1: relational query interface

This type of database machines provides an interface of a relational query. This interface improves the number of interaction because a host computer can get resulting tuple(s) with one interaction. FREND provides Type 1 interface by SQL-like primitives for a host computer. DELTA[SHIB84] also provides Type 1 interface by a query tree which includes primitives of relational algebra operations.

Type 2: stored query interface.

A query is stored in a database machine beforehand and invoked when needed. The concept 'declare cursor statement' and 'open cursor statement' of SQL[ISO87] correspond to this interface. The declare cursor statement defines a query which may include variables with unassigned values like formal parameters of subroutines. When the open cursor statement is executed, assigned values are bound to variables of a query. Since only values of arguments instead of an entire query only have to be transmitted from a host computer to a database machine at its execution, the volume to be transmitted is reduced by this Type 2 interface.

Type 3: Stored primitive interface

Not only primitives for a query, but also a sequence of primitives including control primitives such as transaction controls can be stored and invoked by one command by this interface. The stored command method which IDM500 [UBEL85] [EPST80] adopted corresponds to this interface. Type 3 interface is superior to Type 1 and Type 2 interface because in Type 3 both the number of interaction and the volume of data are much reduced than those interfaces of Type 1 and Type 2 . i.e: interaction is needed at every time of beginning transaction, selection , update and ending transaction in Type 1 and Type 2. On the other hand, the number of interaction is reduced to one by Type 3.

3. CUSTOMIZATION OF DATABASE MACHINE INTERFACE

3. 1 Functions to be needed to enhance performance

Three interface types are discussed in chapter 2. However, there are still problems in the interaction between a database machine and a host computer. For example, FREND, adopted Type 1 interface, has been suffered the interaction overhead in the field experience of transaction oriented applications. An application of semantic data model was experimented using IDM 500 (with Type 3 interface) [TSUR84]. Its conclusion showed much processing was needed at the host computer to support the database machine and suffered communication overhead.

In order to resolve this communication problem, database machines should provide an interface to hosts as high as possible. Easy solution is that an application oriented database machine is to be developed with high level primitives and an interface optimal to a specific application. However, it is not practical because each application requires its own interface and primitives. For example, transaction processing applications, knowledge base applications, statistical database applications require their own interfaces and primitives for reducing communication overhead. This approach is not acceptable from a developer's point of view.

Therefore, authors introduce an idea of customization of database machine interface. Of course, type 3 interface may be said as a kind of customization. However, for an advanced application such as decision support application, type 3 interface is not enough. This is because database machines have not been considered from the viewpoint of customization. According to authors' experiences, functions of primitives required for customization are shown as follows.

(1) Execution control function

In order to execute a function in which a parameter of a query is dependent on former queries, primitives for execution control such as branch instruction must be provided. Type 3 database machine dose not work efficiently in advanced database application area because interaction is needed for condition testing or result testing. Even for transaction processing applications, some conditions such as found/not-found should be tested. Moreover, in AI applications, recursive queries such as "find a least fixed point" are required to support logic programming[CERI86]. More conditions or results are tested to qualify above recursive queries than queries in conventional transaction processing applications. Therefore, primitives for execution control are important to customize an interface for various applications.

(2) Query manipulation

In decision support applications, target information may sometimes be a qualification of a query that selects the specific number of tuples, rather than tuples themselves a query specifies. For such applications, query should be modified in a database machine rather than in a host computer. Type 3 could not resolve this problem. So is it, both in Type 2 and Type 1 interfaces. Therefore, manipulation functions of a query tree such as change a link between query tree etc. are needed.

(3) Arithmetic and logical operations

Arithmetic and logical operations must be arbitrarily introduced to database machines. In Type 1 and Type 2 interface, an aggregate function in relational query can be assumed to be those operations. Of course new aggregate functions could be added to database machines. However, it is impossible to prospect all required aggregate functions because various arithmetic and logical operations are needed in various applications. Moreover aggregate functions can not generally resolve various requirements. Therefore, database machine should provide generic environment for arithmetic and logical operations.

Database machines can have flexible interface by providing functions mentioned above. This customization will remove unnecessary communication overhead. New interface proposed here as Type 4 could be said a function of stored program control.

3.2 Virtual machine approach

In implementing these functions of customizations, database machine must preserve the characteristic of database machines [HIKI85] [STON81] [STON83].
• Efficient task scheduling

Special purpose machines do not suffer from the OS overhead such as context switching because they do not provide general purpose programming environment.
• Efficient data file management

Special purpose machines can provide efficient data file management optimally tuned for relational operations.
• Efficient database buffering

Special purpose machines can provide efficient database buffering which results in enhancement of the performance and in which secondary memories are accessed least frequently.

In order to accomplish purposes mentioned above, authors adopt a virtual machine approach. This virtual machine provides not only primitives for data manipulation database machines already provide, but also new primitives for customization discussed in 3.2. These new primitives are restricted as little as those necessary for customization. By virtue of these restrictions new database machine dose not provide environment of a general purpose processor.

Users can customize an interface of the database machine by defining new commands using the instructions and registering them in the database machine. However, a programmer of database machine can not directly activate system calls and could not directly manipulate the data file in that machine. Programmers may write programs in a high level language like C. The source programs are compiled to object codes of virtual machine instructions at a host computer. Then, those instructions are stored in the database machine. By these procedures Type 4 interface is realized. The virtual machine version of database machine FREND (V-FREND) have been developed according to this conclusion. In chapter 4, V-FREND is explained.

4. V-FREND : VIRTUAL MACHINE VERSION OF FREND
4.1 V-FREND architecture

FREND which has Type 1 interface is a relational database machine and implemented as software backend. Its primitives for data manipulation are based on SQL-like relational query language, in which queries must be represented as an internal format. FREND also provides primitives for transaction control such as start-transaction. If a host computer sends a command to FREND, corresponding primitive is activated internally, and the result is sent back to a host computer.

According to the result of discussion in chapter 3, authors extended FREND to a virtual machine by software. The extended FREND is called V-FREND. The virtual machine has instructions for data manipulation, transaction control, execution control, query manipulation, and arithmetic/logical operation etc. Instructions are explained in 4.2. The architecture of V-FREND is shown in Fig.2. V-FREND consists of virtual CPU, program area and data area. The virtual CPU executes the instructions. Instructions are fetched from the program area which contains the sequence of V-FREND instructions. Data such as variables or retrieval conditions are stored in data area.

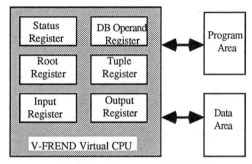

Fig.2 Architecture of V-FREND

Since DBMS is virtualized as internal component of virtual CPU, it is not shown in the figure. Instructions for data manipulation and transaction control are the only ways to access to database.

V-FREND also has special purpose data areas called 'register'. The registers are used in order to reduce the number of operands of the instructions or to contain special purpose data such as machine status. There are following six registers.

•Database Operand Register:
   Operands of data manipulation instructions or transaction control instructions are stored in this register.
•Root register
   This register points the root of a parse tree of search condition. The detail will be mentioned in section 4.3.
•Tuple Register
   A Tuple to be inserted or retrieved is stored in this register.
•Input/Outout register
   Data to be transmitted to/from a host computer are stored in this register.
•Status Register
   This register indicates the state of V-FREND. For example, whether an instruction of retrieval is successful or not is indicated.

4.2 Instructions of Virtual Machine V-FREND

Fig.3 shows some instructions of the virtual machine. In later part of this section, the reason why authors adopted these kinds of functional primitives to the database machine is described.

The instructions of V-FREND are categorized as follows from a functional point of view.

(1)Database Manipulate Instructions.
(2)Operand Manipulate Instructions
(3) Arithmetic / logical Instructions and Move Instructions
(4) Input-Output Instructions
(5) Execution Control Instructions

The conventional database machines[HIKI85][EPST80] only support the primitives that correspond to instructions in group (1). While, database machine V-FREND supports all instructions listed above. This is an implementation of required functions described in chapter 3. The details of instructions are described in followings.

(1) Database Manipulate Instructions

Database Manipulate Instructions of V-FREND are categorized into two classes which are as same as the conventional database machine FREND. The first class is a data manipulation instruction set. Instructions for retrieval(RTRV,RTVN), update(UPDT), delete(DELT), and insert (INST) are provided. The RTRV instruction requires a retrieval condition as its operand. The condition is represented in

database manipulation instructions

RTRV	define cursor and retrieve a tuple
RTVN	retrieve next tuple
UPDT	update current tuple
DELT	delete current tuple
INST	insert tuple into a relation
STRT	start transaction
ENDT	end transaction
ABRT	abort transaction

operand manipulation instructions

CONS	connect a sub-tree to another tree
CNST	connect a sub-tree to another tree
CHVL	change value of node
LEFT	get value of left pointer of node
RGHT	get value of right pointer of node
CHC	change constant
PLANT	plant a condition tree with I/O format from/to the data area
ASTA	set targets of retrieval
ASRE	set relations used in retrieval
ASSO	set sort specification of retrieval

arithmetic and logical instructions

AND	logical and
OR	logical or
NOT	logical not
ADD	add
SUB	subtract
SFTL	shift left
SFTR	shift right

flow control instructions

CJMP	conditional jump for two valued logic
CJPN	conditional jump on null-value tests
CJPT	conditional jump for three valued logic
JMP	jump
RET	return to supervisor
RETT	return and reply a tuple

input/output instructions

IN	receive a message from a host computer
OUT	send a message to a host computer

Fig.3 Instruction Set of V-FREND (extracted)

the form of parse tree. The second class is a transaction control instruction set. Concerning to transaction control, instructions for start transaction(STRT), commit&end(ENDT), and abort&end(ABRT) are provided.

(2) Operand Manipulate Instructions

Modification of query is accomplished by Operand Manipulation Instructions. Instructions we propose make easy to modify operands on Database Operand Register, which contains various operands of database manipulation instructions. For example, changing the target relation of a same retrieval condition, changing target items of a same retrieval condition, can be easily performed. Another important example is an operation against a retrieval condition tree. Using those instructions, the modification of retrieval condition on the database machine side without interaction to a host computer, or recursive query such as parts explosion, can be performed easily. This also works effectively under the circumstances such as statistical databases that various retrieval conditions are tried arbitrarily. The manipulation of a retrieval condition tree is described in section 4.3.

(3) Arithmetic/logical Instruction and Move Instructions

They are used for movement of data on memory, and for logical operations such as AND, OR, NOT of bit string, and for arithmetic operations of add, subtract etc.

(4) Input and Output Instructions

In order to exchange data from/to a host computer, IN and OUT instructions are provided. Executing IN instruction,data from a host computer is set on Input Register. Also, result data to be returned is set to Output Register. After executing OUT instruction, the result is sent back to a host computer.

(5) Execution Control Instructions

Different from conventional database machines, V-FREND has conditional branch instructions. Not only those based on two valued logic, but also those based on three valued logic are supported. This is also one of special features in addition to the operand manipulate instructions already discussed in(2). The basic principle of conditional branch instructions is based on two valued logic shown in the followings.

CJMP   <first operand>, <operation code>, <second operand>,
        <branch destination address for true>

If the result of an operation against first operand and second operand is true, it will branch to the destination specified. Moreover, CJPN instruction, which is the branch instruction for testing null value, is additionally installed. The form is as follows.

CJPN   <first operand>, <operation code>,
          <branch destination address for true>

Operation code is either ISNULL or ISNOTNULL. If this is applied to a parts explosion example, it is possible to define a relation whose final level part is a tuple with null-value. This tuple is retrieved recursively as a result of the retrieval of a certain minor part. In this case, the test for null value at the end of retrieval is required. For example, if the retrieved minor part name is to be stored to the variable named as "minor", the final judgement can be done as follows.

```
LOOP: CJPN minor, ISNULL, FOUND
        /* "minor" to be set as the major part, and further retrieval is performed */
      JMP LOOP /* unconditional jump */
FOUND:  /* current major part results in the final level part to be got */
```

V-FREND also provides branch instruction CJPT which supports the three valued logic including the logic value "unknown", which results by comparison of null value to the other value. The form of it is as follows.

CJPT   <first operand>, <operation code>, <second operand>,
          <destination for true>, <destination for unknown>

The example which treats the NULL value on a comparison of A with B is shown. If the value of A or B is NULL, the result of A>=B is unknown.

```
          CJPT  A>=B , TRUE, UNKNOWN
          /* handle false case */
          • • •
TRUE:     /* handle true case */
          • • •
UNKNOWN: /* handle unknown case */
          • • •
```

The introduction of conditional branch instructions reduces the number of interactions between a host computer and V-FREND. This is because that these instructions make it possible to change the retrieval condition or to change the actions according to the former result without a host computer's judgement.

4.3 Manipulation against the parsed condition tree

This section describes retrieval condition trees of V-FREND and correlated manipulate instructions. An example of a retrieval condition tree is shown in Fig.4. Leaf nodes of the retrieval condition tree have a different structure from other nodes. Here, the leaf node is called the leaf and the other is called the node. The leaf indicates constants and attributes. Each node consists of three fields. Those are the value of a node, the right side sub-tree, and the left side sub-tree. The

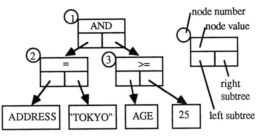

Fig.4 Retrieval Condition Tree

nodes of a tree are identified by the node numbers.The value of a node represents logical operators (AND, OR, NOT) or comparison operators (=, <, != ,etc). Each node has sub-trees of a retrieval condition tree to its right and left. Node No.1 in Fig.4 indicates that the value of the node is AND, and the sub-tree of the right is the tree which represents {ADDRESS = "TOKYO"} starting No.2 node, and the sub-tree of the left is the tree which represents { AGE >= 25} starting No.3 node. The leaf of the tree is either constants or attributes ADDRESS or "TOKYO" correspond to.

A retrieval condition tree in V-FREND is manipulated by using the following four types of instructions.

(a) Change constants or attributes of a node (CHC)
(b) Connect a sub-tree to a node (CONS, CNST)
(c) Change a value of a node (CHVL)
(d) Find a forward node beyond a node (LEFT, RGHT)

(a) is used to change the leaf of a retrieval condition tree, namely to change attributes or constants part. If this instruction is used, the same retrieval condition is able to be applied recursively. For example, in parts explosion, a part 'B' retrieved as a minor part of part 'A' must be the value of major part in the retrieval condition in the next step. In order to substitute a leaf value in a condition tree, CHC (change constant) with the following form is used.

CHC <node number>, <right/left>, <address of the leaf node>

In this example, the current result 'B' is stored at address P. CHC 1,right,P substitutes the value of the current condition 'A' to the value of 'B'. This is shown in Fig.5.

Instructions of (b) are used for either deletion or connection of other condition tree from/to a retrieval condition tree. By

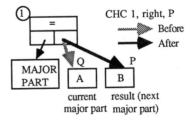

Fig.5 CHC Instruction

preparing a retrieval condition sub-tree in advance, both deletion and addition of retrieval condition can be applied to the former retrieval condition arbitrarily. This instruction set (b) is effective for applications that search a suitable conditions by changing retrieval conditions. In decision support systems, that instruction set (b) would much decrease the number of interaction.

Instructions of (c) change values of a node. Values are ">, =, >=, <, =< <>". This is a complemental function of an instruction set (b). In order to show the effect of the instruction set (b), following example is explained(Fig.6). The condition tree shown in Fig.4 is added as a subtree to a tree with the condition of (level>=70). The sub-tree exists at address P and the condition tree at address Q. In order to link those trees, AND is equipped at the first node of the condition tree at address Q. The sub-tree at address P is to be linked to the left of the first node of the condition tree. Instruction CNST (Construct Tree) is used as follows.

CNST <node number to be linked>, <left /right>, <sub-tree address>
Parameters are specified as follows.

CNST 1, left, P

As a result, condition tree Q has become a condition tree for conjuncted retrieval condition. Root register stores the address of the first node of the tree manipulated.

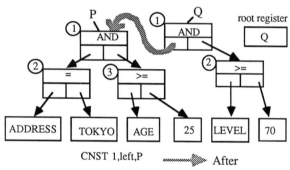

CNST 1,left,P ⟶ After

Fig.6 CNST Instruction

5. EVALUATION

The effect of V-FREND is evaluated using an example of parts explosion in this chapter.The relation named PART consists of those attributes of MAJOR_P and MINOR_P. This is shown in Fig.7. In general parts explosion problem, the goal is to retrieve all parts needed for a given part from PART relation. Procedures to solve this problem are shown in [DATE86]. But in this example, for the simplicity, we assume the goal to

PART

MAJOR_P	MINOR_P
A	B
B	C
C	D
C	E
D	<NULL>
E	<NULL>

Fig.7 PART Relation

retrieve only one part at the final level. Fig.8 shows the procedure for given part "A".

```
current_major = 'A' ;
select MINOR_P into :minor from PART
where MAJOR_P = :current_major;
/* the variable "minor" is assigned to the first level minor part (this case 'B') of current_major part (
this case 'A') */
while(minor != NULL_VALUE) {              /* repeat until the final level */
          current_major = minor; /* this level of minor should be
                                          major in the next level */
          select MINOR_P into :minor  from PART
          where MAJOR_P = :current_major;
}
/* the variable "current_major" is assigned to the part whose MINOR_P is NULL_VALUE. Because
the part has no minor part, this is the result. */
```
Fig. 8 A Procedure for Parts Explosion.

Underlined statements are retrieval operations needed for the database machine. Type 1 interface makes it possible to execute each of these lines with one interaction even when the database machine provides lower level primitives. However, a number of interaction still exist as shown in Fig.9.

In a database machine with type 2 or type 3 interface, the query is executed as follows. The statement

select MINOR_P into :minor where MAJOR_P = :current_major;

can be stored at the database machine before the execution. In the execution time, only values of variables would be sent from a host computer. This eliminate the volume of the data to be transmitted. In this example, however, the terminate condition must be tested by comparing the result with null value. Even with type 3 interface, it is impossible to embed this function of terminate condition check in the database machine. Therefore tests should be executed at the host computer, the number of interaction is as same as the case of type 1 interface.

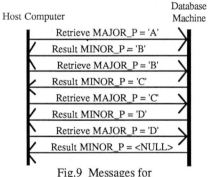

Host Computer — Database Machine

Retrieve MAJOR_P = 'A'
Result MINOR_P = 'B'
Retrieve MAJOR_P = 'B'
Result MINOR_P = 'C'
Retrieve MAJOR_P = 'C'
Result MINOR_P = 'D'
Retrieve MAJOR_P = 'D'
Result MINOR_P = <NULL>

Fig.9 Messages for Conventional Database Machines

V-FREND makes it possible to store an entire procedure in the machine itself. For example, terminate condition of "while (minor != NULL_VALUE)" can be written as similar as to the example of condition branch instruction at section 4.2.

Re-generation of the next step query which condition depends on the result of a former query, can also be written in V-FREND. The substitution of current_major = minor, can be realized by tree manipulation instructions.

Therefore, a user can get results with one interaction (Fig.10); that is the invocation of a procedure from a host computer, and the transfer of results from a database machine. Table 1 shows the comparison of each type interface.

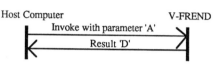

Fig.10 Messages for V-FREND

Table 1. Nuber of Messages in Each Type Interfaces

Type	number of messages	volume of data to be transmitted
Type 1 (query)	8	the entire query and the result
Type 2 (stored query) Type 3 (stored primitive)	8	parameters of the query and the resutl
V-FREND	2	parameters of the procedure and the result

A stored program and extended primitives like condition branch or tree manipulation can improve the interaction between a host computer and a database machine. In the example of parts explosion in this section, it takes four times of retrievals to get to the termination. Generally, it would take more times to get to the termination, which results in interactions of a host computer and a database machine with type 1,2,3 interface. However, V-FREND is much effective even hierarchy of a part explosion is much deeper.

6. CONCLUSION

Total throughput including a database machine and a host computer can be enhanced by improving the interface between them. Key points are extending primitives and the stored program control by the virtual machine architecture.

The customization of interfaces of a database machine is effective in applications of not only conventional database systems, but also semantic data model systems, systems which require recursive queries, and decision support systems. When extending functions of a database machine, a certain rule or an integrated method is inevitable. Authors proposes the virtual database machine technique to extend its functions. In this environment, authors do not expect that the machine would provide compilers nor editors etc. on its machine. The virtual database machine only provide the environment of execution of extended database manipulation functions. This results in preserving various characteristics of database machines, such as efficient task scheduling, efficient database file managements, and efficient database buffering.

Authors have already developed and roughly evaluated V-FREND. In order to refine V-FREND, detailed functional and performance evaluation are planned in future.

REFERENCES

[BITI83]   Bitton,D., et al., "Benchmarking Database Systems A Systematic Approach", Proc. of VLDB, 1983, pp. 8-19.

[CERI86]   Ceri,S., et al "Translation and Optimization of Logic Queries: the Algebraic approach", Proc. of VLDB, 1986, pp. 395 - 402.

[CANA74] Canaday,R.H, et al.,"A Back-end Computer for Data Base Management", CACM, Vol.17. No.10, 1974, pp.575-582.

[DATE86] Date,C.J., "An introduction to Database Systems (Volume I Forth Edition) " ,Addison-Wesley,1986, pp. 203-206.

[ELEC84]   "Multiple 8086s do parallel processing" (An article on DBC/1012 of Teradata Corp.), Electronics report, Electronics Vol.57, No.2 ,1984, pp.50.

[EPST80] Epstein,R. et al., "Design Decisions for the Intelligent Database Machine", Proc. AFIPS, Vol.49,1980,pp.237-241.

[HIKI81]   Hikita,S., et al., "Optimization of the file access method in content-addressable database access machine (CADAM)", Proc . of AFIPS conference 1981, Vol 50, 1981, pp.507-513.

[HIKI85]   Hikita,S., et al., "Database Machine FREND", Database Machines Forth International Workshop, Springer-Verlag, 1985, pp.190-207.

[ISO87]   ISO, "Database Language SQL",ISO-9075,1987.

[SHEM84] Shemer,J., et. al,(conversation) ,"The Genesis of a Database Computer", Computer, vol 17 no. 11 ,IEEE,1984.,pp. 42-56.

[SHIB84]   Shibayama,S. et al., "A Relational Database Machine with Large Semiconductor Disk and Hardware Relational Algebra Processor", New Generation Computing 2, OHMSHA, LTD. and Springer-Verlag, 1984, 131-155.

[STON81] Stonebraker, M., "Operating System Support for Database Management" CACM, Vol.24, No.7, 1981, pp.412-418.

[STON83] Stonebraker, M., "Performance Enhancements to a Relational Database System", ACM TODS, Vol.8, No.2, 1983, pp.167-185.

[TSUR84] Tsur, S., et al., "An Implementation of GEM - Supporting a Semantic Data", Proc. of SIGMOD '84, Vol.14, No.2, 1984, pp.286-295.

[UBEL85] Ubell,M., "The Intelligent Database Machine (IDM)", Query Processing in Database Systems, Springer-Verlag,1985, pp.237-247.